Books by Stanley Edgar Hyman

THE TANGLED BANK   *1962*
Darwin, Marx, Frazer and Freud as Imaginative Writers

POETRY AND CRITICISM   *1961*
Four Revolutions in Literary Taste

THE CRITICAL PERFORMANCE   *1956*
An Anthology of American and British Literary Criticism
of Our Century

THE ARMED VISION   *1948*
A Study in the Methods of Modern Literary Criticism

THE
TANGLED
BANK

Stanley Edgar Hyman

THE TANGLED BANK

DARWIN, MARX, FRAZER AND FREUD AS IMAGINATIVE WRITERS

ATHENEUM

New York

1962

To my children
who are glad to see it done

On the afternoon of October 24th 1917, four days after my marriage, my wife surprised me by attempting automatic writing. What came in disjointed sentences, in almost illegible writing, was so exciting, sometimes so profound, that I persuaded her to give an hour or two day after day to the unknown writer, and after some half-dozen such hours offered to spend what remained of life explaining and piecing together those scattered sentences. "No," was the answer, "we have come to give you metaphors for poetry."

W. B. Yeats, *A Vision*

Preface

To BEGIN on a strong negative note, this book is not a history of ideas nor even a discussion of ideas. It is a work of literary criticism, a study of the writings of Darwin, Marx, Frazer and Freud as imaginative organizations, as though they were poems. It does not attempt to compete with the innumerable studies of their contributions within their fields, but to supplement them in another dimension, and the writer claims only a literary critic's knowledge of the fields concerned. Although there have been a few pioneering articles along these lines, acknowledged below, I am not aware of any previous large-scale treatment. The propriety of a literary study of works not usually classified as literature need not be argued; if *The Tangled Bank* contribute insight into the great books it discusses, I would take its approach to be justified.

The methods are those of modern literary criticism, as I have outlined them in *The Armed Vision*. Within that tradition, the book's heavy reliance is on the ritual theory of Jane Harrison and Gilbert Murray (although most of my "myths" here are necessarily Platonic rather than ritual), William Empson's handling of analogical form, and Kenneth Burke's concept of symbolic action. As much as possible, I have tried to select and present the material to make its own point, with very liberal quotation and a minimum of explicit interpretation, as I would teach it in class. The reader is thus challenged to do his own interpretation and evaluation, which may very well not coincide with mine.

At a few places in the book, for no better reason than human weakness, I have forsaken my principles and ventured a dissenting opinion on a technical matter: that Darwin could not have discovered genetics, that the labor theory of value blinded Marx to other values,

that Frazer went wrong on the origin of myths, that Freud's reconstruction of Moses is preposterous, and others. These are offered as no
more than my personal views, and any reader is privileged to ignore
them. I have made no attempt, for reasons that will be clear in the
course of the book, to correct or even to identify statements by my
subjects that would now universally be accepted as erroneous; but
again there are a few exceptions.

In thirteen years of study, I have read almost every scrap of writing by Darwin, Marx, Frazer and Freud (although only a tiny fraction
of the literature about them). I discuss all of their books, but I treat
their articles and papers in very different fashions: Darwin's are hardly
mentioned, since they have never been collected, they are of relatively
little significance, and practically everything of interest in them went
into his books; Freud's are discussed in great detail, since they are
readily available in the five-volume *Collected Papers*, and they include
things of the utmost importance that never appeared in his other books;
the articles and papers of Marx and Frazer are dealt with in a fashion
somewhere between those extremes.

Darwin, Marx, Frazer and Freud are among the most important
thinkers of the past century, and are significant shapers of the modern
mind and of the present century. (I attempt to sketch in some of that
influence in my conclusion.) It is the thesis of this book that the power
and influence of their ideas is due in some substantial part to their
ability as imaginative writers, and it is that ability which the book attempts to explore. This is not merely a superficial matter of "style,"
nor is the treatment narrowly aesthetic. I believe their books to be art,
but I believe art itself to have an ethical as well as an aesthetic dimension, in that it is the work of the moral imagination, imposing order and
form on disorderly and anarchic experience. That this vision of order
and form is primarily metaphoric makes it no less real, since lines of
force then radiate out from the work of art and order or reorder the
world around, as they do from Wallace Stevens' jar in Tennessee.

Acknowledgments

P A R T S of this book have appeared in *The American Scholar, The Carleton Miscellany, The Centennial Review, The Kenyon Review, New Mexico Quarterly, The Texas Quarterly, and The Virginia Quarterly;* they are reprinted here through the kindness of the editors.

My personal indebtedness, over ten years of reading and three years of writing, has been very great. I owe innumerable insights to the authors and editors of the many works that I quote from and list in the bibliography, and of many more not quoted from or listed. I must particularly acknowledge two American critics who anticipated my approach in pioneering articles, Theodore Baird and Wylie Sypher. I owe thanks to the many different translators of Marx and Freud whose work I use, although that debt has not prevented me from tinkering with their translations on behalf of smoother style and American spelling. I am indebted to many biographers, but the indebtedness of any student of Freud to the late Ernest Jones is so great that it must be individually acknowledged.

My friends and colleagues at Bennington College have helped by sharing my load during a sabbatical leave, providing me with information and correcting some of my misinformation, assisting my poor efforts with the German language, and in many other ways. I must particularly thank the dozen friends who read the manuscript in whole or in part, and gave me the benefit of their ideas, in a few cases acknowledged in the text but in most cases not. My students at Bennington College, particularly the classes who studied this material with me, will find their ideas shamelessly pirated, as will my class at Columbia University. Since individual acknowledgment is impossible in their case, I hope that they will accept this collective acknowledgment.

Mary S. Hopkins and the staff of the Bennington College Library have shown the utmost kindness in providing books, and Louis Scher and the staff of The Seven Bookhunters the utmost ingenuity in finding books. A sabbatical leave from Bennington College and a fellowship from the American Council of Learned Societies made the writing possible, and I cordially thank President William C. Fels and the trustees of the College, President Frederick H. Burkhardt and the officers of the Council. Harry Ford, Simon Michael Bessie, and the staff at Atheneum Publishers have been boundlessly helpful and encouraging. Isabel Sherwood typed the manuscript and read my handwriting with her usual wizardry, Walter Lehrman generously copyread the final draft, and Joan Blake kindly compiled the index. William Shawn and Edith Oliver of *The New Yorker* have been more than kind in every way. And once again my beloved wife, Shirley Jackson, has helped beyond the possibilities of acknowledgment.

S. E. H.

North Bennington, Vermont
December, 1961

Contents

INTRODUCTION

HOWEVER much we affect to scorn it, the nineteenth century had a liveliness of intellectual tone that we might properly envy. Ideas were important. Looking back in 1921, John Morley wrote defiantly, in an epilogue to his essay "On Compromise":

> Some ages are marked as sentimental, others stand conspicuous as rational. The Victorian age was happier than most in the flow of both these currents into a common stream of vigorous and effective talent. New truths were welcomed in free minds, and free minds make brave men.

The motto of the Enlightenment, *Sapere aude,* "dare to know," could still be taken seriously as guidance for a life, a book, or even a review. Ernest Jones writes of what the psychoanalysts call "resistances" in *Free Associations:*

> The most formidable of them—i.e. the greatest impediment to scientific progress—have always been those that had become connected with the idea of the Divinity, so that each step onward signified displacing this idea to a greater distance and to contemporaries could only appear in terms of blasphemy. The mid-nineteenth century saw greater boldness in this direction than any other period had.

Ideas were in a bubbling state of ferment early in the nineteenth century, and among them were all or most of the ingredients that Darwin, Marx, Frazer and Freud needed for their revolutionary visions in the second half of the century.

In *The Death of Adam,* John C. Greene writes of Darwin's theory of the origin of species by means of natural selection:

> All the elements of the theory were present in the scientific world by 1818. Buffon, Kant, and Laplace had derived the origin of the solar system from the operation of a universal system of laws, elements, and forces. Hutton had conceived the surface of the earth as a system of matter in motion millions of years old. Cuvier had applied the resources of comparative anatomy to the reconstruction of extinct species and, with William Smith, had discovered how to read the fossil record embedded in the globe's crust. Buffon had suggested the variability of organic forms, and Lamarck had postulated their gradual evolution from monad to man. Buffon had seen that the extinction of species was related to the struggle for survival among the various creatures produced by nature's endless combinations. Maupertuis, Prichard, and Wells had sensed the possibility that new types

3

might be formed from chance variations thrown up in the course of procreation, and Wells had used the notion of natural selection to explain the origin of the Negro race. Even Malthus' Essay on the *Principle of Population*, the book which Darwin said gave him the clue to the origin of species, was available.

By 1832 there was Charles Lyell's *Principles of Geology*, with its exhaustive demonstration of great change by the slow workings of natural processes. Greene comments:

> If Buffon had had such a discussion available when he first began to question the fixity of species he might well have anticipated Darwin's entire theory, for his thought about the nature and mechanisms of organic change was much closer to Darwin's than was Lamarck's.

Thomas Henry Huxley stated unequivocally: "Darwin's greatest work is the outcome of the unflinching application to Biology of the leading idea and the method applied in the *Principles* to Geology." Darwin himself admitted that his books "came half out of Lyell's brain."

Not only could Darwin's revolutionary theory have been anticipated, it *was* anticipated. In 1844 the anonymous *Vestiges of the Natural History of Creation* appeared, and went through ten editions in ten years. It was the work of the eccentric Scottish publisher Robert Chambers, and its science was so amateur and ludicrous that no one took it seriously, but the essence of Darwin's theory was there. As everyone knows, it was the independent working-out of the theory by another scientist, Alfred Russell Wallace, similarly influenced by Lyell and Malthus, that finally led to Darwin's publishing in 1858, jointly with Wallace, an abstract of the material he had been working on in secret. In *Darwin and Modern Science*, edited by A. C. Seward, the geneticist W. Bateson reprints Darwin's statement from his *Autobiography*:

> It has sometimes been said that the success of the *Origin* proved 'that the subject was in the air,' or 'that men's minds were prepared for it.' I do not think that this is strictly true, for I occasionally sounded not a few naturalists, and never happened to come across a single one who seemed to doubt about the permanence of species.

Bateson comments:

> This experience may perhaps have been an accident due to Darwin's isolation. The literature of the period abounds with indications of 'critical expectancy.'

The phrase is Huxley's. If the idea of the struggle for existence came to Darwin from Malthus, Malthus had in turn probably borrowed it from Buffon, so that in applying conclusions about society to natural history, Darwin was in fact only reapplying them. Perhaps both Malthus and Buffon were merely translating theology. Friedrich Engels wrote in 1844, in "Outlines of a Critique of Political Economy":

> The Malthusian theory is merely the economic expression of the religious dogma of the contradiction between spirit and nature, and of the corruption of both resulting from it.

Karl Marx, who struck up a friendship with Engels because of the degree to which that "Critique" resembled his own views, similarly found the ideas he needed ripe for the plucking all around him. Utopian socialism, another secularization of religious vision, developed in Thomas More's *Utopia* in 1516, Tommaso Campanella's *City of the Sun* in 1623, and James Harrington's *Oceana* in 1656. The vision began to come down to earth in the nineteenth century. Charles Fourier published *Théorie des quatre mouvements* in 1808, Robert Owen his *New View of Society* in 1813, and Count Henri de Saint-Simon *L'Industrie* in 1817. The other two principal ingredients of Marxism, German philosophy and English political economy, attained their ripeness for his purposes with Georg Friedrich Hegel's *Phenomenology of Mind* in 1807 and David Ricardo's *The Principles of Political Economy and Taxation* in 1817. Thus by 1818, the year Marx was born, all his materials were ready for him. Isaiah Berlin, in *Karl Marx: His Life and Environment*, summarizes more fully:

> To trace the direct source of any single doctrine advanced by Marx is, therefore, a relatively simple task which his numerous critics have been only too anxious to perform. It may well be that there is not one among his views whose embryo cannot be found in some previous or contemporary writer. Thus the doctrine of communal ownership founded upon the abolition of private property, has probably, in one or another form, possessed adherents at most periods during the last two thousand years. Consequently the often debated question whether Marx derived it directly from the writings of Mably, or from some German account of French Communism, is too purely academic to be of great importance. As for the more specific doctrines, historical materialism of a sort is to be found fully developed in a treatise by Holbach printed a century before, which in its turn owes much to Spinoza; a modified form of it was restated in Marx's own day by Feuerbach. The view of human history as the history of war between social classes is to be found in Saint-Simon, and was to a large extent adopted by such contemporary liberal French historians as Thierry and Mignet, and equally by the more conservative Guizot. The scientific theory of the inevitability of the regular recurrence of economic crises was probably first formulated by Sismondi; that of the rise of the Fourth Estate was certainly held by the early communists, popularized in Germany in Marx's own day by von Stein and Hess. The dictatorship of the proletariat was adumbrated by

Babeuf in the last decade of the eighteenth century, and was explicitly developed in the nineteenth in different fashions by Weitling and Blanqui; the present and future position and importance of workers in an industrial state was more fully worked out by Louis Blanc and the French State Socialists than Marx is prepared to admit. The labour theory of value derives from Locke, Adam Smith and the classical economists; the theory of exploitation and surplus value, and of its remedy by deliberate State control, is found both in Fourier, and in the writings of early English socialists, such as Bray, Thompson and Hodgskin; the list could easily be continued further.

In another genesis, Berlin writes that historical materialism "derives its structure from Hegel, and its dynamic principle from Saint-Simon, its belief in the primacy of matter from Feuerbach, and its view of the proletariat from the French communist tradition." Marx credited many of these predecessors, who were his sources where Darwin's (except for Malthus and Lyell) were rather anticipators whose work he read later. The only uniqueness Marx claimed was the combination of historical materialism with the dialectic of class struggle.

Later in the century James George Frazer found the same "critical expectancy." One strand of his method, evolutionary anthropology, derives directly from Darwin. I wrote in "The Ritual View of Myth and the Mythic" in *Myth: A Symposium*, edited by Thomas A. Sebeok:

> When Darwin concluded *The Origin of Species* (1859) with a call for evolutionary treatment in the sciences of man, he opened the door to a variety of genetic studies of culture, and when he showed in *The Descent of Man* (1871) that human evolution was insignificant organically although vastly speeded up culturally (we might not be so quick to say 'ethically' as he was), he made cultural studies the legitimate heirs of evolutionary biology. The same year as *The Descent*, in response to *The Origin*, E. B. Tylor's *Primitive Culture* appeared, drawing an immediate fan letter from Darwin. It staked off quite a broad claim to cultural studies in its subtitle 'Researches into the Development of Mythology, Philosophy, Religion, Language, Art and Custom.'

A second strand was the comparative method, independently invented by Baron Charles de Montesquieu in *Esprit des lois* in 1748, and by Johann Gottfried von Herder in *Über den Ursprung der Sprache* in 1772. A series of German philologists, chief among them Franz Bopp, followed Herder in applying the method to the evolution of language in the first half of the nineteenth century. In 1861 Sir Henry Maine published *Ancient Law* and John Ferguson McLennan published *Primitive Marriage*, simultaneous applications of the comparative method to the study of society. In a series of books and articles from 1868 on, William Robertson Smith, a pupil of McLennan's, turned the method into the science of comparative religion. The third strand was the inductive study of myth and cults begun by Wilhelm Mannhardt with *Germanische Mythen* in 1858, and culminating in *Antike Wald- und Feldkulte* in 1877. In short, all the ingredients of Frazer's system were ready for him in his schooldays.

The ideas of Sigmund Freud were similarly bubbling during the nineteenth century. It was Freud who *drove home* the conception of an unconscious mind and its biological nature, Jones writes in *Free Associations*, "just as Darwin had that of evolution, however much both ideas may have been 'in the air.' " Here too we have the secularization of a traditional religious vision, as Jones reminds us by quoting Romans 7:23: "But I see another law in my members, warring against the law of my mind." The popularization of hypnosis by F. Anton Mesmer in the 1770s had focussed attention on the unconscious mind, and resulted in a considerable French movement in the nineteenth century. In 1823 Alexandre Bertrand discovered the psychological nature of hypnotism, by 1864 A. A. Liébault was using deep hypnosis on his patients in Nancy, and by the 1870s Jean Martin Charcot was treating hysterics by means of hypnosis in Paris. Freud later translated Charcot and Liébault's pupil Hippolyte Bernheim into German, studied with Charcot, and visited the Nancy clinic. As late as 1898, when he was working on *The Interpretation of Dreams*, Freud was afraid that Pierre Janet, Charcot's successor, would anticipate him. He writes to a friend:

> I picked up a recent book of Janet's on hysteria and *idées fixes* with beating heart, and laid it down again with my pulse returned to normal. He has no suspicion of the clue.

In Vienna, Freud's friend Josef Breuer had been treating cases by means of hypnosis since 1880.

Philosophically, in one aspect Freud inherits eighteenth-century rationalism, with its conviction that every mental process is determined, meaningful, and explainable. Rousseau's natural man lies behind Freud's id, as Benthamite calculation (as Erich Fromm and David Riesman have shown) lies behind his concept of the pleasure principle. Equally, Freud is the heir of nineteenth-century irrationalism. Thomas Mann has put this most eloquently, in "Freud's Position in the History of Modern Thought." Mann writes:

> As a delver into the depths, a researcher in the psychology of instinct, Freud unquestionably belongs with those writers of the nineteenth century who, be it as historians, critics, philosophers or archaeologians, stand opposed to rationalism, intellectualism, classicism—in a word, to the belief in mind held by the eighteenth and somewhat also by the nineteenth century; emphasizing instead the night side of nature and the soul as the actually life-conditioning and life-giving element; cherishing it, scientifically advancing it, representing in the most revolution-

ary sense the divinity of earth, the primacy of the unconscious, the pre-mental, the will, the passions, or, as Nietzsche says, the 'feeling' above the 'reason.'

Mann educes a long list of German irrationalists, but the significant names are of course Arthur Schopenhauer and Friedrich Nietzsche, two writers Freud made a point of not reading in his formative years because of his recognition of the similarity of their ideas to his. Freud's equal indebtedness to eighteenth-century rationalism and nineteenth-century romanticism is only superficially a paradox. Both are oversimplifications: in another sense Rousseau is a thoroughgoing romantic, and some of Mann's list of chthonic and daemonic spirits, like Bachofen, are as rationalist as they come. As Heinz Hartmann points out in "Rational and Irrational Action" in the first volume of *Psychoanalysis and the Social Sciences,* psychoanalysis necessarily integrates rationalism and irrationalism. By 1880, while Freud was still a physiologist, all the ideas he needed were ready and waiting for him.

DARWIN

If true, it was nothing to be proud of, but rather a humiliating discovery, and the less said about it the better.

THOMAS CARLYLE, *in a letter*

CHARLES ROBERT DARWIN was born on February 12, 1809, in Shrewsbury, England, to Dr. Robert Waring Darwin and his wife Susannah Wedgwood. Robert Darwin was a giant of a man weighing over 300 pounds; he was of tremendous forcefulness and a considerable tyrant. After his death his son recalled: "I think my father was a little unjust to me when I was young, but afterwards I am thankful to think I became a prime favourite with him." Darwin's mother, a sweet and gentle invalid who raised pigeons as a hobby, died in 1817, when Charles was eight. "It is odd," he wrote in his *Autobiography*, "that I can remember hardly anything about her except her death-bed, her black velvet gown, and her curiously constructed work-table." In his boyhood, perhaps after this event, he developed a slight stammer and a difficulty with "r" which remained with him all his life. After his mother's death Charles attended a day school in Shrewsbury, where he was an indifferent scholar. In 1825, at the age of sixteen, he was sent to Edinburgh University, where his older brother Erasmus was, to study medicine. When that did not take, his father transferred him in 1828 to Christ's College, Cambridge, as a student of divinity. Darwin remained there for three years, showing little interest in any academic subject, although his boyhood interest in natural history developed at Cambridge into a passion for collecting. In 1831 Darwin passed the examination for the B.A. degree, without honours, and in August he went on a geologic tour of North Wales with his geology professor, Adam Sedgwick.

In the autumn of 1831 Darwin was invited by Captain Robert FitzRoy to sail as naturalist on *H. M. S. Beagle* in a three-year voyage around the globe, and when his father's objections were overcome by his uncle, Josiah Wedgwood, Darwin sailed just after Christmas. The voyage lasted for five years, and Darwin collected an enormous number of specimens and educated himself in half-a-dozen sciences. Darwin's mysterious illness, which was to dominate the rest of his life, first made its appearance on the *Beagle* voyage in 1834, when he was incapacitated for two weeks in Chile with weakness and nausea (Dr. Darwin proved unable to diagnose the ailment when his son told him the symptoms on his return). Darwin's formal scientific career began during the voyage, when geologic letters and papers he sent home were read by his former teachers to scientific societies. When Darwin returned in 1836 he moved to Cambridge and began work on his Journal of the voyage, his specimens, and his geological observations. Early in 1837 he took lodgings in London, to be near the British Museum, and that summer he began to keep a notebook on the problem of the origin of species. He began to suffer from palpitations of the heart, and his doctors strongly urged him to discontinue all work. Darwin continued to work on the Journal, to produce papers in geology, and to organize his zoological material and edit the accounts of it by zoologists that were published in five volumes from 1839 to 1843. In May of 1838 his health was worse, and he took a summer holiday in Scotland in an effort to recover.

Early in 1839 Darwin was married to his first cousin, Emma Wedgwood, Josiah's daughter, and they settled in a house in London. Their first child, William, was born late that year. Emma, who wrote to her own daughter on a honeymoon many years later that "nothing marries one so completely as sickness," immediately began to tend her husband's health and to mother him.[1] Darwin's health got worse and worse, producing periods when work was impossible, and making any kind of social life extremely difficult. The excitement of going out or having company had to be paid for with insomnia, vomiting, and tremors that night and the next day. In 1842, for reasons of Charles' health, the Darwins retired to the country, buying Down House in the village of Downe in Kent. The rest of Darwin's life is externally uneventful. He wrote up his geological material from the Beagle voyage in three books, then spent the eight years from 1846 to 1854 classifying barnacles, then turned to his mother's hobby of pigeon-breeding, then for the remainder of his life experimented with plants and earthworms. He continued to accumulate material on the problem of the origin of species and related problems, and wrote draft essays on the subject in 1842 and 1844.

In addition to his scientific work, Darwin filled his days walking on the Down grounds, playing with the children (five sons and two daughters survived, of ten), reading, building up his small inherited fortune by shrewd investments, and keeping up a formidable correspondence. He did not attend scientific meetings, rarely came to London, and saw only relatives and a few intimates. After 1842, the year of his moving to Down, Darwin rarely spent a night without severe stomach trouble or a day without periods of prostration.[2] When his

[1] Gwen Raverat, Darwin's granddaughter, recalls in *Period Piece:* "In my grandparents' house it was a distinction and a mournful pleasure to be ill . . . At Down, ill health was considered normal." She was born after her grandfather's death, but recalls her grandmother's "dangerous" interest in illness, the "sympathetic gloating" with which she would say "And have you got a *bad* sore throat, my poor cat?" and the horror and shame with which it filled her as a child.
[2] The cause of Darwin's ill health has been extensively discussed. The only work devoted exclusively to the subject, W. W. Johnston's *The Ill-Health of Charles Darwin: its Nature and its Relation to his Work,* was published in 1901. Johnson concludes, in the vocabulary of the time, that Darwin suffered from "chronic neurasthenia of a severe grade due first to the overstrain of the *Beagle* voyage and second to the life of hard intellectual work begun in 1837 and continued until 1882." Edward J. Kempf's *Psychopathology,* published in 1920, devotes a section to the Darwin case. It diagnoses Darwin's illness as anxiety neurosis, caused by repressed Oedipal hostility to his father and attachment to his mother sublimated into natural history study. Dr. Douglas Hubble, in an article in the *Lancet* in 1943, finds the illness a neurotic reaction to a tyrannical father, encouraged by his wife's neurotic devotion to illness; in summary, "the perfect

father died, in 1849, Darwin was too sick to go to the funeral, and from then on he reduced his working hours to two and a half a day, although he worked seven days a week. Occasionally he went somewhere for a water cure. After the publication of *The Origin of Species* in 1859, Darwin was a famous man, but the pattern of his withdrawn life remained unaltered. From 1860 to 1872 he spent a good deal of time revising the *Origin* for new editions, for the most part weakening it to accommodate to criticism and objections. (Some of the concealed contradictions in the later editions have been studied by Loren Eiseley in *Darwin's Century*). From 1862 on he worked mostly at botany, helped by gardeners and by his sons. In 1863 Darwin's health became markedly worse, and he gave up the burden of shaving and grew his famous beard. In April of 1864 he was recovered enough to work again, until he was prostrated again for most of 1865.

In the course of his life Darwin lost most or all of his Church of England faith. In the *Autobiographical Sketch* he wrote in 1876, not published until after his death, Darwin describes his views as having gradually moved from theism to agnosticism after the publication of the *Origin*, and in the years after 1876 he seems to have progressed to atheism but kept quiet about it, largely to spare his wife's sensibilities. Darwin almost never engaged in scientific controversy or polemic, for temperamental and other reasons, but in his old age in 1880 he wrote at least one letter to *Nature* against a particularly obtuse critic. In 1881 he wrote to Wallace: "I have everything to make me happy and contented, but life has become very wearisome to me." After a series of heart attacks in 1882, he had a severe attack during the night of April 18. "I am not the least afraid to die," he said when he recovered consciousness. The next afternoon he died, at the age of seventy-three. He was buried in Westminster Abbey, a few feet from the grave of Sir Isaac Newton.

---

nurse had married the perfect patient." W. C. Alvarez, in *Nervousness, Indigestion, and Pain*, also published in 1943, argues a hereditary constitutional factor. Since then other Freudian interpretations have been published by Dr. Rankin Good in the *Lancet* in 1954, and Ernest Jones in *Free Associations* in 1959, the latter proposing the theory of natural selection as a symbolic parricide and the lifelong neurosis as its guilty consequence.

The Whole Round World

T H E *Journal of Researches into the Natural History and Geology of the countries visited during the Voyage of H. M. S. Beagle round the world, under the command of Capt. Fitz Roy, R. N.,* hereinafter called the *Journal of Researches,* was Darwin's first book, and always remained his favorite. It was originally published in 1839 as the third of three volumes on the voyage; expanded and reissued independently in 1845, it had an immediate popular success, which has continued to this day. I would imagine that far more people have read it than have read *The Origin of Species.* The book has a great deal of charm, but, to this reader at least, no controlling metaphor or imaginative design. Darwin preferred it to his other books as the most personal of his works, and because the *Beagle* experience was the fulcrum of his life, transforming him from an aimless youth into a committed scientist. Darwin's grand-daughter, Lady Nora Barlow, writes of the experience in *Charles Darwin and the Voyage of the Beagle* as a "conversion," and William Irvine remarks in *Apes, Angels, and Victorians:* "The long voyage of the *Beagle* was his creative period—the withdrawal of the prophet to his wilderness, of the scientist to his laboratory." We can see both the "before" and "after" vividly in the book, but the transformation itself is hardly visible in its pages.

The first thing a reader notices in the *Journal of Researches* is a preoccupation with the poetry of the landscape. The overriding impression is of natural beauty. St. Domingo "possesses a beauty totally unexpected"; around Rio de Janeiro there are "wonderful and beautiful, flowering parasites" and "the forest abounded with beautiful objects"; in Patagonia "it is truly wonderful and beautiful" to see a condor fly; seeing Tierra del Fuego from a boat involves "losing all the beauty of a succession of ridges"; the woods of Chiloe "are incomparably more beautiful" than similar woods, and its volcano is "this most beautiful mountain"; and so on endlessly. In a passage from the notebooks of the voyage that Darwin did not publish in the book (Lady Barlow has since published them as *Charles Darwin's Diary of the Voyage of H. M. S. "Beagle"*), he records his reaction to Brazil in 1832:

14

On the road the scenery was very beautiful, especially the distant view of Rio. As a Sultan in a Seraglio I am becoming quite hardened to beauty. It is wearisome to be in a fresh rapture at every turn of the road. And as I have said before, you must be that or nothing.

When the *Beagle* returned to Brazil in 1836, however, on its way home to England, Darwin was no longer a bored sultan. He writes in the final chapter of the *Journal of Researches:*

> In my last walk I stopped again and again to gaze on these beauties, and endeavoured to fix in my mind forever, an impression which at the time I knew sooner or later must fail. The form of the orange-tree, the cocoa-nut, the palm, the mango, the tree-fern, the banana, will remain clear and separate; but the thousand beauties which unite these into one perfect scene must fade away; yet they will leave, like a tale heard in childhood, a picture full of indistinct, but most beautiful figures.

Darwin was equally profuse in noting natural effects that could not be called beautiful, but accorded with other conventions of romantic landscape. "If the scenery was not beautiful," he writes, "it was remarkable and grand." A town "presents a melancholy, but very picturesque appearance," or "the scene by the dimmed light of the moon was most desolate." Scrambling over rocks at Tierra del Fuego, Darwin "was amply repaid by the grandeur of the scene." Cloud-enveloped mountains are "very sublime," "it was a sublime spectacle to watch the shades of night gradually obscuring the last and highest pinnacles," and so on. These effects call up their proper artistic associations: an old Indian rides "like a Mazeppa on the white horse"; the Andes are like "hearing in full orchestra a chorus of the Messiah"; a vision in Argentina is "a Salvator Rosa scene"; in a comment in the notebooks omitted from the book, after noting the grandeur of desolation in Tierra del Fuego, Darwin adds, "To have made the scene perfect, there ought to have been a group of Banditti." Few things in the book are unpleasantly ugly, and they tend to be creatures whose habits he deplores: a carrion hawk has "a disgusting appearance"; a snake is "hideous," and Darwin comments, "I do not think I ever saw any thing more ugly, excepting, perhaps, some of the vampire bats"; a buzzard is "this disgusting bird, with its bald scarlet head, formed to wallow in putridity." All this beauty, grandeur, picturesqueness, and sublimity has no point beyond communicating "delight" to the observer. Darwin's later doctrine of utilitarian beauty or functional form hardly exists in the *Journal.* He can appreciate the edibility of the tropical scenery: "However seldom the usefulness of an object can account for the pleasure of beholding it, in the case of these beautiful woods, the knowledge of their high productiveness no doubt enters largely into the feeling of admiration." For the most part, however, he finds the grandeur of

desolation just as attractive, although it too comes to surfeit him
at times, and he writes in Chile: "We rode all day over an uninterest-
ing country. I am tired of repeating the epithets barren and
sterile."

The justification for the landscape, in Kenneth Burke's terms, is
to furnish a proper scene for the dramatic action. Darwin was
quite aware of the theatrical parallel. He writes of Brazil: "The general
effect frequently recalled to my mind the gayest scenery of the Opera-
house or the great theatres." He describes the first primitives he saw,
the natives of Tierra del Fuego, thus: "The party altogether closely
resembled the devils which come on the stage in plays like *Der
Freischutz*." Of the Falkland Islands, Darwin comments, "The theatre
is worthy of the scenes acted on it." All the dramatic agons in the book
take place against appropriate backdrops. Amid the lush foliage and
jagged rocks of the Brazilian shore, a little soft fish, the Diodon,
destroys "the great and savage shark" by gnawing through its side. In
more placid coral reefs "the soft and gelatinous body of a polypus"
conquers "the great mechanical power of the waves of an ocean"; here
the struggle is like the slow oxidation of rust rather than the fast
oxidation of burning. In the book's final retrospect scene and act are
one:

> Among the scenes which are deeply impressed on my mind,
> none exceed in sublimity the primeval forests undefaced by the
> hand of man; whether those of Brazil, where the powers of Life
> are predominant, or those of Tierra del Fuego, where Death and
> Decay prevail.

Most of the actors in these dramas are animals, but Darwin humanizes and personifies them to a remarkable extent. Ants are "lion-
hearted little warriors" and their victims are "poor little creatures";
a black and vermilion toad, calling to his mind *Paradise Lost*, "is a fit
toad to preach in the ear of Eve"; the carrion vultures think "Ah!
when the Indians come we shall have a feast"; niata cattle have "the
most ludicrous self-confident air of defiance imaginable"; a tern in-
spires the whimsy, "Little imagination is required to fancy that so light
and delicate a body must be tenanted by some wandering fairy
spirit." Birds, if they do not eat carrion or turn into fairies, are the
lovable clowns of this world: the booby and the noddy are "of a
tame and stupid disposition," as their names suggest, the Argentine
partridge "appears a very silly bird," and, seeing the Chilean Turco,
"It really requires little imagination to believe that the bird is ashamed
of itself, and is aware of its most ridiculous figure." When Darwin
observes a Galapagos lizard burrowing, he cannot resist pulling its
tail. "At this it was greatly astonished, and soon shuffled up to see
what was the matter; and then stared me in the face, as much as to
say, 'What made you pull my tail?' " Darwin played down some of
these personifications for publication. Thus in the notebooks he
writes:

It is rather curious the manner in which the Vegetation *knows* how much rain to expect.

In the first edition of the book, this becomes:

It is curious to observe how the seeds of the grass seem to know, as if by an acquired instinct, what quantity of rain to expect.

In the second edition, it is:

It is curious to observe how the seeds of the grass and other plants seem to accommodate themselves, as if by an acquired habit, to the quantity of rain which falls on different parts of this coast.

A good deal of the *Journal of Researches* is devoted to Darwin's thoughts on the problems of man in society, where the scene-act ratio has none of the fitness of wild life in nature. Darwin is deeply disturbed by the massacres of the Indians in South America: "Who would believe in this age that such atrocities should be committed in a Christian civilised country?"; the South American states will have to learn "that a republic cannot succeed till it contains a certain body of men imbued with the principles of justice and honour."

What most disturbed Darwin on the voyage was the fact of slavery. At first plantation life tempted him. He writes of Brazil: "As long as the idea of slavery could be banished, there was something exceedingly fascinating in this simple and patriarchal style of living; it was such a perfect retirement and independence from the rest of the world." But the idea of slavery cannot be banished, nor can "those atrocious acts which can only take place in a slave country." It is "a degradation lower than the slavery of the most helpless animal"; Brazil is "a land also of slavery, and therefore of moral debasement." At the end of the *Journal of Researches*, Darwin sums up his experience of slavery with some fervor:

I thank God, I shall never again visit a slave-country. To this day, if I hear a distant scream, it recalls with painful vividness my feelings, when passing a house near Pernambuco, I heard the most pitiable moans, and could not but suspect that some poor slave was being tortured, yet knew that I was as powerless as a child even to remonstrate. I suspected that these moans were from a tortured slave, for I was told that this was the case in another instance. Near Rio de Janeiro I lived opposite to an old lady, who kept screws to crush the fingers of her female slaves. I have staid in a house where a young household mulatto, daily and hourly, was reviled, beaten, and persecuted enough to break the spirit of the lowest animal. I have seen a little boy, six or seven years old, struck thrice with a horsewhip (before I could interfere) on his naked head, for having handed me a glass of water not quite clean; I saw his father tremble at a mere glance from his master's eye. These latter cruelties were witnessed by me in a Span-

ish colony, in which it has always been said, that slaves are better
treated than by the Portuguese, English, or other European
nations. I have seen at Rio Janeiro a powerful negro afraid to ward
off a blow directed, as he thought, at his face. I was present
when a kind-hearted man was on the point of separating for ever
the men, women, and little children of a large number of families
who had long lived together. I will not even allude to the many
heart-sickening atrocities which I authentically heard of;—nor
would I have mentioned the above revolting details, had I not
met with several people, so blinded by the constitutional gaiety
of the negro, as to speak of slavery as a tolerable evil.

In Brazil, Darwin was told of an old woman who escaped from
slavery and jumped off a mountain rather than be recaptured. He
comments dryly: "In a Roman matron this would have been called
the noble love of freedom; in a poor negress it is mere brutal ob-
stinacy."
    Darwin's reactions to the primitive peoples he calls "savages"
show less awareness that he and they are members one of another. At
his first sight of a party of Fuegians: "It was without exception the
most curious and interesting spectacle I ever beheld: I could not have
believed how wide was the difference between savage and civilized
man: it is greater than between a wild and domesticated animal." They
are like "very young children," unable to comprehend the simplest
alternative. He writes:

> These poor wretches were stunted in their growth, their hideous
> faces bedaubed with white paint, their skins filthy and greasy;
> their hair entangled, their voices discordant, and their gestures
> violent. Viewing such men, one can hardly make oneself be-
> lieve that they are fellow-creatures, and inhabitants of the same
> world. It is a common subject of conjecture what pleasure in
> life some of the lower animals can enjoy: how much more rea-
> sonably the same question may be asked with respect to these
> barbarians!

Eventually he concludes: "There is no reason to believe that the
Fuegians decrease in number; therefore we must suppose that they enjoy a sufficent share of happiness, of whatever kind it may be, to
render life worth having." By the time he gets to Australia in 1836
he has more sense of cultural relativism; the aboriginals there "appeared far from being such utterly degraded beings as they have
usually been represented," and "In their own arts they are admira-
ble," with examples. His conclusion to the book is that "nothing
is more certain to create astonishment than the first sight in his native
haunt of a barbarian,—of man in his lowest and most savage state."
    Theodore Baird, in "Darwin and the Tangled Bank" in *The
American Scholar*, Autumn 1946, has called Darwin's description of
the Fuegians "pages comparable to Swift on the Yahoo." What

lacerates Swift is that his fellow men *are* Yahoos, but Darwin feels only remoteness. His great imaginative discovery, that these are men like himself, adapted to their environment like Galapagos tortoises or Andean plants, is reserved for the future. "Nature by making habit omnipotent, and its effects hereditary," Darwin concludes, "has fitted the Fuegian to the climate and the productions of his miserable country," but there is no sense that it could have done the same to Darwins and Wedgwoods.

The natural superiority of England is on Darwin's mind all through the *Journal of Researches.* He thinks: "How different would have been the aspect of this river if English colonists had by good fortune first sailed up the Plata! What noble towns would now have occupied its shores!" Tahitian pineapples are "perhaps even better than those cultivated in England; and this I believe is the highest compliment which can be paid to any fruit." Darwin's principal impression of New Zealand is one of familiarity: "It was quite pleasing to behold the English flowers in the gardens before the houses"; elsewhere he saw "every fruit and vegetable which England produces" and farm animals "lying comfortably together, as in every English farm-yard"; even the weeds and rats "I was forced to own as countrymen." His first reaction to Australia was "to congratulate myself that I was born an Englishman," although he later soured somewhat. Darwin concludes in the book's Retrospect: "It is impossible for an Englishman to behold these distant colonies, without a high pride and satisfaction. To hoist the British flag, seems to draw with it as a certain consequence, wealth, prosperity, and civilisation."

In most respects the Darwin of the *Beagle* voyage was a credit to his Whig family tradition. The Chilean miners, for example, "are unthrifty in their habits, and consequently poor"; whereas English miners "from being obliged to think and act for themselves, are a singularly intelligent and well-conducted set of men." Darwin's only uneasiness in the *Journal of Researches* about English institutions appears to be the fact of poverty, and here he suggests as an alternative to guilt the future social Darwinism of Herbert Spencer and some of his own later followers:

> It is often attempted to palliate slavery by comparing the state of slaves with our poorer countrymen: if the misery of our poor be caused not by the laws of nature, but by our institutions, great is our sin; but how this bears on slavery, I cannot see; as well might the use of the thumb-screw be defended in one land, by showing that men in another land suffered from some dreadful disease.

England at least freed its slaves, so that "it is a consolation to reflect, that we at least have made a greater sacrifice, than ever made by any nation, to expiate our sin."

Almost all of Darwin's later scientific ideas are stated or implicit in the *Journal of Researches.* Most of the ingredients of the theory

of evolution by natural selection are here in embryo. The problem of
species is a constant preoccupation. His reaction to Patagonian fossils in 1834 is: "This wonderful relationship in the same continent between the dead and the living, will, I do not doubt, hereafter throw
more light on the appearance of organic beings on our earth, and their
disappearance from it, than any other class of facts." The three
pages following these observations, put in after Darwin returned to
England and read Malthus in 1838, are a brilliant little essay on the
extinction of species by natural selection, some of which was lifted
bodily into the *Origin*. He notes that an argument of Lyell's is
"founded on the assumption of the immutability of species," and that
one might assume "otherwise." At the Galapagos Archipelago, he
comments: "Here, both in space and time, we seem to be brought
somewhat near to that great fact—that mystery of mysteries—the
first appearance of new beings on this earth." Of the Galapagos
birds, he remarks: "Seeing this gradation and diversity of structure in
one small, intimately related group of birds, one might really fancy
that from an original paucity of birds in this archipelago, one species
had been taken and modified for different ends."

It seems fairly certain that from 1834, if not earlier, Darwin was
convinced by such evidence on the *Beagle* voyage as the Patagonian
fossils and the Galapagos birds of the mutability of species. (Darwin's
statement in his *Autobiography* that he began compiling notes for the
Origin in 1837 and "worked on true Baconian principles, and without any theory collected facts on a wholesale scale," apparently
means without any theory of the *method* of evolution, not the *fact*
of evolution.) He is equally aware in the *Journal of Researches* of the
principle of variation, writing in connection with a proto-rattlesnake,
that "every character, even though it may be in some degree independent of structure, has a tendency to vary by slow degrees."
Darwin also notes many instances of ecological adaptation. "Thus we
have a little living world within itself," he writes, "adapted to these
inland lakes of brine." The giraffe's neck is "one of those beautiful
provisions of nature." A crab that lives on coconuts "is as curious a
case of instinct as ever I heard of, and likewise of adaptation in
structure between two objects apparently so remote from each other
in the scheme of nature, as a crab and a cocoanut tree." All of this
needs only the realization that variations are inherited, and that in
conditions of competition the fitter would prevail, to be the evolution of species by natural selection. At least once in the *Journal of
Researches* Darwin comes very close to making the connection: he
realizes that the niata cattle, from the form of their lips, would be
exterminated in a drought before other cattle, and concludes "This
strikes me as a good illustration of how little we are able to judge from
the ordinary habits of life, on what circumstances, occurring only at
long intervals, the rarity or extinction of a species may be determined."

Although early in the voyage Darwin seems to have been convinced that species evolve by natural law, he used the vocabulary of "creation," perhaps with a trace of irony. Thus there is "a grand scheme . . . on which organized beings have been created"; but of an insignificant species, "one is apt to wonder why they were created"; and observing the Galapagos, "one is astonished at the amount of creative force, if such an expression may be used." The last sentence of the book, advice to a hypothetical naturalist interested in voyaging, begins, "Travelling ought also to teach him distrust."

D A R W I N spent the two decades after the *Beagle* voyage trying one scientific field after another. His first task, from 1839 to 1843, was editing the five-volume *Zoology of the Voyage of the Beagle*, by five scientific specialists. Darwin wrote some material on the habits and range of the various species, but otherwise had little opportunity for his own views. He was not a qualified professional scientist in any field, and in the opinion of his son, Sir Francis Darwin, never became one. Sir Francis wrote in *The Life and Letters of Charles Darwin* in 1887:

> In reading his books one is reminded of the older naturalists rather than of the modern school of writers. He was a Naturalist in the old sense of the word, that is, a man who works at many branches of the science, not merely a specialist in one.

What first seemed to emerge as Darwin's specialty was geology, which Nora Barlow calls "his first love among the sciences." Darwin published three books on the subject between 1842 and 1846. Unlike the *Journal of Researches*, each is shaped by an imaginative design, built around a great metaphor.

The first is *The Structure and Distribution of Coral Reefs*, published in 1842, and its vision is the key one of natural selection, that given an enormous duration of time and changed conditions (here subsidence), microcosm becomes macrocosm and life overcomes death. As soon as he got back to England from the voyage, urged on by the geologist Sir Charles Lyell, Darwin read a paper on coral reefs to the Geological Society. He then withdrew it from the society's journal to turn it into the book, although a three-page abstract of the paper was published in the Proceedings in 1837. The book was entirely a matter of assembling evidence in as convincing a fashion as possible. Darwin confesses in his *Autobiography:* "No other work of mine was begun in so deductive a spirit as this, for the whole theory was thought out on the west coast of South America, before I had seen a true coral reef. I had therefore only to verify and extend my views by a careful examination of living reefs."

The title is in a sense misleading. The book is not primarily about structure and distribution, but about *origins*. It begins: "The object of this volume is to describe from my own observation and the works of others, the principal kinds of coral-reefs, and to explain the origin of their peculiar forms." In his re-evaluation "Darwin and Coral Reefs," published in *A Century of Darwin*, edited by S. A. Barnett in 1958, C. M. Yonge writes: "There is some similarity in the broad simplicity of ultimate statement between the subsidence theory of the origin of barrier reefs and atolls and the theory of evolution that appeared seventeen years later. Both represent the bringing together of evidence from many sources and reveal a mind capable of seizing upon the crucial aspects of highly complicated problems and an imagination that ranged freely through both space and time."

In our terms, both are the same poetic vision of struggle, adaptation, and triumph. Struggle is basic. Darwin writes in *Coral Reefs* of "the almost universal law of 'consume and be consumed.'" He tries to show "how severe a struggle is in progress on these low coral-formations between the two nicely balanced powers of land and water," as well as "a struggle for each station between different organisms." The corals "hold their places, like other organic beings, by a struggle one with another and with external nature"; it is "a prolonged struggle against unfavourable conditions." The coral community (rather than the individual coral animals) metaphorically aspires to rise up. When the area subsides, the community dies. Then new coral rises on the skeletons, "like monuments, marking the place of their burial," until a great island, atoll, or reef is formed. "Thus may the history of an atoll be followed from its birth, through the occasional accidents of its existence, to its death and final obliteration." But it is an agon of Bios against Thanatos, and the life force is ultimately triumphant: "the vital energies of the corals conquer the mechanical power of the waves," and the community triumphs.

The next books, *Geological Observations on the Volcanic Islands*, published in 1844, and *Geological Observations on South America*, published in 1846, were logically republished together as *Geological Observations* in 1876. Their common imaginative vision is of emergence, of new birth. Where coral islands arise by triumphing over subsidence, volcanic islands are rising, and the key to South American geology is continental elevation, the mountains all new-born and raw, islands on the land. Years later, in 1853, Darwin wrote to Lyell: "I remember in old days (I may mention the subject as we are on it) often wishing I could get you to look at continental elevations as *the* phenomenon, and volcanic outbursts and tilting up of mountain chains as connected, but quite secondary, phenomena. I became deeply impressed with the truth of this view in S. America." The world of these books is a Heraclitean world in which *panta rhei*, everything flows. The fluidity of lavas is seen in the imagery of water: some "are so rugged, that they may be compared to a sea frozen during a storm," others are "almost as smooth as a lake when ruffled by a breeze." The concern is as aetiological as in the work on coral, "to make out the cause," but now genetic exploration is reinforced by genetic imagery. Where the metaphor for the coral is of a sacrificial dying, here it is a coming to birth, with the landscape as a great maternal body. The volcanoes are like teeming wombs, "orifices of eruption." The land of South America thrown up by the sea contains shell named *labiata, vagina, venus;* everything is fertile and genital. What was a mild tendency in the earlier books for geologic shapes to strike Darwin as mammary ("mammillated projections" of coral, etc.) is here obsessive: "pap-formed hills," "mammiform hillocks," "paps of rock" abound. It is all a great natural genesis, the earth bringing to birth and nourishing.

Darwin's next work is in the field of systematics, his only publication too technical for the layman, and not to our purposes here. It consists of four monographs on the sub-class Cirripedes, published in 1851 and 1854. Darwin worked on his tiny barnacles for eight years, alternately delighting in and cursing their miniscule complexity. He explains the history of the study in the preface to the first volume:

> I had originally intended to have described only a single abnormal Cirripede, from the shores of South America, and was led, for the sake of comparison, to examine the internal parts of as many genera as I could procure. Under these circumstances, Mr. J. E. Gray, in the most disinterested manner, suggested to me making a Monograph on the entire class, although he himself had already collected materials for this same object.

In his *Autobiography*, Darwin gives more detail:

> In October, 1846, I began to work on 'Cirripedia.' When on the coast of Chile, I found a most curious form, which burrowed into the shells of Concholepas, and which differed so much from all other Cirripedes that I had to form a new suborder for its sole reception. Lately an allied burrowing genus has been found on the shores of Portugal. To understand the structure of my new Cirripede I had to examine and dissect many of the common forms; and this gradually led me on to take up the whole group. I worked steadily on this subject for the next eight years, and ultimately published two thick volumes, describing all the known living species, and two thin quartos on the extinct species. I do not doubt that Sir E. Lytton Bulwer had me in his mind when he introduced in one of his novels a Professor Long, who had written two huge volumes on limpets.

He concludes:

> My work on the Cirripedia possesses, I think, considerable value, as besides describing several new and remarkable forms, I made out the homologies of the various parts—I discovered the cementing apparatus, though I blundered dreadfully about the cement glands—and lastly I proved the existence in certain

genera of minute males complemental to and parasitic on the hermaphrodites. This latter discovery has at last been fully confirmed; though at one time a German writer was pleased to attribute the whole account to my fertile imagination. The Cirripedes form a highly varying and difficult group of species to class; and my work was of considerable use to me, when I had to discuss in the 'Origin of Species' the principles of a natural classification. Nevertheless, I doubt whether the work was worth the consumption of so much time.

In the course of the work Darwin got terribly bored. In a letter to Richard Owen in 1848 they were "my beloved barnacles," but by 1852 he was writing to W. D. Fox: "I am at work at the second volume of the Cirripedia, of which creatures I am wonderfully tired. I hate a Barnacle as no man ever did before, not even a sailor in a slow-sailing ship." At another time he observed in a letter that his split interests made him ambivalent: "I had thought the same parts of the same species more resemble (than they do anyhow in Cirripedia) objects cast in the same mould. Systematic work would be easy were it not for this confounded variation, which, however, is pleasant to me as a speculatist, though odious to me as a systematist."

It was the opinion of Thomas Henry Huxley and Sir Joseph Hooker, however, that the work on Cirripedia made Darwin a scientist. Hooker, who had had great influence in persuading Darwin to continue the study, wrote to Francis Darwin after his father's death: "Your father recognized three stages in his career as a biologist: the mere collector at Cambridge; the collector and observer in the *Beagle*, and for some years afterwards; and the trained naturalist after, and only after the Cirripede work." Huxley, who in his obituary notice for the Royal Society called the *Beagle* science "a vast accumulation of useless manuscript," described the Cirripedes as "a piece of critical self-discipline," and concluded: "In my opinion your sagacious father never did a wiser thing than when he devoted himself to the years of patient toil which the Cirripede-book cost him." In the opinion of G. J. Romanes, in his memorial notice of Darwin as a zoologist in *Nature*, the Cirripede work showed "that had Mr. Darwin chosen to devote himself to a life of purely morphological work, his name would probably have been second to none in that department of biology."

One of the fascinations of the Cirripedes was their remarkable forms of sexuality, a Freudian fantasy-world under the microscope. Darwin writes to Lyell in 1849:

> I work now every day at the Cirripedia for 2½ hours, and so get on a little, but very slowly. I sometimes, after being a whole week employed and having described perhaps only two species, agree mentally with Lord Stanhope, that it is all fiddle faddle; however, the other day I got a curious case of a unisexual, instead of a hermaphrodite cirripede, in which the female had the com-

mon cirripedial character, and in two valves of her shell had two little pockets, in *each* of which she kept a little husband; I do not know of any other case where a female invariably has two husbands. I have one still odder fact, common to several species, namely, that though they are hermaphrodite, they have small additional, or as I shall call them, complemental males, one specimen itself hermaphrodite had no less than *seven*, of these complemental males attached to it. Truly the schemes and wonders of Nature are illimitable.

The principal image of the Cirripedes that gets into the *Origin* is that in some genera "the male is a mere sack, which lives for a short time and is destitute of mouth, stomach, and every other organ of importance, excepting those for reproduction." After the monographs were published, Darwin wrote to Huxley in 1854 correcting himself on the cement glands: "I have been able rigorously to confirm in an anomalous species, by the clearest evidence, that the actual cellular contents of the ovarian tubes, by the glandlike action of a modified portion of the continuous tube, passes into the cementing stuff: in fact cirripedes make glue out of their own unformed eggs!" One would have to go far to find a prettier image of sublimation.

The Origin of Species

THE *Origin of Species by Means of Natural Selection or the Preservation of Favoured Races in the Struggle for Life* appeared in 1859, and immediately caught the imagination of the world. The first edition sold out on the day of publication, and the second shortly after. Within a few years most of the thinking world was convinced of the evolution of species, as it had not been by Buffon, Lamarck, Darwin's grandfather Erasmus, Robert Chambers' *Vestiges of Creation*, or anyone else. It has rarely been doubted that this enormous effect was achieved by the power of scientific argument, that is, by the book's rhetorical organization. This was certainly Darwin's view. He begins the book's final chapter: "As this whole volume is one long argument." One of Darwin's latest biographers, Sir Arthur Keith, in *Darwin Revalued,* expresses the prevailing view: "In the *Origin* he had assembled such a solid mass of observation" that conviction followed inescapably.

There can be no doubt that the book's rhetorical effectiveness is great. Darwin states his theories simply and plausibly, bolsters them with a great deal of convincing evidence (beginning close to home with domestic animals) and scrupulously notes the difficulties and puzzles still unsolved. Yet a problem remains. The evidence to establish the idea of evolution by natural selection inductively was not really available in 1859, and many of Darwin's processes turn out on closer examination to be plausible hypotheses, and his causes tautologies. Nor does the vehemence of the reaction pro and con suggest the characteristic effect of a scientific demonstration.

I would submit that *The Origin of Species* caught the imagination of its time as a dramatic poem, and a dramatic poem of a very special sort. This view would certainly have surprised Darwin. He was under no illusions about his literary powers, and although he worked quite hard at the writing and rewriting of this book, he saw its prose as "incredibly bad." His effort was to produce the straightest possible piece of factual writing, and he was only dissuaded by the publisher, John Murray, from calling the book *An Abstract of an Essay on the Origin of Species.* It is the judgment of a popular text-

26

book that Darwin's work "cannot be said to belong to literature, if in the definition of literary work is presupposed an effort toward artistic expression."

Theodore Baird, whose "Darwin and the Tangled Bank" is one of the few published efforts to correct this conventional estimate, boldly claims that the *Origin* is not only a work of literature, but "the complicated literary expression known as tragedy." It is here that any literary consideration should begin. The *Origin* is much less overtly dramatistic than the *Journal of Researches*, with the act-scene fitnesses of the earlier book here confined mostly to the great historical pageant of palaeontology, as when Darwin notes that the geological strata mark "only an occasional scene, taken almost at hazard, in an ever slowly changing drama."

The key term in the *Origin* is "the struggle for existence." Darwin explains:

> In looking at Nature, it is most necessary to keep the foregoing considerations always in mind—never to forget that every single organic being may be said to be striving to the utmost to increase in numbers; that each lives by a struggle at some period of its life; that heavy destruction inevitably falls either on the young or old, during each generation or at recurrent intervals.

All through the book, he refers to "a constant struggle going on," "the constantly-recurring Struggle for Existence," "victory in the battle for life," and so on. From this struggle comes "natural selection," or, in Herbert Spencer's more vivid phrase that Darwin adopted, "the survival of the fittest."

Darwin was quite aware that all these terms were metaphoric, a heightening of much less dramatic processes. He writes of "struggle for existence":

> I should premise that I use this term in a large and metaphorical sense including dependence of one being on another, including (which is more important) not only the life of the individual, but success in leaving progeny. Two canine animals, in a time of dearth, may be truly said to struggle with each other which shall get food and life. But a plant on the edge of a desert is said to struggle for life against the drought, though more properly it should be said to be dependent on the moisture. A plant which annually produces a thousand seeds, of which only one of an average comes to maturity, may be more truly said to struggle with the plants of the same and other kinds which already clothe the ground. The mistletoe is dependent on the apple and a few other trees, but can only in a far-fetched sense be said to struggle with these trees, for, if too many of these parasites grow on the same tree, it languishes and dies. But several seedling mistletoes, growing close together on the same branch, may more truly be said to struggle with each other. As the mistletoe is disseminated by birds, its existence depends on them; and it may methodically

be said to struggle with other fruit-bearing plants, in tempting
the birds to devour and thus disseminate its seeds. In these several
senses, which pass into each other, I use for convenience' sake the
general term of Struggle for Existence.

In the third edition, in 1861, he writes similarly of "natural selection":

In the literal sense of the word, no doubt, natural selection is a
false term; but who ever objected to chemists speaking of the
elective affinities of the various elements?—and yet an acid cannot strictly be said to elect the base with which it in preference
combines. It has been said that I speak of natural selection as an
active power or Deity; but who objects to an author speaking of
the attraction of gravity as ruling the movements of the planets?
Every one knows what is meant and is implied by such metaphorical expressions; and they are almost necessary for brevity.

In fact, these terms are much more than metaphors. They people
the world of nature with protagonists and antagonists where previously we had seen only a solitary cactus or a growing seed. Moreover,
the dramatic action they summon up is tragic. In Gilbert Murray's
terms, the basic ritual stages of tragedy are *agon* or contest, *sparagmos*
or tearing apart, then *anagnorisis* or discovery and *epiphany* or joyous
showing-forth of the resurrected protagonist. Darwin's struggle for
existence is clearly Murray's *agon* and *sparagmos*, and his natural
selection or survival of the fittest, *anagnorisis* and *epiphany*. For the
final exultation that the Greeks felt at the affirmation of Reliving
Dionysus, Darwin substitutes a quieter tragic satisfaction. He writes:

When we reflect on this struggle, we may console ourselves with
the full belief, that the war of nature is not incessant, that no fear
is felt, that death is generally prompt, and that the vigorous, the
healthy, and the happy survive and multiply.

The *Origin* concludes: "Thus, from the war of nature, from famine
and death, the most exalted object which we are capable of conceiving, namely, the production of the higher animals, directly follows.
There is grandeur in this view of life. . . ."

We realize that this dramatic and tragic vision of life comes from
Darwin, rather than from his subject matter, when we see how un-
dramatic most present-day formulations of natural selection are. A
typical one is that of George Gaylord Simpson in *The Meaning of
Evolution* in 1949: "In the modern theory natural selection is differential reproduction, plus the complex interplay in such reproduction
of heredity, genetic variation, and all the other factors that affect
selection and determine its results." Darwin was aware of differential
reproduction as early as his draft for the *Origin* in 1844, but always
within a larger context of struggle: a fleeter fox would survive better
and "rear more young," but "the less fleet ones would be rigidly
destroyed."

The archetypal image of the *Origin* is the war of nature, an image Darwin at first believed he had borrowed from Alphonse de Candolle. The 1842 outline for the book begins the section on "Natural Selection":

> De Candolle's war of nature.—seeing contented face of nature,—may be well at first doubted.

These notes are amplified in the 1844 essay into:

> De Candolle, in an eloquent passage, has declared that all nature is at war, one organism with another, or with external nature. Seeing the contented face of nature, this may at first be well doubted; but reflection will inevitably prove it is too true.

When Darwin had to choose a few pages from his manuscript to accompany Wallace's paper in the historic presentation of the new theory to the Linnean Society in 1858, he began with that passage, which he clearly recognized as the heart of his message. By the time the passage appeared in the *Origin* the next year, Darwin had recognized that De Candolle had no patent on the war of nature, and lumped him in with others. The important thing now was tearing off the pacific mask that life wears, and Darwin writes of the illusion concealing the tragic reality like a Melville narrator:

> We behold the face of nature bright with gladness, we often see superabundance of food; we do not see or we forget, that the birds which are idly singing round us mostly live on insects or seeds, and are thus constantly destroying life; or we forget how largely these songsters, or their eggs, or their nestlings, are destroyed by birds and beasts of prey; we do not always bear in mind, that, though food may be now superabundant, it is not so at all seasons of each recurring year.

The flatness at the end is almost deliberate; Darwin's vision is tragic, but it is not hysterical. It never rises in pitch to melodrama, as in the "Nature, red in tooth and claw" of Tennyson's "In Memoriam," or the Grand Guignol vision of some of Darwin's followers. After millions of years of evolution, Romanes writes typically in 1892,

> We find that more than half of the species which have survived the ceaseless struggle are parasitic in their habits, lower and insentient forms of life feasting on higher and sentient forms; we find teeth and talons whetted for slaughter, hooks and suckers moulded for torment—everywhere a reign of terror, hunger, and sickness, with oozing blood and quivering limbs, with gasping breath and eyes of innocence that dimly close in deaths of brutal torture!

Darwin is aware of the tragic ambivalence of life and death, that for five thousand years "pigeons have been watched and tended with the utmost care, and loved by many people," and for just as long have been as considerately raised and tended for the pot. In the *Journal of*

Researches, Darwin was moved to horror and revulsion by the fact
that the natives of Tierra del Fuego, in times of hunger, kill and eat
the old women of the tribe sooner than their dogs, because "Doggies
catch otters, old women no." By the time of the *Origin,* this is accepted with calm objectivity:

> We see the value set on animals even by the barbarians of Tierra
> del Fuego, by their killing and devouring their old women, in
> times of dearth, as of less value than their dogs.

When the *Origin* appeared, it was reviewed in the *American
Journal of Science and Arts* by Asa Gray, perhaps the shrewdest (as
Huxley was the most brilliant) of the Darwinians. Gray notes that
Darwin's frankness about objections and unsolved problems gives the
book the character of a mythic quest. He writes: "The interest for the
general reader heightens as the author advances on his perilous way
and grapples manfully with the most formidable difficulties." In the
Origin, Darwin tends to make the imperilled knight not himself but
his theory: a difficulty would be "fatal to the whole theory," an argument is "a fatal objection," "Such objections as the above would be
fatal to my views," and so on endlessly. But Darwin's imagery in correspondence makes it clear that the life at stake is Darwin's own.
Sending an advance copy of the book to Hugh Falconer in 1859, he
writes: "Lord, how savage you will be if you read it, and how you will
long to crucify me alive!" He writes to H. G. Bronn in 1860: "The
objections and difficulties which may be urged against my view are
indeed heavy enough almost to break my back, but it is not yet
broken!" When Lyell refused to come out in support of the theory
publicly, Darwin wrote to him: "You cut my throat, and your own
throat; and I believe will live to be sorry for it." In later years Darwin's correspondence is full of "It is clear to me that I ought to be
exterminated," "I know well that I deserve many a good slap on the
face," "If I am wrong, the sooner I am knocked on the head and an-
nihilated so much the better." He seems to have seen himself as the
scapegoat, the sacrificial victim, sometimes the Judaeo-Christian
blameless victim without blemish, but sometimes the guilty pagan
slayer who must himself be slain. When the theory of evolution first
took publishable form, in 1844, Darwin wrote to Hooker "I am almost convinced (quite contrary to the opinion that I started with)
that species are not (it is like confessing a murder) immutable." In
1856 he signed a letter to Hooker "your insane and perverse friend,"
and wrote to Gray, "I know that this will make you despise me."

If Darwin's tragic vision embraces bloodshed and murder, it also
embraces beauty and joy. The *Origin* is as full of the word "beauty"
as the *Journal of Researches,* but now it is a utilitarian beauty. Sometimes it is a "beautiful adaptation" to function, like that of the woodpecker, the mistletoe, or the giraffe; sometimes it has a visual loveliness
too, as in "the beautifully plumed seed of the dandelion"; sometimes it is an abstraction, like the power engaged "in slowly and

beautifully adapting each form to the most complex relations of life";
sometimes it is pure exultant generalization, "There is so much beauty
throughout nature." The last sentence of the book, beginning "There
is grandeur in this view of life," concludes "from so simple a beginning
endless forms most beautiful and most wonderful have been, and are
being evolved." The "wonderful" there is, of course, "wonderfully
adapted to survive." In 1863, Darwin wrote to Huxley: "With a book,
as with a fine day, one likes it to end with a glorious sunset."

The *Origin*, although it resolutely postpones consideration of
human origins for a later work, is oddly anthropocentric. One reason
is that Darwin constantly humanizes animals in what used to be called
the "pathetic fallacy": male alligators have courtship rites "like
Indians in a war dance"; frightened ants "took heart" and a single
ant stood "an image of despair over its ravaged home"; in the con-
solatory statement quoted above, the surviving animals are not only
vigorous and healthy, but "happy." Man is always on Darwin's mind
as he talks of the lower orders. The criteria for an "advance in organization" among the vertebrata are "the degree of intellect and an approach in structure to man." When the *Origin* announces the descent
of man, he is not named, simply lumped in: "According to this view it
may be inferred that all vertebrate animals with true lungs are descended by ordinary generation from an ancient and unknown prototype, which was furnished with a floating apparatus or swim bladder."
Later in the *Origin* Darwin concludes in more detail that the higher
vertebrates "are the modified descendants of some ancient progenitor,
which was furnished in its adult state with branchiae, a swim bladder,
four fin-like limbs, and a long tail, all fitted for an aquatic life." (More
explicitly, Darwin wrote to Lyell in 1860: "*Our* ancestor was an
animal which breathed water, had a swim bladder, a great swimming
tail, an imperfect skull, and undoubtedly was an hermaphrodite! Here
is a pleasant genealogy for mankind.")

The chief thematic metaphor in *The Origin of Species*, consti-
tuting the book's principal imaginative design, is a visual figure that
develops in richness and complexity as it goes through a series of metamorphoses. It begins as the ladderlike polity of life, a form of the
medieval Great Chain of Being (so exhaustively studied by A. O.
Lovejoy in his book of that title). Early in the book Darwin writes of
"places in the polity" of nature, "places which are either unoccupied
or not perfectly occupied by other beings," "a place in the natural
polity of the country," "new places in the polity of nature." Eventually this progresses from simple to complex, and becomes a vision of
"one long and branching chain of life," of which we know from the
past only a few links (the nonsense of the "Missing Link" apeman
seems to be based on this passage). As the book goes on, the figure
modifies from the chain, either simple or complex, to that of a living
tree, in a remarkable extended metaphor (earlier used in a letter to
Gray that was one of the documents presented to the Linnean
Society):

The affinities of all the beings of the same class have sometimes been represented by a great tree. I believe this simile largely
speaks the truth. The green and budding twigs may represent
existing species; and those produced during former years may
represent the long succession of extinct species. At each period
of growth all the growing twigs have tried to branch out on all
sides, and to overtop and kill the surrounding twigs and branches,
in the same manner as species and groups of species have at all
times overmastered other species in the great battle for life. The
limbs divided into great branches, and these into lesser and lesser
branches, were themselves once, when the tree was young, budding twigs, and this connection of the former and present buds
by ramifying branches may well represent the classification of all
extinct and living species in groups subordinate to groups. Of the
many twigs which flourished when the tree was a mere bush, only
two or three, now grown into great branches, yet survive and
bear the other branches; so with the species which lived during
long-past geological periods, very few have left living and modified descendants. From the first growth of the tree, many a limb
and branch has decayed and dropped off; and these fallen
branches of various sizes may represent those whole orders, families, and genera which have now no living representatives, and
which are known to us only in a fossil state. As we here and there
see a thin straggling branch springing from a fork low down in
a tree, and which by some chance has been favoured and is still
alive on its summit, so we occasionally see an animal like the
Ornithorhynchus or Lepidosiren, which in some small degree
connects by its affinities two large branches of life, and which has
apparently been saved from fatal competition by having inhabited
a protected station. As buds give rise by growth to fresh buds,
and these, if vigorous, branch out and overtop on all sides many a
feebler branch, so by generation I believe it has been with the
great Tree of Life, which fills with its dead and broken branches
the crust of the earth, and covers the surface with its ever-
branching and beautiful ramifications.

Darwin continues to use the tree figure, later referring to the variety
of species as being "like the branching of a great tree from a single
stem." Even this image, however, ultimately will not contain the
infinite richness of relationships in nature, which he describes as progressing "onwards in ever-increasing circles of complexity." The
book's final paragraph achieves the ultimate transformation. It begins:

It is interesting to contemplate a tangled bank, clothed with
many plants of many kinds, with birds singing on the bushes, with
various insects flitting about, and with worms crawling through
the damp earth, and to reflect that these elaborately constructed
forms, so different from each other, and dependent upon each

other in so complex a manner, have all been produced by laws acting around us.

With the image of the tangled bank, so reminiscent of Shakespearean lyric, Darwin embraces all the rich complexity of life. The image of the great Chain of Life is ordered, hierarchic, and static, essentially medieval; the great Tree of Life is ordered, hierarchic, but dynamic and competitive, a Renaissance vision; but the great Tangled Bank of Life is disordered, democratic, and subtly interdependent as well as competitive, essentially a modern vision.

The minor metaphors in the work fall into place within this great organizing metaphor. "Struggle for existence" and "survival of the fittest," noted above, are other ways of looking at the tangled bank. The metaphors are epiphanies or showings-forth. For the most part they image process in dramatic action, provide scenes "in an ever slowly changing drama": "as with mariners shipwrecked near a coast"; "to feel no surprise at sickness, but, when the sick man dies, to wonder and to suspect that he died by some deed of violence"; "when we no longer look at an organic being as a savage looks at a ship." A constant metaphor is language itself: "a breed, like a dialect of a language"; "It may be worth while to illustrate this view of classification, by taking the case of languages"; "Rudimentary organs may be compared with the letters in a word"; and so on. J. Arthur Thomson, in *Darwin and Modern Science*, praises Darwin's "clear visions" and they are all metaphors: "visions of the web of life, of the fountain of change within the organism, of the struggle for existence and of its winnowing, and of the spreading genealogical tree." Darwin says of morphology, defined in the *Origin's* Glossary as "The law of form or structure independent of function": "This is one of the most interesting departments of natural history, and may almost be said to be its very soul." Similarly, Aristotle says in the *Poetics* (in Bywater's translation): "But the greatest thing by far is to be a master of metaphor. It is the one thing that cannot be learnt from others; and it is also a sign of genius, since a good metaphor implies an intuitive perception of the similarity in dissimilars." By this criterion Darwin displayed genius as morphologist and metaphorist alike.

Perhaps the most surprising thing in *The Origin of Species*, to those who think of Darwin as the type of the prosaic scientist, is that it repeatedly calls not for an act of understanding but for an act of the imagination. Darwin writes: "It is good thus to try in imagination," "How strange are these facts!" "no one with the most vivid imagination would ever have thought," "no one can have marvelled more than I have done," "the fact is a marvellous one," "But these cases are so wonderful," "Glancing at instincts, marvellous as some are," "We see the full meaning of the wonderful fact," and so on. The call is not only for imagination, marvel, wonder, but for the sort of immersion in nature that led Emerson to say "Books are for the scholar's idle hours." Darwin writes:

It is hardly possible for me to recall to the reader who is not a practical geologist, the facts leading the mind to comprehend the lapse of time. . . . Not that it suffices to study the Principles of Geology, or to read special treatises by different observers on separate formations, and to mark how each author attempts to give an inadequate idea of the duration of each formation, or even of each stratum. We can best gain some idea of past time by knowing the agencies at work, and learning how deeply the surface of the land has been denuded, and how much sediment has been deposited. . . . Therefore a man should examine for himself the great piles of superimposed strata, and watch the rivulets bringing down mud, and the waves wearing away the sea-cliffs, in order to comprehend something about the duration of past time, the monuments of which we see all around us.

Perhaps not so far as it might seem from Proust's comparable venture in comprehending the duration of past time.

I T I S remarkable enough, I suppose, to find that *The Origin of Species* is a work of literature, with the structure of tragic drama and the texture of poetry. Probably, however, the work is even more ambitious than that, and constitutes something like a sacred writing, a scripture. Sometimes the language gets quite Biblical, as when Darwin writes "But assuredly, if this theory be true, such have lived upon the earth," or, like Job, "This was a sore trouble to me." The deeper resemblance, however, is to scriptural form. S. H. Hooke and others have shown that this form, like the form of Greek tragedy, is of ritual origin, deriving from an annual New Year festival in the ancient Near East that began with the reenactment of the creation drama and ended with the fixing of destinies for the coming year. The basic structure of our Bible is thus creation and lawgiving, a Genesis followed by a Leviticus, a rebirth out of the belly of the great fish to prophecy, or an emergence from the bonds of death to redeem the world.

This scriptural form is at the heart of *The Origin of Species*. What Darwin calls "Development and Embryology," that is, genesis, is basic to the book; so much so that Darwin concludes the chapter:

> Finally, the several classes of facts which have been considered in this chapter, seem to me to proclaim so plainly, that the innumerable species, genera and families, with which this world is peopled, are all descended, each within its own class or group, from common parents, and have all been modified in the course of descent, that I should without hesitation adopt this view, even if it were unsupported by other facts or arguments.

At another place, against mutation, "embryology enters a strong protest." In a letter to Gray in 1860, Darwin writes: "It is curious how each one, I suppose, weighs arguments in a different balance: embryology is to me by far the strongest single class of facts in favour of change of forms, and not one, I think, of my reviewers has alluded to this." The *Origin* has a passionate concern with what Darwin calls "genealogy": "all true classification being genealogical," he generalizes; he keeps speaking of "the unknown progenitor" of various forms; and he concludes in the final chapter:

> I believe that animals are descended from at most only four or five progenitors, and plants from an equal or lesser number.
> Analogy would lead me one step farther, namely, to the belief that all animals and plants are descended from some one prototype.

Two pages later: "We possess no pedigrees or armorial bearings." The whole book is thus a quest for primordial ancestry, a drama of continuing creation out of lower forms like the ritual enactment of the mythic first creation. The laws of Darwin's Leviticus that come in consequence are the capitalized abstractions of the book's last paragraph:

> These laws, taken in the largest sense, being Growth with Reproduction; Inheritance which is almost implied by reproduction; Variability from the indirect and direct action of the conditions of life, and from use and disuse: a Ratio of Increase so high as to lead to a Struggle for Life, and as a consequence to Natural Selection, entailing Divergence of Character, and the Extinction of less-improved forms.

More vividly, Darwin's fixing of destinies is the "one general law leading to the advancement of all organic beings" with which he concludes Chapter 8: "Multiply, vary, let the strongest live and the weakest die."

Some of the book's prophetic quality comes from Darwin's predominant tone of personal testimony: I was there, I saw it, this happened to me. Early in the first chapter he writes "Looking to the domestic dogs of the whole world, I have, after a laborious collection of all known facts, come to the conclusion . . ." and the reader realizes with a shock that Darwin is not joking. "Believing that it is always best to study some special group," he explains, "I have, after deliberation, taken up pigeons," and continues, "I have been associated with several eminent fanciers, and have been permitted to join two of the London Pigeon Clubs." He will begin a discussion: "In Staffordshire, on the estate of a relation, where I had ample means of investigation . . ." Experimenting with aphids, as an entomologist, "I then tickled and stroked them with a hair in the same manner, as well as I could, as the ants do with their antennae"; as a botanist, "I have made so many experiments and collected so many facts"; as a geologist, "scarcely any fact struck me more when examining many hundred miles of the South American coasts." There is something formidable and relentless about his active involvement: to find out the proportions of geologic formations on a "beautiful map," he writes, "I have estimated the areas by cutting out and weighing the paper"; to test means of seed dispersal across water, "I picked up in my garden 12 kinds of seeds, out of the excrement of small birds." (Darwin never outgrew the born naturalist of the *Beagle* voyage who drank the contents of a tortoise's bladder to determine that it "had only a very slightly bitter taste").

Darwin writes to Hooker in 1861:

> Here is a good joke: H. C. Watson (who, I fancy and hope, is going to review the new edition of the 'Origin') says that in the first four paragraphs of the introduction, the words 'I,' 'me,' 'my,' occur forty-three times! I was dimly conscious of the accursed fact. He says it can be explained phrenologically, which I suppose civilly means, that I am the most egotistically self-sufficient man alive; perhaps so. I wonder whether he will print this pleasing fact; it beats hollow the parentheses in Wollaston's writing.

Wollaston is not much read these days, and we may be reminded more readily of *Walden*, by Darwin's contemporary Henry Thoreau, which begins firmly: "When I wrote the following pages, or rather the bulk of them, I lived alone," and goes on to snarl:

> In most books, the *I*, or first person, is omitted; in this it will be retained; that, in respect to egotism, is the main difference. We commonly do not remember that it is, after all, always the first person that is speaking.

The effect of this tone of personal testimony is to heighten the immediacy of what is essentially a new religious message, a new testament or covenant. Darwin had written to Hooker in 1848: "But I don't care what you say, my species theory is all gospel." When he was preparing the book for publication, he wrote asking advice of Lyell:

> P. S. Would you advise me to tell Murray that my book is not more *un*-orthodox than the subject makes inevitable. That I do not discuss the origin of man. That I do not bring in any discussion about Genesis, &c., &c., and only give facts, and such conclusions from them as seem to me fair.

Rather disingenuously, in the book itself Darwin writes: "I see no good reason why the views given in this volume should shock the religious feelings of any one." Yet a Christian reader might fairly be shocked. In the *Origin's* testament, God the Father may exist, and may even have created the world, but if so he has long been remote from it, like the otiose high gods of mythology who have tired of the misbehavior of their creatures and deserted them. The *Origin's* first statement on the subject is that the idea of the separate creation of each species "makes the works of God a mere mockery and deception." This God is, moreover, unknowable: "Have we any right to assume that the Creator works by intellectual powers like those of man?" It is perhaps best not even to talk of creation, so that on one page the problem is "whether species have been created at one or more points of the earth's surface," and on the next page this is rephrased as "the view of each species having been produced in one area alone." [1] Darwin complains:

> But many naturalists think that something more is meant by the Natural System; they believe that it reveals the plan of the Creator; but unless it be specified whether order in time or space, or both, or what else is meant by the plan of the Creator, it seems to me that nothing is thus added to our knowledge.

Of the view "that it has pleased the Creator to construct all the animals and plants in each great class on a uniform plan," Darwin comments "but this is not a scientific explanation." He asks rhetorically: "But do they really believe that at innumerable periods in the earth's history certain elemental atoms have been commanded suddenly to flash into living tissue?" If God the Father probably did not create, he does not intervene either: "We may feel certain that the ordinary succession by generation has never once been broken, and that no cataclysm has desolated the whole world." Nor does the *Origin* ever mention the Second Person of God. After some struggle, Darwin had lost his faith in the historical existence of Jesus by 1839, as the *Autobiography* explains:

> But I was very unwilling to give up my belief; I feel sure of this, for I can well remember often and often inventing daydreams of old letters between distinguished Romans, and manuscripts being discovered at Pompeii or elsewhere, which confirmed in the most striking manner all that was written in the Gospels. But I found it more and more difficult, with free scope given to my imagination, to invent evidence which would suffice to convince me. Thus disbelief crept over me at a very slow rate, but was at last complete. The rate was so slow that I felt no distress.

Late in life Darwin wrote to a German student who had questioned him about religion: "Science has nothing to do with Christ, except in so far as the habit of scientific research makes a man cautious in admitting evidence."

The living deity who succeeded these outmoded supernaturals is

---

[1] After the first edition of the *Origin*, Darwin somewhat lost his nerve, and changed his concluding statement about life "originally breathed into a few forms or into one" to "originally breathed by the Creator into a few forms or into one." He also added a defensive epigraph from Bishop Butler's *Analogy of Revealed Religion*.

called Nature, but she is no less than the earth goddess or Great
Mother worshipped everywhere under a variety of names: by the
Greeks as Gaia or Ge, by the Phrygians as Cybele, by the Egyptians
as Isis or Hathor, by the Babylonians as Ishtar. Darwin had first seen
her in an evil or Hecate aspect. "I do not know of any other instance,"
he writes in the *Journal of Researches*, "where Dame Nature appears
so wilfully cruel." There is a key passage in the conclusion to the
drafts of 1842 and 1844 that is not in the *Origin*. I give the more
complete 1844 version:

> It is derogatory that the Creator of countless Universes should
> have made by individual acts of His will the myriads of creeping
> parasites and worms, which since the earliest dawn of life have
> swarmed over the land and in the depths of the ocean. We cease
> to be astonished that a group of animals should have been formed
> to lay their eggs in the bowels and flesh of other sensitive beings;
> that some animals should live by and even delight in cruelty; that
> animals should be led away by false instincts; that annually there
> should be an incalculable waste of the pollen, eggs and immature
> beings; for we see in all this the inevitable consequences of one
> great law, of the multiplication of organic beings not created
> immutable.

In 1856, Darwin wrote to Hooker: "What a book a devil's chaplain
might write on the clumsy, wasteful, blundering, low, and horribly
cruel works of nature!" Sometime between the draft of 1844, in
which he supposes a male "Being" who selects, and that letter to
Hooker, God the Father was replaced by Mother Nature, and Darwin
as *her* chaplain seems to have felt so strongly that *she* could not work
evil that the key passage about parasites, cruelty and waste was not
included in the *Origin*.

Darwin starts by insisting that Nature is not a goddess, but a
metaphor. He writes:

> So again it is difficult to avoid personifying the word Nature; but
> I mean by Nature, only the aggregate action and product of
> many natural laws, and by laws the sequence of events as ascer-
> tained by us.

As soon as he begins to talk about Nature, however, she is transformed
into a female divinity with consciousness and will. Thus:

> Nature, if I may be allowed to personify the natural preservation
> or survival of the fittest, cares nothing for appearances, except in
> so far as they are useful to any being. She can act on every in-
> ternal organ, on every shade of constitutional difference, on the
> whole machinery of life. Man selects only for his own good:
> Nature only for that of the being which she tends. Every se-
> lected character is fully exercised by her, as is implied by the fact
> of their selection.

This deity is not only omnipotent, she is omnipresent, "daily and hourly scrutinising, throughout the world, the slightest variations; rejecting those that are bad, preserving and adding up all that are good; silently and insensibly working." She is also divinely impartial, as Zeus is limited by the Fates and by Themis: "What natural selection cannot do, is to modify the structure of one species, without giving it any advantage, for the good of another species." She is no longer the "Dame Nature" of the *Journal of Researches* and the early letters; here Darwin is scrupulous to call her "a power, represented by natural selection or the survival of the fittest, always intently watching." She is no less a goddess.

This was the new grand design that gave the Victorians faith when the old faith had eroded away. "How great is the power of man in accumulating by his Selection successive slight variations," Darwin writes. Yet in comparison to this omnipotent deity, how poor a thing is man. Darwin writes:

> How fleeting are the wishes and efforts of man! how short his time! and consequently how poor will be his results, compared with those accumulated by Nature during whole geological periods! Can we wonder, then, that Nature's productions should be far 'truer' in character than man's productions; that they should be infinitely better adapted to the most complex conditions of life, and should plainly bear the stamp of far higher workmanship?

Or:

> Slow though the process of selection may be, if feeble man can do much by artificial selection, I can see no limit to the amount of change, to the beauty and complexity of the coadaptations between all organic beings, one with another and with their physical conditions of life, which may have been effected in the long course of time through nature's power of selection, that is by the survival of the fittest.

"Be ye therefore perfect, even as your Father which is in heaven is perfect," Jesus says in the Sermon on the Mount. "And as natural selection works solely by and for the good of each being, all corporeal and mental endowments will tend to progress towards perfection," Darwin writes in the Conclusion to the *Origin*, which we might translate as "Become ye therefore perfect, even as your Mother which is on earth is perfect."

It is, of course, a new teleology, as was immediately recognized by Gray, the only "Nicene" Christian among Darwin's early supporters. Gray wrote in *Nature* in 1874, "Let us recognize Darwin's great service to natural science in bringing back to it Teleology: so that instead of Morphology *versus* Teleology, we shall have Morphology wedded to Teleology." Darwin wrote to him: "What you say about Teleology pleases me especially, and I do not think anyone

else has ever noticed the point. I have always said you were the man to
hit the nail on the head." [2] Francis Darwin writes in *The Life and
Letters:*

> One of the greatest services rendered by my father to the
> study of Natural History is the revival of Teleology. The evolu-
> tionist studies the purpose or meaning of organs with the zeal
> of the older Teleology, but with far wider and more coherent
> purpose.

Sir William Thiselton-Dyer, on the occasion of the Darwin-Wallace
celebration in 1908, identified Darwin's source in Paley's *Natural
Theology:*

> The thought of each age is the foundation of that which follows.
> Darwin was an admirer of Paley, a member of his own College.
> He swept in the whole of Paley's teleology, simply dispensing
> with its supernatural explanation.

The beauty of this apparent secularizing or naturalizing of teleology is that it allowed those like Gray who wanted teleology to
claim that Darwin evidences it (all is designed to progress to perfection), and those like Huxley who wanted to believe that teleology
"had received its deathblow at Mr. Darwin's hands," as he wrote in
1864, to deny its presence (the Great Designer is out).

In reality, of course, Darwin's teleology is as sacred and supernatural as Paley's, but with all-seeing Mother Nature substituted for
God the Father. It was a fit covert religious revolution for Victorian
England, but it also had a particular fitness for Darwin, whose deep
identification with his dead mother and submission to his overwhelming father suggest a classic Oedipal situation. Psychologically,
Darwin's religion is a compensatory mother worship. One of the
oddest themes running through *The Origin of Species* is a kind of
Oedipal natural selection: "There will be a constant tendency in the
improved descendants of any one species to supplant and exterminate
in each stage of descent their predecessors and their original progenitor," so that "the original parent-species itself, will generally
tend to become extinct"; "The principle of competition between
organism and organism, between child and parent," always results in
victory for "the new and improved forms of life."

J. W. Judd writes, in *Darwin and Modern Science:* "Darwin
became the 'Paul' of evolution." I think the comparison with the
epistolary saint is an extremely suggestive one. Darwin's vista of the
future at the end of the *Origin*, "The terms used by naturalists, of
affinity, relationship, community of type, paternity, morphology,
adaptive characters, rudimentary and aborted organs, &c., will cease
to be metaphorical, and will have a plain signification," is clearly the
voice of Paul in I Corinthians, "For now we see through a glass

---

[2] Gray had in fact been hitting that nail on the head in everything he wrote
about Darwin since 1860, but Darwin apparently did not notice until 1874.

darkly; but then face to face." Like Paul, Darwin returns again and again to mystery: the origin of species is "that mystery of mysteries"; the laws of correlation are "mysterious"; the laws of variation are "various, unknown, or but dimly understood"; and so forth. He keeps emphasizing the limits of earthly knowledge: "our profound ignorance," "so profound is our ignorance, and so high our presumption," "seeing how profoundly ignorant we are," "if we make due allowance for our ignorance." Even the old testament of his religion, the record of the rocks, is a tattered and deficient scroll. Borrowing and expanding a metaphor of Lyell's, Darwin writes:

> I look at the geological record as a history of the world imperfectly kept, and written in a changing dialect; of this history we possess the last volume alone, relating only to two or three countries. Of this volume, only here and there a short chapter has been preserved; and of each page, only here and there a few lines.

The story of the Fall in Genesis appears to be a disguised myth of the origin of death. St. Paul returns it to its earlier meaning ("For as in Adam all die, even so in Christ shall all be made alive"); and so, in a fashion, does Darwin. In the *Origin* he is not interested in a moral Fall, but in a Platonic myth of the origin of death that shall be as consoling as the Christian doctrine of *felix culpa*, Adam's happy fault that necessitated Christ. In his doctrine (which is everywhere in the *Origin* implied rather than stated), death is not inherent in the properties of protoplasm (the simplest organisms do not die), but is a trait evolved by natural selection, permitting a speedier improvement of the higher organisms, and thus an advantage in competition and a good for life. Darwin knew this as early as the 1837 notebook, although it was not stated in print until much later. Darwin wrote in a letter to A. Gapitche in 1880 that evolution "depends on a long succession of generations, which implies death." As St. Paul put it, "For since by man came death, by man came also the resurrection of the dead."

The appeal of the *Origin* is not only for imagination, wonder, marvel, rather than ratiocination, but ultimately for belief and faith. Thus, as in Patristic writings, the strongest confirmatory evidence comes from disbelievers: from a Mr. Hudson, "a strong disbeliever in evolution," or the many geologists and palaeontologists who "entirely disbelieve in the change of species." In an 1860 letter he writes of the necessity for "a compact set of believers." Sometimes Darwin got more faith than he bargained for. He writes to Hooker in 1865:

> I have had an enormous letter from Leo Lesquereux (after doubts, I did not think it worth sending) on Coal Flora: he wrote some excellent articles in Silliman against *Origin* views; but he says now after repeated reading of the book he is a convert! But how funny men's minds are! he says he is chiefly

converted because my books make the Birth of Christ, Redemption by Grace, etc., plain to him!

Darwin writes of his own state of mind in the *Origin:* "But I must confess, that, with all my faith in natural selection, I should never have anticipated that this principle could have been efficient in so high a degree." With belief and faith comes a change of heart, and a kind of salvation. Instead of the central Pauline mysteries of Incarnation and Atonement, Darwin's mystery is a kind of totemic brotherhood, a consubstantiality with all organic beings, resembling St. Paul's "every one members one of another." In his contribution to *Darwin and Modern Science*, Frazer notes that when Europeans first landed on one of the Alaskan islands, the natives took them for cuttlefish on account of the buttons on their clothes. In a deeper sense, Darwin identifies Europeans as totemic brothers to cuttlefish, and reminds us that what he calls in an early notebook "animals, our fellow brethren," are as precious as we in the eyes of our common mother.

Like the New Testament, *The Origin of Species* eventuates its mysteries in a new morality of humility. When Darwin's lifelong ill-health first appeared, in his youth, his father did not fail to remind him that "the race is for the strong." *The Origin of Species*, and in fact the whole body of his work, is Darwin's rejoinder that, to the contrary, slow and steady win the race, or, as he quotes from Trollope's Brickmaker in a letter to Romanes, "It is dogged as does it." Darwin writes in the *Origin:* "Natural selection acts only by the preservation and accumulation of small inherited modifications"; Nature "can never take a great and sudden leap, but must advance by short and sure, though slow steps"; in geology, "agencies which apparently have so little power, and which seem to work so slowly, have produced great results." Darwin's own laborious procedures, the infinite pains he took with every fact, show him Nature's fit prophet. He admired Herbert Spencer's "prodigality of original thought," always taking great and sudden leaps like Darwin's father's, but he notes in a letter to Hooker that "each suggestion, to be of real value to science, would require years of work."

Essentially, it is the morality of such Beatitudes as "Blessed are the meek: for they shall inherit the earth"; of "Are not two sparrows sold for a farthing? and one of them shall not fall on the ground without your Father"; of "Take heed that ye despise not one of these little ones." With his Cirripedes in mind, Darwin writes: "Every naturalist who has dissected some of the beings now ranked as very low in the scale, must have been struck with their really wondrous and beautiful organization." Darwin's first book after the *Journal of Researches*, on Coral Reefs, and the last book he published (after fifty years of studying the subject), on Earthworms, both point this moral, that tiny creatures slowly and steadily work great wonders.

The final irony is that Darwin's scripture, written the way the corals build a reef, dealing with transformations so slow in time that they are invisible at any given moment, caught the imagination of the world—converted it if you wish—not in that fashion but in a flash. As M. I. Finley writes in *The World of Odysseus:*

> Never in the history of the known religions, Eastern or Western, was a new religion introduced otherwise than at one stroke. New ideas may have been germinating for a long time, old ideas may have been undergoing constant and slow change, still other notions may have been imported from abroad. But the actual step of transformation, the abandonment of the old faith and the creation of the new, has always been sharp, swift, abrupt.

"Behold," says St. Paul, "I shew you a mystery; We shall not all sleep, but we shall all be changed, In a moment, in the twinkling of an eye."

Man and His Brethren

D ARWIN'S work had always had a remarkable integration, but after the *Origin*, each of his books was consciously planned as an expansion of its material and additional evidence for the origin of species by means of natural selection. Lyell, Huxley, and Murray had independently suggested that method to Darwin, and it was a method extremely congenial to his habits of mind. The first such book was *The Variation of Animals and Plants under Domestication*, which appeared in 1868, an expansion of the first chapter of the *Origin*. Darwin writes in a footnote to the Introduction:

> To any one who has attentively read my 'Origin of Species' this Introduction will be superfluous. As I stated in that work that I should soon publish the facts on which the conclusions given in it were founded, I here beg permission to remark that the great delay in publishing this first work has been caused by continued ill-health.

Variation under Domestication buttresses the *Origin* with enormously more evidence, without much affecting its theory. In a letter to A. R. Wallace, Darwin describes it as "a large accumulation of facts." Using a characteristic technique of rhetorical ingratiation, the *Origin* properly begins with variation in domestic livestock, speaking directly to every reader's experience.[1] *Variation under Domestication* amplifies this rhetorical technique and spreads the net more widely: it begins with the domestic dog and cat. As a symbolic or poetic work, however, it intensifies the key image of the *Origin*, life as a struggle. In civilized man, selecting domestic animals, the war is rather pacific, and becomes "a universal principle in human nature, namely, . . . our rivalry, and desire to outdo our neighbors." Not entirely pacific, however. "Lord Rivers, when asked how he

---

[1] It is amusing to learn from Ray Ginger's account of the Scopes Trial, *Six Days or Forever?*, that the foreman of the grand jury that indicted Scopes had come to believe in evolution through his experience as a farmer, seeing the improvement of potatoes, tomatoes, cattle, and hogs during his lifetime in Tennessee.

44

succeeded in always having first-rate greyhounds, answered 'I breed many, and hang many.' " Experiments have made horses and even pigeons carnivorous. The pigeon breeder "may freely reject inferior birds, as they serve at an early age as excellent food." Among primitive breeders the struggle is even more violent; thus the aborigines of Australia "are all very glad to get a European Kangaroo dog, and several instances have been known of the father killing his own infant that the mother might suckle the much-prized puppy." In nature, the struggle is to the death: "It has truly been said that all nature is at war; the strongest ultimately prevail, the weakest fail."

In the course of *Variation under Domestication*, Darwin promises a future work on genetics, to show "that consanguinity by itself counts for nothing," but in an important sense the whole book is erroneous genetics. Mendel's demonstration of particulate inheritance had been published for three years, but no one was aware of it until 1900, and Darwin was the prisoner of the genetic theory of his time, a "blending" inheritance in which progeny democratically compromised the traits of their parents. This is less of a problem in the *Origin*, where the subject is presented as a mystery of mysteries, but here, with so much ostensibly known about the breeding of domesticated animals and plants, Darwin was severely handicapped. For most of the book he is thoroughly Lamarckian, showing the inherited effects of the use or disuse of parts, although he also presents material to the contrary. He demonstrates Buffon's principle of the direct action of climate and food on inheritance, and in places suggests that they have no inherited effect. He sometimes marvelously anticipates Mendelian genetics, as in a concept of "pre-potency" on the verge of Mendel's "dominance," and sometimes denies even that "Variability must be looked at as an ultimate fact, necessarily contingent on reproduction." He frequently recognizes "leaps" or "saltation," what De Vries was later to call mutations, and periodically insists that they cannot be taken advantage of in a state of nature.[2] Altogether it is no wonder that Darwin sent Hooker instructions for reading *Variation* in 1868: "About my book, I will give you a bit of advice. Skip the whole of Vol. I, except the last chapter, (and that

[2] Most remarkably, Darwin concludes the book with his own genetic theory, the "provisional hypothesis of Pangenesis," a speculation that invisible "gemmules" thrown off by every cell in the organism combine to make up the sexual elements. No theory of Darwin's was more derided on its appearance, even by many of his friends, but he stuck to it, at least as a possibility. Darwin wrote playfully to Hooker in 1868: "It is a comfort to me to think that you will be surely haunted on your death-bed for not honouring the great god Pan." He wrote to J. Jenner Weir in 1870: "Whether it would be prudent to allude to despised pangenesis I cannot say, but I fully believe pangenesis will have its successful day." After the general acceptance in our century of Weismann's theory of the continuity of the germ plasm, this seemed extremely unlikely. Now, in "The Third Stage in Genetics" in *A Century of Darwin*, Donald Michie not only describes Pangenesis as "an arresting and prophetic hypothesis" that fits some present evidence as germline heredity does not, but concludes "I estimate that genetics has about ten years to go before it can claim fully to have caught up with Darwin."

need only be skimmed), and skip largely in the 2nd volume; and then you will say it is a very good book."

The Descent of Man and Selection in Relation to Sex, published in 1871, twelve years after *The Origin of Species*, was the payment on its promise that "light would be thrown on the origin of man and his history" (or, in later editions, "much light"). More boldly, Darwin writes in the new book: "Man must be included with other organic beings in any general conclusion respecting his manner of appearance on this earth." Huxley had written in 1863 that "Man's place in nature" was the most fundamental of all questions, and Darwin wrote to him in 1867: "I am thinking of a chapter on man," presumably in *Variation*. It soon became a separate book. Where Wallace argued a religious dualist view, man's material being descended from earlier mammals, but his higher faculties infused by some other power, Darwin and Huxley went about putting man back in nature with a resolute monism. In 1858, when he was assembling the *Origin*, Darwin had written reassuringly to Wallace:

> You ask whether I shall discuss 'man.' I think I shall avoid the whole subject, as so surrounded with prejudices; though I fully admit that it is the highest and most interesting problem for the naturalist.

For its bulk, the book contains surprisingly little directly on the actual origin or descent of man, and almost three-quarters of the volume is a separate work on sexual selection. That little, however, firmly places man among the mammals, and in provocatively humbling terms. Thus:

> Man is liable to receive from the lower animals, and to communicate to them, certain diseases, as hydrophobia, variola, the glanders, syphilis, cholera, herpes, &c.; and this fact proves the close similarity of their tissues and blood, both in minute structure and composition, far more plainly than does their comparison under the best microscope, or by the aid of the best chemical analysis. Monkeys are liable to many of the same non-contagious diseases as we are; thus Rengger, who carefully observed for a long time the Cebus Azarae in its native land, found it liable to catarrh, with the usual symptoms, and which, when often recurrent, led to consumption. These monkeys suffered also from apoplexy, inflammation of the bowels, and cataract in the eye. The younger ones when shedding their milk-teeth often died from fever. Medicines produced the same effect on them as on us. Many kinds of monkeys have a strong taste for tea, coffee, and spiritous liquors: they will also, as I have myself seen, smoke tobacco with pleasure.

Or:

Man is infested with internal parasites, sometimes causing fatal effects; and is plagued by external parasites, all of which belong to the same genera or families as those infesting other mammals, and in the case of scabies to the same species. Man is subject, like other mammals, birds, and even insects, to that mysterious law, which causes certain normal processes, such as gestation, as well as the maturation and duration of various diseases, to follow lunar periods. His wounds are repaired by the same process of healing; and the stumps left after the amputation of his limbs, especially during an early embryonic period, occasionally possess some power of regeneration, as in the lowest animals.

He writes: "Man, as I have attempted to shew, is certainly descended from some ape-like creature," and refers to "our male ape-like progenitors." Man is not only a mammal, but a rather poor one, weak, slow, and lacking in natural weapons. In 1862, when his wife and children were ill, Darwin wrote to Gray, "We are a wretched family, and ought to be exterminated." He meant the Darwins, but some of *The Descent of Man* reads as though he meant the humans.

Darwin's deliberate aim in the book is to humble "that arrogance which made our forefathers declare that they were descended from demi-gods." He begins the book's penultimate paragraph: "The main conclusion arrived at in this work, namely, that man is descended from some lowly organized form, will, I regret to think, be highly distasteful to many." C. Bouglé, in *Darwin and Modern Science*, fairly remarks of the *Descent:* "One might say that the naturalist had here taken as his motto 'Whoever shall exalt himself shall be abased; and he that shall humble himself shall be exalted.'" As the duality of the quotation from Scripture suggests, however, the aim is not simply a diminishing of mankind, but the familiar tragic rhythm of action, an humbling that will end in exaltation. Thus by putting *homo sapiens* back in nature, reminding him that "man is descended from some lower form," or "an off-shoot from the Old World Simian stem," Darwin offers him "a pedigree of prodigious length," if unfortunately not "of noble quality." Here is a stroll down the ancestral portrait gallery:

The early progenitors of man must have been once covered with hair, both sexes having beards; their ears were probably pointed, and capable of movement; and their bodies were provided with a tail, having the proper muscles. Their limbs and bodies were also acted on by many muscles which now only occasionally reappear, but are normally present in the Quadrumana. At this or some earlier period, the great artery and nerve of the humerus ran through a supra-condyloid foramen. The intestine gave forth a much larger diverticulum or caecum than that now existing. The foot was then prehensile, judging from

the condition of the great toe in the foetus; and our progenitors,
no doubt, were arboreal in their habits, and frequented some
warm, forest-clad land. The males had great canine teeth, which
served them as formidable weapons. At a much earlier period the
uterus was double; the excreta were voided through a cloaca; and
the eye was protected by a third eyelid or nictitating membrane.
At a still earlier period the progenitors of man must have been
aquatic in their habits; for morphology plainly tells us that our
lungs consist of a modified swim-bladder, which once served as a
float. The clefts on the neck in the embryo of man show where
the branchiae once existed. In the lunar or weekly recurrent
periods of some of our functions we apparently still retain traces
of our primordial birthplace, a shore washed by the tides. At
about this same early period the true kidneys were replaced by
the corpora wolffiana. The heart existed as a simple pulsating
vessel; and the chorda dorsalis took the place of a vertebral
column. These early ancestors of man, thus seen in the dim
recesses of time, must have been as simply, or even still more simply organised than the lancelet or amphioxus.

Our ancestors may have been arboreal, tailed quadrupeds, and, still
earlier, primitive fishes like the lancelet, but they long antedate William the Conqueror.

In this Franciscan world, with its Brother Chimpanzee and Little
Sister Amphioxus, we have the magical monism of totemic brotherhood, in which a man wearing bone buttons may very well *be* a
cuttlefish. There are odd surrealist scenes in the *Descent* where
the naturalist becomes magically one with the species he is studying:
Mr. Verreaux of Australia, with a female butterfly in his pocket,
pursued amorously by a crowd of several hundred male butterflies;
Dr. Scudder exciting a cricket to answer him by rubbing on a
file with a quill. The *Descent* gave Freud his basic vision for human
psychological prehistory (borrowed by Darwin in turn from a
Dr. Savage in the *Boston Journal of Natural History*). It is, of
course, the Primal Horde, in which the old male gorilla keeps a
harem of females and drives out the young males until they succeed
in killing and replacing him. It is all an oddly pre-Freudian world, in
which, for example, "the males of several amphipod crustaceans become sexually mature whilst young," inexplicably, since "they have
not as yet acquired their full-developed claspers." One might as
readily call the *Descent* pre-Marxist, it is all so unsettling, and the
London Times quite properly disapproved of its publication at the
very moment of the Paris Commune. In 1877 Rudolf Virchow proposed that the teaching of Darwinism be prohibited in Germany
as tending to socialism.

One contemporary notice penetrated to the essence of *The
Descent of Man*. It is by an anonymous reviewer in the *Spectator*,
March 12, 1871. He writes:

Mr. Darwin finds himself compelled to reintroduce a new doctrine of the fall of man. He shews that the instincts of the higher animals are far nobler than the habits of savage races of men, and he finds himself, therefore, compelled to reintroduce,—in a form of the substantial orthodoxy of which he appears to be quite unconscious,—and to introduce as a scientific hypothesis the doctrine that man's gain of *knowledge* was the cause of a temporary but long-enduring moral deterioration as indicated by the many foul customs, especially as to marriage, of savage tribes. What does the Jewish tradition of the moral degeneration of man through his snatching at a knowledge forbidden him by his highest instinct assert beyond this?

In other words, as the reviewer brilliantly recognized, the *Descent* is precipitous, a Fall out of animal Eden to the savage condition, and then the slow painful climb back. It is the myth of a moral Fall lacking in the *Origin*. In the *Descent*, Darwin shows by a series of anecdotes that animals are loyal, domestic, loving, courageous, and self-sacrificing. Birds, for example, will feed their blind, crippled, and orphaned. Even the lower animals share in this moral goodness. Thus:

> Parental affection, or some feeling which replaces it, has been developed in certain animals extremely low in the scale, for example, in star-fishes and spiders. It is also occasionally present in a few members alone in a whole group of animals, as in the genus Forficula, or earwigs.

Primitive man, on the other hand, gets his moral character blackened regularly in the book. "The licentiousness of many savages is no doubt astonishing"; they have "bad customs and base superstitions"; they are just as apt as not to kill their young and desert their elderly. When comparison is made, animals generally come off best. Thus "Our early semi-human progenitors would not have practiced infanticide or polyandry; for the instincts of the lower animals are never so perverted as to lead them regularly to destroy their own offspring, or to be quite devoid of jealousy." Even when noting that some animals "will expel a wounded animal from the herd, or gore or worry it to death," Darwin extenuates it with human comparison:

> This is almost the blackest fact in natural history, unless, indeed, the explanation which has been suggested is true, that their instinct or reason leads them to expel an injured companion, lest beasts of prey, including man, should be tempted to follow the troop. In this case their conduct is not much worse than that of the North American Indians, who leave their feeble comrades to perish on the plains; or the Fijians, who, when their parents get old, or fall ill, bury them alive.

Darwin's conclusion aggressively picks up the question whether he would admit to simian descent, which Bishop Wilberforce had asked

Huxley at the famous Oxford Meeting when the *Origin* was first published:

> For my own part I would as soon be descended from that heroic little monkey, who braved his dreaded enemy in order to save the life of his keeper, or from that old baboon, who descending from the mountains, carried away in triumph his young comrade from a crowd of astonished dogs—as from a savage who delights to torture his enemies, offers up bloody sacrifices, practises infanticide without remorse, treats his wives like slaves, knows no decency, and is haunted by the grossest superstitions.

Darwin's efforts, in fact, are not to reduce man to a bestial condition, as opponents of the book charged, but to ennoble and humanize animals. Thus "the brain of an ant is one of the most marvelous atoms of matter in the world, perhaps more so than the brain of a man." "The dream is an involuntary art of poetry," Darwin quotes from Jean-Paul, and adds "As dogs, cats, horses, and probably all the higher animals, even birds, have vivid dreams, and this is shewn by their movements and the sounds uttered, we must admit that they possess some power of imagination." Could not "some unusually wise ape-like animal" have imitated the growl of a predator to his fellow-monkeys, and thus have invented speech? "No one with an unbiased mind can study any living creature, however humble, without being struck with enthusiasm at its marvellous structure and properties." "The mental powers of the Crustacea are probably higher than at first sight appears probable." Darwin writes, giving an example of very thoughtful behavior in a shore-crab. Mantises fight "like hussars with their sabres"; ants "have the power of recognising each other after long intervals of time, and are deeply attached"; the male stickleback goes "mad with delight" when the female inspects the nest he has built for her.

As we might expect, this program of humanizing animals and bestializing savages requires sometimes an absolute ethics and aesthetics, sometimes a relative, and Darwin dutifully makes the requisite switches. "Some real and great crimes, such as incest," are absolute; other crimes, such as killing enemies, are moral within their social context; and "some accidental breach of a trifling, though fixed, rule of etiquette" is sometimes made to seem worse than any crime. "Judging from the hideous ornaments, and the equally hideous music admired by most savages," Darwin writes, "it might be urged that their aesthetic faculty was not so highly developed as in certain animals, for instance, as in birds." Savages clearly do not share our aesthetic standards, but Darwin cannot make up his mind whether or not birds do. When he talks of the courting sounds of birds—"the drumming of the snipe's tail, the tapping of the woodpecker's beak, the harsh trumpet-like cry of certain water-fowl, the cooing of the turtle-dove, and the song of the nightingale"—he warns that their beauty must be judged by female birds, not "by the standard of man's taste." Darwin then immediately refers to a "disgusting carrion vulture" male and quotes Audubon on its courtship dance as "extremely ludicrous," although we cannot imagine that they are either disgusting or ludicrous to the female. When he is surprised that the female pheasant "should be able to appreciate fine shading and exquisite patterns" in the plumage of the male pheasant, it is "undoubtedly a marvelous fact that she should possess this almost human degree of taste." Birds that do not share human standards of beauty are rapped over the claws. Darwin asks rhetorically of the macaw: "Have these birds as bad taste for musical sounds as they apparently have for colour, judging by the inharmonious contrast of their bright yellow and blue plumage?" At other times, he remembers his evolutionary relativism: "No doubt it is to us a most grotesque notion that the posterior end of the body should be coloured for the sake of ornament even more brilliantly than the face," but it is not a grotesque notion to the blue-bottomed baboon. An appendix to the book, on "Sexual Selection in Relation to Monkeys," notes that these bright behinds are turned to people "as a sort of greeting," but makes no comment in terms of either ethics or aesthetics.

The human power that will return man to Edenic innocence, and undo the Fall or Descent, is culture, although Darwin precedes the use of the word in its present-day broad anthropological usage for all non-biological inheritance. Thus biological man is a poor mammal, but cultural man is little lower than the angels. Darwin writes:

> Man in the rudest state in which he now exists is the most dominant animal that has ever appeared on this earth. He has spread more widely than any other highly organized form: and all others have yielded before him. He manifestly owes this immense superiority to his intellectual faculties, to his social habits, which lead him to aid and defend his fellows, and to his corporeal structure. The supreme importance of these characters has been proved by the final arbitrament of the battle for life. Through his powers of intellect, articulate language has been evolved; and on this his wonderful advancement has mainly depended. . . . He has invented and is able to use various weapons, tools, traps, &c. with which he defends himself, kills or catches prey, and otherwise obtains food. He has made rafts or canoes for fishing or crossing over to neighboring fertile islands. He has discovered the art of making fire, by which hard and stringy roots can be rendered digestible, and poisonous roots or herbs innocuous.

Darwin makes it clear that this culture is compensatory. He writes:

> The small strength and speed of man, his want of natural weapons, &c., are more than counterbalanced, firstly, by his intellectual powers, through which he has formed for himself weapons, tools, &c., though still remaining in a barbarous state, and, secondly, by his social qualities which lead him to give and receive aid from his fellow-men.

Man's capacity for "incomparably greater and more rapid improvement" than any other animal "is mainly due to his power of speaking and handing down his acquired knowledge." "At the present day civilised nations are everywhere supplanting barbarous nations," he writes, "and they succeed mainly, though not exclusively, through their arts, which are the products of the intellect." Darwin clearly needs the all-embracing term "culture" to oppose to "nature." When he does refer to "culture" it is in the more limited sense:

> Obviously no animal would be capable of admiring such scenes as the heavens at night, a beautiful landscape, or refined music; but such high tastes are acquired through culture, and depend on complex associations; they are not enjoyed by barbarians or by uneducated persons.

Culture does not guarantee man evolutionary victory, it just changes the terms of the competition, and the final vision the *Descent* offers for man is "if he is to advance still higher, it is to be feared that he must remain subject to a severe struggle." The new Eden is, however, in prospect:

> Man may be excused for feeling some pride at having risen, though not through his own exertions, to the very summit of the organic scale; and the fact of his having thus risen, instead of having been aboriginally placed there, may give him hope for a still higher destiny in the distant future.

F O R a book mainly about sex, *The Descent of Man* is oddly reticent in certain areas. It is hard to tell whether this is choice or necessity, and the likeliest guess is that they reinforce each other. We know that the publisher made Darwin delete at least one indecency, a sentence that implied a capacity of female animals to experience sexual desire. One odd distortion fits in so neatly with Darwin's Oedipal identification that it is tempting to see it as a personal expression. This distortion comes up whenever Darwin talks about rudimentary bisexuality in humans. He writes:

> It is well known that in the males of all mammals, including man, rudimentary mammae exist. These in several instances have become well developed, and have yielded a copious supply of milk. Their essential identity in the two sexes is likewise shewn by their occasional sympathetic enlargement in both during an attack of the measles. The *vesicula prostatica*, which has been observed in many male mammals, is now universally acknowledged to be the homologue of the female uterus, together with the connected passage. . . . Some other rudimentary structures belonging to the reproductive system might have been here adduced.

Later he returns to the subject:

> In the mammalian class the males possess rudiments of a uterus with the adjacent passage, in their vesiculae prostaticae; they bear also rudiments of mammae, and some male Marsupials have traces of a Marsupial sack. Other analogous facts could be added.

He is fascinated by male breasts and the prostate as a rudimentary womb, but he seems unable to write down the other analogous facts that "might have been here adduced" or "could be added," that rudimentary male sex organs appear equally in the human female, and with considerably more erotic function. Instead, Darwin goes on to develop an extensive fantasy of the male mother:

> It may be suggested, as another view, that long after the progenitors of the whole mammalian class had ceased to be androgynous, both sexes yielded milk, and thus nourished their young; and in the case of the Marsupials, that both sexes carried their young in marsupial sacks. This will not appear altogether improbable, if we reflect that the males of existing syngnathous fishes receive the eggs of the females in their abdominal pouches, hatch them, and afterwards, as some believe, nourish the young; —that certain other male fishes hatch the eggs within their mouths or branchial cavities;—that certain male toads take the chaplets of eggs from the females, and wind them round their own thighs, keeping them there until the tadpoles are born;— that certain male birds undertake the whole duty of incubation, and that male pigeons, as well as the females, feed their nestlings with a secretion from their crops. But the above suggestion first occurred to me from mammary glands of male mammals being so much more perfectly developed than the rudiments of the other accessory reproductive parts, which are found in the one sex though proper to the other. The mammary glands and nipples, as they exist in male mammals, can indeed hardly be called rudimentary; they are merely not fully developed, and not functionally active. They are sympathetically affected under the influence of certain diseases, like the same organs in the female. They often secrete a few drops of milk at birth and at puberty: this latter fact occurred in the curious case, before referred to, where a young man possessed two pairs of mammae. In man and some other male mammals these organs have been known occasionally to become so well developed during maturity as to yield a fair supply of milk. Now if we suppose that during a former prolonged period male mammals aided the females in nursing their offspring, and that afterwards from some cause (as from the production of a smaller number of young) the males ceased to give this aid, disuse of the organs during maturity would lead to their becoming inactive.

Other reticence in the book seems more characteristically Victorian. Hottentot women "offer certain peculiarities, more strongly marked than those occurring in any other race." These are finally revealed to be that "the posterior part of the body projects in a wonderful manner." There are odd euphemisms for animal rutting: "the season of love," "the final marriage ceremony," "their marriage unions," and so forth. Among the Aymara and Quichua Indians: "The men of these two tribes have very little hair on the various parts of the body where hair grows abundantly in Europeans, and the women have none on the corresponding parts." A summary of primitive physical mutilations omits circumcision, subincision, and cliterectomy, producing a delicious comedy when Darwin notes of tattooing: "This practice was followed by the Jews of old." The oddest euphemism in *The Descent of Man* is Darwin's term "licentiousness," which he keeps speaking of as a check to population: "There is reason to believe that in some cases (as in Japan) it has been intentionally encouraged as a means of keeping down the population"; among savages "utter licentiousness, and unnatural crimes, prevail to an astounding extent," serving "to keep down the numbers of each savage tribe"; the fall of Greece may have been due to "extreme sensuality." By "licentiousness" Darwin apparently means deviant sexuality, since there is nothing else he could mean, and it would be interesting to know who encouraged it in Japan.

A good deal of the eroticism repressed in connection with human sexuality gets released in the accounts of animal sexuality, as it naturally would. Thus male sand wasps "are exceedingly ardent," and male snakes, "though appearing so sluggish, are amorous." Of frogs and toads:

> It is surprising that these animals have not acquired more strongly-marked sexual characters; for though cold-blooded their passions are strong. Dr. Guenther informs me that he has several times found an unfortunate female toad dead and smothered from having been so closely embraced by three or four males.

The sexuality of the lower animals in the *Descent* is wildly surrealist. A cast-off cuttlefish tentacle goes off on its own and mates with the female. Of naked sea-slugs, which are hermaphrodite but couple, "It is conceivable that two hermaphrodites, attracted by each other's greater beauty, might unite." (In 1864, Darwin had written to B. D. Walsh: "What can there be in the act of copulation necessitating such complex and diversified apparatus?") Among the higher animals, there are scenes like nothing so much as French bedroom farce: while two capercailzie cocks fight over a hen, she "sometimes steals away with a young male who had not dared to enter the arena with the older cocks"; "one of a pair of starlings (*Sturnus vulgaris*) was shot in the morning; by noon a new mate was found; this was again shot, but before night the pair was complete; so that the disconsolate widow or widower was thrice consoled during the same day"; "a female zebra would not admit the addresses of a male ass until he was painted so as to resemble a zebra"; some amorous male pigeons, "called by our English fanciers 'gay birds,' are so successful in their gallantries" that they have to be shut up, and some females are equally profligate "and prefer almost any stranger to their own mate."

In the world of the *Descent*, when Darwin or his publisher remembers, males are lustful, and thus morally inferior to pure and innocent females. In human society, in Darwin's prehistoric reconstruction, virtue begins among the wives and then spreads to the unmarried females; "How slowly it spreads to the male sex, we see at the present day." Differential modification is explained by "the males of almost all animals having stronger passions than the females." As Darwin later wrote in the *Autobiography* that his wife was "so infinitely my superior in every single moral quality," so in general "Woman seems to differ from man in mental disposition, chiefly in her greater tenderness and less selfishness; and this holds good even with savages." There are, however, aspects in which males are superior: "Man is more courageous, pugnacious, and energetic than woman, and has a more inventive genius"; "male monkeys, like men, are bolder and fiercer than the females." Or, as Darwin put it in a letter to Wallace in 1868: "As the male is the searcher, he has required and gained more eager passions than the female."

Where Darwin had information to the contrary, he suppressed it, as he did the statement from a correspondent in 1868 that "the common hen prefers a salacious cock, but is quite indifferent to colour." Among the lower animals, however, Darwin could let himself go, and here we clearly see the fantasy image of the dominating, passionate, aggressive female. "Thus the females of certain flies (Culicidae and Tabanidae) are bloodsuckers, whilst the males, living on flowers, have mouths destitute of mandibles." Here of course are his barnacles again: "The complemental males of certain Cirripedes live like epiphytic plants either on the female or the hermaphrodite form, and are destitute of a mouth and of prehensile limbs." The paragraph on domesticity among the spiders is reminiscent of nothing so much as Gulliver in Brobdingnag or Baudelaire's "La Géante":

> The male is generally much smaller than the female, sometimes to an extraordinary degree, and he is forced to be extremely cautious in making his advances, as the female often carries her coyness to a dangerous pitch. De Greer saw a male that 'in the midst of his preparatory caresses was seized by the object of his attentions, enveloped by her in a web and then devoured, a sight which, as he adds, filled him with horror and indignation.' The Rev. O. P. Cambridge accounts in the following manner for the extreme smallness of the male in the genus Nephila. 'Mr. Vinson gives a graphic account of the agile way in which the diminutive male escapes from the ferocity of the female, by gliding about and playing hide and seek over her body and along her gigantic

limbs: in such a pursuit it is evident that the chances of escape would be in favour of the smallest males, whilst the larger ones would fall early victims; thus gradually a diminutive race of males would be selected, until at last they would dwindle to the smallest possible size compatible with the exercise of their generative functions,—in fact probably to the size we now see them, i.e., so small as to be a sort of parasite upon the female, and either beneath her notice, or too agile and too small for her to catch without great difficulty.'

Matching the fantasy of the aggressive, devouring female is inevitably the fantasy of the gentle maternal male, living on flowers. Darwin writes:

The male of the smooth-tailed stickleback (G. *leiurus*) performs the duties of a nurse with exemplary care and vigilance during a long time, and is continually employed in gently leading back the young to the nest, when they stray too far. He courageously drives away all enemies including the females of his own species. It would indeed be no small relief to the male, if the female, after depositing her eggs, were immediately devoured by some enemy, for he is forced incessantly to drive her from the nest.

Among emus we have a reversal of "the usual moral qualities of the two sexes; the females being savage, quarrelsome, and noisy, the males gentle and good."

The Descent of Man is wrongly titled, at least in that its dominant mood is onward and upward. Man fell into the savage state, but he is rising out of it, and he will abolish it. "At some future period, not very distant as measured by centuries, the civilised races of man will almost certainly exterminate, and replace, the savage races throughout the world." Darwin writes quite dispassionately of the organized extermination of the aboriginal Tasmanians by the settlers, calling it "the famous hunt." It is a proper survival of the fittest, and Darwin notes with no visible irony that "The New Zealander seems conscious of the parallelism, for he compares his future fate with that of the native rat now almost exterminated by the European rat."

Teleology is still inherent in Mother Nature, and perfection is visible ahead. Darwin reminds us "what an infinite debt of gratitude we owe to the improvement of our reason, to science, and to our accumulated knowledge." In his vision of man he sees "the standard of his morality rise higher and higher," and he looks to a future in which "the struggle between our higher and lower impulses will be less severe, and virtue will be triumphant." He generalizes from history:

It is apparently a truer and more cheerful view that progress has been much more general than retrogression; that man has risen, though by slow and interrupted steps, from a lowly condition to the highest standard as yet attained by him in knowledge, morals and religion.

"It is not improbable," he writes "that after long practice virtuous tendencies may be inherited." "It is incredible," he exclaims, "that all this should be purposeless."

Darwin's ultimates now go beyond natural selection. In primitive tribes, "The bravest men, who were always willing to come to the front in war, and who freely risked their lives for others, would on an average perish in larger numbers than other men. Therefore it hardly seems probable, that the number of men gifted with such virtues, or that the standard of their excellence, could be increased through natural selection, that is, by the survival of the fittest." However, as soon as we take a social unit the anomaly disappears: "A tribe including many members who, from possessing to a high degree the spirit of patriotism, fidelity, obedience, courage, and sympathy, were always ready to aid one another, and to sacrifice themselves for the common good, would be victorious over most other tribes; and this would be natural selection." Except in this larger sense, "civilisation thus checks in many ways the action of natural selection." It is even an advantage, in the larger sense, to be less than the fittest in the narrower sense (*felix culpa* again). Thus Darwin writes:

> We should, however, bear in mind that an animal possessing great size, strength, and ferocity, and which, like the gorilla, could defend itself from all enemies, would not perhaps have become social: and this would most effectually have checked the acquirement of the higher mental qualities, such as sympathy and the love of his fellows. Hence it might have been an immense advantage to man to have sprung from some comparatively weak creature.

The moral sense, Darwin quotes Mackintosh as saying, "has a rightful supremacy over every other principle of human action." He presumes that even ants have "some feeling of right and wrong, or a conscience." H. Hoeffding writes on "The Influence of the Conception of Evolution on Modern Philosophy" in *Darwin and Modern Science:* "Darwin has, indeed, by his whole conception of nature, rendered a great service to ethics in making the difference between the life of nature and the ethical life appear in so strong a light."

With a morality that is "useless" by his narrow functional criteria, Darwin is now tempted by a beauty similarly "useless." He writes:

> Hardly any colour is finer than that of arterial blood; but there is no reason to suppose that the colour of the blood is in itself any advantage; and though it adds to the beauty of the maiden's cheek, no one will pretend that it has been acquired for this purpose. So again with many animals, especially the lower ones, the bile is richly coloured; thus, as I am informed by Mr. Hancock, the extreme beauty of the Eolidae (naked sea-slugs) is chiefly due

to the biliary glands being seen through the translucent integu-
ments—this beauty being probably of no service to these animals.

Beauty in bird courtship display "is even sometimes more important
than success in battle." Darwin begins by demonstrating that the
horns of stags are efficient weapons, worries about it, and goes on:

> The suspicion has therefore crossed my mind that they may
> serve in part as ornaments. That the branched antlers of stags
> as well as the elegant lyrated horns of certain antelopes, with
> their graceful double curvature, are ornamental in our eyes, no
> one will dispute. If, then, the horns, like the splendid accoutre-
> ments of the knights of old, add to the noble appearance of
> stags and antelopes, they may have been modified partly for this
> purpose, though mainly for actual service in battle; but I have
> no evidence in favour of this belief.

Here, where he uses "purpose" to mean "no purpose," Darwin completely transcends the world of nature of the *Origin* and accepts the
world of culture ("the ethical life," in Hoeffding's vocabulary,
"grace" in St. Augustine's). His final moral imperative is curiously
akin to Freud's concept of civilization as the taming of the instinctual life: "The highest possible stage in moral culture is when we
recognize that we ought to control our thoughts, and 'not even in inmost thought to think again the sins that made the past so pleasant
to us.' " The quotation is from *The Idylls of the King.* It shows as well
as anything could what the anonymous reviewer in the *Spectator* immediately perceived, that *The Descent of Man*, this bold attack on
Victorian orthodoxy, was the salvation of Victorian orthodoxy in
the only terms, imaginative and poetic, in which it could still be
saved.

The Expression of the Emotions in Man and Animals, published
in 1872, as a work of science is an important early venture in be-
havioral psychology or "ethology." As an imaginative construct, it extends *The Descent of Man* (in which, as usual, it had originally been planned as a chapter) in putting man back in nature, in fact,
in developing the mystic consubstantiality of Victorian man with
such lower beings as animals, children, primitives, the insane, and Victorian women. In the introduction, Darwin lists his six principal
sources: (1) he tried "to observe infants"; (2) he obtained notes on
the insane from superintendents of asylums; (3) he used photographs
of a man whose facial muscles were galvanized; (4) he studied "the
great masters of painting and sculpture"; (5) he circulated queries
about primitives; and (6) "I have attended, as closely as I could, to the
expression of the several passions in some of the commoner animals."

The animals in the book are as humanized as those in the *Journal of Researches*. "It is well known that cats dislike wetting their feet, owing, it is probable, to their having aboriginally inhabited the dry country of Egypt." When the puppies of Darwin's terrier bitch were destroyed, "her desire to lick my hands rose to an insatiable passion." Hyenas fight each other, "mutually conscious of the wonderful power of each other's jaws," bent low and all tucked in, sidling or backing toward each other.

Darwin studied his own children with a beautiful dispassion: "With one of my children, under the age of two years, I clearly perceived that his humph of assent was rendered by a slight modulation strongly emphatic; and that by a peculiar whine his negative expressed obstinate determination"; with a Darwin baby, "I repeatedly observed that the first symptom of an approaching passion was the rushing of the blood into his bare scalp"; "I never saw disgust more plainly expressed than on the face of one of my infants at the age of five months"; "I may add, that I have observed a guilty expression, without a shade of fear, in some of my own children at a very early age." Darwin persuaded his friends to observe the emotional reactions of their children too. He wrote to Huxley in 1867, enclosing a query for Mrs. Huxley to fill out: "A dear young lady near here plagued a very young child for my sake, till it cried, and saw the eyebrows for a second or two beautifully oblique, just before the torrent of tears began." He wrote to Sir W. Bowman, a surgeon friend, the same year: "I intended in my former note only to express a wish that if, during your professional work, you were led to open the eyelids of a screaming child, you would specially observe this point about the eye showing signs of becoming gorged with blood, which interests me extremely."

The answers to Darwin's queries about primitives gave him such information as that the men weep copiously and unreasonably, thus "A New Zealand chief cried like a child because the sailors spoilt his favourite cloak by powdering it with flour." He was able somewhat to confirm this from his own experience: "I saw in Tierra del Fuego a native who had lately lost a brother, and who alternately cried with hysterical violence, and laughed heartily at anything which amused him." English women turned out to be even more remarkable, but Darwin had great trouble in observing them or getting reliable information. He writes, "This protrusion of the head and body seems a common gesture with the enraged; and I have noticed it with degraded English women whilst quarrelling violently in the streets. In such cases it may be presumed that neither party expects to receive a blow from the other." With less degraded English women, Darwin had to be much more delicate. He writes of a case of false pregnancy in a woman past the menopause, "which cannot here be related in full," its conclusion being that "a state of things returned, continuing for three days, which had ceased during the six previous years." He studies the sociology of female blushing:

For instance, a lady by herself may give money to a beggar, without a trace of a blush, but if others are present, and she doubts whether they approve, or suspects that they think her influenced by display, she will blush. So it will be, if she offers to relieve the distress of a decayed gentlewoman, more particularly of one whom she had previously known under better circumstances, as she cannot then feel sure how her conduct will be viewed.

The natural history of female blushing is harder to come by:

I was desirous to learn how far down the body blushes extend; and Sir J. Paget, who necessarily has frequent opportunities for observation, has kindly attended to this point for me during two or three years. He finds that with women who blush intensely on the face, ears, and nape of neck, the blush does not commonly extend any lower down the body. It is rare to see it as low down as the collar-bones and shoulder-blades; and he has never himself seen a single instance in which it extended below the upper part of the chest. . . . Dr. Langstaff has likewise observed for me several women whose bodies did not in the least redden while their faces were crimsoned with blushes. . . . Dr. J. Crichton Browne has several times seen the blush extend as far down as the collar-bones, and in two instances to the breasts. . . . The foregoing facts show that, as a general rule, with English women, blushing does not extend beneath the neck and upper part of the chest. Nevertheless Sir J. Paget informs me that he has lately heard of a case, on which he can fully rely, in which a little girl, shocked by what she imagined to be an act of indelicacy, blushed all over her abdomen and the upper parts of her legs. Moreau also relates, on the authority of a celebrated painter, that the chest, shoulders, arms, and whole body of a girl, who unwillingly consented to serve as a model, reddened when she was first divested of her clothes.

Darwin got his information everywhere he could. He writes:

I asked one of my informants, a surgeon, to attend to the effects of retching when nothing was thrown up from the stomach; and, by an odd coincidence, he himself suffered the next morning from an attack of retching, and three days subsequently observed a lady under a similar attack; and he is certain that in neither case an atom of matter was ejected from the stomach; yet the orbicular muscles were strongly contracted, and tears freely secreted. I can also speak positively to the energetic contraction of these same muscles round the eyes, and to the coincident free secretion of tears, when the abdominal muscles act with unusual force in a downward direction on the intestinal canal.

In the same letter that asks Bowman if he could manage to open the eyelids of a screaming child, Darwin explains further:

So, again, when the muscles of the abdomen contract violently in a propelling manner, and the breath is, I think, always held, as during the evacuation of a very costive man, and as (I hear) with a woman during severe labour-pains, the orbicularis contracts, and tears come into the eyes.

Unable to watch a woman contracting her abdominal muscles, Darwin was thrown back on his own equivalents. Since he spent hardly a day of his adult life without severe digestive trouble, vomiting, and retching, Darwin calmly observed his own torment. As dutifully he went to the arts, studying the expression of grief in the Laocoön figures, weeping in the *Odyssey*, anger puffing out "her fairy nostrils" in Tennyson, or fear in Job. His chief literary source is Shakespeare, quoted with great frequency in the book, since he "from his wonderful knowledge of the human mind ought to be an excellent judge." Since Darwin neither enjoyed Shakespeare nor read him for pleasure, we can picture the dutiful researcher plodding through the plays as conscientiously as he studied the corners of his eyes when vomiting.

It is this final impression of the quiet fanatic with which the book leaves us. Darwin goes to the Zoological Gardens with a stuffed snake and upsets the peccary, sneaks a pinch of snuff to an American monkey, terrifies the baboons with a turtle. He persuades a keeper to make the elephants scream and trumpet, to see if they weep like children and primitives. He persuades another keeper to insult the Anubis baboon and put him in a furious rage, then to make up with him, Darwin studying their expressions meanwhile. He writes to the superintendent of the zoo, about a "pretty little monkey" alleged to cry when frightened, "Could you make it scream without hurting it much?" The final sense we get is of a community of feeling and reaction in infant and adult, elephant and keeper, degraded woman and galvanized man, Darwin and a small American monkey sharing his snuff. It is a world as teeming with emotion as the natural world teems with life.

A Tiny Ball of Dirt

FOR the last two decades of his life, Darwin was primarily a botanist, somewhat to the surprise of his friend, the botanist Gray, who as late as 1857 addressed him in a letter as "you geologists." He had never been content to be one of what he called the "blessed gang" of compilers, dependent on the work of others, and even for the *Origin* he had bred pigeons extensively. In botany, incapacitated as he was, he could experiment in his own gardens and greenhouses, even in pots in his study. At the same time, each of his botanical books, as Gray shrewdly wrote him when the first appeared, was "a flank movement on the enemy," a demonstration of one or another kind of adaptation for natural selection. Even here, of course, Darwin was a compiler, using botanical information and specimens sent him by correspondents all over the world, but at least he was able to test every idea experimentally.

The intent of the first botanical book, *The Various Contrivances by which Orchids are Fertilised by Insects*, published in 1862, was thus part of the evolutionary argument, to illustrate, Darwin wrote to Murray, "how Natural History may be worked under the belief of the modification of species." Darwin explained its genesis in his *Autobiography:* "I was led to attend to the cross-fertilisation of flowers by the aid of insects, from having come to the conclusion in my speculations on the origin of species, that crossing played an important part in keeping specific forms constant." At the same time, the book's imaginative impulse was clearly to justify in new terms the utility of beauty, and it constitutes something of a lyric paean to the beauty and wonder of the orchid. Darwin writes in *The Various Contrivances:* "The study of these wonderful and often beautiful productions, with all their many adaptations, with parts capable of movement, and other parts endowed with something so like, though no doubt different from, sensibility, has been to me most interesting." Several years later, Darwin wrote to Lyell commenting on an article by the Duke of Argyll:

> The Duke, who knows my Orchid book so well, might have learnt a lesson of caution from it, with respect to his doctrine of differences for mere variety or beauty. It may be confidently said

that no tribe of plants presents such grotesque and beautiful differences, which no one until lately, conjectured were of any use; but now in almost every case I have been able to show their important service. It should be remembered that with humming-birds or orchids, a modification in one part will cause correlated changes in other parts. I agree with what you say about beauty. I formerly thought a good deal on the subject, and was led quite to repudiate the doctrine of beauty being created for beauty's sake.

The book's characteristic tone is awe. It begins "The object of the following work is to show that the contrivances by which Orchids are fertilised, are as varied and almost as perfect as any of the most beautiful adaptations in the animal kingdom," and continues, "An examination of their many beautiful contrivances will exalt the whole vegetable kingdom in most persons' estimation." Darwin writes of *Orchis pyramidalis*, which ingeniously sticks its pollinia to the probosces of moths: "In no other plant, or indeed in hardly any animal, can adaptations of one part to another, and of the whole to other organisms widely remote in the scale of nature, be named more perfect than those presented by this Orchis." Of *Coryanthes macrantha*, which drops bees into a bucket of fluid and attaches the pollen mass to their backs as they crawl out, its operation "would have appeared utterly incredible had it not been repeatedly witnessed by a careful observer." In this contest of beauty and ingenuity, one would think that "nothing can be more perfect than the contrivance of *pyramidalis* and *Coryanthes*, but *Catasetum*, "the most remarkable of all Orchids," is. This flower (although Huxley flatly refused to believe it) shoots its adhesive pollinia at insects. After weighing the rival claims, Darwin concludes:

> Yet an ill-defined feeling tells me to rank the magnificent Vaneae as the highest. When we look within this tribe at the elaborate mechanism for the ejection and transportal of the pollinia of Catasetum, with the sensitive rostellum so wonderfully modified, with the sexes borne on distinct plants, we may perhaps give the palm of victory to this genus.

Every part of the flower cooperates, and in an unusual flight of fancy Darwin writes: "A poet might imagine that whilst the pollinia were borne through the air from flower to flower, adhering to an insect's body, they voluntarily and eagerly placed themselves in that exact position in which alone they could hope to gain their wish and perpetuate their race."

The objects of all this beauty and contrivance are insects, who are sometimes seen in the role of Paris judging, sometimes as suitors being courted, and sometimes as the priests of an odd marriage rite. "Moths and butterflies perform their office of marriage-priests," Darwin writes, and young flowers "must remain in a virgin condition until they are a little older." In this imaginative design, Darwin is himself a kind of insect: he imitates the proboscis of an insect by pushing "very gently a sharply-pointed common pencil into the nectary," or "I imitated this action with a bristle"; "Accordingly I imitated the action of a retreating insect"; once, carried away, "The walls of this cavity have a pleasant nutritious taste." Even acting and thinking like an insect, Darwin cannot fertilize some flowers and cannot figure it all out: in one case, "How insects perform the act of fertilisation I have failed to understand"; in another, "How this is possible is unintelligible to me." He concludes:

> The more I study nature, the more I become impressed with ever-increasing force, that the contrivances and beautiful adaptations slowly acquired through each part occasionally varying in a slight degree but in many ways, with the preservation of those variations which were beneficial to the organism under complex and ever-varying conditions of life, transcend in an incomparable manner the contrivances and adaptations which the most fertile imagination of man could invent.

The book's last sentence is a message from on high: "It is hardly an exaggeration to say that Nature tells us, in the most emphatic manner, that she abhors perpetual self-fertilisation."

The next work was *The Movements and Habits of Climbing Plants*, published in *The Journal of the Linnean Society* in 1865, and as a separate volume in 1875. Where the orchids were traps with female wiles, these climbing plants are like lively animals. Shoots slither like snakes (if I may extend Darwin's alliteration):

> The straight shoot slowly and gradually slid up the stick, so as to become more and more highly inclined, but did not pass over the summit. Then, after an interval sufficient to have allowed of a semi-revolution the shoot suddenly bounded from the stick and fell over to the opposite side. . . .

Another plant has a tendril "curiously like the leg and foot of a small bird," and it clutches branches "like a bird when perched." Of another tendril: "The whole terminal portion exhibits a singular habit, which in an animal would be called an instinct; for it continually searches for any little crevice or hole into which to insert itself." Darwin concludes:

> It has often been vaguely asserted that plants are distinguished from animals by not having the power of movement. It should rather be said that plants acquire and display this power only when it is of some advantage to them; this being of comparatively rare occurrence, as they are affixed to the ground, and food is brought to them by the air and rain. We see how high in the scale of organization a plant may rise, when we look at one of the more perfect tendril-bearers. It first places its tendrils ready for action, as a polypus places its tentacula.

Clearly hierarchical factors are involved. Darwin writes: "It could not have been anticipated that so lowly a plant as this Fumaria should have been a climber." The movement is always upward, and it is shocking when the roots of a Brazilian philodendron "use their powers to descend, instead of to ascend like twining plants." In this world, unlike the social world, it is possible to have both upward mobility and security. One particularly efficient climber "probably could ascend a polished stem incessantly tossed by heavy storms," and Darwin writes:

> I have more than once gone on purpose during a gale to watch a Bryony growing in an exposed hedge, with its tendrils attached to the surrounding bushes; and as the thick and thin branches were tossed to and fro by the wind, the tendrils, had they not been excessively elastic, would instantly have been torn off and the plant thrown prostrate. But as it was, the Bryony safely rode out the gale, like a ship with two anchors down, and with a long range of cable ahead to serve as a spring as she surges to the storm.

It is almost as though the plants were conscious. Darwin tests some tendrils with a glass tube and a zinc plate, "but they soon recoiled from these objects with what I can only call disgust." He asks, "Why have they been endowed with sensitiveness?" and the answer is that it is all Nature's economy and foresight, in which "nothing superfluous is granted," but everything necessary. What we cannot understand—"These movements, which seemed so nicely adapted for some purpose, were useless," "the habit seems to us in our ignorance useless"—Mother Nature can.

With the next work, *Insectivorous Plants*, published in 1875, Darwin's imaginative vision gets genuinely bizarre. The book begins with a directly confessional tone, like a Gide novel:

> During the summer of 1860, I was surprised by finding how large a number of insects were caught by the leaves of the common sun-dew (*Drosera rotundifolia*) on a heath in Sussex.

This tone of personal engagement continues all through, dominating the tone of scientific detachment with which the book concludes: "Such are the diversified means, as far as at present known, by which higher plants gain their subsistence." These insectivorous plants are like predatory animals: "On one plant all six leaves had caught their prey"; on another "The whole upper surface is covered with gland-bearing filaments, or tentacles, as I shall call them, from their manner of acting." Furthermore, sundews have the power of digestion, and their secretions "act on albuminous compounds in exactly the same manner as does the gastric juice of mammals." When they do not dissolve the coats of pollen grains, "It is well known that the gastric juice of animals does not attack cellulose"; when they do not dissolve fats, "Oily substances are not digested by the gastric juice of animals"; when they fail to affect starch, "I need hardly say that starch is not digested by the gastric juice of animals." Darwin concludes: "There is, therefore, a remarkable parallelism between the glands of Drosera and those of the stomach in the secretion of their proper acid and ferment." Having established true digestion in Drosera, Darwin chortles, "No such power was before distinctly known to exist in the vegetable kingdom." He wrote to Hooker in 1873: "I do not think any discovery gave me more pleasure than proving a true act of digestion in *Drosera*."

Like the climbing tendrils, these insectivorous plants are almost conscious. "If a bit of dry moss, peat, or other rubbish, is blown on to the disc, as often happens, the tentacles clasp it in a useless manner. They soon, however, discover their mistake and release such innutritious objects." Without nerves or muscles, they have "extreme sensitiveness, exceeding that of the most delicate part of the human body, as well as the power of transmitting various impulses from one part of the leaf to another," and they display a contraction very like muscular action. In digesting bone and teeth, a "large quantity of acid is secreted, owing, apparently, to the desire of the plant for phosphorous." Altogether, "the leaf falsely appears as if endowed with the senses of an animal." Darwin reminds himself that their greatest inferiority to animals is the lack of a brain, but he seems neither entirely convinced nor entirely convincing.

In this study, all of Darwin's experimental ingenuity for the first time comes into play, and at times he reminds the reader of nothing so much as a mad scientist in Hawthorne or Poe. He tests the glands of Drosera with saliva, drops of milk, fragments of hard-boiled egg, bits of raw meat, small cubes of albumen and cheese, dead flies, scraps of writing paper, wood, dried moss, sponge, cinders, glass, the quill of a pen, stone, gold-leaf, dried grass, cork, blotting-paper, cotton-wool, hair rolled up into little balls, "the poison of a cobra-snake," human urine, "thick and thin mucus from the bronchial tubes," decoctions of green peas and chopped cabbage leaves, a decoction of chopped grass boiled in distilled water, belladonna, atropine, hyoscyamus, strychnine, quinine, digitaline, nicotine, veratrine, colchicine, theine, curare, morphine, camphor, glycerine, plain water, alcohol, chloroform, sulphuric and nitric ether, carbolic acid, "poison from the fang of a living adder," oil of caraway, oil of cloves, turpentine, twenty different salts and acids in solution, and any number of others. Sometimes he is reminiscent of the witches in Macbeth, going after his sundews with tissue from the visceral cavity of a toad, cartilage from the leg bone of a sheep, bits of the skinned ear of a cat, slivers of the dried bone of a fowl moistened with saliva, and slices of the canine tooth of a dog.

Crazy as this list sounds, the delicacy of Darwin's experiments on the sundew was for his time quite remarkable. He made the tentacles of Drosera "move in a conspicuous manner" by placing on them a particle of human hair $\frac{1}{125}$ of an inch long weighing $\frac{1}{78,740}$ of a grain, He comments:

> A bit of hair, $\frac{1}{50}$ of an inch in length, and therefore much larger than those used in the above experiments, was not perceived when placed on my tongue; and it is extremely doubtful whether any nerve in the human body, even if in an inflamed condition, would be in any way affected by such a particle supported in a dense fluid, and slowly brought into contact with the nerve. Yet the cells of the glands of Drosera are thus excited to transmit a motor impulse to a distant point, inducing movement. It appears to me that hardly any more remarkable fact than this has been observed in the vegetable kingdom.

Using chemicals, he could get a tentacle to move with approximately $\frac{1}{30,000,000}$ of a grain of phosphate of ammonia in solution. "When I read over my notes, in 1873," Darwin writes, "I entirely disbelieved them." He repeated the experiments a number of times over several years, with the greatest care, and got the same results. Darwin concludes:

> I am well aware that this statement will at first appear incredible to almost every one. Drosera is far from rivalling the power of the spectroscope, but it can detect, as shown by the movement of its leaves, a very much smaller quantity of the phosphate of ammonia than the most skilful chemist can of any substance.

Ultimately, in his view, the tribute should not be to his skill but to Drosera's:

> With Drosera, the really marvelous fact is, that a plant without any specialised nervous system should be affected by such minute particles; but we have no grounds for assuming that other tissues could not be rendered as exquisitely susceptible to impressions from without if this were beneficial to the organism, as is the nervous system of the higher animals.

Darwin's next botanical work, *The Effects of Cross and Self Fertilisation in the Vegetable Kingdom*, was published in 1876. He writes in the introduction, "My present work is the complement of that on Orchids, in which it was shown how admirably these plants are constructed so as to permit of, or to favour, or to necessitate cross-fertilisation." His conclusion, after experiments going on for eleven years, is that cross-fertilized plants have an enormous advantage in height, weight, fertility, and hardiness, and that it begins immediately in the first generation, "a surprising conclusion, for from the analogy of domesticated animals it could not have been anticipated." While Darwin's experiments in cross-fertilization were going on, the Moravian abbot Gregor Mendel was similarly crossing plants and determining the principles of inheritance. Darwin used the same plant, the common pea, for some of his experiments, and hit on some of the things Mendel did, but he never got Mendel's results. One problem was that "The colour of the flowers was a point to which I did not at first in the least attend." When he did get around to observing color, as in the sweet pea, it was oddly imprecise:

> The seedlings from both the Purples were chiefly Purples, but with some Painted Ladies and some Scarlets. The seedlings from aberrant Painted Lady were chiefly Painted Ladies with some Scarlets. Each variety, whatever its parentage may have been, retained all its characters perfect, and there was no streaking or blotching of the colours, as in the foregoing plants of crossed origin.

With careful counting and a few more generations here, Darwin could have discovered genetics too, like his model Newton, who incredibly discovered gravitation *and* the calculus *and* the nature of light.

What kept Darwin from making Mendel's discovery was his different purpose, and ultimately, in my view, his different temperament. Darwin was a natural quantifier, but he ignored or was vague about color because it was of little use to the plant. He was interested in, and was thus rigorously quantitative about, competitive advantages: height, weight, fertility, vigor. His language is that of the sporting contest, the cockpit or the prize ring: "One of the self-fertilised plants was for a long time taller by two inches than its opponent, but was ultimately beaten by it"; "this victory was fairly won after a long struggle"; "the seedlings thus raised were put into competition"; others were "not subjected to any competition"; of a seedling with its summit gnawed off by a slug, "so great was its constitutional vigor that it ultimately beat its uninjured self-fertilised rival." A self-fertilized plant that beat all cross-fertilized comers Darwin named "Hero." One can see the same sporting vision when Darwin describes the bees that cheat the flowers' arrangements for cross-fertilization by biting through the corolla to get at the nectar. He calls it "their felonious practice" or getting their nectar "in a felonious manner," as though they were fighters who gouged, and there is little doubt that he would bar them from the ring if he could.

Darwin's correspondence during the botanical period uses the same competitive imagery, for botanist and plant alike. He writes in a letter to Hooker in 1858 that fossil species in competition with modern ones would be "beaten hollow," and that if Australian plants turn out to be successfully naturalized elsewhere, "I must strike my colours." He writes to Lyell in 1860: "Talk of adaptation in woodpeckers, some of the orchids beat it." He baits Gray in 1862, on European weeds overcoming their American counterparts: "Does it not hurt your Yankee pride that we thrash you so confoundedly? I am sure Mrs. Gray will stick up for your own weeds. Ask her whether they are not more honest, downright good sort of weeds." To John Scott the same year: "I have worked like a slave . . . on the meaning of the two sets of very different stamens, yet have been shamefully beaten, and I now cry for aid." To Falconer the next year, on the same problem of dimorphic plants: "There is something very odd, but I am as yet beaten." To D. Oliver in 1864: "Do you know *Coryanthes,* with its wonderful basket of water? See what Crueger says about it. It beats everything in orchids." To Lord Farrar some years later, "You are the man to conquer a *Coronilla.*"

Ultimately, Darwin's viewpoint is that of an English squire, a sporting breeder writing for other breeders. If he writes on one page "We stand in awe before the mystery of life," on the next page he is writing practical advice to horticulturists, suggesting "an incomparably better plan" than the one they follow at present. Darwin, who tells us so proudly in the *Origin* that when he turned to breeding pigeons he was permitted to join two London pigeon clubs, goes into more detail about the experience in a letter to Huxley in 1859:

> For instance, I sat one evening in a gin palace in the Borough amongst a set of pigeon fanciers, when it was hinted that Mr Bull had crossed his Pouters with Runts to gain size; and if you had seen the solemn, the mysterious, and awful shakes of the head which all the fanciers gave at this scandalous proceeding you would have recognised how little crossing has had to do with improving breeds.

Francis Darwin reports in the *Life and Letters:*

> He became a member of two Pigeon Fanciers' Clubs, and was always treated with great civility at their meetings. They called him 'Squire,' and he sat with them in a cloud of smoke. No doubt they agreed with one enthusiast who wrote in a treatise on the Almond Tumbler that 'If it was possible for noblemen and gentlemen to know the amazing amount of solace and pleasure derived from the Almond Tumbler, . . . scarce any nobleman or gentleman would be without their aviaries,' and were pleased to see that my father, at least, understood the truth of these views.

In *Darwin and Modern Science,* H. Hoeffding writes: "In accentuating the struggle for life Darwin stands as a characteristically English thinker: he continues a train of ideas which Hobbes and Malthus had already begun." (For Marx's remarks on the same subject, see below p. 122). There is some truth in this, but there would be more if Hoeffding had written "a characteristically English country squire." The laws of inheritance, however, could only be discovered by someone neutrally interested in studying how variation is inherited, not someone committed to getting the best variations inherited as soon as possible.

Darwin's next botanical book, *The Different Forms of Flowers on Plants of the Same Species,* published in 1877, is almost an exercise in plant eugenics. The last book having shown crossing to be an advantage, this goes a step further to demonstrate that plants with several forms of flowers are most efficiently designed for crossing. (*Beaten for so long by polymorphic plants, Darwin finally conquered.*) Those seedlings fertilized by crossing Darwin invidiously calls "legitimate," those self-fertilized, "illegitimate," and his demonstration is that the legitimate seedlings are more fertile and vigorous than the illegitimate. Plants arrange his legitimate crossings with extreme ingenuity, even to some that are heterostyled, trimorphic, and have remarkably complicated matings. *Lythrum salicaria* is particularly ingenious:

> In short, nature has ordained a most complex marriage-arrangement, namely a triple union between three hermaphrodites,— each hermaphrodite being in its female organ quite distinct from the other two hermaphrodites and partially distinct in its male organs, and each furnished with two sets of males.

"In their manner of fertilisation," he writes ecstatically, "these plants offer a more remarkable case than can be found in any other plant or animal."

The experiments were quite laborious. Darwin writes: "I will give the results of my experiments in detail, partly because the observations are extremely troublesome, and will not probably soon be repeated—thus, I was compelled to count under the microscope above 20,000 seeds of *Lythrum salicaria.*" He notes unhappily that if one were to make hybrids between two such species, "he would be compelled to fertilise 900 flowers and count their seeds. This would probably exhaust the patience of the most patient man." The sexual arrangements of these plants seem to him even more remarkable than those of the Cirripedes, and he tries to explain them in an elaborate metaphor of a hypothetical ant community:

> We shall, perhaps, best perceive the complex and extraordinary nature of the marriage arrangements of a trimorphic plant by the following illustration. Let us suppose that the individuals of the same species of ant always lived in triple communities; and that in one of these, a large-sized female (differing also in other characters) lived with six middle-sized and six small-sized males; in the second community a middle-sized female lived with six large- and six small-sized males and in the third, a small-sized female lived with six large- and six middle-sized males. Each of these three females, though enabled to unite with any male, would be nearly sterile with her own two sets of males, and likewise with two other sets of males of the same size with her own which lived in the other two communities; but she would be fully fertile when paired with a male of her own size. Hence the thirty-six males, distributed by half-dozens in the three communities, would be divided into three sets of a dozen each; and these sets, as well as the three females, would differ from one another in their reproductive powers in exactly the same manner as do the distinct species of the same genus.

In Darwin's hall of fame, along with Catasetum and Coryanthes, Drosera, and "Hero," there surely was a busy heterostyled trimorphic household of Lythrum.

Darwin's last botanical book, *The Power of Movement in Plants*, in which his son Francis collaborated, appeared in 1880. Developing out of the earlier *Climbing Plants*, it deals with movements too slow and slight to be perceived, or reactions to light so dim that it produces no visible shadow. The book is a demonstration that most complicated plant movements, rooting, climbing, heliotropism, and the rest, are modifications of the simple movement Darwin calls "circumnutation," a slight revolving movement continuous in all the growing parts of all plants. In an imaginative vision Darwin returns to the *Origin*'s key metaphor of the Great Tree of Life, but now it is a great tree in motion: "If we look for instance, at a great acacia tree, we may feel assured that every one of the innumerable growing shoots is constantly describing small ellipses; as is each petiole, sub-petiole, and leaflet." Darwin's methods for observing and recording these movements were particularly delicate and ingenious. He and his son glued tiny glass filaments or bits of paper to the part of the plant they were observing, and by means of a black dot at the tip and a black dot on a nearby card were able to record the movement magnified up to forty times. When magnification was unnecessary, they allowed the tips of radicles to make their own tracks on smoked glass-plates. At other times they watched the movements directly under a microscope. As with insectivorous plants, Darwin played mad scientist. He squirted water at plants, whacked their pots with a stick, dropped acid on them, scratched them with needles, cut thin slices off the growing tips, cauterized them with nitrate of silver, greased roots, froze leaves by preventing them from closing at night, and clothed parts of them in little tubes and caps. He wrote to Sir W. Thistleton-Dyer when the book appeared: "It was very good fun bothering the seeds of *Cucurbita* by planting them edgeways."

The book's imaginative vision is of a world seemingly still that is ceaselessly in motion, and its conclusion makes that motion visible by speeding it up, like a botanical film, as Darwin and his reader "in imagination take a germinating seed" and follow its development step by step. These plants are more like animals than ever. Roots "run down the old burrows of worms," "a radicle may be compared with a burrowing animal such as a mole," plants sleep at night and even stir restlessly in their sleep. Seedlings break through the ground arched and wriggling as a man would if he were trying to get up from under a load of hay. The only plant movements that Darwin does not believe are modifications of circumnutation are the movements of plants sensitive to touch and the movements of his insectivorous plants when seizing their prey. Drosera showed no circumnutation, but would go after a bit of raw meat in a matter of seconds; where ordinary plants head for sunlight, water, or other nourishment, carnivorous plants pursue *their* food. Darwin is now prepared to break down his last barrier between plants and animals. He notes that "plants do not of course possess nerves or a central nervous system," but that he has finally come to believe that the tip of the radicle, "having the power of directing the movements of the adjoining parts, acts like the brain of one of the lower animals."

In the course of his botanical writings, Darwin's language gets much more scientific. The earlier books are written in the popular language of the *Journal of Researches* or *The Origin of Species*. By the *Forms of Flowers*, Darwin is avoiding popular terminology; what florists call "pin-eyed" and "thrum-eyed," "I will designate . . . long-styled and short-styled." *The Power of Movement* gets quite technical: "cotyledons, besides being heliotropic, are affected paratonically," or "the movement of the petiole is in all probability due to the varying turgescence of the pulvinus." In 1843, Darwin had written to Hooker: "From my entire ignorance of Botany, I am sorry to say that I cannot answer any of the questions which you ask me." By 1861, he was writing to him: "But I must stop; otherwise, by Jove, I shall be transformed into a botanist. I wish I had been one." The next year he wrote to J. Scott: "Botany is a new subject to me" and "I know only odds and ends of Botany." In 1877, when he published *The Different Forms of Flowers*, Darwin notes in the introduction that the subject "ought to have been treated by a professed botanist, to which distinction I can lay no claim." In fact, by that time he was not only a professional botanist, but in the opinion of some, the greatest since Linnaeus.

Our concern, however, is not with his scientific achievement but with his imaginative designs. Looking at his botanical work as a whole, one of the most striking of these is the sweeping vision of plants as animals. It appears as far back as 1855, when Darwin wrote to Hooker about his plans to train a plant, *Hedysarum:* "I read somewhere that no plant closes its leaves so promptly in darkness, and I want to cover it up daily for half an hour, and see if I can *teach it* to close by itself, or more easily than at first in darkness." In 1860, he wrote to him: "By Jove, I sometimes think *Drosera* is a disguised animal!," and Emma Darwin wrote to Lady Lyell: "At present he is treating Drosera (the sun-dew plant) just like a living creature, and I suppose he hopes to end in proving it to be an animal." Darwin's son William later remembered his father saying he believed he could write a poem about *Drosera.* In 1863 or 1864, Darwin wrote to Gray: "Depend on it you are unjust on the merits of my beloved Drosera; it is a wonderful plant, or rather a most sagacious animal. I will stick up for Drosera to the day of my death." A decade later, working on the power of movement, Darwin reported to Hooker about *Desmodium gyrans:* "The little leaflets never go to sleep, and this seems to me very odd; they are at their games of play as late as 11 o'clock at night and probably later," and his wife wrote to their daughter Henrietta, with equal whimsicality but opposite conclusions: "Father is much absorbed in Desmodium gyrans and went to see it asleep last night. It was dead asleep, all but its little ears, which were having most lively games, such as he never saw in the day-time." A few months later Darwin confessed to Hooker about a mimosa: "If it dies, I shall feel like a murderer." The next year he wrote to Chauncey Wright, about plants in general: "I begin to think that they are more wonderful than animals." In 1880, recognizing his long-term tendency, Darwin wrote to Alphonse de Candolle: "It always pleases me to exalt plants in the organic scale," and he was so taken with the statement that he added it to his *Auto-biography* the next year.[1]

Everywhere in Darwin's later work the distinction between plants and animals tends to disappear. He writes in the *Orchid* book, which first announces that the vegetable kingdom would be exalted, "The flowers of Orchids, in their strange and endless diversity of shape, may be compared with the great vertebrate class of Fish, or still more appropriately with tropical Homopterous insects." In his later experiments with worms, Darwin found that they moisten leaves with a secretion that starts to digest them before they are taken into the alimentary canal, and he writes in the *Worms* book: "Perhaps the nearest analogy may be found in such plants as Drosera and Dionaea; for here animal matter is digested and converted into peptone not within a stomach, but on the surface of the leaves." *Insectivorous Plants* similarly reports a parasitic crustacean that lacks an alimentary canal and absorbs nourishment through "root-like processes," and among Darwin's notes was the comment on termites: "Curiously like cleistogamic flowers."

The other striking quality in this dramatizing of plants, perhaps less conscious in Darwin and his wife than the exaltation of plants as animals, is their sex symbolism. Perhaps Darwin *was* somewhat aware of it, since he wrote to Murray in 1861, about the *Orchid* book: "The subject of propagation is interesting to most people, and is treated in my paper so that any woman could read it." In 1878, near the end of his life, he wrote to Heinrich Mueller:

> I am working away on some points in vegetable physiology, but though they interest me and my son, yet they have none of the

[1] One of the most curious features of this is that the idea of plants as inferior animals was, like evolution, one of the disreputable ideas held by Darwin's grandfather Erasmus Darwin, the author of *Zoonomia* and *The Botanic Garden*. It is as though, after writing scornfully in the Historical Sketch preceding the *Origin* of his grandfather's anticipation of Lamarck's "erroneous views," Darwin had finally come to appreciate the old gentleman as he went further into botany. A footnote in *The Power of Movement* cites the third canto of *The Botanic Garden* for a fact. In 1879 Darwin translated for English publication a study of his grandfather by Ernst Krause, adding a prefatory memoir.

I am indebted to F. T. McGill, Jr., for calling to my attention the remarkable reference in Washington Irving's *Knickerbocker's History of New York* to "the startling conjecture of Buffon, Helvetius, and Darwin, so highly honorable to mankind, that the whole human species is accidentally descended from a remarkable family of monkeys!" Since the *History* was published in 1809, the year of Darwin's birth, the reference is of course to his grandfather.

fascination which the fertilisation of flowers possesses. Nothing in my life has ever interested me more than the fertilisation of such plants as *Primula* and *Lythrum*, or again *Anacamptis* or *Listera*.

So much of the imagery is reptilian, phallic: tendrils climbing, shoots circumnutating warily, roots forcing and penetrating, pollinia erecting and depressing. In one aspect the orchids are serpentine: "a strange, lurid, and almost reptilian appearance," "each horn therefore is tubular, with a slit down one side, like an adder's fang." Much more dramatically, however, both orchids and insectivorous plants are female imagery, vulvar, vaginal: attracting, clutching, catching the probosces of insects, enslaving in their service or mercilessly destroying. The illustrations in the *Orchid* book are more lurid than Georgia O'Keeffe's flower paintings, and the illustrations in *Insectivorous Plants* of Darwin's beloved *Drosera* or the American *Dionaea*, the Venus Fly-trap, are the witchcraft fantasy or nightmare of *vagina dentata*.

In the article "Darwin as a Botanist" in *A Century of Darwin*, J. Heslop-Harrison concludes: "In his technique of experiment, Darwin was irreproachable within the limits of his facilities, and in powers of detailed observation it is doubtful whether any biologist has ever surpassed him." What made Darwin this master of experiment was the patience and fertility of imagination he showed in testing Drosera or tormenting a root tip in every way possible, and what in turn inspired him to do these things was a variety of strong symbolic identifications with his experimental subjects. Plants are not only personalized, they are motivated; when Darwin was testing the resistance of seeds to seawater, he wrote to Hooker in 1855: "The bore is, if the confounded seeds will sink, I have been taking all this trouble in salting the ungrateful rascals for nothing." One of Darwin's childhood memories, recounted in his *Autobiography*, is of telling his schoolfellows "some great falsehoods about being able to colour crocuses as I liked." His botanical work was thus literally what Freud defined (in reference to Schliemann's discovery of Troy) as the only true happiness: the adult gratification of a childhood wish. More and more of his emotional life went into botany. Darwin wrote to Hooker in 1863: "I am like a gambler, and love a wild experiment." To J. Jenner Weir, some years later, he revealed his odds: "I am accustomed with my numerous experiments with plants to be well satisfied if I get any good result in one case out of five." As his health progressively incapacitated him for going out into the world, Darwin became increasingly like his plants, rooted yet subtly active. There is an odd identification at the beginning of *Climbing Plants:* "I kept a potted plant, during the night and day, in a well-warmed room to which I was confined by illness." The whole round world with which he had begun narrowed bit by bit to his own gardens and greenhouses, his sickroom, a little plot of ground. Yet as he never tires of telling us, life is so rich everywhere that the microcosm is the macrocosm. To the fourth edition of the *Origin*, in 1866, Darwin adds: "On a piece of ground three feet long and two wide, dug and cleared, and where there could be no choking from other plants, I marked all the seedlings of our native weeds as they came up." There were 357. From the seeds in a tiny ball of dirt on a partridge foot, 32 plants grew, and from a cupfull of pond mud, planted in a pot in his study, 537 plants of many kinds appeared. As Henry Thoreau, who had his own little microcosm pond, remarked, it is not worth the while to go round the world to count the cats in Zanzibar.

DARWIN'S last book, *The Formation of Vegetable Mould Through the Action of Worms, with Observations on Their Habits*, published in 1881, the year before his death, fittingly combines several of his interests. It is zoology insofar as it studies the worms, geology as it deals with alteration of the earth's surface, ecology in the worms' relationship to environment and other forms of life, and involves a good deal of botany. Worms are tiny burrowing beings like his radicles, a worldwide phenomenon that can be reduced to a tiny ball of dirt, and a triumph of evolutionary adaptation. Darwin had been interested in earthworms all his life. He studied them in South America on the *Beagle* voyage, and when he returned home a remark by his uncle, Josiah Wedgwood, about their action in a Wedgwood field in Staffordshire inspired him to further study. Darwin read a paper, "On the Formation of Mould," to the Geological Society, in 1837. Working on the book in 1880, Darwin wrote to J. Victor Carus: "It is the completion of a short paper read before the Geological Society more than forty years ago, and has revived old geological thoughts. . . . As far as I can judge it will be a curious little book."

In its deepest implications, the *Worms* book is a reassuring Notes from Underground. To the question in Callimachus' epigraph on Charidas of Cyrene, "What is it like below?," Darwin is able in effect to answer: "Good; good little beings working for us." He writes in the book's conclusion:

> Worms prepare the ground in an excellent manner for the growth of fibrous-rooted plants and for seedlings of all kinds. They periodically expose the mould to the air, and sift it so that no stones larger than the particles which they can swallow are left in it. They mingle the whole intimately together, like a gardener who prepares fine soil for his choicest plants.

The imagery, like that of corals, is again "Little David was small, but oh my." Darwin begins with the warning, "The subject may appear an insignificant one, but we shall see that it possesses some interest; and the maxim 'de minimis lex non curat,' does not apply to science." He quotes a critic in the *Gardener's Chronicle* who rejected his conclusions about worms with the statement, "Considering their weakness and their size, the work they are represented to have accomplished is stupendous." Darwin comments: "Here we have an instance of that inability to sum up the effects of a continually recurrent cause, which has often retarded the progress of science, as formerly in the case of geology, and more recently in that of the principle of evolution."

Worms are not only small and weak, but deaf, dumb, blind, and limbless. But they are many, perhaps 54,000 to an acre. They work steadily at their chore, which is running the soil through their alimentary canals, and product from ten to eighteen tons of castings on an acre per year. They have, moreover, been doing it for a long time. Darwin writes: "The result for a country of the size of Great Britain, within a period not very long in a geological sense, such as a million years, cannot be insignificant." Furthermore, worms are much stronger than anyone thinks: their average weight is a gram, but they can drag stones weighing two ounces or fifty-seven times their own weight; and they go down deeper than people imagine, sometimes to a depth of eight feet. When they remodeled a field for several decades, "the transformation was wonderful." Darwin's conclusion is that no one can continue to doubt "that worms play an important part in nature" and "a more important part in the history of the world than most persons would at first suppose." When the book appeared, a reviewer commented:

> In the eyes of most men . . . the earthworm is a mere blind, dumb, senseless, and unpleasantly slimy annelid. Mr. Darwin undertakes to rehabilitate his character, and the earthworm steps forth at once as an intelligent and beneficent personage, a worker of vast geological changes, a planer down of mountain sides. . . . a friend of man . . . and an ally of the Society for the preservation of ancient monuments.

Darwin discovered these values in the earthworm by his usual processes of empathy and identification. He explains in the introduction: "As I was led to keep in my study during many months worms in pots filled with earth, I became interested in them, and wished to learn how far they acted consciously, and how much mental power they displayed." He tested their reaction to various sorts of light and to a hot poker held near. He tried every sort of sound on them without effect, including "the deepest and loudest tones of a bassoon," although when they felt the vibration of a piano they went whipping into their burrows. Sometimes Darwin played worm with them; as he wrote to Romanes in 1881, "I tried to observe what passed in my own mind when I did the work of a worm." At other times he disguised himself as an enemy: "It has often been said that if the ground is beaten or otherwise made to tremble, worms believe that they are pursued by a mole and leave their burrows. I beat the ground in many places where worms abounded, but not one emerged." Sometimes he took the role of god: he made better leaves for the worms than natural leaves, by cutting triangles out of writing-paper and rubbing them with raw fat; he even made an improved variety of rain for them, "the drops from which were closer together than those of rain, but not nearly so large as those in a thunder storm; nor did they strike the ground with nearly so much force as drops during heavy rain." As a result of all this, Darwin is able to give a psychological portrait:

> We have seen that worms are timid. It may be doubted whether they suffer as much pain when injured, as they seem to express by their contortions. Judging by their eagerness for certain kinds of food, they must enjoy the pleasure of eating. Their sexual passion is strong enough to overcome for a time their dread of light. They perhaps have a trace of social feeling, for they are not disturbed by crawling over each other's bodies, and they sometimes lie in contact.

He later adds to that curious test of social feeling that they are cannibal. Most remarkable, they have intelligence of a sort. "When their attention is engaged, they neglect impressions to which they would otherwise have attended; and attention indicates the presence of a mind of some kind." "We can hardly escape from the conclusion that worms show some degree of intelligence in their manner of plugging up their burrows," he writes, since they are able to profit from experience.

The ecological value that worms have is entirely their excretion, and a great deal of *The Formation of Vegetable Mould* naturally concerns itself with castings. Darwin measures and weighs some sent him from India, the largest six inches in height and weighing a quarter of a pound, and prints life-size engravings from photographs. He is very much interested in the texture of castings. Here is a typical discussion:

> Castings when first ejected are viscid and soft; during rain, at which time worms apparently prefer to eject them, they are still softer; so that I have sometimes thought that worms must swallow much water at such times. However this may be, rain, even when not very heavy, if long continued, renders recently-ejected castings semi-fluid; and on level ground they then spread out into thin, circular, flat discs; exactly as would so much honey or very soft mortar, with all traces of their vermiform structure lost.

Here is a description of a worm caught in the act:

> I have watched worms during the act of ejection, and when the earth was in a very liquid state it was ejected in little spurts, and when not so liquid by a slow peristaltic movement. It is not cast indifferently on any side, but with some care, first on one and then on another side; the tail being used almost like a trowel.

It is easy enough to identify this preoccupation as coprophilic, and to note the concern with excrement running all through Darwin's books (one of the earliest scientific notes he made, on the *Beagle* voyage in 1832, was the observation: "Viscache shit as dogs"). So it may be, and we can see some of the repressed peepings of *The Expression of Emotions* later finding their outlet in openly watching the sexuality of trimorphic plants and the excretion of earthworms. A rounder view, however, would see beyond Darwin's personal fantasies and preoccupations to the resounding affirmation that he makes about excrement, from the guanaco dung that the Peruvian Indians use for fuel to the castings of worms: out of dirt and decay come life and value; "Except a corn of wheat fall into the ground and die, it abideth alone: but if it die, it bringeth forth much fruit." The last paragraph of *The Formation of Vegetable Mould* is Darwin's apology, like a deathbed repentance, for ever finding evil behind the face of nature bright with gladness:

> When we behold a wide, turf-covered expanse, we should remember that its smoothness, on which so much of its beauty depends, is mainly due to all the inequalities having been slowly leveled by worms. It is a marvellous reflection that the whole of the superficial mould over any such expanse has passed, and will again pass, every few years through the bodies of worms. The plough is one of the most ancient and most valuable of man's inventions; but long before he existed the land was in fact regularly ploughed, and still continues to be thus ploughed by earthworms. It may be doubted whether there are many other animals which have played so important a part in the history of the world, as have these lowly organized creatures.

When the book appeared, a lady wrote to ask Darwin whether she might still kill snails in her garden, or were they as useful as worms? He had made his point. Everything that lives is holy.

MARX

It must always remain a portent to the historians
of opinion—how a doctrine so illogical and dull
can have exercised an influence over the minds of
men, and through them over the events of history.

LORD KEYNES, *The End of Laissez-Faire*

KARL HEINRICH MARX was born at Trier in the Rhineland on the 5th of May, 1818. His father was Herschel Marx, a lawyer, and his mother was Henrietta Pressburg. Both were Jews, descended from long lines of rabbis. Marx was devoted to his father, who seems to have been unusually intelligent and understanding. He had little intellectual rapport with his mother, although she declared him to be a child of fortune in whose hands everything would go well. In 1824, when Karl was six, his father and the seven children were baptized into the National Lutheran church, his father taking the name Heinrich for Herschel. (The next year, when her parents were dead, Henrietta Marx was baptized.) Karl went to school uneventfully in Trier, and was graduated from the secondary school in 1835. That fall he enrolled as a student of jurisprudence at the University of Bonn, where he seems to have spent most of his time in convivial drinking. Early in 1836 he became engaged to Jenny von Westphalen, the highborn daughter of his friend and mentor, Councillor Ludwig von Westphalen.

In the autumn of 1836, after fighting a student duel, Marx was transferred by his father to the University of Berlin to continue his studies of jurisprudence. Here he settled down to intellectual pursuits, studied history and philosophy, joined the Young Hegelian circle, and began writing verse. In 1838 Heinrich Marx died. Karl Marx remained at the University of Berlin until 1841, but left without taking a degree. Instead he got a doctorate of philosophy *in absentia* from the University of Jena by submitting a thesis on Greek philosophy. In 1842 he became a contributor to the *Rheinische Zeitung* in Cologne, and soon became its editor. He began to study political economy intensively, and in 1843 he married Jenny von Westphalen. When the paper was suppressed by the government later that year, the Marxes went to Paris. In Paris, Marx and Arnold Ruge got out the first and only issue of the *Deutsch-Franzoesische Jahrbücher*, containing articles by Marx as well as a contribution by Friedrich Engels. In 1845, Marx was expelled from Paris at the instigation of the Prussian government. He renounced his Prussian citizenship, and was stateless for the rest of his life. Marx then moved to Brussels, where he began collaborating with Engels in a series of books and articles in a wide variety of periodicals. In 1846 in Brussels he founded the Association of German Workers, and lectured on political economy.

The next year he joined the Communist League, visited London for a conference of its leaders, and was instructed to collaborate with Engels in drafting a communist manifesto. With the publication of the *Manifesto* in February, 1848, Marx was arrested and expelled from

81

Belgium. He moved to France briefly on the invitation of the provisional government, and left in April for Cologne in Prussia, where
he reorganized the Communist League and founded the *Neue Rheinische Zeitung*. In Cologne in 1849 Marx was arrested and tried twice,
first for violating press censorship, then for inciting to armed insurrection. He was acquitted both times, but was nevertheless expelled from
Prussia by the government. The paper was suppressed, the last number
appearing in red as a protest. Marx moved to Paris, but in September
was given the choice by the police of expulsion or internment in
Brittany. He chose expulsion and moved to London, where he remained for the rest of his life.

By 1849, after six years of being hounded and driven across the face
of Europe, Marx was no longer the blithe philosopher or ambitious
journalist he had been in 1843, but a hardened and embittered revolutionary. All the evidence suggests great inner resources of strength.
Berlin writes: "In an age which destroyed its adversaries by methods
not less efficient because they were dignified and slow, which forced
Carlyle and Schopenhauer to seek escape in a remote civilization or an
idealized past, and drove its arch-enemy, Nietzsche, to hysteria and
madness, Marx alone remained secure and formidable." "He is," Berlin
adds, "one of the rare revolutionaries who were neither thwarted nor
persecuted in their early life." An American and a German later to be
an American met Marx in Cologne in 1848 and were struck in different
fashions by his formidable quality. "Behind his moderation and re-
serve," Albert Brisbane later wrote, "one could detect the passionate
fire of a daring spirit." "Never in my life," Carl Schurz later wrote,
"have I met a man whose attitude was so insolent and intolerably
arrogant."

In London, Marx settled down to work on the compendium of
political economy that eventually became *Capital*. In 1850 Engels came
to London. Then, having made peace with his family, he settled in
Manchester to work as a bookkeeper in a branch of the family cotton-
spinning firm, and to live in common-law marriage with a Manchester
working girl, Mary Burns. Without any gainful employment, Marx's
life in London was extraordinarily hard. He could fairly have described
himself as Dryden described himself in the postscript to his translation
of *The Aeneid:* "struggling with wants, oppressed with sickness,
curbed in my genius, liable to be misconstrued in all I write." Sup-
ported by what Engels could spare from the hundred pounds a year
he earned in Manchester, by loans from Henrietta Marx, and by occasional journalism, the Marxes moved from one slum hovel to another,
pawned their clothing to buy food, and hid in the house hungry and
cold while their creditors beat at the door. Marx's letters to Engels
report that he cannot go out because his shoes are in pawn, or that he
cannot write because he has no money for paper, or that he cannot send
off a manuscript because he cannot afford stamps.

In 1850 Marx's son Guido died, in 1852 his daughter Franziska
died, and in 1855 his son Edgar died, all because the family could not

afford adequate food or medicine. When Franziska died there was no money for a coffin, but they managed to borrow two pounds from a French refugee. Three daughters, Jenny, Laura, and Eleanor, survived. When Marx's son, Edgar, gifted but so slight that he was nicknamed *Mouche* ("fly" in French), died at the age of six, Marx was inconsolable, and he had to be restrained from throwing himself into the grave. Marx told his daughter Eleanor in later life that he could forgive Christianity a great deal for teaching the love of children, and there is no doubt that he was an exceptionally devoted father, and that close to the heart of his bitterness against the social order was the deaths of his children. It was certainly augmented, however, by his illness. He suffered first from hemorrhoids, then from a disease of the liver and an inflammation of the eyes, then from carbuncles, during the early years in London. As in Darwin's case, there have been interpretations of his ill health as neurotic, among them Otto Ruehle's in *Karl Marx: His Life and Work*.

Despite the miseries of poverty, the deaths of his children, and his illness, Marx's early years in London were not entirely bleak. He worked at the British Museum from 9 to 7 every day his health and the state of his clothes permitted. His wife was adoring and uncomplaining. In the evenings he played with the children, riding them piggyback or making paper boats with them and having sea fights in a bucket. On Sundays he played with the children all day, and in fair weather the family walked in the country, Marx telling the children stories he made up and carrying one small child or another on his shoulders, her hair decked with anemones. Sometimes while Marx worked at home his children made him play horsie, and his daughter Eleanor recalled that several chapters of *The Eighteenth Brumaire of Louis Bonaparte* were written while three children whipped the author on. Marx could not even resist strange children, and he was regularly found playing with them in the street or walking over to give some ragged child a penny.

With adults, Marx's recreation was chess, which he played desperately, losing his temper when he was pressed and furious when he lost. During the early years in London, he kept up practice with the sabre. "What he lacked in science, he tried to make up in aggressiveness," Wilhelm Liebknecht reports in his memoir, "and unless you were cool, he could really startle you." Marx was once challenged to a pistol duel by an outraged revolutionary named Willich, but a friend fought in his place. Marx himself challenged a German editor to a duel in London in 1851, but got a retraction instead. Liebknecht tells an amazing story of Marx, himself, and another friend engaging in a pub crawl one evening. They broke a row of street lights with paving stones, and had to run from the police.

In 1851 Marx became a correspondent for the *New York Tribune* at five dollars a weekly article, which somewhat improved his financial standing, although Horace Greeley didn't print all his articles, paid only for what he printed, and soon cut Marx's rate. At first Engels did most of the articles over Marx's name. That year the Communist

League broke up in squabbling and was dissolved. Marx wrote to Engels:

> I very much like the public isolation in which we two now find ourselves. It is quite in accordance with our attitude and our principles. The system of mutual concessions, of half-measures tolerated for the sake of appearances, and the necessity of taking one's share of the responsibility in the eyes of the general public together with all those fools, is now at an end.

For the next few years, partyless, Marx worked on his economic material, contributed articles to radical journals, and sent his weekly piece to the *Tribune*. In 1857 the managing editor of the *Tribune*, Charles A. Dana, engaged him to write articles for the *New American Cyclopaedia*, which got as far as "C" before expiring. In 1860, Engels' father died, and he became a partner in the firm of Ermen and Engels. In 1861, the *Tribune* fired Marx. A Prussian amnesty was announced to celebrate the coronation of Prince Wilhelm, and Marx went to Berlin on a forged passport, but, although amnestied, he was refused renaturalization. On that trip he stopped off in Amsterdam and borrowed 160 pounds from his uncle Philip, then stopped off in Trier to see his mother, who gave him no more money but tore up his old notes.

When Marx got back to London, he tried to get a job as a clerk in a railway office, but was not hired because of his poor handwriting. Marx's only known quarrel with Engels occurred in 1863, when Engels was terribly hurt by Marx's cold reaction to the news of the death of Mary Burns. Marx patched it up by writing that his own mother, "full of bodily infirmities," should have died instead. Engels promptly moved in with Mary's sister Elizabeth. Later in 1863 Marx's mother did die, and he went back to Trier to attend her funeral. When he returned to London he enrolled in a course in technology for working men at the Geological Institute. He had a hard time with it, writing to Engels: "I understand the mathematical laws, but the simplest technical reality demanding perception is harder to me than to the biggest blockheads."

In 1864 the International Workingmen's Association, the First International, was founded in London, with Marx drawing up the inaugural *Address to the Working Classes of Europe*. During the next years Marx spent much of his time on correspondence and business of the International. His letters to his friend Dr. Kugelmann show a surprisingly childish vanity about his importance. "I have kept behind the scenes all the time," he writes to him in 1866, adding a week later "Really, I have to lead the whole society." "If I were to leave here at this critical time," he writes in 1868, "the whole labor movement, which I influence from behind the scenes, would fall into very bad hands and go the wrong way." In 1867 the first volume of *Capital* was published, and Marx continued to work on the later volumes. In 1869 Engels sold his share in the firm to Ermen and retired from business on an income large enough to support the Marxes and himself modestly. He moved to London and settled near Marx in 1870. Marx began to work at home instead of at the Museum, and soon wore a path in the study carpet. He took up the study of Russian, he said, to be able to read primary sources about land ownership. Engels suspected that he was using the Russian books to delay the completion of *Capital*, and once told Paul Lafargue, Laura's husband, that he would like to burn them all.

In March, 1871, the first communist government, the Paris Commune, was set up after a revolution. Marx wrote a public Address on behalf of the International encouraging the Commune. After twenty years of obscurity in London, he suddenly found himself notorious, and he wrote to Kugelmann proudly: "I have the honor to be at this moment the best calumniated and the most menaced man in London. That really does one good after a tedious twenty years' idyll in my den." After the bloody collapse of the Commune in May, Marx was still regarded as a dangerous revolutionary, to be carefully watched. The next year Marx had the General Council of the International moved to New York, where it was allowed to expire quietly. He began to suffer from headaches, insomnia, and chronic mental depression. In 1873 Marx had a severe breakdown. He recovered somewhat, later in the year, but continued to suffer from depression. In 1874 he applied for naturalization as a British subject, but his application was rejected on the ground that he had not been a loyal subject to his own sovereign. During the next few summers he sneaked to Carlsbad three times for the cure, and there largely recovered from his liver trouble and depression, although the headaches and insomnia continued. The doctor ordered him to work no more than four hours a day, and for a while he followed orders.

In 1879 Jenny Marx was discovered to be suffering from inoperable cancer, and in 1881 she died. After her death Marx traveled to Algiers and through France trying to recover his health. He suffered severely from pleurisy and bronchitis, then from an abscessed lung. On March 14, 1883, he had a slight hemorrhage of the lung, and that afternoon he died peacefully in his sleep, at the age of sixty-five. He was buried in Highgate Cemetery, in his wife's grave, in unconsecrated ground. "While he still may have many adversaries," Engels said at his funeral, "he has now hardly one personal enemy." Engels survived Marx by twelve years, succeeding him in the leadership of the international communist movement, and editing the second and third volumes of *Capital* for publication. Engels himself died in 1895. His body was cremated and the ashes dropped into the North Sea.

The Gnawing Criticism
of the Mice

I N 1 8 3 7, when he was nineteen years old, Karl Marx, the author of
the drama *Oulanem*, the Sternian novel *Scorpion and Felix*, the
philosophic dialogue *Cleanthus*, and many volumes of verse—all unpublished—gave up the writing of poetry and imaginative prose as
beyond his powers and burned a mass of his manuscripts. Three manuscript volumes of poems, sent to his fiancée Jenny von Westphalen as
The Book of Love, survived the holocaust, but in later years she would
not show them to anyone, and they have since disappeared. With the
verse presumably perished his partial translation of the *Pandects*, hundreds of pages of a philosophy of law, a lengthy system of metaphysics,
and a whopping study of Hegel. Four years later Marx tried a new
direction and wrote his doctoral dissertation on *The Difference Between the Democritean and Epicurean Philosophies of Nature*. This
work boldly takes a stand with Epicurus: "Any explanation is adequate. Only let there be no myths." In the preface, Marx identifies himself even more boldly with Prometheus, "the holiest saint and martyr
in the philosophical calendar," quoting Aeschylus: "In simple words, I
hate the pack of gods." The thesis was not published because Marx
hoped to expand it into a comprehensive study of Epicurean, Stoic,
and Skeptic philosophy, although he never did.

In the next two years, as editor of the *Rheinische Zeitung*, Marx
produced articles on subjects he knew considerably less about, as he
later admitted, among them the problems of the Moselle vintners, the
law against taking wood in the forests, and the question of free trade.
In 1843 and early 1844, in the *Deutsch-Franzoesische Jahrbücher* he
edited with Arnold Ruge, Marx published a number of articles that
pointed more clearly at his future operations. One series, "On the
Jewish Question," flatly announces that the abolition of Judaism was
the solution to the question. "The social emancipation of Jewry is the

86

emancipation of society from Jewry," Marx thundered.[1] Another article, "Introduction to the Criticism of Hegel's Philosophy of Right," contains Marx's famous formulation about religion, "It is the opium of the people," and proclaims the revolutionary slogan: "I am nothing but I must be everything." A third, a spurious travel letter from Holland, announces that Holland shames Germany, and in answer to the rhetorical objection, "You don't start a revolution with shame," replies "Shame is in itself a revolution."

Articles published in the Paris *Vorwaerts* the next year show a developing concern with the condition of the English proletariat, with which Marx challenged the platitudes of English political economy (although at the time he was only able to read it in French translation). Mocking the English economist McCulloch, Marx writes:

> Good *pure air*—the pestilential atmosphere of the English cellar dwellings! *Great beauty of nature*—the fantastic rags of the English poor, and the wilted, shrunken flesh of the women who are wasted with work and poverty; the children who live on refuse; the deformed creatures produced by overwork in the monotonous mechanical processes of the factories! And the most charming *last details of practice*—prostitution, murder and the gallows!

In the spring and summer of 1844, Marx produced three manuscripts on economic and philosophic matters, developing out of his reading notes. Undiscovered until recently, they were published in part in Russian in 1927, complete in German in 1932, and in English only in 1959. Their publication has radically altered opinions of Marx, since for the first time they make explicit the moral basis of his revolutionary communism in humanist and existentialist philosophy. More than any of Marx's later work, the *1844 Manuscripts* are centrally concerned with the moral evil of what Hegel called "alienation" or "estrangement." The principal indictment of *Capital*, that capitalism has transformed men into commodities, is made in the *1844 Manuscripts*, but then Marx goes on to say: "Let us now rise above the level of political economy." On this higher level, the alienation of the worker from his product is an estrangement from his full human identity. "Therefore," Marx writes, "he does not affirm himself but denies himself, does not feel content but unhappy, does not develop

---

[1] In 1959, *On the Jewish Question* was published in English translation in a most sensational and distasteful form by the Philosophical Library as *A World Without Jews*. The anti-Semitic and provocative passages are printed in large type, and Dagobert D. Runes contributes an introduction making Marx in effect responsible for a century of persecution of the Jews following his articles. The introduction concludes with "the sanguinary dream of Karl Marx—a world without Jews," as though Runes cannot understand the difference between the Nazi ideal of the physical extermination of the Jews and Marx's very *unsanguinary* ideal of their eventual renunciation of Judaism. Marx's anti-Semitism is neither attractive nor defensible, but scholarship is not served by distorting his views and blackening his name with crimes he would surely have abhorred.

freely his physical and mental energy but mortifies his body and ruins his mind." "Alienated labor" results in "alienated life," and what has been alienated is "human status and dignity." Private property is thus "the estrangement of man," but socialism will be "a new enrichment of *human* nature."

In short, by 1844, Marx had written millions of words, most of them unpublished, and had settled on most of the ideas he was to make his own. That autumn in Paris, he encountered Friedrich Engels, who had been a contributor to the *Rheinische Zeitung* and whom he had briefly met once before. Unlike Marx, Engels had come to his views after an intense religious struggle. In addition, he knew a great deal at first-hand about the proletariat, having grown up knowing the slums around his family's textile factory in Barmen, and having been sent to work for two years at the family cotton spinnery in Manchester. He had just published the revolutionary and impassioned *Outlines of a Critique of Political Economy* in the *Jahrbuecher*, which Marx regarded as a work of theoretical genius, and he had earlier published two intemperate pamphlets against Schelling and in defense of Hegel. Engels was clearly more advanced in some of Marx's own directions, and the two immediately discovered their absolute community of views and set out to produce a book together as a rite of blood brotherhood. Entitled *The Holy Family, or A Critique of Critical Criticism: Against Bruno Bauer and Company*, it was published in 1845. The book's foreword, dated "Paris, September 1844," makes its ceremonial nature clear. Marx and Engels write:

> We therefore give this polemic as a preliminary to the independent works in which we—each for himself, of course—shall present our positive view and thereby our positive attitude to more recent philosophical and social doctrines.

The Holy Family is thus a negative preliminary work, a killing off of the "speculative idealism" of the Young Hegelians, Bruno and Edgar Bauer and their followers, and their master Hegel with them. It is an oddly schoolboyish polemic, and the wit is mostly ponderous. The Bauers called their movement "Critical Criticism," and Engels opposes to it "the base mass in all its massy massiness." He quotes a letter from a reader to the Bauers with the comment:

> The representative of the *sentimental, soft-hearted Mass pining for salvation* cringes and implores Criticism for a kind word with effusions of the heart, deep bows and rolling of the eyes.

Marx, who wrote most of the book, indulges in a variety of comic devices. He creates Critical "idealistic intestines" to oppose to the "vulgar body," puns on the name "Bauer" ("peasant" in German), interrupts quotations with such asides as "Collect yourself, Reader," or wild calls for help, and creates antitheses on this order: "His art is not that of disclosing what is hidden, but of hiding what is disclosed."

Marx clubs the Bauers and their followers with French realistic socialism and the materialism of Ludwig Feuerbach. Edgar Bauer's translation of Proudhon is mercilessly mocked. Bauer does not understand: that Proudhon "first makes a real science of political economy possible"; that he proceeds not from the realm of ideas but "from the fact of poverty, of misery"; that "his work is a scientific manifesto of the French proletariat and therefore has quite a different historic significance than that of the literary bungling of a Critical Critic." Feuerbach is a hero because his *Theses on the Reform of Philosophy* were banned by the censor, as nothing by Critical Criticism would ever be. Charles Fourier's "masterly" remarks are quoted against Criticism's inanities.

Against the Bauers, and encouraged by Feuerbach's glorification of "love," Marx succeeds in defining (perhaps more eloquently than he ever did again) his own humanistic vision. He writes:

> Here Critical Criticism is not against love alone, but against everything living, everything which is immediate, every sensuous experience, any and every *real* experience.

The French Revolution, which the Bauers denigrate, was a "hammer" of freedom and enlightenment, and its slogans are still full of meaning:

> Equality is the French expression for the unity of human essence, for man's consciousness of his species and his attitude toward his species, for the practical identity of man with man, i.e., for the social or human relation of man to man.

Defending Proudhon's categories against Edgar Bauer, Marx writes:

> But Not To Have is not a mere category, it is a most disconsolate reality; today the man who has nothing is nothing, for he is cut off from existence in general and still more from a human existence. . . . Not To Have is the most desperate *spiritualism*, a complete unreality of the human, a complete reality of the dehumanized, a very positive To Have, a having of hunger, of cold, of disease, of crime, of debasement, of all inhumanity and monstrosity.

The importance of materialism, Marx explains, is that from the empirical world "man experiences and gets used to what is really human and that he becomes aware of himself as man." He sees the proverb "What's done is done" as "the *stoic* and at the same time *epicurean* human principle of a free and strong nature," and elsewhere affirms "human independence" against Christian "debasement."

Marxist editors have tended to scorn *The Holy Family* as "of little general interest today" or "a bit obsolete," and it was not available in English translation until 1956, but it is of great interest in foreshadowing most of Marx's later themes and imaginative designs. Its organizing metaphor is the blasphemous one of the title, that the Bauers are Jesus, Mary and Joseph. Criticism is "holy," "like God" it is almighty and all-wise, Bruno Bauer's treatises are "the annunciation of

the Critical Saviour and Redeemer of the world" (the nasty comedy
here is that Bauer had lost his teaching post for denying the historical
reality of Jesus Christ). The group is endlessly called "the Holy
Family of Charlottenburg" and "the Holy Critical Family," and Marx
explains that it arose out of Bruno Bauer's divine freedom from all human passions:

> That is why he sets up for himself a *holy family*, just as the
> solitary God endeavours to do away with his boring isolation from
> society in the Holy Family.

Bauer can look forward to "the *Critical last judgment* like a second
triumphant *Christ*, and, after defeating the dragon, ascend calmly to
heaven." The last chapter of the book, "The Critical Last Judgment,"
is a wild parody of the Book of Revelation. In his fewer pages, Engels
is even more profuse in blasphemy. He contributes the phrase "Critical
Christ," and begins the book:

> Critical Criticism, however superior to the mass it deems it-
> self, has infinite pity for the mass. And therefore Criticism has so
> loved the mass that it sent it its only begotten son, that all who
> believe in him may not be lost, but that they may have Critical
> life. Criticism was made mass and dwelt amongst us and we beheld
> its glory, the glory of the only begotten of the father.

After their meeting in Paris, Engels had gone back to Barmen, which
he called the "Zion of obscurantism," and had written to Marx: "The
sleepy life in the family—Christian and Prussian through and through
—I cannot stand it any longer. I might in the end become a German
philistine and introduce philistinism into communism." For him, blasphemy was a defensive incantation.

As he attacks the Bauers and their followers, Marx attacks Eugène
Sue's *Mysteries of Paris*, which they had praised, and for many pages
he deserts the Bauers to go after Sue directly. Sue writes to satisfy
"his monkish, bestial lust" and is "the most wretched offal of socialist
literature." His sin, like that of Critical Criticism, seems to lie in falsifying life, and thus denying it. Sue distorts love while Critical Criticism
rejects it and "plays about with prostitutes." In Engels' metaphor,
Criticism is an old woman who "paints and adorns her wrinkled and
repugnant abstraction of a body and ogles all over Germany in search
of a wooer," in Marx's it is "an old maid," or a cow chewing "the old
Hegelian cud." Even worse than their sins against life, however, are
their sins against language. Reichardt misuses foreign words, which are
quoted at length; Faucher creates German words on English principles of word-formation; Edgar Bauer mishandles Proudhon's French,
which is, unlike German, "the language of politics and of thoughtful
observation"; Szeliga mixes his metaphors; Bruno Bauer writes a hopeless jargon of apology and qualification. The primary task of the
writer, Mallarmé said, is to purify the language of the tribe, and Marx
began by purifying it of Bruno Bauer and company.

His next piece of writing was the famous eleven *Theses on Feuerbach*, jotted down in Brussels in the Spring of 1845 and not published until Engels found them among Marx's papers after his death. Since they were not shaped either rhetorically or imaginatively for publication, they require little discussion here, except to note that they constitute another sort of clearing of the boards for action. The first thesis begins:

> The chief defect of all hitherto existing materialism—that of Feuerbach included—is that the object, reality, sensuousness, is conceived only in the form of the *object* or *contemplation* but not as *human sensuous activity, practice*, not subjectively.

They go on to note that "circumstances are changed precisely by men," that changed understanding requires that things be "radically changed in practice," and that "social life is essentially *practical*" as well as sensuous. The standpoint of the new materialism, Marx proclaims, is "*human* society or socialized humanity," and the last thesis announces:

> The philosophers have only *interpreted* the world in various ways; the point however is to *change* it.

Marx's next book, *The German Ideology, a Criticism of Recent German Philosophy and Its Representatives Feuerbach, Bruno Bauer and Stirner, and a Criticism of German Socialism and Its Various Prophets*, was written in collaboration with Engels in 1845 and 1846. It was not published in their lifetime for reasons Marx explains in his preface to *The Critique of Political Economy* in 1859:

> We decided to work out our own standpoint together as against the opinions and the ideology of German philosophy, in fact, to settle accounts with our former philosophic conscience. We did this in the form of a criticism of post-Hegelian philosophy. The manuscript, two big octavo volumes, was already in the hands of a Westphalian publisher when we were informed that altered circumstances rendered publication impossible, whereupon we abandoned our manuscript to the gnawing criticism of the mice. We did so with little regret because our main object had been achieved —we had come to an understanding with ourselves.

Where *The Holy Family* had used Feuerbach's materialism to destroy the idealism of Hegel and the Young Hegelians, this in turn kills off Feuerbach and the Left Hegelians and utopian "True" socialists he influenced, by all the former devices of mockery plus new charges of plagiarism and venality. The wild blasphemous outpouring of *The Holy Family* here is only a sacrilegious trickle: Stirner is "Saint Max" or "Blessed Max" and Bauer is "Saint Bruno"; "The bourgeois attitude towards the institutions of the bourgeois regime is like that of the Jew towards the Law"; True Socialism is founded and builds its Church on "the Rock of Ages," or uses a "stone which the builders have rejected" as its cornerstone, to find it only "a stumbling-block"; Gruen is mocked with a parody of the Parable of the Talents.

Thinkers are now seen not as independent speculators, however misguided, but as spokesmen of a class, "ideologists," defined as those "who make the perfecting of the illusion of the class about itself their chief source of livelihood." They are thaumaturges and charlatans, and Marx and Engels continually expose "the whole trick" or "the following tricks" of their operations. They are again clubbed with the realistic French, with Fourier's "masterly observations" or "Gargantuan view of man," or the demonstration that Gruen has plagiarized from the French communist Cabet. The tone of anti-Germanism is now ferocious. Marx and Engels write an elaborate jape about philosophy as an industry:

> Later when the German market was glutted, and the commodity in spite of all efforts found no response in the world-market, the business was spoiled in the usual German manner by fake and shoddy production, deterioration in quality, adulteration of the raw materials, falsification of labels, fake purchases, bill-jobbing and a credit system devoid of any real basis.

Germans are distinguished for "cretinism," their two most numerous classes are petty bourgeoisie and philosophers, and they "conceal the abject part they have played and continue to play in real history by equating the illusions, in which they are so rich, with reality." Marx explains, "First of all, an abstraction is made from a fact; then it is declared that the fact is based upon the abstraction," and advises, "That is how to proceed if you want to appear German, profound and speculative." One gets the sense that being hounded out of Germany, France and Belgium by the Prussian government had not increased Marx's patriotism, but it is hard to imagine who Marx and Engels expected to read the book other than cretinous Germans. One can detect something like a sigh of relief when they consign it to the mice.

Arid and quibbling as much of it is, *The German Ideology* nevertheless has the first bold imaginative designs in Marx's work. It opens in Marx's preface with a riot of metaphor. He paraphrases the view of the German ideologists: "The phantoms of their brains have gained the mastery" over men; "Let us liberate them from the chimeras, the ideas, dogmas, imaginary beings under the yoke of which they are pining away." Marx announces "the aim of uncloaking these sheep, who take themselves and are taken for wolves." Later Marx and Engels write: "They all imagine that they are weaving the web of history when, as a matter of fact, they are merely spinning the long yarn of their own imaginings"; or, "This great cock of the walk turns out, however, to be a perfectly ordinary capon." Sometimes the language is a fireworks of word-play, as when they write: "There must of necessity be one sacred head, the spearhead of all these philosophical and theological heads, in a word, the speculative unity of all these blockheads."

Behind the fireworks there are a number of comprehensive imaginative visions. One is of capitalism soiling and fouling everything it touches. The philosophers are "industrialists of philosophy," and "each with all possible zeal set about retailing his apportioned share." Trade, "as an English economist says, hovers over the earth like the Fate of the Ancients." Industrial capitalism "destroyed as far as possible ideology, religion, morality, etc., and where it could not do this, made them into a palpable lie." Bourgeois writers are "quacks and quill-drivers," "broken-down literary hacks." Wild nature has somehow been corrupted: there is "the bitterest competition among plants and animals"; tall and stately oaks are "tall and stately capitalists" consuming the nutriment of the tiny shrubs; parasites are "the ideologists of the vegetable world"; there is "open warfare" everywhere in nature. Even the solar system is affected:

> He could see in his 'countless host of worlds' a whole heavenly feudal monarchy complete with tenants and vassals, a few of which, e.g. the moon, lead a very poor life *aere et aqua interdicti;* a feudal system in which even the homeless vagabonds, the comets, have been apportioned their station in life and in which the shattered asteroids bear witness to occasional unpleasant scenes, while the meteors, those fallen angels, creep shamefaced through the 'infinite space,' until they find somewhere or other a modest lodging. In the further distance, he would come upon the reactionaries, the fixed stars.

As for the injunction "Consider the lilies of the field":

> Yes, consider the lilies of the field, how they are eaten by goats, transplanted by man into his button-hole, how they are crushed beneath the immodest embraces of the dairymaid and the donkey-driver!

Opposed to this vision of universal war and corruption is an origin myth of Man Producing. Men become human only as producers: "They themselves begin to distinguish themselves from animals as soon as they begin to *produce* their means of subsistence, a step which is conditioned by their physical organization." Marx and Engels continue:

> But life involves before everything else eating and drinking, a habitation, clothing and many other things. The first historical act is thus the production of the means to satisfy these needs, the production of material life itself.

This primal man producing the necessities of life is a whole man, and his work is meaningful, whereas the alienated modern worker's work "is a matter of indifference to him." The vision is of "real, active men," "men in the flesh." Private property creates partial, specialized men:

For as soon as labor is distributed, each man has a particular, exclusive sphere of activity, which is forced upon him and from which he cannot escape. He is a hunter, a fisherman, a shepherd, or a critical critic, and must remain so if he does not want to lose his means of livelihood; while in communist society, where nobody has one exclusive sphere of activity but each can become accomplished in any branch he wishes, society regulates the general production and thus makes it possible for me to do one thing today and another tomorrow, to hunt in the morning, fish in the afternoon, rear cattle in the evening, criticize after dinner, just as I have a mind, without ever becoming hunter, fisherman, shepherd or critic.

Private property "makes one man into a restricted town-animal, the other into a restricted country-animal," whereas communism will make man whole. "In a communist organization of society there are no painters; at most there are people who, among other things, also paint." Marx and Engels repeatedly quote from Henri de Saint-Simon: "My whole life can be expressed in one thought: all men must be assured the freest development of their natural capacities." Implicit in this vision of Man Producing is Man Cooperating. "A certain mode of production, or industrial stage, is always combined with a certain mode of cooperation, or social stage." It is this that makes man human: "The animal has no 'relations' with anything, cannot have any." They write:

> Only in community with others has each individual the means of cultivating his gifts in all directions; only in the community, therefore, is personal freedom possible.

The integration of these metaphors is a dynamic vision of society in process. The division of labor "was originally nothing but the division of labor in the sexual act"; from it other divisions of labor "develops spontaneously." The first social relationship is the family, with all others arising out of it.[2] Like an organism, the bourgeoisie "develops," "splits," "absorbs." Saltation, the sudden jump, comes in with revolution: "Revolution is the driving force of history." Revolution wipes out the corruption of private property and frees the whole man, and the first part of *The German Ideology* ends with the imperative: "In order, therefore, to assert themselves as individuals, they must overthrow the State." The true imperative is not the commanding voices of Marx and Engels, however, but the need for purgation and rebirth. They write:

> This revolution is necessary, therefore, not only because the ruling class cannot be overthrown in any other way, but also because the class *overthrowing* it can only in a revolution succeed in ridding itself of all the muck of ages and become fitting to found society anew.

[2] This seems to be true, but Marx and Engels later changed their minds about it. See the discussion of Engels' *Origin of the Family* below.

It is this muck that must be washed off in blood, and that bloodbath becomes Marx's tragic vision and lifelong quest.

Marx's next book, *The Poverty of Philosophy: A Reply to* The Philosophy of Poverty *by M. Proudhon,* was published in Paris in 1847, in French. This third polemic, the first one Marx wrote without Engels, is an attempt to demolish Proudhon and the French socialists, once so realistic compared with the woolly Germans, but now seeming equally utopian to Marx. Isaiah Berlin, in *Karl Marx: His Life and Environment,* describes it as "the bitterest attack delivered by one thinker upon another since the celebrated polemics of the Renaissance," but compared to *The Holy Family* and *The German Ideology,* it seems rather moderate. The only new device in Marx's bag of rhetorical tricks is that he corrects Proudhon's arithmetic and keeps reminding him of it. If the Germans are not social thinkers, they are the greatest scientists as well as the greatest musicians, and Marx says in the foreword that he writes as "both German and economist," that is, as a scientific economist. Treating Proudhon's idealism as he had earlier treated Hegel's, Marx stands every statement on its head, beginning with Proudhon's title. Here are two examples from the same page:

> It is then not the commodity that has attained, in gold and silver, the status of 'constituted value,' it is M. Proudhon's 'constituted value' that has attained, in gold and silver, the status of money.
>
> Was it the sovereign who took possession of the gold and silver to make them the universal agents of exchange by affixing his seal to them? Or was it not, rather, these universal agents of exchange which took possession of the sovereign and forced him to affix his seal to them and thus give them a political consecration?

The thinkers quoted against Proudhon are now the realistic English economists, and now Marx rather likes their bluntness. "Sophistication," he says wryly, "as the English call the adulteration of commercial goods." He writes approvingly of Adam Smith, but his particular hero is David Ricardo, the wealthy banker who expounded bourgeois society "scientifically," who "takes his starting point from present-day society," whose "theory of values is the scientific interpretation of actual economic life." Marx writes:

> Doubtless Ricardo's language is as cynical as can be. To put the cost of manufacture of hats and the cost of maintenance of men on the same plane is to turn men into hats. But do not make an outcry at the cynicism of it. The cynicism is in the facts and not in the words which express the facts.

He quotes at length from the Ricardian John F. Bray, to show that Bray anticipated everything of value in Proudhon. Even demand economics, which Marx for the most part ignored because he was interested in an intrinsic "value" in commodities that exists independent of

supply and demand, is here welcomed as a club with which to beat
Proudhon's idealism. He reminds Proudhon that even a unique product
is superfluous "if there is no demand for it," and comments:

> What caps M. Proudhon's difficulty? Simply that he has for-
> gotten about *demand*, and that a thing can be scarce or abundant
> only insofar as it is in demand.

Marx concludes: "He will never find any buyers, so long as he leaves
out demand."

The only thing retained from German philosophy is the
Hegelian dialectic, now purged of Hegel and his idealism. Marx explains and demonstrates the dialectic at length. Poor Proudhon is dismissed as some sort of social climber trying to be a Hegelian philosopher. Marx writes:

> M. Proudhon, in spite of all the trouble he has taken to scale the
> heights of the *system of contradictions*, has never been able to
> raise himself above the first two rungs of simple thesis and an-
> tithesis; and even these he has mounted only twice, and on one of
> these two occasions he fell over backwards.

Instead of Hegel's "language of pure reason, separate from the individual," Marx's dialectic is now grounded in the real sensuous world.
His constant appeal in the book is away from economic theory, abstraction, and category to observed economic behavior: "The old vine-
growers of France in petitioning for a law to forbid the planting of
new vines; the Dutch in burning Asiatic spices, in uprooting clove
trees in the Moluccas," are source materials for studying the relation of
scarcity to value. The consumer is not an abstraction but "the worker
who buys potatoes" or "the kept woman who buys lace." History is
seen as "a continuous transformation of human nature," the "idyll" of
"the good old patriarchal life" on the soil has been "hurled into the
movement of history," and the book ends with "the last word of social
science," which turns out, surprisingly, to be George Sand's call to
revolutionary action: "Combat or death, bloody struggle or extinction."

In Engels' preface to the first German edition of *The Poverty of
Philosophy* in 1884, he makes the curious statement:

> If we now say: that is unjust, that ought not to be so, then that has
> nothing immediately to do with economics. We are merely saying
> that this economic fact is in contradiction to our moral sentiment.
> Marx, therefore, never based his communist demands upon
> this. . . .

Few books, it seems to me, have based their economics more firmly
on moral sentiment than *The Poverty of Philosophy*, and its characteristic tone is the strident voice of ethical outrage. In a passage that
anticipates the great passage in the *Manifesto* on the cash nexus, Marx
writes:

This is the time when the very things which till then had been communicated, but never exchanged; given, but never sold; acquired, but never bought—virtue, love, conviction, knowledge, conscience, etc.—when everything, in short, passed into commerce. It is the time of general corruption, of universal venality, or, to speak in terms of political economy, the time when everything, moral or physical, having become a marketable value, is brought to the market to be assessed at its truest value.

The trouble with traditional economics is that it ignores human realities, which Marx calls "leaving class antagonism out of account." Thus:

It is like saying that because, under the Roman emperors, morays were fattened in artificial fishponds, therefore, there was enough to feed the whole Roman population abundantly. Actually, on the contrary, the Roman people had not enough to buy bread with, while the Roman aristocrats had slaves enough to throw as fodder to the morays.

Or:

But perhaps also, in speaking of improvement, the economists were thinking of the millions of workers who had to perish in the East Indies so as to procure for the million and a half workers employed in England in the same industry, three years' prosperity out of ten.

Some of the great moral themes of *Capital* are announced in miniature: Scottish economy is "the driving out of men by sheep"; the factory system is "children kept at work at the whip's end." Almost the only praise Marx had for Proudhon, when he wrote a memorial notice for him in 1865, is that Proudhon sometimes revealed "a deep and genuine feeling of indignation at the infamy of the existing order."

If this is the first hesitant voice of an Old Testament prophet, some of Marx's indignation with Proudhon in the book is directed at a rival, or false, prophet, a prophet of Baal. *The Poverty of Philosophy* begins with the prefatory statement

M. Proudhon's work is not just a treatise on political economy, an ordinary book; it is a bible, 'Mysteries,' 'Secrets Wrested from the Bosom of God,' 'Revelations'—it lacks nothing. But as prophets are discussed nowadays more conscientiously than profane writers, the reader must resign himself to traversing with us the arid and gloomy erudition of 'Genesis,' in order to ascend later, with M. Proudhon, into the ethereal and fertile realm of *super-socialism*.

"The actual Genesis," Marx snarls later in the book, "shows us God as the world's first manufacturer." The book's dominating metaphor, and one that from this time on distinguishes everything Marx writes, might be called, not "Secrets Wrested from the Bosom of God," but

"Veils Stripped off Jezebel." Proudhon "rediscovers his first hypotheses in all their nakedness"; when he writes something, Marx must "tear the veil from this mystical language." Ricardo is reproached by the innocent French "because it annoys them to see economic relations exposed in all their crudity, to see the mysteries of the bourgeoisie unmasked." Proudhon disguises Society behind the "myth" of Prometheus, but Marx tears the mask away and exposes naked social relations. Most of Marx's mockery and parody of Proudhon's metaphors and "poetic images" stems from his conviction that they *conceal* and *hide*, whereas Marx's own metaphors and poetic images *reveal* and *expose*.

The other feature of the book that foreshadows the direction of Marx's future writing is a semi-dramatic form, not of the theatre, but voices perhaps in a lecture room or meeting hall. Even more than in *The Holy Family*, Marx interrupts quotations with asides, as though he were reading them aloud. He introduces authorities with "Let old Boisguillebert have the floor," or "Let us listen also to a modern economist." He asks and answers rhetorical questions, as though manipulating an audience:

> Does this mean that after the fall of the old society there will be a new class domination culminating in a new political power? No.

In his *Address on the Question of Free Trade*, written at the same time, delivered at a public meeting, and printed as an appendix to the English translation of *The Poverty of Philosophy*, Marx goes directly into a playlet form to write speeches for manufacturers, workers, shopkeepers and farmers. From the dialogues of polemic, Marx was beginning to venture further afield into drama.

In the revolutionary year of 1848, Marx's great masterpiece of rhetoric, *The Communist Manifesto*, appeared. The fog of polemical quibbling suddenly seems to clear, and the opening sentence is like a trumpet blast: "A spectre is haunting Europe—the spectre of communism." The spectral image had always fascinated Marx, and his early writings are full of it. What made this spectre different was that the others were illusions to be exorcised, whereas this concealed a reality that was, for the ruling class, worse than their phantoms. For the first time, Marx was in conformity with his last thesis on Feuerbach, he was no longer interpreting the world but directly attempting to change it. The last sentences of the *Manifesto* are a ringing call to action:

> The proletarians have nothing to lose but their chains. They have a world to win.
> Working men of all countries, unite!

Between this fierce opening and conclusion, a simple polarization of past and present history is offered. "The history of all hitherto existing society is the history of class struggles," Marx writes, and races through history documenting his generalization. The present struggle is sketched in with the same broad strokes: the bourgeoisie is not only wicked but inept, and "unfit any longer to be the ruling class in society," the proletariat is not only "the immense majority" but it has powerful allies like Marx and Engels, "a small section of the ruling class [that] cuts itself adrift, and joins the revolutionary class, the class that holds the future in its hands." Some of this is information addressed to the proletariat, some threats addressed to the bourgeoisie. Marx writes:

In one word, you reproach us with intending to do away with your property. Precisely so; that is just what we intend.

In a running dialogue with bourgeois voices, he writes:

Do you charge us with wanting to stop the exploitation of children by their parents? To this crime we plead guilty.

Before the final slogans to the proletariat, the work threatens:

The Communists disdain to conceal their views and aims. They openly declare that their ends can be attained only by the forcible overthrow of all existing social conditions. Let the ruling classes tremble at a communist revolution.

After all the ferocity, the actual measures proposed are surprisingly moderate. Marx lists them, with the reservation that they would differ in different countries:

1. Abolition of property in land and application of all rents of land to public purposes.
2. A heavy progressive or graduated income tax.
3. Abolition of all right of inheritance.
4. Confiscation of the property of all emigrants and rebels.
5. Centralization of credit in the hands of the state, by means of a national bank with state capital and an exclusive monopoly.
6. Centralization of the means of communication and transport in the hands of the state.
7. Extension of factories and instruments of production owned by the state; the bringing into cultivation of waste lands, and the improvement of the soil generally in accordance with a common plan.
8. Equal obligation of all to work. Establishment of industrial armies, especially for agriculture.
9. Combination of agriculture with manufacturing industries; gradual abolition of all the distinction between town and country by a more equable distribution of the population over the country.
10. Free education for all children in public schools. Abolition of children's factory labor in its present form. Combination of education with industrial production, etc.

Furthermore, it turns out that neither threats to the ruling class nor rallying the workers is actually necessary, since the revolution is historically inevitable. Marx writes:

The advance of industry, whose involuntary promoter is the bourgeoisie, replaces the isolation of the laborers, due to competition, by their revolutionary combination, due to association. The development of modern industry, therefore, cuts from under its feet the very foundation on which the bourgeoisie produces and appropriates products. What the bourgeoisie therefore produces, above all, are its own grave-diggers. Its fall and the victory of the proletariat are equally inevitable.

The Communist Manifesto is almost an anthology of revolutionary rhetoric, and some of its most effective slogans are borrowed. Werner Sombart has shown that "The proletarians have nothing to lose but their chains" and "The workers have no country" are Marat's, and that "the exploitation of men by men" is from Bazard. The nexus of "cash payment" is Thomas Carlyle's, and had been quoted in Engels' *The Condition of the Working Class in England in 1844.* "The free development of each is the condition for the free development of all" is apparently modified from "the consumption of each presupposes the consumption of all," a statement of Karl Gruen's mocked in *The German Ideology.* The *Manifesto* has this composite character because "Citizen Marx" had been directed to draw it up as an official statement by the central committee of the newly-formed Communist League, and had been given three earlier unsatisfactory drafts to work from, the last of them by Engels. This has been published as an appendix to the *Manifesto* in Ryazanoff's scholarly edition, and it makes a fascinating comparison with Marx's.

Engels' document, entitled *Principles of Communism*, is a question-and-answer catechism addressed to workers. It asks, and soberly answers, such questions as "What is the proletariat?," "What have been the later consequences of the industrial revolution?," "Will it be possible to abolish private property at one blow?" Answers are lacking to such questions as "How will the problem of nationalities be dealt with under a communist regime?" and "How will the various religions be dealt with under communism?" as though Engels scrupulously recognized the difficulty of the questions. The tone is pacific, and Engels' characteristic answer to "Will it be possible to bring about the abolition of private property by peaceful means?" begins "It is a thing greatly to be desired, and communists would be the last persons in the world to stand in the way of a peaceful solution." The list of a dozen recommended measures has a lot in common with Marx's list in the *Manifesto,* and is in fact somewhat bolder. One of Engels' proposed measures is "Equal right of inheritance to be enjoyed by illegitimate as by legitimate children," and his statement on the family under communism is: "It will make the relations between the sexes a purely individual, private affair which concerns only the two persons involved; a relationship which is in no way the concern of society." Both of these seem to have been inspired by Engels' lively bachelor life, both undoubtedly outraged Marx's prudish middle-class mores, and both disappeared in his draft.

Marx's positive changes show his mastery of the art of rhetoric. He discarded the question-and-answer form at Engels' own suggestion, changed the tone from earnest and pacific to as provocative a one as possible, and filled the work with dramatic conflict. Where Engels had written:

> Far from inaugurating an era of communal ownership of women, a communistic organization of society puts an end to such a condition of things.

Marx writes:

> But you Communists would introduce community of women, screams the whole bourgeoisie in chorus.
>
> The bourgeois sees in his wife a mere instrument of production. He hears that the instruments of production are to be exploited in common, and, naturally, can come to no other conclusion than that the lot of being common to all will likewise fall to the women. . . .
>
> For the rest, nothing is more ridiculous than the virtuous indignation of our bourgeois at the community of women which, they pretend, is to be openly and officially established by the Communists. The Communists have no need to introduce community of women; it has existed almost from time immemorial.
>
> Our bourgeois, not content with having the wives and daughters of their proletarians at their disposal, not to speak of common prostitutes, take the greatest pleasure in seducing each other's wives.
>
> Bourgeois marriage is in reality a system of wives in common and thus, at the most, what the Communists might possibly be reproached with is that they desire to introduce, in substitution for a hypocritically concealed, an openly legalized community of women. For the rest, it is self-evident, that the abolition of the present system of production must bring with it the abolition of the community of women springing from that system, *i.e.*, or prostitution both public and private.

Where the previous communist slogan had been "All men are brothers," Marx, who said there were lots of men he didn't want as brothers, replaced it with the imperative "Working men of all countries, unite!"

In other words, where Engels aimed at instructing the proletariat and reassuring the bourgeoisie, Marx sets out deliberately to incite the proletariat and provoke the bourgeoisie. This raises the interesting question of the audience for whom the *Manifesto* is written. *The Holy Family*, *The German Ideology*, and *The Poverty of Philosophy* do not really appear to be written with any audience in mind, or at best an audience of a few Hegel-reading radical intellectuals. Engels' draft is written to be read by every literate and serious working man, but Marx's text is written to be read by the world. Workers are to exult in it, but their enemies in chancelleries and bourses, in offices and clubs, are to read it too and shiver. It was published just too late to affect the February, 1848, revolutions in Paris and Germany, but after that it spread vigorously. It was translated into French in 1848 in time for the June riots, it appeared in English in 1850, and within a short time it was available in every Western language. Engels claims, in his introduction to the Polish edition of 1892, that translations of the *Manifesto* are an index to the degree of development of large-scale industry in any country. Harold Laski, in his introduction to a centennial edition of the *Manifesto* put out by the British Labour Party, writes: "In the influence it has exerted it compares with the American Declaration of Independence of 1776, and the French Declaration of Rights of 1789." Joseph Stalin called it "The Song of Songs of Marxism." "If Marx and Engels had never created anything else," Wilhelm Liebknecht wrote in his memoir of Marx, "they had gained immortality." Seldom in history can popular success have been achieved so surprisingly. Anyone who had predicted that the next work by the author of *The Holy Family*, *The German Ideology*, and *The Poverty of Philosophy* would be a spectacular worldwide best seller could have gotten very good odds in the late months of 1847.

Perhaps the explanation is again not rhetorical effectiveness but imaginative design. The key metaphor in the work is the one of stripping away veils that made its first appearance in *The Poverty of Philosophy*. The *Manifesto's* most powerful rhetorical passage is formally organized around that image:

> The bourgeoisie, where it has got the upper hand, has put an end to all feudal, patriarchal, idyllic relations. It has pitilessly torn asunder the motley feudal ties that bound man to his 'natural superiors,' and has left no other nexus between man and man than naked self-interest, than callous 'cash payment.' It has drowned the most heavenly ecstasies of religious fervor, of chivalrous enthusiasm, of philistine sentimentalism, in the icy water of egotistical calculation. It has resolved personal worth into exchange value, and in place of the numberless indefensible chartered freedoms, has set up that single, unconscionable freedom—Free Trade. In one word, for exploitation, veiled by religious and political illusions, it has substituted naked, shameless, direct, brutal exploitation.
>
> The bourgeoisie has stripped of its halo every occupation hitherto honored and looked up to with reverent awe. It has converted the physician, the lawyer, the priest, the poet, the man of science, into its paid wage laborers.
>
> The bourgeoisie has torn away from the family its sentimental veil, and has reduced the family relation to a mere money relation.

In summary:

> All fixed, fast-frozen relations, with their train of ancient and venerable prejudices and opinions, are swept away, all new-formed ones become antiquated before they can ossify. All that is

solid melts into air, all that is holy is profaned, and man is at last compelled to face with sober senses his real conditions of life and his relations with his kind.

It is the bourgeoisie, Marx says, that has pitilessly torn things asunder, drowned them in icy water, torn away the veil and left them naked, stripped them of their halo. In truth, Marx tears away these veils and halos in the bourgeoisie's name. *He* shows the naked reality behind the illusions, as Darwin showed the naked war behind the face of nature bright with gladness.

The other metaphors in the work similarly play on glamorous illusion and bitter reality: the aristocracy waved "the proletarian almsbag," but the people "saw on their hindquarters the old feudal coat of arms"; the aristocracy "pick up the golden apples dropped from the tree of industry," which turn out to be wool, beet-sugar, and potato-spirits; "Christian socialism is but the holy water with which the priest consecrates the heart-burnings of the aristocrat." The most elaborate mixed metaphor in the book is a peculiarly elaborate way of saying "veiling nakedness":

> The robe of speculative cobwebs, embroidered with flowers of rhetoric, steeped in the dew of sickly sentiment, this transcendental robe in which the German Socialists wrapped their sorry 'eternal truth,' all skin and bone. . . .

The accompanying image of action is a fairy-tale one: as capitalism has transformed men into commodities, so communism will transform those commodities back into men. "Laborers, who must sell themselves piecemeal, are a commodity, like every other article of commerce," but the revolution will break the spell and restore them as men, free to develop their human capacities. Marx had written in the *Vorwaerts* in 1844: "One who compares the huge baby-shoes of the proletariat with the dwarfed and down-at-heel political shoes of the bourgeoisie, cannot but prophesy that Cinderella will grow to giant stature."

Four years later, his Cinderella had become Jack the Giant Killer. The great historical drama, on the stage of the world, was finally announced. No more closet dramas, concert readings on the lecture platform, or colloquies before the curtain of history. Marx swings into the last section of the *Manifesto* with impatience: "But let us have done with the bourgeois objections to communism." He announces the great tragic drama of worldwide revolution, in which the proletariat will be bathed in blood, to wash off the bourgeois muck, and will rise in epiphany at the end, immaculate, transformed, glorious and all-powerful. Germany "is on the eve of a bourgeois revolution" which "will be but the prelude to an immediately following proletarian revolution," universal and world-wide. *The Communist Manifesto* is in fact only a stage prologue to the greatest historical drama ever to be performed.

A World to Win

M ARX'S next period begins with a thud. *Wage-Labor and Capital*, published in 1849, has to announce the failure of the 1848 revolutions everywhere. The material of the pamphlet had been delivered as a series of lectures in elementary Marxist economics before the German Workingmen's Club of Brussels in 1847, but by the time they were printed in the *Neue Rheinische Zeitung* in 1849, they had changed from a briefing for the revolution to an apology for its failure. Marx confronts the discouraging situation frankly on the first page:

> It was necessary, beyond everything else, to follow the development of the class struggle in the history of our own day, and to prove empirically, by the actual and daily newly-created historical material, that with the subjugation of the working class, accomplished in the days of February and March, 1848, the opponents of that class—the bourgeois republicans in France, and the bourgeois and peasant classes who were fighting feudal absolutism throughout the whole continent of Europe—were simultaneously conquered; that the victory of the "moderate republic" in France sounded at the same time the fall of the nations which had responded to the February revolution with heroic wars of independence; and finally that, by the victory over the revolutionary workingmen, Europe fell back into its old double slavery, into the *English-Russian* slavery. The June conflict in Paris, the fall of Vienna, the tragi-comedy in Berlin in November, 1848, the desperate efforts of Poland, Italy, and Hungary, the starvation of Ireland into submission—these were the chief events in which the European class struggle between the bourgeoisie and the working class was summed up. . . .

In June, 1848, Marx had written about the defeated workers in the *Zeitung* in a tone of pastoral elegy, calling on the press "to crown their sad brows with laurel." By December of that year he was writing of their betrayers with a mordant sense of their transience. Marx writes of the Prussian bourgeoisie in one tremendous antithesis-crammed sentence:

It had sunk to the level of a sort of *social* estate, as distinctly opposed to the crown as to the people, eager to be in the opposition to both, irresolute against each of its opponents, taken severally, because it always saw both of them before or behind it; inclined from the very beginning to betray the people and compromise with the crowned representative of the old society because it itself already belonged to the old society; representing not the interests of a new society against an old but renewed interests within a superannuated society; at the steering wheel of the revolution not because the people stood behind it but because the people prodded it on before it; in the van not because it represented the initiative of a new but only the rancor of an old social epoch; a stratum of the old state that had not cropped out but been upheaved to the surface of the new state by an earthquake; without faith in itself, without faith in the people, grumbling at those above, trembling before those below, egoistic towards both sides and conscious of its egoism, revolutionary in relation to the conservatives and conservative in relation to the revolutionists, distrustful of its own mottoes, phrases instead of ideas, intimidated by the world storm, exploiting the world storm; no energy in any respect, plagiarism in every respect; common because it lacked originality, original in its commonness; dickering with its own desires, without initiative, without faith in itself, without faith in the people, without a world-historical calling; an execrable old man, who saw himself doomed to guide and deflect the first youthful impulses of a robust people in his own senile interests—sans eyes, sans ears, sans teeth, sans everything—such was the *Prussian bourgeoisie* that found itself at the helm of the Prussian state after the March Revolution.

The moral in *Wage-Labor and Capital* is that consequently "It is time to examine more closely the economic conditions themselves, upon which are founded the existence of the capitalist class and its class rule, as well as the slavery of the workers." Behind the haphazard and anarchic appearance of economic conditions there is law: "In the totality of this disorderly movement is to be found its order." The pamphlet then sketches out this order in bold simplifications. Under capitalism, labor-power is a commodity like sugar, the weaver is an instrument of production "on a par with the loom," and the spinner, like the silkworm, spins to live. Furthermore, the chains that bind the working-class are forged by its own labor. Marx writes:

> Does a worker in a cotton factory produce only cotton goods? No. He produces capital. He produces values which serve anew to command his work and to create by means of it new values.

He explains further:

> When wage-labor produces the alien wealth of dominating it, the power hostile to it, capital, there flow back to it its means of em-

ployment, *i.e.*, its means of subsistence, under the condition that
it again become a part of capital. . . .

The difference between the two worlds is dramatically exaggerated;
the worker weaves silk, mines gold, and builds a palace, but he himself wears a cotton jacket, handles only copper coins, and lives in a
basement. "The interests of capital and the interests of wage-labor are
diametrically opposed to each other," thus "Profit rises in the same
degree in which wages fall; it falls in the same degree in which wages
rise."

Naturally, this state of affairs cannot continue indefinitely, and it
turns out that the great historical tragedy that the *Manifesto* announced, the world-wide revolution, has only been postponed, and is
as inevitable as ever. "Every social reform must remain a Utopia," Marx
writes, "until the proletarian revolution and the feudalistic counter-
revolution have been pitted against each other in a *world-wide war.*"
Conditions are hopefully worsening. Marx writes in the equivalent of
italics: "*In the same measure in which labor becomes more unsatisfactory, more repulsive, do competition increase and wages decrease.*"
He proclaims: "The forest of outstretched arms, begging for work,
grows ever thicker, while the arms themselves grow ever leaner."
Blood flows already, the vampire of capital lives on "fresh exploitable
blood and muscle," and

> Like a master, at once distinguished and barbarous, it drags with
> it into its grave the corpse of its slaves, whole hecatombs of work-
> ers, who perish in the crises.

The resurrection out of this death will be the rising of the revolutionary working class.

Marx's next book, *The Class Struggles in France 1848–1850*, published in 1850, was a venture into contemporary history. It too ran as a
series of articles in the *Neue Rheinische Zeitung*, the revolutionary
newspaper Marx and Engels published in Cologne from June, 1848, to
its suppression in 1849, after which it was briefly edited from London
as the *Neue Rheinische Revue* and printed in Hamburg. Many years
later, in 1881, Engels wrote to Eduard Bernstein that the secret of their
journalistic success had been "the contempt and mockery with which
we treated our opponents." That is a fair description of Marx's slashing
style in *The Class Struggles*. Here is the demise of the Constituent
Assembly:

> This miserable Assembly left the stage, after it had given it-
> self the pleasure, two days before the anniversary of its birthday,
> May 4, of rejecting the motion of amnesty for the June insurgents.
> Its power shattered, held in deadly hatred by the people, re-
> pulsed, maltreated, contemptuously thrown aside by the bour-
> geoisie, whose tool it was, forced in the second half of its life to
> disavow the first, robbed of its republican illusion, without great
> creations in the past, without hope in the future and with its living

body dying bit by bit, it knew how to galvanize its own corpse
only by continually recalling and living through over again the
June victory, substantiating itself by constantly repeated damna-
tion of the damned. Vampire, that lived on the blood of the June
insurgents!

As a work of rhetoric the book is primarily, as its title suggests, an
interpretation of contemporary history in terms of the conflict of
classes. The classes are not the simple bourgeois-proletarian polarity of
Wage-Labor and Capital, but a tangle of interrelating and opposing
groups: the finance aristocracy, the landed aristocracy, the industrial
bourgeoisie, the shopkeepers or petty bourgeoisie, the proletariat, the
lumpenproletariat or declassed, and the peasantry. There is little direct
economic analysis. Engels explains in his 1895 introduction to the
work that this is the difficulty in writing current history ahead of
statistics, and goes on to say:

> Hence, the materialist method has here often to limit itself to
> tracing political conflicts back to the struggles between the in-
> terests of the social classes and fractions of classes encountered as
> the result of economic development, and to show the particular
> political parties as the more or less adequate political expression of
> these same classes and fractions of classes.

Only in the last article in the book, published six months after the rest
and written by both Marx and Engels, has economics caught up, and
the events are explained in terms of the crisis of 1847 and the return
of prosperity in 1849. "The commercial and industrial prosperity,"
they conclude, "prevented any attempt at revolution on the part of the
proletariat." For the future, "A new revolution is only possible in consequence of a new crisis. It is also, however, just as certain as this."
Marx saw his rhetorical task as turning his fleeing troops back to the
fighting, and his tone is that a battle has been lost but that the war will
be won. The book begins:

> With the exception of a few short chapters, every important
> part of the annals of the revolution from 1848 to 1849 carries the
> heading: Defeat of the revolution!
> But what succumbed in these defeats was not the revolution.

Marx's rhetorical emphasis is not, as in *Wage-Labor and Capital,*
on the permanent injustice of capitalism, but on the special and dramatic wickedness, luxuriance and immorality of the French ruling
classes. "The July monarchy was nothing other than a joint stock
company for the exploitation of French national wealth," he writes,
and continues:

> While the finance aristocracy made the laws, was at the head
> of the administration of the State, had command of all the or-
> ganized public powers, dominated public opinion through facts
> and through the press, the same prostitution, the same shameless

cheating, the same mania to get rich was repeated in every sphere, from the Court to the Cafe Borgne, to get rich not by production, but by pocketing the already available wealth of others. In particular there broke out, at the top of bourgeois society, an unbridled display of unhealthy and dissolute appetites, which clashed every moment with the bourgeois laws themselves, wherein the wealth having its source in gambling naturally seeks its satisfaction, where pleasure becomes *crapuleux,* where gold, dirt and blood flow together. The finance aristocracy, in its mode of acquisition as well as in its pleasures, is nothing but the resurrection of the *lumpenproletariat* at the top of bourgeois society.

For putting down the June insurgents, the Mobile Guards "found their reward in the soft arms of the courtesans." Marx's moral is the simple earlier dichotomy: "As against the shameless orgies of the finance aristocracy, the struggle of the people for the first necessities of life!" The thematic metaphor pervading *The Class Struggles in France* is that of a theatrical performance. What the declassed do surreptitiously, the ruling class does publicly and theatrically: "On the most prominent stages of bourgeois society, the same scenes were publicly enacted which regularly lead the *lumpenproletariat* to brothels, to workhouses and lunatic asylums, before the Bench, to prisons, and to the scaffold." New classes of French society were suddenly "forced to leave the boxes, the stalls and the gallery and to act in person upon the revolutionary stage!" The Constituent Assembly "played the principal and state role on the proscenium." The peasants, "for a moment active heroes of the revolutionary drama, could no longer be forced back into the passive and spineless role of the chorus." "With the proletariat removed for the time being from the stage," the bourgeoisie takes over. A period is characterized "not by the phrase but by the accent and the gesture which enliven the phrase." This drama, however, is not the grand historical tragedy for which the *Manifesto* had raised the curtain. Marx tries a variety of theatrical identifications. At one point he calls it "tragi-comic," at another "a melodramatic scene"; at other times he describes it in terms of opera, "many-voiced song" from which "the chest notes were missing," although loudly applauded by a claque. What Marx finally identifies as his dramatic form is straight comedy. Events are a "clumsily constructed comedy," the speeches of Barrot are "worthy of a Beaumarchais," political jockeyings are "this great comedy of intrigues" and "Thus the comedy was played." It is all "an unutterable comedy." In this comedy "the Bourse Jews" or "the Jews of finance" are the stock comic Jew, sinister but harmless, "Bourse wolves" without any teeth. In the action, all the sections of the exploiting class have their masks torn off, "the veil that shrouded the republic was torn to pieces," even the state deficit is rudely disrobed. It is Marx's old metaphor of stripping the veil from wicked Jezebel, but here closer to the throwing off of disguises at the end of the comedy. The party of the Mountain, Marx notes, "instead of tearing

this web of deceit to pieces, took the parliamentary comedy tragically";
but Marx knows that the real tragedy, the great historical drama, will
come later. He writes:

> The revolution which finds here, not its end, but its organizational
> beginning, is no short-lived revolution. The present generation is
> like the Jews, whom Moses led through the wilderness. It has not
> only a new world to conquer, it must go under, in order to make
> room for the men who are fit for a new world.

The proletariat is "the scarred, irreconcilable, unconquerable enemy."
Marx's final comment on the June insurrection makes it a little death
and rebirth, a miniature foreshadowing of the great tragedy:

> Only through the defeat of June, therefore, were all the
> conditions created under which France can seize the initiative of
> the European revolution. Only after baptism in the blood of the
> June insurgents did the tricolor become the flag of the European
> revolution—the red flag.
> And we cry: *The revolution is dead!—Long live the revolu-
> tion!*

Marx's next book, published in 1852, is an even more slashing and
vigorous sequel, *The Eighteenth Brumaire of Louis Bonaparte*. It was
published in Joseph Weydemeyer's New York journal, *Die Revolution*, at a time when Marx and Engels had no periodical of their own,
no party (the Communist League had expired), and delighted in the
freedom. If *The Class Struggles in France* was high-level journalism,
interested in pointing the moral of events for communist readers, *The
Eighteenth Brumaire*, however close in time it is to the events it deals
with, is history, primarily concerned with producing a meaningful
and coherent organization of those events. Marx was testing his materialist theory by history, as his correspondence at the time shows he
was similarly testing Ricardian economics. Engels writes in his preface
to the third German edition in 1885:

> Marx was the first to discover the great law which governs the
> march of history. According to this law, all historical struggles, al-
> though they seem to take place on the political, religious, philo-
> sophical, or any other ideal plane, are, in reality, nothing else than
> the more or less clear expression of struggles between social
> classes. The existence of these classes and their collisions, are
> themselves determined by the degree of development in the eco-
> nomic situation, by the prevailing mode of production, and by the
> methods of exchange which result. This law bears the same
> relationship to history as the law of the conservation of energy
> bears towards the physical sciences. It provides Marx with the key
> to the understanding of the history of the Second Republic in
> France. *The Eighteenth Brumaire* served Marx to test and to prove
> this law. Now, after the lapse of thirty-three years, we have to
> admit that the proof has stood the test of time.

Isaiah Berlin has identified Marx's historical materialism as a radical empiricism, like Darwin's survival of the fittest, affirming that whatever wins is right. Actually, the complex duality of Marx's historical operations proclaims the pun inherent in the word "right," the paradox that whatever wins, like Louis Bonaparte, is right for the situation, but far from right or satisfactory in a value judgment. The rhetorical slant of *The Eighteenth Brumaire* is precisely this double aim, to show Louis Bonaparte's triumph as both inevitable and reprehensible.

The Eighteenth Brumaire announces this dual aim in the preface. Marx writes: "For my part, I prove that the class war in France created circumstances and relationships that enabled a grotesque mediocrity to strut about in a hero's garb." The concept of class identification is now considerably extended. Marx explains:

> Nor must it be supposed that the democratic deputies are all shopkeepers, or enthusiastic champions of the small-shopkeeper class. Culturally and by individual status they may be the polar opposites of members of the shopkeeping class. What has made them become the political representatives of the petty bourgeoisie is this. Intellectually they have failed to transcend the limitations which are, materially, imposed upon the petty bourgeois by the conditions of petty-bourgeois existence. Consequently they are, in the theoretical field, impelled towards the same aspirations and solutions as those towards which, in practical life, the petty bourgeois are impelled by material interests and by their social position. Speaking generally, such is always the relationship between the political and literary representatives of a class and the class they represent.

It is in this sense that "Bonaparte represents a class, the class of those who form a considerable majority in French society, the peasantry." Marx explains:

> But insofar as the tie between the peasants is merely one of propinquity, and insofar as the identity of their interests has failed to find expression in a community, in a national association, or in a political organization, these peasant families do not form a class. They are, therefore, unable to assert their class interests in their own name, whether through parliament or through a congress. They cannot represent themselves, and must be represented. He who is to be their representative must also appear to them as their lord and master, as one holding authority over them, one wielding unrestricted governmental powers, who will protect them against the other classes, and who will send them the rain and the sunshine from above.

The economic analysis is also broadened. It is no longer a simple matter of crisis or recovery, of an event followed by "a rise in the stock-market quotations." Now classes have varying economic needs involving everything from taxes to the price of grain, and these are further complicated by ideas. After explaining that the opposition between the legitimate monarchists and the Orleanists represented the opposition between two different forms of property, landed wealth and industrial capital, Marx continues:

> But at the same time they were loyal to one or other branch of the royal house? They were bound by old memories, personal enmities, hopes and fears, prejudices and illusions, sympathies and antipathies, by convictions and articles of faith and principles? Who denies it! Upon the different forms of property, upon the social conditions of existence, as foundation, there is built a superstructure of diversified and characteristic sentiments, illusions, habits of thought, and outlooks on life in general. The class as a whole creates and shapes them out of its material foundation, and out of the corresponding social relationships. The individual, in whom they arise through tradition and education, may fancy them to be the true determinants, the real origin, of his activities.

The characteristic tone of *The Eighteenth Brumaire*, however, is not dispassionate analysis but moral indignation. Liebknecht writes in *Karl Marx: Biographical Memoirs*:

> Is the *Eighteenth Brumaire* unintelligible? Is the arrow incomprehensible that flies straight at its target and pierces the flesh? Is the spear unintelligible that, hurled by a steady hand, pierces the heart of the enemy? The words of the *Brumaire* are arrows, are spears—they are a style that stigmatizes, kills. If hate, if scorn, if burning love of freedom ever found expression in flaming, annihilating, elevating words, then it is surely in the *Eighteenth Brumaire*, in which the earnestness of Tacitus is united to the deadly satire of Juvenal and the holy wrath of Dante. The style here is what it—the stylus—originally was in the hands of the Romans—a sharp-pointed steel pencil for writing as well as stabbing. The style is the dagger used for a well-aimed thrust at the heart.

Actually, most of Marx's arrows seem aimed at the groin. Louis Bonaparte's *coup* is imaged sexually: "Neither a nation nor a woman can be forgiven for the unguarded hour in which a chance comer has seized the opportunity for an act of rape." His supporters, "the Society of Disorder, Prostitution, and Theft," are "the scum and offal and detritus of all classes." Of his tool, Barrot, finally prime minister after twenty years of effort: "At long last, he had led his bride home, but not until after she had become a prostitute." Marx fumes at "Bonaparte's nightly orgies with swell mobsmen and swell mobswomen." He quotes the words of Madame Girardin: "Many times ere this, France has been under the rule of kept women, but never before under the rule of kept men." In a vision very like the opening lines of Yeats'

"The Second Coming," Marx writes that in his time "truth is without passion; and passion is without truth."

There is a constant organic analogy for politics. "These graded ministries constituted a sort of thermometer, on which parliament could read off the decline in its vital heat." Latent differences appear among the Party of Order "much as when dried infusoria come into contact with water, exhibit renewed vital energy, and promptly undergo division." For the birth of Louis Bonaparte's dictatorship, Marx produces a particularly unlovely image: "All that was needed was a bayonet thrust to burst the bladder, so that the monster could leap into the light of day." In a variant: "The champions of the Party of Order were still seated upon the shoulders of armed force, when they realized, one fine morning, that the seat had become prickly, for the shoulders had turned into bayonets." The revolution has meanwhile burrowed underground, but when it emerges "Europe will leap to her feet and exclaim: 'Old mole! Canst work i' the earth so fast? A worthy pioneer!' "

The theatrical form of *The Eighteenth Brumaire* is even more explicit than that of *The Class Struggles*. The book begins:

> Hegel says somewhere that, upon the stage of universal history, all great events and personalities reappear in one fashion or another. He forgot to add that, on the first occasion, they appear as tragedy; on the second, as farce.

The "great French Revolution" of 1793 was for Marx "a great historic tragedy," an authentic revolution, and its participants "achieved the task of their day—which was to liberate the bourgeoisie and to establish modern bourgeois society." In every epoch of revolutionary crisis, he says, "men are eager to press the spirits of the past into their service, borrowing the names of the dead, reviving old war-cries, dressing up in traditional costumes, that they may make a braver pageant in the newly-staged scene of universal history." It is this impulse to fake a brave historical pageant that led Napoleon the Little to costume himself as Napoleon the Great. The proletarian party is "removed from the stage," or "passed to the back of the revolutionary stage," except for "a few supers from the working class." "The Assembly is always on the boards," when they are "no longer before the footlights" or "on the stage of history," the members lose all identity. After a "crashing overture," the petty bourgeoisie get discouraged and "the actors cease to take themselves seriously." The mergers of the monarchist parties "were conducted upon the public stage instead of as mere private theatricals.

In *The Class Struggles in France*, it had been "the dung heap of history" onto which repudiated parties were thrown. Here the same obsolescence is imaged in a book, "Their page of history was closed," and it is obviously a playbook. Louis Bonaparte is trying to turn back to an earlier page, to revert to an earlier historical drama. "From 1848 to 1851 there was nothing more than a walking ghost of the old revolution," Marx writes. Its present form is "the adventurer who hid his commonplace and unpleasing physiognomy behind the iron death-mask of Napoleon." All sorts of ghosts walk the stage: rumors of a *coup d'etat* are a "spook"; the "Red Spectre" is conjured up and exorcised; even Hamlet's ghost puts in its appearance. In his borrowed mask and costume and the lustre of his stage effects, Louis Bonaparte thinks to put on a brave historical pageant, but he is only the dead walking.

The drama finally performed on the stage, following the historical tragedy of the French Revolution, the prologue of 1848, and the comedy of the period covered in *The Class Struggles*, is farce, as the book's opening announces. With characteristic kindliness, Marx introduced Louis Bonaparte in *The Class Struggles in France* as the peasants' symbol:

> The symbol that expressed their entry into the revolutionary movement, clumsily cunning, knavishly naive, doltishly sublime, a calculated superstition, a pathetic burlesque, a cleverly stupid anachronism, a world historical piece of buffoonery and an undecipherable hieroglyphic for the understanding of the civilized—this symbol bore the unmistakable features of the class that represents barbarism within civilization.

In *The Eighteenth Brumaire*, Louis Bonaparte is the figure of the buffoon. He is "this adventurer, goaded onward by his debts," whose "long career as a vagabond adventurer had equipped him with sensitive feelers which enabled him to perceive the most favorable moment for extorting money." Marx describes his grotesque band of followers:

> Side by side with broken-down profligates of uncertain means of livelihood and questionable antecedents, side by side with decayed adventurers who had dropped out of the ranks of the bourgeoisie, there were vagabonds, disbanded soldiers, discharged prisoners, fugitives from the galleys, sharpers, jugglers, professional beggars, pickpockets, conjurors, gamesters, pimps, brothel-keepers, porters, men of letters, organ-grinders, ragpickers, knifegrinders, tinkers—in a word, all the elements of that vague, dissolute, down-at-heels and out-at-elbows rabble which the French denote by the composite name of *la Bohème*. They were kindred elements to Louis Bonaparte, and it was of them that he formed the substantial framework of his Society of December the Tenth.

Marx continues:

> An old and crafty roué, he regards the historical life of the nations as a comedy in the most ordinary sense of the term; looks upon their most important activities, their actions of State, as a masquerade in which the fine costumes, the high-sounding words, and the dignified postures are nothing but a mask for trifling. Thus it was in the Strasburg affair (1836) when a tame Swiss vulture impersonated the Napoleonic eagle. When he raided Boulogne

(1840) he had some London footmen decked out in French uniform; they represented the army. In his Society of December the
Tenth, he got together about ten thousand loafers and tatterde-
malions to play the people, as Snug the joiner played the Lion. At
the time when the bourgeoisie itself was acting pure comedy, but
was doing so in all seriousness, paying full reverence to the
pedantic conventions of the French stage, itself partly gulled and
partly convinced by the solemnity of its own public acts, the adventurer who played the comedy in full awareness was bound to
win.

In this farcical world where "one fishwife outweighed seventeen
burgraves," "after twenty years' vagabondage and a number of preposterous adventures, this man becomes Emperor of the French."
Napoleon the Little hides behind the death mask of his uncle, a tame
Swiss vulture replacing his uncle's eagle, but it is visibly a masquerade.
The Eighteenth Brumaire of Louis Bonaparte has little of Marx's familiar imagery of unmasking or tearing away the veil. The farce is
all too nakedly visible on the stage.

F R O M 1851 on, Marx wrote a good deal of journalism of a lower
order, much of it published in Horace Greeley's New York *Daily
Tribune*. Many of these articles, with articles by Engels, letters, and
other materials, have been reprinted in book form: *The Eastern Question* in 1897, *The Life of Lord Palmerston* in 1899, *The Civil War in
the United States* in 1937, *Letters on India* in 1937, *Revolution in Spain*
in 1939, *Marx on China* in 1951, *The Russian Menace to Europe*
in 1952. The most popular and famous of these collections, *Revolution
and Counter-Revolution in Germany in 1848* was later discovered to
be entirely the work of Engels. In general, Marx specialized in
diplomacy and politics, and got Engels to write the articles on financial
and military affairs. Marx's source was primarily the press, supple-
mented by *Hansard* and diplomatic reports, private information from
friends and revolutionary connections, and prodigious research in
books. Until 1853, Engels translated the articles for him; after that he
wrote them in English. These *Tribune* articles have much in common
with the current history of his two French books, although their
tone differs for the different audience. Their characteristic effect is
what Marx, in an 1857 article on China, calls "that great historical
irony which does not flow from the wit of individuals, but from the
humor of situations." This humor tends to be professorial rather than
savage. Here is a typical example from an 1854 article on Spain, with
no further explanation:

> It may be observed, *en passant*, that the *boletines* of General
> Blaser bear a wonderful resemblance to the orders of the day of

the Spanish generals of the sixteenth century, which gave such occasion for hilarity to Francis I, and of the eighteenth century, which Frederick the Great turned into ridicule.

Where he can, Marx expounds historical materialism, showing class alignments behind the events and economic realities behind the class alignments. He sometimes displays his familiar indignation: "The whole State machinery of France transformed into one immense swindling and stock-jobbing concern": Spain "exhibited all those symptoms of inglorious and protracted putrefaction so repulsive in the worst times of the Turkish Empire"; and so on. There are rumbles of the old revolutionary threats. "The next European revolution," Marx writes to the *Tribune* in 1856, "will find Spain matured for co-operation with it"; an 1853 letter on India threatens "a great social revolution," as a result of which "then only will human progress cease to resemble that hideous pagan idol, who would not drink the nectar but from the skulls of the slain." In 1853 Marx mixed a fine revolutionary metaphor:

> Under these circumstances, as the greater part of the regular commercial circle has already been run through by British trade, it may safely be augured that the Chinese revolution will throw the spark into the overloaded mine of the present industrial system and cause the explosion of the long-prepared general crisis, which, spreading abroad, will be closely followed by political revolutions on the continent.

In the same article, he explains: "Since the commencement of the eighteenth century there has been no serious revolution in Europe which had not been preceded by a commercial and financial crisis." The next year it was no longer crisis that would bring on the revolution, stepping forth "in shining armor, sword in hand, like Minerva from the brow of the Olympian," but "the impending European war." In 1856, in a speech in the *People's Paper*, Marx compares the revolution to a volcano underfoot (as Frazer was to do later, without the same enthusiasm).

The special villains of Marx's journalism are England and Russia. England forced opium on the Chinese, oppressed Ireland and India, and tried to bully the United States, "the only popular government in the world." Russia was the great champion of world reaction, the oppressor of Poland, the center, as Engels wrote Marx in 1851, of "baseness and Slavonic dirt." In 1848 the principal program of the *Neue Rheinische Zeitung* had been a unified German republic and war with Russia. Some of Marx's liveliest articles, collected in *The Eastern Question* and *The Secret History of Lord Palmerston*, are devoted to his weird conviction that "the vain and unscrupulous Palmerston," the prime minister of England, was in the pay of the Russians. Marx had picked up the idea from a mad Russophobe and Turkophile named David Urquhart. Marx wrote to Engels in 1853: "I am now reading

Urquhart, the crazy M. P., who declares that Palmerston is sold to Russia." A few months later, after studying the matter further, he wrote to Engels: "Curious as it may seem to you, as a result of closely following the footprints of the noble viscount for the past twenty years, I have come to the same conclusion as the monomaniac Urquhart, namely that Palmerston has been sold to Russia for several decades."

In an article on China in 1859, Marx exposes Palmerston's deviousness:

> In all his transactions with the weak Asiatic States, with China, Persia, Central Asia, Turkey, it has always been his invariable and constant rule to ostensibly oppose Russia's designs by picking a quarrel, not with Russia, but with the Asiatic State, to estrange the latter from England by piratical hostilities, and by this roundabout way drive it to the concessions it had been unwilling to yield to Russia.

In his correspondence with Engels at the time, Marx wrote more bluntly that the Anglo-Chinese treaty "was worked out by Palmerston in conjunction with the Petersburg Cabinet." In his *Tribune* correspondence, Marx took to calling him "the Russian Minister Palmerston," and charging him with everything from planning war with the United States to provoking the Hong Kong Chinese into putting arsenic in the bread of the European community. Berlin speaks of the "highly twentieth-century flavour" of Marx's journalism, emphasizing "hidden interests and the sinister activity likely to result from them, rather than the explicit motives furnished by the actors themselves," but only on Palmerston does Marx really have the present-day touch.

A Contribution to the Critique of Political Economy, which appeared in 1859, is Marx's first ambitious publication as an economist. Written for his peers, it indulges in little rhetoric and keeps Marx's poetic imagination in check. It is thus not a very interesting book for our purposes, nor, since it has been superseded by *Capital* as a treatise in economics, for any purposes. Much of its reputation comes from the official statement of the doctrine of historical materialism in the preface, an expansion of the briefer statement in *The Eighteenth Brumaire* about the economic foundation of society and the ideational superstructure. Marx announces the book's intention in the preface with the statement that "the reader who wishes to follow me at all, must make up his mind to pass from the special to the general," and the first chapter explains that he will deal with a diamond as a diamond, whether it is "on the breast of a harlot, or in the hand of a glasscutter."

Marx never regarded it as an easy, popular, or readable work. Much of the argument of the *Critique* is in the form of series of equations, and the style is that of a textbook: "Let one ounce of gold, one ton of iron, one quarter of wheat and twenty yards of silk represent equal exchange values"; or "For the sake of simplicity gold is assumed throughout as the money commodity." Marx's ideal in the book is apparently the "frivolous, rapacious and unprincipled adventurer" Sir William Petty, whose *Preface to Political Arithmetick* in 1699 he quotes approvingly:

> Petty is conscious of being the founder of a new science. His method, he says, 'is not yet very usual, for instead of using only comparative and superlative Words, and intellectual Arguments,' he has undertaken to speak 'in Terms of Number, Weight or Measure; to use only Arguments of Sense, and to consider only such Causes, as have visible Foundations in Nature; leaving those that depend upon the mutable Minds, Opinions, Appetites, and Passions of particular Men, to the Consideration of others.'

In a letter to Weydemeyer in 1852, Marx claims credit for discovering neither the existence of classes nor their struggle, but only that classes evolve with production, that their struggle necessarily leads to the dictatorship of the proletariat, and that this in turn will abolish classes. There is little of this future vision in the *Critique*, perhaps because it was written as the first installment of a larger work never completed. If anything, the book's historical perspective tends to be backward-looking, to a universal primitive communism in the past that was destroyed through the expropriation of men by their fellows in what *Capital* later called "Primitive Accumulation."

The prefatory statement of the theory of historical materialism returns to an old organic metaphor: new productive relations develop "in the womb of the old society" or "in the womb of bourgeois society." In the text, most of the metaphors are resolutely inorganic, as Marx now takes his models from mathematics or physics. Some of them are wonderfully mixed, as in "skilled labor which rises above the level of average labor by its higher intensity, by its greater specific gravity." The only substance which appears to have life is gold coin, which is metamorphosed into a "chrysalis," appears "like a general" on the battlefield, "keeps rather mixed company," is "gradually transformed into a mere phantom," gets "clipped and reduced and the superfluous gold fat lands in the melting pot," is cut up "with oriental cruelty," "has not sold its shadow, but buys with its shadow," is "reduced to the condition of a mere symbolic paper rag" but is soon "restored to its golden glory." Marx quotes Peter Martyr on the advantages of an organic currency, the Mexican use of cacao-beans as a medium of exchange:

> O, happy coin, which furnished mankind with a pleasant and useful beverage and keeps its possessors immune from the hellborn pest of avarice, since it cannot be either buried or preserved long.

The *Critique* constantly suggests scriptural sinfulness: hoarders are searching for "the eternal treasure, which neither moth nor rust can eat"; Luther is quoted against luxury and gluttony; there is even an

odd joking reference to economics before Adam Smith as "pre-
Adamic," with its hint that bourgeois production is a Fall.

In an unfinished and unpublished introduction to the *Critique*,
written in 1857 but not used for the book and printed as an appendix
to an American edition in 1904, Marx discusses the various ways a
critique of political economy might be written. He explains:

> If we start out, therefore, with population, we do so with a chaotic
> conception of the whole, and by closer analysis we will gradually
> arrive at simpler ideas; thus we shall proceed from the imaginary
> concrete to less and less complex abstractions, until we get at the
> simplest conception. This once attained, we might start on our
> return journey until we finally come back to population, but this
> time not as a chaotic notion of an integral whole, but as a rich
> aggregate of many conceptions and relations. The former method
> is the one which political economy had adopted in the past at its
> inception. . . . The latter is manifestly the scientifically correct
> method.

A Contribution to the Critique of Political Economy was written by
the first method, moving from concrete to abstract, but Marx's vision
was of a work of economics that would move from the abstract to the
concrete, "a rich aggregate of many conceptions and relations," Darwin's tangled bank. It is the announcement of *Capital*.

Marx's next work, *Herr Vogt*, published in 1860, is the only one of
his books, so far as I know, that has never been translated into any
other language. It is an answer to a book by Karl Vogt, a German
radical and Darwinian biologist in exile in Switzerland, charging Marx,
among other things, with being the leader of a band of blackmailers
and counterfeiters. Marx worked for a year on his reply and succeeded
in demolishing Vogt, charging that he was a paid agent of Louis Bonaparte (which later turned out, unlike Vogt's charges against Marx, to
be true). Oddly, it is Marx's most literary work, full of quotations from
most of the literatures of Europe. It begins:

> The original of Karl Vogt is the immortal Sir John Falstaff and
> in his zoological resurrection he has lost nothing of his character.

Engels thought *Herr Vogt* was Marx's finest polemic, better than *The
Eighteenth Brumaire*. Liebknecht called it "this laughing humor," and
Jenny Marx said that it was "a fine piece of drollery," but to the modern reader it seems like a curious regression to the schoolboy world of
The Holy Family and *The German Ideology*. One piece of Marx's
mature wisdom stands out in it, the bitter aphorism: "There is only
one antidote to mental suffering, and that is physical pain."

Marx ended the period between *The Communist Manifesto* and
the publication of *Capital* as he had begun it, with a popularization of
his economics for an audience of workers. This is *Value, Price and
Profit*, an address delivered in English to the General Council of the
First International in 1865. (It was not published until after Marx's

death, when his daughter found it among his papers). This graphic and effective work sketches in the facts of Marxist economic life with the bold simplicity of *Wage-Labor and Capital*. It anticipates some of the material in *Capital*, as Marx wrote to Engels, "in an extremely condensed but relatively popular form." Marx keeps reminding his audience that "all of you know" such economic realities as unemployment and the cycle of crises. Rent, interest, and profit, he explains, are only names for parts of surplus value, which is unpaid labor stolen from the worker. "Exploitation," Marx calls it, with the comment "you must allow me this French word." What the economists call "Original Accumulation," he says, replacing one origin myth with another, "ought to be called *Original Expropriation*."

After a ten-hour working day had been standard for two centuries, Marx announces, in the nineteenth century "capital celebrated its bacchanalia, and prolonged the working day from ten to twelve, fourteen, eighteen hours." If the worker "resigned himself to accept the will, the dictates of the capitalist as a permanent economic law, he would share in all the miseries of the slave, without the security of the slave." Marx writes:

> Time is the room of human development. A man who has no free time to dispose of, whose whole lifetime, apart from the mere physical interruptions by sleep, meals, and so forth, is absorbed by his labour for the capitalist, is less than a beast of burden. He is a mere machine for producing foreign wealth, broken in body and brutalised in mind. Yet the whole history of modern industry shows that capital, if not checked, will recklessly and ruthlessly work to cast down the whole working class to this utmost state of degradation.

Instead of "the labour of the man, the head of the family, his wife and perhaps three or four children are now thrown under the Juggernaut wheels of capital." So far as the capitalists are concerned, "A quick succession of unhealthy and short-lived generations will keep the labour market as well supplied as a series of vigorous and long-lived generations." The moral is naturally "a new and fundamental revolution," and the pamphlet concludes with a hope for the workers:

> They ought to understand that, with all the miseries it imposes upon them, the present system simultaneously engenders the *material conditions* and the *social forms* necessary for an economic reconstruction of society. Instead of the *conservative* motto: "*A fair day's wages for a fair day's work!*" They ought to inscribe on their banner the *revolutionary* watchword: "*Abolition of the wages system!*"

It is the same call to the proletariat to rise and bring off the great historical tragedy that had concluded *The Communist Manifesto*, but curiously most of the conviction has gone out of it. Marx had first expected the revolution in 1844, during a weaver's rising in Silesia.

Then 1848 was the year of boundless hopes. In the first number of the *Neue Rheinische Revue* in 1849, Marx predicted that the revolution would certainly break out by "August 1850 at the latest." In the vocabulary of historical materialism, wish always became prediction. Then he and Engels had expected revolution in 1851, again in 1852, then in 1853 as a result of crisis, and in 1854 as a result of the Crimean War. In 1855 Engels foresaw a great trade crisis that would "ruin the whole of European industry, glut all the markets, involve all the possessing classes, and cause the complete bankruptcy of the bourgeoisie." Marx thought in 1855 that the revolution had begun in England with a demonstration in Hyde Park against a bill to prohibit the sale of beer on Sunday. Here the irate proletarians, Marx and his family among them, shouted at the rich riding by, "Go to church!" In 1856 Engels wrote to Marx, "This time the crash will beat anything known before," and Marx replied:

> This time the thing is on a European scale never reached before and I do not think we shall be able to sit here as spectators much longer. The mobilization of our persons is at hand.

When the crisis finally appeared, in 1857, Engels wrote to Marx:

> I feel in magnificent form amidst this general breakdown. In 1848 we said: Now our time is coming, and in a certain sense it came. But now it is really coming, now it will be a fight for life. This makes my military studies more practical at once. I will at once throw myself into the existing organization of the Prussian, Austrian, Bavarian and French armies, and beyond that into nothing but riding, that is, fox-hunting, which is the real school.

Marx wrote back:

> I am working like mad, day and night, at putting my economic studies together so that I may at least have the outlines clear before the deluge comes.

But there was no deluge, and the next year Marx complained of "the favorable turn of world trade at this moment." However, a revolution seemed to be beginning in Russia, which would spread to the Continent and, Marx wrote to Engels, "immediately assume a socialist character." In 1859 it was again war, the French war in Italy, that would trigger the revolution. In 1863, the Polish rising showed "that the era of revolution has at length been reopened in Europe." And so on regularly. By 1865 Marx was somewhat cynical about the imminence, if not the certainty, of the revolution. Meanwhile, instead of the great historical tragedy, there had been the comedy of France after 1848, the nasty farce of Louis Bonaparte, the cloak-and-dagger thrillers of Palmerston's intrigues and *Herr Vogt*. It was time to sweep the stage of all these low clowns and to get the heroic working class back on the boards.

Capital

T H E first volume of *Capital, The Process of Capitalist Production*, was published in 1867. It is the only volume of the book that Marx completed, and for convenience here it will be referred to as *Capital*. As Engels wrote in his preface to the first English translation in 1886, "This first book is in a great measure a whole in itself, and has for twenty years ranked as an independent work." Marx had worked on it for eighteen years, since the failure of the revolutions of 1848, and in some fashion it was to be an answer to that failure and a victory for the proletariat.

The other event that affected it most directly was the publication of *The Origin of Species* in 1859. In *Capital*, Marx quotes from "Darwin in his epoch-making work on the origin of species," and suggests a parallel:

> Darwin has interested us in the history of Nature's technology, *i.e.*, in the formation of the organs of plants and animals, which organs serve as instruments of production for sustaining life. Does not the history of the productive organs of man, of organs that are the material basis of all social organization, deserve equal attention?

In 1860, Marx had written to Engels, after a month spent nursing his wife through a severe illness:

> During my time of trial, these last four weeks, I have read all sorts of things. Among others Darwin's book on Natural Selection. Although it is developed in the crude English style, this is the book which contains the basis in natural history for our view.

The next year, writing to Ferdinand Lassalle, Marx explains more fully:

> Darwin's book is very important and serves me as a basis in natural science for the class struggle in history. One has to put up with the crude English method of development, of course.

In 1862, Marx wrote to Engels:

As regards Darwin, whom I have looked at again, it amuses me
that he says he applies the 'Malthusian' theory *also* to plants and
animals, as if Malthus's whole point did not consist in the fact that
his theory is applied *not* to plants and animals, but only to human
beings—in geometrical progression—as opposed to plants and animals. It is remarkable that Darwin recognizes among brutes and
plants his English society with its division of labor, competition,
opening up of new markets, 'inventions' and Malthusian 'struggle
for existence.' It is Hobbes's *bellum omnium contra omnes*, and it
is reminiscent of Hegel in the *Phenomenology*, where bourgeois
society figures as 'spiritual animal kingdom,' while with Darwin
the animal kingdom figures as bourgeois society.

Later that year, when Thomas Henry Huxley delivered his *Six Lectures to Working Men* on Darwinism, Marx, Liebknecht, and a little
group of German communists sat in the audience, busily taking notes.
Their "expressions of hungry inquiry" impressed Frederic Harrison,
as he later wrote.

The history of Marx's direct relations with Darwin is a confusing
one. For most of their lives they lived less than twenty miles apart,
Darwin at Down, Marx at various addresses in London, but they never
met. When the second edition of *Capital* in German was published in
1873, Marx sent a copy to Darwin with a letter that does not survive.
Darwin's reply apparently does not survive either, but it is reported by
Marx's son-in-law Edward Aveling, and the style seems characteristic
of Darwin:

October 1st, 1873

Dear Sir,—I thank you for the honour which you have done me by
sending me your great work on *Capital*; and I heartily wish that I
were more worthy to receive it, by understanding more of the
deep and important subject of political economy. Though our
studies have been so different, I believe that we both earnestly desire the extension of knowledge; and this, in the long run, is sure
to add to the happiness of mankind.

I remain, dear Sir,
Yours faithfully,
Charles Darwin

Darwin never opened his copy of the great work, and it was found
uncut after his death. In 1880, when they were both near death, Marx
once more wrote to Darwin in a letter that Darwin again did not preserve. Apparently he offered to dedicate the future second volume of
Capital, or the future English edition of the first, to Darwin, offered to
show him proof-sheets, and enclosed something that gave Darwin the
impression that *Capital* was an atheist tract. Marx preserved Darwin's
reply, and it is now in the Marx-Engels-Lenin Institute in Moscow. It
reads in part:

I thank you for your friendly letter and the enclosure. The publication of your observations on my writings, in whatever form they appear, really does not need any consent on my part. . . . I should prefer the part or volume not to be dedicated to me (although I thank you for the intended honour), as that would, in a certain extent, suggest my approval of the whole work, with which I am not acquainted. Although I am a keen advocate of freedom of opinion in all questions, it seems to me (rightly or wrongly) that direct arguments against Christianity and Theism hardly have any effect on the public; and that freedom of thought will best be promoted by that gradual enlightening of human understanding which follows the progress of science. I have therefore always avoided writing about religion and have confined myself to science. Possibly I have been too strongly influenced by the thought of the concern it might cause some members of my family, if in any way I lent my support to direct attacks on religion. I am sorry to refuse you any request, but I am old and have little strength, and the reading of proofs (as I know from present experience) imposes a heavy strain on me.

In his funeral oration over Marx's grave in 1883, Engels said "As Darwin discovered the law of evolution in organic nature, so Marx discovered the law of evolution in human history." In 1888, in his preface to an English edition of *The Communist Manifesto*, Engels prophesied that historical materialism "is destined to do for history what Darwin's theory has done for biology." Apparently Marx shared Engels' view that his work was comparable to Darwin's, and the analogy of historical dialectics with evolutionary biology is everywhere in *Capital*. His preface to the second edition in 1873 announces that capitalism is "a passing historical phase" in the evolution of social production, and quotes from a Russian review of the first edition. I give extracts:

> Marx treats the social movement as a process of natural history, governed by laws not only independent of human will, consciousness and intelligence, but rather, on the contrary, determining that will, consciousness and intelligence.

> In a word, economic life offers us a phenomenon analogous to the history of evolution in other branches of biology.

> The scientific value of such an inquiry lies in the disclosing of the special laws that regulate the origin, existence, development, and death of a given social organism and its replacement by another and higher one.

Marx comments:

> Whilst the writer pictures what he takes to be actually my method, in this striking and (as far as concerns my own application of it) generous way, what else is he picturing but the dialectic method?

In the preface to the first edition, Marx had written, "The present
society is no solid crystal, but an organism capable of change, and is
constantly changing." The book is so organismal that even machines
are seen as "the bone and muscles of production," with pipes and con-
tainers "the vascular system." In place of the war of nature, we have
"a fierce strife of classes." The war of man against nature has "worked
wonders" in such matters as reclaiming land from the sea, but this
only makes the war of man against man more anomalous: "the
cleanly weeded land, and the uncleanly human weeds."

Marx was quite explicit about his analogy with biological science.
In the later volumes of *Capital*, Marx is a systematist very like Darwin with his barnacles, classifying "the small dealer, who represents
a hermaphrodite form," and so forth. He is, as he describes Adam
Smith, "penetrating to the inner relations, the physiology as it
were, of the bourgeois system." Berlin phrases Marx's conception of
the book "as a comprehensive treatise on the laws and morphology
of the economic organization of modern society." George Bernard
Shaw makes a harsh judgment in the preface to *Back to Methuselah:*

> There was nothing about Socialism in the widely read first
> volume of *Das Kapital:* every reference it made to workers
> and capitalists showed that Marx had never breathed industrial
> air, and had dug his case out of bluebooks in the British Museum.
> Compared with Darwin, he seemed to have no power of obser-
> vation: there was not a fact in *Das Kapital* that had not been
> taken out of a book, nor a discussion that had not been
> opened by somebody else's pamphlet.

Shaw exaggerates. Occasionally Marx does report personal observation in a tone very like Darwin's, as in a footnote:

> On the whole, the working population, subject to the Factory
> Act, has greatly improved physically. All medical testimony
> agrees on this point, and personal observation at different
> times has convinced me of it.

His technical details of such crafts as glass manufacture and watch-
making in the book are impressive, and could not have been learned
from books. Marx learned as much as possible about the textile
industries from Engels, and may have drawn out other friends with
industrial experience.

The most striking resemblance of *Capital* to *The Origin of
Species* lies in the method of progressing from simple to complex
that Marx had announced in the introduction to *The Critique of
Political Economy*. Early in the book Marx keeps excluding com-
plexities: "Wages is a category that, as yet, has no existence at the
present stage of our investigation"; "Money based upon credit implies on the other hand conditions, which from our standpoint of the
simple circulation of commodities, are as yet totally unknown to us";
we must "treat the difference as accidental in order that the phe-

nomena may be observed in their purity." As we go along, things begin to get realistic and concrete, and instead of an abstract spinner producing a hypothetical yarn, we suddenly have "10,000 mule spindles, spinning No. 32 yarn from American cotton." Marx keeps reminding us that he is temporarily omitting this or that complicating factor, "despite the important part which this method plays in actual practice." By the third volume, in the chapter entitled "Counteracting Causes," we have complex reality as rich and ambivalent as Darwin's tangled bank.

Early in *Capital* Marx writes, "The relations between debtors and creditors form a sort of chain," but it is a Great Chain of Becoming, as organic and dynamic as Darwin's tree. The elementary form of value "is a mere germ, which must undergo a series of metamorphoses before it can ripen into the Price-form." A commodity is "the social chrysalis state" of labor, and money is the "gold-chrysalis" of the commodity. Everything grows: "The colonial system, like a hot-house, ripened trade and navigation," or "served as a forcing-house" for public credit. Working men are like corals, building a cooperative venture in their lives and deaths. Their future society will supplant capitalism as a new and improved species, as capitalism in turn supplanted its parent forms. Marx writes of capitalism: "It is clearly the result of a past historical development, the product of many economical revolutions, of the extinction of a whole series of older forms of social production." The society that replaces capitalism, communism, will be perfect, in that the proletariat must abolish class antagonism in the process of abolishing classes. In short, Marx inherits Darwin's teleology, the City of God at the end of the evolutionary process. Like Huxley, he denies its existence, writing to Lassalle in 1861 of the *Origin:*

> Despite all deficiencies, not only is the deathblow dealt here for the first time to 'teleology' in the natural sciences but their rational meaning is empirically explained.

Marx denied similarly that his own system was teleological, writing in the *1844 Manuscripts:* "Communism is not itself the aim of human development or the final form of human society." He also regularly affirmed the opposite, writing in the statutes of a new Communist society in 1850 that communism was "the last form of constitution of the human family."

In *Capital*, Marx is conscious of analogy not only with Darwinian biology but with all the natural sciences. He writes in the preface:

> In the analysis of economic forms, moreover, neither microscopes nor chemical reagents are of use. The force of abstraction must replace both. But in bourgeois society the commodity-form of the product of labor—or the value-form of the commodity—is the economic cell-form. To the superficial observer, the analysis of these forms seems to turn upon minutiae. It does in fact deal

with minutiae, but they are of the same order as those dealt with in microscopic anatomy.

He finds analogues with chemistry: "To borrow an illustration from chemistry, butyric acid is a different substance from propyl formate"; a discovery is like "the discovery by science of the component gases of air"; Proudhon's idealism is attacked with "What opinion should we have of a chemist" if he studied "eternal ideas" instead of matter? Marx similarly uses physics, giving as an analogy in the preface: "The physicist either observes physical phenomena where they occur in their most typical form and most free from disturbing influences, or, wherever possible, he makes experiments under conditions that assure the occurrence of the phenomenon in its normality." Value "forcibly asserts itself like an over-riding law of nature," he writes. "The law of gravity thus asserts itself when a house falls about our ears." Dialectics is illustrated by celestial mechanics. In the course of the work, Marx changed his physical vocabulary, as Engels explains in a footnote to the second volume:

> The term 'latent' is borrowed from the idea of latent heat in physics, which has now been almost replaced by the theory of the transformation of energy. Marx therefore uses in the third part, which is of later date, another term borrowed from the idea of potential energy, viz.: 'potential,' or, analogous to the virtual velocities of D'Alembert, 'virtual capital.'

Marx draws extensively on mathematics, from "A simple geometrical illustration will make this clear" to the abstruse equations later in the volume, of which this is a typical one:

$$S = \begin{cases} \frac{s}{v} \times V \\ P \times \frac{\acute{a}}{a} \times n \end{cases}$$

He ventures into astronomy: "Just as the apparent motions of the heavenly bodies are not intelligible to any but him who is acquainted with their real motions, motions which are not directly perceptible by the senses." Sometimes it is optics: "In the same way the light from an object is perceived by us not as the subjective excitation of our optic nerve, but as the objective form of something outside the eye itself." Often Marx has so many scientific analogies in mind that his metaphor mixes hopelessly, as in a description of petty industry: "But it flourishes, it lets loose its whole energy, it attains its adequate classical form, only where the laborer is the private owner of his own means of labor set in action by himself."

Marx wrote in the *1844 Manuscripts* a bold prophecy of unification: "Natural Science will one day incorporate the science of man, just as the science of man will incorporate natural science; there will be a *single* science." Marx always thought of himself as a scientist, and wrote Kugelmann in 1868 that advertising *Capital* was "beneath the dignity of a scientific man." He saw the book as the start of the new science of man that would eventually merge with natural science, and announced on the first page of the preface: "Every beginning is difficult, holds in all sciences." Marx conceived of his work as primarily within the tradition of political economy, but making it truly scientific through dialectical philosophy and materialist history. Yet his concept of scientific method never excluded value-judgments, since the task of the new science was not only to interpret the world, but to change it. Thus the book is political economy, or economics, of a rather special sort. Part I, the first three chapters, summarizes the 1859 *Contribution to the Critique of Political Economy*, and the rest continues and completes its task of correcting traditional (or "bourgeois") economics. Marx had written to Engels optimistically in 1863 that the work would be "100 per cent easier to understand" than the *Critique*, that it was taking on "a bearably *popular* form," but he saw it primarily as an extended *Critique*.

As a work of economics, its theory is surprisingly simple. At its base is the labor theory of value, the idea that the value of commodities is based only on the socially-necessary labor time (not the accidental individual labor time) of their production. Marx claimed no credit for this discovery, attributing it to many earlier economists, among them Benjamin Franklin, but principally to Smith and Ricardo. He did insist on its revolutionary importance. Marx writes:

> The recent scientific discovery, that the products of labor, so far as they are values, are but material expressions of the human labor spent in their production, marks, indeed, an epoch in the history of the development of the human race.

Marx's theoretical contribution, developed from Fourier and English socialism, was the corollary of surplus value, the idea that all profit (whether shared as interest, rent, or anything else) comes from buying the daily labor-power of the worker, who in that time produces both his own cost and a surplus pocketed by the capitalists. Thus labor produces all wealth, is paid for part of it, and is exploited or robbed of the rest of it.

It is not our task here to discuss the truth or falsity of either theory, and perhaps economic theories are not true or false in any determinable sense. For Engels, as for most Marxists, the theory of surplus value was, with historical materialism, Marx's great contribution. He said in Marx's funeral oration: "With the discovery of surplus value, light was suddenly shed on the darkness in which all our economists, both bourgeois and socialist, had lost themselves." For Shaw, as for many non-Marxists, Marxian economics was popular among socialists because simple to understand and explain (as he wrote in the articles collected as *Bernard Shaw and Karl Marx: A Symposium*) but dangerous for socialism because easily refutable. All

we need note here is that neither theory depends on the other, and
that neither is refutable by observation in the market. *Capital* admits
freely that some commodities embodying labor value are unsalable,
that with others "the price realized may be abnormally above or below the value." For the most part, however, it either ignores demand and market price, or assures us that shifts in production
eventually adjust them to reflect real value, that is, labor value. Labor value is an oddly idealistic conception for so materialistic a
thinker, and it alters in meaning disconcertingly through the
work. Berlin best summarizes this ambiguity:

> Whether Marx's concept of value be interpreted as mean-
> ing the actual market price of commodities, or an average norm,
> round which the actual prices oscillate, or an ideal limit toward
> which they tend, or that which in a rationally organized so-
> ciety prices ought to be, or something more metaphysical
> and Hegelian, an impalpable essence, infused into brute matter
> by the creativeness of human labour, or, as unsympathetic
> critics have maintained, a confusion of all these; and again
> whether the notion of a uniform entity called undifferentiated
> human labour (which according to the theory constitutes eco-
> nomic value), different manifestations of which can be com-
> pared in respect of quantity alone, is, or is not, valid—and it is
> not easy to defend Marx's use of either concept—the theory
> of exploitation based on them remains unaffected.

Essentially, "value" for Marx has nothing to do with economics.
It is an intrinsic property of commodities representing the amount
of workers' blood that has gone into them. If told that however
much workers' blood or "value" a commodity possesses, there is no
demand for it in the market, Marx would have replied as Thoreau did
in "A Plea for Captain John Brown": "No doubt you can get more in
your market for a quart of milk than for a quart of blood, but that
is not the market that heroes carry their blood to."

Capital is also a work of history. The first volume gives its subject a historical or genetic explanation in the penultimate section on
"The Accumulation of Capital" and even a speculative prehistory in
the final section on "The So-Called Primitive Accumulation." Both
turn out to be, as one might guess, histories of theft. The third
volume is more traditionally historical, with Marx's dogged genetic
concern, so that a chapter giving an account of the cotton crisis of
1861–1865 begins with a "Preliminary History, 1845–1860." The
fourth volume, *Theories of Surplus Value*, is straight critical history of ideas. If the test of history is accurate prediction (as it is
where history claims to be scientific), *Capital* does not come
off as well as Marx's books on events in France, or even as well as his
Tribune journalism. Marx sees a future of increased piece work,
since "piece-wage is the form of wages most in harmony with
the capitalist mode of production"; of longer hours, since "ma-

chinery is the surest means of lengthening the working day"; of lower wages, since "The constant tendency is to force the cost of labor back towards zero"; of general worsening of conditions, since "In proportion as capital accumulates, the lot of the laborer must grow worse." In short: "Accumulation of wealth at one pole is, therefore, at the same time accumulation of misery, agony of toil, slavery, ignorance, brutality, mental degradation, at the opposite pole."

Toward the end of the century, Eduard Bernstein jotted down his reasons for leading a revisionist movement in Marxism: "Peasants do not sink; middle class does not disappear; crises do not grow ever larger; misery and serfdom do not increase." Sombart wrote similarly in *Capitalism* some years later:

> Karl Marx prophesied: firstly, the increasing misery of hired workers; secondly, general 'concentration,' with the disappearance of the class of artisans and peasants; thirdly, the catastrophic collapse of capitalism. Nothing of the kind has come to pass.

To it Sombart opposed his own prognosis:

> Capitalism will continue to transform itself internally in the same direction in which it has already begun to transform itself, at the time of its apogee: as it grows older, it will become more and more calm, sedate, reasonable.

To the arguments of Bernstein and Sombart, that Marx's predictions do not accord with the plain facts of experience, orthodox Marxism has characteristically chosen one of two rejoinders. One is to say that Marx's predictions have all come true, but that in the age of imperialism these miseries have been visited on the oppressed workers of the colonial countries, as a consequence of which capitalism could afford to become "more calm, sedate, reasonable" in the imperialist countries. The other is to say that Marx's predictions have not come true because, so accurately and convincingly did they foresee increasing misery leading to revolution, that they forced the terrified ruling class to mend its ways and share a tithe of its booty with the workers.

I would suggest that it is more useful to regard Marx's predictions in Kenneth Burke's terms, as symbolic expressions rather than as objective predictions. The constant prophecies of revolution, we have noted, are ways of expressing hopes and wishes in a vocabulary that denies the relevance of the observer's hopes and wishes and insists that it is objective science. Liebknecht adds that Marx continually used to prophesy economic crises to his friends, "and in consequence was subjected to our hearty derision, which made him furious." The visions of the worsening of conditions in *Capital* are not really realistic appraisals of the future, they are dramatizations, what Burke calls "the temporalizing of essence," putting the essence of the present situation as a fated vision of the future (as origin myths put it as a genesis in the past). They demonstrate Burke's "principle of completion," entelechy,

the inevitable tendency to perfect terminology by carrying it to the
end of the line. If capitalism was cruel, it would become crueler,
cruelest; if the lot of the proletariat was bad, it would worsen until it
was worst. As Marx wrote to Engels in 1865, "If you have said 'A' it
follows that you must go on and say 'B.'"

In some respects, like everything Marx wrote, *Capital* is a work of
philosophy. Marx notes indignantly in the preface to the second edition that the Paris *Revue Positiviste* charged him with treating economics metaphysically. He replies that a Russian reviewer refutes the
charge with the statement "The method of Marx is the deductive
method of the whole English school," although why a work cannot be
both metaphysical and deductive he does not say. Sometimes, as Berlin
notes, Marx's concept of value seems very metaphysical, as when he
writes: "The value of commodities is the very opposite of the coarse
materiality of their substance, not an atom of matter enters into its
composition." Most of the philosophy in the book, however, is in the
form of dialectics. In the preface to the second edition, goaded by his
reviewers, Marx explains how his materialist dialectics (what Plekhanov
later named "dialectical materialism") differs from Hegel's idealist and
"mystifying" dialectics. The preface concludes with a snarl:

> That crisis is once again approaching, although as yet but in its
> preliminary stage; and by the universality of its theatre and the
> intensity of its action it will drum dialectics even into the heads of
> the mushroom-upstarts of the new, holy Prusso-German empire.

The reversals and antinomies that so pleased Marx in *The Poverty
of Philosophy* now lead to Hegelian paradoxes and "reflex-categories"
in economics: "Concrete labor becomes the form under which its
opposite, abstract human labor, manifests itself"; "The labor of private
individuals takes the form of its opposite, labor directly social in its
form"; "It must have its origin both in circulation and yet not in circulation"; and so forth. Contradictions arise, interpenetrate, are recon-
ciled, and provoke new contradictions. "Relative surplus value is
absolute," Marx announces like a good dialectician, "Absolute surplus
value is relative." A few pages later, he is indignant with John Stuart
Mill, a bad dialectician:

> After thus proving clearly, that even if capitalist production had
> no existence, still it would always exist, Mill is consistent enough
> to show, on the contrary, that it has no existence, even when it
> does exist."

Earlier in the volume, he had protested: "John Stuart Mill, with his
usual eclectic logic, understands how to hold at the same time the view
of his father, James Mill, and the opposite view." "Eclectic" if *they* do
it, "dialectic" for our side.

After political economy, *Capital* seems to be principally sociology,
although Marx never uses Comte's term. "Speculative sociology,"
H. Stuart Hughes calls it in *Consciousness and Society*, following

Croce's idea that Marx describes an unreal world to cast light on the real one. Alfred G. Meyer in *The Centennial Review,* Fall 1959, discusses the resemblance of Marx's view of societies, as functional systems of action, to Parsonian sociology. A better identification for our purposes might be Georges Sorel's description of Marx's sociology as "social poetry," ideas in "summary and symbolic formulas." As sociology, the book is a bold vision, not of one society, but of Disraeli's "two worlds": the capitalist and working classes as though they were physically different peoples, as in fact in England at the time they were: "the deficiency of fat-forming food among a large part of the working class," contrasted to "the superfluous fat of the bourgeoisie and aristocracy." We will explore this dramatistic sociology in a later consideration of the book as a literary and imaginative organization. Actually, to the extent that Marx was describing conditions of the working class as remote from most of his readers as Darwin's Fuegians, he was writing anthropology, and doing more field work than was conventional for his time.

Whatever *Capital*'s field, Marx was interested in making the study of society scientific. He wanted "the natural laws of capitalist production," defining "laws" as "tendencies working with iron necessity towards inevitable results." It is these over-riding laws that forcibly assert themselves like gravity when a house collapses. The later part of the volume is full of them: "the iron law of proportionality," "the constant tendency to equilibrium," "the law of capitalist production," "the general law of capitalist accumulation," and so on endlessly. In this objective science, "England is used as the chief illustration" not because Marx is interested in the conditions of English life, he insists, but because for capitalist production, England is "classic ground," or only in England has a phenomenon "the classic form." A footnote adds another consideration:

> For the rest England figures here in the foreground because she is the classic representative of capitalist production, and she alone has a continuous set of official statistics of the things we are considering.

More than any sort of social science, *Capital* is preachment, value judgment, moral exhortation, ethical protest and imperative. It seems amazing that this has been a matter of dispute. The first volume of *Capital* "wasted no time either in finding justifications for the capitalists or in reproaching them with their injustice," Rosa Luxemburg writes in Mehring's *Karl Marx.* Berlin in his otherwise excellent biography explains that Marx was endowed with "exceptionally little sensibility, and was repelled as much by the rhetoric and emotionalism of the intellectuals as by the stupidity and complacency of the bourgeoisie"; that he appealed "solely to reason, to the practical intelligence"; that "Marx denounces the existing order by appealing not to ideals but to history: he denounces it not as bad, or unfortunate, or due to human wickedness or folly"; that *Capital* is distinguished by "the almost complete absence from it of explicit moral argument, of appeals to conscience or to principle."

Other readers have seen it very differently. Emile Durkheim wrote of *Capital* (in a passage translated and cut by Hughes):

> What a lot of statistical data, of historical comparisons, of studies would be indispensable to settle a single one of the innumerable questions it treats! . . . The truth is that the facts and observations gathered in it . . . figure there as little more than arguments. The research . . . was undertaken to establish the doctrine . . . , far from the doctrine resulting from research. . . . It was passion that inspired all these systems; what gave birth to them and constitutes their strength is the thirst for a more perfect justice. . . . Socialism is not a science, a sociology in miniature: it is a cry of pain. . . .

Pareto and Sorel more or less concur, and Hughes generalizes: "The critics of the 1890's had agreed that Marx had exerted his influence primarily as an ethical leader." Marx interested Shaw not as an economist but as a great denouncer of the infamies of capitalism.

Everywhere *Capital* reproaches the capitalists for their injustice, denounces the existing order as wicked, explodes with wrath or cries with pain. It is a Manichaean world in which the forces of good and evil are locked in eternal combat. What puts Luxemburg and Berlin off, I think, is Marx's style of ironic protest, as when he writes:

> It is a very cheap sort of sentimentality which declares this method of determining the value of labor-power, a method prescribed by the very nature of the case, to be a brutal method.

Marx has previously made his comment with a quotation from an anonymous 1707 pamphlet: "Such a spirit of cruelty reigns here in England among the men of trade, that is not to be met with in any other society of men, nor in any other kingdom of the world." The book's vision, developing the Carlylean cash-nexus passage in the *Manifesto*, is of everything slimed and corrupted:

> Objects that in themselves are no commodities, such as conscience, honor, etc., are capable of being offered for sale by their holders, and of thus acquiring, through their price, the form of commodities.

As intangibles become commodities, man becomes "a thing, although a living conscious thing." Women, of course, become prostitutes—what better symbol for turning flesh into commodity, people into things? Prostitution is everywhere in the book. "Glasgow pigs together in its wynds and closes" gallant Highlanders along with "prostitutes and thieves." The factory relay-system "drove the youths to the pot-house, and the girls to the brothel." With Australian unemployment, "prostitution in some places there flourishes as wantonly as in the London Haymarket." The ruling class itself Marx divides into "young whores and old nuns." The book quotes the cynical "*Pecunia non olet*" that one of the Roman emperors (Vespasian, I think) replied when charged with living off a tax on urinals. Marx keeps reminding us that in money we cannot smell "a trace of surplus-value," but the final effect is to make the whole of capitalist production stink to heaven. *Capital* has little or nothing to say about communism or socialism, but a vision of the good life shines through it. Marx writes:

> Capital oversteps not only the moral, but even the merely physical maximum bounds of the workday. It usurps the time for growth, development, and healthy maintenance of the body. It steals the time required for the consumption of fresh air and sunlight.

This good life is not only healthy, free, and spontaneous, but it is oddly primitive, rejecting the division of labor. It asks of men, with Goethe and Hegel, that they be able to do everything, that they be whole men. The capitalist world of cruelty, ruthlessness and horror is preparing the way for this better one with iron inevitability, and Marx walks before it with a lantern.

W E G E T closer to the essential nature of *Capital* if we deal with it, not as science, social science, or exhortation, but as imaginative literature. In a letter to Engels in 1865, Marx wrote, "Whatever shortcomings they may have, the merit of my writings is that they are an artistic whole." *Capital* is much more structured than its method of composition would suggest. Part I is brought to a climax with the Rabelaisian prose of Marx's old favorite Sir William Petty:

> Money is but the fat of the Body Politick, whereof too much doth as often hinder its agility, as too little makes it sick. . . . as fat lubricates the motion of the muscles, feeds in want of victuals, fills up the uneven cavities, and beautifies the body; so doth money in the state quicken its action, feeds from abroad in time of dearth at home; evens accounts . . . and beautifies the whole; altho more especially the particular persons that have it in plenty.

The book's periodic descents into the horrors of capitalism are spaced so that each comes as a fresh shock, and each is followed by a deliberate flatness, what Stendhal called "benches for my readers to sit down on." Thus after the ghastliness of "The Working-Day," Part III ends calmly on the bourgeois delusion "that with the shortening of the working-day by 2 hours, the selling price of 12 spinning machines dwindles to that of 10!" The book's effective finish comes at the end of the penultimate chapter, with the famous announcement about outgrown capitalism:

> This integument is burst asunder. The knell of capitalist private property sounds. The expropriators are expropriated.

This is followed by a footnote quoting from *The Communist Manifesto*. The last chapter is a quiet coda, almost an appendix, the sort of anticlimax beloved of the Greek dramatists.

The poetic texture of *Capital* is an amazing richness of image, symbol, and metaphor. One of Marx's principal sources is classical mythology (he took a course in it at the university), which he uses with a surrealist freedom. The preface to *Capital* says that social statistics "raise the veil just enough to let us catch a glimpse of the Medusa head behind it," and explains:

> Perseus wore a magic cap that the monsters he hunted down might not see him. We draw the magic cap down over eyes and ears as a make-believe that there are no monsters.

Marx goes on to talk of "the Furies of private interest"; to quote Petty's creation myth for material wealth, "Labor is its father and the earth its mother"; to describe the "Sisyphus-like labor" of the hoarder; to reveal a law "that rivets the laborer to capital more firmly than the wedges of Vulcan did Prometheus to the rock."

If the laborer is Sisyphus and Prometheus, capital is not only Gorgon and Furies but a whole menagerie of supernatural horrors. It is a monster "that vampire-like only lives by sucking living labor"; possessing a "vampire-thirst for the living blood of labor"; and will not loose its hold, quoting Engels, "so long as there is a muscle, a nerve, a drop of blood to be exploited." It has a "werewolf's hunger for surplus-labor." *Capital's* machines are giants and ogres: "a mechanical monster whose body fills whole factories, and whose demon power, at first veiled under the slow and measured motions of his giant limbs, at length breaks out into the fast and furious whirl of his countless working organs." Two pages on machinery say "cyclopean," "stupendous," "cyclopean," "cyclopean," "cyclopean," "gigantic," "monster," "such a weight that not Thor himself could wield it." The capitalists are ghouls: "coining children's blood into capital"; killing children in silk manufacture so that "the children were slaughtered out-and-out for the sake of their delicate fingers"; exporting "the capitalized blood of children." They are "flesh agents," "dealers in human flesh," and force workmen to become lesser slave dealers, and sell their own wives and children to the factories.

Accompanying these metaphoric myths are metaphoric rites. The most important are of birth and rebirth. Marx's aim, he says in the preface, is to "shorten and lessen the birth-pangs" of the new society. Capital is "value big with value, a live monster that is fruitful and multiplies." "Force is the midwife of every old society pregnant with a new one." Rebirth is a protean metamorphosis even in economics:

> In order, therefore, that a commodity may in practice act effectively as exchange value, it must quit its bodily shape, must transform itself from mere imaginary into real gold, although to the commodity such transubstantiation may be more difficult than to

the Hegelian 'concept,' the transition from 'necessity' to 'freedom,' or to a lobster the casting of his shell, or to Saint Jerome the putting off of the old Adam.

"Classical political economy," Marx writes, cannot formulate true relations "so long as it sticks in its bourgeois skin." As for capital itself, it "likewise arrives in due time at the moment when it must renew its head and limbs, when it casts off its old skin and is likewise born again." Everything is crystallized, congealed, petrified: commodities are "definite masses of crystallized labor-time"; "money is a crystal formed of necessity in the course of the exchanges," "a solid crystal of value"; "as values, all commodities are only definite masses of congealed labor-time"; "money becomes petrified into a hoard"; and so on. But these dead will waken in Marx's world of fairy tale, where capital "has acquired the occult quality of being able to add value to itself. It brings forth living offspring, or, at the least, lays golden eggs." Like the prince in *Sleeping Beauty*, "living labor must seize upon these things and rouse them from their death-sleep."

Marx's favorite metaphor in the early books, stripping away the veil, here finds its place as the ritual of exposing beautiful temptresses as the loathly hags they are. His preface announces not only raising the veil so we can see the Medusa head, but "the ultimate aim of this work, to lay bare the economic law of motion of modern society." In a sense, it has already been done for him: "Modern Industry rent the veil that concealed from men their own social process of production." Marx will expose the gods worshipped as things of wood and stone. In a section on "The Fetishism of Commodities and the Secret Thereof," he explains that a commodity is "something transcendent," that it has a "mystical character," that it is "a mysterious thing," and explains: "In order, therefore, to find an analogy, we must have recourse to the mist-enveloped regions of the religious world." Marx then deals with commodities in terms of "fetishism," "magic," "necromancy." The hoarder is a worshipper who "makes a sacrifice of the lusts of the flesh to his gold fetish." Marx quotes S. Laing: "Every large town may be looked upon as a place of human sacrifice, a shrine where thousands pass yearly through the fire as offerings to the moloch of avarice." The colonial system was " 'the strange God' who perched himself on the altar cheek by jowl with the old Gods of Europe, and one fine day with a shove and a kick chucked them all of a heap."

Like a poet, Marx strives to summon up an immediacy of sensation, to make the reader feel the experience itself. Adulteration is a good example. He begins with a footnote early in the book, remarking that those selling cheap bread below its value sell it "adulterated with alum, soap, pearl ashes, chalk, Derbyshire stone-dust, and suchlike agreeable, nourishing, and wholesome ingredients." When he returns to the topic a few chapters later it is with increased fury, and the reader can taste the awfulness on his tongue:

Englishmen, always well up in the Bible, knew well enough that
man, unless by elective grace a capitalist, or landlord, or sinecur-
ist, is commanded to eat his bread in the sweat of his brow, but
they did not know that he had to eat daily in his bread a certain
quantity of human perspiration mixed with the discharge of
abscesses, cobwebs, dead black-beetles, and putrid German
yeast, without counting alum, sand, and other agreeable mineral
ingredients.

Marx adds a footnote:

The French chemist, Chevallier, in his treatise on the 'so-
phistications' of commodities, enumerates for many of the 600
or more articles which he passes in review, 10, 20, 30 different
methods of adulteration. He adds that he does not know all the
methods, and does not mention all that he knows. He gives 6
kinds of adulteration of sugar, 9 of olive oil, 10 of butter, 12 of
salt, 19 of milk, 20 of bread, 23 of brandy, 24 of meal, 28 of
chocolate, 30 of wine, 32 of coffee, etc. Even God Almighty does
not escape this fate. See Ronard du Card, on the falsifications of
the materials of the Sacrament.

Later in the book Marx similarly forces the reader down into the filth
and squalor of English workingclass life, into the choking factory
room where "it is exceptionally unpleasant to stand even 10 minutes,"
and children work 10 hours or more a day. He produces an oppressive
sense of claustrophobia using nothing more than images based on
statistics on the space workers are allotted: children working in a
space of 12⅔ cubic feet, "less space than the half of what a child would
occupy if packed in a box measuring 3 feet in each direction," or bed-
rooms in which each adult had as much air as "he would have if he
were shut up in a box of 4 feet measuring each way, the whole night."
Marx was somewhat defensive about the style of *Capital*. He
writes in the preface to the second edition:

The mealy-mouthed babblers of German vulgar economy fell
foul of the style of my book. No one can feel the literary
shortcomings in *Capital* more strongly than I myself.

Marx quotes in his defense the *Saturday Review*, which said, "The
presentation invests the driest economic questions with a certain
peculiar charm" (he did not quote the beginning of the sentence,
which is "The author's views may be as pernicious as we conceive
them to be"), and the St. Petersburg *Journal*, which said the book
was distinguished by "an unusual liveliness." Along with the richness
of imagery, the outstanding characteristics of Marx's style and language in the book are its polyglot and polymathic learning, and the
vigor of its abuse. Besides the technical references to almost every
science and branch of knowledge, the book is full of untranslated
quotations in Greek and Latin, French and Italian, and English, as

though Marx were writing not for an audience of workers but for German Ph. D.'s, as perhaps he was. Just after the publication of *Capital*, Marx wrote to Kugelmann: "One submits to the public a book worked out with painstaking care (and never perhaps has a work of that kind been written in more difficult circumstances) in order to raise the Party as high as possible and to disarm even the vulgar by the manner of presentation." *Capital* has references and quotations, identified and unidentified, involving Homer, Greek drama, and the Bible (sometimes in the Vulgate Latin), Plato and Aristotle, Shakespeare and Cervantes, Goethe and Balzac, Dante and innumerable others. The German of *Capital*, according to people qualified to judge, is masterful, if somewhat pedantic and slightly anglicized by Marx's years in England (Liebknecht gives the example of "*zusammengehudelten Menschen*," "people huddled together," which is the English "huddle" rather than the German "*hudeln*," "to praise fawningly").

The other barrier to the reader, Marx's polemic style, was natural to him and lifelong, if augmented during the composition of *Capital* by his miseries and physical ailments. Sending off proofs of the book to Engels, Marx wrote, "I hope the bourgeoisie will remember my carbuncles all the rest of their lives," saying nothing about the liver trouble and the rest. Marx's language is in fact restrained in the book, as compared to his correspondence with Engels, which crackles with invective and abuse. Henry Mayers Hyndman, a British socialist leader who met Marx in the last years of Marx's life, gives us a sense in *The Record of an Adventurous Life* of how shocking this invective was in the England of the time. Hyndman writes:

> Accustomed as we are nowadays, especially in England, to fence always with big soft buttons on the point of our rapiers, Marx's terrible onslaughts with naked steel upon his adversaries appeared so improper that it was impossible for our gentlemanly shamfighters and mental gymnasium men to believe that this unsparing controversialist and furious assailant of capital and capitalists was really the deepest thinker of modern times.

Michael Bakunin, the recipient of some of Marx's worst abuse, said that everything that came from Marx's pen was weighty, earnest, and profound, "when he was not engaged in personal polemic." In the first volume of *Capital*, invective and learning combine at times to produce an amazing rhetoric, as in a ferocious attack on "the greed for gold." It begins quoting Columbus:

> Gold is a wonderful thing! Whoever possesses it is lord of all he wants. By means of gold one can even get souls into Paradise.

and ends:

> Modern society, which soon after its birth pulled Plutus by the hair of his head from the bowels of the earth, greets gold as its Holy Grail, as the glittering incarnation of the very principle of its own life.

Meanwhile Marx throws off footnotes on Henry III of France robbing cloisters to sell the relics, the despoiling of the Delphic temple by the Phocians, Phoenician temple prostitution combined with banking, and bitter passages against gold from *Timon of Athens* and the *Antigone*.

Marx had a shrewd sense of the truth that the raised voice betrays insecurity. He remarks of S. Bailey: "That he laid his finger on some serious defects in the Ricardian theory is proved by the animosity with which he was attacked by Ricardo's followers." In his letter, written against Proudhon, to Annenkov in 1846, Marx writes:

> He himself is so thoroughly conscious of the emptiness of his arguments, of his utter incapacity for speaking about these things, that he hurls himself head over heels into explosions of rage, vociferation and righteous wrath, foams at the mouth, curses, denounces, cries shame and murder, beats his breast and boasts before God and man that he is unspotted by these socialist infamies!

None of it applied to Marx himself, though. In letters to Engels he keeps referring to his work on *Capital* as "the whole of the economic shit" or "the whole shit," but his scatology, with which the letters teem, is only the faithful reflection of that vast dung-heap the capitalist world. In 1850 Marx had written to Ferdinand Freiligrath about the problem of disreputable recruits to the cause:

> Storms always raise a certain amount of dirt and dust, and a revolutionary period does not smell of attar of roses. It is clear that occasionally one is spattered with all sorts of muck. It is impossible to be too particular at such a moment.

The basic form of *Capital* is dramatic. Recommending that Engels study the Irish history of 1779 and 1780, Marx wrote to him: "This period is of the highest interest, scientifically and dramatically." Although it was now balanced with science, his interest in the world stage of history remained as strong as it had ever been. Marx begins the book with an apology in the preface for making dramatic characters out of abstractions, like Darwin on Nature:

> To prevent possible misunderstanding, a word. I paint the capitalist and the landlord in no sense *couleur de rose*. But here individuals are dealt with only in so far as they are the personifications of economic categories, embodiments of particular class-relations and class-interests.

In fact, everything is personified in the book. Linen tells us things and "betrays its thoughts," a table "evolves out of its wooden brain grotesque ideas," any commodity is "a born leveller and a cynic," "commodities are in love with money, but 'the course of true love never did run smooth,'" prices are "wooing glances cast at money by commodities," "circulation sweats money from every pore."

Capital is crammed with heroes and villains. A few of the heroes are real men. The factory inspectors are honorable and heroic men, particularly their chief, Leonard Horner, who "rendered undying service to the English working class," and for it "was persecuted and maligned by the manufacturers in every conceivable manner." At least one political economist, Ricardo, wrote "with the scientific impartiality and love of truth characteristic of him." A few individual workingmen stand out of the anonymous hordes to become individual heroes, probably the most vivid of them G. Apsden, who told an investigating commission in unforgettable words:

> That boy of mine . . . when he was 7 years old I used to carry him on my back to and fro through the snow, and he used to have 16 hours a day . . . I have often knelt down to feed him as he stood by the machine, for he could not leave it or stop.

The true dramatic hero of *Capital*, however, is the personified Proletariat, whose voice is suddenly heard addressing the Capitalist in the "Working-Day" chapter. After a long speech explaining surplus value, he concludes:

> I demand, therefore, a working-day of normal length, and I demand it without any appeal to your heart, for in money matters sentiment is out of place. You may be a model citizen, perhaps a member of the Society for the Prevention of Cruelty to Animals, and in the odor of sanctity to boot; but the thing that you represent face to face with me has no heart in its breast. That which seems to throb there is my own heart beating. I demand the normal working-day because I, like every other seller, demand the value of my commodity.

Elsewhere in the book, the Proletariat is silent victim rather than protesting voice, his role to suffer rather than act, and if the work is not a tragedy, its failure would seem to lie in the failure of its protagonist to be an active force.[1]

The villainous real men in the book are rarely capitalists, almost always hireling political economists, and they tend to be rather ludicrous villains as Marx's invective heats up and begins to glow. In the preface to the second edition, Marx describes the field:

> In place of disinterested enquirers, there were hired prize fighters; in place of genuine scientific research, the bad conscience and evil intent of apologetic.

They are "sophists and sycophants of the ruling-classes," the Germans particularly "petty retailers and hawkers in the service of the great foreign wholesale concerns." In the text Marx gets specific. MacLeod is "a successful cross between the superstitious mercantilists, and the enlightened Free Trade bagman." Bastiat is "truly comical," a "dwarf

---

[1] Just seventy years later, George Orwell wrote in *The Road to Wigan Pier:* "A thousand influences constantly press a working man down into a *passive* role. He does not act, he is acted upon."

economist." "The learned Professor Roscher" is the author of "eclectic professorial twaddle," a combination of ignorance and apologetics. Mueller is a "romantic sycophant." Pinto is "the Pindar of the Amsterdam Stock Exchange." Ganilh is the author of a "miserable work," and "It is not possible to bring out the cretinism of his standpoint." An anonymous author is "an uncommonly self-satisfied wiseacre." Senior is a "sycophant doctrinaire" motivated by "the love of lucre." Ure, in a re-use of the formula for Pinto, is "the Pindar of the automatic factory," and Marx bitterly quotes his description of the machinery Marx found cyclopean: "In these spacious halls the benignant power of steam summons around him his myriads of willing menials." Burke is "the celebrated sophist and sycophant." Commenting on Burke's "The laws of commerce are the laws of Nature, and therefore the laws of God," Marx says, "No wonder that, true to the laws of God and of Nature, he always sold himself in the best market." McCulloch is "a past master in this pretentious cretinism." Malthus is "that master in plagiarism," and the sensation he created "was due solely to party interest." A book by Watts is "a very sink of all long-ago-rotten, apologetic commonplaces." Bentham is "that insipid, pedantic, leather-tongued oracle," the Martin Tupper of philosophers. Destutt de Tracy is "the fish-blooded bourgeois doctrinaire." Macaulay is a "systematic falsifier of history." Aikin is, in the third variant, "the Pindar of the slave-trade."

The only capitalists who emerge as dramatic personalities in *Capital* are landowners. The chief of these is the Duchess of Sutherland, who infuriated Marx by entertaining Harriet Beecher Stowe in London to show her sympathy for the Negro slaves in the United States. Marx promptly sent the *Tribune* the facts about the Sutherland "slaves" in Scotland, published them in a pamphlet, and summarized them in the book. He writes:

This person, well instructed in economy, resolved, on entering upon her government, to effect a radical cure, and to turn the whole country, whose population had already been, by earlier processes of a like kind, reduced to 15,000, into a sheep-walk. From 1814 to 1820 these 15,000 inhabitants, about 3000 families, were systematically hunted and rooted out. All their villages were destroyed and burnt, all their fields turned into pasturage. British soldiers enforced this eviction, and came to blows with the inhabitants. One old woman was burnt to death in the flames of the hut, which she refused to leave. Thus this fine lady appropriated 794,000 acres of land that had from time immemorial belonged to the clan. She assigned to the expelled inhabitants about 6000 acres on the sea-shore—2 acres per family. The 6000 acres had until this time lain waste, and brought in no income to their owners. The Duchess, in the nobility of her heart, actually went so far as to let these at an average rent of 2s. 6d. per acre to the clansmen, who for centuries had shed their blood for her family.

The whole of the stolen clan-land she divided into 29 great sheep farms, each inhabited by a single family, for the most part imported English farm-servants. In the year 1835 the 15,000 Gaels were already replaced by 131,000 sheep. The remnant of the aborigines, flung on the sea-shore, tried to live by catching fish. They became amphibious and lived, as an English author says, half on land and half on water, and withal only half on both.

But the brave Gaels must expiate yet more bitterly their idolatry, romantic and of the mountains, for the 'great men' of the clan. The smell of their fish rose to the noses of the great men. They scented some profit in it, and let the seashore to the great fishmongers of London. For the second time the Gaels were hunted out.

Marx notes that Senior naturally called "the proceedings in Sutherlandshire one of the most beneficent clearings since the memory of man." The other landowner who emerges as an individual villain, if a considerably more honest one, is Lord Leicester. Marx quotes:

'It is a melancholy thing to stand alone in one's country,' said Lord Leicester, when complimented on the completion of Hookham. 'I look around and not a house is to be seen but mine. I am the giant of Giant Castle, and have eat up all my neighbors.'

The true villain of the book is the Capitalist, defined as "capital personified and endowed with consciousness and a will." He is "our friend, Moneybags," or "his holiness, Freetrade," or "Rent-roll." "His soul is the soul of capital," and his body is naturally "the syphilitic and scrofulous" body of the upper classes. In one dramatic vision, after an account of children working 36 consecutive hours in the glass works, Marx sees:

Meanwhile, late at night perhaps, self-denying Mr. Glass-Capital, primed with port wine, reels out of his club homeward, droning out idiotically, 'Britons never, never shall be slaves!'

In the book's final dramatic apocalypse, "capital comes dripping from head to foot, from every pore, with blood and dirt."

The subsidiary personified villain in the book is the Jew. Marx loses few opportunities for a sneer or innuendo at Jews. The language spoken by commodities is Hebrew, and they are "inwardly circumcised Jews"; the quantity of precious metals in a country is not changed by "a Jew selling a Queen Ann's farthing for a guinea"; capital speaks in the voice of Shylock; "The chosen people bore in their features the sign manual of Jehovah." An old joke of Bruno Bauer's about the Jews, that they live "in the pores of Polish society" the way the gods of Epicurus live in the Intermundia, charmed Marx so much that he repeats it in every volume of the book. There are one or two sneers at Christians, on the order of "The sheep's nature of a Christian is shown in his resemblance to the Lamb of God," but the Jews are Marx's especial butt.

Marx's correspondence with Engels is as obsessively anti-Semitic as scatological, with much of it directed at their friend and rival Lassalle, whose misfortune it was that his father had remained a Jew when Marx's father converted. Lassalle is "Yiddle Brown" or "Ephraim Smart," "Itzig" or "Baron Itzig." To Engels he is "a typical Jew from the Slav frontier," "a greasy Jew from Breslau," or "Oi, oi, the great Lassalle." In 1862, Marx wrote to Engels explaining Lassalle: "It is perfectly obvious from the shape of his head and the way his hair grows that he is descended from the Negroes who joined Moses on the journey out of Egypt, unless perhaps his mother or his grandmother had relations with a nigger."

Marx's relations to the Jews are a subject of considerable complexity. His articles on *The Jewish Question* had advised the Jews to emancipate themselves from Judaism by emancipating themselves from capitalism. Other revolutionists treated him to the same sort of anti-Semitism to which he treated Lassalle. "M. Marx is by origin a Jew," Bakunin wrote. "He unites in himself all the qualities and defects of that gifted race. Nervous, some say, to the point of cowardice, he is immensely malicious, vain, quarrelsome, as intolerant and autocratic as Jehovah, the God of his fathers, and like Him, insanely vindictive." Feuerbach, Bruno Bauer, and Eugen Duehring were all anti-Semites, and Duehring viciously attacked Marx as a Jew, as did many of Bakunin's followers. In Marx's view, Judaism is a matter of cultural identification; he had repudiated it with Lutheran baptism (which he despised equally), and he was thus no Jew. Unlike Freud, who deserted the religion but not the cultural identification, Marx was aloof or hostile all his life to everything Jewish. To the best of my knowledge, neither Marx nor Engels ever mentioned Marx's Jewish origins in correspondence until after Marx's death, when Engels wrote to an unknown correspondent in 1890, in a letter against anti-Semitism, "Marx was of purest Jewish blood."

Sometimes, with a reverse racism, many approving writers have identified Marx with inherited Jewish qualities. For Shaw, his power lay in his "fine Jewish literary gift, with terrible powers of hatred, invective, irony." Hyndman saw Marx as combining "the righteous fury of the great seers of his race, with the cold analytical powers of Spinoza and the Jewish doctors." In John Middleton Murry's *Heroes of Thought*, Marx's doctrine of salvation by the proletariat is "Jewish apocalyptic Messianism" and the revolution is "a completely secularized Jewish eschatology." Murry writes:

> The element of primitive Jewish Messianism with regard to the future in Marx is very great, though it is paradoxically concealed behind an excessive realism with regard to the present. It is the Jew in Marx, the inheritor of centuries of racial oppression, who proclaims anew the inevitable millennium of the despised and rejected: and the true commentary on the passionate emotional bias of *Das Kapital* (as distinct from the economic analysis which

hides it) is the *Book of Revelation*. This powerful bias is apparent, not merely in the strange, catastrophic conception of the redemptive proletariat, wherein the Proletariat *is* the Messiah, but also in Marx's signal failure to imagine "the classless society." It was, for him, simply the millennium: the Kingdom of Heaven on earth.

For Waldo Frank in *In the American Jungle*, Marx is a traditional Jewish prophet who must be interpreted like Moses or Isaiah. Hughes, too, sees Marx as "the Old Testament prophet" and notes "In the 1890's it was not yet possible to discern the unconscious revelations of ancestral thought-patterns that lay scattered through the Marxian writing." One can doubt the inheritance of Jewish thought-patterns, but some cultural transmission is certain. Both Marx's parents were descended from rabbis, his mother was not "enlightened" like his father, and one can doubt that Marx's childhood was as antiseptic as he would have had it. If Marx's adult stance was that of an Old Testament prophet or a Talmudic disputant, if he saw the world peopled with the Golems and Dybbuks of capitalism, we can suspect nurture. When Marx quotes Luther against usury in *Capital*, he may be, like Luther, bitterly anti-Semitic, but like Luther he is the cultural heir of an Old Testament tradition of moral indignation.

The dramatic movement of *Capital* consists of four descents into suffering and horror, which we might see as four acts of a drama. At first Marx writes as though he were taking the reader on a guided tour:

> Accompanied by Mr. Moneybags and by the possessor of labor-power, we therefore take leave for a time of this noisy sphere, where everything takes place on the surface and in view of all men, and follow them both into the hidden abode of production, on whose threshold there stares us in the face 'No admittance except on business.' Here we shall see, not only how capital produces, but how capital is produced. We shall at last force the secret of profit-making.

By the next page, we realize that we are actually being taken to the play. Marx continues:

> We think we can perceive a change in the physiognomy of our dramatis personae. He, who before was the money owner, now strides in front as capitalist; the possessor of labor-power follows as his laborer. The one with an air of importance, smirking, intent on business; the other timid and holding back, like one who is bringing his own hide to market and has nothing to expect but—a hiding.

The first act is "The Working-Day" chapter. Its theme is announced a few pages before it begins when Marx reminds the capitalists of "the boys and girls whom you employ," and its action is

mostly the mistreatment of women and children. Marx quotes a
magistrate of the lace trade:

> Children of nine or ten years are dragged from their squalid
> beds at two, three, or four o'clock in the morning and compelled
> to work for a bare subsistence until ten, eleven, or twelve at
> night, their limbs wearing away, their frames dwindling, their
> faces whitening, and their humanity absolutely sinking into a
> stonelike torpor, utterly horrible to contemplate.

In the Staffordshire potteries, "a branch of industry by the side of
which cotton-spinning appears an agreeable and healthful occupation,"
children of seven work fifteen hours a day. A twenty-year-old mil-
liner in London was literally worked to death during the busy season,
sewing thirty hours at a stretch in an overcrowded workroom, kept
awake with sherry and coffee, getting snatches of sleep in a parti-
tioned stall in a bedroom, until she died of exhaustion. The silk manufacturers make their profit "spinning silk 10 hours a day out of the
blood of little children who had to be placed upon stools for the
performance of their work." And so the nightmare goes for almost a hundred pages: children are bled, women are driven. Opposed
to it there is a contrasting image stated early in the chapter: "A
horse . . . can only work 8 hours from day to day." No horse would
be treated like these women and children.

The next act is the "Machinery and Modern Industry" chapter, its theme announced in the preceding chapter with a footnote
about "abnormal development of some muscles, curvature of bones,
etc.," and the statement that manufacture "converts the laborer into
a crippled monstrosity." Its dual preoccupation is the mutilation of
men and the deaths of children. Marx gives chilling figures on infant
death-rate, listing towns in England where more than one-fourth
of the babies die annually. The Birmingham steel-pen industry employed girls from the age of 5, and the tile-making industry employed
children of 4, working them as long or longer than adults. In a decade
of lace-making, the tuberculosis rate went up from one in 45 to one
in 8. Infants were given opiates and "shrank up into little old men" or
became "wizened like little monkeys." Men are warped into freaks by
industry, stunted, deformed, prematurely aged, crippled, and paralyzed. In a summary of this chapter later in the book, Marx makes it
clear that these literal mutilations are also metaphoric for the
existential mutilations of capitalism: alienation and estrangement.

The third act is the "The General Law of Capitalist Accumulation" chapter. Here working men are slain like the children, with the
average life-span in Manchester 38 for the upper middle class and 17
for the workers, in Liverpool 35 for the upper middle class and 15 for
the workers. The chapter sets its tone with a quotation from a Dr.
Hunter: "It is not too much to say that life in parts of London and
Newcastle is infernal." The Inferno we go down into is packed with
the damned, a Bosch hell of bodies obscenely heaped together, where

working people live up to 18 in a room, up to 10 in a cellar, 5 or 6 to a bed. "Adult persons of both sexes, married and unmarried," Marx writes, "are huddled together in single small sleeping rooms." "Decency must always be outraged, and morality almost of necessity must suffer," he concludes, adding a few choice details of bastardy and incest. As "The Working-Day" opposed the conditions of the horse, this chapter has a contrasting image of cattle, from the placards that appeared in London reading "Fat oxen! Starving Men!" to Marx's conclusion about English agriculture: "Of all the animals kept by the farmer, the laborer, the *instrumentum vocale,* was thenceforth the most oppressed, the worst nourished, the most brutally treated."

The last act of Marx's drama is the book's final part, "The So-Called Primitive Accumulation." Here we go back into the origins of the capitalists' economic power: "In actual history it is notorious that conquest, enslavement, robbery, murder, briefly force, play the great part." Marx summarizes:

> The spoliation of the church's property, the fraudulent alienation of the State domains, the robbery of the common lands, the usurpation of feudal and clan property, and its transformation into modern private property under circumstances of reckless terrorism, were just so many idyllic methods of primitive accumulation. They conquered the field for capitalistic agriculture, made the soil part and parcel of capital, and created for the town industries the necessary supply of a 'free' and outlawed proletariat.

There are two sections of horrors. The first is a summary of the bloody legislation against vagabondage in England, concluding, "Thus were the agricultural people, first forcibly expropriated from the soil, driven from their homes, turned into vagabonds, and then whipped, branded, tortured by laws grotesquely terrible, into the discipline necessary for the wage system." The second is a recital of the crimes against the aboriginal peoples in the colonies. Marx writes:

> The discovery of gold and silver in America, the extirpation, enslavement and entombment in mines of the aboriginal population, the beginning of the conquest and looting of the East Indies, the turning of Africa into a warren for the commercial hunting of black skins, signalized the rosy dawn of the era of capitalist production. These idyllic proceedings are the chief momenta of primitive accumulation.

Describing the stealing of men into slavery in Java, which reduced one province from a population of 80,000 to 18,000 in sixty years, Marx comments, "Sweet commerce!" He illustrates "the Christian character of primitive accumulation" with the bounties Puritan Massachusetts put on Indian scalps, including 50 pounds apiece for scalps of women and children. As with the earlier horse and cattle, here the living conditions of sheep are opposed to those of the British farmers they replaced. Marx quotes the terrible image from an early translation of More's *Utopia:* "Your shepe that were wont to be so meke and tame, and so smal eaters, now, as I heare saye, be become so great devourers and so wylde that they eate up, and swallow downe, the very men themselfes."

All this is very far from the great historical tragedy Marx had been pursuing for twenty years. *Capital* has a pathetic rather than a tragic protagonist. Marx notes: "And just as in society, a general or a banker plays a great part, but mere man, on the other hand, a very shabby part, so here with mere human labor." The dramatic form of *Capital*, I would submit, is Victorian melodrama. Bernard Shaw comes close to realizing this in "The Illusions of Socialism" when he describes Marx's theory of class struggle:

> the dramatic illusion of struggle . . . which presents the working-class as a virtuous hero and heroine in the toils of a villain called the capitalist; suffering terribly and struggling nobly, but with a happy ending for them, and a fearful retribution for the villain, in full view before the curtain on a future of undisturbed bliss.

Wylie Sypher fully realizes it in a brilliant article in *The Kenyon Review* in 1948 on "Aesthetic of Revolution: The Marxist Melodrama." I would suggest that we see Marx's book as a melodrama called something like *The Mortgage on Labor-Power Foreclosed*. In the first act the villain mistreats the virtuous wife and injures her poor little child; in the second act the young laboring hero himself is maimed and sits paralyzed in a wheelchair while the child dies; in the third act they are thrown out into the snow and take refuge in a miserable hovel; in the fourth act the discovery is made that the villain stole the mortgage originally and has no legal or moral rights over our heroes. It needs a fifth act in which the working-class family is rescued and restored to its happy home, but only the proletarian revolution could produce that final curtain, and Marx could not finish *Capital* without it.

Capital is a synthesis of many things. As Marx drew on a wide range of thinkers for his ideas, so he drew on many traditional forms in the culture besides drama. A comparison with scriptural form has frequently been made. Engels announces in his preface to the first English translation " 'Das Kapital' is often called, on the Continent, 'the Bible of the working class,' " and it seems to have been so defined in a resolution at one of the congresses of the International. Pareto said *Capital* possessed "to a high degree the characteristics that one

encounters in all holy books, vagueness and obscurity." In the sense
that it could be quoted to all purposes and contains something for
everybody, as the later history of communism and socialism shows,
Capital is certainly a Bible. In terms of basic scriptural form, it is
much less a Bible than *The Origin of Species*. Where scriptural
form is a reenactment of creation followed by a fixing of destinies, or
Genesis and Leviticus, Marx's laws arise out of the dynamic processes to which most of his book is devoted, with the myths and rites
of Genesis appended in the history of accumulation at the end. "Accumulate, accumulate!" he writes. "That is Moses and the prophets!"
—but it is not a law for *his* chosen people. Marx's genetic concern
in the final chapters, one of them even called "Genesis of the Capitalist
Farmer," is not the myth for the rites of revolution he wants. Only in
the history of successful proletarian revolution could he get a Genesis-
Exodus for his Leviticus, and that never came in his lifetime.[2]

Marx draws extensively on the Bible and Christian theology, but
in a secularized and parodied form. He accepts as inevitable the consequences of the Fall in Genesis, Hegel's first negation, that labor is
"the everlasting nature-imposed condition of human existence," but
denies the Edenic myth, the negation of the negation, insisting that
no human existence could or should be exempt from labor. Capitalism,
he notes, has its own myth of original sin, the fable of the grass-
hopper and the ant:

> In times long gone by there were two sorts of people; one,
> the diligent, intelligent, and, above all, frugal elite; the other,
> lazy rascals, spending their substance, and more, in riotous liv-
> ing. . . . Thus it came to pass that the former sort accumulated
> wealth, and the latter sort had at last nothing to sell except their
> own skins. And from this original sin dates the poverty of the
> great majority that, despite all its labor, has up to now nothing
> to sell but itself, and the wealth of the few that increases con-
> stantly although they have long ceased to work. Such insipid
> childishness is every day preached to us in the defense of prop-
> erty.

Marx simply substitutes the story of Jacob and Esau, and dates
man's fallen condition from the time one brother stole another's
birthright. He mocks the theological vocabulary by using words
like "incarnation" and "transubstantiation" for the embodiment of
labor in commodities or money (with just a suggestion of seriousness in the sacrificial role of the working class). Marx takes a positive pleasure in blasphemy, parodying scriptural quotations: "As the
hart pants after fresh water, so pants his soul after money, the only

[2] It is the view of Harry W. Pearson, expressed in conversation, that the
Bible form does not obtain for *Capital* alone, but for the whole of Marx's work
as a unit, in which Genesis would have its proper place at the beginning. In his
interpretation, Marx's true Genesis is labor, and his true Fall is the alienation of
labor, its transformation into commodity form.

wealth"; "It is the old story: Abraham begat Isaac, Isaac begat Jacob, and so on. The original capital of £10,000 brings in a surplus-value of £2000, which is capitalized"; "Want of faith in the national debt takes the place of the sin against the Holy Ghost, which may not be forgiven"; "The birth of the latter [Modern Industry] is heralded by a great slaughter of the innocents"; "What then becomes of the ten commandments, of Moses and the prophets, of the law of supply and demand?"

In one of its aspects, Capital is sometimes quite funny, in a sardonic fashion. Marx remarks that Robinson Crusoe, as soon as he gets on the island, "commences, like a true-born Briton, to keep a set of books." He illustrates exchange with a Bible-seller who puts the proceeds into brandy, and comments "Our Hotspur is enabled to sell his Bible, and only because the latter has sold the water of everlasting life is the distiller enabled to sell his *eau-de-vie.*" Marx characterizes the market economy: "There alone rule Freedom, Equality, Property, and Bentham." Of working women unemployed by a crisis: "They had time to learn to cook. Unfortunately, the acquisition of this art occurred at a time when they had nothing to cook." Of the ancient Greeks:

> Oh! those heathen! . . . They perhaps excused the slavery of one on the ground that it was a means to the full development of another. But to preach slavery of the masses, in order that a few crude and half-educated parvenus might become 'eminent spinners,' 'extensive sausage-makers,' and 'influential shoeblack dealers,' to do this, they lacked the bump of Christianity.

Capital is a tissue of puns and word-play, most of them untranslatable. An encounter between linen and a coat becomes a comic courtship because the German "*zugeknoepften*" means not only "buttoned-up" but "reserved," and because linen is a feminine word and coat a masculine. The few puns that can be translated come through without much distinction, like the worker taking his hide to market and due for a hiding, or, of the Indian cotton-weavers who starved to death when the power-loom was introduced:

> No doubt, in turning them out of this 'temporal' world, the machinery caused them no more than 'a temporary inconvenience.'

English translation seems to have improved at least one, a lawsuit over soot that was non-suited.

An important question *Capital* suggests is Engels' role in it. His *The Condition of the Working Class in England in 1844,* which will be discussed below, is the primary determinant of the book's sociology, and seems to have been used as a scaffolding the way Marx used Engels' draft for *The Communist Manifesto.* Marx cites and quotes Engels by name a few times, and sometimes credits him transparently, as when he writes "The above data, which may be relied on, were given me by a Manchester spinner." In some sense the whole work, and all of Marx's writing, is a collaboration. Berlin calls them Moses and Aaron, with Marx as Moses, but perhaps Chang and Eng would be more accurate. Mehring reminds us that Engels pioneered in the economic field, with his *Outlines of a Critique of Political Economy* in 1844, as well as in the sociological, and concludes, "He was much too modest about his own contributions." In 1869, Marx was shown a reading list on socialism prepared by a Dr. Held, Professor of Political Economy at Bonn. It said:

> Engels—*The Condition of the Working Class in England* etc. The best product of German socialist-communist literature. Closely connected with Engels is Karl Marx, the author of the most scientific and most erudite work which Socialism as a whole can boast of, *Das Kapital*. Although it has only recently appeared, this book is still an echo of the movement of 1848. That is why I mention it here in connection with Engels.

Marx noted, in a letter to Kugelmann: "His comments show the terrible limitations of these learned mandarins."

The ultimate question about *Capital* is the one Engels asks in his preface to the second volume: "How is it that Marx's theory of surplus value struck home like a thunderbolt out of a clear sky, in all modern countries, while the theories of all his socialist predecessors, including Rodbertus, remained ineffective?" The poet Freiligrath thought that it was the book's appeal to businessmen, rather than economists "in sentiment" like himself, and wrote to Marx in 1868: "I know that in the Rhineland many young merchants and factory owners are enthusiastic about the book." Shaw's answer to Engels' question, in the preface of *Back to Methuselah*, is in terms of his own mystique: "Like Darwin, he had for the moment the World Will by the ear." I would submit that it was not Marx's theory but Marx's book as a powerful imaginative construct, like Darwin's, that struck home or seized the great ear. Perhaps the final irony was that of the Russian censorship, which permitted the publication of a Russian translation in 1872 on the ground that although the book showed a pronounced socialist tendency, it was not written in a popular style and was unlikely to find many readers. Nor was Marx any more prophetic about his Russian public. He wrote to Kugelmann in 1868:

> It is an irony of fate that the Russians, whom I have fought for twenty-five years, and not only in German, but in French and English, have always been my 'patrons.' In Paris in 1843 and 1844 the Russian aristocrats there treated me most tenderly. My book against Proudhon (1847) and the one published by Duncker (1859) have had a greater sale in Russia than anywhere else. And the first foreign nation to translate *Capital* is the Russian. But too much should not be made of all this. The Rus-

sian aristocracy is, in its youth, educated at German universities and in Paris. They always run after the most extreme that the West can offer.

It is pure *gourmandise*, such as a part of the French aristocracy practiced during the eighteenth century.

The Will of History

THE remaining volumes of *Capital* are of considerably less interest. After Marx's death, Engels found the manuscripts in a terrible state, and he spent most of his remaining years working on them. (Marx once told his son-in-law, Paul Lafargue, that "he would rather burn his manuscripts than leave them behind him unfinished," and Engels may sometimes have wished that he had.) For volume two there were eight fragmentary manuscripts, only one in a final draft, and that made obsolete by some of the others. For the remaining two volumes there was only one manuscript, but that very incomplete, a first draft full of notes for later expansion. The handwriting was impossible, and parts of the manuscripts showed clear evidence of Marx's breakdown. Engels put the books together as best he could, adding or altering what seemed necessary (with scrupulous notation that he had done so), and showing in footnotes which manuscript he was using, where Marx's figures were inconsistent, and what Marx later came to believe about one or another matter. Engels' preface to the third volume suggests the difficulties. He writes of the manuscript:

> The beginnings of the various sections were, as a rule, pretty carefully elaborated, or even polished as to style. But the farther one proceeded, the more sketchy and incomplete was the analysis, the more excursions it contained into side issues whose proper place in the argument was left for later decision, the longer and more complex became the sentences, in which the rising thoughts were deposited as they came. In several places, the handwriting and the treatment of the matter clearly revealed the approach and gradual progress of those attacks of ill health, due to over-work, which at first rendered original work more and more difficult for the author and finally compelled him from time to time to stop work altogether.

The second volume, *The Process of Circulation of Capital*, was published by Engels in 1885. A good part of it is formulas and equations, some of them more complicated than anything in the

first volume. They abstract and simplify economic relations "in order
not to complicate the formula." Periodically the real world breaks
through, and Marx will stop saying "C—M—C" and remark "In the
building business of London, for instance, which is carried on mainly
on credit," or return to the details of cotton-spinning. He quotes occasionally from the testimony before a parliamentary Committee investigating bank acts and a royal commission on railways. A sad par-
enthetical note by Engels, who had been a bookkeeper in Manchester,
shows the limits of Marx's empiric knowledge:

> The preparation of this chapter for publication has given me
> no small amount of difficulty. Expert as Marx was in algebra, the
> handling of figures in arithmetic nevertheless gave him a great
> deal of trouble and he lacked especially the practice of commer-
> cial calculation, although he left behind a ponderous volume of
> computations in which he had practiced by many examples the
> entire variety of commercial reckoning. But a knowledge of the
> various modes of calculation and a practice in the daily practical
> calculations of the merchant are by no means the same. Con-
> sequently Marx entangled himself to such an extent in his com-
> putation of turnovers, that the result, so far as he completed his
> work, contained various errors and contradictions.

The second volume probably has less sparkle than anything
Marx wrote. One has only to compare the ferocious chapter on "The
Working-Day" in the first volume with Marx's account of the same
subject here:

> The circumstances which augment the product of the indi-
> vidual working-day, such as cooperation, division of labor, em-
> ployment of machinery, shorten at the same time the working
> period of connected acts of production.

In place of the imagery and metaphor of the first volume we have
such bold ventures as: "metamorphoses (materially considered, exchanges)." There are a few weak attempts at invective: a hierarchy
of vocations, "king, priest, professor, prostitute, soldier"; a mention of
Mill's "usual pomposity" and Destutt de Tracy's "confused and at the
same time boastful thoughtlessness." Only at the very end of the book,
in two pages mocking some remarks by a Mr. Drummond, the Secretary of the British Legation in Washington, does Marx recover some
of the first volume's mordant style. There are few quotations and extracts in the book (they would have been put into the final draft) and
thus little of Marx's drama, which always comes from an interplay of
voices. In her chapter in Mehring's biography, adopting Marx's own
dramatistic metaphor, Luxemburg put her finger on another difficulty:

> The contents of the second and third volumes take us to a
> different plane. In the first volume we are in the factory, in the
> deep social pit of labor where we can trace the source of capitalist
> wealth. In the second and third volumes we are on the surface, on

the official stage of society. Department stores, banks, stock exchanges, finance, and the troubles of the 'needy' agriculturalists take up the foreground. The worker has no role on this stage, and in fact he shows little interest in the things which happen behind his back after he has been skinned. We see the workers in the noisy mob of business people only when they troop off to the factories in the grey light of the early morning or hurry home again in the dusk as the factories eject them in droves after the day's work.

The third volume, *The Process of Capitalist Production as a Whole*, was published by Engels in 1894. Although the working class still remains offstage, this volume has a good deal more life than the second. It is here that Marx briefly reveals his vision of the Realm of Freedom beyond the Realm of Necessity. Chapter V, "Economies in the Employment of Constant Capital," displays all the vigor and fury of the first volume, since the economies are naturally at the expense of the worker's health and life. Marx writes: "These sacrifices of human beings are mostly due to the groveling greed of the mine owners"; capitalism is "more than any other mode of production prodigal with human lives, with living labor, wasting not only blood and flesh, but also nerves and brains"; "The issue was to prove that killing is no murder when done for profit." A subsection entitled "Utilization of the Excrements of Production" wastes none of its opportunity to relate its subject to human excrement. The third volume also returns to some of the evolutionary concerns of the first, again resorting to organic metaphors. In Marx's theory of the way competition brings about an average rate of profit on invested capital despite varing amounts of surplus value (which Luxemburg said was the basic problem of Marxist economics), it produces an automatic system very like natural selection.

In the course of writing the third volume, Marx clearly got fascinated by the financial world. Where the characteristic quotation in the first volume is a manufacturer telling a parliamentary commission how long he works a nine-year-old child, the characteristic quotation in the third volume is a banker telling a similar commission why interest rates fluctuate. Marx's tone becomes almost admiring, as when he notes "Meteorological reports do not register the stand of the barometer and thermometer more accurately than the reports of the Bourse do the stand of the rate of interest." This is not the Marx who called down fire and brimstone on Sodom, but the Marx who wrote wryly to Engels that he knew everything about capital except how to acquire some. In going from the microcosm to the macrocosm, from the barter of one simple commodity for another to the complicated transactions of the world of finance and credit, Marx moved into a region where he felt imaginatively at home, as though he were David Ricardo the wealthy banker or Sir William Petty the unprincipled adventurer. Where Darwin began his investigations with a pure impulse to understand nature and only late in life became its affirmative propagandist, Marx began his investigations impure, desiring primarily to alter the system, and by the third volume of *Capital* had acquired something like a pure interest in its operations.

One curious point in the third volume is worth noticing. Marx attacks an agriculturalist:

> That Mr. Lavergne is not only familiar with the advantages of English agriculture, but also believes in the prejudices of the English tenants and landlords, is proved by him on page 48: 'One great disadvantage is generally connected with grain plants . . . they exhaust the soil that bears them.' Mr. Lavergne believes not only that other plants do not do so, but he also believes that leguminous crops and root crops enrich the soil: 'Leguminous plants draw the principal elements of their growth out of the air, while they give back to the soil more than they take from it; therefore they help both directly and indirectly through their return in the shape of animal manure to make good in a double way the damage caused by grain crops and other exhausting crops; hence it is a matter of principle that they should alternate with such crops; in this consists the Norfolk rotation." (Pages 50 and 51.)
>
> No wonder that Mr. Lavergne, who believes these fairy tales of the English rural mind, also believes. . . .

Why should Marx, who kept up fanatically with scientific discoveries, dismiss a faultless statement of modern soil chemistry as "prejudices" and "fairy tales," and why did Engels not correct it for him or note its error? Other places in the volume show that Marx is fully aware that agricultural soil loses fertility. I would submit that both were blinded by the dogma of the labor theory of value, which insists that all value is produced by human labor, not by the labor of clover. "Uncultivated land," Marx writes in the first volume, "is without value, because no human labor has been incorporated in it." "No soil yields any product," he writes in the third, "without an investment of capital." To recognize the natural value of the nitrogen that one soybean could put into the soil might have toppled the labor theory of value, the theory of surplus value, and the whole vast edifice of Marxist theory.

The fourth volume of *Capital, Theories of Surplus Value,* was edited from Marx's manuscript by Karl Kautsky, after Engels' death, and published between 1905 and 1910. It is a history of ideas, very unlike the rest of *Capital,* and Kautsky sensibly published it as a separate work rather than as another volume to *Capital.* Because it deals principally with economic theorists, it returns to some of the bold invective of the first volume, and in fact it seems to have been written between 1861 and 1863, when Marx was at work on the first volume. Here again are "the inane Say," "the wretched McCulloch," "the contemptible Malthus," and the usual "twaddle" and "nonsense" of "bourgeois thick-headedness." Otherwise the book has little not clearer and sharper in the first volume. Marx writes a long dialogue between Worker and

Capitalist in which the former educates the latter in the theory of surplus value, and shows a few other traces of dramatistic metaphor, mostly on this order: "At last, however, Ricardo comes on the stage, and calls to science: Halt!" The bourgeois system of production is identified as a matter of religious faith, and Ricardo heralds its Day of Judgment or "Twilight of the Gods." For the first time Marx seems to accept man as Fallen: "Is not the tree of evil also the tree of knowledge, since the time of Adam?" It is all surprisingly moderate.

AFTER the publication of the first volume of *Capital*, Marx spent the rest of his life, when illness allowed, working on the other volumes. He interrupted it chiefly for two important brief works, both occasional in inspiration. The first was *The Address of the General Council of the International Working Men's Association on The Civil War in France, 1871*. The Commune in Paris gave up the struggle on May 28, 1871, and on May 30 Marx read his address, in English, to the General Council. It was printed later that year in radical periodicals in Geneva and Leipzig as *The Civil War in France*. The proletarian revolution that the Paris Commune represented in its meteoric two months was, however briefly, the real tragedy on the stage of history that Marx had been calling for since 1848. He writes indignantly of the idle rich of Paris going to watch the streetfighting as they might go to the theatre:

> Considering the civil war but an agreeable diversion, eyeing the battle going on through telescopes, counting the rounds of cannon, and swearing by their own honour, and that of their prostitutes, that the performance was far better got up than it used to be at the Porte St. Martin. The men who fell were really dead; the cries of the wounded were cries in good earnest; and, besides, the whole thing was so intensely historical.

In his second address of the General Council on the Franco-Prussian War, in September 1870, Marx had foreseen the rising and warned against it. "Any attempt at upsetting the new government in the present crisis," he wrote, "when the enemy is almost knocking at the doors of Paris, would be a desperate folly." At the same time he wrote to Engels: "The whole French branch has set off for Paris today, to commit imbecilities in the name of the International. They wish to . . . proclaim the Paris Commune." At the height of the Commune, on April 12, Marx had written to Kugelmann foreseeing its fall, "crushed by the wolves, swine, and vile curs of the old society."

Convinced as he was that the Commune should not have been attempted and was likely to fail, Marx bowed to history and accepted the Commune as the most glorious event of all time. "History has no like example of a like greatness," he wrote to Kugelmann, than "these

Parisians, storming heaven." He accepted the measures that the Commune improvised empirically as the revelation of what the seizure of power by the working class entailed: government by a council of workingmen elected through universal suffrage, for short terms and subject to recall; abolition of the standing army and the police; an elective judiciary, responsible and subject to recall; universal free secular education; and so on. How far these measures are from the *Communist Manifesto*'s graduated income tax, state bank, and agricultural armies! Then Marx had been guessing at the future, now he had seen "the political form at last discovered under which to work out the economical emancipation of labor." Never before had Marx been so lyric. He writes:

> Working, thinking, fighting, bleeding Paris—almost forgetful, in its incubation of a new society, of the cannibals at its gates— radiant in the enthusiasm of its historic initiative!

Here, finally, was the tragic drama for which Marx had kept the curtain up for almost a quarter of a century. French history was no longer comedy or farce, as it still was in Marx's addresses of the General Council on the Franco-Prussian War, in 1870, when he wrote of Louis Bonaparte costuming his followers in workmen's blouses to demonstrate in the streets, predicted that the Second Empire "will end, as it began, by a parody," and described the King of Prussia exhibited by his "stage managers." With the appearance of the Commune, the proletarian hero took the stage in earnest, and acted rather than suffered. Inevitably, the antagonists are not clowns like Louis Bonaparte, nor the ludicrous villains of melodrama, the Ures and Seniors in *Capital*, but represent something genuinely evil and monstrous. The chief of them is Louis Adolphe Thiers, the betrayer and executioner of the Commune, whose physique happily coincided with Marx's need. In *The Civil War in France* Thiers is "that monstrous gnome," "a parliamentary Tom Thumb permitted to play the part of a Tamerlane," Voltaire's "monkey allowed for a time to give full fling to his tigerish instincts." Marx rises to a Ciceronian height of invective against him:

> A master in small state roguery, a virtuoso in perjury and treason, a craftsman in all the petty stratagems, cunning devices, and base perfidies of parliamentary party warfare; never scrupling, when out of office, to fan a revolution, and to stifle it in blood when at the helm of the state; with class prejudices standing him in the place of ideas, and vanity in the place of a heart; his private life as infamous as his public life is odious—even now, when playing the part of a French Sulla, he cannot help setting off the abomination of his deeds by the ridicule of his ostentation.

One of Marx's most useful rhetorical discoveries, from the American Civil War, was that the forces of good are never responsible for bloodshed, which is always caused by the forces of evil fighting to restore their wicked domination. The civil war in France is thus repeatedly "a slaveholders' rebellion," and it too had its firing on Fort Sumter: "Thiers opened the civil war by sending Vinoy . . . to seize, by surprise, the artillery of the National Guard." [1]

The imagery and tone of *The Civil War in France* is no longer the thundering wrath of the Old Testament prophet, but the New Testament's glad tidings that salvation and redemption have come. Paris, he writes, "had to stand forward as the self-sacrificing champion of France, whose salvation from ruin and whose regeneration were impossible without the revolutionary overthrow of the political and social conditions that had engendered the Second Empire." The suggestion is of primitive Christianity, even ironically, as when the Commune disendows the churches and sends the priests back, Marx says, "to feed upon the alms of the faithful in imitation of their predecessors, the apostles." The revolting atrocities committed against the Commune, described by Marx in considerable detail, are proper sacrificial ritual, a "tearing to pieces" of "the living body of the proletariat." Marx is, as always, violent against French bourgeois immorality, writing typically: "Galifet, the kept man of his wife, so notorious for her shameless exhibitions at the orgies of the Second Empire." Now, however, all has been morally transformed and regenerated:

> Wonderful, indeed, was the change the Commune had wrought in Paris! No longer any trace of the meretricious Paris of the Second Empire! . . . The *cocottes* had refound the scent of their protectors—the absconding men of family, religion, and, above all, of property. In their stead, the real women of Paris showed again at the surface—heroic, noble, and devoted, like the women of antiquity.

The doctrine of the withering away of the state after the proletariat seizes power, first discovered by Marx in the Commune's experience, is like Jesus' "Render unto Caesar." "While the merely repressive organs of the old governmental power were to be amputated," he wrote, its few "legitimate functions" would be properly performed by "society." Here the God-Caesar opposition is between "the social body" and "the state parasite" on it. The sharpest possible dichotomy exists between the sacred and the profane: there is bourgeois internationalism, "Even at this moment the right hand of Thiers is Ganessco, the foul Wallachian, and his left hand is Markovsky, the Russian spy"; and proletarian internationalism, "The Commune admitted all foreigners to the honour of dying for an immortal cause." "Opposed to this new world at Paris, behold the old world at Versailles," Marx writes. "Paris all truth, Versailles all lie." The living body of the

<hr>

[1] Taking the hint, Engels concludes his preface to the first English translation of *Capital* in 1886 with the statement that Marx believed that:
England is the only country where the inevitable social revolution might be effected entirely by peaceful and legal means. He certainly never forgot to add that he hardly expected the English ruling classes to submit, without a 'pro-slavery rebellion,' to this peaceful and legal revolution.

proletariat is dismembered and scattered, like that of Dionysus, yet it will rise anew. Marx concludes, with more faith than he has had in decades: "But the battle must break out again and again in ever-growing dimensions, and there can be no doubt as to who will be the victor in the end." He begins the last paragraph of the address: "Working men's Paris, with its Commune, will be for ever celebrated as the glorious harbinger of a new society."

Marx wrote *The Civil War in France*, Liebknecht says, "with his own life-blood and that of the Commune." The next year he and Engels wrote a preface to a new edition of *The Communist Manifesto*, noting the places where it had been outmoded by the Commune's experience. They conclude: "But then, the *Manifesto* has become a historical document which we have no longer any right to alter."

Marx's last work was a public letter, *Marginal Notes to the Program of the German Workers Party*, written in 1875, and published by Engels in 1891 as *Critique of the Gotha Program*. Its occasion was a conference in Gotha to unite the Social-Democratic Workers' Party of Germany, which followed Marx, and the General Association of German Workers, which followed Lassalle. Marx wrote the letter to persuade his followers not to accept the joint program, which seemed to him entirely Lassallean and harmful. He wrote unsuccessfully, it turned out, since his letter was suppressed by Liebknecht on the grounds that Marx was too remote from conditions in Germany, and not shown around; and unnecessarily, because the united party adopted a pure Marxist program in 1891. The *Critique of the Gotha Program* is an important work of Marxist theory because it is Marx's only sustained venture in predicting the actual shape of socialism-communism. In terms of imaginative organization, if *The Civil War in France* is a Gospel, telling of the crucifixion and resurrection of the proletariat, the *Critique* is like the Revelation of St. John the Divine, giving the vision of apocalypse at the second coming. Writing entirely in this spirit of personal testimony, Marx concludes the *Critique*, "*Dixi et salvavi animam meam*," "I have spoken and saved my soul."

In the work Marx goes into detail about the way the proletarian society will administer production, will provide for schools and health services, will care for those unable to work, etc. In his vision, the first communist society (now in Marxist theory more generally called "socialism"), as it emerges from capitalism, will be "still stamped with the birthmarks of the old society from whose womb it emerges." That is, it will be unequal, and will return to producers the differing values of their products. The "higher phase" of communist society of the future will leave all that behind and inscribe on its banners, "From each according to his ability, to each according to his needs."

It was, of course, the experience of the Commune that made Marx, always so reluctant to describe the future social order, suddenly able to see it in a revelation. It is now clear to him that the demand in the Gotha Program (as in *The Communist Manifesto*) for "a single progressive income tax" is outmoded: "Income tax presupposes the various sources of income of the various social classes, and hence capitalist society." Writing to August Bebel in March, 1875, while Marx was working on his critique, Engels stated one of their criticisms of the Gotha Program:

> The whole talk about the state should be dropped, especially since the Commune, which was no longer a state in the proper sense of the word. . . . We would therefore propose to replace the word 'state' everywhere by the word *Gemeinwesen*, a good old German word, which can very well represent the French word *commune*.

Marx could be comically unable to predict the future of capitalism, as in his criticism of the Gotha Program's demand for the abolition of child labor: "A *general prohibition* of child labor is incompatible with the existence of large-scale industry and hence an empty, pious aspiration." He had, however, seen his vision of future communism in the two blazing months of the Commune; the bush burned and was not consumed.

This Judgment Day quality of the Revolution was shrewdly perceived by Shaw and Murry. The fullest account of Marx's eschatology with which I am familiar is that of Mircea Eliade in *The Sacred and the Profane*. Eliade writes:

> Marx takes over and continues one of the great eschatological myths of the Asiatico-Mediterranean world—the redeeming role of the Just (the 'chosen,' the 'anointed,' the 'innocent,' the 'messenger'; in our day, the proletariat), whose sufferings are destined to change the ontological status of the world. In fact, Marx's classless society and the consequent disappearance of historical tensions find their closest precedent in the myth of the Golden Age that many traditions put at the beginning and the end of history. Marx enriched this venerable myth by a whole Judaeo-Christian messianic ideology: on the one hand, the prophetic role and soteriological function that he attributes to the proletariat; on the other, the final battle between Good and Evil, which is easily comparable to the apocalyptic battle between Christ and Anti-christ, followed by the total victory of the former. It is even significant that Marx takes over for his own purposes the Judaeo-Christian eschatological hope of an *absolute end to history;* in this he differs from other historicistic philosophers (Croce and Ortega y Gasset, for example), for whom the tensions of history are consubstantial with the human condition and therefore can never be completely done away with.

The withering away of the state, the key image from the *Critique* that seems in realistic political terms so clearly a sop to the Bakuninists, is, in mythological terms, the final binding and casting into the pit of the great dragon (as in Freudian terms it might be the wish of paternal impotence). It is also a characteristic image from evolutionary biology.

V. I. Lenin comments, in *The State and Revolution:* "The expression 'the state *withers away*' is very well chosen, for it indicates both the gradual and the spontaneous nature of the process." More generally: "Marx treats the question of communism in the same way as a naturalist would treat the question of the development of, say, a new biological species, if he knew that such and such was its origin, and such and such the direction in which it was changing." To some extent, as Leopold Schwartzchild points out in *The Red Prussian* (and as Soviet Russian experience certainly confirms),[2] the withering-away of the state is a semantic trick; you call the oppressive functions "state" and the rest "administration" or "society." The accompanying myth, however, the triumph of the saints, is the "dictatorship of the proletariat," a term that first appears in *The Class Struggles in France* in 1850, replacing the negative concept, "proletarian revolution," in the *Manifesto.* Marx had kept it under wraps for two decades, but now that the Commune had performed its rites, briefly setting up such a dictatorship, it became the myth of the Second Coming, first as a lamb to the slaughter, but in the last days as a lion in judgment.

The ultimate question is the relation between historical inevitability and effort. The eventual victory of the proletariat was ordained, is inevitable in history, but men have to act as though human initiative makes the difference, as perhaps it does in any given time or place. Along with Marx's revelation of the communist millenium in the *Critique of the Gotha Program*, his niggling attention to the wording of slogans shows how much room was left for human effort. "Men make their own history, but not just as they please," Marx had written in *The Eighteenth Brumaire*, neatly combining free will and predestination. Shaw saw it, in *The Intelligent Woman's Guide to Socialism and Capitalism*, as a deliberate compromise, like the Thirty-nine Articles:

> Two of their tenets contradict one another as flatly as the first two paragraphs of Article 27 of the Church of England. One is that the evolution of Capitalism into Socialism is predestined, implying that we have nothing to do but sit down and wait for it to occur. This is their version of Salvation by Faith. The other is that it must be effected by a revolution establishing a dictatorship of the proletariat. This is their version of Salvation by Works.

Engels had written to Bebel about the Gotha Program: "It is of such a character that if it is accepted Marx and I can *never* give our

[2] The state of Soviet dialectics is best illustrated by Joseph Stalin's remarks on the subject in *Leninism*. Stalin writes:

We are in favor of the state withering away and at the same time we stand for the strengthening of the dictatorship of the proletariat, which represents the most powerful and mighty authority of all forms of state which have existed up to the present day. The highest possible development of the power of the state, with the object of preparing the conditions for the withering away of the state: that is the Marxist formula. Is it 'contradictory'? Yes, it is 'contradictory.' But this contradiction is a living thing, and completely reflects Marxist dialectics.

adherence to the *new* party established on this basis." When it was accepted nevertheless, he wrote to Bebel six months later:

> The asses of the bourgeois papers have taken this program quite seriously, have read into it what is not there and interpreted it in a communist sense. The workers appear to do the same. It is *this circumstance alone* which has made it possible for Marx and myself not to dissociate ourselves publicly from such a program. So long as our opponents and the workers likewise insert our views into this program it is permissible for us to keep silent about it.

Perhaps after all the Gotha Program was the will of history, so blind she couldn't tell a Lassallean demand from a Marxist one. Marx's comment was more direct. He quoted Heine: "I have sown dragons and reaped a harvest of fleas."

In 1877, for the first time in his life, Marx wrote articles for conservative newspapers, attacking Gladstone's Russian policy in the London press. He regained some of his old spirit writing a chapter against Duehring for Engels' book. In 1880 he compiled a remarkable questionnaire for the *Revue Socialiste*, addressing 100 detailed questions to French workers. Some are as loaded as "Have you ever known any ordinary workers who were able to retire at the age of 50 and live on the money acquired in their capacity as wage earners?", but most are neutral and skillfully designed to elicit information. Unfortunately, too few French workers answered the questionnaire for anything to be done with the results. In 1881, Marx wrote to Domela Nieuwenhuis with melancholy hindsight about the Parisians storming heaven:

> With a small amount of common sense the Commune could have attained all that was attainable at that time, namely a compromise that would have been useful to the whole mass of the people.

In 1882, a year before he died, Marx wrote to his daughter Laura that he was coming to Paris to find peace, adding:

> By peace I mean family life, children's voices, the whole of that 'microscopic little world' which is so much more interesting than the 'macroscopic' world.

The Second Fiddle

N O   A C C O U N T   of Marx's writings can be complete without a discussion of Engels'. In a real sense, every work either of them wrote was a collaboration. For more than a decade after Marx's death, Engels released new writings by Marx to the world, reinterpreted old ones with new prefaces, and himself wrote at least one book, *The Origin of the Family*, that carries Marx's imaginative vision some distance further. Engels' own writings are an essential part of the picture.

Engels had written one book before the collaboration began, *The Condition of the Working Class in England in 1844*, published in 1845, when Engels was 25. No one familiar with *Capital* can read *The Condition of the Working Class*, which preceded it by twenty-two years, without some degree of shock. Here, the reader discovers to his amazement, is a remarkable foreshadowing of the sociology of *Capital*. Engels too quotes from Nassau W. Senior, "a fanatical opponent of all independent movements of the workers." He gives examples Marx later repeats of the appalling ignorance of working-class children, boys of sixteen or seventeen who did not know that twice two are four, had never heard the name of the Queen, or thought Christ was a former king of London. He quotes and praises Leonard Horner. He even anticipates Marx's favorite fable in *Capital*, Menenius Agrippa's story of the contention of the parts of the body, and Marx's favorite image, "the vampire property-holding class."

Engels' particular butt in *The Condition of the Working Class* is Dr. Andrew Ure, the man *Capital* was to call "the Pindar of the manufacturers." Engels calls him "a bourgeois *pur sang*, a man after the heart of the Anti-Corn Law League"; speaks of his "falsehood" and "hypocrisy"; describes him as the "chosen apostle" of the bourgeoisie, who "sings a dithyramb" on their themes; and concludes, "Beyond all other bourgeois is our friend Dr. Ure, the most furious enemy of the Unions." Engels quotes some gems from Ure. One is on the standard of living of cotton spinners:

> In fact, it was their high wages which enabled them to maintain a stipendiary committee in affluence, and to pamper them-

selves into nervous ailments, by a diet too rich and exciting for
their indoor employments.

Here is Ure on the conditions of factory children in the vicinity of
Manchester:

> They seemed to be always cheerful and alert; taking pleasure in
> the light play of their muscles, enjoying the mobility natural to
> their age. The scene of industry, so far from exciting sad emotions,
> in my mind, was always exhilarating. It was delightful to observe
> the nimbleness with which they pieced broken ends, as the mule
> carriage began to recede from the fixed roller beam, and to see
> them at leisure, after a few seconds' exercise of their tiny fingers,
> to amuse themselves in any attitude they chose, till the stretch and
> winding on were once more completed. The work of these lively
> elves seemed to resemble a sport, in which habit gave them a
> pleasing dexterity.

After interrupting Ure with mocking asides like these Marx later used
in *Capital*—"Oh! Wisdom, thou speakest as the dove!"—Engels concludes: "The language of Dr. Ure alone, which I have quoted, would
be yet more revolting if it were not so preposterous."

The Condition of the Working Class in England in 1844 is a
uniquely powerful book, a neglected masterpiece pushed aside by
Marx's later work. Marx himself thought it was vitally important, and
labored to get Engels to write a second volume carrying things down
into the 1860s. In some respects the book comes out very well in a
comparison with *Capital*, particularly in Engels' direct testimony from
experience. He had lived in Manchester less than two years when he
wrote it, but he accurately says: "I know it as intimately as my own
native town, more intimately than most of its residents know it." He
takes us on harrowing walks through the streets, wading through
filthy alleys, climbing over foul debris, crawling into hovels and dank
cellars where the working class lives. Like a good field ethnographer,
Engels pries everywhere, studying the clothes on the washlines, noting
just what items peddlers stock, naming the patent medicines that contain laudanum and are thus responsible for the deaths of children,
writing knowledgeably of sex habits. His tone is always personal: "I
once heard a manufacturer ask a foreman," or:

> I once went into Manchester with such a bourgeois, and spoke to
> him of the bad, unwholesome method of building, the frightful
> condition of the working-people's quarters, and asserted that I had
> never seen so ill-built a city. The man listened quietly to the end,
> and said at the corner where we parted: "And yet there is a great
> deal of money made here; good morning, sir.'

Engels concludes the book: "Such is the state of the British working-
class as I have come to know it in the course of twenty-one months,
through the medium of my own eyes, and through official and other
trustworthy reports."

Some of *The Condition* is a deliberate effort to rub his well-off readers' noses in proletarian reality, as Marx later similarly tried to get his readers to taste the pus in their bread or break into a claustrophobic sweat. Here is one account:

> She lay dead beside her son upon a heap of feathers which were scattered over her almost naked body, there being neither sheet nor coverlet. The feathers stuck so fast over the whole body that the physicians could not examine the corpse until it was cleaned, and then found it starved and scarred from the bites of vermin. Part of the floor of the room was torn up, and the hole used by the family as a privy.

In one place Engels takes the reader, "the inhabitants can pass into and out of the court only by passing through foul pools of stagnant urine and excrement"; in another, sixteen people live in a tiny damp cellar, along with their pigs "and other disgusting things of the most revolting kind." Near the end of the book, in a nightmarish image of resurrection, he describes the digging up of the pauper cemetery in Manchester to run a railroad through it:

> If it had been a respectable cemetery, how the bourgeoisie and the clergy would have shrieked over the desecration! But it was a pauper burial-ground, the resting-place of the outcast and super-fluous, so no one concerned himself about the matter. It was not even thought worth while to convey the partially decayed bodies to the other side of the cemetery; they were heaped up just as it happened, and piles were driven into newly-made graves, so that the water oozed out of the swampy ground, pregnant with putre-fying matter, and filled the neighborhood with the most revolting and injurious gases. The disgusting brutality which accompanied this work I cannot describe in further detail.

The sharpest metaphor in the book is one explicitly stated: "the social war, the war of each against all." Fourteen years before the publication of *The Origin of Species,* Engels writes of "a battle for life, for existence, for everything, in case of need a battle of life and death." Here the war is not in nature but in society, between classes and within them. This battle is, moreover, rapidly polarizing. "Society is already in a state of visible dissolution," and "The enemies are dividing gradu-ally into two great camps—the bourgeoisie on the one hand, the workers on the other." Even more pervasive than the imagery of war is the metaphor of a deceptive outside concealing a horrible inside. If a working man starves to death in England, Engels notes, "the police take care that he does so in a quiet and inoffensive manner." On a fine Sunday, Bradford "offers a superb picture, when viewed from the sur-rounding heights," but when you get down inside its working-class districts, there is the same filth, misery, disease, and crime. South Lancashire offers "beautiful hill country, sloping gently from the watershed westwards towards the Irish Sea, with the charming green valleys of the Ribble, the Irwell, the Mersey, and their tributaries," but at its heart is the blight of Manchester, and at the heart of Manchester, hidden away, the horrors of working class life. "I have never seen so systematic a shutting-out of the working class from the thoroughfares," Engels writes, "so tender a concealment of everything which might affront the eye and the nerves of the bourgeoisie, as in Manchester."

Engels' task was thus to reveal what had been hidden, to make the covert overt, to bring it out of darkness into the light of day. Some of his imagery is as terrifying as anything in *Capital*. Here is a working woman:

> M. H. twenty years old, has two children, the youngest a baby, that is tended by the other, a little older. The mother goes to the mill shortly after five o'clock in the morning, and comes home at eight at night; all day the milk pours from her breasts, so that her clothing drips with it.

One Lancashire working man, identified only as Jack, comes through with all the unforgettable quality of G. Apsden in *Capital*. When the men were replaced by women and children in the mills, he found himself staying at home while his wife worked in the factory from five-thirty in the morning to eight at night. In Engels' account we see him sitting by the fire, trying to hide from a friend the fact that he is mending his wife's stockings, weeping, cursing, and damning "the factories, and the masters, and the Government, with all the curses that he had learned while he was in the factory from a child." Here are children as young as five employed sixteen hours a day, night work that immediately doubles the number of bastards, all the cripplings, stuntings, and deformities we know so well from *Capital*. A child of *two* turns up working in a lace factory.

The cutlery-grinders of Sheffield are all doomed to die early from grinders' asthma, and Engels shows us their existentialist desperation pervading the whole of Sheffield's life. Since ten years ago, he writes,

> the number of grinders and the violence of the disease have increased, though attempts have been made to prevent it by covering grindstones and carrying off the dust by artificial draught. These methods have been at least partially successful, but the grinders do not desire their adoption, and have even destroyed the contrivance here and there, in the belief that more workers may be attracted to the business and wages thus reduced; they are for a short life and merry one. Dr. Knight has often told grinders who came to him with the first symptoms of asthma that a return to grinding means certain death, but with no avail. He who is once a grinder falls into despair, as though he had sold himself to the devil. . . . Immorality among young people seems to be more prevalent in Sheffield than anywhere else. . . . The younger generation spend the whole of Sunday lying in the street tossing coins or fighting dogs, go regularly to the gin palace. . . . No

wonder then, that, as all the witnesses testify, early, unbridled sexual intercourse, youthful prostitution, beginning with persons of fourteen to fifteen years, is extraordinarily frequent in Sheffield. Crimes of a savage and desperate sort are of common occurrence; one year before the commissioner's visit, a band, consisting chiefly of young persons, was arrested when about to set fire to the town, being fully equipped with lances and inflammable substances. We shall see later that the labor movement in Sheffield has this same savage character.

Sometimes the reader is reminded of Swift. Engels writes:

The cottages are old, dirty, and of the smallest sort, the streets uneven, fallen into ruts and in part without drains or pavement; masses of refuse, offal and sickening filth lie among standing pools in all directions, the atmosphere is poisoned by the effluvia from these, and laden and darkened by the smoke of a dozen tall factory chimneys. A horde of ragged women and children swarm about here, as filthy as the swine that thrive upon the garbage heaps and in the puddles.

At other times the vision suggests Blake's *Songs of Experience:*

These pale, lank, narrow-chested, hollow-eyed ghosts, whom one passes at every step, these languid, flabby faces, incapable of the slightest energetic expression, I have seen in such startling numbers only in London.

When Engels falls into sentimentality, which is not infrequently, we may think of Dickens. Here is Engels redoing the death of Little Nell:

Yet one is left in doubt whether even this terribly torturing death is not a blessing for the children in rescuing them from a long life of toil and wretchedness, rich in suffering and poor in enjoyment.

Engels praises Thomas Hood's "beautiful poem," "The Song of the Shirt," and tries his own lyric hand on the subject of the London needlewomen:

These women usually live in little garret rooms in the utmost distress, where as many crowd together as the space can possibly admit, and where, in winter, the animal warmth of the workers is the only heat obtainable. Here they sit bent over their work, sewing from four or five in the morning until midnight, destroying their health in a year or two and ending in an early grave, without being able to obtain the poorest necessities of life meanwhile. And below them roll the brilliant equipages of the upper bourgeoisie, and perhaps ten steps away some pitiable dandy loses more money in one evening at faro than they can earn in a year.

The strongest literary influence on *The Condition of the Working Class in England* is Thomas Carlyle, about whom Engels is thoroughly ambivalent. Engels quotes him on the Irish and comments, "If we except his exaggerated and one-sided condemnation of the Irish national character, Carlyle is perfectly right." Of Carlyle on the miseries of the cotton spinners, Engels remarks: "Carlyle is perfectly right as to the facts and wrong only in censuring the wild rage of the workers against the higher classes." Engels praises his *Chartism* and his "splendid description of the English bourgeoisie and its disgusting money greed" in *Past and Present.* He quotes Carlyle's "Cash Payment is the only nexus between man and man," and improvises on the theme:

> Only when estranged from his employer, when convinced that the sole bond between employer and employee is the bond of pecuniary profit, when the sentimental bond between them, which stood not the slightest test, had wholly fallen away, then only did the worker begin to recognize his own interests and develop independently; then only did he cease to be the slave of the bourgeoisie in his thoughts, feelings, and the expression of his will.

(From here, the idea went into *The Poverty of Philosophy*, then into *The Manifesto*, and finally into *Capital*.) Engels' fullest appraisal of Carlyle comes in a footnote at the end of the book:

> Wholly isolated is the half-German Englishman, Thomas Carlyle, who, originally a Tory, goes beyond all those hitherto mentioned. He has sounded the social disorders more deeply than any other English bourgeois, and demands the organization of labor.

What Engels' style in *The Condition* has most in common with Carlyle's (as with Marx's) is moral indignation. Engels writes:

> There is, therefore, no cause for surprise if the workers, treated as brutes, actually become such; or if they can maintain their consciousness of manhood only by cherishing the most glowing hatred, the most unbroken inward rebellion against the bourgeoisie in power. They are men so long only as they burn with wrath against the reigning class. They become brutes the moment they bend in patience under the yoke, and merely strive to make life endurable while abandoning the effort to break the yoke.

"The employment of children must be forbidden," he proclaims; of the cottage system, "It is clearly unjust," "It implies a double wrong." In a long comparison he shows that the "free" laborer is worse off than the serf, as, for example: "The serf owed his master the *jus primae noctis*, the right of the first night—the free workingman must, on demand, surrender to his master not only that, but the right of every night." Engels' slogans are aggressively humanistic: "They, as human beings, shall not be made to bow to social circumstances, but social conditions ought to yield to them as human beings." Ultimately, they appeal to the Christian virtues Engels had absorbed in his childhood. "It is infamous,

this charity of a Christian bourgeois!," Engels writes, and opposes to
it: "Such relief given by an honest proletarian who knows himself
what it is to be hungry, for whom sharing his scanty meal is really a
sacrifice, but a sacrifice borne with pleasure, such help has a wholly
different ring to it from the carelessly-tossed alms of the luxurious
bourgeois." In his work on *The Housing Question*, written in 1872,
Engels writes of *The Condition of the Working Class:*

> As far as I know, I was the first to describe in German these condi-
> tions in their classical form as they exist in England. I did not do
> that, as Muelberger suggests, because they 'violated my *sense of
> justice*'—whoever insisted on writing books about all the facts
> which violated his sense of justice would have a lot to do—but, as
> can be read in the introduction to my book, by describing the
> social conditions created by modern large-scale industry, to pro-
> vide an actual basis for German socialism, which was then arising
> and was expending itself in empty phrases.

All one can say about this defensive disclaimer of morality is that it
isn't true, that Engels probably copied it from Marx, and that it wasn't
true of Marx either.

The conclusion of *The Condition of the Working Class* is an indictment. "The property-holding, manufacturing class must bear the
moral responsibility for this distress," Engels writes. He defines his
aim as demonstrating that bourgeois society daily and hourly commits
murder, and that it commits it knowingly. "I broadly accuse it of
social murder," he proclaims. The motive? "The greater pecuniary
profits of the bourgeoisie!" In his last chapter Engels turns to address
the bourgeoisie in bitter fury:

> Philanthropic institutions forsooth! As though you rendered the
> proletarians a service in first sucking out their very life-blood and
> then practicing your self-complacent, Pharisaic philanthropy upon
> them, placing yourselves before the world as mighty benefactors
> of humanity when you give back to the plundered victims the
> hundredth part of what belongs to them! Charity which degrades
> him who gives more than him who takes; charity which treads the
> downtrodden still deeper in the dust, which demands that the de-
> graded, the pariah cast out by society, shall first surrender the last
> that remains to him, his very claim to manhood, shall first beg for
> mercy before your mercy deigns to press, in the shape of an alms,
> the brand of degradation upon his brow.

As his remarks about "true manliness" and "true womanliness," or the
need of an infant for maternal love during the first year, show, Engels
had a characteristically twentieth-century theory of the personality, in
which the good life requires dignity and love as much as the amel-
ioration of social conditions, deny it however he might.

The faults and limitations of *The Condition of the Working Class
in England in 1844* are lesser matters. One of the things that distin-

guishes it from *Capital* is that Engels lacks Marx's blithe assurance of universal certainty. He will admit that he doesn't really know whether piecework raises or lowers total wages, "It is hard to get to the bottom of the matter," or ruin his case against dangerous machinery with the realistic comment that these devices "are rarely used now." He is torn by ambivalence. On one hand he yearns for the old pre-industrial England with its workmen "leading a righteous and peaceful life in all piety and probity; and their material position far better than that of their successors." On the other hand there is his evolutionary faith that this intellectual vegetation was death, and that "but for the industrial revolution they would never have emerged from this existence, which, cosily romantic as it was, was nevertheless not worthy of human beings." We see the same ambivalence in the imagery: the warmth of the factories, like a tropical climate, brings on premature female puberty; the hardship of the factories delays female puberty or prevents it altogether.

Shaw wrote in "The Illusions of Socialism": "It is perverse stupidity to declare in one breath that the working-classes are starved, degraded, and left in ignorance by a system which heaps victuals, education, and refinements on the capitalist, and to assume in the next that the capitalist is a narrow, sordid scoundrel, and the working-man a high-minded, enlightened, magnanimous philanthropist." It is precisely this "perverse stupidity" that Engels is caught up in, torn between his desire to show the terrible brutalizing of the proletarians, and his pastoral vision in which they embody all value. Suddenly they are not desperate Sheffield savages or filthy Yahoos, but "industrious and worthy people—far worthier and more to be respected than all the rich of London." Engels writes, forgetting his complaint that they are given no leisure to think:

> The English working-man who can scarcely read and still less write, nevertheless knows very well where his own interest and that of the nation lies. He knows, too, what the especial interest of the bourgeoisie is, and what he has to expect of that bourgeoisie. If he cannot write he can speak, and speak in public; if he has no arithmetic, he can, nevertheless, reckon with the Political Economists enough to see through a Corn-Law-repealing bourgeois, and to get the better of him in argument; if celestial matters remain very mixed for him in spite of all the effort of the preachers, he sees all the more clearly into terrestrial, political, and social questions.

A few pages later Engels has even forgotten that his pastoral hero can scarcely read, and informs us that "the epoch-making products of modern philosophical, political, and poetical literature are read by working-men almost exclusively," among them Helvetius, Holbach, Diderot, Strauss, Proudhon, Bentham, Godwin, Shelley "the genius, the prophet," and Byron "with his glowing sensuality."

Directly opposed to this pastoral romanticizing of the English workingman is a boundless contempt for the Irish, "comfortable only in the dirt." The Irish ruin working-class housing by using the wood-work for firewood; along with pigs they introduce filthiness, "which is the Irishman's second nature," and drunkenness, which is his only form of self-expression: "The southern facile character of the Irishman, his contempt for all humane enjoyments, in which his very crudeness makes him incapable of sharing, his filth and poverty, all favor drunk-enness." In short, Engels writes of the Irish as slavery apologists write of the Negroes, seeing them as subhuman. (In 1891, after a visit to Ireland, in a note to the fourth edition of *The Origin of the Family*, Engels explains the demoralized condition of the Irish in England as a problem in acculturation rather than as one of innate depravity, and thus corrects the strictures of his youth.) What the Irish were for Engels, the lumpenproletariat was for Marx, simply scum; "that pas-sively rotting mass," as the *Manifesto* called it. Of that, there is no trace in Engels before he collaborated with Marx. In *The Condition*, thieves and prostitutes are poor oppressed working people like any other.

A weakness the book shares with Marx's writings is its wishful prediction of revolution, although in 1845 Engels had far more justifi-cation than Marx had after 1848. Engels threatens "before too long a time goes by," a revolution "in comparison with which the French Revolution, and the year 1794, will prove to have been child's play." He mutters ominously that "the decisive battle between bourgeoisie and proletariat is approaching," and proclaims "The only possible solution is a violent revolution, which cannot fail to take place." Engels announces: "The war of the poor against the rich will be the bloodiest ever waged," then explains:

> Prophecy is nowhere so easy as in England, where all the compo-nent elements of society are clearly defined and sharply sepa-rated. The revolution must come; it is already too late to bring about a peaceful solution; but it can be made more gentle than that prophesied in the foregoing pages.

On the next page, he concludes the book with Georg Buechner's slogan:

> The classes are divided more and more sharply, the spirit of resist-ance penetrates the workers, the bitterness intensifies, the guerilla skirmishes become concentrated in more important battles, and soon a slight impulse will suffice to set the avalanche in motion. Then, indeed, will the war-cry resound through the land: 'War to the palaces, peace to the cottages!'—but then it will be too late for the rich to beware.

ENGELS' books written during his collaboration with Marx need not occupy us in the same detail. *The Peasant War in Germany*, published in 1850 in two issues of the *Neue Rheinische Revue*, was written, Engels wrote in a preface, "under the vivid impression of the counter-revolution that had just been completed." As an application of Marx's theory of historical materialism, it is principally concerned with class analysis. Behind the religious issues of the wars Engels shows class struggles, he reveals the economic interests underlying heresies, and he demonstrates that the wars resulted in a permanent change in German class alignments. Engels never relaxes the historical parallels. "Those classes and fractions of classes which everywhere betrayed 1848 and 1849," he writes, "can be found in the role of traitors as early as 1525, though on a lower level of development." Further: "Between 1517 and 1525, Luther had gone through the same transformations as the German constitutionalists between 1846 and 1849"; "In 1848 as in the Peasant War, the interests of the opposition classes clashed with each other and each acted of its own accord." Engels rides his military hobby horse: admiring the strategy and tactics of Georg Truchsess, who smashed the peasant armies; regretting that Thomas Muenzer, the peasant leader, "possessed no military knowledge whatsoever"; approving the "splendid campaign" and "brilliant battles" of Geismaier, "the only noted military talent among all the peasant chiefs."

In *The Peasant War in Germany*, Engels spares his readers no details of the atrocities against the peasants and their leaders: "Dózsa was captured, roasted on a red hot throne, and his flesh eaten by his own people, whose lives were granted to them only under this condition"; Truchsess had Rohrbach "chained to a post, surrounded by firewood and roasted to death on a slow fire, while he, feasting with horsemen, gloated over this noble spectacle"; "Muenzer was put on the rack in the presence of the princes, and then decapitated." When the peasants commit atrocities, they are played down: "Then followed Sicilian Vespers for all the nobility who fell into the hands of the peasants"; Rohrbach had knights run the gauntlet, "this being the most humiliating death he could invent for them." The moral of *The Peasant War* is somewhat ambiguous: Muenzer was too far in advance of his time, preaching communism before the material conditions were ready for it; if the peasants had struck at Truchsess when they were most powerful and he weakest, "they could have ended the entire war." In other words, conditions must be ripe, but conditions are always ripe for something if men are ready. Battles had failed in 1525 and 1848, but the war was still to be won.

Engels' next work, *Revolution and Counter-Revolution in Germany in 1848*, is a study of that second lost battle. Written in English, it appeared as a series of articles in the New York *Tribune* in 1851 and 1852 over Marx's name, was published in book form as Marx's, edited by his daughter Eleanor Aveling, and was only discovered to be Engels' with the revelation of their correspondence. (Marx had asked Engels to do the articles because his English was imperfect, because he was busy with political economy, and because he lacked Engels'

military knowledge.) The first article announces, "If, then, we have
been beaten, we have nothing else to do but to begin again from the
beginning." What was now necessary was "the study of the causes that
necessitated both the late outbreak and its defeat." Here is the same
class analysis, with the principal factor the special importance of the
petty bourgeoisie, the small trading and shop-keeping class, in Germany and Austria. Again we get military second-guessing: "In war,
and particularly in revolutionary warfare, rapidity of action until
some decided advantage is gained is the first rule, and we have no
hesitation in saying that upon *merely military grounds* Perczel ought
not to have stopped until his junction with the Viennese was effected."

   Where *The Peasant War* never achieves any particular imaginative
vision, here Engels' loathing for the King of Prussia, Frederick William IV, gives the book something of the character of a Grail romance,
with the impotent old Fisher King awaiting the stroke of the lance.
Compared with Louis XVI of France, Frederick William "certainly
surpassed his French original in weakness of character"; he is "the poor
king," appearing in public "while in a state which elsewhere would
come under the Maine Liquor Law." The general imagery of inadequacy and impotence is overwhelming: a ministry is "poor deluded
wretches"; an assembly displays "total impotency" or is "a stage
where old and worn-out political characters exhibited their involuntary ludicrousness and their impotence of thought, as well as action";
"The petty bourgeoisie, great in boasting, is very impotent for
action, and very shy in risking anything"; and so on.

   In 1850, need forced Engels back to "fiendish commerce," working
for the family firm in Manchester again, and for the next two decades
he wrote no more books. Through the period of Marx's contributions to the New York *Daily Tribune*, Engels wrote many articles
and parts of articles for him, on military and other subjects. Engels
had always been a military specialist. He had done his service as an
artilleryman in the Prussian army before going to Manchester in 1842,
he had fought in the insurrection in the Palatinate in 1849, and since
then he had studied military science with such enthusiasm that his
friends called him "General." His articles on the Crimean War
in the *Tribune* were so knowledgeable that their author was taken to
be General Winfield Scott, and writing on the American Civil War in
1862, Engels had proposed a march through Georgia as the key to
Union victory. During the 1860s Engels wrote on military topics for
the *Volunteer Journal* and the *Manchester Guardian*, and in 1870 and
1871 he published sixty articles on the Franco-Prussian war in the
Pall Mall Gazette. Several of these series were issued at the time as
pamphlets. A collection of Engels' military writings was published in
two volumes by the East German Ministry of National Defense in
1957, and the ones from the *Volunteer Journal* and the *Guardian*, including a technical series on "The History of the Rifle," were published
in a volume, *Engels as Military Critic*, by W. H. Chaloner and W. O.

Henderson in 1959. This book makes it clear that Engels had the spirit of an old army man, but he always maintained that his military studies were only training for the revolution, because of (as he wrote to Marx) "the enormous importance which the *partie militaire* must have in the coming movement."

With the publication of the first volume of *Capital* in 1867, Engels interrupted his military studies long enough to write nine separate reviews of it. The most ambitious of them, written for the British liberal magazine *The Fortnightly Review*, was not printed. One that was printed in a Leipzig paper, the *Demokratisches Wochenblatt* in 1868, opens with a curious appeal to German patriotism:

> The relation between capital and labor, the hinge on which our entire present system of society turns, is here treated scientifically for the first time, and with a thoroughness and acuity possible only for a German. Valuable as the writings of an Owen, Saint-Simon, Fourier, are and will remain—it was reserved for a German to climb to the height from which the whole field of modern social relations can be seen clearly and in full view just as the lower mountain scenery is seen by an observer standing on the topmost peak.

Engels was, as about so many things, ambivalent about Germany. In *Revolution and Counter-Revolution* he praises the "physical and intellectual power of the German nation to subdue, absorb, and assimilate its ancient eastern neighbors," arguing that "this tendency of absorption on the part of the Germans had always been, and still was, one of the mightiest means by which the civilization of Western Europe had been spread in the east of that continent." In later works, he calls Marxism "German scientific socialism," credits Leibniz rather than Newton with the calculus, credits Kepler rather than Newton with celestial mechanics, credits Wolff, Oken and Baer for anticipating evolution, and in general boasts of the German scientific tradition wherever possible. At the same time his writings continue a running series of sneers against the Germans: they are "unbeatable" in the field of quality deterioration; Germany is the country where "everything happens too late." In the preface to a book he wrote in 1878, Engels summarizes:

> Sublime nonsense in poetry, in philosophy, in politics, in economics, in the writing of history; sublime nonsense in the lecture-room and on the platform, sublime nonsense everywhere; sublime nonsense which lays claim to a superiority and depth of thought distinguishing it from the simple, commonplace nonsense of other nations; sublime nonsense the most characteristic mass-product of Germany's intellectual industry, cheap but bad—just like other German products.

Other than his pride in German social science, there is not much worth noting in Engels' reviews of *Capital*. He is trying very hard to be

someone else (the one for the *Fortnightly* was signed "Samuel Moore")
and the tone is deadly: "Mr. Marx gives some interesting examples
from Parliamentary papers, for which we refer to the book itself."

Engels' next work was *The Housing Question*, which appeared as
three articles in the Leipsig *Volksstaat* in 1872. He explains in the
preface to the second German edition:

> As a consequence of the division of labor that existed between
> Marx and myself, it fell to me to present our opinions in the
> periodical press, that is to say, particularly in the fight against
> opposing views, in order that Marx should have time for the elabo-
> ration of his great basic work. Thus it became my task to present
> our views, for the most part in a polemical form, in opposition to
> other kinds of views. So also here. . . . Marx would have accom-
> plished all this much better and more convincingly.

The remarkable feature of *The Housing Question* is its extremism,
its bold vision of the free alienated proletarian, desperate in his ownership of nothing, the hope of the future. The Commune experience had
revived Engels as much as Marx. Thus "the ownership of house, garden
and field, and security of tenure in the dwelling-place, is becoming today, under the rule of large-scale industry, not only the worst
hindrance to the worker, but the greatest misfortune for the whole
working class." Engels writes:

> In order to create the modern revolutionary class of the proletariat
> it was absolutely necessary to cut the umbilical cord which still
> bound the worker of the past to the land. The hand weaver who
> had his little house, garden and field along with his loom, was a
> quiet contented man 'in all godliness and respectability' despite
> all misery and despite all political pressure; he doffed his cap to
> the rich, to the priests and to the officials of the state; and in-
> wardly was altogether a slave. It is precisely modern large-scale
> industry, which has turned the worker, formerly chained to the
> land, into a completely propertyless proletarian, liberated from all
> traditional fetters and *free as a bird*; it is precisely this eco-
> nomic revolution which has created the sole conditions under
> which the exploitation of the working class in its final form, in the
> capitalist mode of production, can be overthrown.

It is the authentic voice of primitive Christianity, calling on converts to
renounce the world and follow the Christ. The foxes have holes, and
the birds of the air have nests, but this new Son of man hath not where
to lay his head. Engels asks, "Will the troglodyte with his cave, the
Australian aborigine with his clay hut, and the Indian with his hearth
ever accomplish a June insurrection and a Paris Commune?" Should we
therefore look backward longingly? "On the contrary." Giving the
worker "hearth and home" would "put back the clock of world history
by a hundred years," and thereby "make the present-day workers

into just such narrow-minded, crawling, sneaking slaves as their great-grandfathers were."

Engels' tireless insistence in the book is that nothing but revolution will solve *any* social problem. "In order to make an end of *this* housing shortage there is only *one* means," he writes, "to abolish altogether the exploitation and oppression of the working class by the ruling class." He gives the same answer to "all so-called social reforms." "It is not," Engels writes, "the solution of the housing question which simultaneously solves the social question, but only by the solution of the social question, that is, by the abolition of the capitalist mode of production, is the solution of the housing question made possible." Engels will not, however, define the future society except to say that all these problems will be solved. "It is not our task to create utopian systems for the arrangement of the future society," he writes scornfully, or "To attempt to answer such a question in advance and for all cases would be utopia-making, and I leave that to others." The answers to all social questions are implied in the first volume of *Capital*, by Dr. Karl Marx: "He spent twenty-five years in investigating them from all angles, and the results of his criticism contain throughout the kernels of so-called solutions, insofar as they are possible at all today."

Retired in 1870, Engels began an eight-year intensive study of mathematics and natural science. From 1872 on, he worked on a book called *Dialectics of Nature*, putting it aside unfinished at Marx's death in 1883 to work on the manuscripts of *Capital*. *Dialectics of Nature* was published in the twentieth century, and an English translation appeared with a preface and notes by J. B. S. Haldane. The editing must have been a feat comparable to Engels' on the later volumes of *Capital*, since the order of the four bundles of manuscript was uncertain, some of it was in rough notes, and it was written in the composite language in which Engels apparently thought, as for example:

> Wenn Coulomb von particles of electricity spricht, which repel each other inversely as the square of the distance, so nimmt Thomson das ruhib hins als bewiesen.

Or:

> In der heutigen Gesellschaft, dans le méchanisme civilisé, herrscht duplicité d'action, contrariété de L'interêt individuel avec le collectif; es ist une queue universelle des individus contre les masses.

Dialectics of Nature is of interest for our purposes chiefly in two respects. The first is Engels' extension of Darwin's speculations about what constitutes a biological individual. Engels' notes read:

> *The Individual.*—This concept also has been dissolved into something purely relative. Cormus, colony, tapeworm—on the other hand, cell and segment as individuals in a certain sense (anthropogeny and morphology).

He adds:

> Among lower animals the concept of the individual cannot be
> established at all sharply. Not only as to whether a particular ani-
> mal is an individual or a colony, but also where in development
> one individual ceases and the other begins (nurses).

Like Darwin's metaphors, Marx's "giant body of the proletariat" had
finally become scientific plain-seeing. The other matter of interest is
the remarkable modernity of some of Engels' formulations. The English translator, Clemens Dutt, has helped. Engels' word "Kraft" has
been translated not "force," in the older usage of his time, but
"energy." The amazing definition "Life is the mode of existence of
protein bodies" loses some of its twentieth-century sound in the German, which says "*Eiweiss*," "albumen." Haldane's footnote casually
explains that "*Eiweiss*" is translated "protein" throughout, since
albumens are now known to be only one group of proteins. The
chief reason Engels' science seems so advanced is that his dialectic
places the emphasis on dynamics, process, and becoming rather than
being, in a fashion characteristic of twentieth-century science. Finally, Engels had, if not a naturally scientific mind, at least a naturally
skeptical one, and the book's final chapter, an article on "Natural Science and the Spirit World," is one of the funniest demolitions of
spiritualism ever written.

Herr Eugen Duehring's Revolution in Science, commonly known
as *Anti-Duehring*, was published in 1877 and 1878 in the Leipzig
Vorwaerts, the successor to the *Volksstaat*. Three chapters from it, reprinted as the pamphlet *Socialism: Utopian and Scientific*, have had
an enormous circulation and influence as an introduction to Marxism.
The rest of the book consists of the development of a materialism
more absolute than Marx's, the expansion of the dialectic to claim one
area of science after another, and a running polemic with Duehring,
who had had the insolence to set up as a rival socialist philosopher and
system-builder. The preface to the first edition begins wonderfully:
"The following work is by no means the fruit of any 'inner urge.' On
the contrary." The book concludes on what Engels gaily calls "a note
of raillery and reconciliation" in "our comprehensive judgment on
Herr Duehring," which is "*mental incompetence due to megalomania.*"

In between, *Anti-Duehring* plays all the stops of polemical abuse:
"ignorant arrogance," "quite an extraordinary creature, who claims to
be not less infallible than the Pope," "the Richard Wagner of philosophy—but without Wagner's talents," a "mish-mash of platitudes and
oracular sayings, in a word, . . . simple balderdash," "Herr Duehring's persistent habit of quoting falsely," "plagiarism," and so forth.
Austin Lewis, who translated and edited an abridgement of *Anti-
Duehring* published as *Landmarks of Scientific Socialism* in the
United States in 1907, keeps protesting Engels' invective in his
introduction. "Engels pursues him somewhat too closely and much too
bitterly," he writes. "Much of the work is valueless today because of

Engels' eagerness to score a point off his adversary." Lewis protests "the elaborate ridicule with which he covers his opponent, and which is by no means a recommendation to the book." Lewis, with the sweet reasonableness of American Socialism, is simply too far from the Golden Bough world of German radicals exiled in Victorian England, where each guardian of the grove has slain his predecessor and must himself be slain. While Engels was at work on *Anti-Duehring*, Marx wrote to him: "Ruthlessness—the first condition of all criticism," and himself set the example in the one chapter, on Duehring's economics, that he wrote for the book. Marx writes: "It would be better to read Herr Duehring's chapter on Mercantilism in the 'original,' that is, in F. List's *National System*, Chapter 29." Duehring writes that Hume, in connection with a felicitous idea, "does not even claim to have originated it." "This would certainly not have happened to Herr Duehring," Marx adds. Otherwise, Hume was "the Duehring of the eighteenth century." Marx sums up, over Engels' name, the final value of Duehring's work

> And just as in philosophy he could not find hard words enough for the very Hegel whom he was so constantly exploiting and at the same time emasculating, so in the *Critical History* the most baseless calumniation of Marx only serves to conceal the fact that everything in the *Course* about capital and labor which has any sense in it at all is likewise an emasculated plagiarism of Marx.

Duehring had been foolish enough to attack Marx, writing of his "Chinese erudition," "philosophical and scientific backwardness," "buffoonery pretending to be witty," "dialectical frills and mazes," "the nebulous hybrids of Marx's conceptions," "bastards of historical and logical fantasy." Duehring was a ferocious anti-Semite, and Engels, who was a milder anti-Semite, seems to have been driven by the logic of the dialectic, the negation of the negation, to philo-Semitism. He writes of Duehring's "hatred of Jews, exaggerated to the verge of absurdity," and his acceptance of "the popular prejudice against the Jews, inherited from the bigotry of the Middle Ages." From *Anti-Duehring* on, to the best of my knowledge, the sneers against the Jews disappear from Engels' correspondence, until in 1890 he wrote the letter against anti-Semitism (published in the Vienna *Arbeiterzeitung*) in which he spoke of Marx's "purest Jewish blood." Duehring had also attacked Darwin, describing his theory as "a piece of brutality directed against humanity." Here, with no personal involvement, Engels defends Darwin against Duehring's strictures while extending his own developing criticism, that Darwin "attributed to his discovery too wide a field of action." The way out of the Darwinian world of capitalism is the understanding and control of social forces; otherwise "The forces operating in society work exactly like the forces operating in Nature: blindly, violently, destructively, so long as we do not understand them and fail to take them into account." He wants a Darwin without Malthus: "No Malthusian spectacles are required in order to perceive the struggle for existence in nature."

The positive part of *Anti-Duehring* is Engels' fullest statement of Marxism. Earlier socialism, he writes, could not explain capitalism and its consequences, "and thus could not get the mastery over them." With Marxism everything is different.

> These two great discoveries, the materialist conception of history and the revelation of the secret of capitalist production by means of surplus value, we owe to *Marx*. With these discoveries socialism became a science, which had in the first place to be developed in all its details and relations.

For the first time, Engels sketches out some details of the future society. Theft will be negligible "in a society in which the motive for stealing has been done away with." Man will be free in an "existence in harmony with the established laws of Nature," freedom being Hegel's (and earlier, Spinoza's) "recognition of necessity." "The abolition of the antithesis between town and country," the demand of the utopians Fourier and Owen, is not utopian but feasible and essential; "the great towns will perish" and man will be whole again.

Engels has great fun with Duehring's myth of a Fall, the first use of force by man against man. "The famous original sin," he sneers, "when Robinson Crusoe made Friday his slave." For Duehring, force is "historically the fundamental fact." Engels writes:

> For Herr Duehring force is the absolute evil; the first act of force is for him the original sin; his whole exposition is a jeremiad on the contamination, which this brought about, of all subsequent history by this original sin; a jeremiad on the shameful perversion of all natural and social laws by this diabolical power, force.

Naturally Marxism has no such theological superstition.

In 1883, Marx died, and in 1884 Engels published *The Origin of the Family, Private Property, and the State, in the Light of the Researches of Lewis H. Morgan.* Its preface announces:

> The following chapters are, in a sense, the execution of a bequest. No less a man than Karl Marx had made it one of his future tasks to present the results of Morgan's researches in the light of the conclusions of his own—within certain limits, I may say our—materialistic examination of history, and thus to make clear their full significance. For Morgan in his own way had discovered afresh in America the materialistic conception of history discovered by Marx forty years ago, and in his comparison of barbarism and civilization it had led him, in the main points, to the same conclusions as Marx. And just as the professional economists in Germany were for years as busy in plagiarizing *Capital* as they were persistent in attempting to kill it by silence, so Morgan's *Ancient Society* received precisely the same treatment from the

spokesmen of 'prehistoric' science in England. My work can only provide a slight substitute for what my departed friend no longer had the time to do. But I have the critical notes which he made to his extensive extracts from Morgan, and as far as possible I reproduce them here.

(Marx's *Abstract of Morgan's "Ancient Society"* was published in Russian translation in 1945, but so far as I know is not otherwise available.)

The *Origin of the Family* is far more than the execution of Marx's bequest. Actually it is the capping of Marx's great imaginative vision of the human condition with an adequate origin myth. What Morgan had done for Marx and Engels was to find "the key to the most important and hitherto insoluble riddles of earliest Greek, Roman and German history." Engels writes in his preface to the fourth edition:

> This rediscovery of the primitive matriarchal gens as the earlier stage of the patriarchal gens of civilized peoples has the same importance for anthropology as Darwin's theory of evolution has for biology and Marx's theory of surplus value for political economy.

Morgan had produced an evolutionary prehistory, in which the family "advances from a lower to a higher form as society advances from a lower to a higher condition," and the development of incest taboo affords "a good illustration of the operation of the principle of natural selection." (It was, in fact, too mechanical an operation for Engels, who keeps referring to "the urge toward the prevention of inbreeding" and to a point at which natural selection "had accomplished its task" and stopped operating.) What Morgan offered, in fact, was a myth of prehistoric original sin or primal crime more suitable for Marxism than Duehring's enslavement: the theft of rights from the ancient mother.

In *Capital*, Marx had put the crime back into earlier history: capital was stolen from the working class in primitive accumulation (or, in Pearson's terms, labor fell into commodity form). Now, using Morgan and carrying out Marx's wish, Engels showed that that theft was merely the ritual repetition of the great primal theft. It is a true myth of the fall out of Eden, what Engels calls "a fall from the simple moral greatness of the old gentile society." The supremacy of women "was general in primitive times," as Bachofen had shown before Morgan. The patriarchal or patrilineal revolution was thus the primal crime: "The overthrow of mother-right was the *world historical defeat of the female sex.*" With patriliny came all the evils of the fallen condition, the monogamous family and private property: "Monogamous marriage comes on the scene as the subjugation of the one sex by the other." Monogamy was "the first form of the family to be based, not on natural, but on economic conditions—on the victory of private property over primitive, natural communal property." From this in turn stem all the later evils of the social and economic condition: "The first class oppression coincides with that of the female sex by the male." Engels quotes from Marx's notes:

> The modern family contains in germ not only slavery (*servitus*), but also serfdom, since from the beginning it is related to agricultural services. It contains *in miniature* all the contradictions which later extend throughout society and its state.

The bourgeois family, Engels adds, "is a conjugal partnership of leaden boredom, known as 'domestic bliss.' " The husband enslaves and exploits the wife: "Within the family he is the bourgeois and the wife represents the proletariat."

It is hard to know, without access to Marx's abstract, how much of this is Engels going beyond Marx. Some of it seems to represent Marx's deepest wishes, like the emphasis on Morgan's accounts of adoption into the Iroquois gens with full acceptance as son and brother, as Marx felt he had been ceremonially adopted into the proletariat by his change of identity when he took up political economy in 1843. (The formula for himself in Marx's later writings is "working men, or acknowledged representatives of the working class"—in response to baiting by opponents of unimpeachable proletarian origins.) Some of Engels' book seems to be very uncharacteristic of Marx, particularly the scorn for the bourgeois family—Marx was as classic a bourgeois paterfamilias as Darwin before him or Freud after him (when his daughter Laura married Lafargue, he was very particular about the property settlement). The *Origin of the Family* has a tone of authority and a quality of greatness missing in Engels' works since *The Condition of the Working Class*, and it is ironic that his two major books should have been written the year before he began the collaboration with Marx and the year after Marx died. In some sense, Engels was freed to an independence very like genius. Schwartzchild describes Engels as "a fundamentally feminine intellect: an intellect with a longing for someone stronger than himself, a longing to cling and to submit." "I am meant to play second fiddle," Engels wrote. After Marx's death he was first fiddle with no choice.

Some of *The Origin of the Family* seems very much Engels on his own. Where Marx had despised Rousseau's primitivism, Engels recreates it in prehistory. He writes:

> And a wonderful constitution it is, this gentile constitution, in all its childlike simplicity! No soldiers, no gendarmes or police, no nobles, kings, regents, prefects, or judges, no prisons, no lawsuits—and everything takes its orderly course.

Man was born free, in other words, but is everywhere in chains. Here too is Rousseau's noble savage: among the Iroquois, "the personal dignity, uprightness, strength of character, and courage of these barbarians"; Zulus and Nubians doing "what no European army can do"; "The Gilyaks still preserve in their moral character many of the virtues of a primitive tribe." "This is what men and society were like before the division into classes," Engels concludes. The ancient Germans "breathed new life into a dying Europe" by means of "their barbarism, their gentile constitution." In an ideal state reminiscent of Plato's myth of the origin of the sexes, "Within the tribe there is as yet no difference between rights and duties." Engels had come a long way in the decade since *The Housing Question,* when he sneered at Proudhon: "On what historical knowledge the book is based can be judged from the fact that it believes in the historical existence of the Golden Age."

The future utopia of socialism is naturally the Golden Age of primitive communism rewon with improved technology and material plenty. Engels writes of the good old days:

> Production was limited in the extreme, but—the producers controlled their product. That was the immense advantage of barbarian production, which was lost with the coming of civilization; to reconquer it, but on the basis of the gigantic control of nature now achieved by man and of the free association now made possible, will be the task of the next generation.

He concludes the book on Morgan's vision of "The next higher plane of society," which he places in italics: *"It will be a revival, in a higher form, of the liberty, equality and fraternity of the ancient gentes."* An important ingredient in the future utopia will be a sexual freedom that we can only believe would have shocked and repelled Marx, who blushed, Liebknecht says, "like a girl six years old" at any indelicacy in mixed company. "If strict monogamy is the height of all virtue," Engels writes nastily, "then the palm must go to the tapeworm, which has a complete set of male and female sexual organs in each of its 50–200 proglottides, or sections, and spends its whole life copulating in all its sections with itself." "The Australian aborigine, wandering hundreds of miles from his home among people whose language he does not understand," Engels wrote, perhaps thinking of Mary Burns, the Manchester working girl who had welcomed the German exile to her bed, "nevertheless often finds in every camp and every tribe women who give themselves to him without resistance and without resentment."

In modern saturnalian rites, Engels explains, "for a short time the old freedom of sexual intercourse is again restored." Historically, "the old comparative freedom of sexual intercourse by no means disappeared with the victory of pairing marriage or even of monogamous marriage." Its rites have been preserved by the class that embodies all moral value: "Sex-love in the relationship with a woman becomes, and can only become, the real rule among the oppressed classes, which means today among the proletariat—whether this relation is officially sanctioned or not." After the social revolution: "Prostitution disappears; monogamy, instead of collapsing, at last becomes a reality—for men also." Eventually monogamy too disappears:

> Society looks after all children alike, whether they are legitimate or not. This removes all the anxiety about the 'consequences,'

which today is the most essential social—moral as well as economic—factor that prevents a girl from giving herself completely to the man she loves. Will not that suffice to bring about the gradual growth of unconstrained sexual intercourse and with it a more tolerant public opinion in regard to a maiden's honor and a woman's shame?

Sex under communism will in fact be wild and free and wonderful:

> What we can now conjecture about the way in which sexual relations will be ordered after the impending overthrow of capitalist production is mainly of a negative character, limited for the most part to what will disappear. But what will there be new? That will be answered when a new generation has grown up: a generation of men who never in their lives have known what it is to buy a woman's surrender with money or any other social instrument of power; a generation of women who have never known what it is to give themselves to a man from any other considerations than real love, or to refuse to give themselves to their lover from fear of the economic consequences. When these people are in the world, they will care precious little what anybody today thinks they ought to do; they will make their own practice and their corresponding public opinion about the practice of each individual—and that will be the end.

At which point Engels adds: "Let us, however, return to Morgan, from whom we have moved a considerable distance."

The other dimension in which Engels let himself go after Marx's death was in his learning, particularly linguistic learning. Marx had been the polymath and polyglot, and Engels' works during Marx's lifetime have none of the coruscation of quotation and reference, in half a dozen tongues, of Marx's. But Engels had been teaching himself languages along with science and military affairs: first Russian and the Slavic languages; then Persian and some other oriental languages; then the Germanic languages, Gothic, Old Norse, Anglo-Saxon; then "a little Frisian-English-Jutish-Scandinavian philology"; finally Gaelic and others. "Engels stutters in twenty languages," Mehring reports a friend's saying. *The Origin of the Family* quotes the *Elder Edda* in Icelandic and the *Völuspà* in Old Norse, introduces Serbian and Bulgarian kinship terms and Danish boundary words. Some pages are a riot of linguistics and comparative philology. Engels "was probably the most widely educated man of his day," says Haldane in his preface to *Dialectics of Nature:*

> Not only had he a profound knowledge of economics and history, but he knew enough to discuss the meaning of an obscure Latin phrase concerning Roman marriage law, or the processes taking place when a piece of impure zinc was dipped into sulphuric acid. And he contrived to accumulate this immense knowledge, not by

leading a life of cloistered learning, but while playing an active part in politics, running a business, and even fox-hunting!

Engels' last book, *Ludwig Feuerbach and the Outcome of Classical German Philosophy*, was published in 1888. It is very like a final settling of accounts. Since the unpublished *German Ideology*, Engels writes in the foreword, Marx and he had never returned to Feuerbach. "A full acknowledgment of the influence which Feuerbach, more than any other post-Hegelian philosopher, had upon us during our period of storm and stress, appeared to me to be an undischarged debt of honor." Where Feuerbach is inadequate:

The blame for this falls solely upon the wretched conditions in Germany, in consequence of which cobweb-spinning eclectic flea-crackers had taken possession of the chairs of philosophy, while Feuerbach, who towered above them all, had to rusticate and grow sour in a little village.

Secondarily, the book is belated justice to Hegel. "We have expressed ourselves in various places regarding our relation to Hegel," Engels writes in the foreword, "but nowhere in a comprehensive connected account." In some respects, as the book makes clear, Hegel continues to tower over everyone, Feuerbach included. *Ludwig Feuerbach* has a curiously serene tone, like emotion recollected in tranquillity, and might remind a reader of the final benignity of *The Tempest*. Austin Lewis, in his appendix to *Landmarks of Scientific Socialism*, writes of Engels:

He started with a heart inflamed with the wrongs of the suffering, as the damning pages of the work above cited [*The Condition of the Working Class in 1844*] show; he ends with a calm and dispassionate enquiry (apart from what he considered to be the exigencies of controversy) into the fundamental causes of economic and social progress.

In *Ludwig Feuerbach*, Engels notes the teleology in Hegel's system:

According to this, history worked unconsciously but with necessity towards a certain pre-determined, ideal goal—as, for example, according to Hegel, towards the realization of his absolute idea—and the unalterable trend towards this absolute idea formed the inner inter-connection in the events of history.

If there was ever such a teleology in the Marxist system, in the ultimate classless society, it is there for Engels no longer. He writes:

With all philosophers it is precisely the 'system' which is perishable; and for the simple reason that it springs from an imperishable desire of the human mind—the desire to overcome all contradictions. But if all contradictions are once and for all disposed of, we shall have arrived at so-called absolute truth: world history will be at an end.

Elsewhere:

> Just as knowledge is unable to reach a complete conclusion in a
> perfect, ideal condition of humanity, so is history unable to do so:
> a perfect society, a perfect 'State,' are things which can only
> exist in imagination.

What there is for Engels, as for Heraclitus, is only ceaseless flux,
process, change. He writes of Marxist materialism: "With each epoch-
making discovery even in the sphere of natural science it has to change
its form." In his and Feuerbach's time, Engels notes, the three decisive
discoveries of this sort were the nature of the cell, the transformation
of energy, and evolution by natural selection. "The great basic
thought," he writes, is "that the world is not to be comprehended as
a complex of ready-made *things*, but as a complex of processes."

The end-product is a kind of ultimate skepticism:

> If, however, investigation always proceeds from this standpoint, the
> demand for final solutions and eternal truths ceases once for all;
> one is always conscious of the necessary limitation of all acquired
> knowledge, of the fact that it is conditioned by the circum-
> stances in which it was acquired. On the other hand, one no
> longer permits oneself to be imposed upon by the antitheses, un-
> superable for the still common old metaphysics, between true
> and false, good and bad, identical and different, necessary and acci-
> dental. One knows that these antitheses have only a relative va-
> lidity; that that which is recognized now as true has also its latent
> false side which will later manifest itself, just as that which is now
> regarded as false has also its true side by virtue of which it could
> previously have been regarded as true. One knows that what is
> maintained to be necessary is composed of sheer accidents and
> that the so-called accidental is the form behind which necessity
> hides itself—and so on.

From this comes a kind of pragmatism or empiricism: "The most telling refutation of this as of all other philosophical fancies is practice,
viz., experiment and industry." The final value is humanism: one must
"accept mutual relations based on reciprocal inclination between human beings, such as sex love, friendship, compassion, self-sacrifice,
etc.," while remaining wary of Feuerbach's "extravagant deification of
love." One accepts mortality with the human condition, and Engels
snarls at "the tedious notion of personal immortality."

In a footnote to *Ludwig Feuerbach*, Engels makes his final statement on his relation to Marx. He writes:

> Here I may be permitted to make a personal explanation.
> Lately repeated reference has been made to my share in this the-
> ory, and so I can hardly avoid saying a few words here to settle
> this particular point. I cannot deny that both before and during
> my forty years' collaboration with Marx I had a certain independ-
> ent share in laying the formulations, and more particularly in

elaborating the theory. But the greater part of its leading basic principles, particularly in the realm of economics and history, and, above all, its final, clear formulation, belong to Marx. What I contributed—at any rate with the exception of a few special studies—Marx could very well have done without me. What Marx accomplished I would not have achieved. Marx stood higher, saw farther, and took a wider and quicker view than all the rest of us. Marx was a genius; we others were at best talented. Without him the theory would not be what it is today. It therefore rightly bears his name.

In 1893, two years before his death, Engels wrote to Mehring:

> If I find anything to object to it is that you attribute more credit to me than I deserve, even if I count in everything which I might possibly have found out for myself—in time—but which Marx with his more rapid *coup d'oeil* and wider vision discovered much more quickly. When one has the good fortune to work for forty years with a man like Marx, one does not usually get the recognition one thinks one deserves during his lifetime. Then if the greater man dies, the lesser easily gets overrated, and this seems to me to be just my case at present; history will set all this right in the end and by that time one will be safely round the corner and know nothing more about anything.

In the final paragraph of *Ludwig Feuerbach*, Engels called, not for the overthrow of capitalism, but for "the understanding of the whole history of society." To the book he appended, for their first publication, Marx's 1845 Theses on Feuerbach, concluding "The philosophers have only *interpreted* the world in various ways; the point however is to *change* it." It was the neatest possible statement of how far he had come from that revolutionary optimism.

After *Ludwig Feuerbach*, Engels spent his remaining years tidying up. In 1890 he wrote to J. Bloch explaining the materialist conception of history. The letter concludes:

> Marx and I are ourselves partly to blame for the fact that younger writers sometimes lay more stress on the economic side than is due to it. We had to emphasize this main principle in opposition to our adversaries, who denied it, and we had not always the time, the place or the opportunity to allow the other elements involved in the interaction to come into their rights. But when it was a case of presenting a section of history, that is, of a practical application, the thing was different and there no error was possible. Unfortunately, however, it happens only too often that people think they have fully understood a theory and can apply it without more ado from the moment they have mastered its main principles, and those even not always correctly. And I cannot exempt many of the more recent 'Marxists' from this reproach,

for the most wonderful rubbish has been produced from this quarter too.

In his preface to the English translation of *The Condition of the Working Class in England in 1844*, issued in 1892, Engels wrote that conditions had greatly improved in the half-century since the book's time, "and glad and proud I am to have lived to see it." He explained:

> I have taken care not to strike out of the text the many prophecies, amongst others that of an imminent social revolution in England, which my youthful ardour induced me to venture upon.

In 1894, in an article in *Neue Zeit*, he criticizes the peasant program adopted by the Marseilles Congress of French Marxists with something of the acerbity Marx had shown toward the Gotha Program. "How easy and pleasant it is to keep on coasting once you are on the toboggan slide!" he writes, proposing an uncompromising stand that would leave the reactionary peasants to their natural spokesmen, the anti-Semites. In 1895 he wrote an introduction to a new edition of Marx's *The Class Struggles in France*, proclaiming boldly "But we, too, have been shown to have been wrong by history, which has revealed our point of view of that time to have been an illusion." He explains:

> History has proved us, and all who thought like us, wrong. It has made it clear that the state of economic development on the Continent at that time was not, by a long way, ripe for the removal of capitalist production.

Engels goes on to compare the communist movement with that "dangerous party of revolt," the early Christians (a subject he had been writing about with increasing fascination since Marx's death). The only effect of Roman persecution had been to ensure Christian triumph, and suddenly one day, after countless martyrdoms, Christianity was proclaimed the state religion. It was oddly where he had begun, and within three months, before he could negate his negation, Engels was dead.

FRAZER

In social studies, the evolutionist comparative method had achieved a kind of massive futility in the vast tomes of Frazer.

E. R. Leach, *Man and Culture*

JAMES GEORGE FRAZER was born in Glasgow on January 1, 1854. His father, Daniel Frazer, was an apothecary and justice of the peace, descended from a line of Free Church ministers. His mother, Katherine Brown, was descended from well-to-do Glasgow merchants who became country gentry. In his old age, when he wrote "Memories of My Parents," Frazer recalled his father as a strong-minded and devout man whom no one called "Dan," and his mother as loving and warm, dying in 1899 "with her arms resting on the volumes of my *Pausanias*." Frazer could not recall any of the children ever having been punished, adding: "Indeed they had no occasion to punish us, for we were dutiful and obedient children who never dreamed of questioning their authority or thwarting their wishes." The family was staunchly Presbyterian. They had daily worship, "the whole family and the servants kneeling devoutly," and Church twice on Sundays, followed by family hymn singing and a reading from an edifying book.

At the age of six or so James attended Mr. Munsie's school in Glasgow, learning nothing he could later remember. Shortly afterwards the Frazers moved out of town to Helensburgh, to a house at the mouth of the Gareloch looking across the Firth of Clyde. James attended Springfield Academy, then Larchfield Academy, which he recalled as his happiest schooldays and where he acquired a taste for classical studies. In November, 1869, almost sixteen, Frazer matriculated at Glasgow University as a candidate for the Master of Arts degree. He studied a rigidly fixed curriculum consisting of Greek and Latin, Mathematics, Natural Philosophy, Logic and Metaphysics, Moral Philosophy, and English Literature. "I have always been glad," he wrote in retrospect many years later, "that in my sixteenth year I was allowed no discretion, but was shepherded into the fold of knowledge by wiser and more experienced heads than my own." Here the Professor of Humanity, George Gilbert Ramsey, inspired Frazer to choose classical studies as his career. Two other teachers, John Veitch, the Professor of Logic and Metaphysics, and Lord Kelvin, whose physics lectures Frazer attended, were later acknowledged as giving his mind its permanent bias toward rationalism and exact law. At Glasgow University Frazer intended to compete in the Snell Exhibition, in which the winner received a scholarship to Balliol College at Oxford. His father was wary of the High Church tendencies of Oxford, Frazer later wrote, "and fearing to expose me to the contagion he sent me to Cambridge instead."

Late in 1873 Frazer competed for an entrance scholarship at Trinity College, Cambridge. He won it, and in the autumn of 1874 he

189

entered Trinity as a student. He never left Trinity. For his thesis on Plato's ideal theory in 1879, Frazer received a fellowship at Trinity, which was renewed three times, the last time for life. He qualified for the bar in accord with his father's wish and was admitted to the Middle Temple in 1881, but he never practised law. At Cambridge Frazer first became interested in anthropology through reading Tylor's *Primitive Culture*. This interest was greatly augmented in 1883 when Robertson Smith was appointed Reader in Arabic at Cambridge and became a member of the High Table at Trinity. Smith's views about the date of Deuteronomy had scandalized the Free Church of Scotland and caused his removal for heresy from the Chair of Hebrew at Aberdeen. He soon became friendly with Frazer, who regarded him as the greatest man he had ever known, after his father. As editor of the ninth edition of the *Encyclopaedia Britannica*, that monument of Scottish enlightenment, Smith commissioned articles on classical and anthropological subjects from Frazer. Frazer soon found that anthropology was his real interest, and he began collecting material for articles that turned into books, and books that turned into larger books.

His outer life was entirely without incident. "The facts of Frazer's life," writes his biographer R. Angus Downie, "consist essentially of a list of books." For more than fifty years, twelve or fifteen hours a day, seven days a week, Frazer read with steel pen in hand, copying out passages of anthropological interest into notebooks, or worked at compiling the notebooks into books. Only a relatively small amount of lecturing, walking and travel interrupted this lifetime of industry, in which Frazer literally read and wrote himself blind. In his "Memories of My Parents," looking back more than seventy years, Frazer writes of a dangerous flood in the stream in their garden during his childhood.

> We children had been playing on the banks of the swollen stream a few minutes before the catastrophe, but were saved from imminent death by the hurried and timely intervention of a kind friend. This was perhaps the nearest approach to an adventure which I have had in my uneventful life.

Frazer read books in Greek and Latin, French and German, Spanish, Italian and Dutch, in addition to English. He studied Hebrew at Cambridge, in a class with Jane Harrison, Francis Cornford (who married Darwin's granddaughter Frances), and A. B. Cook, although he did not get very far with it. As his fame increased, Frazer did more lecturing, although he was a poor public speaker and an indifferent lecturer, suffering terribly from stage fright.

Apart from reading, writing, editing and lecturing, the only events in Frazer's life were social and recreational. He kept up a vast correspondence, probably as enormous as Darwin's, with travelers and explorers, missionaries, anthropologists, colonial officials, in fact with anyone involved with primitive peoples anywhere in the world. Some of these correspondences turned into friendships, particularly those with Sir Baldwin Spencer and Canon John Roscoe. Apart from these, most of Frazer's social contacts were with Cambridge and Trinity scholars, first Smith, then a series of contemporaries and younger Fellows, among them A. E. Housman, who succeeded to Frazer's rooms in Whewell's Court. In 1884 Frazer took a walking tour of the Highlands with Smith and John Sutherland Black, and in 1890 a more melancholy trip taking the invalid Smith to Edinburgh. During vacations he travelled widely in Great Britain and parts of the continent, walking up to thirty miles a day. He got as far as Greece, where he sailed among the islands. Despite a life-long ambition, he never got to the Holy Land.

In 1896, at the age of forty-five, Frazer varied his uneventful life considerably by marrying Lilly Grove, a widow with a son and a daughter. She mothered him even more resolutely than Emma Darwin did her invalid husband. In 1901, Jane Harrison wrote acerbly to Lady Mary Murray:

> Mrs. Frazer (your double!) has been sitting on my bed for two hours, telling me 'who not to know,' i.e. who has not paid Mr. Frazer 'proper attention'! This is the price I pay for a few shy radiant moments under the Golden Bough.

Bronislaw Malinowski, who knew Frazer in the years after 1910, writes in his biographical appreciation:

> His mundane glory was largely due to the activities of Lady Frazer, who took upon herself the management of his worldly career. Personally, Frazer despised and detested the limelight and glare of public acclamation, which he endured somewhat grudgingly but with resignation. Lady Frazer's word was the last one. Those of us who came to know the capable, energetic, though somewhat redoubtable life companion of Frazer became as devoted to her as to him. Orders, titles, and honorary degrees apart, she also cooperated with him, had his books translated, and managed for him his extensive correspondence and his relations with other scholars. With all this Lady Frazer was unquestionably a puzzling element to most of Frazer's friends as well as in his position in the academic world.

The Frazers had no children. After their marriage they agreed that Frazer should be at work at the college every morning by eight, and he was, sometimes working until two the next morning and returning again at eight. Although Lilly Frazer sometimes traveled on the continent with her daughter, leaving her husband in Cambridge, and he deserted her each working day, the Frazers were extremely close, and Frazer had no other intimate friend after his marriage.

In 1908 Frazer was appointed to the chair of Social Anthropology at the University of Liverpool. In 1914, he was knighted. In 1921 his friends established the annual Frazer Lectureship in Social Anthropology in his honor (Housman delivering the Address). In 1925 he was awarded the Order of Merit. He received many other honors, many more than Darwin, refusing only professorships and chairs that required lecturing (after the Liverpool experience), and turning down the editorship of the Loeb Classical Library on the grounds that it would take him away from his work. In the 1930s Frazer's sight began to fail and by 1936 it was too far gone for him to read and write. He continued to work, relying on a series of secretaries, until 1939, when he became paralyzed. A remarkable and devastating portrait of Frazer's last years was published in *The New Statesman and Nation* for January 13, 1951, entitled "Autumn of an Anthropologist." It is by Sarah Campion, who, in the spring of 1940, a year before his death, served briefly as Frazer's secretary. She describes Sir James and Lady Frazer, he quite blind and paralyzed, she stone deaf, seated in two thronelike chairs in Cambridge, holding hands. Miss Campion's principal job was reading aloud to Frazer. She writes:

> These readings were always from his own works, and he would listen with the greatest attention, as if hearing for the first time the words of a promising colleague. His favourite tale was that of the Witch of Endor, taken from his own version of the Old Testament.

On May 7, 1941, when Frazer was eighty-seven, his heart failed. Lady Frazer died a few hours later. A joint funeral was held for them in Trinity Chapel, and they were buried in one grave in St. Giles Cemetery in Cambridge.

The Volcano Underfoot

J AMES GEORGE FRAZER's first book, *The Growth of Plato's Ideal Theory*, is a dissertation written in competition for a fellowship at Trinity College, Cambridge, in 1879. Frazer, who had taken his degree at Trinity in 1878, won the fellowship, which developed into a lifetime of study at the college. The dissertation was not published until 1930, when Frazer issued it with a preface apologizing for neglecting his Platonic studies in the half century since. *The Growth of Plato's Ideal Theory* had effectively announced their suspension with:

> I had intended to examine in equal detail the later dialogues in which Plato expands and modifies his theory of Ideas, but the results reached by the preceding investigations are not sufficiently encouraging to induce me to carry out the plan.

Despite the "growth" of the title, Frazer is more interested in Plato's decay, tracing "that gigantic and yet splendid error" whereby his epistemology became ontology, or, "Plato's fundamental error, the bestowal of objective existence on subjective abstractions." Plato's theory of knowledge is "the more manly and hopeful" than Wordsworth's, but eventually "the theory broke down." Frazer concludes with a greater metaphor of disenchantment:

> The fact is, there is no use mincing matters, the Ideal world has collapsed; the sky has fallen and down tumble the Ideas, then pick themselves up and walk about trying to look as like ordinary beings as possible. They drop their titles of honour; would you believe it, there is not an *auto*- anything among them, they are plain Justice, Motion, and so on. It is true that in an earlier part of the dialogue they still dwell aloft, for we find the Eleatic stranger holloing to them, and their answer comes faintly back from the height. They had been warned before by Parmenides to come down, and now the remorseless stranger lays the axe to the root of the tree, and it is all over with the Ideas. And we shall meet them no more in Plato. Half smilingly, half tearfully, we bid them farewell. So fade the dreams of youth.

Frazer next published articles in the ninth edition of the *Encyclopaedia Britannica*. The earlier volumes were already complete, but he wrote on topics from "Penates" to "Totemism" between 1885 and 1888. These articles, some of which appear in the eleventh edition in revised form, display many of Frazer's qualities and later preoccupations. Primarily, they exhibit the comparative method. Thus the article on "Penates" relates them as "a remnant of fetishism or animism" to analogous customs of the Hindus, Germans, Lapps, Russians, Serbians and Chinese; the article on "Saturn" finds parallel myths in New Zealand, India, and China, and among the Bushmen, Kaffres, Basuto, Indians of Guiana, and Eskimos; the article on "Pericles" finds Whigs and Tories among the Athenians, and identifies Ceramicus as "the Westminster of Athens." Frazer's later scenic preoccupation appears in his one article on a place, "Praeneste." "The modern town of Palestrina, a collection of narrow and filthy alleys, stands on the terraces once occupied by the temple of Fortune," he writes, but from a nearby hill a "magnificent view" may still be seen.

Frazer's articles stand out even in the ninth *Britannica* for the boldness and vigor of their language. In the article on "Province" he writes of the "two classes of harpies joined in wringing the uttermost farthing from the unhappy provincials." Frazer compares "the excesses of these blood-suckers" with, in modern times, "the blind rapacity which has turned the empire of the Turk from a garden into a wilderness." A reference to Gibbon in the same article shows that he had already found his stylist. By the time he got to "Thesmophoria" in 1888, Frazer was an authority on obscene and curious rites, as his two dozen learned footnotes make clear. The article concludes with a tiny forecast of *The Golden Bough*:

> The Thesmophoria would thus form one of that class of rites, widely spread in Western Asia and in Europe, in which the main feature appears to be lamentation for the annual decay of vegetation or a rejoicing at its revival. This seems to have been the root, *e. g.*, of the lamentations for Adonis and Attis. See W. Mannhardt, *Antike Wald- und Feld-Kulte*.

The article on "Taboo," written the same year, focusses on the fundamental duality of the magical that was to underlie all of Frazer's later work. He writes:

> On the other hand, it is true that the opposition of sacred and accursed, clean and unclean, which plays so important a part in the later history of religion, did in fact arise by differentiation from the single root idea of taboo, which includes and reconciles them both and by reference to which alone their history and mutual relations are intelligible.

"It was a moot question with the Greeks," he adds, "whether the Jews abhorred or worshipped pigs."

In 1884 Frazer had revised an edition of Sallust, his first classical editing. From then on he published widely in periodicals, on classical, literary, and folklore subjects. Almost all of these articles were collected in *Sir Roger de Coverley and Other Literary Pieces* (1920) and its amplified edition *The Gorgon's Head and Other Literary Pieces* (1927), *Garnered Sheaves* (1931), and *Creation and Evolution in Primitive Cosmogonies and Other Pieces* (1935). Frazer changed the titles of his articles, the titles of his collections, and reprinted articles in a number of forms in addition to using them in later books, but the mare's nest has been unravelled up to 1934 in an excellent bibliography by Theodore Bestermann.

The most important of Frazer's early articles is "On certain Burial Customs as illustrative of the Primitive Theory of the Soul," read before the Anthropological Institute in 1885, printed in its *Journal* the next year, and reprinted in *Garnered Sheaves*. It displays Frazer's fully developed method, and in its appended summary of the discussion of the paper at the meeting, the final ingredient of his theoretical system is acknowledged.

> Dr. E. B. Tylor remarked that Mr. Frazer's original and ingenious treatment of the evidence must materially advance the study of animistic funeral customs. . . . Dr. Tylor concluded by expressing his satisfaction at the excellent results of Mr. Frazer's study of classical authors, not as mere ancient texts, but as repertories of real facts full of anthropological value. . . .
>
> Mr. Frazer, in reply, expressed his deep gratification at the interest which Mr. Tylor had expressed in his paper. It was the writings of Mr. Tylor which had first interested him in anthropology, and the perusal of them had marked an epoch in his life.

Tylor's *Primitive Culture*, which he read as an undergraduate, had introduced Frazer to anthropology, but to a specific sort of anthropology, the application to the history of culture of Darwin's evolution by natural selection. Frazer refers to Tylor in a later book as "my revered master," but the synthesizing nature of Frazer's mind kept Tylor from ever being more than one such. R. R. Marett strikes a fairer balance in his 1927 Frazer Lecture: "It is to be observed that he is vilified as the intellectual bondslave of Tylor, as if his association with Robertson Smith had in no wise affected the orientation of his thought." By 1885 Frazer had woven together Mannhardt's inductive study of cults, Tylor's evolutionary anthropology, Smith's comparative religion, and Gibbon's irony. He had a method he was to use for the next half century.

In 1887 Frazer published his first book and his first pamphlet. The book was the tiny volume *Totemism*, reprinted as a small part of *Totemism and Exogamy* in 1910. *Totemism* was the first of a long line of Frazer's works to burst its original confines. It had been written as a *Britannica* article, grew too long, and Smith had it published as a book, using an abridgement for the encyclopaedia. The subject was

very important to Smith, who believed totemic brotherhood to underlie Semitic religion, and thus Christianity. He wrote to J. S. Black: "I
have taken much personal pains with it, guiding Frazer carefully in his
treatment." Frazer disparages *Totemism* in the preface to the later re-
print: "The book comprised little more than a classified collection of
facts, for when I wrote it I had as yet formed no theory either of
totemism or exogamy." *Totemism*, however, is considerably more than
Frazer says. It brings together the theoretical researches of Bachofen,
McLennan, Mannhardt, and others; as well as the new field work of
Fison and Howitt among the Australians, Morgan among the Iroquois,
and other pioneer ethnographers; along with the classical authors
Tylor had congratulated Frazer on using. It classifies totemism into
minute subdivisions, and explores each classification at length. *Totemism* gives an origin theory for some of these varieties, but on the larger
problem, after dismissing all the theories, Frazer concludes: "No satisfactory explanation of the origin of totemism has yet been given."

Tylor's general principle, that the functional cultural usages of
earlier stages survive as "fossils" in later stages, is the book's underlying theory. Thus: "Oaths were originally ordeals, and some of
them are of totem origin"; the magic obstacles of folk tales suggest
descent from totemic origin myths; and so forth. Social institutions are
seen in a great life cycle. Frazer writes:

> Combining this important evidence as to the growth of
> totems with the evidence already noticed of the process by which
> clans tend to become phratries, we get a view of the growth,
> maturity, and decay of totems. As subtotems they are growing; as
> clan totems they are grown; as subphratric and phratric totems
> they are in successive stages of decay.

In 1899, in the *Fortnightly Review*, Frazer was to write of Australia:

> Here, then, in the secluded heart of the most secluded continent
> the scientific inquirer might reasonably expect to find the savage
> in his very lowest depths, to detect humanity in the chrysalis
> stage, to mark the first blind gropings of our race after freedom
> and light.

As the identification of "our race" suggests, *Totemism*'s embracing vision is of brotherhood, of Ainus with bears, of Samoans with cuttlefish, of Australians with kangaroos, of Omahas with buffalo, of all with
each other and with us. Do not married persons of the Booandik tribe
in South Australia "talk to each other in a low whining voice and use
words different from those in common use," for all the world as though
they were British couples?

The 1887 pamphlet is *Questions on the Manners, Customs, Religions, Superstitions, &c., of Uncivilized or Semi-Civilized Peoples*, revised and enlarged in 1907 as *Questions on the Customs, Beliefs, and
Languages of Savages*. In its enlarged form it is a pamphlet containing

507 questions (many more than Marx's *Questionnaire*), some with multiple parts. Frazer's preface explains that "the questions make no pretence to be exhaustive," and that:

> I would point out that they are intended not so much to be put directly to the savage as to indicate to the civilised enquirer in the field those subjects on which investigators at home would be glad to have information.

The preface makes Frazer's assumptions about primitives very clear. They are not to be asked leading questions, not because it would be unscientific, but because they would politely give the answer they think is expected, having a characteristic "indifference of savage man to abstract truth." From this absurdity follows the sensible suggestion: "So every one who questions savages as to their ways should make it a rule to let them speak as much and himself as little as possible." The questions themselves are neutral and objective, but they cluster thickly around belief and custom, and delve for such Frazerian concerns as totemism, rites of passage, and scapegoats. There are hardly any questions about material culture, and the concept of acculturation, or any historical change in the culture, is entirely missing.

Primitive culture is assumed to be a timeless entity, consisting of social organization and traditional customs, with accompanying beliefs. The section on "relationship" asks for kinship terms rather than the actual kinship organization, probably assuming that the "savage" would not understand it, but that it could be reconstructed from his terms. The question of motivation is, however, continually raised. A typical pair of questions is: "Does he visit his wife only by stealth for some time after marriage? If so, why?" The preface acknowledges the help of such field ethnographers as A. C. Haddon, W. H. R. Rivers, and the Rev. John Roscoe, in formulating the questions, and they are probably typical of the ethnography of the time, with two significant exceptions. No cross-cultural comparisons are suggested, those being the province of the library anthropologist like Frazer who has access to materials from different cultures, and no historical reconstructions are requested, those being a matter of evolutionary hierarchy better worked out theoretically.

Between the two editions of the pamphlet, Frazer worked at one of his little articles on custom, this one on a curious ancient priesthood at Nemi in Italy. It oddly refused to stay within the confines of a magazine article, and soon became a focus for many of his preoccupations: totemism and taboo, fertility cults and rites of passage, scapegoats and sacrificial gods. In 1890, the first installment of the material was published as *The Golden Bough: A Study in Comparative Religion*, in two volumes. It will be discussed in a later chapter, with its subsequent enlargements. Before the publication of the first edition of *The Golden Bough*, Frazer had been an obscure classical scholar who dabbled in anthropology. After it he was merely a less obscure classical scholar who dabbled in anthropology. No one immediately hailed him as the Darwin of comparative religion. Joseph Jacobs reviewed the book with three other books, among them Smith's *The Religion of the Semites*, in *Folk-Lore*. He finds Smith's book "perhaps the more important," although Frazer's shows much more literary skill. Jacobs concludes that *The Golden Bough* is really "a series of monographs on folk-lore and mythological subjects" rather than a unified work, and that its facts outweigh its theories. In at least one case, the first edition of *The Golden Bough* had an effect that was primarily decorative. It was read to Tennyson while his portrait was being painted by Watts, and Watts worked a bit of mistletoe into the background.

In 1894 Smith died, and Frazer wrote an obituary notice for *The Fortnightly Review*, reprinted in *The Gorgon's Head*. It gave him an opportunity for his first systematic evaluation of the comparative method. Frazer writes:

> The method which in his hands proved so powerful an instrument in opening up new and rich veins of thought was what is known as the comparative method. As few, perhaps, even of educated readers have a definite notion of the principles of the comparative method in its applications to the study of religion, and of its bearing on many profound practical problems which are pressing on us for solution now, and which loom still larger in the future, some general observations on the subject may not be out of place here, in so far as they enable the reader to apprehend more clearly Robertson Smith's place in the rapidly moving stream of contemporary thought.
>
> The idea of regarding the religions of the world not dogmatically but historically—in other words, not as systems of truth or falsehood to be demonstrated or refuted, but as phenomena of consciousness to be studied like any other aspect of human nature—is one which seems hardly to have suggested itself before the nineteenth century. Certainly the systematic development of the conception is a product of that unparalleled analytic or scientific activity which in the course of the present century has enlarged enormously the boundaries of knowledge. Now when, laying aside as irrelevant to the purpose in hand the question of the truth or falsehood of religious beliefs, and the question of the wisdom or folly of religious practices, we examine side by side the religions of different races and ages, we find that, while they differ from each other in many particulars, the resemblances between them are numerous and fundamental, and that they mutually illustrate and explain each other, the distinctly stated faith and circumstantial ritual of one race often clearing up ambiguities in the faith and practice of other races. Thus the comparative study of religion soon forces on us the conclusion that the course of religious evolution has been, up to a certain point, very similar among all men, and that no one religion, in all

events in its earlier stages, can be fully understood without a comparison of it with many others.

Regarded thus far, the comparative study of religion possesses a purely historical or antiquarian interest. It explains what the religious beliefs and practices of mankind have been and are, but it supplies no answer to the questions, Are these beliefs true? Are these practices wise? But though it cannot answer these questions directly, it often furnishes us indirectly with at least a probable answer to them; for it proves that many religious doctrines and practices are based on primitive conceptions which most civilized and educated men have long agreed in abandoning as mistaken. From this it is a natural and often a probable inference that doctrines so based are false, and that practices so based are foolish. It should be observed, however, that this inference, though natural and often probable, is never necessary and certain, ...

Frazer goes on to explain that the comparative study of religion "calls for a reconsideration of the speculative basis of ethics as well as of theology." Smith's qualities, with which he advanced the comparative study of religion, were "great fertility of ideas and a vivid historical imagination, fed by a memory stored with a prodigious array of facts and kept under strict control by an unvarying soundness and sobriety of judgement." Finally, Smith saw "that religion cannot properly be isolated from the other sides of human life and treated as if it were independent of them." It was, altogether, a perfect prescription for the author of *The Golden Bough*. In a tribute to Smith published in *The Quarterly Review* in 1911, Salomon Reinach wrote that Smith's ultimate achievement was *"Genuit Frazerum."*

The next year Frazer published a book with an unprepossessing title, *Passages of the Bible Chosen for Their Literary Beauty and Interest*. The preface explains that Frazer is somewhat handicapped in his approach to the Hebrew text "since I know no Hebrew" (by 1918, when he published *Folk-Lore in the Old Testament*, Frazer had read the Old Testament through in Hebrew, and the footnotes show him to be an aspiring textual critic). *Passages of the Bible* at first seems literary-amateurish, another Victorian book of Posies. The preface proposes the reading of the Authorized Version "simply for the sake of the enjoyment which as pure literature it is fitted to afford," and states Frazer's purpose: "that a service might be rendered to lovers of good literature by disengaging these gems from their setting." The notes are full of literary comparisons. For the Song of Deborah, Frazer quotes Virgil, Burke, Napier, Macaulay, Heine, Scott, and "Sir Patrick Spens." Notes on Canticles quote other ballads, Goethe, Longfellow, Hood, Burns, and a long list of ancient writers. This is one form of the comparative method; for the more familiar one, the notes cite parallels from the folklore of the world for Bible legends and customs.

The viewpoint is for the most part old-fashioned rationalist. On flood legends: "The origin of all such legends is to be sought, partly in the recollection of real but local floods, partly in inferences drawn from the discovery of shells and fossil fish on the tops of hills and other spots remote from the sea." [1] *Historical Geography of the Holy Land* is quoted to show that the destruction of Sodom and Gomorrah was a spontaneous explosion of natural gas in the bituminous soil, and that a pillar of rock salt was transformed into the legend of Lot's wife. One note says bluntly: " 'Behemoth and leviathan,' i.e. the hippopotamus and the crocodile."

The only quality that raises *Passages of the Bible* above the level of its fellows is Frazer's dramatistic vision of the Bible, which makes it, not a scrapbook of lyric beauties, but a sequence of dramatic actions and agons. The preface concludes:

> Apart from all questions of its religious and historical import, which do not here concern us, the Bible is an epic, if not a history, of the world; or, to change the metaphor, it unrolls a vast panorama in which the ages of the world move before us in a long train of solemn imagery, from the creation of the earth and the heavens onward to the final passing away of all this material universe and the coming of a new heaven and a new earth wherein shall dwell righteousness. Against this gorgeous background, this ever shifting scenery, now bright with the hues of heaven, now lurid with the glare of hell, we see mankind strutting and playing their little part on the stage of history. We see them taken from the dust and returning to the dust; we see the rise and fall of empires: we see great cities, now the hive of busy multitudes, now silent and desolate, a den of wild beasts. All life's fever is there—its loves and hopes and joys, its high endeavours, its suffering and sin and sorrow. And then, last scene of all, we see the great white throne and the endless multitude gathered before it: we hear the final doom pronounced; and as the curtain falls we catch a glimpse of the fires of hell and the glories of heaven—a vision of a world (how different from this!) where care and sin and sorrow shall be no more, where the saints shall rest from their labours, and where God himself shall wipe away all tears from their eyes. This may not be science and history, but is at least an impressive pageant, a stately drama: without metaphor, it is noble literature; and like all noble literature it is fitted to delight, to elevate, and to console.

Frazer liked that passage so much that he reprinted it as a prose gem in *Sir Roger de Coverley* and in *The Gorgon's Head*.

In 1898 Frazer published a masterpiece of scholarship, his six-

---

[1] It would be hard to find a neater conjunction of the two theories of myth chiefly opposed to the ritual theory with which Frazer was mainly identified— the euhemerist view that myths derive from history, and the cognitionist view that they are erroneous scientific speculation.

volume edition of Pausanias's *Description of Greece,* of which the first
volume is Frazer's translation and the other five are commentary, maps,
and scholarly apparatus. Frazer reprinted the introduction and selec-
tions from his commentary as *Pausanias and Other Greek Sketches* in
1900, and reprinted it again as *Studies in Greek Scenery, Legend and
History* in 1917. This little book is not so much a commentary on
Pausanias as Frazer's own guidebook to Greece. His preface says:
"Slight and fragmentary as these sketches are, I am not without hope
that they may convey to readers who have never seen Greece something of the eternal charm of its scenery." The tone is passionately
phil-Hellenic: "No other people has exerted so deep and abiding an
influence on the course of modern civilisation as the Greeks"; Greece
is "freedom" where Macedonia is "slavery." Opposed to the glories of
Mycenae and Athens there was the shabbiness of Doric Sparta:

> On the other side we see an open unfortified city with insignifi-
> cant buildings, where art and poetry never flourished, where gold
> and silver were banned, and where even the kings prided them-
> selves on the meanness of their attire.

Modern Greece is the triumph of those nineteenth-century Spartans
the Turks, "a few dirty hamlets." At a "fairy grotto," Frazer writes,
"But alas! the women who may be seen any day washing their dirty
linen at the mouth of the cave break the spell."

The comparative method is everywhere. Of a Greek religious
custom: "A ruder conception of religion than is revealed by this
practice of adoring and feeding a staff it might be hard to discover
among the lowest fetish-worshippers of Western Africa." Aristomenes
is "the William Tell or Sir William Wallace of Messenia," Pausanias
"the Camden of ancient Greece," the Minyans of Orchomenus are
"the Dutchmen of antiquity," for miraculous Greek battles there are
parallels with Scotland and Mexico.

The dominant imaginative organization of *Pausanias and Other
Greek Sketches* is what Kenneth Burke would call the scene-act ratio,
similarly the imaginative core of *The Golden Bough* (Pausanias had
seen the grim priest in his sacred grove at Aricia!) Frazer reports
the scenery in a tone of personal testimony very like Darwin's: "Perhaps I may be allowed to say that having repeatedly sailed along the
coast in question I can testify from personal experience. . . ." Certain
scenes at certain times have fitnesses for certain acts: "It was when the
sunset glow was on Hymettus that Socrates drained the poisoned cup";
"The scene, if it indeed be so" of the sacrifice of Iphigenia at Aulis
"was somewhat bleak and cheerless as I saw it under a leaden sky on a
dull November afternoon"; "On a grey November morning, with the
mists down on the distant mountains," the plain of Chaeronea "wears
a cheerless aspect that well becomes a battlefield where a nation's
freedom was lost." The play enacted against these backdrops is once
more a tragedy. It is neither Darwin's tragedy of natural selection nor

202 FRAZER

Marx's of proletarian revolution, but a new historical tragedy of the destruction of civilization by barbarism. Frazer writes:

> It is not indeed to be supposed that the Dorians swept over Greece in one unbroken wave of conquest. The tide of invasion probably ebbed and flowed; raids were met and repelled, but were followed by incursions of fresh swarms of invaders, the newcomers steadily gaining ground, encroaching on and enveloping the ancient Mycenaean kingdoms till, the last barrier giving way before them, the capitals themselves were stormed, their treasures plundered, and the palaces given to the flames. The conflict between civilisation and barbarism, the slow decline of the former and the gradual triumph of the latter, may have lasted many years. It is thus that many, if not most, permanent conquests have been effected. It was thus that the Saxons step by step ousted the Britons, and the Danes obtained a footing in England; it was thus that the Turks slowly strangled the Byzantine empire. Events like the fall of Constantinople and the expulsion of the Moors from Granada are only the last scenes in tragedies which have been acting for centuries.

Frazer defines his ideal of prose style in attacking Pausanias. He writes:

> The literary style of Pausanias is no exception to the rule that the style of a writer reflects the character of the man. Pausanias was neither a great man nor a great writer. He was an honest, laborious, plodding man of plain good sense, without either genius or imagination, and his style is a faithful mirror of his character. It is plain and unadorned, yet heavy and laboured, as if the writer had had to cast about for the proper words and then fit them painfully together like the pieces in a Chinese puzzle. There is a sense of strain and effort about it. The sentences are devoid of rhythm and harmony. They do not march, but hobble and shamble and shuffle along. At the end of one of them the reader is not let down easily by a graceful cadence, a dying fall; he is tripped up suddenly and left sprawling, till he can pull himself together, take breath, and grapple with the next. It is a loose, clumsy, ill-jointed, ill-compacted, rickety, ramshackle style, without ease or grace or elegance of any sort.

Pausanias tries hard—"Such attention is a simple duty which every author owes to his readers"—and "he occasionally rises to a fair level of literary merit." Meanwhile Frazer too tries hard, with more success. Many of the book's gorgeous passages are dramatic actions called forth by the scenes. The imaginative reconstruction of the performance of the mysteries in describing the great Hall of Initiation at Eleusis is typical:

> Suddenly the curtain rose and revealed the vast hall brilliantly illuminated, with the gorgeously attired actors in the sacred drama

moving mazily in solemn procession or giddy dance out and in amongst the forest of columns that rose from the floor of the hall, while the strains of grave or voluptuous music filled the air. Then, when all was over, the curtain would as suddenly descend, leaving the spectators in darkness and silence, with nothing but the memory of the splendid pageant that had burst upon them and vanished like a dream.

If Frazer's vision seems to have more in common with the Radio City Music Hall than with anything that could have transpired at Eleusis, it is nevertheless an equivalent for him of the initiatory experience, as the mountain-citadel of Aliphera inspired him to recite, not a lyric from the Greek Anthology, but Keats' "Ode on a Grecian Urn." In short, by 1900 Frazer had developed an individual method and style, had a vision of the menace of barbarism and a dramatic scene in the sacred grove in Aricia. It was time to embody his myth in other rites.

THE second edition of *The Golden Bough* appeared in 1900, expanded to three volumes, with the material approximately doubled and many new theories and interpretations. One could see how Frazer had grown in importance over a decade by the different treatment the editions got in *Folk-Lore*. In 1890, Jacobs had reviewed the book as one of four; in the issue of June, 1901, *Folk-Lore* printed eight different reviews of the new edition by prominent folklorists and anthropologists, including the president of the society and the editor and the publisher of the journal. Contention was violent, particularly from Rabbi Moses Gaster, who found Frazer's hypothesis of ritual murder at ancient Purim festivities infuriating. Charlotte S. Burne, the editor, closed the discussion with the suggestion: "We may even think the Golden Bough itself too slender a twig to sustain the weight of learning hung upon it." With a monumental stubbornness that, if nothing else did, would put him in the company of Darwin, Marx, and Freud, Frazer went back to assembling more material for a third edition.

In 1905 he delivered a series of lectures at Trinity on "The Sacred Character and Magical Function of Kings in Early Society." They consist of new material from the forthcoming third edition of *The Golden Bough*, and were published separately that year as *Lectures on the Early History of the Kingship*. The material need not detain us, since it later appeared in *The Golden Bough* almost unchanged, but Frazer began his first lecture with an eight-page discussion of the science of anthropology, which was not reprinted in the big book, and which is of great interest. Here Frazer defines his field as the history of institutions, "an important branch" of the tree of anthropology, "the study of man." He writes:

Now, if we are to pursue this study in a scientific spirit, we must endeavour to investigate the beliefs and customs of mankind with the same rigorous impartiality with which, for example, the zoologist investigates the habits of ants and bees.[2]

Along with the new insistence on scientific rigor comes a new humility. "Now anthropology in general and the history of institutions in particular are still in the collecting stage," Frazer writes. "The prime want of the study is not so much theories as facts." He continues:

The most urgent need of anthropology at present is to procure accurate accounts of the existing customs and ideas of savages before they have disappeared. When these have been obtained, when the records existing in our libraries have been fully scrutinised, and when the whole body of information has been classified and digested, the philosophic historian will be able to formulate, with a fair degree of probability, those general laws which have shaped the intellectual, social, and moral evolution of mankind.

That will not be done in our day. The great thinkers, the Newtons and Darwins of anthropology, will come after us. It is our business to prepare for them by collecting, sifting, and arranging the records in order that when, in the fulness of time, the master-mind shall arise and survey them, he may be able to detect at once that unity in multiplicity, that universal in the particulars, which has escaped us. The duty at present incumbent on the investigator is therefore to rake together the facts, whether, like some of my friends, he goes for them at the peril of his life to savage lands, or merely unearths them at his ease from the dust of libraries. The time has gone by when dreamers like Rousseau could reconstruct the history of society out of their own minds, and their dreams could be accepted as visions of a golden age to come, their voices listened to like angel trumpets heralding the advent of a new heaven and a new earth. It is not for the anthropologists of to-day to blow these high notes, to build these gay castles in the clouds. His task is the soberer, duller one of laying, in the patient accumulation of facts, the foundations of a structure more solid and enduring than the glittering fantasies of Rousseau's dream.

Some hypotheses are necessary even to the compiler, Frazer writes, "but these provisional hypotheses should be held very loosely; we must always be ready to modify or discard them when they are found to conflict with fresh evidence." Almost the only hypothesis Frazer does not hold loosely in the discussion, but takes as the theoretical basis of his approach, is evolution, "the intellectual, social, and moral evolution of mankind" above. He writes:

[2] We may be amused to recall that Dr. Kinsey turned to studying human sexuality with the same rigorous objectivity he had previously devoted to the study of gall-wasps.

The continuity of human development has been such that most, if not all, of the great institutions which still form the framework of civilised society have their roots in savagery, and have been handed down to us in these later days through countless generations, assuming new outward forms in the process of transmission, but remaining in their inmost core substantially unchanged. Such, for example, to take a few conspicuous instances, are the institution of private property, the institution of marriage, the institution of war, and the worship of a god. Differences of opinion may exist, and have existed, as to the precise value of the inheritance; as to the fact of it there can be none.

Lectures on the Early History of the Kingship shows Frazer engaged in the process of modifying his theory on the basis of fresh evidence or argument. The preface acknowledges the influence of A. B. Cook in forcing him to reconsider his theory of the Arician kingship, by convincing him that the temple at Nemi had had a sacred fire. He now puts the kingship at Nemi as a typical example of the evolution of kingship, choosing it for "the greater definiteness and precision which we attain by considering an abstract problem in a concrete form." The question it raises "can only be adequately answered by the comparative method." One of the new field ethnographers Frazer cites for a fact is Franz Boas, writing on the Eskimo of Baffin Land in 1901. Boas was only four years younger than Frazer, had been to Baffin Land as early as 1883, and had been publishing for two decades, but his is the characteristic voice of twentieth-century anthropology, as Frazer's is of nineteenth. Frazer's plea to stop generalizing until more evidence is in, and his concept of the primary task as getting accurate accounts of primitive peoples before they disappear, are word for word what Boas was saying and continued to say all his life, across the Atlantic. There is no evidence that Frazer was familiar with any of Boas' theoretical writings. Frazer reached the Boas position in 1905, and quickly departed from it, in each case for reasons we do not know.

In 1908 Frazer was appointed to the chair of Social Anthropology at the University of Liverpool. His inaugural lecture, *The Scope of Social Anthropology*, was published later that year. It shows a considerable falling away from the ideal of empiricism and the tone of humility in the earlier statement. Now anthropology is defined in aggressively Darwinian terms, its aim "to follow as far as may be the evolution of human thought and institutions from the earliest times." Frazer divides social anthropology into two departments, "one of which embraces the customs and beliefs of savages, while the other includes such relics of these customs and beliefs as have survived in the thought and institutions of more cultured peoples." He calls them "the study of savagery" and "the study of folklore." Custom and belief are now "mental variations," their origin "just as obscure as in the origin of those physical variations on which, if biologists are right, depends the evolution of species, and with it the possibility of progress." In this evolution of custom and belief, "the strongest at last prevails, the fittest survives." The aim of anthropology is "discovering the general laws which have regulated human history in the past, and which, if nature is really uniform, may be expected to regulate it in the future." Frazer would like to limit social anthropology, or at least his concern with it, to "the origin, or rather the rudimentary phases, the infancy and childhood, of human society."

With study should come some measure of prediction and control, and "it may reasonably be hoped that a deeper and wider acquaintance with the past history of mankind will in time enable our statesmen to mould the destiny of the race in fairer forms than we of this generation shall live to see." The methods used resemble Darwin's embryology and palaeontology. Frazer writes:

> The study might accordingly be described as the embryology of human thought and institutions, or, to be more precise, as that inquiry which seeks to ascertain, first, the beliefs and customs of savages, and, second, the relics of these beliefs and customs which have survived like fossils among peoples of higher culture.

"In short, the definition assumes that civilisation has always and everywhere been evolved out of savagery," Frazer adds, and "if any one disputes it I do not think it worth while to argue with him." "By comparison with civilised man the savage represents an arrested or rather retarded stage of social development," Frazer explains, although this retardation is not absolute but relative to us: "they are not primitive by comparison with truly primaeval man." The two limitations Frazer now accepts are that the remote prehistoric past and the improved future are alike inaccessible. "About the social conditions of primaeval man, I repeat, we know absolutely nothing, and it is vain to speculate," he says of the first. Of the second:

> But if you wish to shatter the social fabric, you must not expect your professor of Social Anthropology to aid and abet you. He is no seer to discern, no prophet to foretell a coming heaven on earth, no mountebank with a sovran remedy for every ill, no Red Cross Knight to head a crusade against misery and want, against disease and death, against all the horrid spectres that war on poor humanity. It is for others with higher notes and nobler natures than his to sound the charge and lead it in this Holy War.

Frazer's sidenote adds at that point: "At least the present lecturer limits himself to these phases."

The imaginative design underlying this abstract theory and dramatizing it into immediacy is a vision of the thin veneer of civilization over savagery. Superstitions are "transmitted from truly savage ancestors through many generations of outwardly though not really civilised descendants." "The smooth surface of cultured society is sapped and mined by superstition," Frazer writes, adding:

Only those whose studies have led them to investigate the subject are aware of the depth to which the ground beneath our feet is thus, as it were, honeycombed by unseen forces. We appear to be standing on a volcano which may at any moment break out in smoke and fire to spread ruin and devastation among the gardens and palaces of ancient culture wrought so laboriously by the hands of many generations. After looking on the ruined Greek temples of Paestum and contrasting them with the squalor and savagery of the Italian peasantry, Renan said 'I trembled for civilisation, seeing it so limited, built on so weak a foundation, resting on so few individuals even in the country where it is dominant.'

When the savagery of "the ignorant and foolish multitude" is not a volcano underfoot, it is the sea around us: "The surface of society, like that of the sea, is in perpetual motion; its depths, like those of the ocean, remain almost unmoved." Primitive peoples are thus a priceless clue to our own inner natures, a record we cannot afford to lose. "The savage is a human document," Frazer writes, but "many savages have either been totally exterminated or so changed by contact with Europeans that it is no longer possible to obtain trustworthy information as to their old habits and traditions." Frazer's final appeal in the essay is for expeditions to study our perishing brothers, in a blare of metaphor:

For soon, very soon, the opportunities which we still enjoy will be gone for ever. In another quarter of a century probably there will be little or nothing of the old savage life left to record. The savage, such as we may still see him, will then be as extinct as the dodo. The sands are fast running out: the hour will soon strike: the record will be closed: the book will be sealed. And how shall we of this generation look when we stand at the bar of posterity arraigned on a charge of high treason to our race, we who neglected to study our perishing fellow-men, but who sent out costly expeditions to observe the stars and to explore the barren ice-bound regions of the poles, as if the polar ice would melt and the stars would cease to shine when we are gone? Let us awake from our slumber, let us light our lamps, let us gird up our loins.

What is surely Frazer's most curious book was published in 1909. Entitled *Psyche's Task: A Discourse Concerning the Influence of Superstitions on the Growth of Institutions*, it is nothing less than a defense of the volcano and the depths of the sea by a very reluctant barrister. The book was reissued in 1913, enlarged with additional examples, and it is from the second edition that I quote. The book's title epigraph is from Milton's *Areopagitica*:

Good and evil we know in the field of this world grow up together almost inseparably; and the knowledge of good is so involved and interwoven with the knowledge of evil and in so many cunning resemblances hardly to be discerned, that those confused seeds, which were imposed on Psyche as an incessant labour to cull out and sort asunder, were not more intermixt.

The dedication is: "To all who are engaged in Psyche's task of sorting out the seeds of good from the seeds of evil I dedicate this discourse." The book's bold thesis is that superstition is not an unmitigated evil, but that "among certain races and at certain stages of evolution some social institutions which we all, or most of us, believe to be beneficial have partially rested on a basis of superstition."

Frazer chooses four secular institutions as examples and announces that he will attempt to prove the following propositions:

I. Among certain races and at certain times superstition has strengthened the respect for government, especially monarchical government, and has thereby contributed to the establishment and maintenance of civil order.

II. Among certain races and at certain times superstition has strengthened the respect for private property and has thereby contributed to the security of its enjoyment.

III. Among certain races and at certain times superstition has strengthened the respect for marriage and has thereby contributed to a stricter observance of the rules of sexual morality both among the married and the unmarried.

IV. Among certain races and at certain times superstition has strengthened the respect for human life and has thereby contributed to the security of its enjoyment.

After the introduction, the book consists of four chapters, each devoted to proving one of the propositions. The first chapter argues that superstitious awe of rulers has increased obedience to them; the second chapter argues that superstitious fear has served to deter men from stealing; the third chapter argues that fear of magical consequences has deterred men from adultery, fornication, and incest; the fourth chapter argues that the dread of the ghost has served to protect human life.

The author of *The Golden Bough* knew better than anyone that the divinity of kings is as apt to cost them their lives as to preserve them, that primitive beliefs are sometimes as destructive of property as the ones he adduces are conservative, that magic has often demanded adultery, fornication and incest, and that dread of the ghost has saved no more lives than desire to satisfy the ghost has cost. But superstition is his client. Even in *Psyche's Task* Frazer gives enough contradictory evidence to wreck his case, but he pleads against it. One can see Frazer's ambivalence most clearly when he thinks of reforming custom. The Thonga hippopotamus hunter, Frazer shows us, empowers himself for the hunt in a thoroughly disreputable fashion. Frazer writes:

Perhaps the same train of thought partially explains the incest which the hunter has to commit with his own daughter before he sets out for the chase. Can it be that by this violence done to his offspring he is supposed to acquire power over the beast? It may be so, yet it is difficult to see why the violence should take this particular form, and why, on the principles of homeopathic or imitative magic, a pretence of wounding and killing the girl with a spear would not have served his turn better.

Frazer is in the position of those twentieth-century applied anthropologists encouraging initiatory pig-sticking instead of head-hunting. He knows that custom cannot be abolished without demoralization, but he hopes that an imposed substitute can keep the effectiveness in the form without the content. One can see what underlies the ambivalence most clearly when Frazer writes: "Thus taboo became a powerful instrument for strengthening the ties, perhaps our socialist friends would say riveting the chains, of private property." Frazer abhorred Marx, his evolutionary predecessor, as much as he did Freud, his evolutionary successor. The volcano underfoot, the sea around him, are the revolution and the id as well as the blind superstition of the masses, and forced to a choice Frazer will find conservative allies where he can.

It seems to me, however, that *Psyche's Task* reveals the unresolved ambivalence without forcing to a choice. The first paragraph of the introduction sets the defense of superstition in an ironic frame: "Without posing as the Devil's Advocate or appearing before you in a blue flame and sulphureous fumes, I do profess to make out what the charitable might call a plausible plea for a very dubious client." When Frazer reissued the book in 1928, he changed the title to *The Devil's Advocate: A Plea for Superstition*, without further alteration. In all its editions the book ends:

> That, ladies and gentlemen, is my plea for Superstition. Perhaps it might be urged in mitigation of the sentence which will be passed on the hoary-headed offender when he stands at the judgment bar. Yet the sentence, do not doubt it, is death. But it will not be executed in our time. There will be a long, long, reprieve. It is as his advocate, not as his executioner, that I have appeared before you to-night. At Athens cases of murder were tried before the Areopagus by night, and it is by night that I have spoken in defense of this power of darkness. But it grows late, and with my sinister client I must vanish before the cocks crow and the morning breaks grey in the east.

The *advocatus diaboli* in sanctification proceedings is, of course, on God's side, making a case to be demolished. Some of *Psyche's Task* suggests that Frazer is writing a mock-defense, a Modest Proposal, not only for superstition generally but for religion specifically. He writes in the introduction:

> The institutions to which I refer are purely secular or civil. Of religious or ecclesiastical institutions I shall say nothing. It might perhaps be possible to shew that even religion had not wholly

escaped the taint or dispensed with the support of superstition;
but I prefer for to-night to confine myself to those civil institutions which people commonly imagine to be bottomed on nothing
but hard common sense and the nature of things.

It is religion, as Frazer makes clear at the end of *The Golden Bough*,
that is sentenced to death after our time.

Somewhere beneath the surface of *Psyche's Task* there is a sociology of institutions, as Bronislaw Malinowski points out in "Sir James
George Frazer: A Biographical Appreciation" in *A Scientific Theory
of Culture and Other Essays*. Frazer concludes his introduction:

> No institution founded wholly on superstition, that is on false-
> hood, can be permanent. If it does not answer to some real human
> need, if its foundations are not laid broad and deep in the nature
> of things, it must perish, and the sooner the better.

For Malinowski, these words are the germ of his own functional
anthropology, continuing the sociological line of Smith's thinking to
which Frazer had not usually been sympathetic. "Sociology was quite
alien to him," Franz Steiner says of Frazer, in *Taboo*. In terms of
Frazer's own approach, his formulation seems less like a scientific
question for further study than like an absolute judgment: some insi-
tutions are founded wholly on falsehood, some answer a real human
need. If government and marriage, respect for human life and private
property, are examples of the latter, religion, *Psyche's Task* seems to be
implying, is our prime example of the former.

Frazer's other important publication of 1909 is "Some Primitive
Theories of the Origin of Man" in *Darwin and Modern Science*, already noticed in connection with Darwin. This essay was reprinted
in 1935 as "Creation and Evolution in Primitive Cosmogonies," in the
volume of that title. As the later title shows, Frazer is again ambivalent,
but here his ambivalence consists not in making one point on the
surface and a contrary one beneath, or running in different directions
at different times, but in maintaining a majestic impartiality. Frazer
concludes the essay:

> I have confined myself to collecting examples of two radically
> different views, which may be distinguished as the theory of
> creation and the theory of evolution. According to the one, man
> was fashioned in his existing shape by a god or other powerful
> being; according to the other he was evolved by a natural process
> out of lower forms of animal life. Roughly speaking, these two
> theories still divide the civilised world between them. The parti-
> sans of each can appeal in support of their view to a large con-
> sensus of opinion; and if truth were to be decided by weighing
> the one consensus against the other, with *Genesis* in the one scale
> and *The Origin of Species* in the other, it might perhaps be found,
> when the scales were finally trimmed, that the balance hung very
> even between creation and evolution.

As an essay for a Darwin centenary volume, of course, this is a powerful example of trimming, but in the context of Frazer's own imaginative constructions the dualism is essential. Creation is the Western myth, Faustian or Promethean. It places act in its scene and in time, so that Frazer begins the essay describing his visit to the hill of Panopeus in Greek Phocis, where, "they say, the sage Prometheus created our first parents by fashioning them, like a potter, out of clay." Frazer found the very clay, "a reddish crumbling earth." By this impious act of wrenching man out of nature, in some of the cosmogonies Frazer synopsizes, human death came into the world. In creationist cosmogonies man has been made above and beyond nature, a striving and sinful being, and the wages of sin is death.

Evolution is the comparable Eastern myth, Buddhist or Hindu. Here there is "none of that high notion of the transcendent dignity of man" of the creationists, man is in nature, part of the endless natural cycle of metamorphosis and change. Here we have totemic fraternal monism, "which unites by a mystic bond a group of human kinsfolk to a species of animals or plants." Quoting a missionary in South Africa, Frazer describes a Bushman of more than average intelligence who "could not state any difference between a man and a brute—he did not know but a buffalo might shoot with bows and arrows as well as a man, if it had them." In this world without time and place, there is neither act nor scene, and as there is no dividing line between man and nature there is no death. In the cycle of nature, evolutionary man is immortal. Thus not only do creation and evolution lie equal in the balance, but so do all our famous antitheses—time and eternity, grace and nature, free will and determination, corruption and incorruption. For Frazer, a balancing of their claims, like putting belief on trial, was an essential prelude to decision. His image of the balance hung very even does not adequately convey the tension. We might prefer Santayana's image of the pendulum perfectly at rest, upward.

What Do You Dance?

IN 1910 Frazer published his first ambitious work after *The Golden
Bough*, the four sizeable volumes of *Totemism and Exogamy: A
Treatise on Certain Early Forms of Superstition and Society*. He
explains in the preface that the subjects of his title, totemism and
exogamy, are entirely unrelated. John Ferguson McLennan had discovered them both in primitive societies and had combined them;
since then Spencer and Gillen in Australia and Rivers among the
Melanesians had shown them to be independent. Frazer's aim in the
book is no less than collecting all the evidence on both subjects, and
deriving a theory of origin and function from it inductively. One
theory would suffice for both origin and function, since Frazer habitually approached social institutions with the rationalist assumption that
they have been originated to function as they do; thus he speaks of
"those marriages of brothers with sisters and of parents with children
which it was apparently the intention of exogamy to put an end to."
As late as 1941, when he wrote his biographical appreciation, Malinowski took the book seriously as anthropology. He writes:

> In many ways Frazer's *Totemism and Exogamy* is about the best
> introductory reading for the young student of anthropology,
> because it gives an easier, more attractive, and better integrated
> picture of a whole series of tribal cultures than any book I know.

Like *Capital*, *Totemism and Exogamy* insists that it is primarily
a work of science. In the preface Frazer takes account of the charges
beginning to be made by anthropological critics that his method consists of wrenching traits out of their cultural contexts. He writes:

> The facts are arranged in ethnographical order, tribe by tribe,
> and an attempt has been made to take account of the physical
> environment as well as of the general social conditions of the
> principal tribes which are passed in review. In this way I have
> sought to mitigate the disadvantages incidental to the study of any
> institution viewed abstractedly and apart from the rest of the social
> organism with which it is vitally connected. Such abstract views

are indeed indispensable, being imposed by the limitations of the human mind, but they are apt to throw the object out of focus, to exaggerate some of its features, and to diminish unduly others which may be of equal or even greater importance. These dangers cannot be wholly avoided, but they may be lessened by making our study as concrete as is compatible with the necessary degree of abstraction.

Frazer concludes the preface:

> As a plain record of a curious form of society which must soon be numbered with the past, the book may continue to possess an interest even when, with the progress of knowledge, its errors shall have been corrected and its theories perhaps superseded by others which make a nearer approach to truth. For though I have never hesitated either to frame theories which seemed to fit the facts or to throw them away when they ceased to do so, my aim in this and my other writings has not been to blow bubble hypotheses which glitter for a moment and are gone; it has been by a wide collection and an exact classification of facts to lay a broad and solid foundation for the inductive study of primitive man.

As befits a scientist, Frazer gives the negative evidence as fully as the positive. "Indeed," he writes in the middle of the second volume, "the English missionary and scholar, the Rev. Dr. R. H. Codrington, who is our best authority on Central and Southern Melanesia, doubts whether the term totemism is applicable to the beliefs and customs of the islanders with which he is acquainted." Tylor having objected to Frazer's use of the term "totemism" for the sacred animals and plants of Samoa, Frazer now writes: "I so far agree with him that I think I should not have spoken of them as totems without qualification." Frazer has a proper scientific sense of the human limitations of the field-worker. He notes:

> In all investigations of savage life the mental capacity, intelligence, tact, and sympathy of the observer are of the first importance; and as the union of these qualities is rare, so the number of first-rate observers of savages is few indeed. Where these personal qualities of head and heart are wanting, no liberal subvention of money, no costly apparatus, no elaborate machinery will supply their place.

Frazer often writes tentatively: "But this is merely a conjecture, I know of no evidence to support it"; or, "But so far as I have studied the evidence adduced to support these conclusions I have to confess that it leaves me doubtful or unconvinced." Criticizing Edward Westermarck for mechanical materialism, for his ultra-Darwinian attempt to explain the growth of institutions "too exclusively from physical and biological causes without taking into account the facts

of intelligence, deliberation, and will," Frazer produces an eloquent
passage against oversimplification:

> For true science reckons with all the elements of the problem
> which it sets itself to solve, and it remembers that these elements
> may differ widely with the particular nature of the subject under
> investigation. It does not insist on reducing the heterogeneous at
> all costs to the homogeneous, the multiformity of facts to the
> uniformity of theory. It is cautious of transferring to one study
> the principles and methods which are appropriate to another. In
> particular the science which deals with human society will not,
> if it is truly scientific, omit to reckon with the qualities which
> distinguish man from the beasts.

Sometimes Frazer is less scientific in *Totemism and Exogamy*
than his principles would suggest. He carries on a curious war against
phonetic symbols, "setting some of the consonants on their feet instead
of on their heads," upending them much as Marx upended Hegel.
Sometimes when he encounters negative evidence he does not discard
or modify his theory, but merely presents the contradiction with "It
is interesting to find." When Frazer learns that the custom of the
sororate, marriage to the wife's younger sister, does not exist among
some peoples during the wife's lifetime, he simply assumes that things
were as he would have them in the past: "In these cases we can hardly
doubt that the restriction is a comparatively late modification of an
older custom which allowed a man to marry the sisters of his living
as well as of his deceased wife."

If the test of science, however, is discarding theories when they
no longer seem to fit the facts, *Totemism and Exogamy* is probably
the most scientific work in history. At times we are hip deep in discarded theories. Frazer writes in the preface:

> That my conclusions on these difficult questions are final, I am
> not so foolish as to pretend. I have changed my views repeatedly,
> and I am resolved to change them again with every change of the
> evidence, for like a chameleon the candid enquirer should shift
> his colours with the shifting colours of the ground he treads.

Frazer explains in the summary "The Origin of Totemism" in the
fourth volume:

> Three different theories of the origin of totemism have at
> different times occurred to me as possible or probable. Two of
> them I have seen reason to abandon; the third I still regard as
> probably true.

Frazer's first theory, developed after he published *Totemism* in 1887,
appears in the first edition of *The Golden Bough*. It originates
totemism in a belief in the external soul. A widespread belief in external
souls that must be deposited in a safe place had been announced by
Edward Clodd in *Myths and Dreams*, and Frazer adopted it as an

origin theory for totemism. As field studies began appearing that showed no such thing, Frazer discarded the theory. His next theory, published in "The Origin of Totemism" in *The Fortnightly Review* in 1899, and reprinted in *Totemism and Exogamy*, is that totemism is an organization for the magical increase of food. This came from the researches of Baldwin Spencer and F. J. Gillen among the Arunta of Central Australia, and their account of the *intichiuma* ceremonies, in which opossum-men or witchetty-grub-men make their totemic brothers increase. Frazer hit on the theory reading the proofs of their book *The Native Tribes of Central Australia* in 1898. About 1906, Frazer discarded this second explanation, on the grounds that "the motive which the theory assigns for the origin of the institution is too rational, and the social organization which it implies is too complex, to be primitive." Keeping the *intichiuma* idea as a functional development, Frazer soon worked out a third theory of totemic origins, based on a magical theory of conception. This was confirmed for him in 1909 by Rivers' discovery among the Melanesians of Banks Island of just the sort of belief in human fertilization by the spirit of the totem animal or plant that Frazer had decided was "absolutely primitive totemism." Since "the tap-root of totemism" was thus "the sick fancies of pregnant women," in Frazer's latest theory, "totemism may be described as a creation of the feminine rather than of the masculine mind."

Totemism and Exogamy is a hodge-podge of those three theories and others. At the same time, Frazer repeatedly chips away at his theory of the origin of exogamy as a contrivance designed to prevent incest. An article by Andrew Lang in 1906 had convinced him that primitives were not geneticists, which left him with no actual motive for incest avoidance. The Bachofen view that marriage and other ceremonies are designed to replace matriliny with patriliny comes to seem less and less likely as the book goes on. As the evidence increased, avoidance and taboo seemed to make less and less sense as incest precautions. Thus the Navajo have a strong avoidance custom between mother-in-law and son-in-law. "To avoid these embarrassments," Frazer adds, demolishing his theory, "a man will sometimes marry the mother first and then the daughter so as to make the mother-in-law also a wife, thus disarming her of her terrors." He concludes about his theory of incest-prevention:

> At least if that is not the origin of exogamy I must confess to being completely baffled, for I have no other conjectures to offer on the subject.

All of Frazer's theories evolved similarly, leaving their fossils in *Totemism and Exogamy*. The theory of myth he inherited from Mannhardt and Smith is that of ritual origin or at least association, myth as a story that accompanies, directs and sanctions a rite. That theory runs all through the book. Frazer tells a Cherokee myth of Mother Corn and relates it to the Green Corn dance. He describes Northwest

Coast drama as "accompanied by a chorus of women who sing the myth which is being acted by the performers." A Kwakiutl dance "must be considered a dramatic performance of the myth." When he is in this mood, Frazer's typical entry on a myth is: "probably reflects a real custom."

In "The Golden Bough" in *The New Statesmen and Nations* in 1941, H. N. Brailsford writes of Frazer: "His interest in ritual was always slighter than his interest in myth, yet ritual is certainly the more fundamental of these two." Frazer was never content with the theory of ritual origins, as he was never content with any theory of origins; in addition some of its implications were emotionally unsettling. Frazer very much wanted a euhemerist theory that would base myths on the exploits of real men. He first got it from Haddon, who revealed to the world the warrior-hero Kwoiam in the lore of one of the peoples of the Torres Straits. Frazer writes of Kwoiam in *Totemism and Exogamy:*

> From the accounts given of him, this personage appears to have been an Australian by descent, either a pure-bred or a half-bred native of North Queensland, who so signalised himself by his prowess, that myths gathered round his memory, blurring and transfiguring the man into a cloudy being of fairyland.

Haddon had actually visited the ruins of Kwoiam's house on the island of Mabuiag, and "rescued the dusky hero and his story from oblivion." Haddon thus established that Kwoiam had been a real man (since Haddon had seen the ruins of a real house) although "on his death he was raised by the people of Mabuiag to something that approached to the rank of divinity." This was fine, but not perfect, since Frazer himself hadn't seen the ruins, and the myths appeared to have been told of Kwoiam, not originated in his doings.

Sometime around 1907, exactly what Frazer wanted appeared. His friend the Rev. John Roscoe, a missionary among the Baganda of Uganda, presented to the Ethnological Museum at Cambridge the mummified jawbone, genitalia, and naval cord of Kibuka, the war god of the Baganda, which had been preserved for centuries by the Baganda and acquired from them by Roscoe. (These objects, tastefully decorated with cowrie shells, are pictured on p. 381 of Sir William Ridgeway's *The Dramas and Dramatic Dances of Non-European Races.*) Since these were unquestionably real human remains, and the Baganda assured Roscoe that they were the god's, then it followed with inexorable logic that gods had once been real men.[1] Frazer writes in *Totemism and Exogamy:*

> It becomes highly probable that many, if not all, of the great national gods of the Baganda are simply men who have been

[1] In *Totemism,* Frazer later made fun of the argument that if you do not believe the story that one of the Solomon Islands was raised from the sea by a turtle, you have only to go look at the rock where his hook slipped on the first attempt.

raised to the rank of deities after their death or possibly even in
their life. The inference is confirmed by the tradition that the
greatest of all the Baganda gods, Musaka, was a brother of the
war-god Kibuka, and that two other powerful deities, Nende and
Musoke, were sons of Musaka; for if one of the divine brothers,
Musaka and Kibuka, was once a man, as we know him for certain
to have been, a presumption is raised that the other brother and
his two sons were originally men also.

In his 1923 Frazer Lecture, Roscoe said: "I am proud to call myself
a disciple of Sir James, to whose inspiration I owe my first love for
this important branch of study." In a more important sense Frazer
might have called himself a disciple of Roscoe, since Roscoe was
instrumental in Frazer's exhanging the one indisputably sound theory
of myth he ever held for a mummified scrotum.

Evolution is the only theory Frazer holds to consistently in
Totemism and Exogamy. Since "it is now generally admitted that all
the civilised races of mankind have at some time passed through
the stages of savagery," a record "of the thoughts and habits of a people
so low down in the scale of humanity must possess the highest scientific
interest." Frazer automatically assumes that everything evolves into
greater reasonableness, writing:

> In this last respect it can hardly be disputed that the central tribes
> have preserved the more primitive beliefs and customs, and that
> the gradual transition from a purely fortuitous determination of
> the totem to a strict inheritance of it in the paternal line marks
> a social and intellectual advance in culture. To imagine that the
> change had taken place in the opposite direction, in other words,
> that tribes which had once derived their totems invariably from
> their fathers afterwards abandoned the hereditary principle in
> favour of one which left the determination of their totems to the
> sick fancies of pregnant women—this would be a theory too pre-
> posterous to be worthy of serious attention.

At one point Frazer suggests that incest taboos develop by natural
selection, tribes that do not have them suffering competitively in
breeding. He concludes:

> In acting as they did, these poor savages blindly obeyed the
> impulse of the great evolutionary forces which in the physical
> world are constantly reducing higher out of lower forms of exist-
> ence and in the moral world civilisation out of savagery.

At his best, Frazer believes in the sort of neo-evolutionist doctrine
anthropologists have been returning to in our time, the insistence that
all cultures evolve similarly, although not necessarily through the
same stages. Frazer writes:

> But in the absence of proof that the Semites and the Aryans in
> general ever practised exogamy and counted kinship on the

classificatory system we are not justified in concluding that these institutions have at one time been common to the whole human race. Nor, apart from the want of direct evidence, does there appear to be any reason in the nature of things why these institutions should be necessary stages in the social evolution of every people.

Elsewhere:

> Thus the totemism of the Baganda should serve as a warning against the supposition that totemism almost necessarily develops, first, into a worship of sacred animals and plants, and afterwards into a worship of anthropomorphic deities with sacred animals and plants for their attributes.

It was the hierarchy of evolution that Frazer never rejected. Totemism's "main interest for us lies in the glimpse which it affords into the working of the childlike mind of the savage; it is as it were a window opened up into a distant past." Frazer describes the hill tribes of Bengal: "Here, therefore, the rude children of nature could maintain their freedom and preserve their simple habits with but little change from generation to generation." He generalizes:

> Haziness is characteristic of the mental vision of the savage. Like the blind man of Bethsaida he sees men like trees and animals walking in a thick intellectual fog.

The book is studded with: "the infantine intelligence of the primitive savage"; "the inevitable haziness and confusion of savage"; "the undeveloped intelligence of the low savages."

The characteristic weakness of Tylor and Smith is the rationalist assumption of the social contract, that primitives think as we do and consciously arrange institutions to achieve desired ends. Commenting on Tylor's phrase "the ancient savage philosophers," R. R. Marett in *Tylor* snaps, "There never was a 'savage philosopher'." Frazer was able to see this fault clearly in his masters. As early as 1889 he wrote to Black about Smith's *Religion of the Semites:*

> What I mean is that primitive man looks at the world from such a totally different point of view from us, that what seems simple and obvious to us almost certainly did not appear so to him; and, *vice versa*, what seems simple and obvious to him is almost always so entirely remote from our ways of thought that we should never have dreamed of it. Accordingly, any explanations of the origin of religion or society which commend themselves at once to us as entirely agreeable to reason and probability ought always, in my opinion, to be regarded with the greatest distrust. Their inherent probability (from our point of view) is a strong presumption against them. Rousseau's views (to take an extreme example) on the origin of society commended themselves to the most reasonable people last century, just because, if *they* had to

reconstruct society from the foundations, they would have proceeded much as Rousseau supposes that primitive man did. But
from primitive man to a French Encyclopaedist is a very long
interval. I do not say that Smith has fallen into the mistake of
making the early Semites reason like nineteenth-century people;
all I would say is that the very simplicity and obviousness of the
deductions inspire me with a somewhat vague and perhaps un-
justifiable distrust.

A decade later Frazer gave up his distrust, having decided from
Spencer and Gillen's *The Native Tribes of Central Australia* that
primitives *did* operate like nineteenth-century social planners.

In an article written while he still believed totemism to be Spencer
and Gillen's magical food-production, reprinted in the book, Frazer
writes:

> Viewed in this light, Totemism is a thoroughly practical
> system designed to meet the everyday wants of the ordinary man
> in a clear and straightforward way. There is nothing vague or
> mystical about it, nothing of that metaphysical haze which some
> writers love to conjure up over the humble beginnings of human
> speculation, but which is utterly foreign to the simple, sensuous,
> and concrete modes of thought of the savage.

The article emphasizes the effects of "public opinion" and concludes
that totemism "may have begun in a humble way by the union of a
few neighbouring groups under the influence of some able men." The
later sections of *Totemism and Exogamy* do not essentially differ. "Men
of a more original and ingenious turn of mind than the rest," Frazer
writes, "may have simply invented some of the ceremonies and then
palmed them off as inspirations of the higher powers upon their credu-
lous fellows." In this rationalist mood, Frazer will deny even his natural
processes of social evolution:

> The truth is that all attempts to trace the origin and growth of
> human institutions without the intervention of human intelligence
> and will are radically vicious and foredoomed to failure.

"There are strong grounds for thinking," he continues, "that the system of exogamy has been deliberately devised and instituted by the
Australian aborigines for the purpose of effecting just what it does effect." "The reformers who devised and introduced these great social
changes were probably," he explains, "the council of old men."
Frazer continually reaffirms this process: "Every now and again
there arises a man of superior ability to his fellows"; or, "It may accordingly have occurred to some primitive sages." His genesis of stories of
the type of "The Swan Maiden" and "Beauty and the Beast" reads like
a parody of Victorian rationalism:

> Such stories are explained naturally and simply on the supposition
> that they referred originally to husbands and wives who, under a

system of totemism and exogamy, would claim kindred with animals or plants of different kinds, the husband assimilating himself
to one sort of creature and the wife to another. In such households,
husband and wife would naturally resent any injury done to their
animal kinsfolk as a wrong done to themselves; and domestic jars
would easily arise whenever one of the couple failed to respect the
humble relations of the other.

One of Frazer's rationalist assumptions in *Totemism and Exogamy* became a major tenet in Freud's *Totem and Taboo*. Frazer writes:

> Instead of assuming, therefore, from the legal prohibition of incest
> that there is a natural aversion to incest, we ought rather to assume
> that there is a natural instinct in favour of it, and that if the law
> represses it, as it represses other natural instincts, it does so because
> civilised men have come to the conclusion that the satisfaction of
> these natural instincts is detrimental to the general interests of
> society.

At another point Frazer drags out Paley's old argument for design,
which one would have thought had been laid to rest by *The Origin of
Species'* reconstruction of the evolution of the eye:

> It is hardly too much to affirm that no other human institution
> bears the impress of deliberate design stamped on it more clearly
> than the exogamous classes of the Australian aborigines. To sup-
> pose that they have originated through a series of undesigned co-
> incidences, and that they only subserve by accident the purpose
> which they actually fulfil and which is cordially approved of by
> the natives themselves, is to tax our credulity almost as heavily as
> it would be to suppose that the complex machinery of a watch has
> come together without human design by a mere fortuitous con-
> course of atoms, and that the purpose which it serves of marking
> time on the dial, and for the sake of which the owner of the watch
> carries it about with him, is simply an accidental result of its
> atomic configuration.

Frazer pictures the designers of social organization as men essentially like himself. He writes: "Thus whichever way the founders of
the two-class system of exogamy arranged descent," they were dis-
concerted by finding that incest was still possible. Consequently, "It
appears to have struck some inventive genius" that a four-class system
would improve things further. As for the ultimate eight-class system:

> The scheme no doubt took shape in the minds of a few men of
> sagacity and practical ability above the ordinary, who by their
> influence and authority persuaded their fellows to put it in prac-
> tice.

Here is Frazer entering into the mind of an Australian woman:

> It would be easy for her either to frequent places haunted by spir-
> its of her own totem only in order to receive one of them into her

womb, or at all events, if she were unscrupulous, to fib that she had done so, and in this way to satisfy the longing of her mother's heart by getting children of her own totem.

Periodically, in *Totemism and Exogamy*, Frazer recognizes the inadequacy of this sort of rationalism, as he had recognized it in the letter to Black. Frazer writes:

> This error has probably arisen from considering a savage as a human being who in a rude exterior thinks much as does a civilised man. Such an idea cannot have a sound foundation. We see its results perhaps in the most marked form in the writings of Rousseau, but even later writers are not free from it.

Or, of a theory of the origin of exogamy no more rationalistic than his own, he will write: "McLennan appears to have greatly overrated the intelligent foresight of primitive man." Of another: "It may well be doubted whether the Australian aborigines are capable of conceiving or executing so elaborate a system of fraud."

Totemism and Exogamy, for the first time in Frazer's writing, has something of a historical perspective, as the field-workers he used began to record change. Frazer recognizes that one Australian tribe, the Biduelli, is "a medley composed of refugees who had fled from the neighbouring tribes," with mixed language and totems. Others have such acculturated totems as the English bee. In one tribe he recognizes that the custom of killing elopers is transforming into an ordeal ceremony, and among others that circumcision is being replaced by tying a ligature around the upper arm at initiation. Of Melanesia he writes: "The very raising of this question of zoological classification suggests that totemism is here breaking down." In Fiji and Samoa "the sacred animals had become gods."

Frazer is somewhat inhibited by two characteristic Victorian factors, prudishness and ethnocentrism. The first faithfully reflects his sources, many of them ordained missionaries. The Dieri of Australia have ceremonies for the multiplication of wild dogs and of snakes, "but both of these are reported to be so obscene that they are indescribable." A description of initiation ceremonies among the natives of Kiwai Island by the Rev. J. Chalmers, reprinted by Frazer, concludes: "The more secret and immoral practices I cannot here repeat." The Rev. Lorimer Fison, a distinguished pioneer anthropologist, published the following description of a Fijian ceremony:

> Then follows a great feast, which ushers in a period of indescribable revelry. All distinctions of property are for the time being suspended. Men and women array themselves in all manner of fantastic garbs, address one another in the most indecent phrases, and practice unmentionable abominations openly in the public square of the town. The nearest relationships—even that of own brother and sister—seem to be no bar to the general license, the extent of

which may be indicated by the expressive phrase of an old Nandi chief who said, 'While it lasts, we are just like the pigs.'

Frazer adds:

> Fuller accounts of the license permitted on these occasions, based in part on a written statement taken down by Mr. Edward O'Brien Heffernan, Native Advocate and Stipendiary Magistrate, from the lips of a native in presence of the principal chiefs of Nandi, Vunda, and Sambeto, were sent in manuscript by Mr. Fison to Professor E. B. Tylor, who writes on the subject as follows: 'The details of indecent dances and rites referred to may be left in MS.'

Frazer's own problem was his inability to keep from outraged comment, the result of his ethnocentric morality. In two adjacent pages on ceremonial behavior in India one notes: "They practise various forms of fervent but misguided piety"; "highly disgusting to all sensible and cleanly men"; "An unmarried, but not necessarily chaste, woman"; "the filthy eructations of this tipsy maniac"; "The two sets of ragamuffins squabble with each other." Of the Todas, Frazer writes: "So lax, or rather so perverted, according to our ideas, is their standard of morality." Haida ceremonies "consisted of the usual medley of savagery and fraud." African peoples who knock out or file teeth persist in "maiming and mutilating themselves in this absurd fashion," and all such bodily mutilations are "these worse than needless tortures, which savages inflict on each other and submit to with a misplaced heroism."

AS THESE quotations make clear, *Totemism and Exogamy* is exhortation as well as social science. In our terms, it has equally strong components of symbolic action and imaginative design. Symbolically, the changes of theory are neither scientific scrupulosity nor weakness of character combined with extreme suggestibility, but shifting psychological needs. Thus one might look for connections between the theory that totems are external souls and the remnants of Frazer's childhood Presbyterianism, the theory that totemic magic has an economic function and Frazer's own need for self-justification, the theory that the totems fertilize and Frazer's adjustment to his own childlessness. "If it was not the mother," Frazer writes of totemism, "it has been the foster-mother of painting and sculpture." Also, we might add, of literature. The Christian religion is never far from his mind as he writes of the fervent and misguided piety of savages, and it breaks through occasionally. "In short a belief that a virgin can conceive and bring forth a son is one of the last lingering relics of primitive savagery," Frazer writes at one point.

As for the concern with history, it is immediately obvious that it is a concern with historical drama, and that in *Totemism and Exogamy*

Frazer has readily to hand the historical tragedy Marx vainly pursued. Frazer writes in the preface.

> Our contemporaries of this and the rising generation appear to be hardly aware that we are witnessing the last act of a long drama, a tragedy and a comedy in one, which is being silently played, with no fanfare of trumpets or roll of drums, before our eyes on the stage of history. Whatever becomes of the savages, the curtain must soon descend on savagery for ever.

Totemic ceremonies are not only sacred dramas but historical dramas:

> It is thus that the past history, or what he believes to be the past history, of his people is stamped upon every young man's imagination and memory for life. He does not read it in books: he sees it acted before his eyes.

All of Frazer's metaphors in *Totemism and Exogamy* dramatize similarly. Three decades before it occurred, he intimates his own death in images of the natural cycle:

> Today the totemic harvest still stands white to the sickle in many fields, but it may be left for others hereafter to see the sheaves brought home. My sun is westering, and the lengthening shadows remind me to work while it is day.

Frazer later uses the same image for the decline of the American aborigine: "The long Indian day draws fast to evening." Cultural evolution is seen in a metaphor of organic growth. Frazer writes:

> Nowhere among the aborigines of North America have such miracle plays, as we may call them, been staged and acted with so elaborate, indeed so gorgeous an apparatus of costumes and scenic effects as among the Pueblo Indians of Arizona and New Mexico and the coast tribes of British Columbia; nowhere, accordingly, is it so likely that these solemn religious rites would gradually have shrivelled or blossomed into a purely secular drama, if the course of evolution had not been cut short by the advent of the whites. The seed was sown; it needed only time and favourable circumstances to spring up and bear the fine flower of art, whether in the desert air and under the blue skies of Arizona or in the rain-saturated forests of British Columbia.

While art grows naturally, it also grows by artifice. In a cinematic metaphor that may remind us of Plato's cave, Frazer writes.

> If we compare the face of nature to an illuminated screen on which figures pass to and fro, we may liken magicians to men gesticulating and shouting at the figures and imagining that they come and go at their bidding; while all the time the phantasmagoria is worked by a Master of the Show smiling invisible behind the screen.

If God runs a magic lantern show, history does an alchemical turn.
Frazer writes:

> If that is so, exogamy has been an instrument in the hands of that
> unknown power, the masked wizard of history, who by some mys-
> terious process, some subtle alchemy, so often transmutes in the
> crucible of suffering the dross of folly and evil into the fine gold
> of wisdom and good.

Frazer's common metaphor for science is light. In the case of some observers, facts "loom dimly from their writings like lamps seen through
a fog." The causes of some customs "lie deeper down in some dark
abyss of superstition, which the plummet of science has not yet
sounded nor its lamp illuminated." There are more directly scientific
metaphors. Exogamy seems an essential part of totemism but only as
"people who had never met with copper and tin might easily mistake
bronze for a single pure metal until they discovered it to be an alloy by
finding its two components separately." Perhaps the most curious metaphor for the distinction between magic and science, and a good example of how Frazer draws metaphor out, is a figure from night-time gun-
nery:

> Magical rites may be compared to shots discharged at random in the
> dark, some of which by accident hit the mark. If the gunner learns
> to distinguish between his hits and his misses, he will concentrate
> his hitherto scattered fire in the right direction and accomplish his
> purpose. If he fails to make the distinction, he will continue his
> random discharges with as little result as before. A scientific
> farmer is an artilleryman of the former sort; an Australian headman
> of the grass-seed totem is an artilleryman of the latter sort.

The dominating metaphor of the book, as one might expect from
the subject, is mystic brotherhood, communion, consubstantiation.
Like Engels on the English working class, when Frazer is not reviling
his primitives as childlike and revolting savages, he displays them as
philosophers on a par with the Greeks. Thus Canadian Indians have a
concept of the Platonic archetype, the Haida name children as the ancient Greeks did, and the Hidatsa have a ceremony rather like the
Eleusinian mysteries. Frazer writes of the latter:

> In this simple worship of the mother-corn we may see as it were in
> miniature the origin of some of the great goddesses of classical an-
> tiquity, Isis, Demeter, and Ceres, the only substantial difference
> between them being that whereas the corn-goddess of America
> was a personification of maize, the corn-goddesses of the old world
> were personification of wheat or barley.

As Frazer embraces the primitives in fraternity and equality, they embrace lower orders. He writes:

> Apparently the Tlingits thought that this common rule of avoid-
> ance observed by a man and his wife's mother was a great law of

nature which was recognized also by the lower animals; for when they were digging for clams, which withdraw rapidly into the sand, they used to say, 'Do not go down so fast or you will hit your mother-in-law in the face.'

Of primitives in general:

They thought less of themselves as animals and more of the animals as men. The result was a more humane and considerate treatment of their totems, which manifested itself chiefly in the refusal to kill and eat the totemic animals or plants. On the whole the new attitude to the totem is kindlier, less crude and savage, than the old one; it shews some consideration for the feelings, or supposed feelings, of others, and such consideration is invariably a mark of a certain refinement of nature.

"The relation between a man and his totem," Frazer says in the summary and conclusion of the book, "is one of simple friendly equality and brotherhood."

The book's other great imaginative design is of course the relationship of scene to act. The difference between totemism in central and northern Australia and in south-eastern Australia "is probably to be explained in large measure by the different physical configuration of the countries which they occupy." Frazer's account of the physical nature of the interior of Australia, which he had never seen but knew from descriptions by Spencer and Gillen, is a considerable feat in the creation of mood. He writes:

The aspect of country covered with such scrub is very gloomy. From any eminence you can perceive nothing on earth but a sea of sombre brown bushes stretching as far as the eye can reach, above which a solitary tree rising at rare intervals seems only to deepen the melancholy of the scene, especially on a dull day when a grey clouded sky broods over the mournful silence of the landscape. Even sunshine hardly cheers the prospect, for if it lightens a little the sad colouring of the endless shrubbery, it at the same time extends the view of it further and further, and so seems to render escape from it still more hopeless.

"In this dismal and monotonous scenery," he writes, "a wretched diversity is here and there created by the remains of what once were lakes." If the scene is ominous and foreboding, the heat and aridity are a felt terror:

The mercury in a thermometer, sheltered both from sun and wind, has been known to rise till it burst the tube, which was graduated to 127° Fahrenheit. Such fervent heat probably does not last for a long time together; yet for three months Captain Sturt found the mean temperature to be over 101° Fahrenheit in the shade; and the drought was such that every screw dropped out of the boxes, combs and horn handles split up into fine flakes, the lead fell out of pencils, the finger-nails of the explorers became as brittle as glass, and the hair of men and the wool of sheep ceased to grow.

Only in these scenes can we understand Australian ceremonies, just as we can only understand Toda custom if we know the Todas' idyllic country. Frazer describes it in a characteristic purple passage:

> But in all this lovely land it is the prospect from the sharp edge of the tableland which travellers dwell upon with the most rapturous delight. The scene is perhaps most impressive early in the day, when the white sea of morning clouds at the feet of the spectator gradually opens up and rolls away like a curtain with the growing heat of the sun, revealing in its gaps now a vast crimson plain veined with dark lines of wood, now a long rocky ridge gleaming like fire in the sunlight, till a purple cloud-shadow blots it out and fresh line of crags and ravines starts into view beyond. Jagged peaks hung with woods frame the nearer landscape and in the distance faint blue mountains melt like dreams into the azure of the sky. Under the shifting lights and shadows of the morning sun struggling with mist and cloud the scene is a phantasmagoria, a perfect dissolving view, all the colours glowing with gemlike radiance in the intense tropical sunshine and the keen thin mountain air.

The Todas are the proper actors for such a scene:

> They are a tall, well-built, athletic people, with a rich brown complexion, a profusion of jet black hair, a large, full speaking eye, a Roman nose, and fine teeth. The men are strong and very agile, with hairy bodies and thick beards. Their countenances are open and expressive; their bearing bold and free; their manners grave and dignified; their disposition very cheerful and friendly.

Frazer sees the scene as so determining that his strongest comparison for the baleful effect of superstition is "like a foul exhalation from a marshy soil, it may poison unseen the whole life of a people." The actions that occur on these stages are primarily acts of identification and self-identification. "When you wish to ascertain to what tribe a man belongs," Frazer explains, "you ask him 'What do you dance?'." The "great laxity in matters of sexual morality" of these rites makes Frazer uneasy, but they seem to be a consequence of the scene. "There is something in the pastoral life," he writes, "which favors the growth of abnormal relations between the sexes." When Frazer repeats the statement in the book's conclusion, he adds, "in a peculiar way which we do not understand." Malinowski writes:

> Frazer, somewhat prudish in his reaction to psychoanalysis, insisted that his primitives must be both promiscuous and incestuous. With an almost maternal attitude of concern, he delighted in their pranks and pleasures, while regretting their naughtiness.

Frazer's typical attitude toward promiscuity can be seen in his discussion of the Oraons of Bengal. He writes:

> However, the charitable view which the gallant colonel took of the relations between Oraon maids and bachelors is not shared by other experienced authorities on the Indian people. Thus Sir Herbert Risley observes that among the Oraons 'sexual intercourse before marriage is tacitly recognized, and is so generally practised that in the opinion of the best observers no Oraon girl is a virgin at the time of her marriage. To call this state of things immoral is to apply a modern conception to primitive habits of life.'

He adds a footnote quoting another authority:

> Risley is certainly right about premarital communism amongst the Oraons. I have been told that if an Oraon girl is thought unduly coy all the youths of the village combine against her and get her deflowered by one or more of their number.

Frazer's attitude toward incest can best be seen in his quotation from Fison on Fijian ritual brother-sister incest in the Nanga ceremonies:

> We cannot for a moment believe that it is a mere licentious outbreak, without an underlying meaning and purpose. It is part of a religious rite, and is supposed to be acceptable to the ancestors.

Actually, Frazer's third theory of totemism, human-conception magic, was not so far from his second theory, food-increase magic, as he thought. Primitive sexuality is a rite of increase too, a magical identification with the great cycle of nature. These acts in the primitive scene are life-giving, and thus for Frazer ultimately good. *Totemism and Exogamy* affirms the same teeming fertility of life that Darwin affirmed in the *Origin*.

The crop that grows luxuriantly for Frazer as a result of these fertility rites is principally his prose. His irony swells with the tones of public address, as in a sentence about the Reddis of Madras:

> However, these fine, powerful, well-dressed men, these gentlemen farmers, these substantial steady-going yeomen, these leaders of society with their neat well-built houses and jewels of fine gold, nevertheless retain the primitive institutions of exogamy and to some extent of totemism. So false is the popular notion that these ancient customs are practised only by vagrant savages with no house over their heads and little or no clothing on their backs.

Frazer synopsizes myths with a new jazziness: in an African story about the origin of death the chameleon tells men "not to believe the lies of that shallow sceptic the thrush"; of a Baganda ordeal, "No true born Elephant-man, they thought, could suffer in his stomach the melted butter in which the king's jawbone had been steeped." When a Nandi of the elephant clan shoots an elephant for the tusks, in Frazer's phrasing, he goes up to the corpse and says, "So sorry, old fellow, I thought you were a rhinoceros." Frazer quotes Bartram's account of the happy and prosperous Seminoles in 1792, "as blithe and free as the birds of the air," and adds bitterly, "Since Bartram thus wrote, the birds to which he compared the Seminole are mostly flown and their nests are empty." If there are no outstanding purple passages in *Totemism and Exogamy*, other than those summoning up landscapes Frazer had never seen, it is because color pervades his prose everywhere. In earlier books he might have written "dead rooster" but here only "deceased chanticleer" will do.

S O M E of the most important writing Frazer did from 1897 to 1913 was not published until 1932. It is a series of letters to Sir Baldwin Spencer in Australia, published with Spencer's replies in *Spencer's Scientific Correspondence with Sir J. G. Frazer and Others*, edited by R. R. Marett and T. K. Penniman. The correspondence is a fascinating one, and shows a remarkable symbiosis, what the introduction calls "a close and constant co-operation between the anthropologist of the study and the anthropologist of the field." Marett and Penniman explain:

> If it should be asked why any of this correspondence should be published at all, since so great a part of the material contained in the letters has appeared in its final form in the various books of Spencer and Frazer, the answer is that methods of arriving at truth have value for the student, as well as the truth itself thereby resulting; and never so much as when we are privileged to watch two such master minds at work, the one at home, the other in the field. Thereupon we can see how the new facts collected in Australia are brought into relation with evidence from other parts of the world, and instantly suggest fresh theories concerning the origins of human institutions. These theories are then referred back to the field worker, accompanied by many questions in regard to points that may have been overlooked, or left obscure. Thus the theoretical scheme is tested, and at the same time new lines of research are opened up by means of a constant process of action and reaction.

We see Spencer writing to Frazer the details of Arunta totemism, and Frazer writing back for more facts: "It is all the more important that the system should be described as fully as possible." Frazer asks specific questions—"Is there in any case a purification of the slayer?"—and Spencer answers them and corrects Frazer's misapprehensions, while Frazer lectures Spencer on theory. Meanwhile, Frazer worries, like Darwin's friends, that Spencer and Gillen's conclusions will be anticipated if they do not publish quickly; he finds them a publisher, reads the manuscript and makes suggestions, reads the proofs and makes corrections.

Frazer writes to Spencer about the division of labor:

> You are most well advised in eschewing comparisons. Nothing (short of gross inaccuracy) is apt to spoil a work of descriptive ethnology so much as an attempt to combine the description with comparisons. Descriptive and comparative ethnology should be kept most rigidly apart; to try to combine both is to spoil both. I think that all the finest descriptions of individual races that we possess are wholly free from the comparative element and are written (as they should be) just as if the writer was unaware of the existence of any race but the one he is describing.

In a further subdivision of labor, Gillen was keeping himself even purer. "By mutual agreement," Spencer writes to Frazer, "he reads no one else's work so as to keep him quite unprejudiced in the way of theories." Frazer writes to Spencer in 1902:

> I am delighted to hear that in the midst of all your other work you find time to go on with the writing of your book. I pant for the time when I should be allowed (as I hope I shall be) to read it in proof. Remember, I expect to be allowed the privilege of reading your proofs. If you allow me, I should like to do just as I did for the former book—look out for printer's errors and for occasional obscurities or awkwardnesses of expression, of which I might sometimes suggest amendments to be approved or rejected by you at your discretion. As to omitting or cutting out a single fact or opinion, however apparently unimportant, I hope I would rather cut off my hand.

At the same time, Frazer was laboring in England for the support of field work. He writes to Spencer in 1908, in connection with his forthcoming plea in *The Scope of Social Anthropology:* "I am anxious to establish at Liverpool an institute for the prosecution of anthropological work in the field, and should like to inaugurate it by an expedition by you and Gillen to Western Australia, for there is nothing that I have more at heart than that."

Frazer himself never got out into the field or encountered any people more primitive than Cambridge undergraduates. Edward Westermarck, in his 1928 Frazer Lecture, announces:

> I have heard Sir James himself regret that he has derived his facts from books without supplementing them through personal work in the field. This was really the main reason why I wanted to point out the enormous importance of his research just for the field anthropologist. A commander *should* not expose himself to the dangers attending action on the field. And in Social Anthropology Sir James Frazer is the supreme commander.

Westermarck goes on to point out how taking along a copy of *The Golden Bough*—"luckily enough for my pack-mule" then in two volumes—when he first went into the field in Morocco had done wonders for him, by way of showing him what to look for and how to interpret it. When the suggestion was made that an expedition leaving for New Guinea take Frazer along, the Governor of New Guinea protested: "Frazer must stay at home, for he is the brains, and we are merely the feelers." After Frazer's death Malinowski wrote in his biographical appreciation: "The letters which I received from Frazer during my sojourn in New Guinea and Melanesia helped me more by suggestion, query and comment than any other influence."

William James reports that he once asked Frazer about natives he had known, and Frazer exclaimed, "But Heaven forbid!" It was not that he was too much of a humanist to go into the field, but, in his own conception of anthropology, too much of a scientist. Just as the field workers must not be corrupted by comparisons or analogues, so the study worker must not be corrupted by one cultural context and its special features, and if he were to take the time to familiarize himself with a number of cultures in the field, who would meanwhile read all the books and make all the comparisons and generalizations? There is some evidence that Frazer resented his lack of experience in the field. In his memorial tribute, "Fison and Howitt," published in *Folk-Lore* in 1909 and reprinted in *The Gorgon's Head*, Frazer sneers at those "who study savages at a safe distance, and have never perhaps seen one of them in their lives," and "all who view savages through a telescope, whether from a club or a college window." The division of labor between study and field, which had been invented by McLennan, was nevertheless Frazer's basic conception of proper anthropological method. His brief reviews of ethnographies in the *Times Literary Supplement* never forget to praise the field worker for his "prudent abstention" from speculation, generalization, and comparison, "which only tend to impair the value of a descriptive work on a definite ethnical area," and for which abstention "the anthropologist at home can hardly be too grateful to him." In plain truth, Spencer and Gillen's *The Native Tribes of Central Australia*, Frazer's ideal ethnography, does briefly venture into comparison with other peoples, origin theory, and evolutionary generalization, but, Frazer apparently felt, not fatally.

Frazer admired Spencer with an impressive humility that appears to be quite sincere. "Books like mine, merely speculative," he wrote to him in 1898, "will be superseded sooner or later (the sooner the better for the sake of truth) by better inductions based on fuller knowledge; books like yours, containing records of observation, will never be superseded." That same year he presents a problem to Spencer with the explanation: "I can only state this difficulty without solving it." He even complains to Spencer in 1903 about the "stiffness and artificiality" of his own writing. Spencer fully returned the admiration. In his 1897 letter beginning the correspondence, he writes, "I need hardly say that the *Golden Bough* has been most useful to me." (Poor Gillen probably wasn't allowed to read it.) Two years later, Spencer writes to Frazer that he is "appreciating more and more your wealth of knowledge and power of intuition, and envying you much your delightful style of writing." The next year, after receiving a copy of the second edition of *The Golden Bough*, Spencer writes to Frazer: "The knowledge that there is some one like you who can piece together the odd fragments of information which isolated workers can acquire is a great stimulant." In 1903 Spencer writes denying that Frazer's writing is either stiff or artificial, adding: "After receiving your letter to-day, I just went and read the ending of the *Golden Bough* once more, and thought that if ever I could write in that way I should die happy!"

Spencer and Gillen had both been initiated into the Arunta witchetty-grub totem. Both had a solid knowledge of the Australian aborigines, Spencer from three ambitious expeditions and his training as a natural scientist (he was a professor of biology at the University of Melbourne), Gillen from his years as a Sub-Protector in the native administration. Somewhat to our amazement, both accepted Frazer as equally conversant with aboriginal thinking and behavior, through the power of his imagination. Thus Frazer writes to Spencer in 1898, reconstructing the thinking of a kangaroo-man and improvising a soliloquy for him. Spencer writes, correcting him, "I find a difficulty in regard to your suggested train of thought," but the difficulty lies in facts Frazer did not yet know, not in the way he has his kangaroo-man think. In 1897, before the friendship with Frazer began, Spencer wrote to Henry Balfour:

> It is astonishing how, when once you have spent any time among savages, you divide Anthropological writers up as you read them, into those who understand savages and those who don't. Tylor pre-eminently does, so does Frazer.

We might note that Tylor, although primarily another study anthropologist, *had* been in the field. In *James George Frazer: the Portrait of a Scholar*, R. Angus Downie writes:

> Whether, as part of his Scottish heritage, he has inherited enough of the clan spirit and of dialectic subtlety to sympathize with and to understand the workings of the savage mind, or whether he has, like other great men, retained much that is child-like in his character, it is certain that he has attained wonderful intimacy with the peculiar logic of primitive people in all parts of the globe.

We may legitimately doubt that Frazer's ability to understand the minds of primitive men, if we accept the testimony to it sometimes in defiance of our own impressions, came either from his Scots-clan-mind or his child-mind. If he had such a power, it was the power of the aesthetic imagination, the same power that lets a writer into the mind of Tamerlane or Joan of Arc.

Frazer never entirely gave up his straight literary studies. In 1912 he published an edition of the *Letters of William Cowper* with a memoir, and in 1915 he published a selected *Essays of Joseph Addison* with a preface. Neither seems a fount of insight. Frazer's memoir of Cowper, his favorite poet and a fellow barrister of the Middle Temple, is typi-

cally, "He came of a good stock on both sides," or "The poet had to
put up with the incessant screaming of children and barking dogs."
The preface to Addison is an elaborate whimsy about "A visit to Coverley Hall," with little of Addison's freshness. Apparently primitive
custom and belief caught Frazer's imagination as no literature ever did,
and we can see the range and complexity of his poetic imagination, not
in his tepid essays on literary subjects, but in his compilations on magic
and religion. Late in his life Frazer defined "the highest poetry" as
characterized by "that flight of imagination, that outburst of lyrical
rapture." For him, the highest poetry was the curious behavior of man.

The Golden Bough

T HE third edition of *The Golden Bough*, subtitled *A Study in Magic and Religion*, appeared in twelve volumes from 1911 to 1915, the work now of "Sir" James George Frazer. The author apologizes for its bulk in the new preface:

> When I originally conceived the idea of the work, of which the first part is now laid before the public in a third and enlarged edition, my intention merely was to explain the strange rule of the priesthood or sacred kingship of Nemi and with it the legend of the Golden Bough, immortalised by Virgil, which the voice of antiquity associated with the priesthood. The explanation was suggested to me by some similar rules formerly imposed on kings in Southern India, and at first I thought that it might be adequately set forth within the compass of a small volume. But I soon found that in attempting to settle one question I had raised many more: wider and wider prospects opened out before me; and thus step by step I was lured on into far-spreading fields of primitive thought which had been but little explored by my predecessors. Thus the book grew on my hands, and soon the projected essay became in fact a ponderous treatise, or rather a series of separate dissertations loosely linked together by a slender thread of connexion with my original subject.

The principles on which he would explain the priesthood at Nemi are defined by Frazer in the first chapter:

> Accordingly, if we can shew that a barbarous custom, like that of the priesthood of Nemi, has existed elsewhere; if we can detect the motives which led to its institution; if we can prove that these motives have operated widely, perhaps universally, in human society, producing in varied circumstances a variety of institutions specifically different but generically alike; if we can shew, lastly, that these very motives, with some of their derivative institutions, were actually at work in classical antiquity; then we may fairly infer that at a remoter age the same motives gave birth to the priesthood

233

of Nemi. Such an inference, in default of direct evidence as to
how the priesthood did actually arise, can never amount to a demonstration. But it will be more or less probable according to the
degree of completeness with which it fulfils the conditions I have
indicated. The object of this book is, by meeting these conditions,
to offer a fairly probable explanation of the priesthood of Nemi.

That statement had been carried by Frazer through all the editions, as
chapters expanded into sections and sections into volumes. The volume, *Taboo and the Perils of the Soul*, for example, was "merely an
expansion of the corresponding chapter in the first edition," and it in
turn could have been expanded still further, since its footnotes list
books giving examples "in addition to those which have been cited in
the previous pages."

The superficial form of *The Golden Bough*, the raising of a problem that leads the reader a merry chase before it can be answered, was
apparently Frazer's natural form. His first important article, "On certain Burial Customs as illustrative of the Primitive Theory of the Soul,"
published in 1886, begins with an apparently trivial problem from
Plutarch's *Roman Questions:*

When a man who has been falsely reported to have died abroad, returns home alive, why is he not admitted by the door, but gets up
on the tiles and so lets himself down into the house?

After many pages of comparative material on custom and belief, Frazer
interjects:

All this time, however, Plutarch has been waiting for his answer, but, perhaps, as he has already waited two thousand years, he
will not object to be kept in suspense for a very few more minutes.

The paper concludes with an explanation, and the comment, "And this
is an English answer to a Roman question." The priesthood at Nemi in
Aricia, that odd custom whereby the priest took office by slaying his
predecessor, was another Roman question that would have an English
answer, and this one after a chase of prodigious length.

As Frazer's conditions for his demonstration suggest, the primary
claim of *The Golden Bough*, like that of *Totemism and Exogamy*, is to
be scrupulously scientific. The preface to the first edition in 1890 says
that the author has discovered some facts that "suggested an explanation" of the rule of the Arician priesthood, and that if he has pushed
the theory too far, "I will readily acknowledge and retract my error as
soon as it is brought home to me." The preface to the second edition in
1900 adds:

Hypotheses are necessary but often temporary bridges built to
connect isolated facts. If my light bridges should sooner or later
break down or be superseded by more solid structures, I hope that
my book may still have its utility and its interest as a repertory of
facts.

Frazer continues:

> As the scope and purpose of my book have been seriously mis-
> conceived by some courteous critics, I desire to repeat in more
> explicit language, what I vainly thought I had made quite clear in
> my original preface, that this is not a general treatise on primitive
> superstition, but merely the investigation of one particular and
> narrowly limited problem, to wit, the rule of the Arician priest-
> hood, and that accordingly only such general principles are ex-
> plained and illustrated in the course of it as seemed to me to throw
> light on that special problem.

"No one will welcome further evidence," he writes, "more warmly
than I shall," and he continues, "I hold myself ready to follow the evidence wherever it may lead." The preface to the third edition, written
in 1910, shows Frazer growing more tentative with each decade. He
writes:

> Similarly, should my whole theory of this particular priesthood
> collapse—and I fully acknowledge the slenderness of the founda-
> tions on which it rests—its fall would hardly shake my general
> conclusions as to the evolution of primitive religion and society,
> which are founded on large collections of entirely independent
> and well-authenticated facts.

As a scientist, Frazer makes use of analogy with the natural sciences: "In magic, as I believe in physics, action and reaction are equal
and opposite." Magic is seen as a kind of primitive erroneous science.
"If he claims a sovereignty over nature," Frazer writes of the magician,
"it is a constitutional sovereignty rigorously limited in its scope and
exercised in exact conformity with ancient usage. Thus the analogy between the magical and the scientific conceptions of the world is close."
To both are opposed religion. Insofar as it "assumes the world to be
directed by conscious agents who may be turned from their purpose
by persuasion, it stands in fundamental antagonism to magic as well as
to science, both of which take for granted that the course of nature is
determined, not by the passions or caprice of personal beings, but by
the operation of immutable laws acting mechanically."

Metaphors drawn from Darwinian science appear everywhere,
from "The magician is the humble grub or chrysalis which in due time
bursts and discloses that gorgeous butterfly the rajah or king," to "a
clearly marked religious stratification." Frazer writes, in language very
like Darwin's, of "the marvelous order and uniformity with which Nature conducts her operations, the wheels of her great machine revolving with a smoothness and precision." Like Darwin, Frazer sat at the
center of a great web of communications, with everyone supplying information to him. Much more than Darwin, he lived by books and the
written word, but like him he habitually appealed from them to immersion in nature. Frazer writes:

If only students would study the little black and white books of men less and the great rainbow-tinted book of nature more; if they would more frequently exchange the heavy air and the dim light of libraries for the freshness and the sunshine of the open sky; if they would oftener unbend their minds by rural walks between fields of waving corn, beside rivers rippling by under grey willows, or down green lanes, where the hedges are white with the hawthorn bloom or red with wild roses, they might sometimes learn more about primitive religion than can be gathered from many dusty volumes, in which wire-drawn theories are set forth with all the tedious parade of learning.

The two even had a common vision of annihilation. In the book's conclusion Frazer writes: "In the ages to come man may be able to predict, perhaps even to control, the wayward courses of the winds and clouds, but hardly will his puny hands have strength to speed afresh our slackening planet in its orbit or rekindle the dying fire of the sun." He footnotes a passage from a letter of Darwin's:

I quite agree how humiliating the slow progress of man is, but every one has his own pet horror, and this slow progress or even personal annihilation sinks in my mind into insignificance compared with the idea or rather I presume certainty of the sun some day cooling and we all freezing.

Frazer never directly compared himself with Darwin, so far as I know. As he had written in *Lectures on the Early History of the Kingship*, he believed that "The great thinkers, the Newtons and Darwins of anthropology, will come after us." As an anthropological scientist, however, his method was, like Darwin's, evolutionary, inductive, and comparative. The cultural evolution he had acquired from Tylor, and its assumptions, underlie everything in *The Golden Bough*. Mostly it is a sophisticated neo-evolutionism: "I am far from affirming that the course of development has everywhere rigidly followed these lines: it has doubtless varied greatly in different societies"; "But in the progress upward from savagery men of the same generation do not march abreast"; "It seems likely that a similar overlapping of the various strata takes place in every instance." A constant in the book is what might be called Tylor's Law, that the functional usages of early stages survive as the playthings of later, as the hunter's bow and arrow and the shaman's rattle become the toys of children. Frazer writes of "the tenacity of life possessed by folk-custom and its tendency, with the growth of civilisation, to dwindle from solemn ritual into mere pageant and pastime"; "Magic regularly dwindles into divination before it degenerates into a simple game"; "It is thus that religious or magical rites dwindle away into the sports of children."

The inductive method Frazer owed particularly to Mannhardt, along with most of the European lore in the book and some theory. The preface to the first edition acknowledges, "I have made great use of the works of the late W. Mannhardt, without which, indeed, my book could scarcely have been written." Collecting sowing and harvest beliefs and customs "in great abundance," Mannhardt had discovered inductively that their function was to make the crops grow. Frazer wrote, as he says, "following in the footsteps of W. Mannhardt," convinced that Mannhardt's inference had been confirmed by the evidence of the Arunta *intichiuma* ceremonies. Part V of *The Golden Bough*, *Spirits of the Corn and of the Wild*, is almost an anthology of Mannhardt's writings, and Frazer keeps reminding the reader that "according to Mannhardt, whose theory I am expounding, the spirit of the corn manifests itself not merely in vegetable but also in human form." He continually makes Mannhardt's basic assumption: "Wherever a like custom has been practised . . . we may conjecture that the motive has been similar." By the third edition Frazer had largely discarded one of Mannhardt's theories, that fire festivals are attempts at restoring the sun's heat, for a poorer theory of Westermarck's, that they are purificatory in origin. He kept the former theory in the book anyway, in part because he never discarded anything, in part "out of deference to Mannhardt, for whose work I entertain the highest respect."

"Much as I owe to Mannhardt," Frazer acknowledges in the preface to the first edition, "I owe still more to my friend Professor W. Robertson Smith." From Smith came a refined comparative method and a most important idea. Frazer writes, "Indeed the central idea of my essay—the conception of the slain god—is derived directly, I believe, from my friend." By the time of the preface to the second edition, Smith was dead, and Frazer writes:

> Messrs. H. Hubert and M. Mauss have represented my theory of the slain god as intended to supplement and complete Robertson Smith's theory of the derivation of animal sacrifice in general from a totem sacrament. On this I have to say that the two theories are quite independent of each other. I never assented to my friend's theory, and so far as I can remember he never gave me a hint that he assented to mine.

More boldly than Smith, Frazer delights in parallels as far apart culturally as possible. "But it is a far cry to Italy from the forests of Cambodia and the sources of the Nile," he writes early in *The Golden Bough*. It is a rhetorical protest only, and the reader will go much further afield before he is finished. The fire customs of the Herero of Africa throw light on those of the ancient Latins, Fijian ceremonies of catching in scarves the souls of criminals explain Athenian cursing of the sacrilegious, the Kikuyu use a scapegoat very like that of the ancient Jews, and so forth.

In one aspect, *The Golden Bough* is a vast argument from analogy. Beyond that, it is hard to classify as to field. In the preface to the final part, *Balder the Beautiful*, Frazer identifies the work as a kind of comparative anatomy of the mind. He writes:

If there is one general conclusion which seems to emerge from the mass of particulars, I venture to think that it is the essential similarity in the working of the less developed human mind among all races, which corresponds to the essential similarity in their bodily frame revealed by comparative anatomy.

"*The Golden Bough* reveals a profound continuity in the human mind," John Peale Bishop writes in his essay on the book. At other times Frazer sees his field as anthropology, whether "social" or "mental." "The savage does not understand the thoughts of the civilised man," he writes, "and few civilised men understand the thoughts of the savage." For this insight specific knowledge of the cultural context is required. For example:

> To explain the ultimate reason why any particular food is prohibited to a whole tribe or to certain of its members would commonly require a far more intimate knowledge of the history and beliefs of the tribe than we possess.

The movement of thought, he writes, following Comte, "so far as we can trace it, has on the whole been from magic through religion to science." Science is not the end, however. "As science has supplanted its predecessors, so it may hereafter be itself superseded by some more perfect hypothesis, perhaps by some totally different way of looking at the phenomena—of registering the shadows on the screen—of which we in this generation can form no idea."

Sometimes Frazer phrases his book's field as speculative prehistory, as in the preface to the second edition, where he writes: "I offer my book in its new form as a contribution to that still youthful science which seeks to trace the growth of human thought and institutions in those dark ages which lie beyond the range of history." Sometimes it is more a sociological history of ideas or institutions. He has emphasized magic, Frazer writes in the preface to the third edition, "because it seems to have been overlooked by writers on the origin of political institutions, who, themselves sober and rational according to modern standards, have not reckoned sufficiently with the enormous influence which superstition has exerted in shaping the human past." When *The Golden Bough* first appeared, it was subtitled "A Study in Comparative Religion." For the second and third editions, Frazer substituted "A Study in Magic and Religion," having decided that Comparative Religion did not embrace all of his subject matter. In the preface to Part II, *Taboo and the Perils of the Soul*, written in 1911, Frazer suggests Comparative Ethics. He writes:

> Few things, perhaps, can better guard us from narrowness and illiberality in our moral judgments than a survey of the amazing diversities of ethical theory and practice which have been recorded among the various races of mankind in different ages; and accordingly the Comparative Method applied to the study of ethical phenomena may be expected to do for morality what the same method

applied to religious phenomena is now doing for religion, by enlarging our mental horizon, extending the boundaries of knowledge, throwing light on the origin of current beliefs and practices, and thereby directly assisting us to replace what is effete by what is vigorous, and what is false by what is true. The facts which I have put together in this volume as well as in some of my other writings may perhaps serve as materials for a future science of Comparative Ethics. They are rough stones which await the master-builder, rude sketches which more cunning hands than mine may hereafter work up into a finished picture.

At less ambitious times Frazer saw the book as a work within the field of folklore, a category which then as now took in almost anything homeless elsewhere.

A major concern of *The Golden Bough*, if not its primary concern, is to produce a theory of mythology. Here Frazer changes his mind so frequently that the third edition of the book is like the palimpsest Frazer often uses as an image for human morality, with statement after statement written over the last on the same document. The theory of the origin of myths with which he began is the simple and convincing one that they arise out of rites distorted and misunderstood. It was clearly implicit in Tylor and explicit in Smith and Mannhardt, and early in the twentieth century it was powerfully reinforced by Jane Harrison, F. M. Cornford and A. B. Cook at Cambridge and by Gilbert Murray at Oxford. This explanation in various phrasings runs all through *The Golden Bough*: "Clearly they belong to that large class of myths which are made up to explain the origin of a religious ritual"; "The legend is plainly a fiction devised to explain the ritual"; "Now the institution of a festival is often explained by a mythical story, which relates how upon a particular occasion those very calamities occurred which it is the real object of the festival to avert"; "may well be a reminiscence of a real custom"; "these traditions may very well reflect a real custom"; "we may reasonably ask whether Ariadne's Dance of the Game of Troy may not have had its origin in religious ritual"; "Such stories may well reflect a custom"; "The narrative has all the air of a fiction devised to explain an old custom, of which the real meaning and origin had been forgotten."

The legends of Pentheus and Lycurgus, Frazer suggests, may be "distorted reminiscences of a custom of sacrificing divine kings in the character of Dionysus." He writes:

We shall probably not err in assuming that many myths, which we now know only as myths, had once their counterpart in magic; in other words, that they used to be acted as a means of producing in fact the events which they describe in figurative language. Ceremonies often die out while myths survive, and thus we are left to infer the dead ceremony from the living myth.

"If we could trace these stories back to their origin," he writes, "we might find that in every case a human couple acted year by year the

parts of the loving goddess and the dying god." Frazer never maintained that *all* myths originate in ritual, and at best his ritual theory is
flawed by the sort of rationalism that saw social institutions deliberately created to produce desired effects, and similarly sees myths as
fictions "made up" or "devised" to explain rites.

Running alongside these ritual explanations of myth, sometimes on
the same page, are cognitionist explanations that have some myths
originate as attempts to explain natural phenomena. Frazer writes: "It
occurred to me that this myth of the demon lover may have been based
on some physical phenomenon, electrical, lunar, or otherwise, which
is periodically seen at night in the Maldive Islands." "These natural
conditions would easily suggest a fable of giants who had taught the
gods and had been slain by thunderbolts," Frazer suggests, and quotes
Tylor, "Tales of giants and monsters, which stand in direct connexion
with the finding of great fossil bones, are scattered broadcast over the
mythology of the world." Elsewhere:

> But we have still to ask, how did the conception of such a compos-
> ite deity originate? Did it arise simply through observation of the
> great annual fluctuations of the seasons and a desire to explain
> them? Was it a result of brooding over the mystery of external
> Nature? Was it the attempt of a rude philosophy to lift the veil and
> explore the hidden springs that set the vast machine in motion?
> That man at a very early stage of his long history meditated on
> these things and evolved certain crude theories which partially
> satisfied his craving after knowledge is certain; from such medita-
> tions of Babylonian and Phrygian sages appear to have sprung the
> pathetic figures of Adonis and Attis; and from such meditations of
> Egyptian sages may have sprung the tragic figure of Osiris.

Frazer repeatedly denies that customs and taboos are rational precautions, proto-hygiene, because of their inconsistency: if the abstinences
imposed on hunters were to keep up their strength for the chase, they
would not continue after the chase; if a fish were taboo because the
people knew it came from polluted water, it would not be reserved for
the king on solemn occasions; and so forth. But his primitives are otherwise proto-scientists in that they produce myths as hypotheses to explain why the water is phosphorescent, or where all those big bones
came from, or why crops spring up and die.

Frazer's third inconsistent strand of myth explanation in *The
Golden Bough* is the euhemerist theory, mostly inspired by Roscoe,
that some myths are distorted recollections of history. "The memories
of great battles linger long among the peasantry of the neighborhood,"
he writes. Of the Romans: "It is quite possible that the uncertainty as
to their fathers may not have arisen till long after the death of the
kings, when their figures began to melt away into the cloudland of
fable, assuming fantastic shapes and gorgeous colouring as they passed
from earth to heaven." "As gods are often merely men who loom large
through the mists of tradition," he writes; or, "Under favourable cir-

cumstances the worship of a dead king may develop into the dominant religion of a people"; or, "The magic touch of time, which distorts and magnifies the past, especially among peoples who see it only through the haze of oral tradition, has glorified and transfigured many a dead man into a deity."

Frazer sometimes holds one or another of these origin theories as a universal, sometimes holds that some or all of them are true for different sorts of myths, sometimes strikes a point midway between two, and sometimes argues for one under the impression that it is one of the others. Thus when he is finally persuaded "to incline the balance to the side of Euhemerism" and believe that Balder was once a real man, he writes:

> The acceptance of this hypothesis would not necessarily break the analogy which I have traced between Balder in his sacred grove on the Sogne fiord of Norway and the priest of Diana in the sacred grove of Nemi; indeed, it might even be thought rather to strengthen the resemblance between the two, since there is no doubt at all that the priests of Diana at Nemi were men who lived real lives and died real deaths.

Here the distinction between the myth as history, where the god was once a real man, and the myth as rite, where the god never existed but is annually personified by men, is hopelessly muddled by the fact that in both cases men "lived real lives and died real deaths."

Elsewhere in the book, with the same confusion, Frazer identifies his own ritual interpretations of myths as euhemerism. Occasionally, he sees the difference clearly, and writes, for example:

> The story of Pygmalion points to a ceremony of a sacred marriage in which the king wedded the image of Aphrodite, or rather of Astarte. If that was so, the tale was in a sense true, not of a single man only, but of a whole series of men.

Sometimes Frazer seems to know exactly what euhemerism is, as when he writes: "In this version a Euhemeristic turn has been given to the myth by representing Jupiter and Juno (Zeus and Hera) as a king and queen of Crete." A dozen pages later "this legend was not a mere myth" because it was apparently based on a real ritual, and myth is some sort of baseless fiction or fabrication. In a pacific, or dialectic, mood, Frazer denies that these incompatible theories are incompatible, writing:

> The personages about whom all the marvels of mythology have been told may have been real human beings, as the Euhemerists allege; and yet they may have been at the same time personifications of natural objects or processes, as the adversaries of Euhemerism assert.

A long paragraph of monumental confusion offers justification. At other times Frazer solves the problem by making euhemerism the origin of the myth, and ritual its function. He writes:

Whatever may be thought of an historical kernel underlying a mythical husk in the legend of Balder, the details of the story suggests that it belongs to that class of myths which have been dramatized in ritual, or, to put it otherwise, which have been performed as magical ceremonies for the sake of producing those natural effects which they describe in figurative language.

In *The Dramas and Dramatic Dances of Non-European Races*, published in 1915, Ridgeway took advantage of what seemed to be Frazer's defection to euhemerism in the third edition of *The Golden Bough* to storm the redoubts of the ritual theory. On the assumptions of Sir James Frazer, "one of my oldest and best friends," Ridgeway writes, "Miss Harrison, Mr. F. M. Cornford, and Professor G. Murray have based the latest theory of the origin of Tragedy." "From the seed sown by Mannhardt in the rich soil of Eleusis," he continues, "has sprung a goodly crop of tares." "Under the spell of the Mannhardt-Frazer theory, my friends Mr. A. B. Cook and Mr. F. M. Cornford have sought to prove that the great games of Greece, such as those at Olympia, arose out of a contest similar to that for the priesthood at Nemi." Since Frazer has renounced ritual origins for euhemerism, Ridgeway exults, "What now becomes of Professor Murray's theory of the origin of Tragedy" and the rest? "With Sir James Frazer's failure of faith in his leading doctrine, what becomes of the flimsy edifices reared by his followers upon his former theories?" To which Harrison and Murray, Cornford and Cook, could fairly reply that Frazer had never been of their party long enough, nor consistently enough, to entitle him to defect from it.

The Golden Bough similarly shuttles between the opposed theories of polygenesis and diffusion for the origin of custom and myth. Generally Frazer believes that customs arise independently because of similar human nature and needs. He writes of the similar fire rites of Rome, Peru, and the Herero of Africa: "There seems to be every reason to think that all three sets of customs originated independently in the simple needs and superstitious fancies of the savage." Frazer argues elsewhere:

> We need not, with some enquirers in ancient and modern times, suppose that these Western peoples borrowed from the older civilisation of the Orient the conception of the Dying and Reviving God, together with the solemn ritual, in which that conception was dramatically set forth before the eyes of the worshippers. More probably the resemblance which may be traced in this respect between the religions of the East and the West is no more than what we commonly, though incorrectly, call a fortuitous coincidence, the effect of similar causes acting alike on the similar constitution of the human mind in different countries and under different skies.

The similarity of the worships of Dionysus and Osiris, he adds, "is sufficiently explained by the similarity of the ideas and customs on which they were founded." Christian and Roman Saturnalia "may well have been parallel and independent deductions from a like primitive philosophy of nature." On the other hand, there is no reason to believe that similar myths and stories arose independently out of similar rites, "for it is certain that popular tales spread by diffusion from tribe to tribe and nation to nation, till they may be handed down by oral tradition among people who neither practise nor even understand the customs in which the stories originated." By the preface to the last part, *Balder the Beautiful*, Frazer has again reached a compromise. He writes:

> To sift out the elements of culture which a race has independently evolved and to distinguish them accurately from those which it has derived from other races is a task of extreme difficulty and delicacy, which promises to occupy students of man for a long time to come; indeed so complex are the facts and so imperfect in most cases is the historical record that it may be doubted whether in regard to many of the lower races we shall ever arrive at more than probable conjectures.

Writing as an anthropological scientist, Frazer naturally plumps for cultural and ethical relativism. He identifies "the commonest of all errors in dealing with the past, that, namely, of interpreting the customs of other races and other generations by reference to modern European standards." Frazer continues:

> In order to understand an alien religion the first essential is to divest ourselves, as well as we can, of our own familiar prepossessions, and to place ourselves at the point of view of those whose faith and practice we are studying. To do this at all is difficult; to do it completely is perhaps impossible; yet the attempt must be made if the enquiry is to progress instead of returning on itself in a vicious circle.

Elsewhere Frazer proclaims:

> The old view that the principles of right and wrong are immutable and eternal is no longer tenable. The moral world is as little exempt as the physical world from the law of ceaseless change, of perpetual flux. Contemplate the diversities, the inconsistencies, the contradictions of the ethical ideas and the ethical practice, not merely of different peoples in different countries, but of the same people in the same country in different ages, then say whether the foundations of morality are eternally fixed and unchanging.

"We can as little arrest the process of moral evolution," he concludes, "as we can stay the sweep of the tides or the courses of the stars." Later Frazer writes of

> the common, the perpetually repeated mistake of judging the savage by the standard of European civilisation. If any of my readers set out with the notion that all races of men think and act much

in the same way as educated Englishmen, the evidence of superstitious belief and custom collected in the volumes of this work
should suffice to disabuse him of so erroneous a prepossession.

"It would be to misjudge ancient religion," Frazer warns us, "to de-
nounce as lewd and profligate the emblems and the ceremonies which
the Egyptians employed for the purpose of giving effect to this conception of the divine power." Part IV ends on his final statement of
relativism:

> If we would understand the early history of institutions, we must
> learn to detach ourselves from the prepossessions of our own time
> and country, and to place ourselves as far as possible at the stand-
> point of men in distant lands and distant ages.

Frazer's faith in cultural and ethical relativism never falters, but his
practice rarely comes up to it. Ethnocentric reactions are too deeply
ingrained. His constant comment is "these crazy wretches," "these
foolish Indians," "these misguided savages," "the muzzy mind of the
Sicilian bumpkin," "the cunning and selfish savage." "Some such train
of thought," he writes, "if these gropings and fumblings of a mind in
darkness deserve the name of thought." Of Isis: "Hence her beautiful
Madonna-like figure reflects a more refined state of society and of
morals than the coarse, sensual, cruel figures of Astarte, Anaitis,
Cybele, and the rest of that crew."

WHEN he assembled the third edition of *The Golden Bough*, Frazer
presented the book as a work of literature. With characteristic ambivalence, he denies that this means giving up its scientific pretensions.
Frazer writes in the preface:

> By discarding the austere form, without, I hope, sacrificing the
> solid substance, of a scientific treatise, I thought to cast my ma-
> terials into a more artistic mould and so perhaps to attract readers,
> who might have been repelled by a more strictly logical and
> systematic arrangement of the facts.

More and more, Frazer keeps referring to his theories as playful fancies
rather than as scientific conjectures, writing typically: "I put forward
the hypothesis for no more than a web of conjectures woven from
the gossamer threads of popular superstition." Brailsford saw this as
primarily a matter of artistry, writing:

> With a plodding industry that no Teutonic scholar ever surpassed,
> he managed to combine an artist's sense of form, and even when it
> grew into twelve big volumes, packed with innumerable notes,
> *The Golden Bough* moved from the intriguing question of its
> opening pages to the triumphant solution in its last book with a

sureness and grace that resembled rather a musical composition in strict sonata form than a scientific treatise.

Others, like Ridgeway, saw it as primarily the renunciation of the views with which Frazer had been identified. Marett writes in his 1927 Frazer lecture:

> Surely, of all the great pioneers of anthropology, Sir James Frazer has been the foremost in proclaiming the purely provisional character of his working principles. Not to speak of that drastic reconstruction of the theoretical framework which caused the second edition of *The Golden Bough* when it replaced the first to read almost like a different work, I know nothing in the history of science more dramatic, and at the same time more indicative of the true spirit of research, than the *peripeteia* that awaits one in the third edition.

Frazer's *peripeteia* came when he decided that gods were not the embodiment of fertility rites but deified real men. As a consequence he decided to stop taking any theory seriously and to renounce the idea that these phenomena were ultimately explicable, at least by him. Frazer went back to being a literary man.

Precisely what sort of literary form the book has gets as many different replies as the earlier question about what sort of social science it is. Frazer's first insistence is that he is writing an epic of humanity's ascent to rationality and perfection, a Paradise First-Gained rather than Regained. In the preface to the second edition, he speaks of "enabling us to follow the long march, the slow and toilsome ascent, of humanity from savagery to civilisation." The assumption of unlimited perfectibility is never dealt with explicity in *The Golden Bough*, but Frazer faced it later as the central theme of his two essays on the Marquis of Condorcet. In "Condorcet on Human Progress," in 1922, Frazer writes: "He was among the first, perhaps the very first, to proclaim as a doctrine, and almost as a dogma, the endless perfectibility of human nature." Frazer adds: "He regarded perfectibility as a general law of nature applicable alike to all organic beings, whether animal or vegetable." In "Condorcet on the Progress of the Human Mind," in 1933, this is restated as: "The course which humanity may be expected to follow hereafter in its progress towards that goal of absolute perfection which it will continually approach without ever actually reaching."

What Frazer does face in *The Golden Bough* is man's limitations as a rational animal, that is, the problem he calls "superstition." "Even in Europe many people still believe," is his characteristic introduction to a superstition, and "So indestructible are the crude fancies of our savage forefathers" is his characteristic conclusion. Frazer's tone is generally mocking and sarcastic, with such comments as "So hard is it for the straining wings of fancy to outstrip the folly of mankind." Here is his typical irony:

It would be superfluous to point out in detail how admirably these measures are calculated to arrest the ravages of disease; but for the sake of those, if there are any, to whom the medicinal effect of crawling through a hole on hands and knees is not at once apparent, I shall merely say that the procedure in question is one of the most powerful specifics which the wit of man has devised for maladies of all sorts.

Frazer finished the third edition of *The Golden Bough* on the eve of the first World War, and some of his disquiet about man as a rational animal apparently came from those gathering tensions. Bishop writes:

Sir James Frazer, writing before the war of 1914–1918, was aware as were few living men of the primitive substructure of modern civilization. But what was frightening in the aftermath of the war was not that the conflict shattering the walls had revealed old and almost forgotten foundations; it was that an advancing civilization should so terribly emulate savagery. It was society in its most modern form that had insisted on returning to that democracy in arms of savage tribes. It was the advance in technics that had made troglodytes of armies. If we were dying, it was not from our vices but from an excess of our virtues. If there was a revolt from reason, it was not against reasoning as an instrument of living, but against the rationalism of the eighteenth century which, after being transformed into the materialism of the nineteenth century, had in our own become dynamism. A faith in progress had become a most unreasonable faith in motion for its own sake. And its works were not good.

Unnerved about his paradise in the present and unsure of it in the future, Frazer violently wrenches it out of time and history entirely, to produce a Platonic idea or ideal of culture. Epic is not history, Frazer had reminded us in *Passages of the Bible*. In this Platonic view, culture-contact does not result in a changing shape for the culture, but in the destruction of the record. In a key metaphor, Frazer writes,

We are like heirs to a fortune which has been handed down for so many ages that the memory of those who built it up is lost, and its possessors for the time being regard it as having been an original and unalterable possession of their race since the beginning of the world.

The title-deed is almost indecipherable, an evolutionary palimpsest, but the epic Frazer records is the quest for that grail of culture, and we inherit both the fortune and the traditions about it. Like all mythic quests, this involves a timeless essentializing out of history. Frazer's primary evolution of human thought in *The Golden Bough*, Comte's "from magic through religion to science," is not a development in history, but a temporalizing of essence. As far back as the reviews of the second edition of *The Golden Bough* in *Folk-Lore* in 1901, F. B. Jevons wrote: "That magic is distinct from religion, I hold with Dr. Frazer. But that magic is prior to religion, Dr. Frazer produces no evidence to show." Forty years later, with Frazer dead, Malinowski found himself repeating the same basic truth:

> In all this we find that evolution, as a metamorphosis of one type of belief or activity into an entirely different one, is not acceptable. We have to assume here, as in many other evolutionary problems, the existence of all the fundamental principles of human thought, belief, custom, and organization from the very beginnings of culture. Magic, religion, and science must be examined as active forces in human society, in organized cult and behavior, and in human psychology. In this we follow Frazer when he affirms that the simple truths derived from observation of nature have always been known to man.

Frazer knew realistically, as Malinowski says, that primitive tribes did not evolve from one to the other, but the essence of these modes is that of a graded series, and their Platonic ideas so evolve. *Man*, not any *men*, had progressed from magic through religion to science, and *The Golden Bough* is the epic of that idealized ascent, as *The Aeneid* is the similar epic idealization of the rise of Rome.

When Frazer actually came to describe the ascent, he sometimes saw the tragic features more sharply than the hopeful. He writes:

> We may feel some natural regret at the disappearance of quaint customs and picturesque ceremonies, which have preserved to an age often deemed dull and prosaic something of the flavour and freshness of the olden time, some breath of the springtime of the world; yet our regret will be lessened when we remember that these pretty pageants, these now innocent diversions, had their origin in ignorance and superstition; that if they are a record of human endeavour, they are also a monument of fruitless ingenuity, of wasted labour, and of blighted hopes and that for all their gay trappings—their flowers, their ribbons, and their music—they partake far more of tragedy than of farce.

In the preface to the last part, *Balder the Beautiful*, Frazer writes of "the long tragedy of human folly and suffering which has unrolled itself before the readers of these volumes, and on which the curtain is now about to fall." He concludes the preface more hopefully, promising in future books "fresh subjects of laughter and tears drawn from the comedy and the tragedy of man's endless quest after happiness and truth." By 1937, when he published *Aftermath: A Supplement to The Golden Bough*, Frazer was back to identifying the whole work as "a dark, a tragic chronicle of human error and folly, of fruitless endeavour, wasted time, and blighted hopes."

The imaginative design of the work is built around several key metaphors for the ascent to rationality and its dangers. The most dramatic of these is one that runs through Frazer's earlier writing, the volcano underfoot. In *The Golden Bough* we see its fullest development:

> It is not our business here to consider what bearing the permanent existence of such a solid layer of savagery beneath the surface of society, and unaffected by the superficial changes of religion and culture, has upon the future of humanity. The dispassionate observer, whose studies have led him to plumb its depths, can hardly regard it otherwise than as a standing menace to civilisation. We seem to move on a thin crust which may at any moment be rent by the subterranean forces slumbering below. From time to time a hollow murmur underground or a sudden spirt of flame into the air tells of what is going on beneath our feet.[1]

By the time of the preface to *Balder the Beautiful*, this metaphor has modified into a vision of man himself deceptively masked. Frazer writes:

> The truth seems to be that to this day the peasant remains a pagan and savage at heart; his civilisation is merely a thin veneer which the hard knocks of life soon abrade, exposing a solid core of paganism and savagery beneath. The danger created by a bottomless layer of ignorance and superstition under the crust of civilised society. . . .

"He knew, as he often said," Brailsford wrote in 1941, conscious of Hitler and the war, "that the primitive savage whose thinking he traced in our still surviving superstitions is alive in the dark places of our hearts." Frazer's common image for culture is of a great fabric, an orderly tangled bank. He writes of having touched only the fringe, having "fingered only a few of the countless threads that compose the mighty web." In this fabric, if magic is the darkness of ignorance, religion is the crimson stain of blood. In the penultimate paragraph of the book, perhaps influenced by Darwin's great tree, Frazer extends the fabric metaphor:

> Without dipping so far into the future, we may illustrate the course which thought has hitherto run by likening it to a web woven of three different threads—the black thread of magic, the red thread of religion, and the white thread of science, if under science we may include those simple truths, drawn from observation of nature, of which men in all ages have possessed a store.

---

[1] Darwin wrote in his diary in 1835, after experiencing an earthquake in Chile on the *Beagle* voyage:

> An earthquake like this at once destroys the oldest associations; the world, the very emblem of all that is solid, moves beneath our feet like a crust over a fluid; one second of time conveys to the mind a strange idea of insecurity, which hours of reflection would never create.

Could we then survey the web of thought from the beginning, we should probably perceive it to be at first a chequer of black and white, a patchwork of true and false notions, hardly tinged as yet by the red thread of religion. But carry your eye further along the fabric and you will remark that, while the black and white chequer still runs through it, there rests on the middle portion of the web, where religion has entered most deeply into its texture, a dark crimson stain, which shades off insensibly into a lighter tint as the white thread of science is woven more and more into the tissue. To a web thus chequered and stained, thus shot with threads of diverse hues, but gradually changing colour the farther it is un-rolled, the state of modern thought, with all its divergent aims and conflicting tendencies, may be compared. Will the great movement which for centuries has been slowly altering the complexion of thought be continued in the near future? or will a reaction set in which may arrest progress and even undo much that has been done? To keep up our parable, what will be the colour of the web which the Fates are now weaving on the humming loom of time? will it be white or red? We cannot tell. A faint glimmering light illumines the backward portion of the web. Clouds and thick darkness hide the other end.

As the last sentences suggest, a Manichaean conflict between light and dark pervades the book. The dark ages were literally so, "a dark cloud" over "the intellectual horizon of Europe." Before us is a "yawning chasm," or a prospect seen fitfully "whenever the mist rises and unfolds the far horizon." Frazer writes:

The domain of primitive superstition, in spite of the encroachments of science, is indeed still to a great extent a trackless wilderness, a tangled maze, in the gloomy recesses of which the forlorn explorer may wander for ever without a light and without a clue.

Of the primitive as thinker:

In attempting to track his devious thought through the jungle of crass ignorance and blind fear, we must always remember that we are treading enchanted ground, and must beware of taking for solid realities the cloudy shapes that cross our path or hover and gibber at us through the gloom.

At other times Frazer writes of plunging "into the labyrinth of magic." If ignorance, magic and superstition are dark, gloomy, misted-over, trackless jungle, and tangled maze or labyrinth, so science, truth and rationality are light, clearings or pathways, clues. Sometimes the book combines imagery of a path with that of light. Here the image is not very hopeful:

It is unlikely that the student's search-light will ever pierce the mists that hang over these remote ages. All that we can do is to follow the lines of evidence backward as far as they can be traced, till, after growing fainter and fainter, they are lost altogether in the darkness.

Many of Frazer's reservations throughout the book show this dual imagery. He writes:

However, I am fully sensible of the slipperiness and uncertainty of the ground I am treading, and it is with great diffidence that I submit these speculations to the judgment of my readers. The subject of ancient mythology is involved in dense mists which it is not always possible to penetrate and illumine even with the lamp of the Comparative Method.

Sometimes there is no path, but light itself makes a clearing in the jungle, or does not. "Drawing together the scattered rays of light," Frazer writes, he proposes "to turn them on the dark figure of the priest of Nemi." Elsewhere he writes:

The circle of human knowledge, illuminated by the pale cold light of reason, is so infinitesimally small, the dark regions of human ignorance which lie beyond that luminous ring are so immeasurably vast, that imagination is fain to step up to the border line and send the warm richly coloured beams of her fairy lantern streaming out into the darkness; and so, peering into the gloom, she is apt to mistake the shadowy reflections of her own figure for real beings moving in the abyss.

Frazer speaks of Demeter and Persephone, "one of the few myths in which the sunshine and clarity of the Greek genius are crossed by the shadow and mystery of death." Great ideas radiate from great minds "like shafts of light from high towers." "In every age," Frazer writes, "cities have been the centres and as it were the lighthouses from which ideas radiate into the surrounding darkness, kindled by the friction of mind with mind in the crowded haunts of men; and it is natural that at these beacons of intellectual light all should partake in some measure of the general illumination." At other times there is no light, and the image is only of a clearing or path. Frazer writes:

To recur to a metaphor which I have already made use of, we of this age are only pioneers hewing lanes and clearings in the forest where others will hereafter sow and reap.

He begins the book's last chapter:

We are at the end of our enquiry, but as often happens in the search after truth, if we have answered one question, we have raised many more; if we have followed one track home, we have had to pass by others that opened off it and led, or seemed to lead, to far other goals than the sacred grove at Nemi. Some of these paths we have followed a little way; others, if fortune should be kind, the writer and the reader may one day pursue together.

For the present we have journeyed far enough together, and it is time to part.

In 1936, when he wrote the preface to *Aftermath*, Frazer saw *The Golden Bough* primarily as a clue in the maze. He writes:

At the best the chronicle may serve as a warning, as a sort of Ariadne's thread, to help the forlorn wayfarer to shun some of the snares and pitfalls into which his fellows have fallen before him in the labyrinth of life.

In Frazer's epic of ascent, two other metaphors seem significant. One is the use of electricity or explosive for the dangerous powers of magic or *mana*. The savage regards his chiefs and kings, Frazer writes, "as charged with a mysterious spiritual force which so to say explodes at contact." Elsewhere: "In short, primitive man believes that what is sacred is dangerous; it is pervaded by a sort of electrical sanctity which communicates a shock to, even if it does not kill, whatever comes in contact with it." More elaborately:

Apparently holiness, magic virtue, taboo, or whatever we may call that mysterious quality which is supposed to pervade sacred or tabooed persons, is conceived by the primitive philosopher as a physical substance or fluid, with which the sacred man is charged just as a Leyden jar is charged with electricity; and exactly as the electricity in the jar can be discharged by contact with a good conductor, so the holiness or magic virtue in the man can be discharged and drained away by contact with the earth, which on this theory serves as an excellent conductor for the magical fluid.

The other metaphor is a military one, and involves no less than a war against Giant Superstition. Frazer writes in the preface to the second edition:

Yet sooner or later it is inevitable that the battery of the comparative method should breach these venerable walls, mantled over with the ivy and mosses and wild flowers of a thousand tender and sacred associations. At present we are only dragging the guns into position: they have hardly yet begun to speak.

In the new preface to *Spirits of the Corn and of the Wild* in 1912, still hopeful, Frazer writes of various things that "combine to draw men into communities, to drill them into regiments, and to set them marching on the road to progress with a concentrated force to which the loose skirmishers of mere anarchy and individualism can never hope to oppose a permanent resistance."

Running all through *The Golden Bough* is a sniping at Christianity, particularly in its Roman Catholic form. If the volcano underfoot is pagan superstition, the bloodstain of religion in the fabric is Christian history, and the darkness and mist, the trackless forest and labyrinth, the dangerous force or besieged enemy, are as apt to be the one as the other. "We must follow truth along," Frazer writes in the preface to the second edition, substituting it for the Cross; "It is our only guiding star: *hoc signo vinces.*" Sometimes Frazer makes his point against Christianity by suggestion. In India a human god started in life "as the son of a carpenter." Of an absurd remark by the divine king of Iddah in Nigeria: "But such confusion, or rather obscurity, is almost inseparable from any attempt to define with philosophic precision the profound mystery of incarnation." Of the early Romans: "Thus the doctrine of the divine birth of kings presents no serious difficulty to people who believe that god may be made flesh in a man, and that a virgin may conceive and bear him a son."

Sometimes Frazer points more directly at Christianity. Lumping together temple prostitutes and nuns, "It is thus that the folly of mankind finds vent in opposite extremes alike harmful and deplorable." Frazer writes generally:

> In the light of the foregoing evidence, stories of the miraculous birth of gods and heroes from virgin mothers lose much of the glamour that encircled them in days of old, and we view them simply as relics of superstition surviving like fossils to tell us of a bygone age of childlike ignorance and credulity.

Or:

> Such tales of virgin mothers are relics of an age of childish ignorance when men had not yet recognized the intercourse of the sexes as the true cause of offspring.

Delighted to learn that the religion of Attis centered in Vatican Hill in Rome, Frazer writes: "From the Vatican as a centre this barbarous system of superstition seems to have spread to other parts of the Roman empire." After describing the unselfish social values of the ancient world, Frazer continues:

> All this was changed by the spread of Oriental religions which inculcated the communion of the soul with God and its eternal salvation as the only objects worth living for, objects in comparison with which the prosperity and even the existence of the state sank into insignificance. The inevitable result of this selfish and immoral doctrine was to withdraw the devotee more and more from the public service, to concentrate his thoughts on his own spiritual emotions, and to breed in him a contempt for the present life which he regarded merely as a probation for a better and an eternal. The saint and the recluse, disdainful of earth and rapt in ecstatic contemplation of heaven, became in popular opinion the highest ideal of humanity, displacing the old ideal of the patriot and hero who, forgetful of self, lives and is ready to die for the good of his country. The earthly city seemed poor and contemptible to men whose eyes beheld the City of God coming in the clouds of heaven. Thus the centre of gravity, so to say,

was shifted from the present to a future life, and however much the other world may have gained, there can be little doubt that this one lost heavily by the change.

Citing an example of god-eating by a pariah caste in India, Frazer writes, without mentioning the Eucharist:

> In Europe the Catholic Church has resorted to similar means for enabling the pious to enjoy the ineffable privilege of eating the persons of the Infant God and his Mother. For this purpose images of the Madonna are printed on some soluble and harmless substance and sold in sheets like postage stamps. The worshipper buys as many of these sacred emblems as he has occasion for, and affixing one or more of them to his food swallows the bolus.

Some pages later he gets more direct:

> Yet a time comes when reasonable men find it hard to understand how any one in his senses can suppose that by eating bread or drinking wine he consumes the body or blood of a deity. 'When we call corn Ceres and wine Bacchus,' says Cicero, 'we use a common figure of speech; but do you imagine that anybody is so insane as to believe that the thing he feeds upon is a god?' In writing thus the Roman philosopher little foresaw that in Rome itself, and in the countries which have derived their creed from her, the belief which he here stigmatises as insane was destined to persist for thousands of years, as a cardinal doctrine of religion, among peoples who pride themselves on their religious enlightenment by comparison with the blind superstitions of pagan antiquity. So little can even the greatest minds of one generation foresee the devious track which the religious faith of mankind will pursue in after ages.

Bishop paraphrases a statement of Murray's to the effect that *The Golden Bough* "represented the most devastating attack anyone had made on Christianity since William Godwin." Bishop agrees that it does, and that it does so deliberately. "The author's strategy is conceived with great cunning and carried out with great art," he writes:

> For however wide we wander, however deep we delve into the records of the past, we are always coming up against one being, the Vegetable God, who as the decapitated Texcatlipoca or the dismembered Osiris is strange, but who is not strange at all, once our astonished gaze has recognized the likeness, as Jesus.
>
> Christianity is seldom mentioned; there is no need it should be, for Sir James naturally assumes that the main articles of the Christian faith are known to his readers.

Bishop's rejoinder to Murray is that for Bishop's generation *The Golden Bough* has not demolished Christianity, but glamorized it. He writes:

For it is also possible for us, regarding Christianity in the light
cast from the sacred tree at Nemi, to find that it has gained as
much as it has lost. Since it had already forfeited in our minds
any special claims it may once have had as a supernatural revelation, these should be counted an inconsiderable loss. By extending
its existence into the dark backward and abysm of time, it has
gained, not only the respectability of age, but another au-
thenticity. A religion less than two thousand years old had always
troubled us; but now its tradition stretches as far as any imaginable race of man. It is shown as a heritage, not from Judea and
Greece only, but from the earth.

If Frazer read Bishop's article in 1936, one wonders what his reaction
was. To have written his epic of humanity's ascent to rationality,
climbing past the superstition and folly of Christianity, only to discover that he was preaching a more attractive syncretistic Christianity,
might well have given him pause.

"Tragic" is the word Frazer frequently uses for his epic of humanity, and in some respects the work seems not so much epic as
tragic drama, death and rebirth in the cycle of nature. *The Golden
Bough* begins with Macaulay's doggerel,

> The priest who slew the slayer,
> And shall himself be slain,

along with Turner's picture of the scene at Nemi, which is reproduced
as the book's frontispiece. Frazer continues: "In antiquity this sylvan
landscape was the scene of a strange and recurring tragedy." He gives
the rule of succession for the kingship or priesthood at Nemi
dramatically:

> In the sacred grove there grew a certain tree round which at any
> time of the day, and probably far into the night, a grim figure
> might be seen to prowl. In his hand he carried a drawn sword,
> and he kept peering warily about him as if at every instant he
> expected to be set upon by an enemy. He was a priest and a mur-
> derer; and the man for whom he looked was sooner or later to
> murder him and hold the priesthood in his stead. Such was the
> rule of the sanctuary.

Later Frazer talks of "a tragic practice" of sacrifice and one or another
sacrificial "tragic figure."

As always with Frazer, the relationship of act to scene is of
vital importance. He writes of the priesthood at Nemi:

> In order to understand it aright we must try to form in our minds
> an accurate picture of the place where it happened; for, as we shall
> see later on, a subtle link persisted between the natural beauty of
> the spot and the dark crimes which under the mask of religion
> were often perpetrated there, crimes which after the lapse of so
> many ages still lend a touch of melancholy to these quiet woods

and waters, like a chill breath of autumn on one of those bright September days 'while not a leaf seems faded.'

Frazer then spends several pages describing the scene, panning down from the Alban hills to a stretch of flat ground near the lake: "This was the scene of the tragedy." Frazer then creates the figure of the protagonist and improvises effects to go with him, writing:

> The post which he held by this precarious tenure carried with it the title of king; but surely no crowned head ever lay uneasier, or was visited by more evil dreams, than his. For year in and year out, in summer and winter, in fair weather and in foul, he had to keep his lonely watch, and whenever he snatched a troubled slumber it was at the peril of his life. The least relaxation of his vigilance, the smallest abatement of his strength of limb or skill of fence, put him in jeopardy; grey hairs might seal his death-warrant. His eyes probably acquired that restless, watchful look which, among the Esquimaux of Bering Strait, is said to betray infallibly the shedder of blood; for with that people revenge is a sacred duty, and the manslayer carried his life in his hand. To gentle and pious pilgrims at the shrine the sight of him might well seem to darken the fair landscape, as when a cloud suddenly blots the sun on a bright day. The dreamy blue of Italian skies, the dappled shade of summer woods, and the sparkle of waves in the sun, can have accorded but ill with that stern and sinister figure. Rather we picture to ourselves the scene as it may have been witnessed by a belated wayfarer on one of those wild autumn nights when the dead leaves are falling thick, and the winds seem to sing the dirge of the dying year. It is a sombre picture, set to melancholy music—the background of forest shewing black and jagged against a lowering and stormy sky, the sighing of the wind in the branches, the rustle of the withered leaves under foot, the lapping of the cold water on the shore, and in the foreground, pacing to and fro, now in twilight and now in gloom, a dark figure with a glitter of steel at the shoulder whenever the pale moon, riding clear of the cloud-rack, peers down at him through the matted boughs.

The appropriateness of the scene is always important for Frazer. Even when it is only a meteorological station built on the site of an ancient temple, it provokes his comment, "It is fitting enough that the atmospheric phenomena should be observed by modern science on the spot where they were worshipped by ancient piety." In the preface to the first edition of *Adonis Attis Osiris* in 1906, Frazer writes:

> In studying afresh these three Oriental worships, akin to each other in character, I have paid more attention than formerly to the natural features of the countries in which they arose, because I am more than ever persuaded that religion, like all other institutions, has been profoundly influenced by physical environment,

and cannot be understood without some appreciation of those aspects of external nature which stamp themselves indelibly on the thoughts, the habits, the whole life of a people.

Frazer dramatizes everything. A reconstruction of the conservative magical mind becomes an elaborate Colonel Blimp music-hall turn:

> The sceptical doubts would naturally be repelled by the other with scorn and indignation as airy reveries subversive of the faith and manifestly contradicted by experience. 'Can anything be plainer,' he might say, 'than that I light my twopenny candle on earth and that the sun then kindles his great fire in heaven? I should be glad to know whether, when I have put on my green robe in spring, the trees do not afterwards do the same? These are facts patent to everybody, and on them I take my stand. I am a plain practical man, not one of your theorists and splitters of hairs and choppers of logic. Theories and speculation and all that may be very well in their way, and I have not the least objection to your indulging in them, provided, of course, you do not put them in practice. But give me leave to stick to facts; then I know where I am.' The fallacy of this reasoning is obvious to us, because it happens to deal with facts about which we have long made up our minds. But let an argument of precisely the same calibre be applied to matters which are still under debate, and it may be questioned whether a British audience would not applaud it as sound, and esteem the speaker who used it a safe man—not brilliant or showy, perhaps, but thoroughly sensible and hard-headed.

Frazer reconstructs many primitive theological debates similarly, the most interesting of them one in *Adonis Attis Osiris*, in which a primitive worshipper defends, against a skeptic, killing his god "to make him live for ever." The believer concludes passionately: "We eat of his broken body in bread. We drink of his shed blood in the juice of the grape." Behind the dramatic dialogues, in other words, there is the real drama, which is the death and resurrection of the god offstage, with the speakers serving like messengers in Greek tragedy. This death and resurrection is the underlying dramatic action of *The Golden Bough*, from the king of the woods at Nemi in the first volume, to the death of Balder in the last. For Frazer, the most important thing about it is that it is life-giving: "The corn-god produced the corn from himself: he gave his own body to feed the people: he died that they might live."

The problem here is that Frazer's tragic drama is the cycle of death and rebirth in nature, but that on it he imposed a pattern of pseudo-history after Roscoe convinced him that gods and religious leaders were deified dead men, and E. Wallis Budge and C. G. Seligmann appeared to confirm it with arguments that Osiris and

Nyakang, a mythic culture hero of the Shilluks, had been early kings. Since "Nyakang, as we know, was an historical personage," perhaps Osiris was. Frazer writes:

> The example of Nyakang seems to show that under favourable circumstances the worship of a dead king may develop into the dominant religion of a people. There is, therefore, no intrinsic improbability in the view that in ancient Egypt the religion of Osiris originated in that way. Certainly some curious resemblances can be traced between the dead Nyakang and the dead Osiris.

Another language, or the Roman Catholic distinction between *dulia*, the reverence accorded the saints, and *latria*, the worship accorded God, might have prevented Frazer from lumping together these various dissimilar meanings implied in the English word "worship." Frazer writes of the Bantu peoples:

> And just as the members of his family whom a man worships privately are not mythical beings conjured up by imagination out of a distant past, but were once real men like himself whom he knew in life, it may be his father, or uncle, or elder brother, so we may be sure that in like manner the dead chiefs revered by the whole tribe are not creations of the mythical fancy, but were once real men of flesh and blood, who ruled over the tribe, and whose memory has been more or less faithfully preserved by tradition.

In his move to euhemerize Western mythology, Frazer begins with Osiris. He writes in the preface to the third edition of *Adonis Attis Osiris:*

> Following the example of Dr. Wallis Budge, I have indicated certain analogies which may be traced between the worship of Osiris and the worship of the dead, especially of dead kings, among the modern tribes of Africa. The conclusion to which these analogies appear to point is that under the mythical pall of the glorified Osiris, the god who died and rose again from the dead, there once lay the body of a dead man. Whether that was so or not, I will not venture to say.

In the text, he does venture to say, in the purest imaginable statement of the euhemerist argument:

> And when we consider that from the earliest to the latest times Egyptian kings were worshipped as gods both in life and in death, there appears to be nothing extravagant or improbable in the view that one of them by his personal qualities excited a larger measure of devotion than usual during his life and was remembered with fonder affection and deeper reverence after his death; till in time his beloved memory, dimmed, transfigured, and encircled with a halo of glory by the mists of time, grew into the dominant religion of his people.

Furthermore, we may have his skull. Frazer writes:

> It is possible, though it would be very rash to affirm, that Osiris
> was no other than the historical King Khent of the first dynasty;
> that the skull found in the tomb is the skull of Osiris himself;
> and that while it reposed in the grave the missing jawbone was
> preserved, like the jawbone of a dead king of Uganda, as a holy
> and perhaps oracular relic in the neighbouring temple.

And if Osiris, why not Isis? "If that were so, we should be almost
driven to conclude that the bejewelled woman's arm found in the
tomb of Osiris is the arm of Isis." Perhaps "they are originally a real
man and woman about whom after death the myth-making fancy wove
its gossamer rainbow-tinted web." And if Isis, why not Semiramis?
"The legend of Semiramis appears to have gathered round the person of a real Assyrian queen, by name Shammuramat." Unfortunately
we do not have her arm. Naturally "the upstart David" was a real
man, although his name may have been Elhanan or Elhanah. Even
Balder may have been a real personage, since "it is also possible that
the myth was founded on the tradition of a hero, popular and beloved
in his lifetime, who long survived in the memory of the people,
gathering more and more of the marvelous about him as he passed
from generation to generation of story-tellers." An appendix tacked on
to the last volume says "we are confirmed in the suspicion that Balder
himself may have been a real man," explaining: "The facts which seem
to incline the balance to the side of Euhemerism reached me as my
book was going to press and too late to be embodied in the volumes."
They turn out to be only more African analogues.

Where all this points, of course, is to the historical reality of Jesus
Christ. For the second edition in 1900, Frazer managed to have it both
ways by the theory that the crucifixion of Christ was an annual mock-
kingship sacrificial rite, which got as its criminal victim one year a
political prisoner, Rabbi Jesus of Nazareth. For the third edition, since
"the hypothesis which it sets forth has not been confirmed by subsequent research," Frazer removed this whimsy from the text but kept
it as an appendix, "The Crucifixion of Christ," to the *Scapegoat* volume. A footnote assures the reader:

> As my views on this subject appear to have been strangely mis-
> understood, I desire to point out explicitly that my theory as-
> sumes the historical reality of Jesus of Nazareth as a great reli-
> gious and moral teacher, who founded Christianity and was cruci-
> fied at Jerusalem under the governorship of Pontius Pilate. . . .
> The doubts which have been cast on the historical reality of Jesus
> are in my judgment unworthy of serious attention. Quite apart
> from the positive evidence of history and tradition, the origin of a
> great religious and moral reform is inexplicable without the per-
> sonal existence of a great reformer. To dissolve the founder of
> Christianity into a myth, as some would do, is hardly less absurd

than it would be to do the same for Mohammed, Luther, and Calvin. Such dissolving views are for the most part the dreams of students who know the great world chiefly through its pale reflection in books.

In a footnote to *Adonis Attis Osiris*, Frazer tries a variant of the argument:

> The historical reality both of Buddha and of Christ has sometimes been doubted or denied. It would be just as reasonable to question the historical existence of Alexander the Great and Charlemagne on account of the legends which have gathered round them. The great religious movements which have stirred humanity to its depths and altered the beliefs of nations spring ultimately from the conscious and deliberate efforts of extraordinary minds, not from the blind unconscious cooperation of the multitude. The attempt to explain history without the influence of great men may flatter the vanity of the vulgar, but it will find no favour with the philosophic historian.

Why so nervous, we might ask, why so desperately muddying the water with shifting examples and increasing invective, confusing religious reformers with the gods of their religions, making the choice only Buddha or "blind unconscious"? Because, we might answer, Frazer feels caught in the middle, a Straussite Unitarian fending off the Trinitarian worshippers in one direction and the Bauerite atheists in the other. Frazer's Jesus is one of "a multitude of other victims of a barbarous superstition, . . . a moral teacher, whom the fortunate accident of his execution invested with the crown, not merely of a martyr, but of a god." Frazer does not want the god, but he must have the man. Thus he constructs a sorry chain, arguing from one divine figure to another by pretending in each case that the historical reality of the former has been established. "If Christ lived the life and died the death of a man on earth," he writes, "may not Osiris have done so likewise?" It is where we came in. The skin of the satyr Marsyas, who piped for Cybele to console her for the death of Attis, and was vanquished by Apollo in a musical contest, "was shown at Celaenae in historical times," Frazer writes. We are surprised that he does not therefor affirm Marsyas' historical existence. Of St. Denys, he notes, "no less than seven heads, all equally genuine, are extant." Should not that have inclined the balance to the euhemerist position that there were seven such saints? On the foreskins of Christ preserved in the churches of Christendom, Frazer is tactfully silent.

Beneath all this nonsense in *Adonis Attis Osiris* there remains Frazer's earlier view, the imaginative design of *The Golden Bough's* inception, that the spirit of vegetation dies and is reborn annually in myth and rite, whether his name be Adonis, Attis, Osiris, or Jesus. "We may surmise," he writes, "that the Easter celebration of the dead and risen Christ was grafted upon a similar celebration of the dead and risen Adonis, which, as we have seen reason to believe, was celebrated in Syria at the same season." Frazer adds:

> In this connexion a well-known statement of Jerome may not be without significance. He tells us that Bethlehem, the traditionary birthplace of the Lord, was shaded by a grove of that still older Syrian Lord, Adonis, and that where the infant Jesus had wept, the lover of Venus was bewailed. Though he does not expressly say so, Jerome seems to have thought that the grove of Adonis had been planted by the heathen after the birth of Christ for the purpose of defiling the sacred spot. In this he may have been mistaken. If Adonis was indeed, as I have argued, the spirit of the corn, a more suitable name for his dwelling-place could hardly be found than Bethlehem, 'the House of Bread,' and he may well have been worshipped there at his House of Bread long ages before the birth of Him who said, 'I am the bread of life.' Even on the hypothesis that Adonis followed rather than preceded Christ at Bethlehem, the choice of his sad figure to divert the allegiance of Christians from their Lord cannot but strike us as eminently appropriate when we remember the similarity of the rites which commemorated the death and resurrection of the two.

Frazer's description of the Festival of Joy, the Easter Sunday of the religion of Attis, would have given St. Jerome conniptions:

> But when night had fallen, the sorrow of the worshippers turned to joy. For suddenly a light shone in the darkness: the tomb was opened: the god had risen from the dead; and as the priest touched the lips of the weeping mourners with balm, he softly whispered in their ears the glad tidings of salvation. The resurrection of the god was hailed by his disciples as a promise that they too would issue triumphant from the corruption of the grave.

Frazer makes the same parallel with the nativity of Mithra on December 25, and its glad cry: "The Virgin has brought forth!"

In Frazer's view, as in Marx's, real human bloodshed and death are essential to historical tragedy. Frazer writes of the primitive's attitude to the plants and animals that feed him:

> To him the conception of the death of these worshipful beings is naturally presented with singular force and distinctness; since it is no figurative or allegorical death, no poetical embroidery thrown over the skeleton, but the real death, the naked skeleton, that constantly thrusts himself importunately on his attention.

This primitive immediacy of real life and death is still essential for ritual. "In short," Frazer writes, "after the serious meaning of the custom had been forgotten, and the substitute was allowed to escape with his life, the high tragedy of the ancient ceremony would rapidly degenerate into farce." The author of the Epistle to the Hebrews put it more directly: "And almost all things are by the law purged with blood; and without shedding of blood is no remission." One part of Frazer's mind insistently sees sacrificial ritual, not as a cooperative life-giving act, but as the slaying of innocent victims by wicked priests. Balder the good, Jesus the teacher, the nameless host of martyrs—*their* blood is the crimson stain in the fabric, *their* blood is on the guilty priest's hands and conscience.

The emotional climax of *The Golden Bough* is Chapter VII of *The Scapegoat*, "Killing the God in Mexico." Here we get a detailed, dramatic, and genuinely harrowing account of Aztec sacrifice, with its profusion of hearts, still pumping, torn out of living bodies. Young girls are flayed and priests deck themselves with the warm bloody skins. Frazer writes vividly of one such, parading "incommoded as he was by the tight and clammy skin of the girl and by her clothes, which must have been much too small for a grown man." It is the purest example of dying to make the crops grow, to keep the sun hot, to renew life, even to the priest reborn in a young skin like a snake, but in its concreteness it disgusts Frazer, and he writes:

> The scene of the slaughter was the platform on the summit of the god Huitzilopochtli's temple. Some of the poor wretches fainted when they came to the foot of the steps and had to be dragged up the long staircase by the hair of their heads. Arrived at the summit they were slaughtered one by one on the sacrificial stone by the high priest, who cut open their breasts, tore out their hearts, and held them up to the sun, in order to feed the great luminary with these bleeding relics. Then the bodies were sent rolling down the staircase, clattering and turning over and over like gourds as they bumped from step to step till they reached the bottom. There they were received by other priests, or rather human butchers, who with a dexterity acquired by practice slit the back of each body from the nape of the neck to the heels and peeled off the whole skin in a single piece as neatly as if it had been a sheepskin.

When the ceremony was over, one of the hypocrite priests preached a sermon, "in which he dwelt with pathetic eloquence on the meanness and misery of human existence," and exhorted his hearers to lead a gentle and virtuous life.

As the chronicler of the evolution of rational man, Frazer sees Aztec sacrifice as the unfortunate effects of an erroneous theory of the sun's combustion. As a tragic dramatist, however, he can see only the wickedness and blood-lust of his villains, the priests and prelates of religion. The murderous priest at Nemi embodies them all; like him they slew their predecessors but like him they will be slain by their successors. Their time is growing shorter with each movement. A climactic sequence in Part III, *The Dying God*, on the tenure of divine kingship, rings their knell. First we have kings killed when their strength fails, then the king of Calicut fighting for his life every twelve years, then ancient Swedish kings sacrificed every nine years, ancient Greek kings every eight, Yoruba chiefs every three, an annual tenure of the kingship in Babylon and Hawaii, and a Congo king killed at the end of a day's reign. Frazer comments on the last: "The right of succession lies with the chief of the Musurongo; but we need not wonder that he does not exercise it, and that the throne stands vacant." We shiver with the priest of Nemi at approaching doom.

As THIS tragic cycle is the fertility cycle of nature, there is no ascent out of it, and as its crimes are the crimes of nature, there can be no blame. Frazer is caught in this dilemma. With no faith in the afterlife and no posterity on earth, he is bound to the wheel and can find immortality only by going back into nature at his death and by leaving a progeny of books, including *The Golden Bough*, bound in green, festooned with mistletoe like a living branch. Insofar as he proclaims that the guilty must be found, Frazer produces not a tragic or a dramatic form, but something more like a detective story. It is this form that gives the book its quality of suspense, of carrying the reader to the solution along a trail of clues. Frazer will characteristically ask a question and then say, "The answer must be deferred for the present," or even, when he is about to explain something, tease the reader for a few more pages. In these terms, Frazer's plea for field anthropology would translate simply. "We need more detective work in the field."

In other moods, Frazer has no interest in indicting the guilty, and little patience with tragedy either in epic or dramatic form. *The Golden Bough* can readily be seen as a comic or ironic mock-epic of human absurdity, and perhaps ultimately its perspective is hopeful. Frazer's poetic imagination here insulates himself and the reader from the horrors, or disarms them stylistically. It is in this sense that Frazer felt that Plato had gone wrong, his later dialogues "guided by the pale cold light of Reason instead of by the purple glow of Imagination." This is the Frazer whose models were Addison and Gibbon, writers who had somehow gone right where Plato had gone wrong. In the series of sketches about Sir Roger de Coverley that Frazer published in imitation of Addison, we see him struggle to achieve Addison's lighthearted mockery and Christian charity for human folly. Frazer's essay "Gibbon at Lausanne" in *Creation and Evolution* emphasizes not the bite of Gibbon's history but its serenity, a "golden bridge along which he led his enchanted readers from ancient to modern times," and "the wizardry of Gibbon, who by his alchemic touch could turn the lead and dross of the dreary Byzantine annals into the liquid gold of his stately periods."

Seen in this perspective of acceptance, *The Golden Bough*'s dying god neatly balances the highest spirituality with the lowest practical utility. "It was one of Frazer's advances," Murray writes, "to make us realize that human religion was much more concerned with man's permanent needs of food and drink than with anything like sunshine and scenery." This was a proper enough reaction in 1890, but seems too simple in a wider perspective. Frazer protests, in one of the prefaces:

> But having said so much in this book of the misty glory which the human imagination sheds round the hard material realities of the food supply, I am unwilling to leave my readers under the impression, natural but erroneous, that man has created most of his gods out of his belly.

Alfred Nutt seems more accurate than Murray, reviewing the second edition in *Folk-Lore*, when he writes: "Man lives by bread—man does not live by bread alone: these two statements contain in germ the Mannhardt-Frazer hypothesis." So much in *The Golden Bough* is over-determined in precisely that fashion. Primitive peoples do not mention the name of the dead out of "fear of evoking the ghost, although the natural unwillingness to revive past sorrows undoubtedly operated also." The ambivalence in *Psyche's Task* represents the same sort of over-determination: institutions serve both a practical and a superstitious need.

It is this dualistic conception of man that gives Frazer what faith he has that the dark scene at Nemi can grow light. The aim of understanding is, as Marx says it must be in the *Theses on Feuerbach*, to change society. Frazer's changes would not be Marx's, but both ultimately see knowledge as power. Frazer writes:

> But the comparative study of the beliefs and institutions of mankind is fitted to be much more than a means of satisfying an enlightened curiosity and of furnishing materials for the researches of the learned. Well handled, it may become a powerful instrument to expedite progress.

In his *Lectures on the Early History of the Kingship* in 1905, Frazer had written: "If the time should ever come when what we merely suspect should prove to be true, and the truth should be recognised by all, it may involve a reconstruction of society such as we can hardly dream of." In the preface to *The Dying God*, Frazer gently mocks the primitive ritual quest for immortality with a wealth of metaphor, but seems to place his own similar hopes in science. He writes:

> Hence, if there is any measure of truth in this theory, the practice of putting divine men and particularly divine kings to death, which seems to have been common at a particular stage in the evolution of society and religion, was a crude but pathetic attempt to disengage an immortal spirit from its mortal envelope, to arrest the forces of decomposition in nature by retrenching with ruthless hand the first ominous symptoms of decay. We may

smile if we please at the vanity of these and the like efforts to stay the inevitable decline, to bring the relentless revolution of the great wheel to a stand, to keep youth's fleeting roses for ever fresh and fair; but perhaps in spite of every disillusionment, when we contemplate the seemingly endless vistas of knowledge which have been opened up even within out own generation, many of us may cherish in our heart of hearts a fancy, if not a hope, that some loophole of escape may after all be discovered from the iron walls of the prison-house which threatens to close on and crush us; that, groping about in the darkness, mankind may yet chance to lay hands on 'that golden key that opes the palace of eternity,' and so to pass from this world of shadows and sorrow to a world of untroubled light and joy.

When Frazer renounces science in the course of producing the third edition, it is only for his own writing, not in regard to his hopes for mankind. The sad prefaces, in other words, abdicate everything except what is really important, the conviction of a happier and more rational human future. It is this unquenchable faith in mankind underlying the failure of faith in his own activities, I think, that gives these statements their poignancy. The latest of the prefaces, to the third edition of *Adonis Attis Osiris*, written in January, 1914, on the eve of the war, shows both the deepest despair Frazer's spirits reached and his stubborn humanism. He writes:

> The longer I occupy myself with questions of ancient mythology the more diffident I become of success in dealing with them, and I am apt to think that we who spend our years in searching for solutions of these insoluble problems are like Sisyphus perpetually rolling his stone up hill only to see it revolve again into the valley. or like the daughters of Danaus doomed for ever to pour water into broken jars that can hold no water. If we are taxed with wasting life in seeking to know what can never be known, and what, if it could be discovered, would not be worth knowing, what can we plead in our defense? I fear, very little. Such pursuits can hardly be defended on the ground of pure reason. We can only say that something, we know not what, drives us to attack the great enemy Ignorance wherever we see him, and that if we fail, as we probably shall, in our attack on his entrenchments, it may be useless but it is not inglorious to fall in leading a Forlorn Hope.

Epic and tragic drama, mystery story and comic poem, do not exhaust *The Golden Bough*'s formal structuring. If Frazer imposed one deliberate organization on the book, it is that of a travelogue. He ends the first chapter:

> To that wider survey we must now address ourselves. It will be long and laborious, but may possess something of the interest and charm of a voyage of discovery, in which we shall visit many

strange foreign lands, with strange foreign peoples, and still stranger customs. The wind is in the shrouds: we shake out our sails to it, and leave the coast of Italy behind us for a time.

The style is sometimes, as Frazer goes along, the purest travelogue:

In late autumn, when storms rage over the land and break the icy fetters by which the frozen sea is as yet but slightly bound, when the loosened floes are driven against each other and break with loud crashes, and when the cakes of ice are piled in wild disorder one upon another, the Esquimaux of Baffin Land fancy they hear the voices of the spirits who people the mischief-laden air.

The book could take as its epigraph Frazer's statement: "So curiously does it often happen that the savage reaches the goal of his wishes by a road which to civilised man might appear at first sight to lead far away from it." Finally, beginning the last book, Frazer heads the voyage home. He writes:

We have travelled far since we turned our backs on Nemi and set forth in quest of the secret of the Golden Bough. With the present volume we enter on the last stage of our long journey.

The book's last paragraph arrives home:

Our long voyage of discovery is over and our bark has dropped her weary sails in port at last. Once more we take the road to Nemi. It is evening, and as we climb the long slope of the Appian Way up to the Alban Hills, we look back and see the sky aflame with sunset, its golden glory resting like the aureole of a dying saint over Rome and touching with a crest of fire the dome of St. Peter's. The sight once seen can never be forgotten, but we turn from it and pursue our way darkling along the mountain side, till we come to Nemi and look down on the lake in its deep hollow, now fast disappearing in the evening shadows. The place has changed but little since Diana received the homage of her worshippers in the sacred grove. The temple of the sylvan goddess, indeed, has vanished and the King of the Wood no longer stands sentinel over the Golden Bough. But Nemi's woods are still green, and as the sunset fades above them in the west, there comes to us, borne on the swell of the wind, the sound of the church bells of Ariccia ringing the Angelus. Ave Maria! Sweet and solemn they chime out from the distant town and die lingeringly away across the wide Campagnan marshes. *Le roi est mort, vive le roi! Ave Maria!*

Most of the individual books and volumes similarly conclude with a passage of rolling periods, usually scenic. It is the voice of the old-time tour leader, what Malinowski calls "the cicerone guiding our steps." This impressive figure cannot simply say "We no longer believe in spirits." He says:

For ages the army of spirits, once so near, has been receding further and further from us, banished by the magic wand of science
from hearth and home, from ruined cell and ivied tower, from
haunted glade and lonely mere, from the riven murky cloud that
belches forth the lightning, and from those fairer clouds that
pillow the silver moon or fret with flakes of burning red the
golden eve. The spirits are gone even from their last stronghold
in the sky, whose blue arch no longer passes, except with children,
for the screen that hides from mortal eyes the glories of the
celestial world. Only in poets' dreams or impassioned flights of
oratory is it given to catch a glimpse of the last flutter of the
standards of the retreating host, to hear the beat of their invisible
wings, the sound of their mocking laughter, or the swell of angel
music dying away in the distance.

What Frazer finally settled on as the form of *The Golden Bough*
is a bundle of facts hung on a peg of theory. He writes in the
preface to the last book:

In this as in other branches of study it is the fate of theories to be
washed away like children's castles of sand by the rising tide of
knowledge, and I am not so presumptuous as to expect or desire
for mine an exemption from the common lot. I hold them all very
lightly and have used them chiefly as convenient pegs on which to
hang my collection of facts. For I believe that, while theories are
transitory, a record of facts has a permanent value, and that as a
chronicle of ancient customs and beliefs my book may retain its
utility when my theories are as obsolete as the customs and beliefs themselves deserve to be.

Varying the metaphor:

Thus Balder the Beautiful in my hands is little more than a stalking-
horse to carry two heavy pack-loads of facts. And what is true of
Balder applies equally to the priest of Nemi himself, the nominal
hero of the long tragedy of human folly and suffering which
has unrolled itself before the readers of these volumes, and on
which the curtain is now about to fall. He, too, for all the quaint
garb he wears and the gravity with which he stalks across
the stage, is merely a puppet, and it is time to unmask him before laying him up in the box.

Later in the volume Frazer reprints an old theory, "partly," he says,
"because I still think it may contain an element of truth, and partly
because it serves as a convenient peg on which to hang a collection of
facts which are much more valuable than any theories of mine."

If the form is what Frazer says it is, many readers will agree with
Burne that the Golden Bough is "too slender a twig to sustain the
weight of learning hung upon it." Some of Frazer's long digressive
essays have only the most remote relevance to his topic. In the midst

of his dramatic shrinking of the tenure of the kingship, Frazer mentions the fear of shooting stars and meteors. "It may be well, even at the cost of a digression, to illustrate this primitive superstition by examples," he writes, and so he does, for nine pages. The topic of primitive indifference to death takes him off on another byway for a dozen pages. After a sizable section on the worship of volcanoes, Frazer confesses:

> On the whole, then, we conclude that the Asiatic custom of burning kings or gods was probably in no way connected with volcanic phenomena. Yet it was perhaps worth while to raise the question of the connexion, even though it has received only a negative answer. The whole subject of the influence which physical environment has exercised on the history of religion deserves to be studied with more attention than it has yet received.

Other digressions apparently have no more justification than that Frazer had notes on a topic that something suggested. Similarly he tells myths, legends, folk tales, and similar stories on every occasion, whether or not they are relevant. In this activity we eventually see him tiring, and by the twelfth volume of the book Frazer is skimping the stories: "As usual the egg is broken and the beast dies."

As a record of Frazer's changes of mind on almost every subject over a quarter of a century, *The Golden Bough* might more accurately be described as a bundle of theories hung on a peg of facts. "I have seen reason to change my views on several matters," he writes in the preface to *Balder the Beautiful*, producing one of the historic understatements. The palimpsest effect is sometimes very strong. Frazer will give an explanation, then write:

> Yet it may be that this explanation does not apply to all the cases, and that certain of them may admit and even require another interpretation, in favour of which I formerly argued as follows:—

He then gives his differing theory from an earlier edition, concluding, "On the foregoing argument, which I do not now find very cogent, I would remark that we must distinguish the cases," and we are off again. A ceaseless internal debate is spread out before us, and recognizing it we can understand the paradox Malinowski describes in Frazer: "Always ready to revise his opinions if these were contradicted by factual evidence, he could never brook personal contradiction or even engage in an argument."

There is a sense in which no one and no evidence ever convinced Frazer, but in which his ambivalent and shifting mind each time found statements and evidence to reinforce positions it had already reached. Thus Mannhardt and Smith appear when Frazer is moving away from the Trinitarian Christianity of his Presbyterian upbringing, Roscoe and Budge when he is moving back to a Unitarian Christianity of his own devising. Before Roscoe arrived with the war god's mummified paraphernalia, Frazer was collecting Corn Maidens for the Cambridge Museum, with the same desire to have something tangible to show for all the foolishness. They were the material embodiments of Manhardt's rites rather than of Roscoe's history, but they were not too far in spirit from pieces of the true Cross.

When the Seligmans discovered a Golden Bough king among the Shilluk of the Sudan while Frazer was working on the third edition, and communicated the information to him, Frazer's mind simply transferred his actor from the Lake of Nemi to the Nile. He writes of the Shilluk king:

> The hours of darkness were therefore the season of peril for the king. It is said that he used to pass them in constant watchfulness, prowling round his huts fully armed, peering into the blackest shadows, or himself standing silent and alert, like a sentinel on duty, in some dark corner.

"On the whole," he writes, "the theory and practice of the divine kings of the Shilluk correspond very nearly to the theory and practice of the priests at Nemi, the Kings of the Wood, if my view of the latter is correct." As well they might, since he had animated both. In his 1933 Frazer Lecture, "Egypt and Negro Africa: A Study in Divine Kingship," Seligman makes it clear that he had gone into the Sudan a Frazerian. In 1948, in *his* Frazer Lecture, E. E. Evans-Pritchard brought the whole matter around full circle. He writes:

> This would seem to be the reasoning behind Shilluk statements that the king may be strangled, or suffocated, or walled up in a hut and left to die there, if he fails to satisfy his wives or shows signs of illness or senility. In view of the great importance Sir James Frazer and others have attached to these statements I must confess that I consider them of interest more as an indication of the mystical nature of the kingship than as evidence that the kings were, in fact, ever killed in the ways mentioned or for the reasons given. It is true that Professor and Mrs. Seligman state categorically that 'there is not the least doubt that kings of the Shilluk were killed with due ceremony when they began to show signs of old age or ill health,' but I have failed to find convincing evidence that any Shilluk king was put to death in either circumstance, although some of the kings must have qualified long before they died for execution on the grounds alleged; and I am persuaded that the story of kings being walled up in a hut is a confusion arising from the usual walling up of the remains of a dead king, the bones being buried after decomposition of the flesh. In the absence of other than traditional evidence of royal executions in Shilluk history and in view of the contradictory accounts cited I conclude that the ceremonial putting to death of kings is probably a fiction.

We are again in the world of the first edition of *The Golden Bough*, with the evidence once more suggesting that myths concretize out of ritual practice rather than commemorate events in history, but Frazer had been dead for seven years.

Sometimes Frazer's metaphors show the strain of his striving after unity. He writes: "In attempting to draw these fragmentary data together, to bridge the chasms, and to restore the shattered whole, we must beware of mistaking hypothesis for the facts which it only professes to cement." As early as 1890, Jacobs had recognized the two-volume *Golden Bough* as a series of independent monographs. Jacobs adds: "One quite envies Mr. Frazer the hours of happy work which must have been passed in compiling this mass of information." By the time of the third edition, as we noted, Frazer was prepared to take the same view of the form as "a series of separate dissertations loosely linked together." For all our analogies with epic, tragedy, comedy, and other literary forms, perhaps the vastness of the book really does break it down, as the author came to believe, into a series of separate works.

What Is Your Dreaming?

A F T E R the third edition of *The Golden Bough* in 1915, when he was sixty-one, Frazer published many books, but he produced little that was new either in conception or in execution. We can examine his later work in less detail, since much of it merely repeats and amplifies Frazer's previous themes. The first such work, and the most ambitious, is *Folk-Lore in the Old Testament*, subtitled *Studies in Comparative Religion, Legend, and Law,* published in three volumes in 1918. It is an expansion of an article of the same title that Frazer had published in *Anthropological Essays Presented to Edward Burnett Tylor* in 1907, and Frazer had worked on and off over a decade filling it out. The preface announces Frazer's intention with the usual scientific analogy. He writes:

> The instrument for the detection of savagery under civilisation is the comparative method, which, applied to the human mind, enables us to trace man's intellectual and moral evolution, just as, applied to the human body, it enables us to trace his physical evolution from lower forms of animal life. There is, in short, a Comparative Anatomy of the mind as well as of the body, and it promises to be no less fruitful of far-reaching consequences, not merely speculative but practical, for the future of humanity.

Frazer adds the familiar disclaimer that his theories are "mere pigeonholes in which temporarily to sort the multitude of facts." There are beliefs and practices in the Old Testament, he explains, "that can hardly be explained except on the supposition that they are rudimentary survivals from a far lower level of culture," that is, "fossils." Thus Frazer is using what Marett in his book *Tylor* defines as "a folklore method—one that works backward from the 'survival.' "

Frazer's assumption, unstated in the book, is that Old Testament stories are distorted, misunderstood, or deliberately misused myths. Thus, to take a typical example, he restores the story of the Fall in Eden to "the true original story," a myth of the origin of death. Frazer tells it as follows:

270

He sent the serpent to the man and woman and charged him to deliver this message: 'Eat not of the Tree of Death, for in the day ye eat thereof ye shall surely die; but eat of the Tree of Life and live for ever.' Now the serpent was more subtle than any beast of the field, and on his way he bethought him of changing the message; so when he came to the happy garden and found the woman alone in it, he said to her, 'Thus saith God: Eat not of of the Tree of Life, for in the day ye eat thereof ye shall surely die; but eat of the Tree of Death, and live for ever.' The foolish woman believed him, and ate of the fatal fruit, and gave of it to her husband, and he ate also. But the sly serpent himself ate of the Tree of Life. That is why men have been mortal and serpents immortal ever since, for serpents cast their skins every year and so renew their youth. If only the serpent had not perverted God's good message and deceived our first mother, we should have been immortal instead of the serpents; for like the serpents we should have cast our skins every year and so renewed our youth perpetually.

Frazer gets this "original form of the story" by identifying the Genesis account as a combination of two widespread myths of the origin of death, the Perverted Message and the Cast Skin. He makes no attempt to explain how it, or any other story he believes to be distorted, got into the Old Testament in its present form. Any reader familiar with the Higher Criticism can readily supply the process in this case: the Priestly compilers, tacking on Genesis last (despite its ancient material), use an old myth of the origin of death to point a moral more relevant to the rest of their story, making it an origin myth of human disobedience to divine command. The New Testament writers, promising immortality, restore the story to its earlier form: the Old Serpent stole eternal life from man under the tree, but Jesus stole it back from him on that same tree.

Frazer is thus entirely unconcerned with history, along the lines of his distinction between Scriptural epic and history, until he gets to the figure of Moses. Here, unwilling to abandon the historicity of religious founders and reformers, he trots out his old arguments. They have a new tone of waspishness, however, against egalitarianism:

> Because little or nothing of the so-called Mosaic legislation in the Pentateuch can be proved to have emanated from Moses, it by no means follows that the great lawgiver was a mere mythical personage, a creation of popular or priestly fancy, invented to explain the origin of the religious and civil constitution of the nation. Any such inference would do violence, not only to the particular evidence which speaks in favour of the historical reality of Moses, but to the general laws of probability; for great religious and national movements seldom or never occur except under the driving force of great men. The origin of Israel and Judaism without Moses would be hardly more intelligible than the origin of

Buddhism without Buddha, the origin of Christianity without Christ, or the origin of Mohammedanism without Mohammed. There is, indeed, a tendency in some quarters at the present day to assume that history is made by the blind collective impulses of the multitude without the initiative and direction of extraordinary minds; but this assumption, born of or fostered by the false and pernicious doctrine of the natural equality of men, contradicts both the teaching of history and the experience of life. The multitude needs a leader, and without him, though it possesses a large faculty of destruction, it possesses little or none of construction. Without men great in thought, in word, in action, and in their influence over their fellows, no great nation ever was or ever will be built up.

Most of Frazer's sarcasm in *Folk-Lore in the Old Testament* is reserved for Biblical fundamentalists. Commenting on a clergyman who found the appearance of the soil of Palestine to confirm the story of the creation of Adam, Frazer writes: "So remarkably does nature itself bear witness to the literal accuracy of Holy Writ." Frazer speaks of "the irascible but really kind-hearted deity," and takes the mocking position of being God's advocate this time, rather than Satan's. He writes:

> This explanation of the mark of Cain has the advantage of relieving the Biblical narrative from a manifest absurdity. For on the usual interpretation God affixed the mark to Cain in order to save him from human assailants, apparently forgetting that there was nobody to assail him, since the earth was as yet inhabited only by the murderer himself and his parents. Hence by assuming that the foe of whom the first murderer went in fear was a ghost instead of a living man, we avoid the irreverence of imputing to the deity a grave lapse of memory little in keeping with the divine omniscience. Here again, therefore, the comparative method approves itself a powerful *advocatus Dei*.

At the same time, Frazer shows a capacity for judging the behavior of Biblical figures not unworthy of the most fundamentalist sermon. He accuses Jacob of "very sharp practice" in buying Esau's birthright, and follows the charge with a paragraph boasting of the superiority of our morals to ancient morals. Samson similarly is "an utterly selfish and unscrupulous adventurer, swayed by gusts of fitful passion and indifferent to everything but the gratification of his momentary whims."

Frazer never lost his ethical absolutism—in a comparative section he indicts cannibalism, indignant that "that certain depraved wretches should gratify their hereditary craving after human flesh in this disgusting manner"—but I think another factor is at work here. Judging the mythic heroes of the Bible as one might judge a disreputable neighbor, Frazer manages to bring them to life, and ultimately his impulse seems more that of the frustrated historical novelist than the frustrated justice of the peace. Here is Jacob at the well:

> Under the charm of the hour and of the scene even the hard mercenary character of Jacob melted into something like tenderness; he forgot for once the cool calculations of gain and gave way to an impulse of love, almost of chivalry: for at sight of the fair damsel approaching with her flocks, he ran to the well and rolling away the heavy stone which blocked its mouth he watered the sheep for her. Then he kissed his cousin's pretty face and wept. Did he remember his dream of angels at Bethel and find the vision come true in love's young dream? We cannot tell. Certainly for a time the selfish schemer appeared to be transformed into the impassioned lover. It was the one brief hour of poetry and romance in a prosaic and even sordid life.

Here is Samson evaluated:

> Among the grave judges of Israel the burly hero Samson cuts a strange figure. That he judged Israel for twenty years we are indeed informed by the sacred writer, but of the judgments which he delivered in his judicial character not one has been recorded, and if the tenor of his pronouncements can be inferred from the nature of his acts, we may be allowed to doubt whether he particularly adorned the bench of justice. His talent would seem to have lain rather in the direction of brawling and fighting, burning down people's corn-ricks, and beating up the quarters of loose women; in short, he appears to have shone in the character of a libertine and a rakehell rather than in a strictly judicial capacity.

Saul:

> Under a showy exterior, this dashing and popular soldier concealed some fatal infirmities,—a jealous and suspicious disposition, a choleric temper, a weakness of will, a vacillation of purpose, and, above all, a brooding melancholy under which his intellect, never of a high order, sometimes trembled on the verge of insanity.

Samuel:

> The prophet was indeed one of those masterful natures, those fanatics cast in an iron mould, who, mistaking their own unbending purpose for the will of heaven, march forward unswervingly to their goal, trampling down all opposition, their hearts steeled against every tender emotion of humanity and pity.

Frazer even writes two pages inside the mind of an Israelite peasant distressed by the Deuteronomic reforms.

Frazer's next important work is "The Scope and Method of Mental Anthropology," a lecture delivered at Trinity in 1921 and reprinted in *Garnered Sheaves*. It shows that Frazer had come some distance since his two earlier statements on the subject. He now seeks, almost whimsically, to rename social anthropology "mental" anthropology. The anthropological science he describes is still evolutionary ("It is this conception of evolution which supplies a basis for the modern science of anthropology"); comparative ("This comparative study of the mind of man is thus analogous to the comparative study of his body which is undertaken by anatomy and physiology"); and inductive ("The method is neither more nor less than induction"). It now assumes for the mind nothing less than Haeckel's principle, Ontogeny Recapitulates Phylogeny:

> That the intelligence of children in normal cases undergoes a process of development from infancy to maturity is too obvious and notorious to need proof; and it is a reasonable inference that, just as the development of their bodies in the womb reproduces to some extent the corporeal evolution of their remote ancestors out of lower forms of animal life, so the development of their minds from the first dawn of consciousness in the embryo to the full light of reason in adult life reproduces to some extent the mental evolution of their ancestors in ages far beyond the range of history.

Children thus represent the thinking of our ancestors, savages think like children, and the insane have "wild fancies" like those of savages. Thus mental anthropology would operate "by a study of the uncivilized races, by a study of children, and by a study of mental pathology."

All of this must have had a curiously archaic sound in 1921, and Frazer seems very much on the defensive. "Some well-meaning but injudicious friends of anthropology," unnamed, have criticized the comparison of traits in widely different cultures, proposing that comparison be restricted within a culture area. Frazer cannot understand the criticism, nor why it is any more illegitimate to compare American and Asian shamans than it is to compare American and Asian sedimentary rocks, and he rails:

> A little reflexion may convince us that any such restriction, even if it were practicable, would be unwise; nay, that, were it enforced, it would be disastrous. We compare things on the ground of their similarity, and similarity is not affected by distance. . . .
> The futility, nay, the inherent absurdity, of the proposed restriction is so manifest that simply to state the proposal explicitly should suffice to expose it.

At the same time he is full of optimistic visions for anthropology, and these are imaged, not with the moderation of *The Golden Bough* as illuminating or clearing a path, but in boldly life-giving terms:

> It is because the question of human origins was till lately a sort of no man's ground, untrodden by the foot of science but tram-

pled by the hoofs of ignorance and superstition, that anthropology has come forward to reclaim this desert from the wild asses which roamed over it, and to turn it into a garden of knowledge. Her efforts have not been wholly in vain. Already the desert has begun to bear fruit and to blossom as the rose.

In a counter-offensive against the new methods of anthropology, Frazer lists those who make the best field-workers in order of preference: first missionaries, then government officials, finally travelers and explorers, among whom he includes professional anthropologists. Frazer defends this hierarchy by the fact that his first two groups live for years among a native people and learn its language thoroughly, but in 1921 his list would seem mostly bravado, a deliberate call to set the clock back half a century. At the same time, Frazer reaffirms the need for armchair anthropology: making comparisons impairs observation in the field, requires different faculties, and can be better done by the student at home. It is, moreover, essential; "without it there could be no true science of man." "It is the application of the comparative method to the heap," Frazer writes, "which evolves order out of chaos by eliciting the general principles or laws which underlie the mass of particulars." "Thus everything hinges on the work of comparison," he reminds his critics. "Only with its help can we rise to those generalizations which are the goal of science." Frazer works up to a vision of an institutionalized spider-web at Cambridge to dwarf Darwin's network as well as his own:

> As an alumnus of this ancient university, I should wish to see established in Cambridge a sort of central bureau or clearinghouse, which would receive and examine anthropological reports from all parts of the world, and from which questions, hints, suggestions, and, if you please, theories, would radiate in return to observers stationed in the remotest regions of the earth. Thus a perpetual circulation of facts and ideas would be maintained between the central bureau and the outlying stations; observation would quicken theory, and theory would stimulate observation. You would possess in the University, as it were, a lighthouse from which the rays of science would stream out to illuminate many dark corners of the earth. *Hinc lucem et pocula sacra.*

The same year Frazer published his translation of Apollodorus' *The Library* in the Loeb Classical Library. He used the introduction to state his final position on myth, and this amazingly turns out to be neither the ritual view nor the euhemerist one that replaced it in the last *Golden Bough*, but the cognitionist theory of his youth. Frazer writes:

> By myths I understand mistaken explanations of phenomena, whether of human life or of external nature. Such explanations originate in that instinctive curiosity concerning the causes of things which at a more advanced stage of knowledge seeks satis-

faction in philosophy and science, but being founded on ignorance and misapprehension they are always false, for were they true, they would cease to be myths.

In a footnote, he finally dismisses Harrison and Murray, Cornford and Cook. Frazer announces:

> By a curious limitation of view, some modern writers would restrict the scope of myths to ritual, as if nothing but ritual were fitted to set men wondering and meditating on the causes of things. No doubt some myths have been devised to explain rites of which the true origin was forgotten; but the number of such myths is small, probably almost infinitesimally small, by comparison with myths which deal with other subjects and have had another origin.

He adds:

> It might have been thought that merely to open such familiar collections of myths as the Theogony of Hesiod, the Library of Apollodorus, or the *Metamorphoses* of Ovid, would have sufficed to dissipate so erroneous a conception; for how small is the attention paid to ritual in these works!

Ultimately, the charge against the ritual theory is that it spoils the fun. Frazer writes:

> The zealous student of myth and ritual, more intent on explaining them than on enjoying the lore of the people, it too apt to invade the garden of romance and with a sweep of his scythe to lay the flowers of fancy in the dust. He needs to be reminded occasionally that we must not look for a myth or a rite behind every tale, like a bull behind every hedge or a canker in every rose.

Most comprehensively, Frazer protests against "the vice inherent in all systems which would explain the infinite multiplicity and diversity of phenomena by a single simple principle, as if a single clue, like Ariadne's thread, could guide us to the heart of this labyrinthine universe." [1]

In 1922 Frazer published a glowing preface to Malinowski's *Argonauts of the Western Pacific*, one of the books of theorizing ethnography that were driving study anthropology out of business. The preface is chiefly remarkable for Frazer's curious approximation of Marx's doctrine of historical materialism. Frazer writes:

---

[1] This argument that it is somehow more scientific to explain a phenomenon in a variety of ways than in a single way has again become popular, if I may judge by Stith Thompson's criticism of myself and others in his contribution to *Myth: A Symposium* in 1955. I confess myself unable to understand its logic. It seems to me like believing that it is more scientific to say that some apples come from apple trees, some from berry bushes, and some from melon vines, than it is to say that all apples come from apple trees, and that if they did not they would be berries or melons.

Little reflection is needed to convince us of the fundamental importance of economic forces at all stages of man's career from the humblest to the highest. After all, the human species is part of the animal creation, and as such, like the rest of the animals, it reposes on a material foundation; on which a higher life, intellectual, moral, social, may be built, but without which no such superstructure is possible.

That same year Frazer published his one-volume condensation of *The Golden Bough*, the form in which most readers know it. It includes a new brief preface, denying sharply that Frazer is any sort of arboreal fanatic. He writes:

> But I am so far from regarding the reverence for trees as of supreme importance for the evolution of religion that I consider it to have been altogether subordinate to other factors, and in particular to the fear of the human dead, which, on the whole, I believe to have been probably the most powerful force in the making of primitive religion. I hope that after this explicit disclaimer I shall no longer be taxed with embracing a system of mythology which I look upon not merely as false but as preposterous and absurd. But I am too familiar with the hydra of error to expect that by lopping off one of the monster's heads I can prevent another, or even the same, from sprouting again.

The first volume of *The Belief in Immortality and the Worship of the Dead* appeared in 1913, but the second volume did not arrive until 1921, the third appeared in 1924, and the fourth never came out. The book arose out of a series of lectures at Trinity and St. Andrews on primitive religion, with the material organized geographically. Frazer's introductory justification for "prosecuting the study of savagery with ardour and diligence" is a development out of his earlier image of the primitive as a written record:

> We are like an heir whose title-deeds must be scrutinised before he can take possession of the inheritance, but who finds the handwriting of the deeds so fading and evanescent that it threatens to disappear entirely before he can read the document to the end. With what keen attention, what eager haste, would he not scan the fast-vanishing characters? With the like attention and the like haste civilised men are now applying themselves to the investigation of the fast-vanishing savages.

The preface to the first volume announces the book's theme as "a vast one," no less than the question of survival after death, and it equivocates in Frazer's characteristic fashion:

> Of all the many forms which natural religion has assumed none probably has exerted so deep and far-reaching an influence on human life as the belief in immortality and the worship of the dead; hence an historical survey of this most momentous creed

and of the practical consequences which have been deduced from it can hardly fail to be at once instructive and impressive, whether we regard the record with complacency as a noble testimony to the aspiring genius of man, who claims to outlive the sun and the stars, or whether we view it with pity as a melancholy monument of fruitless labour and barren ingenuity expended in prying into that great mystery of which fools profess their knowledge and wise men confess their ignorance.

The hard reality that the book confronts is the universal fact of human death, which "concerns us all alike, since simpletons as well as sages must die." Frazer concludes the first volume with a resounding one-handed rhetorical plea for man's grandeur and necessary immortality:

> On the one hand, there are those who love to dwell on the grandeur and dignity of man, and who swell with pride at the contemplation of the triumphs which his genius has achieved in the visionary world of imagination as well as in the realm of nature. Surely, they say, such a glorious creature was not born for mortality, to be snuffed out like a candle, to fade like a flower, to pass away like a breath. Is all that penetrating intellect, that creative fancy, that vaulting ambition, those noble passions, those far-reaching hopes, to come to nothing, to shrivel up into a pinch of dust? It is not so, it cannot be. Man is the flower of this wide world, the lord of creation, the crown and consummation of all things, and it is to wrong him and his creator to imagine that the grave is the end of all.

Frazer then answers this at every point with an "On the other hand," and concludes that these are the two views, of which "I do not presume to adopt the one or the other."

Actually, Frazer comes closer in *The Belief in Immortality* to committing himself to a statement of his own religious beliefs than at any time before or after. As he defines his views, they are what Huxley called "agnostic":

> To speak plainly, the question of the existence of a God is too deep for me. I dare neither affirm nor deny it. I can only humbly confess my ignorance.

Frazer hints rather strongly that the question is not really quite so open as it seems to be in his presentation:

> Even the question of the validity or truth of religious creeds cannot, perhaps, be wholly dissociated from the question of their origin. If, for example, we discover that doctrines which we had accepted with implicit faith from tradition have their close analogies in the barbarous superstitions of ignorant savages, we can hardly help suspecting that our own cherished doctrines may have originated in the similar superstitions of our rude fore-

fathers; and the suspicion inevitably shakes the confidence with
which we had hitherto regarded these articles of our faith. . . .
This weakening of religious faith as a consequence of a closer
scrutiny of religious origins is unquestionably a matter of great
importance to the community; for society has been built and
cemented to a great extent on a foundation of religion, and it is
impossible to loosen the cement and shake the foundation without
endangering the superstructure.

He concludes in the hope "that there is no ultimate incompatibility
between the good and the true." One of the consolations for death
that Frazer produces is the Darwinian argument, from Weismann and
Wallace, that death is an advantageous evolutionary adaptation, rather
than a necessary property of protoplasm. Frazer describes the line
between religion and naturalism as a "Rubicon," crossable in a sudden
bold move.

Early in *The Belief in Immortality*, Frazer says that here his
treatment will be descriptive rather than comparative, although he will
not entirely eschew comparisons. Each method, he adds, has its advantages and disadvantages. Later he lectures field anthropologists on
their "deplorable" habit of combining comparison and generalization
with description. For the first time, Frazer seems to recognize the
danger of analogy, denying that the mortuary dramas of the Torres
Straits Islanders tell us anything about Greek tragedy "so long as we
are ignorant of the precise significance which the natives themselves
attached to these remarkable performances." That is, like customs do
not necessarily have like self-evident motivations. He even quotes a
mocking description by two field ethnographers of "the anthropologist
who has spent all the days of his life in a stiff collar and a black coat
upon the well-paved ways of civilised society." In the presence of the
serried ranks of the dead, Frazer seems much more relaxed about his
operations. Only in regard to evolution does he retain his rigidity:
savages "occupy a state of culture analogous to that of our rude progenitors"; "the various stages of savagery and barbarism" correspond
"to similar stages which the ancestors of the civilised races may be
supposed to have passed through"; "the course of religious development has on the whole been uniform among mankind." Primitive rites
are still dramatic, and Frazer describes tribal ceremonies as one or another "act in the drama," but now he is prepared to draw aesthetic
distinctions. Frazer writes:

> Great indeed is the gulf which divides the beautiful creations of
> Greek fancy from the crude imaginings of the Australian savage,
> whose legendary tales are for the most part a mere tissue of
> trivial absurdities unrelieved by a single touch of beauty or poetry.

Some of Frazer's totemic brothers were finally beginning to weary
him.

The Belief in Immortality announced a fourth volume and never
got to it, but Frazer's next book, *The Worship of Nature*, appeared as

"Volume I" in 1926 and never got any further. Its introduction divides "the natural religion of primitive peoples" into the worship of nature and the worship of the dead, reserving the latter, where it was not handled by *The Belief in Immortality*, for a later work. *The Worship of Nature* is the sort of material that, written before 1915, would have become a part of *The Golden Bough*. As an independent work, it seems to be an attempt to imitate its predecessor's form in smaller compass. Like *The Golden Bough*, *The Worship of Nature* begins with an actor in a scene, but instead of the terrified manslayer in the stormy grove, we have a rustic ploughman "pacing behind the plough drawn by the patient horses up and down the long furrows of up-turned brown earth." The problem here is not why a king must die, but why our minds seek a world beyond the material one.

Despite its very different start, *The Worship of Nature* works up to the same dramatic climax, Aztec priests reborn in the flayed skins of female sacrificial victims. The ghastliness is intensified with new material, Khond ceremonies of cutting up a living victim and carrying the flesh, "quivering, warm, and bleeding" (that is, with the life still in it), to fertilize the fields, or roasting the victim alive to produce rain in proportion to his tears. Where *The Golden Bough* transcends all the horror with the great natural cycle of death and rebirth, *The Worship of Nature*, in its unfinished state, merely breaks off abruptly. Frazer carefully restrains himself from calling the Khond sacrificers "human butchers" or making any protest at their deluded meteorology. When he is aware of it, Frazer is a relativist. He speaks of African beauty varying "from the tall handsome Hamite, with almost perfect features, to the squat, dwarf-like pigmy with spread nose and protruding eyes," but adds that this is "according to our European standards."

An odd bitterness sometimes appears in Frazer's tone about things never before questioned, among them rational inquiry. "The fair-seeming fruit of knowledge," he writes, "too often turns out to be apples of Sodom." In an eloquent passage that may remind us of Matthew Arnold's more melancholy verse, Frazer concludes:

> Thus it is that thought perpetually outstrips sense in the infinitely little as in the infinitely great; however far we extend the field of vision, whether to stars of unimaginable distance, or to corpuscles of unimaginable minuteness, thought still passes beyond them in the endless search after the real, the invisible, the eternal. We stand as it were at a point between two infinities neither of which we can ever hope to reach, yet both of which, by the pressure of some force unknown, we are perpetually urged to pursue. Thought is poised on a knife-edge between two abysses, into the unfathomable depths of which she is for ever peering, till her sight grows dim and her brain reels in the effort to pierce the thick gloom that closes the vista on either hand. Yet we understate the mystery that compasses about our little life

when we speak of it as if it were only twofold, the mystery of the infinitely great and the infinitely small in space; for is there not also the twofold mystery of time, the mystery of the infinite past and the mystery of the infinite future? Thus our metaphor of thought poised between two abysses needs to be corrected and expanded: not two, but four infinities, four gulfs, four bottomless chasms yawn at her feet; and down into them some Tempter— or is it some bright angel?—whispering at her ear, perpetually lures her to plunge, only, it would seem, to beat and flutter her ineffectual wings in the impenetrable darkness.

For the first time, Frazer acknowledges his awareness that "the description of beliefs and customs which the enlightened portion of mankind has long agreed to dismiss as false and absurd, if not as monstrous, vicious, and cruel, is apt to be somewhat tedious and repellent."

In 1929 Frazer published his last major work as a classical scholar, his translation of Ovid's *Fasti* in five volumes, three of them commentary, in which he adds his own treasury of custom and belief to Ovid's elegiac calendar of Roman rites. Frazer's next work, *Myths of the Origin of Fire: An Essay*, appeared in 1930. It is another example of the sort of thing that earlier would have been included in *The Golden Bough* as a digression. In fact, except for its geographical order, it most resembles the sections on myths of the origin of death in several earlier books. Frazer is now insistent on myth as primitive speculation, and he begins the preface, "Mythology may perhaps be defined as the philosophy of primitive man." As in the introduction to Apollodorus, myths differ from philosophical speculations or scientific theories only by being erroneous, and Frazer concludes the preface by offering his arrangement of "these fossils of the mind" as a contribution to "that great palaeontology of the human mind that remains to be written." Although "myths never explain the facts which they attempt to elucidate," they are true historical documents of what the mythmakers believed. Thus myths are lies which contain an essential truth, a subjective rather than an objective truth. Frazer concludes the book:

> Thus, in spite of the fantastic features which distort many of them, the myths of the origin of fire probably contain a substantial element of truth, and supply a clue which helps us to grope our way through the darkness of the human past in the unnumbered ages which preceded the rise of history.

One of the psychological truths that emerges from the book is a primitive sexual and urethral association with fire not unlike that which Freud found in his patients. Frazer dissembles it half-heartedly with euphemism: "she took fire from between her legs"; "some say that an old woman had hidden it under her grass *rami*." Eventually it comes out: in Australia, fire originates from the urethra of a euro or the genitals of a woman; in New Guinea the fire-drill is seen as an act of copulation; and so forth.

In 1930 Frazer published his 1879 dissertation, *The Growth of Plato's Ideal Theory: An Essay*, with a new preface. The preface protests Plato's transformation with a sharpness nowhere in the essay, as though Frazer could only see it from the perspective of half a century. He writes:

> And with the marked change for the worse in the construction of the sentences there goes a still deeper change in the whole cast and setting of the pieces; for in the later dialogues, always with the exception of the *Phaedrus*, the dramatic element has really disappeared, though the form of a dialogue is preserved. The vivacious manner of a great dramatist, enthralling his hearers by the alternate play of high tragedy and light comedy, is exchanged for the dryasdust manner of a professor lecturing to docile pupils, who have little more to do than to assent passively to the doctrines inculcated on them by their master. It is a transformation like that of a Shakespeare into a Kant.

That same year Frazer republished the maps and plans from his edition of Pausanias in a separate volume, with an explanatory text by A. W. Van Buren. Van Buren explains in his preface: "Sir James expressed his desire that it should be reissued separately, accompanied by the modicum of text required to bring its meaning into relief, as a portable atlas for travellers following literally or in spirit in the footsteps of Pausanias." In 1932, in a brief foreword of two dozen lines to J. A. MacCulloch's *Medieval Faith and Fable*, Frazer writes of "those earlier faiths which appeal to our curiosity by their quaint solutions of many dark problems, and touch our hearts by their pathetic attempts to furnish the pilgrim on life's rough way with comfort and consolation for his journey." The moral is somehow a plea for "the solemn music of church bells, that lingering relic of the Middle Ages from which it is to be hoped the modern world will be loth to part."

In this mood of reconciliation with the lying purple glow of imagination, in the ominous year of 1933, Frazer went back to reconsider the Marquis of Condorcet. In 1922 he had published "Condorcet on Human Progress" in the *Times Literary Supplement*. Now, for the Zaharoff Lecture at Oxford, with ironic fitness, he expanded it as "Condorcet on the Progress of the Human Mind." In the preface to *Creation and Evolution in Primitive Cosmogonies*, Frazer explains the relevance of the Condorcet essay:

> The troubled times in which we live, distracted between conflicting ideals, wavering between democracy and despotism, dreaming of universal peace, yet feverishly preparing for universal war, resemble in many respects the stormy times in which Condorcet lived and wrote his famous treatise on the progress of the human mind, and the resemblance adds fresh interest to the

proposals which in that work he put forward for remedying some of the evils of his day and hastening the advent of a new and happier era for mankind. Even if from his pages we could glean no practical hint for our guidance, it would still be a gain to escape for a little from the anxieties and forebodings of the present into serene communion with a spirit so lofty and noble as that of Condorcet. Of the literary arts not the least beneficent is that necromancy which can conjure up from the dusty past the spirits of the wise and good who dedicated their genius and their lives to the service of humanity, and by their silent presence can still minister comfort and encouragement to the sad and weary among the living. Of such, we may say in the language of Scripture, is the kingdom of heaven, and of such was Condorcet.

The essay balances a concern for Condorcet's ideas with a concern for the man behind the book. The ideas are those we have seen stated or implied in so much of Frazer's work: teleological evolution ever aspiring to perfection, the rationality of man, an assumption of enlightened self-interest in which "immoral actions are often simply the fruit of ignorance," and so forth. Before discussing Condorcet's book, Frazer writes, "it may be well to look a little closer at the life and character of the writer, since these are always the determining factors in the composition of a book." He then goes extensively into biography before examining Condorcet's *Sketch of an Historical Picture of the Progress of the Human Mind*. Two biographical details stand out sharply. The first is Frazer's account of Condorcet's religious views:

> Another of the disastrous errors which has retarded the progress of mankind he believed to be religion. On this subject the humane and gentle Condorcet was as fierce and uncompromising an iconoclast as Lucretius himself, as firmly convinced of the countless and unspeakable calamities which faith in the supernatural had inflicted on a suffering humanity.

The second is the drama of Condorcet's betrayal during the French revolution, when, hiding out from a death sentence, he was captured in a tavern when he was asked how many eggs he wanted in an omelette and answered offhand "Twelve" (as though one of them should betray him). For Frazer, Condorcet was the image of the secular and rationalist sacrificial savior, and toward the end of Frazer's life Condorcet was his strongest self-image.

Emboldened by Condorcet's pure and disinterested criticism of the French Revolution, which he helped to make and which decreed his death, Frazer for the first time becomes explicit against Marxism, socialism, and the Russian Revolution. Frazer had often been given to sarcasm about the social injustice of his own society. In *Folk-Lore in the Old Testament*, he writes typically of an African people: "From this we may perhaps infer that among these benighted heathen the spheres of justice and property do not coincide with that rigid and inflexible accuracy which happily characterizes them in Christian Europe." By 1921, in "The Scope and Method of Mental Anthropology," he is enough disturbed by the Russian Revolution to sketch out a dual application for anthropology: to "facilitate the work of the modern legislator and social reformer"; and at the same time to refute the fallacies of socialism, which seeks to confiscate private property on the basis of savage practice, and to expose "visions of a Golden Age of universal equality and universal wealth in the future, modelled on the baseless fancy of a like Golden Age in the past."

By 1926, in *The Worship of Nature*, Frazer is muttering ominously of "the number of crucifixes which would be found in the ruins of Europe by the hordes of infidel and iconoclastic invaders which may one day lay the whole fabric of western civilization in the dust." Finally, in 1933, in the Condorcet essay, Frazer launches a full-scale diatribe:

> For we of this generation and of the generation which is passing away have witnessed, and indeed are still witnessing, though happily at a safe distance, a revolution in Russia which presents many points of similarity to the first great Revolution in France. The words of fiery eloquence in which Edmund Burke, the wisest of political thinkers, branded the Jacobins of his day are applicable, with hardly a change but that of names, to the Bolsheviks of our day. In Russia of to-day, as in France of the day before yesterday, we see the same systematic and determined attacks on those institutions which hitherto had been regarded as the very pillars of civilised society; I mean the institutions of private property, the family, and religion; we see the destruction of these institutions proclaimed as a new gospel to be preached to all nations, established at home by wholesale confiscations, robberies, murders, and massacres, and propagated abroad to the ends of the earth by the apostles and emissaries of disorder, sedition, and civil war. And like the Revolution in France this monstrous brood of political locusts has been hatched in the brains of a few purely speculative thinkers or dreamers, whose glaring fallacies, though they have often been exposed and refuted, still furnish plausible demagogues and glib mountebanks with levers whereby to turn the world upside down. For unhappily in the scales of human judgement the clear dictates of reason are too often outweighed by the blind impulse of the passions.
>
> But from the gloomy spectacle of the thundercloud, pregnant with infernal fire, which now in Europe darkens the eastern horizon and threatens to engulf the whole heavens, it is a relief to turn for a little to the bright, if visionary, picture of the future of humanity which Condorcet painted. . . .

The collection, *Creation and Evolution in Primitive Cosmogonies and Other Pieces*, published in 1935, includes other matters of interest in addition to the Condorcet essay. One is a preface making Frazer's boldest effort to date at reconciling all oppositions. Where the title essay had divided primitive origin myths into those which evolved man out of lower forms and those which created him in an instant, Frazer now sees the difference as no difference. He writes:

> Perhaps in the end the two hypotheses may be found to be not so irreconcilable as at first sight they appear to be. Creative evolution or evolutionary creation, like the Pre-established Harmony of Leibniz, may after all be the expression of that great cosmic process which has wrought, and is still working, all the wonders of this mysterious universe, in its majestic progress eternally moulding the forms and directing the courses alike of atoms and of stars.

Spencer and Roscoe had at one time been influences who led Frazer off in different directions, one toward ritual, the other toward history. Now they are merged in a joint tribute, with Frazer laying his remaining scientific pretensions on their graves with the familiar metaphors of building and light:

> I am proud to have been honoured with their personal friendship and to know that they both believed me to have helped to stimulate and direct their researches. Their books may long survive my own; for a foundation of fact, such as they solidly laid in their writings, is always permanent, while a superstructure of theory is always transitory, being constantly superseded by fresh theories which make nearer and nearer approaches to the truth without ever reaching it. On the shore of the great ocean of reality men are perpetually building theoretical castles of sand, which are perpetually being washed away by the rising tide of knowledge. I cannot expect my own speculations to be more lasting than those of my predecessors. The most that a speculative thinker can hope for is to be remembered for a time as one of the long line of runners, growing dimmer and dimmer as they recede in the distance, who have striven to hand on the torch of knowledge with its little circle of light glimmering in the illimitable darkness of the unknown.

The other important matter in *Creation and Evolution* is the final piece, previously unpublished, entitled "Memories of My Parents." Frazer, as reticent about his private life as about his religious beliefs, finally brought himself, at the age of eighty, to write about his childhood, and to summon up, like Odysseus in Hades, the shades of his parents from "the undistinguished crowd of the nameless and forgotten dead."

Frazer's next book, *The Fear of the Dead in Primitive Religion*, was published in three volumes from 1933 to 1936. It deals with a part of natural religion not covered by *The Worship of Nature*, was begun as yet another series of lectures, and constitutes one more digression in the great *Golden Bough* of Frazer's total works. Its theme is Frazer's old imaginative vision of terror just beneath the deceptive appearance. "Under the polished surface of civilised society," he writes, "there exists a deep stratum of savagery, which finds vent in eruptions of crime as well as in the comparatively, or even wholly, harmless and generally picturesque form of folklore." Frazer cites his 1885 article, "On certain Burial Customs as illustrative of the Primitive Theory of the Soul," and we realize with a start that he has spent half a century ceaselessly placating the dangerous dead. Here again is the universal totemic brotherhood: "So like is human nature in all latitudes and under all varieties of culture"; "So similar is the rut in which error has flowed in ancient Greece and in modern India." Since the emphasis now is openly on fear of the dead rather than on their worship, Frazer turns up precisely the negative euhemerism his system had needed to complete itself: as gods are the ghosts of dead men worshipped, so demons are the ghosts of dead men feared. Frazer writes:

> The general attitude of primitive man—and by primitive man I mean the savage—towards the spirits of the dead is very different from ours in that, on the whole, it is dominated by fear rather than by affection. We think of our beloved dead with sorrow and fond regret, and we can hardly conceive of any greater happiness than that of being reunited to them for ever in a better world beyond the grave. It is far otherwise with the savage.

It is as though the "savage" were Frazer's id, acting out all the hostility, anxiety and guilt that Frazer himself suppressed in regard to his parents.

On the subject of immortality, Frazer commits himself to an unusual extent. "An impartial observer might be tempted to conclude," he writes in the preface, "that the spirits of the dead exist only in the imagination of the fond and foolish portion of mankind," nevertheless "it seems probable that the great majority of our species will continue to acquiesce in a belief so flattering to human vanity and so comforting to human sorrow." The immortality of the soul is impossible to disprove at present: "But the batteries of science have an ever longer range, and on this side they may yet make a deep breach in the frowning bastions of faith." The towering structures of theology in Buddhism, Christianity, and Mohammedism, he writes, "would topple over and crash to the ground if the belief in immortality were to be proved baseless." A belief in the malevolence of ghosts, Frazer writes, "is indeed one of the commonest articles of savage religion, and in the mind of primitive man throws a dark shadow on the bright vision of immortality." In the preface to the third volume, Frazer writes:

> Throughout we are dealing with some of the answers which primitive man has given to the great enigma of death—of death in the widest sense, as the inevitable end, not only of man, but of every living thing. We may smile at some of his answers as childish and absurd, but do we of this generation read the riddle better

than he? May it not be that posterity will smile at some of the solutions of the problem to which our contemporaries, with all the resources of modern science at their disposal, cling as tenaciously as does primitive man to his phantasmagoria of the dead?

The volume, and the book, ends with the melancholy moral that fear of the spirits of the dead has haunted the mind of primitive man from time immemorial, "and we may surmise that the same fear has gone far to shape the moulds into which religious thought has run ever since feeble man began to meditate on the great mysteries by which our little life on earth is encompassed."

In this world of primitive terror, even more than in *The Golden Bough*, everything is overdetermined. The Kiwai Papuans avoid mentioning the names of the dead, for example, because it summons the ghost and is bad manners toward the survivors. One cause is magical and the other practical, or one is reason and the other rationalization, or one shows the surface love and the other exposes the underlying hostility. These primitives more and more become types of human behavior, and less and less remain concrete primitive peoples. Never, even in his earliest work, had Frazer written about belief and custom so much outside of space and time. "On the evening of the day on which they had tortured a prisoner to death," he writes, "the American Indians used to run through the village with hideous yells, beating with sticks on the furniture," etc., with never a word about *what* American Indians or *when?* "Tribes are known to have actually extinguished themselves by their blind faith in sorcery and their infatuated devotion to the poison ordeal as an infallible test of truth," Frazer writes, but he neither names these tribes nor gives his sources. "It is customary," he writes, about a burial custom that his text makes clear died out a long time ago. "Modern Jews put potsherds on the eyes of a corpse," he writes, citing a 1748 publication.

As time and place become dreamlike and insubstantial, so motivation becomes less and less what any specific people gives as the reason for its acts, and more and more what Frazer can dream up. Where a ghost is not mentioned, "on the analogy of the customs described above he may be inferred with a high degree of probability." The third volume, a compilation of all the material that did not get into the lectures in the first two, is particularly a tissue of: "but we may conjecture that," "but more probably the motive is," "but probably their motive was the usual one," "but probably we shall not err in supposing that their aim is," "probably the true original motive of the custom was," "we may surmise that the intention is," "we may conjecture that it was supposed to," "we may safely infer that," and so on. The conjecture, supposition, surmise, and inference is invariably that the action was motivated by fear of ghosts. In this mood, Frazer would have seen the priest at Nemi, unconcerned about his murderous successor, cowering in terror from the shade of his deceased predecessor.

In 1937, Frazer published *Aftermath: A Supplement to The Golden Bough*, containing all the material he had accumulated in the years since the third edition. Some of the book emphasizes Frazer's old themes, or adds new examples to former compilations, or even forgetfully repeats the old material. Some of it freshens things up considerably, with material drawn from important fieldwork done since 1915, including the new British school of social anthropologists, Géza Róheim's Freudian ethnology, and, of course, Malinowski's work. The central image of *The Golden Bough* is, as it were, renewed for us with new kings. The king of the Fung in the Sudan, Evans-Pritchard reports, for fear of being speared, changed his sleeping hut several times a night, and so "he slept and woke, slept and woke, slept and woke." Strengthened by the new evidence, Frazer regains some of his old conviction. "This explanation of the rule of the priesthood of Nemi is necessarily no more than an hypothesis," he writes, "but in the light of the parallels which I have adduced the hypothesis appears legitimate, if not probable." By the time he wrote the preface, in August 1936, Frazer had returned to doubt again, and produced another of his typical statements that "I hold all my theories very lightly," and that he hopes for the survival of his writings "less for the sake of the theories which they propound than for the sake of the facts which they record." The preface concludes: "Such as it is, with all its shortcomings, I now submit *The Golden Bough* in its completed form to the judgment of my contemporaries, and perhaps of posterity."

Later in 1937 Frazer did the same for his other major work, in *Totemica: A Supplement to Totemism and Exogamy*, containing the material that had been published on the subject since 1910. Here there is a sharp and visible change. In the quarter of a century between the books, so much primitive custom had eroded that Frazer could no longer slight problems of culture contact, acculturation, and demoralization. He prints Spencer's warning, in connection with some information:

> Unfortunately, I was unable to gain as complete and minute information as I should have liked. The Warrai tribe is now decadent, having been ruined by coming into contact with the mining fields, and it is always unsafe to rely implicitly upon information in regard to matters concerned with the organisation of a tribe derived from natives who are thus, more or less, demoralised.

Frazer recognizes "the present disintegrated society" in many parts of Australia. From New Caledonia he reports an acculturated ceremony:

> When this dance of the mullet clan was performed for the last time a rifle-shot rang out at the close, at which the dancers fell as if dead to the ground, the report of the rifle signifying at once the explosion of dynamite among the fish, and the extinction of the mullet clan by civilisation.

From Nigeria, Frazer quotes C. K. Meek's account of a Jokun skeptic who ate his totemic brother the python out of hunger, suffered no ill effects; "so he has not hesitated to break the other taboos when opportunity occurred." Frazer quotes a resident in Southern Nigeria: "The people have now outgrown the beliefs, mainly infantile, connected with such ideas of plants and animals."

Accompanying the breakdown of the native cultures, there is a breakdown in Frazer's theory. He still believes that:

> The very primitive aborigines of Australia have adopted so decided an opinion of the extremely prejudicial tendency of close inbreeding that they have actually, to all appearances, unanimously and from time immemorial, instituted an elaborate and very effective form of social organisation for the express purpose of preventing it.

Consciously instituted it may be, but Frazer can no longer believe that it is beneficial. He writes:

> We may be disposed to doubt whether they have really benefited by the institution, and whether it may not rather have served as a clog than a spur to progress. Certainly the innumerable bars which the rigorous system of exogamy characteristic of their social organisation opposes to the legitimate union of the sexes in marriage must have often retarded, if it did not positively arrest, that natural increase of population which is one of the most obvious features of a progressive population.

After all the labors of *Totemism and Exogamy* to demonstrate that the two institutions are unrelated, in *Totemica* Frazer comes back to where he began, and defines exogamy as "one of the most important characteristics of true totemism." He bravely quotes Smith and Dale mocking his conceptional theory of totemism, which "would now only provoke the Ba-ila to ridicule."

All that really survives from *Totemism and Exogamy*, and that intensified, is its imaginative design, Frazer's great vision of the consubstantiality of man and nature. He quotes A. P. Elkin's definition of totemism as "a philosophy which regards man and Nature as one corporate whole." Frazer writes of the Australian aboriginal:

> In the rites he not only expresses his desires in words and actions, but, as in so many of the rites, he often gives of his own life, that is, his own sacred blood, to the species, through its sacramental symbol, so that Nature, or at least some particular natural species, may continue to live and increase.

"The life of the performers," he writes, "is given to, or shared with, the totem." As words like "sacred" and "sacramental" make clear, Frazer now sees primitive religion as more a matter of spiritual identification than of the materiality of rite. Where the characteristic question for determining someone's totem in *Totemism and Exogamy* was

"What do you dance?," in *Totemica* it is "What is your dreaming?"

From the third volume of *The Fear of the Dead* on, Frazer's eyesight had been too far gone for him to write with his famous steel pen, and that volume, *Aftermath*, and *Totemica* had been dictated to his secretary, Downie. In 1938 and 1939 the contents of Frazer's manuscript notebooks, the records of a lifetime of anthropological reading and transcribing, were published in four volumes as *Anthologia Anthropologica*, edited by Downie. The organization is geographical, and after the first volume Downie confines himself almost entirely to material Frazer had not used in any of his books. Frazer's preface to the first volume announces boldly that he is preserving grubs in imperishable amber. He begins:

> *Habent sua fata libelli.* Books, like men, have their fates, and like men they perish. Of none of them, not even of the very greatest, can we affirm with confidence that it is immortal.

He continues:

> The books from which I have drawn the contents of this anthology are written for the most part in a plain straightforward way, the authors contenting themselves with describing in simple language the things which they have seen, or had heard reported by competent native informants. Few, if any, of them possess that magic charm of style which, by firing the imagination or touching the heart, can alone confer what we fondly call immortality upon a work of literature.

Frazer's sources for his notebooks are not only the whole world of published anthropology, formal and informal, that he hopes to immortalize, but unpublished manuscripts by field-workers, private letters, and notes of conversations with such travelers as Mary Kingsley. When his sources are prudish, going into Latin for the details of sex rites or genital mutilations, Frazer is prudish enough to leave it in the Latin, but when they are frank about such matters in English, he is frank enough to leave it in the English. When they give a sense of time and change, Frazer dutifully records it: "Dr. Krapf says that he is expected to kill someone before the ceremony is over; but this seems not to be the case now"; "The foregoing description of the Masai applies to them as they were before 1891." Frazer does not reshape the material at all, except to note obvious comparisons suggested. Thus for the Tonga Islands he will note, "Judgment of Solomon"; or for the Nias of Indonesia: "Story of a mighty man whose strength was in his hair, but was betrayed by his wife, and conquered, after his hair had been cut off." One note, on Malaya, would have been marvelously useful to Marx: "the *pěnanggalan* is a sort of monstrous vampire which delights in sucking the blood of children."

Frazer's last piece of writing, besides the prefaces for *Anthologia Anthropologica*, was fittingly a preface to a reissue, in 1938, of

Spencer and Gillen's by-then-classic *The Native Tribes of Central Australia*. It is like a last whisper of defiance. Of his old theory that totemism is based on ignorance of physical paternity, now derided even by the Ba-ila, Frazer reaffirms: "I regard this as on the whole the most probable explanation of the Mystery of Totemism." Of his Platonic evolution, rejected by everyone, from an age of magic to an age of religion, Frazer remarks stubbornly: "We may fairly conclude that these facts lend some support to the theory."

FREUD

*Ah, how embarrassing Freud is! And how easily
it seems to me we should have discovered his
America without him!*

André Gide, *Journals*

SIGMUND FREUD was born on May 6, 1856, in Freiberg, Moravia, now a part of Czechoslovakia. His father, Jakob Freud, a forty-year-old widower with two grown sons, had married twenty-year-old Amalie Nathanson in 1855. Sigmund was thus his mother's first-born, not his father's. He was named Schlomo in Hebrew, after his dead grandfather Rabbi Schlomo Freud. Jakob Freud was a wool merchant and textile manufacturer from Galicia, and at the time of Sigmund's birth was fairly prosperous. Jakob's elder son Emanuel was the father of a son, John, born not long before Sigmund, and a daughter, Pauline, born not long after, so that Freud's earliest playmates were a nephew and a niece approximately his age. Sigmund always regarded himself as his mother's favorite of her eight children, as he later told the world on several occasions, and Jones reports hearing her refer to him in her old age as *mein goldener Sigi.* As an infant Freud was cared for by an elderly Czech Roman Catholic nurse, who used to take him to church, and who was dismissed and sent to jail for theft when he was two and a half. When he was about a year and a half old, his baby brother Julius died.

In 1859, when Freud was three, the business in Freiberg deteriorated and the family moved to Leipzig and then to Vienna, where Freud was to live for the next eighty years. Emanuel and his family moved to Manchester, and settled in the textile business there as Engels had a decade before (Engels and Freud's half-brothers must have known each other, although no record of contact exists). Young Sigmund was at first educated by his father, then sent to a private school. From the first he was studious and ambitious, interrupting his reading only to take long walks. After the age of seven he was given some education in Judaism and the Hebrew language, but the effort was half-hearted, since Jakob Freud seems to have been himself a free-thinker. In 1865, when Freud was nine, he passed an examination that admitted him to the secondary school. He stood at the head of his class for the last six of his eight years there, and he was graduated *summa cum laude* in 1873. That autumn he entered the University of Vienna as a medical student. In addition to the regular medical curriculum he took a course in Darwinism, and a number of courses in philosophy. In 1875 he visited his relatives in Manchester, the trip a reward from his father for the *summa cum laude*.

In 1876, Freud embarked on his first original research, under the direction of Karl Claus, his instructor in "Biology and Darwinism." It was an amusingly Freudian problem in locating the testes of the eel, and Freud worked at the marine zoology laboratory at Trieste, dissecting four hundred eels. His inconclusive paper was presented to the

295

Academy of Sciences by Claus in 1877 and later published in its Bulletin. Freud spent some of his time in Ernst Bruecke's physiology laboratory, where he found greater satisfaction, and he soon reduced his studies to the regular medical curriculum (no more philosophy) and research under Bruecke. Freud approved Bruecke's emphasis—positivist, dynamic, and evolutionary—and was attracted to Bruecke's austere and Prussian personality. Freud remained at the Bruecke Institute for six years, as a research scholar. He first worked on the problem of the histology of the nerve cells in the spinal cord of a primitive fish called *Ammocoetes*. Bruecke presented Freud's first paper on the subject to the Academy of Sciences in 1877, and it was published in its *Bulletin* in January, with a drawing by Freud. It was Freud's first publication, although his second piece of research. He continued working on the problem, invented an improved method of staining, and published a second paper. He then switched to the nerve cells of crayfish.

In 1879 Freud was called up for a year's military service, which meant only being on call in a hospital, and he spent some of the time translating a volume of John Stuart Mill for a German collected edition. While working on anatomy with Bruecke, he also did some work in experimental physiology in the pathology laboratory. Freud took his medical examinations in 1880 and 1881, and in March, 1881, he was awarded an M.D. degree, at the age of twenty-five. He continued to work at the Institute for another year, finishing his work on the crayfish and being promoted to the position of Demonstrator, with some teaching responsibility. He also worked on the analysis of gases in the chemical laboratory. In 1882 Bruecke advised Freud, because of his poverty, to give up research and practise medicine. At the same time Freud became engaged to Martha Bernays, whose brother Eli was married to Freud's sister Anna. The next month he enrolled in the General Hospital of Vienna, and he moved into the hospital in May, 1883. In June, Martha Bernays' family moved to Wandsbeck, Germany. For the next three years Freud courted her by mail, with occasional visits, in an amazing series of letters recently published.

While at the hospital Freud tried a number of medical specialties, from surgery to psychiatry in Theodor Meynert's clinic, did research in brain anatomy, and was a pioneer experimenter with cocaine. In 1884 he was appointed Lecturer in Neuropathology, and received a six months' traveling grant to study under Charcot in Paris. In August, 1885, he left the General Hospital for good. That autumn and winter he worked under Charcot in the Salpêtrière clinic in Paris. He visited Martha in Wandsbeck on his way to and from Paris, and also stopped off for a few weeks in Berlin on the way back to study children's diseases at the Baginsky Clinic. Back in Vienna in 1886 he became head of the new neurological department in Kassowitz's Children's Institute, where he worked three days a week and studied cerebral paralysis and aphasia. He finally married Martha Bernays that year. Freud had been taking private patients since his days in the

General Hospital, and doing occasional private teaching and scientific abstracting. He now turned to translating seriously, and in the next few years translated two books by Charcot and two by Bernheim.

In 1886 Freud read papers to medical meetings on hypnosis and hysteria, based on material from Charcot's clinic, which promptly resulted in Meynert's barring him from *his* clinic. He soon developed a private practice consisting of neurotic patients, whom he treated with electrotherapy. At the end of 1887 he gave up electrotherapy and turned to hypnosis, which his friend Breuer had been using with success since 1880. In 1889 Freud visited Nancy in France to perfect his hypnotic technique under Liébault and Bernheim, and he began using Breuer's cathartic method (getting the patient under hypnosis to talk out the genesis of her symptoms) for the first time in May, with the patient he called "Emmy v. N." Over the next few years this gradually developed into the method of free association and psychoanalysis. Breuer and Freud began publishing jointly in 1893, their papers culminating in a book in 1895. By this time Freud had three sons and three daughters. He continued publishing papers, lecturing, and treating patients, mostly women at first. Summers the family left Vienna, generally going to the mountains or to the seashore. Freud's son Martin later recalled a vacation on the Adriatic in 1895 when his father (who swam breaststroke, to keep his beard out of water) used to swim out so far that it was impractical for him to swim in for lunch, and a waiter swam out with lunch and cigars. Freud travelled extensively with his wife, and, when she was pregnant or unwell, with his brother Alexander, her sister Minna, or a medical friend.

In 1896 Jakob Freud died, and Freud began analyzing his dreams and himself, using the techniques he used with his patients. He gradually settled into the regular routine he was to follow for the rest of his life: analytic patients all day and evening, then writing and reading until late at night. From 1896 on he suffered severely from constipation. Except for vacations, the only breaks in his routine were attending a meeting of the B'nai B'rith on alternate Tuesdays, and Saturday nights, when he played tarock, a Viennese four-handed card-game, with three other doctors. He began to collect Egyptian, Greek and other antiquities on his travels. In 1899 Berchtesgaden in Bavaria became his favorite summer resort, as it was later to be Hitler's. In 1901 he first visited Rome, long his ambition, with his brother. In 1902 the few Viennese interested in psychoanalysis, including several doctors practising it, began meeting in Freud's office Wednesday evenings. Around 1905 a number of foreigners began to practise psychoanalysis under the influence of Freud's publications, and they soon began to correspond with him and to visit Vienna. In 1908 the first International Psychoanalytic Congress was held in Salzburg. Later in the year Freud again visited his half-brothers in England, and the next year he traveled to the United States for the only time, to lecture at Clark University, which gave him the only honorary degree he was ever to get.

In 1910 the International Psychoanalytic Association was founded, and in 1911 there was the first defection, Alfred Adler resigning from the Vienna society. In 1912 a secret society of loyal lieutenants, the "Committee," was founded by Ernest Jones, consisting of himself and five other stalwarts, and Freud gave them cameos set in gold rings. The Committee held firm, but Wilhelm Stekel broke away in 1912, and Carl G. Jung in 1913. During the war Freud continued to practise and lecture as though nothing had changed, although he worried about his sons Martin and Ernst in the Austrian army. Many of his patients were now analysts undergoing didactic analysis. Former patients and friends in allied and neutral countries smuggled him cigars through Switzerland. The war hurt Freud's practice badly, and the postwar inflation destroyed his savings, but in 1919 foreign patients began to return, and in 1920 there was an International Psychoanalytic Congress at the Hague. Early that year Freud was deeply disturbed by the death of his daughter Sophie, a young mother of two children. In 1922 he attended his last Congress, in Berlin. In April, 1923, his jaw cancer was discovered, and he had a harrowing operation. In June his grandson Heinz, Sophie's younger child and in Freud's opinion the most intelligent child he had ever encountered, died of tuberculosis at the age of four and a half. It was the only occasion on which Freud was known to cry, it brought on the first serious depression of his life, and it was a blow from which he never recovered.

In October, 1923, Freud had a radical operation on his jaw. It took away some of the palate and necessitated an acutely uncomfortable prosthesis, from which he suffered for the rest of his life. The device made his speech defective, like that of someone with a cleft palate. Freud was only once heard to complain about the cancer, with the words "most uncalled-for," although he complained regularly about what he called "the permanent, never-to-be-ended misery of the prosthesis." His doctor at one time thought his difficulty with it was "mainly nervous." In 1924 Otto Rank broke with Freud, and was replaced on the Committee by Freud's daughter Anna, who had become his close companion and nurse. Three years later the Committee was dissolved. In 1929 the analyst closest to Freud, Sandor Ferenczi, deviated from orthodoxy, although without the sharp public break of earlier defectors.

In the summer of 1930 Freud took his last holiday away from Vienna, traveling to Rebenburg in the Salzkammergut. That year his mother died. He was awarded the 1930 Goethe prize, in honor of his prose style. The next year, Freud's seventy-fifth birthday, there was a ceremony at his birthplace in Freiburg, a bronze tablet was put up on the house where he was born, and the street was renamed *Freudova ulice* in his honor. Freud continued to practise, but taking fewer patients. In 1933 the Nazis burned his books in Berlin. In 1936, the year of his eightieth birthday, he was made a Fellow of the Royal Society, and there was a recurrence of his cancer. In 1938 the Nazis invaded Austria, and Freud was finally persuaded to leave Vienna with his family. Strings were pulled by U.S. Ambassador William C. Bullitt and the analyst Marie Bonaparte (Princess George of Greece), and the Freud family was allowed to emigrate to England in June. That fall Freud had the last of his thirty-three operations for the cancer, and in February, 1939, it was found to be so widespread as to be inoperable. On September 23, 1939, in London, Freud died in his sleep, after months of agony very little relieved by narcotics. He was cremated and his ashes deposited in one of his favorite Greek vases.

Imperfect Instruments

IN 1888, when he was thirty-two, Dr. Sigmund Freud published a translation into German of Hippolyte Bernheim's book, *De la suggestion et de ses applications á la thérapeutique*, as *Die Suggestion und ihre Heilwirkung*. His preface, an essay on hypnotism and suggestion, is his earliest published writing in the field of psychology. He is still on the borderline of physiology, explaining: "We possess no criterion which enables us to distinguish exactly between a mental process and a physiological one." Freud boldly announces that "hysterical phenomena are governed by laws," although he does not yet know the laws, nor realize how profoundly his discovery of the laws will revolutionize psychology. The tone of authority from an unknown young Viennese doctor who had published a few papers in physiology and neurology may have surprised the translation's few readers.

Freud's first published book, *On Aphasia*, a contribution to neurology, appeared in 1891. Subtitled "A Critical Study," it is an attack on the localizing theory of aphasia (muteness) then fashionable, and it proposes an alternative functional theory. Freud wrote to his friend, Dr. Wilhelm Fliess:

> In a few weeks I look forward to sending you a paper on aphasia, for which I have a good deal of feeling. I have been very cheeky in it, and have crossed swords with your friend Wernicke, as well as with Lichtheim and Grashey, and have even scratched the high and mighty idol Meynert.

The book's basic approach is evolutionary, influenced by the American neurologist Hughlings Jackson, who had in turn been influenced by Herbert Spencer's Darwinian psychology. Aphasia is seen as a devolution or regression to an earlier stage of mental functioning, with the later genetic and dynamic emphasis of psychoanalysis implicit.

The book's form suggests the running dialogue or debate with an enlightened reader that Freud was to use in many of his later works. He writes: "I have to consider an objection which has no doubt occurred to every reader"; or he asks "How is it to be explained?" and answers, "I can do no more than recognize the difficulty and point to another one in reply." Freud remarks: "How this apparent contradiction can be resolved I am at present unable to state; but I believe that its clarification will also provide the answer to the earlier question," and adds: "Perhaps some observations to be presented later in this book will contribute to the clarification of this difficulty." At various points he summarizes "possible objections against the validity of our views" and answers them. The book's great metaphor is of mental functioning as an evolving organism. Two minor metaphors are of interest: theorizing imaged as physical building, so that an observation "ought to be the cornerstone of a new theory"; and an odd image of nerve tracts containing the body periphery the way "a poem contains the alphabet." The most characteristic foreshadowing of the later Freud is the tone of dogged honesty with which he begins the book's Conclusions:

> I am well aware that the considerations set out in this book must leave a feeling of dissatisfaction in the reader's mind. I have endeavoured to demolish a convenient and attractive theory of the aphasias, and having succeeded in this, I have been able to put into its place something less obvious and less complete. I only hope that the theory I have proposed will do more justice to the facts and will expose the real difficulties better than the one I have rejected. It is with a clear exposition of the problems that the elucidation of a scientific subject begins.

The same year Freud's other neurological book was published. Written in collaboration with Dr. Oskar Rie, then Freud's assistant in the special department of Kassowitz's Children's Institute, it is a sizable monograph, *Klinische Studie über die halbseitige Cerebrallähmung der Kinder* (*Clinical Studies on the Unilateral Cerebrospinal Paralysis of Children*). The work apparently bears little relation to psychology, it has never been translated, and I have not seen a copy of it. It would seem to be, like Darwin's monographs on the Cirripedes, the author's one work too technical for the lay reader.

The next year, 1892, Freud began writing a series of psychological papers devoted to his developing ideas in the field. The first of these, written in collaboration with Dr. Joseph Breuer, entitled "On the Psychical Mechanism of Hysterical Phenomena," was published in 1893. It recognizes "a symbolic relation between the cause and the pathological manifestation, such as normal people also fashion in dreams." With some excitement, it reports the germ of psychoanalytic cure. The authors write:

> The discovery that we made, at first to our own great surprise, was that when we had succeeded in bringing the exciting event to clear recollection, and had also succeeded in arousing with it the accompanying affect, and when the patient had related the occurrence in as detailed a manner as possible and had expressed his feeling in regard to it in words, the various hysterical symptoms disappeared at once, never to return.

They conclude, in the German equivalent for italics: "*Hysterical patients suffer principally from reminiscences.*" The same year Freud published an obituary tribute to his teacher, J. M. Charcot, praising him not primarily as a thinker but as "an artistically gifted temperament," "a seer." He saw Charcot in a mythic role:

> But to his pupils, who made the rounds with him through the wards of the Salpêtrière—that museum of clinical facts for the greater part named and defined by him—he seemed a very Cuvier, as we see him in the statue in front of the Jardin des Plantes, surrounded by the various types of animal life which he had understood and described; or else he reminded them of the myth of Adam, who must have experienced in its most perfect form that intellectual delight so highly praised by Charcot, when the Lord led before him the creatures of Paradise to be named and grouped.

In recognizing the hysteric to be genuinely ill rather than malingering, Charcot was a liberator, Prometheus as well as Adam. He was also a vision of Freud's future.

That year Freud published "A Case of Successful Treatment by Hypnotism," in which he describes in strongly dramatic terms the sort of conflict within the psyche on which his later work would concentrate. Freud writes:

> The emergence of a counter-will is chiefly responsible for the characteristic which often gives to hysterics the appearance almost of being possessed by an evil spirit—the characteristic, that is, of not being able to do something precisely at the moment when they want to most passionately, of doing the exact opposite of what they have been asked to do, and of being obliged to cover what they most value with abuse and contempt.

Freud also published in 1893 "Some Points in a Comparative Study of Organic and Hysterical Paralyses," a task Charcot had assigned to him eight years before. The hallmark of hysterical paralysis, he notes, is the extravagance of its symptoms, always more complete than organic paralysis, and violating the facts of anatomy. To explain a point, Freud gallantly asks his reader's permission "to pass over into the field of psychology," and his conclusion is that psychological rather than neurological explanations must be found.

The next year Freud published "The Defense Neuro-Psychoses," subtitled "An endeavor to provide a psychological theory." Here, for the first time, the evil spirit possessing hysterics and neurotics is given its name. Freud writes:

> In all the cases I have analyzed it was in the sexual life that a painful affect—of precisely the same quality as that attaching to the obsession—had originated. On theoretical grounds it is not impossible that this affect may at times arise in other spheres; I have merely to state that hitherto I have not discovered any other origin of it.

Freud refers to "the unbearable sexual idea," "the intolerable sexual idea," and believes the anxiety this produces to cause the obsession or phobia. Freud's final image for what he was later to call "libido" is electricity: "like an electric charge," "a fluid electric current."

Written the same year and published in 1895 was "The Justification for Detaching from Neurasthenia a Particular Syndrome: The Anxiety-Neurosis." Here Freud is almost offhand about the "sexual aetiology of the anxiety-neurosis," since he has now tested it therapeutically by advising patients to change their sex relations, and finding that "the anxiety is removed and does not return again without a fresh cause of a similar nature." More important, he is now able to see the neurosis dramatistically, and to recognize that the shortness of breath and palpitations of anxiety attacks are a miming of coitus "in an isolated and exaggerated form." Later in 1895 he published "A Reply to Criticisms of the Anxiety-Neurosis," in which he generalizes further: "The aetiology of the neuroses lies in sexuality"; *all* the neuroses, that is. The predominant part played by sexual factors has been "hitherto far too little appreciated." Freud's tone is modestly arrogant. "I wish at once," he writes, "to combat the idea that my theory is to be overthrown so very easily by the first casual and impromptu objections." He is sardonic about the confusions of his medical critics and the lies of their patients, and he writes at one point of his "worthy opponent": "I too have had exactly the same experience, but I was not misled by it."

Freud's first important book, *Studies in Hysteria*, was written in collaboration with Breuer and published in 1895. It was an uneasy collaboration, with Breuer deeply ambivalent about the sexual aetiology of the neuroses, supporting it in public but revealing his dissent to Freud privately. Several months after the book appeared, Breuer wrote to Fliess: "Freud's intellect is soaring; I struggle along behind him like a hen behind a hawk." The book, and in fact the whole later method of psychoanalysis, originated in Breuer's experience with the patient he called "Anna O.," whom he had treated for hysteria between 1880 and 1882. "Anna O." was a girl named Bertha Pappenheim who later became the first social worker in Germany. She discovered that her symptoms (a lively bundle including, among others, paralyses of three limbs, dissociated personalities, and a hacking nervous cough) were relieved when, under hypnosis, she talked out her fantasies and oppressions to Breuer. Her method, which Breuer called "cathartic," was wonderfully successful until Miss Pappenheim revealed by means of a phantom pregnancy that she was in love with Breuer, and he fled the case in dismay. Thus between the two of them they discovered not only the basic principle of psychoanalytic therapy, but its inevitable emotional attachment, the transference, even if Breuer failed to understand it (Freud himself did not fully understand the role of the transference until 1900). Freud never met Miss Pappenheim, who was a friend of his wife's, but one hopes that he recognized his indebtedness to her. Miss Pappenheim called her therapy, so characteristically

Viennese, the "talking cure," since the symptom disappeared when the originating experience was "talked out."

Studies in Hysteria is a substantial revelation of later Freudian psychoanalysis. In it Freud first mentions "resistance," describes "transference" (although without the term), and explains "repression." From its publication, Ernest Jones says in *Sigmund Freud: Life and Work*, "it is customary to date the beginnings of psychoanalysis." Many of the great metaphors that constitute Freud's imaginative vision are also here introduced for the first time. The personality is seen as a geologic stratification, with the earlier layers beneath the later, and Freud elaborately describes a "triple stratification" in hysteria with the comment, "I hope soon to be able to justify this figurative expression." This stratigraphy is soon replaced by an elaborate metaphor of dynamic topography. Freud writes:

> The whole spatially extended mass of the pathogenic material is thus drawn through a narrow fissure and reaches consciousness as if disjointed into fragments or strips. It is the task of the psychotherapist to put it together again into the conjectured organization. He who desires still more comparisons may think here of a Chinese puzzle.

The book's concluding metaphor is drawn from a branch of medicine that always attracted Freud. He writes:

> I have often compared the cathartic psychotherapy to surgical measures, and designated my cures as psychotherapeutic operations; the analogies follow the opening of a pus pocket, the curetting of a carious location, etc.

The concept of symbolic action is basic to the book. "I had to assume," Freud writes of "Elisabeth v. R.," "that she directly sought a *symbolic* expression for her painfully accentuated thoughts and had found it in the aggravation of her pains." However, the cathartic treatment can be as adequate a symbolic action as the symptoms. Freud explains:

> The reaction of an injured person to a trauma has really only then a perfect 'cathartic' effect if it is expressed in an adequate reaction like revenge. But man finds a substitute for this action in speech through the help of which the affect can well-nigh be abreacted.

Freud's chapters are insistently dramatistic. He writes: "The most important explanations are frequently ushered in as superfluous accessories, just like the princes of the opera who are dressed as beggars." Insights are obtained from "a detailed discussion of the psychic processes, as one is wont to hear it from the poet." Freud describes a scene:

> But she gave me no definite answer. She smiled perplexed, as if convinced, and like one who must admit that as we have now

come to the bottom of the thing, there is nothing more to be said about it. I can imagine the kind of tactile sensation that she later learned to interpret. Her features, too, seemed to express that she agreed with my assumption. But I could not penetrate any deeper into her.

The year *Studies in Hysteria* was published Freud wrote to Fliess about the progress of a case:

Meanwhile the time has not yet come to enjoy the climax and then sit back and relax. The later acts of the tragedy will still demand a lot of work from

Your
Sigm.

Freud's first case in the book, his earliest attempt at Breuer's method, was the lady he called "Mrs. Emmy von N." She gave him almost as much trouble as "Anna O." had given Breuer. Among other symptoms, she kept interrupting her remarks to make a sound like the mating call of the woodcock. Freud's concept of the therapist's duties at the time included not only hypnosis and cathartic conversations, but massage and regulating the patient's menstruation by post-hypnotic suggestion. In his early practice Freud seems to have had female patients almost exclusively, and he wrote sharply in a draft essay sent to Fliess early in 1895: "There are two kinds of women patients: one kind who are as loyal to their physician as to their husband, and the other who change their physicians as though they were lovers." Late in 1898 Freud wrote triumphantly to Fliess: "Half my patients are now men." The sexual aetiology of hysteria is affirmed all through the book. "The sexual element . . . is more responsible for traumas than anything else," Freud writes flatly. He reports his discovery of the sexual aetiology of anxiety and hysteria, considerably to his surprise, in the case of "Emmy von N." Even Breuer announces in *Studies in Hysteria:* "Most of the rejected and converted ideas, or the most important of them, have a sexual content," and adds:

I do not think that I exaggerate when I assert that the *great majority of severe neuroses in women originate in the marriage bed.*

Breuer seems to have accepted adult sexuality as causative, but boggled at childhood sexuality. Freud boggled at nothing.

A number of papers published after *Studies in Hysteria* continue and amplify its themes. "Obsessions and Phobias: Their Psychical Mechanisms and Their Aetiology," published in 1895, goes into Pascal's obsession and Lady Macbeth's phobia along with those of patients. "Heredity and the Aetiology of the Neuroses," published the next year, first uses the term "psychoanalytic method" for Breuer's "probing procedure." "Further Remarks on the Defense Neuro-Psychoses," also published in 1896, defines psychoanalysis as "the method of making conscious what was previously unconscious." It works things out very neatly. The two simple neuroses, neurasthenia and anxiety-neurosis, arise respectively from masturbation and sexual frustration; the two defense-neuroses, obsessional neurosis and hysteria, arise respectively from active and passive childhood sex experience. This paper first uses the term "projection." It makes something dynamic of the metaphor of stratification, with "the return of the repressed" seen as an impulse bursting its way back up after it has been forcibly put down below in the substratum.

Freud's next paper, "The Aetiology of Hysteria," was published in 1896 after being delivered as a lecture at the Society of Psychiatry and Neurology in Vienna earlier that year. In it Freud describes the analytic method in a most elaborate archaeological metaphor. He writes:

> Imagine that an explorer comes in his travels to a region of which but little is known and that there his interest is aroused by ruins showing remains of walls, fragments of pillars and of tablets with obliterated and illegible inscriptions. He may content himself with inspecting what lies there on the surface and with questioning the people who live near by, perhaps semi-barbaric natives, about what tradition tells of the history and meaning of these monumental remains, and taking notes of their statements —and then go his way. But he may proceed differently; he may have come equipped with picks, shovels and spades, and may press the inhabitants into his service and arm them with these tools, make an onslaught on the ruins, clear away the rubbish and, starting from the visible remains, may bring to light what is buried. If his work is crowned with success, the discoveries explain themselves; the ruined walls are part of the ramparts of a palace or a treasure-house, from the ruined pillars a temple can be constructed, the many inscriptions, which by good luck may be bilingual, reveal an alphabet and a language, and when deciphered and translated may yield undreamed-of information about the events of the past, to commemorate which these monuments were built. *Saxa loquuntur!*

The fact that in psychoanalysis the scenes are discovered in reverse chronological order "justifies our comparison with the excavation of ruins." Freud uses, apparently without conscious awareness, the key metaphoric progression of Darwin's *Origin of Species*, the development from chain to tree to tangled bank. He writes:

> Taking a case which presents several symptoms, from whatever symptom we start we arrive by means of analysis at a series of experiences the memories of which are linked together by association. At first the memory-chains are distinct from one another as they lead backwards, but, as we said before, they branch out; from a single scene two or more memories may be reached at the same time, and from these again there issue side-chains the single

links of which may in their turn be joined by association to links of the main chain. The metaphor of a family tree of which the members have also intermarried is really not a bad one.

Eventually this becomes the complex bank:

The chains of associations for the separate symptoms then begin to enter into relation with one another; the family trees intertwine.

Another major metaphor is the one Freud later used to organize *The Interpretation of Dreams*, that of an exploratory walk. "This path alone, after our many delays," he writes, "can lead us to the goal." The goal is "the discovery of a *caput Nili* of neuropathology," the source of the Nile in the inaccessible jungle of the psyche. The last important metaphor is one he had tried out earlier in *Studies in Hysteria*. Freud writes:

Just as when putting together children's picture-puzzles, we finally after many attempts become absolutely certain which piece belongs to the gap not yet filled—because only that particular piece at the same time completes the picture and can be fitted in with its irregular edges to the edges of the other pieces in such a way as neither to leave a space nor to overlap—so the content of the infantile scenes proves to be an inevitable completion of the associative and logical structure of the neurosis; and only after they have been inserted does the origin become evident—one might often say, self-evident.

Addressing a real audience, Freud becomes highly dramatistic. He writes: "From previous experience I can foresee that it is just against this conclusion or against its universal validity that your opposition will be directed." All his eighteen cases of hysteria having shown the same thing, Freud protests: "Nobody picked them out to please me." Later he writes, "Two objections which contradict each other are sure to be raised from different quarters against this statement," and proceeds to raise and answer them. To clinch the case for the aetiology of hysteria in passive childhood sexual experience, Freud creates a wildly melodramatic family scene:

Now the feeling of a sexually normal human being recoils from the idea of these infantile sexual scenes, containing, as they do, all the abuses known to libertines and impotent persons, whose sexual practices include the improper use of the mouth and the rectum. The physician's astonishment at this soon gives place to complete understanding. We cannot expect that people who do not scruple to gratify their sexual desires upon children will be repelled by any lack of refinement in the manner of that gratification, and the natural sexual impotence of childhood inevitably impels towards those surrogate activities to which the adult degrades himself in the case of acquired sexual impotence. All the peculiar circumstances in which the ill-matched pair carry on their love-

relation: the adult—who cannot escape his share in the mutual de-
pendence inherent in a sexual relation and yet is endued with complete authority and the right of punishment, and can exchange the
one role for the other in unbridled gratification of his moods; the
child—helpless victim of this capriciousness, prematurely awak-
ened to every kind of sensation and exposed to every kind of
disappointment, often interrupted in the practice of the sexual activities assigned to him by his imperfect control of his natural needs
—all these grotesque, yet tragic, incongruities become stamped
upon the further development of the person concerned and his
neurosis, manifesting themselves in innumerable lasting consequences which deserve to be carefully traced out.

"Heredity," Freud wrote sternly to Fliess at the end of 1896, "is seduction by the father."

In the fall of 1897, as the result of a summer of self-analysis, Freud
made the great discovery that inaugurated mature psychoanalysis, that
these melodramas of infant seduction by a perverted father were
mostly fantasies, not real events. He reports it triumphantly to Fliess
in a letter dated September 21: "I no longer believe in my neurotica,"
and explains the discrepancies that convinced him. He writes: "Between ourselves I have a feeling more of triumph than of defeat
(which cannot be right)," and continues, confusing his Shakespeare
plays, "I vary Hamlet's remark about ripeness—cheerfulness is all."
Where Frazer's reaction to new discovery each time was to discard
his theory, Freud, after "a period of absolute helplessness," simply
modified *his* theory to make fantasy-gratification and wish-fulfilment as
significant as overt acts. Belief in the stories had in turn been Freud's
own neurotic fantasy, gratifying what he had earlier confessed to
Fliess as "my wish to pin down a father as the originator of neurosis."

Freud's first paper after the discovery was "Sexuality in the Aetiology of the Neuroses," published in 1898. This begins with the familiar
generalization:

> Detailed investigations during the last few years have led me
> to the conviction that factors arising in sexual life represent the
> nearest and practically the most momentous causes of every single
> case of nervous illness.

This causation, Freud continues, although ignored by medical science,
"seems actually never to have quite passed out of the consciousness of
the laity." He now boasts that his remarks are based on "more than
two hundred cases." Of the psychoanalytic method, he writes, "I owe
countless successes to it and may reasonably hope to increase its effectiveness considerably yet." Admitting some limitations, he concludes proudly:

> I was obliged to attack at once the hardest tasks with imperfect
> instruments; the test has therefore proved all the more convincing.

Mocking the charge that doctors should not meddle with the sex lives of their patients, Freud concludes sarcastically: "His clumsy hand would only ruin family happiness." For the first time, Freud goes beyond the problem of the individual to make some public statements about the culture, foreshadowing his later indictments. He writes:

> As far as civilization is concerned, too, it is possible that these authorities may be judging correctly in so often reckoning the causation of neurasthenia in the list of its crimes (although this probably comes about in a very different way from that which they suppose); yet the state of our civilization again is unalterable for the individual.

(The year before, Freud had written in a draft to Fliess: "Civilization consists in a progressive renunciation. Contrariwise, the 'Superman'.") Freud concludes his discussion of culture in the paper:

> And so there still remains plenty of work in this direction for the next century—in which our civilization will have to learn to become compatible with the claims of our sexuality!

Freud's tone to his medical colleagues displays a new toughness. He writes:

> A physician can always do harm if he is clumsy or unscrupulous, no more and no less in probing into the sexual life of his patients than in other directions. Naturally, if anyone discovers by a meritorious endeavor to arrive at self-knowledge that he is deficient in the tact, seriousness and discretion necessary for interrogating neurotic patients, if anyone knows that revelations of a sexual character will evoke in himself only lewd thoughts instead of scientific interest, he will do right to keep away from the subject of the aetiology of the neuroses. We only ask in addition that he should avoid treatment of nervous patients altogether.

Freud demands more honesty and tolerance in sexual matters generally, summing it up as "sincerity on the part of physicians and tractability in the public."

The next year, 1899, Freud published "Screen Memories," later included in *The Psychopathology of Everyday Life*, in which he goes into case histories (including his own, disguised) and gives some of his dialogue with patients:

Patient: But I still cannot grasp your point.

Freud: I am coming to it at once.

It sounds rather like Holmes and Watson. The Great Detective was about to appear.

The Interpretation of Dreams

F REUD'S masterwork, *The Interpretation of Dreams,* was published late in 1899, postdated 1900. Freud had discovered the core of the theory, that dreams are wish-fulfilments, early in 1895, and in July, 1895, he first fully analyzed a dream of his own in the new terms, the dream he called "Irma's injection." Freud later recognized the book as his most important, and in his preface to the third English edition in 1931, he writes:

> It contains, even according to my present-day judgement, the most valuable of all the discoveries it has been my good fortune to make. Insight such as this falls to one's lot but once in a lifetime.

The book, then, at least on the surface, is an account of the origin, structure, and function of dreams, along with a method for their interpretation.

In Freud's view, the dream is a distortion of unsuitable thoughts to make them unrecognizable. The processes of distortion, elaborately described in the book's longest chapter, "The Dream-Work," are principally four. They are: "condensation," a combining of a number of thoughts into economical composites, so that each element of a dream will have several meanings and be what Freud called "over-determined"; "displacement," a substitution of one identification for another; "considerations of representability," the replacement of abstractions by concrete images; and "secondary revision," a further tendentious disguising. All this complicated labor results from a conflict between two psychical forces ("or," as Freud says, "we may describe them as currents or systems"), which he first calls the "unconscious" and the "preconscious," and later the "repressed" and the "ego" (a quarter of a century later, he called the "repressed" the "id."). The motive for the labor lies in two major factors Freud named "repression," the act of refusing infantile impulses and related material admission to consciousness, and "resistance," the visible effort that keeps them unconscious. In "The History of the Psychoanalytic Movement," published in 1914, Freud wrote: "The theory of repres-

sion is the pillar upon which psychoanalysis rests," and the observed
fact of resistance is its principal evidence.

The other principal discovery in *The Interpretation of Dreams* is
the "Oedipus complex," which Freud first noticed in his patients, confirmed in analyzing his own dreams in 1897, and promptly recognized
as universal. He explains it fully in the book, without the term (which
he did not use until 1910.) The Oedipus complex, as it is described in
The Interpretation of Dreams (the theory was later modified in the
case of girls), is an infantile erotic attachment to the parent of the opposite sex and rivalry with the parent of the same sex. Freud discusses
Sophocles' *Oedipus the King* (which he had translated for his second-
ary-school graduation examination), and says of its protagonist, for
whom he named the complex:

> His destiny moves us only because it might have been ours—
> because the oracle laid the same curse upon us before our birth as
> upon him. It is the fate of all of us, perhaps, to direct our first sexual
> impulse towards our mother and our first hatred and our first mur-
> derous wish against our father. Our dreams convince us that that
> is so. King Oedipus, who slew his father Laius and married his
> mother Jocasta, merely shows us the fulfilment of our own child-
> hood wishes.

All dreams are thus wish-fulfilments, Freud says, and wish-fulfilment
is the "key" to the understanding of dreams. The simplest wish dreams
fulfill is the wish to sleep, which by the distorting processes of the
dream-work they guard from inner and outer disturbances that would
awaken the sleeper. On a deeper level, dreams gratify the greedy wishful impulses of the unconscious in a symbolic form, and their function
is to serve as a safety-valve discharging its excitation. In their deepest
meaning, dreams fulfill the infantile Oedipal wish, repressed and unconscious. Freud writes: "Dreaming is a piece of infantile mental life
that has been superseded."

The form of *The Interpretation of Dreams* is a controlled gradual
revelation of Freud's theory, progressing from didactic oversimplification to full and rich complexity, like *The Origin of Species* or *Capital*.
Freud will state a principle, then move on to "a first denial of this
assertion," or write, "my earlier statement requires correction." He reminds us each time that things are still being kept too simple, with
such remarks as "Later on I shall have to disclose a factor in dream-
formation which I have not yet mentioned." We can see the development most neatly in the series of summary formulations, of progressive
complication, of the book's main point. The second chapter concludes:
"When the work of interpretation has been completed, we perceive
that a dream is the fulfilment of a wish." The fourth chapter concludes: "a dream is a (disguised) fulfilment of a (suppressed or repressed) wish." The fifth chapter adds: "a succession of meanings or
wish-fulfilments may be superimposed on one another, the bottom one
being the fulfilment of a wish dating from earliest childhood." By the

last chapter, this becomes: "a wish which is represented in a dream must be an infantile one." Thus the simple formula, a dream is the disguised fulfilment of a repressed infantile wish, gradually unfolds over hundreds of pages. If we had any doubt that this form was the work of conscious craft, it would be dissipated by Freud's statement about Sophocles' play:

> The action of the play consists in nothing other than the process of revealing, with cunning delays and ever-mounting excitement —a process that can be likened to the work of a psychoanalysis— that Oedipus himself is the murderer of Laius, but further that he is the son of the murdered man and of Jocasta.

The Interpretation of Dreams is thoroughly dramatistic, sometimes in the form of debate, sometimes in other fashions. Freud writes a running dialogue with an imaginary critic: "I shall meet with the most categorical contradiction," "I shall be told," "an objection may be raised," "Is it not more probable," "I can give only limited assent to this argument," "I cannot accept this objection," and so on. Dreams themselves are dramatic, as Freud notes, in that they reproduce an idea as though we were experiencing it. Neurosis is even more dramatic, in that hysterics "act all the parts in a play single-handed"; and Freud in fact defines hysteria as the conflict of two incompatible wishes, as Hegel defined tragedy as the conflict of two incompatible necessities. Freud quotes Havelock Ellis approvingly in an account of secondary revision that is a little playlet. Ellis writes:

> Sleeping consciousness we may even imagine as saying to itself in effect: 'Here comes our master, Waking Consciousness, who attaches such mighty importance to reason and logic and so forth. Quick! gather things up, put them in order—any order will do —before he enters to take possession.'

With the psyche full of agonists, Freud's psychology must be comparably dramatic, and as we might expect it is full of voices, struggles, soliloquies and colloquies, and stage movement.

As he follows the quicksilver associations of dreams, Freud's style is sometimes a kaleidoscope of verbal puns, what he calls "syllabic chemistry," perhaps reminding the reader of *Finnegans Wake*. In a footnote, Freud quotes the criticism of Fliess when he read the proofs, that "the dreamer seems to be too ingenious and amusing" (Freud does not quote his own reply, that "All dreamers are insufferably witty"). The dream-work is in fact very like the composition of poetry. One dream has "a particularly amusing and elegant form"; another, "remarkable among other things for its form," alternates idea and image as a poem does. Like the poem-work the dream-work "does not think, calculate or judge in any way at all; it restricts itself to giving things a new form." Freud was not pleased with his book's style. He writes to Fliess:

The matter about dreams I believe to be unassailable; what I dislike about it is the style. I was quite unable to express myself with noble simplicity, but lapsed into a facetious, circumlocutory straining after the picturesque. I know that, but the part of me that knows it and appraises it is unfortunately not the part that is productive.

In answer to Fliess' reassurances, Freud replies ten days later:

But I do not think that my self-criticism was wholly unjustified. Somewhere inside me there is a feeling for form, an appreciation of beauty as a kind of perfection; and the tortuous sentences of the dream-book, with its high-flown, indirect phraseology, its squinting at the point, has sorely offended one of my ideals.

A more interesting matter than the book's style (which is, by general agreement, much better than Freud thought) is its tone. There are in fact two tones. The first is the tone of Sherlock Holmes, the Great Detective: assured, intolerant, firm and strong. Of a difference of opinion between himself and a patient, Freud remarks: "Soon afterwards it turned out that I was right." When a dreamer protests over revealing a delicate circumstance behind the dream, Freud says with all of Holmes' forcefulness. "Nevertheless I shall have to hear it." His comment on an "innocent" dream he interprets as a masturbation fantasy is: "Altogether *far* from innocent." He announces vigorously, "Whatever interrupts the progress of analytic work is a resistance," recognizing no calamities or catastrophes, from a broken leg to a war, that are not the patient's devilment. We can see Conan Doyle's hand in the titles Freud gives the dreams, so like Holmes cases: The Dream of Irma's Injection, The Dream of the Botanical Monograph; and Doyle as well as Sophocles has had a clear influence on Freud's form of delayed revelation and suspense.[1] Freud writes typically: "We shall find later that the enigma of the formation of dreams can be solved by the revelation of an unsuspected psychical source of stimulation." The book's contrasting tone is a modest, scientific humility, rather like Darwin's in the *Origin*. Freud writes: "I shall further endeavour to elucidate," "I have been driven to realize," "I did not expect to find my guess at an interpretation justified," and so on. It is as though behind the manifest book, like the manifest dream-content, there were a latent book, like the latent dream-content, making a very different sort of statement.

O F C O U R S E there is. Only on the surface is this a book about the objective interpretation of dreams. Not only is there a subjective book

[1] When Theodor Reik suggested this comparison with Holmes (for Freud's technique, not his tone) in 1913, Freud said he would prefer a comparison with Giovanni Morelli, a nineteenth-century art scholar who specialized in detecting fakes.

beneath the surface, the account of Freud's own neurosis, self-analysis
and cure, but Freud clearly calls our attention to it in *The Interpretation of Dreams*, with no more dissembling than an "as it were." Interpreting a dream about the dissection of his own pelvis, he writes:

> The dissection meant the self-analysis which I was carrying out,
> as it were, in the publication of this present book about dreams
> —a process which had been so distressing to me in reality that I
> had postponed the printing of the finished manuscript for more
> than a year.

In the preface to the second edition in 1908, Freud makes this even
clearer. He writes:

> For this book has a further subjective significance for me person-
> ally—a significance which I only grasped after I had completed it.
> It was, I found, a portion of my own self-analysis, my reaction to
> my father's death—that is to say, to the most important event, the
> most poignant loss, of a man's life. Having discovered that this
> was so, I felt unable to obliterate the traces of the experience.

Despite these clear statements, to the best of my knowledge no one
recognized the autobiographical extent of the book until the publication of Freud's letters to Fliess, in German in 1950 and in English as
The Origins of Psychoanalysis in 1954.

Wilhelm Fliess was a Berlin nose-and-throat specialist and biological theorist,[2] with whom Freud had a close friendship in the years between 1895 and 1900. Freud destroyed his letters from Fliess, but
Fliess kept his from Freud, and after his death in 1928 they were sold
to a bookseller in Berlin and were eventually bought by Marie Bonaparte, who bravely defied Freud when he insisted they be destroyed,
and published them after his death. The 284 documents, ranging in
time from 1887 to 1902, are a uniquely fascinating one-sided correspondence to read, and a remarkable insight into the origins of psychoanalysis generally and the genesis of *The Interpretation of Dreams* specifically.

In his letters to Fliess we can see the agonized stages of Freud's
self-analysis, which resulted in the emergence of what Jones in his
biography calls "the serene and benign Freud" of the twentieth century. In June, 1897, Freud reports to Fliess: "I have never yet imagined
anything like my present spell of intellectual paralysis. Every line I
write is torture." He continues:

> Incidentally, I have been through some kind of a neurotic experi-
> ence, with odd states of mind not intelligible to consciousness—

[2] Fliess' weird cyclic theories apparently still have followers. *Biorhythm*, by
Hans J. Wernli, was published in this country in 1960. It is a popular account of
the Fliess system, with instructions to the reader for making his own Biorhythmic
chart, and it includes sample rhythmograms of Tyrone Power, Louis Bromfield,
George Gershwin, and Henry Ford.

cloudy thoughts and veiled doubts, with barely here and there a ray of light.

In July, he reports:

I still do not know what has been happening to me. Something from the deepest depths of my own neurosis has ranged itself against my taking a further step in understanding of the neuroses, and you have somehow been involved.

In August, he writes:

After a spell of good spirits here I am now having a fit of gloom. The chief patient I am busy with is myself. My little hysteria, which was much intensified by work, has yielded one stage further. The rest still sticks. That is the first reason for my mood. This analysis is harder than any other.

In October, things are going easier, and Freud reports:

For the last four days my self-analysis, which I regard as indispensable for clearing up the whole problem, has been making progress in dreams and yielding the most valuable conclusions and evidence. . . . I cannot give you any idea of the intellectual beauty of the work.

Some days later he writes:

My self-analysis is the most important thing I have in hand, and promises to be of the greatest value to me, when it is finished. When I was in the very midst of it it suddenly broke down for three days, and I had the feeling of inner binding about which my patients complain so much, and I was inconsolable.

Freud continues:

So far I have found nothing completely new, but all the complications to which by now I am used. It is no easy matter. Being entirely honest with oneself is a good exercise. Only one idea of general value has occurred to me. I have found love of the mother and jealousy of the father in my own case too, and now believe it to be a general phenomenon of early childhood.

Later in the month Freud writes:

I am now experiencing myself all the things that as a third party I have witnessed going on in my patients—days when I slink about depressed because I have understood nothing of the day's dreams, fantasies or moods, and other days when a flash of lightning brings coherence into the picture, and what has gone before is revealed as preparation for the present. . . . Resistance has thus become an objectively tangible thing for me, and I only wish that I had also grasped what lies behind repression.

In November, Freud again hit trouble. He explains:

> My self-analysis is still interrupted. I have now seen why. I
> can only analyze myself with objectively-acquired knowledge (as
> if I were a stranger); self-analysis is really impossible, otherwise
> there would be no illness.

Early in December, Freud writes:

> On stagnant days such as yesterday and today everything inside
> me is stagnant and terribly lonely. I cannot talk about it to anyone,
> and I cannot force myself to work, as other workers can.

By February of 1898 it was over, and Freud writes to Fliess: "Self-
analysis has been dropped in favor of the dream book."

The Interpretation of Dreams constantly informs us of the author's reticence about revealing his dreams and their background. He
writes:

> There is some natural hesitation about revealing so many intimate
> facts about one's mental life; nor can there be any guarantee
> against misinterpretation by strangers. But it must be possible to
> overcome such hesitation. . . . And it is safe to assume that my
> readers too will very soon find their initial interest in the indiscre-
> tions which I am bound to make replaced by an absorbing im-
> mersion in the psychological problems upon which they throw
> light.

He continues in a footnote:

> I am obliged to add, however, by way of qualification of what
> I have said above, that in scarcely any instance have I brought for-
> ward the *complete* interpretation of one of my own dreams, as it
> is known to me. I have probably been wise in not putting too
> much faith in my readers' discretion.

At a sexually-suggestive detail in his dream of Irma's injection, Freud
breaks off with "Frankly, I had no desire to penetrate more deeply at
this point." [3] In a 1909 footnote to the interpretation of the dream, he
adds:

> Though it will be understood that I have not reported every-
> thing that occurred to me during the process of interpretation.

In concluding the chapter, he challenges the reader:

> But considerations which arise in the case of every dream of my
> own restrain me from pursuing my interpretive work. If anyone
> should feel tempted to express a hasty condemnation of my

[3] The dream of Irma's injection is brilliantly reanalyzed in terms of ego
psychology by Erik H. Erikson in "The Dream Specimen of Psychoanalysis" in
the *Journal of the American Psychoanalytic Association*, January 1954. Erikson
goes much more fully into the dream than Freud did in the book, making explicit
a good deal of the sexuality that Freud left implicit.

The Interpretation of Dreams

reticence, I would advise him to make the experiment of being franker than I am.

Starting on another dream, Freud writes:

Once again this will involve me in a variety of indiscretions; but a thorough elucidation of the problem will compensate for my personal sacrifice.

Of the dream of the botanical monograph, he writes:

For reasons with which we are not concerned, I shall not pursue the interpretation of this dream any further, but will merely indicate the direction in which it lay.

Describing a memory of his father's giving him a book with colored plates to destroy when he was five, Freud says:

Moreover I can assure my readers that the ultimate meaning of the dream, which I have not disclosed, is intimately related to the subject of the childhood scene.

Of another dream, he writes:

I might pursue the intricate trains of thought further along these lines and explain fully the part of the dream which I have not analyzed; but I must desist at this point because the personal sacrifice demanded would be too great.

Of still another dream:

I must also refrain from any detailed analysis of the two remaining episodes of the dream. I will merely pick out the elements leading to the two childhood scenes on whose account alone I embarked upon a discussion of this dream. It will rightly be suspected that what compels me to make this suppression is sexual material.

Later he speaks of a dream "which I had to leave almost uninterpreted on account of its gross indecency."

We learn from a number of surprising letters to his fiancée the very considerable extent of Freud's own repression and prudishness. We must thus recognize Freud's impressive heroism in making these revelations. He is in fact the bravest sort of hero, a hero of the ludicrous. Men can confess with relative ease to rapes and murders they have committed, but it takes much more courage for Freud to begin the interpretation of one of his dreams with the announcement that at the time of the dream "a boil the size of an apple had risen at the base of my scrotum." At the same time that we recognize Freud's honesty, we must recognize its limits. He admits that he is not telling us the whole truth about himself, and that he is falsifying some of what he does tell. Explaining that "the politeness which I practise every day is to a large extent dissimulation," he adds, "and when I interpret my dreams for my readers I am obliged to adopt similar distortions." Freud acknowledges this more fully in the preface. He writes:

> But if I were to report my own dreams, it inevitably followed that I should have to reveal to the public gaze more of the intimacies of my mental life than I liked, or than is normally necessary for any writer who is a man of science and not a poet. Such was the painful but unavoidable necessity; and I have submitted to it rather than totally abandon the possibility of giving the evidence for my psychological findings. Naturally, however, I have been unable to resist the temptation of taking the edge off some of my indiscretions by omissions and substitutions.

In August of 1899, Freud writes to Fliess:

> I am deep in the chapter on the "dream-work" and have replaced —I think to advantage—the complete dream that you deleted by a small collection of dream-fragments.

The next month he assures Fliess: "I have avoided sex, but 'dirt' is unavoidable." In short, Freud has consciously disguised the material of the book as the dream-work unconsciously disguises, by a censoring process very like secondary revision.

Anyone who reread *The Interpretation of Dreams* after reading the Fliess correspondence must have had an uncanny experience: where Fliess had been invisible in the book before, he was suddenly omnipresent. In his superb new variorum translation of *The Interpretation of Dreams*, published in 1954, James Strachey identifies many of these references. What had on first reading seemed to be a hundred friends all turn out to be Wilhelm Fliess. As the hidden subject of the dream of Irma's injection, Fliess is: "another friend who had for many years been familiar with all my writings during the period of my gestation, just as I had with his"; "a person whose agreement I recalled with satisfaction whenever I felt isolated in my opinions"; "this friend who played so large a part in my life." As the disguised subject of the dream of the botanical monograph, Fliess is involved in a tender fantasy:

> If ever I got glaucoma, I had thought, I should travel to Berlin and get myself operated on, incognito, in my friend's house, by a surgeon recommended by him.

One of the events inspiring the dream was "a letter from my friend in Berlin the day before." When Freud returns to Irma's injection, two more Fliesses turn up: "a friend who was seriously ill" in Munich a year before, and "my friend in Berlin, who *did* understand me, who would take my side, and to whom I owed so much valuable information, dealing, amongst other things, with the chemistry of the sexual processes."

As the concealed subject of other dreams, Fliess appears variously:

"a friend of mine was stopping in Italy and I had been without his address for a considerable time"; "my friend who might be met in Prague"; "a man of importance" who had been attacked by "an unknown young man"; a friend before whom Freud laid "a difficult and long-sought theory of bisexuality"; a friend "I was afraid I might not find alive if I made the journey to him"; and so on endlessly. The effort to disguise the identity of Dr. Fliess of Berlin can only be called ingenuous: when Berlin is named, Fliess is not; on the one occasion when Fliess is named, Berlin is called "B."; at one point Freud says "my friend in Berlin, whom I have referred to as 'Fl.'." Fliess also comes into the book in the peculiar form of "Rome." Freud describes "a series of dreams which are based upon a longing to visit Rome," which at the time he wrote *The Interpretation of Dreams* he regarded as an unattainable longing. Of one of them he writes: "The instigation of this dream had been a proposal made by my friend in Berlin that we should meet in Prague at Easter." "If Rome occurred in one of my dreams," Freud explains in a later chapter, "it was necessary for me to find a substitute for it from some locality known to me." The letters to Fliess make it abundantly clear that a wished-for meeting with Fliess is the Roman association. "Think of a congress on Italian soil!" he writes, using the peculiar word that he used for their vacationing together. "You know my Roman dreams," he adds.

The relationship with Fliess seems to have had, as Freud recognized, a strong homosexual component. (In one letter, he even addresses Fliess as "Dearest.") For the self-analysis, the attachment performed the vital function of an analytic transference, enabling Freud to project onto Fliess his infantile relations with his parents and other relatives. The success of the self-analysis not only cured Freud of his neurosis, but of the transference, and the friendship inevitably came to an end. During the composition of *The Interpretation of Dreams*, Freud writes to Fliess:

> So you see what happens. I live gloomily and in darkness until you come, and then I pour out all my grumbles to you, kindle my flickering light at your steady flame and feel well again; and after your departure I have eyes to see again, and what I look upon is good.

In 1900 Freud writes: "But there can be no substitute for the close contact with a friend which a particular—almost a feminine—side of me calls for." When their friendship turned into bickering in 1901, Freud writes to Fliess, "I was sorry to lose my 'only audience.'" Nine years later, Freud showed in a letter to Sandor Ferenczi that he understood the Fliess relationship. He writes, somewhat over-optimistically:

> You not only noticed, but also understood, that I *no longer* have any need to uncover my personality completely, and you correctly traced this back to the traumatic reason for it. Since Fliess's case, with the overcoming of which you recently saw me

occupied, that need has been extinguished. A part of homosexual cathexis has been withdrawn and made use of to enlarge my own ego. I have succeeded where the paranoiac fails.

He adds:

My dreams at that time were concerned, as I hinted to you, entirely with the Fliess affair, which in the nature of things would be hard to arouse your sympathy.

According to *Glory Reflected*, a memoir by Freud's son Martin, Fliess' photograph continued to occupy a place of honor in his father's study after the break.

Beneath the attachment to Fliess in *The Interpretation of Dreams* is of course the Oedipus complex. The infantile relation that Freud found, and projected onto Fliess, was with his nephew John. Freud writes in *The Interpretation of Dreams:*

It may even be that the development of this martial ideal is traceable still further back into my childhood: to the times when, at the age of three, I was in a close relation, sometimes friendly but sometimes warlike, with a boy a year older than myself, and to the wishes which that relation must have stirred up in the weaker of us.

Later he finds underlying a dream "some scenes of quarrelling from my very early childhood which must have occurred between me and a nephew of mine, a year my senior, who is at present living in England." [4] Later he writes:

Strange to say, I really did once play the part of Brutus. I once acted in the scene between Brutus and Caesar from Schiller before an audience of children. I was fourteen years old at the time and was acting with a nephew who was a year my senior. He had come to us on a visit from England; and he, too, was a *revenant*, for it was the playmate of my earliest years who had returned in him. Until the end of my third year we had been inseparable. We had loved each other and fought with each other; and this childhood relationship, as I have already hinted above, had a determining influence on all my subsequent relations with contemporaries. Since that time my nephew John has had many reincarnations which revived now one side and now another of his personality, unalterably fixed as it was in my unconscious memory. There must have been times when he treated me very badly and I must have shown courage in the face of my tyrant; for in my later years I have often been told of a short speech made by me in my own defense when my father, who was at the same time John's grandfather, had said to me accusingly: 'Why are

---

[4] The lifelong wish to move to England, gratified only in the last two years of Freud's life, would thus be the desire to be with John, as the wish for Rome was the desire to be with Fliess.

you hitting John?' My reply—I was not yet two years old at the time—was 'I hit him 'cos he hit me.'

Of a demonstration of hostility in a dream, Freud says: "This hostility must therefore certainly have gone back to my complicated childhood relations to John." Further on he explains:

In the dream of my uncle which I have just mentioned, the antithetical, affectionate effect probably arose from an infantile source (as was suggested by the later part of the dream), for the uncle-nephew relationship, owing to the peculiar nature of the earliest experiences of my childhood, had become the source of all my friendships and all my hatreds.

When Fliess had a daughter and named her Pauline, the name of his beloved dead sister, and also the name of John's sister, Freud writes, "the associative links between the contradictory components of the dream-thoughts were drawn closer." Freud's account of the relationship with John in a letter to Fliess during the self-analysis in 1897 hints that it involved overt sexuality. Freud writes:

I have long known that my companion in crime between the ages of one and two was a nephew of mine who is a year older and now lives in Manchester; he visited us in Vienna when I was fourteen. We seem occasionally to have treated my niece, who was a year younger, shockingly. My nephew and younger brother determined, not only the neurotic side of all my friendships, but also their depth.

The same thing is perhaps suggested by a remark in the 1896 paper "The Aetiology of Hysteria." Freud writes:

Where the relation is one between two children, the character of the sexual scenes is still repulsive, since every relation of the sort between children postulates a previous seduction of one of them by an adult. The psychic consequences of such a childhood relation are quite extraordinarily far-reaching; the two persons remain all their lives united by an invisible bond.

The relationship with John thus became the prototype for all of Freud's later emotional attachments. He states this most fully at another place in *The Interpretation of Dreams*, writing:

I have already shown how my warm friendships as well as my enmities with contemporaries went back to my relations in childhood with a nephew who was a year my senior; how he was my superior, how I early learned to defend myself against him, how we were inseparable friends, and how, according to the testimony of our elders, we sometimes fought with each other and made complaints to them about each other. All my friends have in a certain sense been re-incarnations of this first figure who 'long since appeared before my troubled gaze': they have been *reve-*

nants. My nephew himself reappeared in my boyhood, and at that time we acted the parts of Caesar and Brutus together. My emotional life has always insisted that I should have an intimate friend and a hated enemy. I have always been able to provide myself afresh with both, and it has not infrequently happened that the ideal situation of childhood has been so completely reproduced that friend and enemy have come together in a single individual —though not, of course, both at once or with constant oscillations, as may have been the case in my early childhood.

He continues, to a stern conclusion:

But the *revenants* were a series of reincarnations of the friend of my childhood. It was therefore also a source of satisfaction to me that I had always been able to find successive substitutes for that figure; and I felt I should be able to find a substitute for the friend whom I was now on the point of losing: no one was irreplaceable.

When Alfred Adler and Wilhelm Stekel broke with Freud, Jones says, Ferenczi suggested that Freud was "living over again the unpleasant experience of Fliess's desertion of him ten years ago, and Freud confirmed this." "I had quite got over the Fliess affair," Freud writes to Ferenczi, "Adler is a little Fliess come to life again. And his appendage Stekel is at least called Wilhelm." In 1912, when C. G. Jung signalled his approaching break by remissness in answering Freud's letters, Freud was reminded, Jones says, "of the same course of events with Fliess where the first sign of Fliess's cooling towards him was his delay in answering Freud's letters" (although in the case of Fliess, Freud had cooled first).

Before Fliess there had been a number of such ambivalent or soon-souring attachments. One of them was with Freud's brother-in-law and old friend, Eli Bernays. Another was with Freud's teacher, Theodor Meynert, of whom Freud tells a very dramatic story in *The Interpretation of Dreams.* He writes:

I had carried on an embittered controversy with him in writing, on the subject of male hysteria, the existence of which he denied. When I visited him during his fatal illness and asked after his condition, he spoke at some length about his state and ended with these words: 'You know, I was always one of the clearest cases of male hysteria.' He was thus admitting, to my satisfaction and astonishment, what he had for so long obstinately contested.

Another such was Breuer, who gets into a Fliess dream in the book. Freud broke with Breuer in 1896, at the beginning of the period Jones calls "the more passionate phase of his relations with Fliess," and in letters to Fliess at the time Freud reviles Breuer bitterly. Jones writes:

Breuer was failing in his role as father-protector by repudiating Freud's researches and rejecting his conclusions. Yet how could one with an easy conscience turn against a person who for fifteen years had done so much to help and support one? In early life Freud had found it impossible to hate his father, and had concealed his hostility by love. The same solution was the only feasible one now, but the outer reality forbade it except by the device of 'decomposing' the father-person into two, one 'good,' the other 'bad.' So hatred was directed against Breuer, and love towards Fliess—both in an excessive degree out of proportion to the merits or demerits of the persons themselves. We know that with Freud intense love and hate were specially apt to go hand in hand.

Without the intense hate, Freud was similarly swept off his feet by Charcot, of whom he writes his fiancée in 1885:

> Charcot, who is one of the greatest of physicians and a man whose common sense borders on genius, is simply wrecking all my aims and opinions. I sometimes come out of his lectures as from out of Notre Dame, with an entirely new idea about perfection. But he exhausts me; when I come away from him I no longer have any desire to work at my own silly things; it is three whole days since I have done any work, and I have no feelings of guilt. My brain is sated as after an evening in the theater. Whether the seed will ever bear any fruit I don't know; but what I do know is that no other human being has ever affected me in the same way.

Less intensely, Freud had been similarly involved with another teacher, Ernst Bruecke, and with Bruecke's assistant, Ernst Fleischl von Marxow. After Fliess there were many others among the more imaginative of Freud's psychoanalytic followers, particularly Jung, Stekel, Otto Rank, and Ferenczi. The passionate letters to Jung are as embarrassing to read as the earlier ones to Fliess. Freud writes to Jung in 1907 "of the calm assurance that finally took possession of me and bade me wait until a voice from the unknown answered mine. That voice was yours." The successive editions of *The Interpretation of Dreams* are like a stratification of developing friendships and favoritisms: Jung appears in the second edition in 1909; Stekel dominates the third in 1911; and Ferenczi and Rank take over from the fourth in 1914 on.

The ambivalent relationship toward Stekel in the book is particularly interesting. Freud began as a relativist in dream interpretation, insisting that images have a unique meaning for each dreamer in the context of his associations. Stekel was an absolutist, insisting that dreams use universal symbols that can be listed in a handbook, as he did so list them in *Die Sprache des Traumes* in 1911 and in later works. Over the years Freud became more and more convinced by Stekel (who had first come to him as a patient), and *The Interpretation of Dreams* expanded to include more and more general dream symbolism. In the 1909 edition Freud lists all sorts of objections to the

Stekel approach, admits "we shall feel tempted to draw up a new 'dream-book' on the decoding principle," and then writes: "Subject to these qualifications and reservations I will now proceed." He goes on to compile a moderate gypsy dream book: the emperor and empress "as a rule" are the father and mother, umbrellas "may" stand for the male organ, ovens usually represent the uterus, etc. In later editions this was enormously expanded, became a new section, and lost much of its tentative tone. In the 1925 collected edition, long after the break with Stekel, Freud wrote an acknowledgment of his influence, still deeply ambivalent: Stekel "has perhaps damaged psychoanalysis as much as he has benefited it," and the intuitive method by which he gets his readings "must be rejected as scientifically untrustworthy"; yet Stekel is ultimately right, and on the subject of absolute symbolism Freud concedes: "It was only by degrees and as my experience increased that I arrived at a full appreciation of its extent and significance, and I did so under the influence of the contributions of Wilhelm Stekel."

Years after the break with Fliess, International Psychoanalytic Congresses were held in four of the six towns where Freud and Fliess had held their "congresses," and a return to a fifth was scheduled but prevented by the first World War. At a meeting with Jung and a few other followers in Munich in 1912, while lunching at a hotel, Freud suddenly fainted. Two weeks later he had an explanation. He writes to Jones:

> I cannot forget that six and four years ago I suffered from very similar though not such intense symptoms in the *same* room of the Park Hotel. I saw Munich first when I visited Fliess during his illness and this town seems to have acquired a strong connection with my relation to that man. There is some piece of unruly homosexual feeling at the root of the matter.

One earlier fainting in the dining room of the Park, Jones says in *Free Associations*, was during a painful scene with Rie, Freud's lifelong friend, family doctor, and tarock-crony. Freud had also fainted at Bremen in 1909, in the presence of Jung and Ferenczi.

Even deeper in Freud's psyche than his nephew John was the figure concealed by displacement, the figure of his father. As Freud says in the 1908 preface, it was guilts connected with his father's death in 1896 that inspired the self-analysis and the book. Freud discusses typical dreams "containing the death of some loved relative," and says of at least one group of them, those with a painful affect, that their meaning is "a wish that the person in question may die." As examples of absurd dreams he gives "two or three dreams which deal (by chance, as it may seem at first sight) with the dreamer's dead father." Freud introduces the second of them: "Here is another, almost exactly similar, example from a dream of my own. (I lost my father in 1896.)" Another is introduced:

For instance, a man who had nursed his father during his last illness and had been deeply grieved by his death, had the following senseless dream some time afterwards.

The dream is a very brief one of the father being dead and not knowing it, and Freud goes on to interpret it. He writes:

> While he was nursing his father he had repeatedly wished his father were dead; that is to say, he had had what was actually a merciful thought that death might put an end to his sufferings. During his mourning, after his father's death, even this sympathetic wish became a subject of unconscious self-reproach, as though by means of it he had really helped to shorten the sick man's life. A stirring up of the dreamer's earliest infantile impulses against his father made it possible for this self-reproach to find expression as a dream; but the fact that the instigator of the dream and the daytime thoughts were such worlds apart was precisely what necessitated the dream's absurdity.

If this is not Freud's own dream, it is one he powerfully identified with, since he repeats it in a 1911 paper, and tells another like it in his *Introductory Lectures*. Freud readily admits to such identification in *The Interpretation of Dreams*. He writes of a patient:

> I knew that the root of his illness had been hostile impulses against his father, dating from his childhood and involving a sexual situation. Insofar, therefore, as I was identifying myself with him, I was seeking to confess to something analogous.

Freud generalizes about absurd dreams and dead fathers, in a clearly autobiographical statement:

> Nor is it by any means a matter of chance that our first examples of absurdity in dreams related to a dead father. In such cases, the conditions for creating absurd dreams are found together in characteristic fashion. The authority wielded by a father provokes criticism from his children at an early age, and the severity of the demands he makes upon them leads them, for their own relief, to keep their eyes open to any weakness of their father's; but the filial piety called up in our minds by the figure of a father, particularly after his death, tightens the censorship which prohibits any such criticism from being consciously expressed.

He then begins "Here is another absurd dream about a dead father," and gives one more dream of his own. Freud's father seems to have been kind but somewhat strict. Jones writes:

> On the other hand, the father was after all a Jewish patriarch and so demanded corresponding respect. Moritz Rosenthal, the pianist, tells a story of how one day he was having an argument

with his father in the street when they encountered Jakob Freud, who laughingly reproved him thus: 'What, are you contradicting your father? My Sigmund's little toe is cleverer than my head, but he would never dare to contradict me!'

We know something of Freud's reaction to his father's death from a series of letters to Fliess. He writes the day after the funeral:

> The old man died on the night of the 23rd, and we buried him yesterday. He bore himself bravely up to the end, like the remarkable man he was.

In response to Fliess's letter of condolence, Freud writes:

> I find it so difficult to put pen to paper at the moment that I have even put off writing to you to thank you for the moving things you said in your letter. By one of the obscure routes behind the official consciousness the old man's death affected me deeply. I valued him highly and understood him very well indeed, and with his peculiar mixture of deep wisdom and imaginative light-heartedness he meant a great deal in my life. By the time he died his life had long been over, but at a death the whole past stirs within one.
>
> I feel now as if I had been torn up by the roots.

He goes on to tell Fliess about "a very pretty dream I had on the night after the funeral." In 1899, while at work on *The Interpretation of Dreams*, Freud writes to Fliess, in connection with some thoughts about death: "My father knew that he was dying, did not speak about it and retained his composure to the end." A few weeks after the book was published, he reports to Fliess:

> Two of my patients have almost simultaneously arrived at self-reproach over the nursing and death of their parents, and shown me that my dreams about this were typical. The guilt is in such cases connected with revenge feelings, malicious pleasure at the patient's sufferings, the patient's excretory difficulties (both urine and stools). Truly an unsuspected corner of mental life.

This is the heart of Freud's revelation about his ambivalence toward his father. In explaining a dream inspired by his father in *The Interpretation of Dreams*, Freud gives us the traumatic childhood scene. He writes:

> When I was seven or eight years old there was another domestic scene, which I can remember very clearly. One evening before going to sleep I disregarded the rules which modesty lays down and obeyed the calls of nature in my parents' bedroom while they were present. In the course of his reprimand, my father let fall the words: 'The boy will come to nothing.' This must have been a frightful blow to my ambition, for references to this scene are still constantly recurring in my dreams and are

always linked with an enumeration of my achievements and successes, as though I wanted to say: 'You see, I *have* come to something.' [5] This scene, then, provided the material for the final episode of the dream, in which—in revenge, of course—the roles were interchanged. The older man (clearly my father, since his blindness in one eye referred to his unilateral glaucoma) was now micturating in front of me, just as I had in front of him in my childhood. In the reference to his glaucoma I was reminding him of the cocaine, which had helped him in the operation, as though I had in that way kept my promise. Moreover I was making fun of him; I had to hand him the urinal because he was blind, and I revelled in allusions to my discoveries in connection with the theory of hysteria, of which I felt so proud.

Freud mentions in a footnote

the tragic requital that lay in my father's soiling his bed like a child during the last days of his life.

In a sense, the whole of psychoanalysis stems from that bedroom scene at seven or eight. Freud later gives a dream of his own, about washing away feces with urine, with the introductory statement that it "will fill every reader with disgust." He interprets it as a boast about his scientific achievements, and sees himself in the role of the cleansing father: "I had discovered the infantile aetiology of the neuroses and had thus saved my own children from falling ill." The day before the dream he had "longed to be away from all this grubbing in human dirt," and the dream reassured him. Analyzing an absurd dream about his father, Freud writes:

These elevated thoughts prepared the way for the appearance of something which was common in another sense. My father's *post mortem* rise of temperature corresponded to the words 'after his death' in the dream. His most severe suffering had been caused by a complete paralysis (*obstruction*) of the intestines during his last weeks. Disrespectful thoughts of all kinds followed from this. One of my contemporaries who lost his father while he was still at his secondary school—on that occasion I myself had been deeply moved and had offered to be his friend—once told me scornfully of how one of his female relatives had had a painful experience. Her father had fallen dead in the street and had been brought home; when his body was undressed it was found that at the moment of death, or *post mortem*, he had passed a stool. His daughter had been so unhappy about this that she could not prevent this ugly detail from disturbing her memory of her father.

[5] Martin Freud tells an anecdote that shows how thoroughly Freud later came to fill all of his father's roles. When Martin's son Walter, Freud's grandson, was four, he cranked up a truck parked on the street and got the motor started. Furiously angry, Freud said that "there was not the slightest sense in becoming attached to a boy who must sooner or later kill himself in dangerous escapades."

Here we have reached the wish that was embodied in this dream. 'To stand before one's children's eyes, after one's death, great and unsullied'—who would not desire this?

He continues:

> The little boy's right to appear in the context of this dream was derived from the fact that he had just had the same misadventure —easily forgivable both in a child and in a dying man—of soiling his bed-clothes.

Along with the major excretory theme, a few minor themes related to Freud's father run through *The Interpretation of Dreams.* One is gray hair. In reaction to the misdeeds of a brother, Freud believed, his father's hair "turned gray from grief in a few days." At the time of the self-analysis, Freud was displeased to find his own beard graying. In a dream, he writes, "the beard further involved an allusion to my father and myself through the intermediate idea of growing gray." In interpreting the dream of dissecting his own pelvis, he explains:

> But I should also have been very glad to miss growing gray— '*Grauen*' in the other sense of the word. I was already growing quite gray, and the gray of my hair was another reminder that I must not delay any longer. And, as we have seen, the thought that I should have to leave it to my children to reach the goal of my difficult journey forced its way through to representation at the end of the dream.

Another father image is fur. Freud reports a story that his father told him when he was ten or twelve:

> 'When I was a young man,' he said, 'I went for a walk one Saturday in the streets of your birthplace; I was well dressed, and had a new fur cap on my head. A Christian came up to me and with a single blow knocked off my cap into the mud and shouted "Jew! get off the pavement!" ' 'And what did you do?' I asked. 'I went into the roadway and picked up my cap,' was his quiet reply. This struck me as unheroic conduct on the part of the big, strong man who was holding the little boy by the hand.

A few pages later a *coat* trimmed with fur appears in a dream involving his mother, but Freud either does not recognize the image or does not comment on it. A third theme is his father's glaucoma, which comes up in the dream of the botanical monograph as well as in the revenge dream of handing his blind father the urinal, and in the fantasy of himself getting glaucoma and putting himself in the hands of Fliess.

The principal guilt dream involving Freud's father in the book is the dream of the burning child. It does not appear until the last chapter, although it is foreshadowed earlier by a dream of a patient about sitting before a child's coffin surrounded by candles. The dream of the burning child opens the last chapter, and Freud goes to great pains to make it clear that it is *not* his own dream. He begins:

> Among the dreams which have been reported to me by other people, there is one which has special claims upon our attention at this point. It was told to me by a woman patient who had herself heard it in a lecture on dreams: its actual source is still unknown to me. Its content made an impression on the lady, however, and she proceeded to 're-dream' it, that is, to repeat some of its elements in a dream of her own, so that, by taking it over in this way, she might express her agreement with it on one particular point.
>
> The preliminaries to this model dream were as follows. A father had been watching beside his child's sick-bed for days and nights on end. After the child had died, he went into the next room to lie down, but left the door open so that he could see from his bedroom into the room in which his child's body was laid out, with tall candles standing round it. An old man had been engaged to keep watch over it, and sat beside the body murmuring prayers. After a few hours' sleep, the father had a dream that *his child was standing beside his bed, caught him by the arm and whispered to him reproachfully: 'Father, don't you see I'm burning?'* He woke up, noticed a bright glare of light from the next room, hurried into it and found that the old watchman had dropped off to sleep and that the wrappings and one of the arms of his beloved child's dead body had been burned by a lighted candle that had fallen on them.

If this dream was not Freud's originally (and the explanation of insistent denials as confirmations that he published in the 1925 paper "Negation" suggests that it was), or if he did not re-dream it, he indentified with it so strongly that it becomes the key image of his guilt. Applied to Freud, it would be the dream of the burning father, with Jakob Freud whispering reproachfully: "Son, don't you see I'm burning?" [6] Freud keeps returning to it all through the chapter: "Its interpretation was not given fully in our sense"; "The unusually subordinate part played in this dream by wish-fulfilment is remarkable"; "The dream of the burning child at the beginning of this chapter gives us a welcome opportunity of considering the difficulties with which the theory of wish-fulfilment is faced"; finally, "Other wishes, originating from the repressed, probably escape us, since we are unable to analyze the dream."

The dream of the burning child helps us to understand the most peculiar single image in the book. Talking of the innocent wishes of children that some rival might die, Freud suddenly writes: "Children know nothing of the horrors of corruption, of freezing in the ice-cold grave, of the terrors of eternal nothingness." (Brill, more dramatically

[6] Richard Blake suggests additional confirmation: Freud's father's *post mortem* rise of temperature, and the urethral associations of fire.

but less accurately, translates this: "The child knows nothing of the horrors of decay, of shivering in the cold grave, of the terror of the infinite Nothing.") The image is of course the paradox of sentient death, and since Freud did not believe in life after death, or really think that the corpse feels the horrors of cold and decay, these can only be the shudders and shivers of the guilty living: himself. His father died because Freud's omnipotent infantile wish had wished him dead. Freud tells another dream in the book beginning:

> During the night before my father's funeral I had a dream of a printed notice, placard or poster—rather like the notices forbidding one to smoke in railway waiting-rooms. . . .

In a letter to Fliess written at the time, and thus obviously more accurate, he says that he dreamed it the night *after* the funeral. Since the dream suggested a prohibition of "smoking" with his father dead (lest he burn him), Freud remembered it as *before* the funeral, and interpreted it in very different terms.

The part of Freud's Oedipus complex more repressed than the hostility to the father in *The Interpretation of Dreams* is the erotic attachment to the mother. Freud describes it openly (except for the comic Latin) in a letter to Fliess written during the self-analysis. He writes:

> At certain points I have the impression of having come to the end, and so far I have always known where the next night of dreams would continue. To describe it in writing is more difficult than anything else, and besides it is far too extensive. I can only say that in my case my father played no active role, though I certainly projected on to him an analogy from myself; that my 'primary originator' was an ugly, elderly but clever woman who told me a great deal about God and hell, and gave me a high opinion of my own capacities; that later (between the ages of two and two-and-a-half) libido towards *matrem* was aroused; the occasion must have been the journey with her from Leipzig to Vienna, during which we spent a night together and I must have had the opportunity of seeing her *nudam* (you have long since drawn the conclusions from this for your own son, as a remark of yours revealed); and that I welcomed my one-year-younger brother (who died within a few months) with ill wishes and real infantile jealousy, and that his death left the germ of guilt in me.

We see a number of these themes in the book. The nurse's early role in giving Freud a high opinion of his own capacities clearly continued his mother's favoritism. Freud writes:

> What, then, could have been the origin of the ambitiousness which produced the dream in me? At that point I recalled an anecdote I had often heard repeated in my childhood. At the time of my birth an old peasant-woman had prophesied to my proud mother that with her first-born child she had brought a great man

into the world. Prophecies of this kind must be very common: there are so many mothers filled with happy expectations and so many old peasant-women and others of the kind who make up for the loss of their power to control things in the present world by concentrating it on the future. Nor can the prophetess have lost anything by her words. Could this have been the source of my thirst for grandeur?

To a discussion of Oedipus dreams, "in which the dreamer has sexual intercourse with his own mother," Freud adds the footnote in 1911:

I have found that people who know that they are preferred or favored by their mother give evidence in their lives of a peculiar self-reliance and an unshakable optimism which often seem like heroic attributes and bring actual success to their possessors.

Less favorably, Freud later refers to his mother-induced self-confidence as "an absurd megalomania which had long been suppressed in my waking life."

On the actual Oedipal desire, he is more reticent in the book. "Love and hunger," writes Freud, who was himself breast-fed, "meet at a woman's breast." If the account of undisguised Oedipus dreams does not admit to Freud's having any, Freud does tell a disguised Oedipus dream, which he says was his last true anxiety-dream, at the age of seven or eight. He writes:

It was a very vivid one, and in it I saw *my beloved mother, with a peculiarly peaceful, sleeping expression on her features, being carried into the room by two (or three) people with birds' beaks and laid upon the bed.*

His brief and quite reticent analysis concludes:

The anxiety can be traced back, when repression is taken into account, to an obscure and evidently sexual craving that had found appropriate expression in the visual content of the dream.

The other ingredient of the Oedipus complex, the child's fear that the forbidden indulgence with his mother will bring death or castration, comes in oddly, in an anecdote of how his mother taught him to accept mortality at six. Beneath its apparent triviality, it makes an intimate association of death with the mother's flesh. Freud writes:

When I was six years old and was given my first lessons by my mother, I was expected to believe that we were all made of earth and must therefore return to earth. This did not suit me and I expressed doubts of the doctrine. My mother thereupon rubbed the palms of her hands together—just as she did in making dumplings, except that there was no dough between them—and showed me the blackish scales of *epidermis* produced by the friction as a proof that we were made of earth. My astonishment at this ocular demonstration knew no bounds and I acquiesced in the belief.

The whole of Freud's Oedipus complex is indirectly revealed in two adjacent cases a page or so from the end of the book. One is of a girl whose hysteria transparently mimed copulation, although the girl's mother could not recognize it. The other is of a boy whose daydream of a sickle and scythe concealed a wish to castrate his father. Freud is clearly a composite of both children: driven by an infantile sexuality his mother failed to recognize, torn by an infantile murderous hostility his father never discovered.

With the recognition comes release; with confession, absolution. Early in the book, Freud quotes Plato's idea "that the best men are those who only *dream* what other men *do* in their waking life." His positive slogan in *The Interpretation of Dreams* (anticipating the later "Where id was, there shall ego be") is: "Psychotherapy can pursue no other course than to bring the Unconscious under the domination of the Preconscious." When these repressed infantile guilty wishes were brought to consciousness by the ego, they could be dismissed: wishes are not omnipotent, they do not kill; my father did not die because I wished him dead as a child, or even as an adult. The last four paragraphs of the book finally get around to the ethical question and absolve Freud. Recalling Plato's formulation, Freud writes, "I think it is best, therefore, to acquit dreams." "Actions and consciously expressed opinions," he decides, "are as a rule enough for practical purposes in judging men's characters." Freud concludes: "It is in any case instructive to get to know the much trampled soil from which our virtues proudly spring."

The Interpretation of Dreams, we learn from a letter Freud wrote to Fliess in 1899, has a planned imaginative organization. He writes:

> The whole thing is planned on the model of an imaginary walk. First comes the dark wood of the authorities (who cannot see the trees), where there is no clear view and it is very easy to go astray. Then there is a cavernous defile through which I lead my readers—my specimen dream with its peculiarities, its details, its indiscretions, and its bad jokes—and then, all at once, the high ground and the prospect, and the question: 'Which way do you want to go?'

Freud first makes the walk metaphor visible at the beginning of the third chapter, after the lengthy analysis in the second chapter of the dream of Irma's injection. He writes:

> When, after passing through a narrow defile, we suddenly emerge upon a piece of high ground, where the path divides and the finest prospects open up on every side, we may pause for a moment and consider in which direction we shall first turn our

steps. Such is the case with us, now that we have surmounted the first interpretation of a dream. We find ourselves in the full daylight of a sudden discovery.

Beginning the fifth chapter, Freud writes:

Having followed one path to its end, we may now retrace our steps and choose another starting-point for our rambles through the problems of dream-life.

The seventh chapter announces, near the beginning:

But before starting off along this new path, it will be well to pause and look around, to see whether in the course of our journeys up to this point we have overlooked anything of importance. For it must be clearly understood that the easy and agreeable portion of our journey lies behind us. Hitherto, unless I am greatly mistaken, all the paths along which we have travelled have led us towards the light—towards elucidation and fuller understanding. But as soon as we endeavor to penetrate more deeply into the mental process involved in dreaming, every path will end in darkness.

Two things should be noticed. First, we are going circuitously only because dreams do, and we follow their movements. The "paths" leading to the unconscious cross "verbal bridges," and so forth. Freud writes:

Superficial associations replace deep ones if the censorship makes the normal connecting paths impassable. We may picture, by way of analogy, a mountain region, where some general interruption of traffic (owing to floods, for instance) has blocked the main, major roads, but where communications are still maintained over inconvenient and steep footpaths normally used only by the hunter.

Second, all of these dark woods, narrow defiles, high grounds and deep penetrations are unconscious sexual imagery, and we are exploring a woman's body, that of Freud's mother. In the first chapter, Freud speaks of someone's failure to follow the path that would have led him to "the very heart" of an explanation, and we know that path that leads to the heart. If it seems unlikely that the discoverer of unconscious sexual imagery should have missed his own, we can only observe that such are the devious workings of the unconscious, remembering that Freud wrote innocently to Fliess, just after his father's death: "I am busy thinking out something which would cement our work together and put my column on your base."

As the book's paths leave the light for the darkness in the last chapter, lit only by the fitful flames of that curious torch, Freud's father, the organizing metaphor switches from walking to digging or mining. Freud had earlier remarked in a footnote: "There is at least one spot in every dream at which it is unplumbable—a navel, as it were, that is its point of contact with the unknown." In the last chapter Freud picks up that image and expands it in a tangle of metaphor (perhaps what he meant by "straining after the picturesque" in the letter to Fliess). Freud writes:

> There is often a passage in even the most thoroughly inter-
> preted dream which has to be left obscure; this is because we
> become aware during the work of interpretation that at that point
> there is a tangle of dream-thoughts which cannot be unravelled
> and which moreover adds nothing to our knowledge of the con-
> tent of the dream. This is the dream's navel, the spot where it
> reaches down into the unknown. The dream thought to which we
> are led by interpretation cannot, from the nature of things, have
> any definite endings; they are bound to branch out in every direc-
> tion into the intricate network of our world of thought. It is at
> some point where this meshwork is particularly close that the
> dream-wish grows up, like a mushroom out of its mycelium.

A few pages later he says:

> It is true that in carrying out the interpretation in the waking state
> we follow a path which leads back from the elements of the dream
> to the dream-thoughts and that the dream-work followed one in
> the contrary direction. But it is highly improbable that these paths
> are passable both ways. It appears, rather, that in the daytime we
> drive shafts which follow along fresh chains of thought and that
> these shafts make contact with the intermediate thoughts and the
> dream-thoughts now at one point and now at another.

What we do down there in the tunnel or mine, oddly, is build. "We have been obliged," Freud writes movingly, "to build our way out into the dark," and adds that the time may come "when we shall find our-selves more at home in it." Freud talks of his psychological or con-ceptual "scaffolding," and warns us not to mistake it for the finished building; "our edifice is still uncompleted."

Freud qualifies his metaphors in a passage very reminiscent of Darwin's in *The Origin of Species*. He writes:

> I see no necessity to apologize for the imperfections of this or
> any similar imagery. Analogies of this kind are only intended to
> assist us in our attempt to make the complications of mental func-
> tioning intelligible.

Later he remarks: "Let us replace these metaphors by something that seems to correspond better to the real state of affairs." Since this turns out to be only a better metaphor, we realize once again that his meta-phors *are* his vision of reality.

Besides the key one of the walk that climbs down and then goes up again, there are a number of other thematic metaphors in *The Inter-*

pretation of Dreams. Perhaps the most pervasive of them is of warfare. Freud says of the dream of the botanical monograph that it has "an indifferent ring about it," and explains: "This reminds one of the peace that has descended upon a battlefield strewn with corpses; no trace is left of the struggle which raged over it." Of another dream: "The state of things is what it was after some sweeping revolution in one of the republics of antiquity or the Renaissance." He speaks of where "our defensive weapons lie," of resistance as "guarding the frontier," and so forth. The warfare is seen primarily as the storming of a fortress: "The state of sleep guarantees the security of the citadel that must be guarded"; in psychosis "the watchman is overpowered"; a phobia "is like a frontier fortification"; the unconscious even has "a kind of sally-gate" so that it can take the offensive against the besiegers. Freud explains in summary that these images are "derived from a set of ideas relating to a struggle for a piece of ground." Again, in Freudian terms, we know what ground, what fortress.

Freud's theories were always deeply dualistic. Jones explains:

> One is naturally tempted to correlate this tendency with its manifestations in Freud's own personality. There was the fight between scientific discipline and philosophical speculation; his passionate love urge and his unusually great sexual repression; his vigorous masculinity, which shines through all his writings, and his feminine needs; his desire to create everything himself and his longing to receive stimulation from another; his love of independence and his needs of dependence. But such thoughts assuredly bring the risk of falsification from the lure of simplistic solutions.

For a divided personality dealing with an ambivalent subject-matter, what better metaphor than warfare?

Another metaphor, visible in many of the quotations above, is light. The book begins with the promise of an endeavor to "elucidate," it endlessly attempts to "throw light" on something or enlighten, and at a key point Freud typically remarks: "We can now see our way a little further." If the paths that first led us toward the light end in darkness in the last chapter, it is a darkness that will eventually be lighted by knowledge, and the whole book (like Freud's self-analysis) can be seen as an act of bringing that which was buried in the dark up into the light. There is also a range of metaphors from natural science. Freud's hope was that his psychology would eventually be grounded in neurology, that "deeper research will one day trace the path further and discover an organic basis for the mental event," or "find a means of picturing the movements that accompany excitation of neurones." He produces a series of metaphors for the mind from mechanical instruments: "a compound microscope or a photographic apparatus, or something of that kind." The dream is "that most marvelous and most mysterious of all instruments," and seen in scientific imagery the censorship is no longer a watchman or guardian of a fortress, but is comparable to "the refraction which takes place when a ray of light passed into a new medium." Another metaphor is electricity, and dream formation makes new connections like "short-circuits," wishes are "currents in the apparatus," etc. Still another series of analogies is drawn from various sorts of picture language. Dream expression is "a pictographic script," "a picture-puzzle, a rebus," "hieroglyphic script," and so on. Dreams "present no greater difficulties to their translators than do the ancient hieroglyphic scripts to those who seek to read them."

A variety of minor metaphors enliven the book. Dream-thoughts are jammed up, "almost like pack-ice"; a dream is like a scrambled "algebraic equation"; analysis results in cure as though "the assertions made in the text are borne out by the accompanying illustrations"; day thoughts need unconscious wishes invested in them as entrepreneurs need capitalists; a repressed idea is like an American dentist in Austria, unable to practice without a local "front"; a dream "is like a firework, which takes hours to prepare but goes off in a moment."

Our best clue to the imaginative form of the book is the epigraph from *The Aeneid* on the title page, *Flectere si nequeo superos, Acheronta movebo* ("If I cannot bend the higher powers, I will stir up the infernal regions"). Freud borrowed it from a book by Ferdinand Lassalle, and first intended it, we learn from an 1896 letter to Fliess, to be the epigraph for a chapter on symptom-formation in a work of general psychology he intended to write. Freud explains in a note in his collected works: "This line of Virgil is intended to picture the efforts of the repressed instinctual impulses." When it is quoted near the end of *The Interpretation of Dreams,* that is its obvious reference, and Freud always denied that it had any other. Nevertheless, it clearly refers to Freud himself as well as to repressed wishes, and is his ultimate answer to his father's prophecy that he would never amount to anything. Freud is a mythic hero who has made the dangerous journey into the underworld and come back with the treasure, and in this aspect the book's form is that of a successful mythic quest. Freud writes:

> The respect paid to dreams in antiquity is, however, based upon correct psychological insight and is the homage paid to the uncontrolled and indestructible forces in the human mind, to the 'daemonic' power which produces the dream-wish and which we find at work in our unconscious.

The Interpretation of Dreams is full of these daemonic powers. Freud writes:

> These wishes in our unconscious, ever on the alert and, so to say, immortal, remind one of the legendary Titans, weighed down since primeval ages by the massive bulk of the mountains which were once hurled upon them by the victorious gods and which are still shaken from time to time by the convulsion of their limbs.

He adds in a footnote:

> If I may use a simile, they are only capable of annihilation in the same sense as the ghosts in the underworld of *The Odyssey*— ghosts which awoke to new life as soon as they tasted blood.

Freud continues: "Indeed it is a prominent feature of unconscious processes that they are indestructible. In the unconscious nothing can be brought to an end, nothing is past or forgotten." The last sentence of the book reminds us of "the indestructible wish."

Mircea Eliade, in *The Sacred and the Profane*, compares psychoanalysis to primitive initiation. He explains:

> The patient is asked to descend deeply into himself, to make his past live, to confront his traumatic experiences again; and, from the point of view of form, this dangerous operation resembles initiatory descents into hell, the realm of ghosts, and combats with monsters. Just as the initiate was expected to emerge from his ordeals victorious—in short, was to 'die' and be 'resuscitated' in order to gain access to a fully responsible existence, open to spiritual values—so the patient undergoing analysis today must confront his own 'unconscious,' haunted by ghosts and monsters, in order to find psychic health and integrity and hence the world of cultural values.

As Freud's was the first analysis, so was he the proto-initiate, the primeval hero of the quest.

Some literary analogues immediately suggest themselves. Freud suggests the comparison with *Oedipus the King* of Sophocles, but since *The Interpretation of Dreams* ends in final triumphant affirmation, we would have to see it as somehow including both *Oedipus the King* and *Oedipus at Colonus*, or progressing from one to the other. Freud similarly brings up *Hamlet* (he quotes or refers to it at least six times in the book, even more often than *Faust*), but the same objection would make Shakespeare's progress from *Hamlet* to *The Tempest* a better analogy. Or, remembering the "dark wood" in which they both begin, we may compare *The Interpretation of Dreams* structurally with *The Divine Comedy;* at least *Inferno, Purgatorio,* and a page of the *Paradiso.* In another sense, recognizing the dream to be a kind of poem, the book is a poem about poetry, a highly imaginative sort of literary criticism. It is Freud's best book because it is his most intimate book, far more revealing than his *Autobiographical Study. The Interpretation of Dreams* was one of the two books (*Three Contributions to the Theory of Sex* was the other) that Freud regularly kept up to date. This was done almost entirely by additions, many in the form of footnotes, almost never by alteration of the text, even where the statement was absurdly outmoded. Freud explains in the preface to the fifth edition of *The Interpretation of Dreams,* in 1918:

I have not been able to bring myself to embark upon any fundamental revision of this book, which might bring it up to the level of our present psychoanalytic views but would on the other hand destroy its historic character.

That "I have not been able to bring myself" is interesting. When we remember Freud's reluctance to publish the book, the year's delay, and all his resistances in it, we realize its enormous importance to him. *The Interpretation of Dreams* is a relentless and unsparing *Confessions*, and its powerful self-revelation underlies its greatness.

The Wicked Fellow
at the Picnic

U NLIKE *The Origin of Species, The Interpretation of Dreams* occasioned no excitement whatsoever on its publication. The half dozen notices it got were almost all unfavorable. In the six weeks after publication, 123 copies were sold, and it took eight years to sell out the edition of 600 copies. In the private joke that Freud and Fliess shared, "the public enthusiasm was immense." Nevertheless, there was some talk about the book, and early in 1900 Freud was asked to write a condensed version of it for a popular psychological series. This appeared as *On Dreams* in 1901, and sold well enough to be re-issued in a revised second edition in 1911, an English translation in 1914, and a third edition in 1921. As a simplified synopsis of *The Interpretation of Dreams*, almost impersonal in style, *On Dreams* contains little that need occupy us. It includes one important new dream of Freud's, introduced as "a dream which I actually had last night," and analyzed in some detail as demonstrating his jealousy in regard to his wife. The only other new material consists of a few brief dreams and fragments, and one homely new metaphor. Freud writes:

> We have gathered an impression that the formation of obscure dreams occurs *as though* one person who was dependent upon a second person had to make a remark which was bound to be disagreeable in the ears of this second one.

While he was working on the popular book, Freud also wrote up his first detailed case history of the girl he called "Dora," and submitted it to a journal for publication. He then changed his mind, withdrew it, and put it aside. Freud did not publish again until 1904, when a chapter he wrote on "Freud's Psychoanalytic Method" appeared in a psychiatric book by Ludwig Loewenfeld. Summarizing what Freud had published in other works, it has few novelties, although it uses one metaphor, of smelting, that clearly continues the mining imagery of *The Interpretation of Dreams*. Freud writes:

Freud has developed on this basis an art of interpretation which takes on the task of freeing, as it were, the pure metal of the repressed thoughts from the ore of the unintentional ideas.

The same year Freud published *The Psychopathology of Every-day Life*. It too had been postponed. In 1901, Freud had written to Fliess:

I am correcting the first pages of the everyday life, which has turned out to be about sixty pages long. I have taken a tremendous dislike to it, and I hope others will take an even bigger dislike to it. It is entirely formless and contains all sorts of forbidden things.

The new conception of *Everyday Life* is that of symbolic action. For a decade, Freud had dealt with the symptoms of neurotics, particularly hysterics, as symbolic actions, but this was his first bold identification of the phenomenon in such normal behavior as slips of the tongue, forgetting, and errors. Freud speaks of something like losing one's keys as a "symptomatic act" or a "symbolic action." Like dreams, these symptomatic or symbolic acts are ways of dramatizing, of acting out the inner impulse in a disguised form. Freud begins the second chapter with a fascinating little dramatic dialogue of his own, in which he convinces a young stranger in his railroad compartment of his general contention by demonstrating the considerable personal significance of a word the young man had omitted from a Virgil quotation. Freud is again the Great Detective, gently leading the culprit to expose himself.

Most of the book's exposure, however, like that of *The Interpretation of Dreams*, is of Freud himself. He writes:

Most of the examples of psychic disturbances of daily life that I have here compiled, I was obliged to take from observation of myself. I endeavored to evade the far richer material furnished me by my neurotic patients because I had to preclude the objection that the phenomena in question were only the result and manifestation of the neurosis.

As befits a hero of the ludicrous, Freud admits to telling tiny lies to his wife which are immediately exposed by slips. He explains:

Perhaps it is a result of my occupation with psychoanalysis that I can scarcely lie any more. As often as I attempt a distortion, I succumb to an error or some other faulty act, which betrays my dishonesty.

Freud admits that the selection of examples of his slips "was partial from the first, and aimed at the exclusion of sexual matters." Otherwise he confesses to every sort of small discreditable behavior, from childish vanity to petty cheating. Freud takes *The Psychopathology of Everyday Life* as an opportunity to correct several errors in *The In-*

terpretation of Dreams: a wrong birthplace for Schiller, a wrong name for Hannibal's father, and a confusion of Zeus with Kronos. Explaining how he missed these blatant mistakes through "three carefully-executed proof-readings," Freud writes:

> Indeed, each of the three examples given is based on the same theme: the errors are the results of repressed thoughts which occupy themselves with my deceased father.

The mechanism producing errors is thus another device for significant distortion, analogous to the dream-work, and through errors too the truth can be read. Furthermore, Freud's quarrel with his own style is now recognizable in terms of symbolic action, not as a failure in literary ability, but as unresolved ambivalence. He writes:

> Even in criticizing an author's style, we are allowed and accustomed to follow the principle of explanation, which we cannot miss in the origin of a single speech-blunder. A clear and unequivocal manner of writing shows us that here, the author is in harmony with himself, but where we find a forced and involved expression, aiming at more than one target, as appropriately expressed, we can thereby recognize the participation of an unfinished and complicated thought, or we can hear through it the stifled voice of the author's self-criticism.

The principal emphasis in *The Psychopathology of Everyday Life* is on vastly increasing the area of the determined. "Certain performances which are apparently unintentional prove to be well-motivated," Freud writes. "Determinism reaches farther than we suppose," he adds, concluding boldly: "There is nothing arbitrary or undetermined in the psychic life." Freud explicitly raises the old philosophic debate. He writes:

> As is known, many persons argue against the assumption of an absolute psychic determinism by referring to an intense feeling of conviction that there is a free will. This feeling of conviction exists, but it is not incompatible with the belief in determinism. Like all normal feelings, it must be justified by something.

A few pages later he resolves the problem: "I believe in outer (real) chance, but not in inner (psychic) accidents." It is thus no accident, as Freud would say, that the book's epigraph is the line from *Faust:* "The air is now so full of such a bogy."

Later in 1904 Freud delivered a lecture, "On Psychotherapy," before the College of Physicians in Vienna, and he published it in 1905. This is an odd defense of psychoanalysis, not primarily in terms of its truth or its practical results, but as "the most ancient form of therapy in medicine," and as a difficult form of art, since, paraphrasing Hamlet, "It is not so easy to play upon the instrument of the soul." In 1905 Freud wrote an essay for a Loewenfeld anthology, "My Views on the Part Played by Sexuality in the Aetiology of the Neuroses." This swung to the opposite extreme, justifying his theories in terms of their evolution out of therapeutic experience, and concluding back in biochemistry. Freud writes of sexuality:

> One can scarcely avoid, in the last analysis, picturing those processes as chemical, so that we might recognize the so-called actual neuroses as the somatic effects of disturbances in sexual metabolism, and the psychoneuroses as, in addition, the psychical effects of these disturbances. The similarity of the neuroses to the phenomena of intoxication and abstinence following upon certain alkaloids, as well as to Graves' and to Addison's diseases, is readily apparent on the clinical side.

In 1905 Freud finally published the pioneer case history he had put away for four years, as "Fragment of an Analysis of a Case of Hysteria." It is the case of an eighteen-year-old girl he calls "Dora," who came to him in 1900, just after his last meeting with Fliess. The abortive analysis ended on the last day of 1900, and Freud wrote it up in the next few weeks. He writes to Fliess on January 25, 1901:

> I finished 'Dreams and Hysteria' yesterday, and the consequence is that today I feel short of a drug. It is a fragment of an analysis of a hysteria, in which the interpretations are grouped round two dreams, so it is really a continuation of the dream book. It also contains resolutions of hysterical symptoms and glimpses of the sexual-organic foundation of the whole. All the same, it is the subtlest thing I have so far written, and will put people off even more than usual. But one does one's duty, and does not write just for the day alone.

The analysis lasted less than three months, when it was spitefully broken off by the patient. Freud had intended to call it "Dreams and Hysteria," but when he went about publishing it four years later he decided to emphasize the fragmentary nature of the results. It is, for many readers, Freud's finest case history. He writes in his postscript:

> Its great merit, namely, the unusual clarity which makes it seem so suitable as a first introductory publication, is closely bound up with its great defect, which led to its being broken off prematurely. I did not succeed in mastering the transference in good time.

Freud also admits in the postscript: "I failed to discover in time and to inform the patient that her homosexual (gynaecophilic) love for Frau K. was the strongest unconscious current in her mental life." Nevertheless, Freud's conclusion makes it clear that he was rather pleased with his achievements in the case.

The emphasis of the Dora case, as its first title shows, is on dream analysis, and much of it is taken up with elaborate and quite beautiful analyses of two dreams. Freud warns the reader in his prefatory remarks: "It would be wrong to suppose that dreams and their inter-

pretation occupy such a prominent position in all psychoanalyses as
they do in this example." The first dream is a rather transparent one
about rescuing mother's jewel-case from a house on fire, and the second is of Dora's trying to get home when her father died. Freud makes
it clear that he is using Dora to test his theories in practice. He writes:

> From the very beginning I took the greatest pains with this pa-
> tient not to introduce her to any fresh facts in the region of sexual
> knowledge; and I did this, not from any conscientious motives,
> but because I was anxious to subject my assumptions to a rigor-
> ous test in this case.

The motivation of the case history is explained: "I wished to supplement my book on the interpretation of dreams by showing how an
art, which would otherwise be useless, can be turned to account for
the discovery of the hidden and repressed parts of mental life."

We see the Great Detective in all his glory in the Dora case, introducing Dora to *all sorts* of fresh facts in the region of sexual knowledge. When she fails to understand her mother's role in her dream,
Freud says to her sternly, "I will explain that to you later." There is
the following delicious interchange:

> Freud: Perhaps you do not know that 'jewel-case' is a favorite
> expression for the same thing that you alluded to not long
> ago by means of the reticule you were wearing—for the
> female genitals, I mean.
> Dora: I knew you would say that.
> Freud: That is to say, you knew that it was *so*.

He continues, in the very voice of Baker Street:

> As you say, the mystery turns upon your mother. You ask how
> she comes into the dream? She is, as you know, your former rival
> in your father's affections.

Freud explains his technique:

> When I set myself the task of bringing to light what human beings
> keep hidden within them, not by the compelling powers of hyp-
> nosis, but by observing what they say and what they show, I
> thought the task was a harder one than it really is. He that has
> eyes to see and ears to hear may convince himself that no mortal
> can keep a secret. If his lips are silent, he chatters with his finger-
> tips; betrayal oozes out of him at every pore.

Unlike Marx's similar image in *Capital* of Capital dripping blood and
dirt from every pore, Freud's image of betrayal oozing out at the pores
prepares not for a verdict of "Guilty" but for an exoneration. Freud
charges bluntly that Dora's nervous coughing is a hysterical fantasy
of "sucking at the male organ," but insists that this is ultimately an
infantile regression to nursing, and explains: "So we see that this
excessively repulsive and perverted fantasy of sucking at a penis has

the most innocent origin." Like Freud himself in *The Interpretation of Dreams*, Dora goes down through nightmares of guilt to be ultimately proclaimed innocent.

Taking the trial and judgment of Dora to be the case history's underlying imaginative structure, we find its texture to be a series of varied metaphors. Freud talks of putting together a synthesis of the case "like a conscientious archaeologist" restoring "mutilated relics of antiquity." Of Dora's life story:

> This first account may be compared to an unnavigable river whose stream is at one moment choked by masses of rock and at another divided and lost among shallows and sandbanks.

Her life story is an unnavigable river, it turns out, because her libido is the same. Freud writes, of Dora's sexuality:

> A stream of water which meets with an obstacle in the river-bed is dammed up and flows back into old channels which had formerly seemed fated to run dry.

Her mental processes, varying the image, are a railroad train. Freud writes:

> Now, in a line of associations ambiguous words (or, as we may call them, 'switch-words') act like points at a junction. If the points are switched across from the position in which they appear to lie in the dream, then we find ourselves upon another set of rails; and along this second track run the thoughts which we are in search of and which still lie concealed behind the dream.

Even when Freud uses a static metaphor for these processes, it becomes dynamic. He writes:

> I suspect that we are here concerned with unconscious processes of thought which are twined around a pre-existing structure of organic connections, much as festoons of flowers are twined around a wire; so that on another occasion one might find other lines of thought inserted between the same points of departure and termination.

Probably the most important of these textural metaphors is demonological. Like an incubus, "the neurosis had seized upon this chance event and made use of it for an utterance of its own." Freud comments:

> No one who, like me, conjures up the most evil of those half-tamed demons that inhabit the human breast, and seeks to wrestle with them, can expect to come through the struggle unscathed.

The question of how consciously Freud is using these metaphors is an interesting one. After making it clear that the key and lock of Dora's dreams are genital symbols, he concludes the account in all apparent innocence:

A single case can never be capable of proving a theorem so general as this one; but I can only repeat over and over again—for I never find it otherwise—that sexuality is the key to the problem of the psychoneuroses and of the neuroses in general. No one who disdains the key will ever be able to unlock the door.

On the other hand, Freud is certainly being coy when he writes, after the expenditure of an impressive amount of artistry:

I must now turn to consider a further complication, to which I should certainly give no space if I were a man of letters engaged upon the creation of a mental state like this for a short story, instead of being a medical man engaged upon its dissection.

Freud's next book, also published in 1905, is *Jokes and Their Relation to the Unconscious.* Freud had been interested in the problem of jokes at least since 1899, when Fliess had complained that *The Interpretation of Dreams* made the dreamer too ingenious and amusing. In answering that dreamers are always insufferably witty, Freud had added: "The ostensible wit of all unconscious processes is closely connected with the theory of jokes and humor." Moreover, many of the jokes Freud uses in the book are the jokes he had exchanged with Fliess in their correspondence, including some with which he strongly identified.

At least one of Freud's impulses in writing the book is simply to tell jokes, the funniest he knows, and in that the book is surprisingly successful, even in translation. "It is quite natural," Freud writes, "that we should select such examples of jokes as objects for our investigation as have produced the deepest impression upon our own lives and which have caused us the greatest amount of laughter." Despite a disclaimer—"When one laughs very heartily at a joke, he is not in the best mood to investigate its technique"—Freud has no way of identifying the material other than as what makes him laugh. He writes:

The opportunity now presents itself for making a not unimportant confession. We are here busying ourselves with an investigation of techniques of wit by means of examples, and we ought to be sure that the examples which we have selected are really true witticisms. The facts are, however, that in a series of cases, we fall into doubt as to whether or not the example in question may be called a joke.

He explains further:

The feeling which usually tells me—and I dare say a great many others under the same conditions—this is a joke, this may be written down as witty before even the hidden and essential character of the wit has been uncovered—this feeling I lack most in witty comparisons. If I first have no hesitation in declaring the comparison as witty, then the next instant I seem to think that the pleasure

I thus found was of a different quality than that which I am accustomed to ascribe to a joke. Moreover, the fact that witty comparisons seldom evoke the explosive variety of laughter by which a good joke proves itself, makes it impossible for me to cast aside the existing doubts, even when I limit myself to the best and most effective examples.

Freud's theoretical explanation of humor in the book does not seem very satisfactory, but it should fairly be admitted that no one else's does either. Humor, he decides, lies not in the content but in the economical form of expression. Harmless wit may produce "a slight ripple of laughter" by its compression, but the wit that evokes an "irresistible outburst of laughter" is always hostile or obscene in tendency, a veiled aggression or symbolic seduction, made pleasurable by "economy in the expenditure of inhibitions or suppressions." [1] Freud's conclusion, in the book's last paragraph, is this:

> It has seemed to us that the pleasure of wit originates from an *economy of expenditure in inhibition,* of the comic from an *economy of expenditure in thought,* and of humor from an *economy of expenditure in feeling.* All three modes of activity of our psychic apparatus derive pleasure from economy. All three present methods strive to bring back from the psychic activity a pleasure which has really been lost in the development of this activity. For the euphoria which we are thus striving to obtain is nothing but the state of a bygone time, in which we were wont to defray our psychic work with slight expenditure. It is the state of our childhood in which we did not know the comic, were incapable of wit, and did not need humor to make us happy.

The best of Freud's examples, and the ones obviously with greatest meaning for him, are Jewish jokes. He explains:

> We demand no patent of nobility for our examples nor do we make inquiries about their origin. The only qualifications we require are that they should make us laugh and serve our theoretical interest. It is to be remarked that both these demands are satisfied best by Jewish jokes.

We then get a series of jokes, introduced as "of the coarse kind," about the reluctance of Jews to bathe, to clean food out of their beards, to respect other Jews; about the absurdities of Jewish marriage-brokers and the arrogance of Jewish *schnorrers* (spongers). Freud finds an ambivalence in the stories, and notes: "But the same conflict is found in the national spirit which has given rise to these and similar stories." He explains in more detail:

---

[1] C. L. Barber suggests, in conversation, that Freud's "economy" is itself a metaphor, related to domestic economy and political economy, and that it runs all through his work.

A particularly favorable case for tendency-wit results if the intended criticism of the inner resistance is directed against one's own person, or, more carefully expressed, against a person in whom one takes interest, that is, a composite personality such as one's own people. This determination of self-criticism may make clear why it is that a number of the most excellent jokes (of which many specimens have been displayed) should have sprung into existence from the soil of Jewish national life. They are stories which were invented by Jews themselves and which are directed against Jewish peculiarities. The Jewish jokes made up by non-Jews are nearly all brutal buffooneries in which the wit is spared by the fact that the Jew appears as a comic figure to a stranger. The Jewish jokes which originate with Jews admit this, but they know their real shortcomings as well as their merits, and the interest of the person himself in the thing to be criticized produces the subjective determination of the wit-work which would otherwise be difficult to bring about. Incidentally I do not know whether one often finds a people that makes merry so unreservedly over its own shortcomings.

"It is the manifold hopeless misery of the Jews," Freud concludes, "to which these pessimistic stories allude."

It is interesting to note that Freud's theory of humor offers no explanation for this pleasure in self-mockery, nor does it explain why Freud, who at forty-four described himself to Fliess as "a rather shabby old Jew," should have so powerfully identified with uncrushable commercial travelers and *schnorrers*. (All his life, apparently, Freud had what he called "*schnorrer* fantasies"). If on the superficial level the book, at least in English, is *Ziggy Freud's Joke Book as Told to Abie Brill;* if more seriously it is a theory of the psychic mechanism of humor that does not really explain it; on the deepest level *Jokes and Their Relation to the Unconscious* is a cry from Freud's own uncrushable spirit. Despite his admission that he knows no other people so merry in its self-destructive humor, similar jokes are characteristic of all oppressed peoples. Negro humor is so similar that the Negro poet Melvin Tolson characterizes it in a poem with the Yiddish phrase *lachen mit yastchekes*, "laughing with needles stuck in you." Freud talks of what the Germans call *Galgenhumor*, "gallows-humor," gives some classic examples of jests by condemned men, and comments:

> We must say that there is something like greatness of soul in this *blague*, in this clinging to his usual nature and in deviating from that which would overthrow and drive this nature into despair.

Ultimately, then, the essence of humor has little to do with economies of expenditure. It is life-affirming, and greatness of soul consists in cracking a joke with the needles in you, or the noose around your neck, or life almost impossible to endure.

FREUD'S other book published in 1905 is *Three Contributions to the Theory of Sex*, his fullest statement of infantile sexuality and its consequences. Here we see another form of Freud's dualism, best expressed in his statement in the first essay:

> The highest and lowest in sexuality are everywhere most intimately connected. ('From heaven through the world to hell.')

More than anything else Freud wrote, *Three Contributions* is a book in the tradition of Darwinian evolution.[2] Normal sexual history is seen as an evolutionary progress from oral through anal to genital sexuality, from narcissistic through homosexual to heterosexual attachments. In this development, adult perversions and neuroses are arrested developments or fixations at earlier stages, exactly like Darwin's living fossils. Freud speaks of "that development which is desirable for civilized man," its goal "the so-called normal sexual life of the adult in whom the acquisition of pleasure has been put into the service of the function of propagation"; that is, "it becomes, so to say, altruistic." What Freud calls in another connection "this teleological mode of thinking," here shows that at least for the individual, Freud saw progress as ever onward and upward.

Freud's attitude toward women becomes somewhat comic in the book. Male sex life is accessible to investigation, Freud writes, "whereas in the woman it is veiled in impenetrable darkness, partly because of cultural stunting and partly on account of the conventional reticence and insincerity of women." (What Freud could have done with that "veiled in impenetrable darkness" and "stunting" if a patient had said it!) Of the moral and intellectual inferiority of women, Freud has no doubts. He writes:

> In this respect, the child perhaps does not behave differently from the average uncultured woman in whom the same polymorphous-

[2] Freud shows little sign of familiarity with Darwin's works. The only ones he quotes, to the best of my knowledge, are *The Descent of Man*, from which he got the Primal Horde, and *The Expression of Emotions*. According to Jones, Freud owned only the former. Freud reports in his *Autobiographical Study* that in his youth "the theories of Darwin, which were then of topical interest, strongly attracted me," and we know that he took a course in Darwinism at the university. There is no evidence that he ever read *The Origin of Species*. Freud's orientation was strongly evolutionary, but he seems to have distrusted the theory of natural selection, as he learned it from Weismann and Haeckel, because it excluded the inheritance of acquired characteristics. He was, in short, a thorough Lamarckian, and he once planned to write a work with Ferenczi on the relation of Lamarckism to psychoanalysis, although he never did. (A reading of the last edition of the *Origin* would have shown Freud that in his later years Darwin had become fully as Lamarckian as Freud was.)

Darwin, by means of introspection, discovered the Freudian principle of wishful forgetting, as he notes in his *Autobiography*, and took steps to prevent such forgetting in his work. When Jones called this passage to Freud's attention, Freud printed it as a footnote to *The Psychopathology of Everyday Life* with the comment that it "does equal credit to his scientific honesty and his psychological acumen."

perverse disposition exists. Such a woman may remain sexually normal under usual conditions, but under the guidance of a clever seducer, she will find pleasure in every perversion and will retain it as her sexual activity.

Freud's odd reticence keeps appearing. Of lesbianism he says: "greater variation will be found on more intimate investigation." "The genitals," he writes, "can never really be considered 'beautiful.' " Coprophilia and necrophilia are "surprising results" of the sexual instinct. The child's genital zone "is destined for great things in later life." Freud reports "all that I have been able to discover about masturbation in little girls," which is not much.

The important new term that appears in *Three Contributions* is "sublimation," the transformation of sexual instincts into something more acceptable. It is this process that produces not only civilized adults, but culture itself. Freud writes:

> The historians of civilization seem to be unanimous in the opinion that such deflection of sexual motive powers from sexual aims to new aims, a process which merits the name of *sublimation,* has furnished powerful components for all cultural accomplishments.

Neurosis and sublimation are the alternatives, so that society sets up barriers to instinctual gratification, but those barriers then offer opportunities for achievement as well as for illness.

The tone of *Three Contributions* is remarkably tentative and moderate. We have to recognize the "deficient clearness of our understanding"; "Psychology is still groping in the dark"; "It seems to me impossible to shed more light and certainty on these general propositions." The book's last paragraph reads:

> The unsatisfactory conclusions which have resulted from this investigation of the disturbances of the sexual life are due to the fact that as yet we know too little concerning the biological processes of which the nature of sexuality consists, to form from our desultory views a satisfactory theory for the explanation of what is normal or pathological.

The metaphors of *Three Contributions* include familiar and unfamiliar ones. Carried over from the Dora case is the water image: "The libido behaves like a stream the principal bed of which is dammed; it fills the collateral roads which until now have perhaps been empty"; psychic forces "act as inhibitions on the sexual life, and narrow its direction like dams." The organizing metaphor of *The Interpretation of Dreams,* walking along a path, appears here comically as what one would say if one gave up metaphor. Freud writes:

> Since we are now dropping the figurative manner of expression hitherto employed, by which we spoke of *sources* of sexual excitement, we may now assume that all the connecting paths lead-

ing from other functions to sexuality must also be passable in
the reverse direction.

He continues:

> The normality of the sexual life is guaranteed only by the exact
> concurrence of the two streams directed to the sexual object
> and sexual aim. It is like the piercing of a tunnel from opposite
> sides.

Along with these familiar Freudian metaphors there are two bold new
ones. Instead of being reticent, concealed in darkness, or an unknown mystery, women actually burn with the fire of passion. Freud
writes:

> If the woman finally submits to the sexual act, the clitoris becomes
> stimulated and its role is to conduct the excitement to the adjacent
> genital parts; it acts here like a chip of pinewood, which is utilized
> to kindle the harder wood.

Finally, the nursing child and the sexually satisfied adult are dramatically equated. Freud writes:

> He who sees a satiated child sink back from the mother's breast
> and fall asleep with reddened cheeks and blissful smile, will have
> to admit that this picture remains as typical of the expression of
> sexual gratification in later life.

It is not hard to recognize that woman on fire with passion (as
opposed to the father on fire because of his son's hostility) and the
gratified child as wishful figures from the author's Oedipus complex,
and to realize why dualism is the book's characteristic effect and tenta-
tiveness its characteristic tone.

After the remarkable publication of three major works in 1905—
the Dora case, *Jokes*, and *Three Contributions*—Freud briefly slack-
ened off. In 1906 he published only one paper, entitled "Psychoanalysis
and the Ascertaining of Truth in Courts of Law," a lecture delivered
at a law school seminar. The whole lecture is structured on an analogy
between the criminal and the neurotic, with the analyst in the position
of detective, lawyer, or judge, faced with the additional difficulty that
the neurotic is hiding "a secret he himself does not know." The next
year Freud published an even bolder analogy, "Obsessive Acts and Religious Practices," in which he equates the neurotic with the worshipper. Freud notes that an obsessional act is called "ceremonial" and that
it has "the character of a sacred rite," and after a number of disclaimers
about "sacrilege" and "travesty," he concludes bluntly that religion
could be described as a "universal obsessional neurosis." Later that
year Freud published an open letter on "The Sexual Enlightenment of
Children," pleading that "from the very beginning everything sexual
should be treated like everything else that is worth knowing about."

Like Engels on the housing question, Freud argues that partial reform is no answer. He concludes:

> Here again we clearly see the unwisdom of putting new wine into old bottles, and perceive the impossibility of carrying through a reform in one particular without altering the foundations of the whole system.

Freud recognizes the harsh effects of what Ruth Benedict was later to call discontinuity in cultural conditioning. He asks, of the misled children: "Is it genuinely and seriously intended that later on they should consider everything connected with sex as something despicable and abhorrent?"

Also in 1907, Freud published a book hardly anyone would have predicted, *Delusion and Dream in Wilhelm Jensen's* Gradiva. It is an analysis of a rather absurd little novel, subtitled "A Pompeiian Fancy," by a German novelist. Like the Dora case, it supplements *The Interpretation of Dreams* by concentrating on dream interpretation, in this case "those dreams which have never been dreamed, those created by authors, and attributed to fictitious characters in their productions." To explain dreams in *Gradiva*, Freud writes, "we must decide to borrow from *The Interpretation of Dreams* by the present writer, and to use some of the rules given there for the solution of dreams." Explaining why he turned to analyzing fictitious dreams in a novel, Freud writes:

> Story-tellers are valuable allies, and their testimony is to be rated high, for they usually know many things between heaven and earth that our academic wisdom does not even dream of. In psychic knowledge, indeed, they are far ahead of us, ordinary people, because they draw from sources that we have not yet made accessible for science.

"As, however, we have not access to the psychic life of the author," Freud writes, "we leave to him the undiminished right of building up a thoroughly valid development on an improbable supposition." He continues:

> Otherwise, we wish to repeat, Wilhelm Jensen has given us an absolutely correct study in psychiatry, in which we may measure our understanding of psychic life, a story of illness and cure adapted to the inculcation of certain fundamental teachings of medical psychology. Strange enough that he should have done this! What if, in reply to questioning, he should deny this intention?

Freud later reveals that that is precisely what happened. He writes:

> One of the circle who, as was explained at the beginning, was interested in the dreams of *Gradiva* and their possible interpretation, put the direct question to Wilhelm Jensen, whether any

such theories of science had been known to him. Our author answered, as was to be expected, in the negative, and rather testily.[3]

Freud's conclusion is that Jensen learned about dreams the way Sophocles (and Freud originally) learned about the Oedipus complex. He writes:

> We are probably drawing from the same source, working over the same material, each of us with a different method, and agreement in results seems to vouch for the fact that both have worked correctly. Our procedure consists of the conscious observation of abnormal psychic processes in others, in order to be able to discover and express their laws. Our author proceeds in another way; he directs his attention to the unconscious in his own psyche, listens to its possibilities of development and grants them artistic expression, instead of suppressing them with conscious critique. Thus he learns from himself what we learn from others, what laws the activity of the unconscious must follow, but he does not need to express those laws, need not even recognize them clearly; they are, as a result of his intelligent patience, contained incarnate in his creatures.

In short, artists are analysts, not neurotics. Jensen not only hit on the nature of the dream-work, but his cure in the novel "shows a considerable resemblance, no, complete agreement" with Freud's therapy, and he even describes the transference. The important corollary to Freud's proposition, that analysts are artists, was one he was still too deeply ambivalent to admit.

In the next two years, 1908 and 1909, Freud published a number of papers, including two important case histories. "Character and Anal Erotism," his first venture into character-typing, boldly identifies cleanliness, orderliness and reliability (Freud's own characteristics) as reaction-formations against an infantile fecal interest, and even goes so far as to explain "Kiss my ass!" (or, as Freud more delicately puts it, "a challenge referring to a caress on this part of the body") as representing "a tender feeling which has undergone repression." "Hysterical Fantasies and Their Relation to Bisexuality" goes beyond the problem of bisexuality to produce an extensive account of hysterical symptoms in dramatic terms. "On the Sexual Theories of Children" displays a vivid imaginative empathy with the child, reminiscent of Darwin's with Drosera or the worm.

---

[3] After the book appeared Freud himself heard from Jensen, whose reaction this time was far from testy. Freud wrote to Jung:

> What Jensen himself has to say? He wrote very warmly about it. In his first letter he expressed his pleasure, etc., and declared that the analysis agreed in all important points with the purpose of the story. Of course he wasn't referring to our theory, since as an old gentleman he seems altogether incapable of entering into any other but his own poetic intentions. He suggested the agreement could be ascribed to poetic intuition, and partly perhaps to his early medical studies.

Freud's most important early criticism of the culture, " 'Civilized' Sexual Morality and Modern Nervousness," was published in 1908. Its emphasis is on the old dualism, the choice between sublimating the sex instincts or becoming fixated at one or another abnormality. Sublimation, made possible by the ability of the sex instinct "to displace its aim without materially losing its intensity," is the source of energy for "cultural activities," activities of "value for civilization." Complete sublimation, however, is as unrealistic a hope as complete "transmutation of heat into mechanical power in the case of machines." "A certain degree of direct sexual satisfaction seems to be absolutely necessary for by far the greater number of natures," Freud writes. The celibate or pre-marital state is pathogenic, but even marriage is not satisfactory sexually, and Freud adds sharply, "A girl must be very healthy to 'stand' marriage." He recurs to his old conception of "the intimate relation existing between all our civilized institutions," and notes "the difficulty of altering any part of them irrespective of the whole." Nevertheless, Freud concludes:

> We may thus well raise the question whether our 'civilized' sexual morality is worth the sacrifice which it imposes upon us, the more so if we are still so insufficiently purged of hedonism as to include a certain degree of individual happiness among the aims of our cultural development. It is certainly not the physician's business to come forward with proposals for reform, but it seemed to me that, by pointing out what significance the injurious results of our sexual morality, enumerated by von Ehrenfels, have in connection with the increase of modern nervousness, I could supplement the account he gives of them, and could thus support the urgency of such reform.

Freud's next paper is a venture into applied psychoanalysis, "The Relation of the Poet to Day-Dreaming." It maintains that poems originate like day-dreams, as a substitute for infantile play, and that poetic form is a "fore-pleasure" enticing us to the greater pleasure of the poem's wish-fulfilment. Freud's essay on "Family Romances," written as a preface to Otto Rank's *The Myth of the Birth of the Hero*, ignores the myth of the hero to describe the analogous romantic fantasy of childhood, that one's *true* parents are highborn, serving as revenge and retaliation for parental punishment. "General Remarks on Hysterical Attacks," published soon after, reiterates Freud's dramatistic vision of hysterical fits as a miming of coitus.

The first of the 1909 case histories is "Analysis of a Phobia in a Five-Year-Old Boy," the classic case of Little Hans. The boy Freud called Hans had been discussed in the 1907 paper "The Sexual Enlightenment of Children" as "Little Herbert," "a splendid boy" who had been brought up with minimal sexual inhibition by his intelligent parents. By 1908, Hans' obsessive concern with his *wiwimacher* (brilliantly translated "widdler" by Alix and James Strachey) had turned into a neurotic phobia of horses, and Freud, who met the boy only once, got elaborate reports on the case from the child's father, who was treating him under Freud's direction. One of the most interesting features of the case history is Freud's constant emotional loading (what he might call "a cathexis of affect") in place of his normal objectivity. Noting that "little Hans seems to be a positive paragon of all the vices," and calling him "the little Oedipus," and "our young libertine," Freud finally corrects the record by "vindicating little Hans' honor":

> But Hans was not by any means a young blackguard; he was not even one of those children in whom at his age the propensity toward cruelty and violence which is part of human nature still has free play. On the contrary, he had an unusually kind-hearted and affectionate disposition.

Hans, like Freud himself in *The Interpretation of Dreams*, is ultimately absolved: he had the Oedipal wishes, but he is innocent of acting on them. Hans is, in fact, an extremely touching figure in the case history, trying to persuade his mother to fondle his widdler by quoting his aunt's remark "He *has* got a dear little thingummy," or telling his father:

> I'd *so* much like to have children; then I'd do everything for them —take them to the bathroom, clean their behinds, and do everything one does with children.

Freud clearly recognizes the enormity of the child's problem in attaining to civilization, "when in the course of his cultural training he is called upon to overcome the innate instinctual components of his mind," and in the name of little Hans he produces a revolutionary slogan:

> Hitherto education has only set itself the task of controlling, or, it would often be more proper to say, of suppressing the instincts. The results have been by no means gratifying, and where the process has succeeded it has only been to the advantage of a small number of favored individuals who have not been required to suppress their instincts. Nor has any one inquired by what means and at what cost the suppression of the inconvenient instincts has been achieved. Supposing now that we substitute another task for this one, and aim instead at making the individual capable of becoming a civilized and useful member of society with the least possible sacrifice of his own activity.

Freud's strong identification with Hans in the case history must in part be his identification with his own Oedipal childhood, but in part it is that Hans, strikingly intelligent and perceptive, is oddly like the adult Freud. When Hans tells his father that his wishing the death of his little sister is good, not bad, because it can be reported to the Professor, Freud comments:

> Well done, little Hans! I could wish for no better understanding of psychoanalysis from any grownup.

When his parents failed in their understanding, "Hans had by a bold
stroke taken the conduct of the analysis into his own hands." Hans
even discovers Freud's profoundest truth, the epiphany at the end of
The Interpretation of Dreams, when he tells his father: "But wanting's
not doing, and doing's not wanting." Freud's only comment is "(!!)."
Hans is not only the infant culture hero, bringing civilization by mastering his instinctual impulses, he is the infant savior, bringing glad
tidings of redemption and forgiveness to those in bondage.

The second case history, "Notes Upon a Case of Obsessional Neurosis," the story of the Rat Man, is much less satisfying. Freud seems
to have felt this, and he introduces it with an unusual amount of depre-
cation. "I shall make some disconnected statements of an aphoristic
character"; Viennese prying "forbids my giving a faithful picture of
the case"; "In these circumstances there is no alternative but to report
the facts in the imperfect and incomplete fashion in which they are
known and in which it is legitimate to communicate them"; and so
forth. The Rat Man is an interesting enough character, addressing
Freud as "Captain," paying for the analysis in a rat currency, which
he obtained by translating "So many florins, so many rats"; and con-
tributing a fascinating record of obsession, but Freud seems never to
identify with it. Freud's tone toward other authorities is as sarcastic
as his introductory statements are self-deprecatory. He interjects an
indignant footnote:

> Yet attempts have been made to explain obsessions without
> taking affectivity into account!

When the Rat Man reports that his father prophesied, "The child will
be either a great man or a great criminal!," Freud comments:

> These alternatives do not exhaust the possibilities. His father
> had overlooked the commonest outcome of such premature pas-
> sions—a neurosis.

At another point, Freud interjects:

> It would be a most desirable thing if the philosophers and psy-
> chologists who develop brilliant theoretical views on the uncon-
> scious upon a basis of hearsay knowledge or from their own
> conventional definitions would first submit to the convincing
> impressions which may be gained from a first-hand study of the
> phenomena of obsessional thinking. We might almost go to the
> length of requiring it of them, if the task were not so much more
> laborious than the methods of work to which they are accus-
> tomed.

Freud's next venture, also in 1909, was a series of five lectures delivered at Clark University in Worcester, Massachusetts, on the
occasion of Clark's twentieth anniversary. The lectures were published the next year as "The Origin and Development of Psychoanalysis," and as Freud's only production for an American audience are of

particular interest. He uses the gradually-complicating form of *The Interpretation of Dreams*, so that the third lecture begins:

> Ladies and Gentlemen: It is not always easy to tell the truth, especially when one must be brief, and so today I must correct an incorrect statement that I made in my last lecture. . . . Now this is not always so; I represented it as being so simple only for purposes of abbreviation.

The lectures are thick with metaphor: Hysterical patients are contemporaries bewailing calamities centuries old instead of going about their present business; Pierre Janet's hysteric is a lady shopper dropping one bundle when she stoops to pick up another; the unconscious is a rowdy ejected from the lecture hall of consciousness for laughing and scraping his feet; associations are ore that the psychologist can refine into valuable metal; psychoanalytic technique is an "arsenal"; men wear "a thick overcoat—a fabric of lies" to conceal their sexuality, "as though it were bad weather in the world of sex"; the sexual impulse does not enter into the child at puberty "as the devils in the gospel entered into the swine"; "the high tide of sexual desire" finds "dams"; symptoms, "to use a simile from chemistry, are the precipitates of earlier love experience," with the physician playing the role of catalyst; hypnosis "cleared away the psychic resistances from a certain field, only to pile them up in an unscalable wall at the boundaries of this field"; "the patient has sore places in his soul life, and one is afraid to touch them, lest his suffering be increased," but like the surgeon, the analyst must hurt to heal.

Freud is sharply aware of his American audience, which included such distinguished figures as William James, Adolf Meyer, and Franz Boas, and which constituted his first real international recognition. He had first planned to address them on the interpretation of dreams, but decided against it because of "a purely subjective and apparently secondary motive." Freud explains:

> It seemed rather an impropriety that in this country, so devoted to practical pursuits, I should pose as 'interpreter of dreams.'

His slant in the lectures is fittingly practical. "The energetic and successful man," Freud writes, "is he who succeeds by dint of labor in transforming his wish fancies into reality." The artist comparably transforms his fancies into art, "so he escapes the fate of a neurosis and wins back his connection with reality by this roundabout way." For the un-American failures, there is only neurosis: "the neurosis takes, in our time, the place of the cloister, in which were accustomed to take refuge all those whom life had undeceived or who felt themselves too weak for life." Freud concludes the lectures characteristically with the anecdote of the old horse that had its ration progressively cut down until it could work without food, although just when the experiment was a success the ungrateful horse died. He meant the joke to apply to the need of the sexual instincts for at least a little gratification, although we can see a personal significance too: the "shabby old Jew" needed at least a feedbag of recognition to keep going.

A NUMBER of papers were published in 1910. The first of them, "Psychogenic Visual Disturbance According to Psychoanalytic Conceptions," has little that is novel other than a dramatic dualism: "Psychoanalysis is a dynamic conception, which reduces mental life to the interplay of reciprocally urging and checking forces." In *"The Antithetical Sense of Primary Words,"* Freud reviews a pamphlet by Karl Abel published more than a quarter of a century before. He begins by repeating a statement from *The Interpretation of Dreams*, that dreams have no negatives, explaining that at the time of writing it he had not understood it. Now, from Abel's book, he understands that dreams resemble archaic languages in representing antitheses in one ambiguous formation. Freud concludes the brief review:

> And we cannot dismiss the conjecture, which forces itself on us psychiatrists, that we should understand the language of dreams better and translate it more easily if we knew more about the development of language.

Freud's next paper, the first of a series of Contributions to the Psychology of Love, is subtitled "A Special Type of Choice of Object Made by Men." Here Freud, as ambivalent as an archaic word, alternately identifies himself with art and with science. He begins the paper in the guise of promising to take the subject away from the artists, while actually describing his own operations in aesthetic terms. He writes:

> Hitherto we have left it to poets and imaginative writers to depict for us the 'conditions of love' under which men and women make their choice of an object, and the way in which they reconcile the demand expressed in their fantasy with the exigencies of real life. Writers indeed have certain qualities which fit them for such a task; more especially, a sensitiveness of perception in regard to the hidden feelings of others, and the courage to give voice to their own unconscious minds.

He then immediately argues that the writer must inevitably distort reality, and that science must therefore take over the subject, "although its touch must be clumsier and the result in pleasure less." "For science," he concludes sternly, "betokens the most complete renunciation of the pleasure-principle of which our minds are capable." Freud then defines the features of his special type of object-choice as "love for a harlot," accompanied by the "need for an injured third party," de-

scribes it with the richness of texture of a nineteenth-century French
novelist, and explains that this is all due to "penetrating psychoanalytic
study."

In an address, "The Future Prospects of Psychoanalytic Therapy,"
delivered before the Second International Psychoanalytic Congress
in 1910, Freud shows an equal alternation between hard-headed realism
and an optimism close to fantasy. Marching boldly into the future,
Freud tells the assembled psychoanalysts that the fixed symbolic meanings of dreams are all being worked out, and adds:

> The dream-material from which these newly-recognized symbols
> are derived will in due time be put before you by the committee
> we are about to form for collecting and studying symbols.

"Our medical practice," he promises them, "will reach a degree of
precision and certainty of success which is not to be had in all the
medical specialties." He promises, with the general recognition of psychoanalytic truth, no less than an end to all neurosis, and explains
(choosing an unfortunate example seven years before Fatima):

> If this hope seems utopian to you, you may remember that
> certain neurotic phenomena have already been dispelled by this
> means, although only in quite isolated instances. Think how com-
> mon hallucinations of the Virgin Mary were in peasant girls in
> former times. So long as such a phenomenon brought a flock of
> believers and resulted perhaps in a chapel being built on the sacred
> spot, the visionary state of these maidens was inaccessible to in-
> fluence. Today even the priesthood has changed its attitude to
> such things; it allows police and medical men to visit the seer,
> and since then the Virgin appears very seldom.

Freud then goes on to produce an analogy for the future psychoanalytic good society that seems childlike in its innocence. He writes:

> Suppose that a number of ladies and gentlemen in good society
> had planned a picnic at an inn in the forest one day. The ladies
> make up their minds that if one of them wants to relieve a
> natural need she will say aloud that she is going to pick flowers;
> but a wicked fellow hears of this secret and has printed on the
> programme which is sent round to the whole party—'If the
> ladies wish to retire they are requested to say that they are go-
> ing to pick flowers.' Of course after this no lady will think of
> availing herself of this flowery pretext, and other freshly devised
> formulas of the same kind will be seriously compromised by it.
> What will be the result? The ladies will own up to their natural
> needs without shame and none of the men will take exception to it.

Side by side with this visionary tone is a contrasting tone of impressive realism. Freud recalls the extensive ignorance and hostility
that surrounded psychoanalysis. He writes:

I will not let myself go to the extent of describing to you the agreeable things that happened during the time when I alone represented psychoanalysis. I know that when I assured my patients that I knew how to relieve them permanently of their sufferings they looked round my modest abode, thought of my want of fame and honors, and regarded me like a man who possesses an infallible system in a gambling-place, of whom people say that if he could do what he professes he would look very different. Nor was it really at all pleasant to operate on people's minds while colleagues whose duty it was to assist took a pleasure in spitting into the field of operation, and while at the first signs of blood or restlessness in him the patient's relatives threatened one. An operation may surely cause reactions; in surgery we became used to that long ago. Nobody believed in me, in fact, just as even today very few believe in us; under such conditions many an attempt was bound to fail.

He explains this as inevitable resistance, writing:

> But now, to be sure, I must damp the ardor of your expectations. The community will not hasten to grant authority to us. It is bound to offer resistance to us, for we adopt a critical attitude towards it; we accuse it of playing a great part itself in causing the neuroses. Just as we make any single person our enemy by discovering what is repressed in him, so the community cannot respond with sympathy to a relentless exposure of its injurious effects and deficiencies; because we destroy illusions we are accused of endangering ideals.

Freud expects all the resistance to collapse eventually, but he warns: "It will not come very quickly; we must be able to wait." Finally, he recognizes that the ultimate limit to his dream of wiping out neurosis is human nature itself. Freud writes:

> Let us remember, however, that it is not for us to advance upon life as fanatical hygienists or therapeutists. We must admit that this ideal prevention of all neurotic illness would not be advantageous to every individual. A good number of those who now take flight into illness would not support the conflict under the conditions we have assumed, but would rapidly succumb or would commit some outrage which would be worse than if they themselves fell ill of a neurosis. The neuroses have in fact their biological function as defensive measures and their social justification; the 'advantage through illness' that they provide is not always a purely subjective one. Is there one of you who has not at some time caught a glimpse behind the scenes in the causation of a neurosis and had to allow that it was the least of the evils possible in the circumstances? And should one really require such sacrifices in order to exterminate the neuroses, while the world remains full of other inextinguishable miseries?

Freud's next paper, "Observations on 'Wild' Psychoanalysis," is an argument against blurting out truths rather than slowly helping to overcome resistances, and it has one striking metaphor. "Such measures,"
Freud writes, "have as little effect on the symptoms of nervous disease
as distributing menus in time of famine has on people's hunger."

Freud's next book, *Leonardo da Vinci: A Study in Psychosexu-
ality*, also appeared in 1910. Freud calls it, varying the subtitle, "a
biographical effort," and remarks in another place: "Readers in general
find every pathography unsavory." He is very careful to "fix the
limits of what psychoanalysis can accomplish in biography." Freud
had always been interested in "the great Leonardo da Vinci" and quotes
from him often, almost certainly for the reasons Jones advances in
Sigmund Freud: Life and Work:

> Much of what Freud said when he penetrated into Leonardo's
> personality was at the same time a self-description; there was
> surely an extensive identification between Leonardo and himself.
> There we learned that Leonardo was torn by two impulses: the
> passion for scientific knowledge and the passion for creating
> works of art.

The problem *Leonardo da Vinci* sets for itself is "to explain the inhibitions in Leonardo's sexual life and in his artistic activity." Freud
roots these in an infantile fantasy of a vulture (actually a kite—according to Strachey, Freud mistranslates) opening Leonardo's mouth with
its tail and striking him in the lips. Freud analyzes the fantasy elaborately, and in terms of it explains various features of Leonardo's career.
He credits Leonardo with a stunted sexual life of "ideal homosexuality," fixated on his mother, and it is thus his mother's ambiguous
Oedipal smile that characterizes Mona Lisa. At that point, apparently
thrown back into his self-analysis and the roots of his own genius,
Freud suddenly refuses to go any further. He writes: "We would
gladly report in what way his artistic activity depends on the primal
forces of his psyche, if our material had not here proved inadequate."
"The nature of artistic attainment," he concludes "is psychoanalyti-
cally inaccessible to us." In 1914 Freud wrote to the portrait painter
Hermann Struck that the artist "is actually a being of a special kind,
exalted, autocratic, villainous, and at times rather incomprehensible."
His Leonardo book, he added, is "partly fiction."

Freud published an enormous number of papers between 1911
and 1913. The first of them is the fourth of the case histories, "Psychoanalytic Notes upon an Autobiographical Account of a Case of
Paranoia (Dementia Paranoides)," the case of Judge Schreber. In 1903,
Schreber had published *Memoirs of a Neurotic*, an account of his
paranoiac illness and partial recovery. Freud never met Schreber, but
he found his delusional system so useful in confirming his own theories of the origin of paranoia in repressed homosexuality that he wrote
up the case entirely from the book. Schreber believed, to put it briefly,
that after other physical tribulations he had been or was being trans-

formed into a woman by God, in order to redeem mankind. This involved: a divine language, consisting of antiquated euphemistic German; a very low opinion of God, who struck Schreber in almost all his activities as "ridiculous or childish"; and many other engaging features. The case history is intensely dramatic, as befits the study of one first-class imagination by another. Its greatest interest in literary terms is an amazing passage where Freud, like an early Kenneth Burke, generates all the principal forms of paranoia linguistically, out of the possible variations of the verbal formula: "*I* (a man) *love him* (a man)." For the first time, Freud shows signs of recognizing the predictability of his explanations. He writes:

> The sun, therefore, is nothing but another sublimated symbol for the father; and in pointing this out I must disclaim all responsibility for the monotony of the solutions provided by psychoanalysis.

Later in 1911 Freud published the first of his "metapsychological" papers. He had first used the term in a letter to Fliess in 1896, writing: "Far beyond these considerations lurks my ideal and problem child, metapsychology." By 1904, in *The Psychopathology of Everyday Life*, the word implied a translation of religious ideas into psychological processes. Freud writes:

> One could venture in this manner to resolve the myths of Paradise, the Fall of Man, of God, of Good and Evil, of Immortality, and so on, thus transforming *Metaphysics* into *Metapsychology*.

During the second decade of the century, Freud used "metapsychology" much more modestly. "I propose that," he writes in 1911, "when we succeed in describing a mental process in all its aspects, dynamic, topographic, and economic, we shall call this a *metapsychological* presentation." At one point he had planned to include some or all of them in a book, *Preliminary Material for a Metapsychological Theory*, but he never did. The first such paper is "Formulations Regarding the Two Principles in Mental Functioning," the two principles being the pleasure-principle and the reality-principle. As we might expect, the essay places the symbolic action of art in a very ambiguous position. Freud writes:

> *Art* brings about a reconciliation of the two principles in a peculiar way. The artist is originally a man who turns from reality because he cannot come to terms with the demand for the renunciation of instinctual satisfaction as it is first made, and who then in fantasy-life allows full play to his erotic and ambitious wishes. But he finds a way of return from this world of fantasy back to reality; with his special gifts he moulds his fantasies into a new kind of reality, and men concede them a justification as valuable reflections of actual life. Thus by a certain path he actually becomes the hero, king, creator, favorite he desired to be,

without pursuing the circuitous path of creating real alterations in the outer world.

In 1912 Freud published another Contribution to the Psychology of Love, on "The Most Prevalent Form of Degradation in Erotic Life," which turns out to be psychic impotence. Here Freud is unsparing of the reader. He writes:

> It has an ugly sound and a paradoxical as well, but nevertheless it must be said that whoever is to be really free and happy in love must have overcome his deference for women and come to terms with the idea of incest with mother or sister. Anyone who in the face of this test subjects himself to serious self-examination will indubitably find that at the bottom of his heart he too regards the sexual act as something degrading, which soils and contaminates not only the body.

He once more reminds us of St. Augustine's harsh vision, "*Inter urinas et faeces nascimur*," and adds, recurring to an old obsession:

> The genitals themselves have not undergone the development of the rest of the human form in the direction of beauty; they have retained their animal cast; and so even today love, too, is in essence as animal as it ever was.

"The purpose of science," he concludes, "is neither to alarm nor to reassure." Freud also began the publication of a series of Papers on Technique with "The Employment of Dream-Interpretation in Psychoanalysis" in 1912. Here more strongly than ever before Freud recognizes the psychoanalytic variant of Heisenberg's Uncertainty Principle, that the study of the psyche inevitably alters it. He writes:

> The more the patient has learnt of the method of dream-interpretation the more obscure do his later dreams become, as a rule. All the acquired knowledge about dreams serves also as a warning to the dream-work.

Even copious and rich dreams can be a form of resistance, Freud recognizes, as the Devil learns to counterfeit a clerical collar.

The second of the Papers on Technique, "The Dynamics of the Transference," returns to some of the metaphors of *The Interpretation of Dreams*. Freud writes:

> Whenever in our analytic delving we come upon one of the hiding-places of the withdrawn libido, there ensues a battle; all the forces which have brought about the regression of the libido will rise up as 'resistances' against our efforts in order to maintain the new condition.

Every thought and act of the patient's "represents a compromise between the forces urging towards the cure and those gathered to oppose it." If the war metaphor was not clear before, Freud makes it explicit, writing in a footnote:

From which, however, one need not infer in general any very particular pathogenic importance in the point selected for resistance by transference. In warfare, when a bitter fight is raging over the possession of some little chapel or a single farmhouse, we do not necessarily assume that the church is a national monument, or that the barns contain the military funds. Their value may be merely tactical; in the next onslaught they will very likely be of no importance.

The next paper, "Types of Neurotic Nosogenesis," goes back to Freud's familiar water metaphor to speak of the conflict between the ego and the libido as "a damming-up of the libido which the ego is not able to master with the means at its disposal without some damage."

The third Paper on Technique, "Recommendations for Physicians on the Psychoanalytic Method of Treatment," returns to still another favorite image of Freud's, the psychoanalyst as surgeon. He writes:

I cannot recommend my colleagues emphatically enough to take as a model in psychoanalytic treatment the surgeon who puts aside all his own feelings, including that of human sympathy, and concentrates his mind on one single purpose, that of performing the operation as skilfully as possible.

Freud adds:

The justification for this coldness in feeling in the analyst is that it is the condition which brings the greatest advantage to both persons involved, ensuring a needful protection for the physician's emotional life and the greatest measure of aid for the patient that is possible at the present time.

"The physician," Freud concludes, "should be impenetrable to the patient, and, like a mirror, reflect nothing but what is shown to him." The following paper, "A Note on the Unconscious in Psycho-Analysis," was written in English for the proceedings of the Society for Psychical Research. In it Freud reverts to still another metaphor from *The Interpretation of Dreams*, the camera, explaining: "A rough but not inadequate analogy to this supposed relation of conscious to unconscious activity might be drawn from the field of ordinary photography." The unconscious is like a negative, from which consciousness can make a positive print.

The next year Freud published "The Excretory Functions in Psychoanalysis and Folklore" as a preface to a German translation of John G. Bourke's *Scatalogic Rites of All Nations*. Calling the material, in a phrase from *Faust*, the "distressing trace of the Earth" that mankind denies or suppresses, Freud concludes that from a different approach comparative folklore "has reached the same results as psychoanalysis." In his next paper, "A Dream Which Bore Testimony," Freud returns to the subject of dream-interpretation, translating a dream so stylishly that even he comments at one point: "We thus have here an overdetermination which detracts somewhat from the elegance of the interpretation." This was followed by "Further Recommendations in the Technique of Psychoanalysis," subtitled "On Beginning the Treatment. The Question of the First Communications. The Dynamics of the Cure." This essay demonstrates in the first paragraph the degree to which it will be metaphoric. Freud begins:

> He who hopes to learn the fine art of the game of chess from books will soon discover that only the opening and closing moves of the game admit of exhaustive systematic description, and that the endless variety of the moves which develop from the opening defies description; the gap left in the instructions can only be filled in by the zealous study of games fought out by master-hands. The rules which can be laid down for the practical application of psychoanalysis in treatment are subject to similar limitations.

Neurosis is "rooted in mental strata that were never penetrated by intellectual study," and thus, when it comes, seems to be "a sort of 'maiden from afar.' " Freud's war image becomes even more dramatic, now hand-to-hand combat with a giant. He writes:

> A formidable resistance has come out into the open in order to defend the neurosis; one takes up its challenge then and there, and grips it by the throat.

On the old problem of the infantile guilts not amenable to adult reason, Freud produces an elaborate legal metaphor for the personality. He writes:

> It is just as if a decree were promulgated by the Ministry of Justice to the effect that juvenile misdemeanors should be dealt with by certain lenient methods. As long as this concession has not come to the knowledge of the individual migistrates, or in the event of their not choosing to make use of it but preferring to deal justice according to their own lights, nothing will be changed in the treatment accorded to youthful delinquents.

Freud's next paper, "The Occurrence in Dreams of Material from Fairy Tales," goes back to folklore, to analyze one dream using associations from "Rumpelstiltskin," and another (dreamed by the Wolf Man, who was to be the fifth and last of Freud's case histories) using "Little Red Riding Hood" and "The Wolf and the Seven Little Goats." It was followed by one of Freud's most important papers for literary and mythological study, "The Theme of the Three Caskets." This begins with the suitor's choice from among three caskets—of gold, silver, and lead—to win the hand of Portia in *The Merchant of Venice*. Freud finds it to be an astrological myth, with the three suitors the sun, moon, and stars. He then explains that such myths are "projected on to the heavens after having arisen quite otherwise under purely human conditions," and proceeds to bring it back down to earth. Freud writes:

> With one wave of the wand, such as usually only happens in fairy tales, we have stripped the astral garment from our theme; and now we see that the subject is an idea from human life, a man's choice among three women.

It can then be equated with another Shakespeare scene, Lear's test of his three daughters, and now the third daughter, Cordelia, the leaden casket, is recognizable. Through her disguise as a wishful antithesis, she is the figure of Death.[4] Freud's final statement of the moral of *King Lear* anticipates his own later philosophic stance. He writes:

> Eternal wisdom, in the garb of the primitive myth, bids the old man renounce love, choose death and make friends with the necessity of dying. . . . the third of the Fates alone, the silent goddess of Death, will take him into her arms.

Another paper, "Infantile Mental Life: Two Lies Told by Children," concludes on Freud's familiar exoneration for the child—passionate, but innocent. He writes:

> We should not think lightly of such episodes in child-life. It would be a grave misconception to read into such childish errors the prognosis of a developing immoral character. Nevertheless, they are intimately connected with the most powerful motivations of the childish soul, and are prophetic of tendencies which will take shape either in the later destiny or in a future neurosis.

A paper read before the International Psychoanalytic Congress in 1913 and published that year, "The Predisposition to Obsessional Neurosis," is strongly evolutionary. It emphasizes that mental functions "have to go through a long and complicated process of development before they reach the state characteristic of a normal adult," and that fixations and regressions lie in wait at every stage. The last of the series of papers, "*Fausse Reconnaissance ('Déjà Raconté')* in Psychoanalytic Treatment" explains the phenomenon, the patient's sense of having already told something to the analyst, as an intention to tell it nullified by resistance. Freud begins by saying that in these arguments as to whether or not something has been said, "it may just as well be the physician as the patient who has fallen a victim to a paramnesia." By the time he finishes, it is of course the patient who is invariably wrong.

Freud's next book, published in 1913, is his first ambitious confrontation of society, *Totem and Taboo*. This aims at nothing less than "a comparison of the psychology of primitive races as taught

---

[1] In 1883 Freud had addressed his fiancée as "Cordelia," with himself in the role of the loyal suitor France. Now thirty years later he was Lear and his daughter Anna had replaced her mother as Cordelia, as Freud admitted in a letter to Ferenczi.

by folklore, with the psychology of the neurotic as it has become known through psychoanalysis." Using the Australian aboriginals as the type of the primitive, and drawing much of his information from Frazer's writings, Freud finds that totemic organization and the incest taboo relate to the two principal features of the Oedipus complex, hostility toward the father and desire for the mother. Freud then creates a Platonic myth of the origin of these social institutions. In the prehistoric days when men lived in a horde like the higher apes, with the old male keeping all the females and driving away his sons when they became rivals, a group of brothers once banded together, slew and ate their father, and seized their mothers and sisters. Freud continues:

> After they had satisfied their hate by his removal and had carried out their wish for identification with him, the suppressed tender impulses had to assert themselves. This took place in the form of remorse, a sense of guilt was formed which coincided here with the remorse generally felt. The dead now became stronger than the living had been, just as we observe it today in the destinies of men. What the father's presence had formerly prevented they themselves now prohibited in the psychic situation of 'subsequent obedience' which we know so well from psychoanalysis. They undid their deed by declaring that the killing of the father substitute, the totem, was not allowed, and renounced the fruits of their deed by denying themselves the liberated women. Thus they created two fundamental taboos of totemism out of the *sense of guilt of the son*, and for this very reason this had to correspond with the two repressed wishes of the Oedipus complex. Whoever disobeyed became guilty of the only two crimes which troubled primitive society.

This primal deed and the accompanying remorse thus became the origin of culture and social organization. "The beginnings of religion, ethics, society and art meet in the Oedipus complex," Freud concludes grandly.

As a theory of historical origins, of course, this is nonsense. Men never lived in any such primal hordes, nor do the higher apes. Eating the totem and committing incest are not the only two crimes that trouble primitive society, nor the worst, nor necessarily crimes at all. Many primitive peoples do not have and never have had totemism, and their incest taboos and ours do not remotely coincide. As a literal origin theory, we must throw all of this out, but Burke's concept of the "temporalizing of essence" allows us to rescue it in other terms if we wish. In Burke's view, the characteristic mental habit of the nineteenth century was translating "essence" into "origin," so that the statement "This is the essence of the situation" becomes "This is how it began." We need only translate back, and Freud's origin theory transforms into "Culture and society have the sort of defensive emphases they might have had had they originated in a prehistoric parricide and incest." Freud is somewhat aware of this possibility, which is essentially the sort of translation he made when he turned his primal seductions in infancy into primal fancies. Freud suggests the possibility, writing:

> According to this the mere impulses of hostility towards the father and the existence of the wish fantasy to kill and devour him may have sufficed to bring about the moral reaction which has created totemism and taboo.

He argues that the difference here between act and wish is not really important, but decides anyway for the act. The book's last sentence ends, quoting *Faust:*

> I think we may as well assume in the case we are discussing, though without vouching for the absolute certainty of the decision, that 'In the beginning was the deed.'

In his comparison of the primitive and the neurotic, a sense of metaphor saves Freud from similar overstatement. He writes in a famous formulation:

> We may say that hysteria is a caricature of an artistic creation, a compulsion neurosis a caricature of a religion, and a paranoiac delusion a caricature of a philosophic system.

Here the relation is clearly analogical; Freud does not mean that any antecedent art work was caricatured by the hysteric, or any antecedent philosophy by the paranoiac. From Frazer's *Totemism and Exogamy*, Freud gets the "valuable argument" that the existence of a taboo shows the existence of an impulse to commit the act, so that presumably the strongest taboos signify the strongest impulses. This is the ultimate in Freud's universalizing of his own Oedipal guilt. His infantile fantasy of killing his father and marrying his mother is first performed solo in the letters to Fliess, then with a few supporting actors in his practice, then with crowds of supers throughout the world, finally on the great scriptural stage of In the Beginning. Our ancestors sinned, as in Eden, and all subsequent history arose from their Fall.

When the book was in proof Freud suddenly lost faith in it, and told Abraham, Ferenczi, and Jones that he was full of doubts about the theory. When Jones saw Freud in Vienna in June, 1913, he asked him how the author of *The Interpretation of Dreams* could now doubt. Freud replied:

> Then I described the wish to kill one's father, and now I have been describing the actual killing; after all it is a big step from a wish to a deed.

Jakob Freud had been dead for seventeen years, but from his corpse, as from the corn god's, nourishing crops continued to appear regularly.

War and Peace

DURING the years of the First World War, Freud published a wide range of papers. "On Narcissism: An Introduction," another effort in metapsychology, appeared in 1914. In his characteristic dynamic or organic topography, Freud sees the libido as a kind of amoeba, putting out object-cathexes like pseudopodia. An equally vivid burst of metaphor describes the paradox of mortality-immortality. Freud writes:

> The individual himself regards sexuality as one of his own ends; while from another point of view he is only an appendage to his germ-plasm, to which he lends his energies, taking in return his toll of pleasure—the mortal vehicle of a (possibly) immortal substance—like the inheritor of an entailed property who is only the temporary holder of an estate which survives him.

In terms of narcissism, Freud presents an unusually cynical view of the family. "The charm of a child," he writes, "lies to a great extent in his narcissism, his self-sufficiency and inaccessibility, just as does the charm of certain animals which seem not to concern themselves about us, such as cats and the large beasts of prey." In this view, the child is "His Majesty the Baby," and parental love, "which is so touching and at bottom so childish, is nothing but parental narcissism born again." "On Narcissism" is important historically in Freud's writings because it includes his first approximation of the superego, called the "ego-ideal." It is equally important in terms of imaginative organization for the resourcefulness of its universalizing of the myth of Narcissus.

In 1914 Freud published his first considerable work of polemic, "On the History of the Psychoanalytic Movement," with the bold epigraph, *Fluctuat nec mergitur*, "It is tossed but does not sink." The tone is extremely personal. In its second sentence, the *History* announces: "For psychoanalysis is my creation, for ten years I was the only one occupied with it." As a consequence of which, Freud adds, he feels entitled to define its character. He describes the loneliness of those early years: "An empty space soon formed itself about my person."

Of his discovery of infantile sexuality, Freud notes that his triumph "gradually became tarnished on reflecting that the discovery was of such a nature that one really ought to be ashamed of having made it." "The interpretation of dreams," he writes, "became a solace and support to me in those difficult first years of analysis." The concept of "resistance" kept him from becoming embittered, Freud explains, but he did not develop "any particular respect for the opinion of the world." Accepting that he was one of those who "have disturbed the world's sleep," Freud writes, he accepted that his fate was to be ignored by science during his lifetime. "When I look back to those lonely years, from the perplexities and pressure of the present," he concludes surprisingly, "it seems to me like a beautiful and heroic era."

The ambivalent tone of this introductory statement, in which Freud looks back on his early isolation with such mixed feelings, is partly the result of the defection of two of his principal followers, Jung and Adler, in the years around 1912. Much of the "History of the Psychoanalytic Movement" is taken up with polemic against them. Jung's approach to myth is "no longer free from objection, yet very interesting," and in his recent work "one is more likely to find that religion becomes injected into the analysis rather than rationally explained by it." Freud reports:

> In 1912, Jung boasted, in a letter to me from America, that his modifications of psychoanalysis had overcome the resistances to it in many persons, who hitherto wanted to know nothing about it. I replied that this was nothing to boast about, that the more he sacrificed of the hard-won truths of psychoanalysis, the fewer resistances he would encounter.

His judgment of Jung is a harsh alternative:

> When one thinks of the disagreements between Jung's various private and public utterances, one is obliged to ask to what extent this is due to his own lack of clearness and how much to a lack of sincerity.

That is, he is either a fool or a liar, and instead of psychoanalysis he has produced "a new religio-ethical system."

Adler is dealt with even more harshly. He is reproached with "the great number of mean outbursts of anger which distort his writings, and by the feeling of an ungovernable mania for priority which pervades his work." His system is only a "secondary revision," and Freud characterizes it:

> It consequently consists of three elements of quite dissimilar value: first, good contributions to the psychology of the ego, which are superfluous but admissible; second, translations of analytical facts into new jargon; and thirdly, distortions and twistings of these facts when they do not fit into his ego theories.

"His theory thus does exactly what all patients do," Freud concludes, "and what our conscious thinking always does; it rationalizes." What Adler asserts is "pitiful and devoid of substance"; his system is "radically false"; and his followers "hail him as the Messiah, for whose appearance waiting humanity had been prepared by so and so many forerunners."

The consequence is excommunication. "My confidence in the honesty and distinction of my opponents was always slight," Freud admits, although he adds later, "I am not to any active degree revengeful." Freud explains that since "analysis is not suitable for polemic use," he will not use it against Jung and Adler, "thereby limiting my indiscretion and aggression against my opponents." He will neither debate the truth of their theories nor refute them, only show that they may not be called psychoanalysis and (despite his protestations) motivate them in unconscious resistances, that is, "use analysis only to make clear how these deviations from analysis could take place among analysts." The Jungian and Adlerian systems show themselves to have been "forced to new interpretations, distortions, and eliminations of the actual results of analysis." Freud concludes:

> As a matter of fact, they have caught a few cultural overtones from the symphony of life, but have once more failed to hear the most powerful melody of the impulses.

Neither, in short, "has the slightest claim to call itself psychoanalysis." Freud's final vision for himself, in the book's concluding paragraph, finds him back in the mineshaft of *The Interpretation of Dreams*, building out into the dark. He writes:

> I can only conclude with the wish that fate may grant an easy ascension to those whose sojourn in the underworld of psychoanalysis has become uncomfortable. May it be vouchsafed to the others to bring to a happy conclusion their work in the depths.

The same year, Freud printed in *Imago* his only anonymous publication, "The Moses of Michelangelo." It appeared with the curious prefatory editorial note:

> Although this paper does not, strictly speaking, conform to the conditions under which contributions are accepted for this Journal, the editors have decided to print it, since the author, who is personally known to them, belongs to psychoanalytical circles, and since his mode of thought has in point of fact a certain resemblance to the methodology of psychoanalysis.

Freud begins the essay with the disclaimer: "I may say at once that I am no connoisseur in art, but simply a layman." He makes ingenuous efforts to dissemble his identity, writing at one point, "I have followed the literature of psychoanalysis closely," and at another, "Long before I had any opportunity of hearing about psychoanalysis." Actually, no one familiar with Freud's writings could have had any doubt about the authorship. His pretence that he is a minor follower of psychoanalysis is immediately exposed by the sort of ironic negative boast about the field that only Freud presumed to make. He writes of the art detective Morelli:

> It seems to me that his method of inquiry is closely related to the technique of psychoanalysis. It, too, is accustomed to divine secret and concealed things from unconsidered or unnoticed details, from the rubbish-heap, as it were, of our observations.

Even more unmistakable are such characteristic Freudian formulations as: "the highest mental achievement that is possible in a man, that of struggling successfully against an inward passion for the sake of a cause to which he has devoted himself." Why then the secrecy? The reasons Freud gave his friends were unsatisfactory. He writes to Jones: "Why disgrace Moses by putting my name to it? It is a joke, although perhaps not a bad one." Jones' theory, which seems convincing, is that Freud insisted on anonymity because of his strong symbolic identification at the time with Moses. The essay interprets Michelangelo's statue as Moses in the act of mastering his fury at his backsliding followers. The essay, written at the same time as "On the History of the Psychoanalytic Movement," shows Freud trying to restrain himself like his mythic progenitor, to go on with his prophetic mission. By 1924, when the essay was published in the collected work, Freud was enough recovered to admit to it.

Later in 1914, Freud published another paper in the series of Further Recommendations in the Technique of Psychoanalysis, this one on "Recollection, Repetition, and Working Through." Its vision of neurotic illness is the dramatistic one of the patient unable to recall the repressed but *acting* it out in the analysis and transference. Freud even writes dramatic dialogue for the resistance. He explains:

> It seems to say: 'See what happens when I really let myself go in these things! Haven't I been right to relegate them all to repression?'

The next paper in the series, "Observations on Transference-love," appeared the following year. Here Freud, for the first time confronting the analytic transference at length, tries a variety of imaginative approaches. First he sees the analyst as a figure like the witch of Endor. Of failing to use the transference, he writes:

> It would be the same thing as to conjure up a spirit from the underworld by means of a crafty spell and then to dispatch him back again without a question.

At the same time, "It is not permissible to disavow the indifference one has developed." Freud is visibly tempted by the vision of "women of an elemental passionateness" in the analytic relationship. "In spite of neurosis and resistance," he admits, "there is an incomparable fascination about a noble woman who confesses her passion." Freud adds:

It is not the grossly sexual desires of the patient that constitute the temptation. These are more likely to repel and to demand the exercise of toleration in order to regard them as a natural phenomenon. It is perhaps the finer impulses, those 'inhibited in their aim,' which lead a man into the danger of forgetting the rules of technique and the physician's task for the sake of a wonderful experience.

Freud's advice to his colleagues consists of two metaphors:

> He must not let the scene of the race between the dogs be enacted, in which the prize was a chaplet of sausages and which a funny fellow spoilt by throwing one sausage onto the course; the dogs fell upon it and forgot about the race and the chaplet in the distance luring them on to win.

> The psychoanalyst knows that the forces he works with are of the most explosive kind and that he needs as much caution and conscientiousness as a chemist. But when has it ever been forbidden to a chemist, on account of its danger, to occupy himself with the explosives which, just because of their effectiveness, are so indispensable?

In short, the analyst must conjure up love and use it in a series of controlled explosions, not fall for a tidbit on the track.

A very important essay in the cultural applications of psychoanalysis appeared in 1915, entitled "Thoughts for the Times on War and Death." It begins with the image of being "swept into the vortex" of the war, goes on to explain that the war is not the "chivalrous crusade" that had been anticipated, but a considerable disillusionment. War comes to seem a natural phenomenon, Freud writes, in which "nations still obey their immediate passions far more readily than their interests," and "the primal man in each of us" is laid bare. "War is not to be abolished," he concludes regretfully. Freud, who had greeted the declaration of war in 1914 with the statement "All my libido is given to Austro-Hungary," by 1915 can only hope that the side on which his sons are fighting has "least transgressed the laws of civilization." The only good consequence of the war is to produce an "altered attitude towards death." "At bottom," he writes, "no one believes in his own death." This disbelief in death produces an impoverishment of life, but war restores the tragic richness. Freud writes:

> It is evident that the war is bound to sweep away this conventional treatment of death. Death will no longer be denied; we are forced to believe in him. People really are dying, and now not one by one, but many at a time, often ten thousand in a single day. Nor is it any longer an accident. To be sure, it still seems a matter of chance whether a particular bullet hits this man or that; but the survivor may easily be hit by another bullet; and the accumulation puts an end to the impression of accident. Life has,

in truth, become interesting again; it has regained its full significance.

The essay concludes: "If you would endure life, be prepared for
death."

Underlying this somewhat operatic vision is Freud's dualist view
of the conflict between civilization and the instincts. "The sense of order and fixed law" that the war had dissipated was only, in Frazer's
mixed metaphor, the thin veneer of civilization over the volcano. "Civilization," Freud reminds us, "is the fruit of renunciation of instinctual
satisfaction," and just as the sex instincts periodically break out of con-
finement, so do what he would later call the death instincts. Freud
concludes:

> From the foregoing observations we may already derive this
> consolation—that our mortification and our grievous disillusion-
> ment regarding the uncivilized behavior of our world-compatriots
> in this war are shown to be unjustified. They were based on an
> illusion to which we had abandoned ourselves. In reality our fel-
> low-citizens have not sunk so low as we feared, because they had
> never risen so high as we believed. That the greater units of hu-
> manity, the peoples and states, have mutually abrogated their
> moral restraints naturally prompted these individuals to permit
> themselves relief for a while from the heavy pressure of civiliza-
> tion and to grant a passing satisfaction to the instincts it holds in
> check.

Another metapsychological paper published in 1915, "Instincts
and Their Vicissitudes," is interesting for the drastic polarization
(somewhat reminiscent of Marx's dialectic) of Freud's charting of the
vicissitudes. In addition to repression and sublimation, an instinct may
be transformed into its opposite or turned round on the subject. Loving
admits of three antitheses: loving-hating, loving-being loved, passion-
indifference. Mental life is governed by three polarities: ego-external
world, the "real"; pleasure-pain, the "economic"; active-passive, the
"biological." Within all these dichotomies, terms dance, as in the following typical ballet:

> So we see that love and hate, which present themselves to us
> as essentially antithetical, stand in no simple relation to each
> other. They did not originate in a cleavage of any common pri-
> mal element, but sprang from different sources and underwent
> each its own development before the influence of the pleasure-
> pain relation constituted them antitheses to each other.

A paper the same year on "Repression" is equally dynamic. Of a repressed instinctual impulse, Freud writes: "It ramifies like a fungus, so
to speak, in the dark." Of the difference between repressing conscious
and unconscious instincts, he writes:

The difference, after all, is not important; it amounts to much the same thing as the difference between ordering an undesirable guest out of my drawing-room or out of my front hall, and refusing to let him cross my threshold once I have recognized him.

Freud adds in a footnote:

I need only add that I have to place a sentinel to keep constant guard over the door which I have forbidden this guest to pass, lest he should burst it open.

Freud's metapsychological paper "The Unconscious," published in 1915, is an elaborate exercise in topography. He later came to regard it as one of his three most important pieces of work (the others being the last chapters of *The Interpretation of Dreams* and *Totem and Taboo*). Freud insists on the metaphoric nature of his chart, writing:

Our mental topography has for the present nothing to do with anatomy; it is concerned not with anatomical locations, but with regions in the mental apparatus, irrespective of their possible situation in the body.

The essay's most striking metaphors show Freud oddly ethnocentric, identifying the content of the unconscious with "a primitive population," and writing of fantasy-formations:

We may compare them with those human half-breeds who, taken all round, resemble white men, but betray their colored descent by some striking feature or other, on account of which they are excluded from society and enjoy none of the privileges of white people.

Freud next published "A Case of Paranoia Running Counter to the Psycho-Analytic Theory of the Disease," which beneath the apparent contradiction found the case to confirm Freud's theory of paranoia as developing out of repressed homosexuality.

The next paper, "Some Character-Types Met With in Psychoanalytic Work," is another venture in characterology. Since resistances relate to character, Freud explains, the analyst soon reaches a point where character "acquires the first claim on his interest." The three principal types he deals with are "the 'exceptions'" (so self-proclaimed), "those wrecked by success" (a category into which Jones puts the fainting Freud of the pre-war years), and those who illustrate "criminality from a sense of guilt." Here Freud anticipates his later divine Eros, writing: "By the side of the necessities of existence, love is the great teacher." In the discussion of "the 'exceptions,'" Freud extends his use of the Shakespearian archetype from Hamlet and Lear to a much less attractive figure, Richard III. He writes:

Now we feel that we ourselves could be like Richard, nay, that we are already a little like him. Richard is an enormously magnified representation of something we can all discover in ourselves.

A slight essay, "On Transience," was also written in 1915 as a contribution to a volume published by the Berlin Goethebund. It is considerably less consoling about the war than the essay written earlier in the year, seeing it now as having simply "shattered our pride in the achievement of our civilization."

After several brief notes on symbolism, Freud published another essay in characterology, "On the Transformation of Instincts with Special Reference to Anal Erotism," in 1916. It further develops the ideas of the 1908 "Character and Anal Erotism." In it Freud first describes female "penis-envy," although not yet universalizing it. He illustrates the transition from anal to genital erotism with a wild diagram, presented with the characteristic apology:

> Unfortunately, this technical device is not sufficiently plastic for our purpose, or possibly we have not yet learned to use it with effect. In any case we ask the reader not to expect too much from it.

Another ambitious paper of 1916, "Metapsychological Supplement to the Theory of Dreams," goes beyond *The Interpretation of Dreams* in attempting a symbolic definition of sleep as "an act that reproduces intra-uterine existence." Dreams are seen even more dramatically than before, as "an externalization of an internal process."

In 1917, Freud published, in Hungarian, a paper on "One of the Difficulties of Psychoanalysis." Its subject is the resistance aroused by libido theory. In it Freud repeats his image of the amoeba for the libido, and develops his metaphor of the analyst as chemist. He writes:

> Our one-sidedness is like that of the chemist who traces all compounds back to the force of chemical attraction. In doing so, he does not deny the force of gravity; he leaves that to the physicist to reckon with.

With visible pride, Freud writes an elaborate account of how "the general narcissism of man, the self-love of humanity, has up to the present been three times severely wounded by the researches of science." The first was the destruction by Copernicus of "the narcissistic illusion" that the earth was at the center of the solar system. The second was Darwin's end to man's presumption in thinking himself superior to the animals. The third and "probably the most wounding" is the revelation by psychoanalysis that "the ego is not master in its own house." Freud concludes a long apostrophe to the ego with the wisdom of the Delphic Oracle. He writes:

> Even if you are not ill, who can tell all that is stirring in your mind of which you know nothing or are falsely informed? You conduct yourself like an absolute sovereign who is content with the information supplied him by his highest officials and never goes among the people to hear their voice. Look into the depths of your own soul and learn first to know yourself, then you will understand why this illness was bound to come upon you and perhaps you will thenceforth avoid falling ill.

That same year Freud published "A Childhood Recollection from *Dichtung und Wahrheit*," in which Goethe's childhood memory of throwing crockery out the window is explained as a symbolic action, "or, let us say more correctly, a magic action," by which the infant Goethe expressed his resentment at the birth of a younger brother. Freud's strong personal identification with Goethe comes through clearly in the essay, particularly in the last paragraph, with its reference to Freud's explanation for his own success in *The Interpretation of Dreams:*

> I have, however, already declared elsewhere that he who has been the undisputed darling of his mother retains throughout life that victorious feeling, that confidence in ultimate success, which not seldom brings actual success with it. And a saying such as 'My strength has its roots in my relation to my mother' might well have been put at the head of Goethe's autobiography.

Later in 1917, Freud published the last of the metapsychological papers, "Mourning and Melancholia." It is chiefly remarkable for our purposes because of a metaphor of the sort that Freud had earlier described to Fliess as one of his "*schnorrer*-fantasies." He writes:

> . . . for instance, when some poor devil, by winning a large sum of money, is suddenly relieved from perpetual anxiety about his daily bread, when any long and arduous struggle is finally crowned with success, when a man finds himself in a position to throw off at one blow some heavy burden, some false position he has long endured, and so on.

THE only book Freud published during the war is *Introductory Lectures on Psychoanalysis*, in 1917, consisting of two series of lectures he had delivered at the Psychiatric Clinic of the University of Vienna in the winter terms of 1915–16 and 1916–17. His audience consisted of medical students and a variety of academic laymen. The first series was improvised and written down afterwards, the second was composed and memorized. Freud aimed again at metapsychology in the more limited sense, admitting to the audience in a late lecture: "I let go of descriptive explanation and took up the dynamic aspect and dropped this again for a so-called economic one." The *Introductory Lectures* is a most remarkable work, in which we see Freud, at sixty, at the height of his powers as a dialectician and rhetorician, not abstracting or popularizing his subject but engaging in dramatic interplay with his hearers, a Socrates who writes all the voices. The form of colloquy or debate is the outstanding feature of the book. Freud remarks typically:

> I am now going to ask you to consider these phenomena. But you will object, with annoyance: 'There are so many tremendous

puzzles both in the wide world and in the narrower life of the soul, so many mysteries in the field of mental disorder which demand and deserve explanation, that it really seems frivolous to waste labor and interest on these trifles. If you could explain to us how it is possible for anyone with sound sight and hearing, in broad daylight, to see and hear things which do not exist, or how anyone can suddenly believe that his nearest and dearest are persecuting him, or can justify with the most ingenious arguments a delusion which would seem nonsensical to any child, then we might be willing to take psychoanalysis seriously. But if psychoanalysis cannot occupy us with anything more interesting than the question why a speaker uses a wrong word or why a *Hausfrau* mislays her keys and similar trivialities, then we shall find something better to do with our time and our interest.'

My reply is: Patience! Your criticism is not on the right track.

At another place:

But now I can well understand that you want to overwhelm me with a flood of questions and doubts, which must be answered and resolved before we can enjoy this first result of our efforts. I certainly do not want to press any hasty conclusions upon you. Let us coolly consider everything in turn.

What would you like to say?

Of course the audience is not actually to say anything. Freud goes on to badger it: "It is remarkable how little respect you have, in your hearts, for a mental fact"; "I regret to say that on this point I find myself in sharpest opposition to your views"; "Now you will break off here only to take up your resistance at another point." "Oh, so he must?," Freud answers another imaginary objection, "That is perhaps still open to question." He encourages his audience with spurious retreats: "Yes, this time you have lighted upon something formidable"; "Now you think you have me in a trap." He challenges it: "Well, if you like, give up the attempt. But if you are not so minded, you can accompany me." He lets them accept nothing uncritically, saying typically:

This technique is certainly very simple, nevertheless I am afraid it will provoke most strenuous opposition in you. You will say: 'Another assumption, the third! And the most improbable of all!'

Freud often scolds his hearers. "You are right in all the unessentials," he says, adding, "In regard to the main issue, however, you are wrong," or "On closer consideration you will admit that you are wrong." At other times he eggs them on: "You may think this a good opportunity to force me to make further reservations." Sometimes the debate is a stand-off. Freud asks:

Can I expect you to believe this exceptionally significant statement on the strength of two examples? No. But can you expect me to go on quoting examples to you until you declare yourselves convinced? Again, no.

On a few occasions, Freud addresses his hearers with real rather than mock humility, as when he admits:

You will certainly have judged the information that I gave you in the last lecture about ordinary nervousness as the most fragmentary and most inadequate of all my accounts. I know that it was.

At the end, he apologizes:

It is more than a conventional formula when I say that I myself am heavily oppressed by the many defects of the lectures I have delivered before you.

In symbolic terms, Freud's colloquy with the audience reflects an obvious ambivalence, the author going into agonistic form whenever he is of divided mind. Within his agonistic form, Freud is constantly aware of drama. He quotes G. Th. Fechner on "the stage whereon the drama of the dream is played out," writes a farce he calls "On the Ground Floor and in the Mansion" about infantile sexuality and social class, and compares the factors underlying neurosis with repertory actors. In rhetorical terms, however, the book is a highly effective device for catching, holding, and converting the audience, and Freud never forgets that he is on the lecture platform. The book begins with the rhetorical challenge: "I am bound to proceed as though you knew nothing of the subject and needed instruction even in its primary elements." At the end of a lecture, Freud will sometimes tack on a teaser for the next, such as: "At the next lecture we will see whether we can agree with the poets in their conception of the meaning of psychological errors." He rhetorically exaggerates his own reactions, as: "A shudder went over me as I heard the story, but I dared not draw the inference."

At times Freud carefully explains his rhetorical techniques, remarking:

You are right: this is indeed striking and requires an explanation. But I will not give it to you; I will rather guide you slowly towards the connections by which the explanation will be forced upon you without any aid from me.

Sometimes Freud is broadly ironic: "To occupy oneself with dreams, however, is not merely impractical and superfluous, but positively scandalous: it carries with it the taint of the unscientific and arouses the suspicion of personal leanings towards mysticism." At other times he tries frankness:

Well, I have not brought you here either to delude you or conceal anything from you. True, I announced that I would give a course of lectures entitled Introductory Lectures on Psychoanalysis; but it was no part of my purpose to show you an easy sequence of facts, whilst carefully concealing all difficulties, filling up gaps, and glossing over doubtful points, so that you might comfortably enjoy the belief that you have learnt something new.

Freud asks the audience: "Now do you think you can summon up courage to venture on the interpretation of a whole dream?" After trying one, he comments: "I really think that as yet we are not properly equipped for interpreting a dream and that we need further instruction and preparation first."

One of Freud's devices is to admit his audience into the conspiracy with him as fellow-victims of the world's scorn. He asks: "If our conception of the existence of any kind of unconscious is already regarded as fantastic, what will people say if we admit that to reach our solution we have had to assume two kinds?" Sometimes he takes the audience seriously, as when he writes: "I mention all these discoveries of new general characteristics of dreams in order to warn you against them, or at least to leave you in no doubt about my own opinion of them." When Freud returns to the lectures after a year's interval, he warns his audience:

I must tell you before I begin, however, that I cannot concede you the same attitude towards me as I did last year. Then I endeavored to take no step without being in agreement with your judgment; I debated a great deal with you, submitted to your objections, in fact, recognized you and your 'healthy commonsense' as the deciding factor. That is no longer possible.

He follows this with another kind of rhetorical consideration: "Although my intention is to conceal nothing from you and to gloss over nothing, I do not need to confuse you and stupefy you at the outset of our studies together." A few pages later he interrupts himself:

Now I must really stop and ask you whether all that I have been saying is not too obscure and complicated? Am I confusing you by so often qualifying and restricting, spinning out trains of thought and then letting them drop? I should be sorry if it were so.

Freud is soon back to his old tricks, however. When he reaches the subject of the perversions, he exclaims: "What distressing emotions these astonishing and grotesque revelations will provoke in you!" A few pages later:

I know that for some time you have been longing to interrupt me with cries of 'Enough of these monstrosities! The motions of the bowels a source of pleasurable sexual satisfaction exploited even by infants! Feces a substance of great value and the anus a

kind of genital organ! We do not believe it; but we understand
why children's physicians and educationists have emphatically rejected psychoanalysis and its conclusions!'

Freud even warns his hearers against his own rhetorical exaggeration.
He advises:

> You must not be led away by my eagerness to defend my-
> self against the accusation that in analytic treatment neurotics are
> encouraged to 'live a free life' and conclude from it that we influ-
> ence them in favor of conventional morality. That is at least as
> far removed from our purpose as the other.

At the end of the penultimate lecture, Freud sets up the last lecture
as a clincher. He explains:

> But now I will pause and let you take up the thread. I ob-
> serve that an objection is invading your thoughts with such vio-
> lence that it would deprive you of all power of attention if it were
> not given expression.

Freud gives their imaginary objection, then answers:

> What you charge me with in this way is exceedingly interest-
> ing and must be answered. But I cannot do that today, our time
> is up. Till next time, then. You will see that I shall be answerable
> to you.

The *Introductory Lectures* is extremely rich in metaphors, some
symbolic in that they are Freud's way of seeing the phenomenon, some
primarily rhetorical in that they are a way of explaining what he sees
in other terms. He says of his metaphors:

> Now I know very well that you will say that these concep-
> tions are as crude as they are fantastic and not at all permissible
> in a scientific presentation. I know they are crude; further indeed,
> we even know that they are incorrect, and unless I am mistaken,
> we have something better ready as a substitute for them; whether
> you will then continue to think them so fantastic, I do not know.
> At the moment they are useful aids to understanding, like Am-
> père's manikin swimming in the electric current, and, insofar as
> they do assist comprehension, are not to be despised. Still, I should
> like to assure you that these crude hypotheses, the two chambers,
> the doorkeeper on the threshold between the two, and conscious-
> ness as a spectator at the end of the second room, must indicate
> an extensive approximation to the actual reality.

Psychoanalysis, Freud tells his hearers, has "incurred the suspicion of
being a fantastic cult that wishes to build in the dark and fish in
murky waters." The mechanism producing slips of the tongue is like
a robber in the dark; concealment shows significance, as "when a child
will not open his clenched fist to show what is in it"; efforts to evade
the censorship are "spies and smugglers"; sexuality is "a well-organized

tyranny" in which one ruling family or another "has usurped all the power." Libido develops like a dicotyledonous plant, or like a prehistoric migration, or like the dorsal nerve roots of *Ammocoetes*, the fish Freud studied under von Bruecke; Freud comments, "Closer consideration will soon show you the weak points of these comparisons."

Neuroses have a double causation as children have two parents; fantasies are like "the establishment of reservations and parks in places where the inroads of agriculture, traffic, or industry threaten to change the original face of the earth rapidly into something unrecognizable"; excitations "play the part of the grain of sand which the oyster envelops in mother-of-pearl." In Freud's habitual imagery phobias are fortresses, libido is an amoeba, neurotics are like those who used to withdraw to the cloister, the unconscious is an apartment, narcissism is a stone wall, analysis produces a violent battle in the soul of the patient, transference is a battlefield or a key to unlock the closed doors in the soul. Freud describes psychoanalysis by contrasting simple mechanics with explosions, and plastic surgery with surgery. He develops his familiar analogy further:

> Psychoanalytic treatment is comparable to a surgical operation and, like that, for its success it has the right to expect to be carried out under the most favorable conditions. You know the preliminary arrangements a surgeon is accustomed to make—a suitable room, a good light, expert assistance, exclusion of the relatives, and so on. Now ask yourselves how many surgical operations would be successful if they had to be conducted in the presence of the patient's entire family poking their noses into the scene of the operation and shrieking aloud at every cut.

Concluding the last lecture, he says:

> Misuse of analysis is possible in various ways: the transference especially, in the hands of an unscrupulous physician, is a dangerous instrument. But no medical remedy is proof against misuse; if a knife does not cut, it will not serve a surgeon.

If Freud assures his audience that his metaphors "approximate to the actual reality," he also keeps warning them that they are metaphors. He says at one point:

> I hope you are not taking the expression 'censorship' in too anthropomorphic a sense, picturing to yourselves the censor as a stern little manikin or a spirit, who lives in a little chamber of the brain and there discharges the duties of his office.

Which is, of course, very much as Freud pictures it. Lecturing at the University and being a professor is clearly of great importance to Freud (afterwards his followers always referred to him as "Professor," never as "Doctor"). His real hopes for the series emerge in the statement: "It might be said of psychoanalysis that if you give it your little finger it will soon have your whole hand." Late in the lectures

Freud reveals that his conscious craft has not been entirely in control. In response to some hypothetical objections, he answers:

> Indeed, I cannot deny any of this or say that you are wrong. I am not so much in love with my powers of presentation as to imagine that every blemish in it is a peculiar charm. I think myself that I might with advantage to you have proceeded differently, and, indeed, such was my intention. But one cannot always carry through a reasoned scheme; something in the material itself often intervenes and takes possession of one and turns one from one's first intentions.

Some of Freud's comments on the perversions, for example, are obviously not rhetorical manipulations of his audience, but his own reactions. "But enough of these horrors!" he says at one point; "these mad, extraordinary and horrible things," at another. As he restrains the audience, we can sense Freud restraining himself, warning: "Indignation and expressions of our personal disgust, together with assurances that we do not share these appetites, will obviously not carry us very far." For Freud, there is an unusually strong sense of disquiet in the book: in the unconscious ("These censored wishes seem to rise up from a veritable hell"); in social organization ("Then there is all that unhappiness in life which we have included under 'frustration in reality,' from which all the absence of love in life proceeds—namely, poverty, family strife, mistaken choice in marriage, unfavorable social conditions, and the severity of the demands by which moral convention oppresses the individual"); and in history ("Think of the colossal brutality, cruelty and mendacity which is now allowed to spread itself over the civilized world").

The three major imaginative designs of the *Introductory Lectures* are subtly related. The first is Freud's earlier metaphor of the analyst as detective. He says:

> Or suppose you are a detective engaged in the investigation of a murder, do you actually expect to find that the murderer will leave his photograph with name and address on the scene of the crime? Are you not perforce content with slighter and less certain traces of the person you seek? So let us not undervalue small signs; perhaps from them it may be possible to come upon the tracks of greater things.

Some pages afterwards, the audience rhetorically asks him: "Well, but are you a judge, and is the person who commits a slip to be accused before you?" Freud soon returns to being a detective, finding "clues" and "signs." The second imaginative vision, also one he has used before, is of the analyst as a kind of detective in scholarship, a palaeographer. Freud writes:

> Practice and experience alone can determine the extent to which dreams can in actual fact be understood. My own opinion is that this is possible to a very great extent; and a comparison

of the results obtained by properly trained analysts confirms my view. It is well known that the lay public, even in scientific circles, delights to make a parade of superior skepticism in the face of the difficulties and uncertainties which beset a scientific achievement; I think they are wrong in so doing. You may possibly not all know that the same thing happened at the time when the Babylonian and Assyrian inscriptions were being deciphered. There was a point at which public opinion was active in declaring that the men deciphering the cuneiform writing were victims of a chimera and that the whole business of investigation was a fraud. But in the year 1857 the Royal Asiatic Society made a conclusive test. They challenged four of the most distinguished men engaged in this branch of research—Rawlinson, Hincks, Fox Talbot and Oppert—to send to the Society in sealed envelopes independent translations of a newly-discovered inscription, and, after comparing the four versions, they were able to announce that there was sufficient agreement between the four to justify belief in what had been achieved and confidence in further progress. The mockery of the learned laity then gradually came to an end, and certainty in the reading of cuneiform documents has advanced enormously since then.

The third image, new to Freud, is of himself as escape artist, a criminal Houdini who challenges the forces of law and order to bind and chain him, then bursts free. It is this that underlies all the arguments Freud writes for the opposition, some of them extremely telling. His characteristic tone is "Heap on more chains!," as when he writes: "First of all, we can make the case against our interpretations even stronger." When he is completely bound, there is a sudden tensing of his powerful chest and forearms, "Even this stronger argument falls to pieces," and the chains lie shattered on the floor. Freud is not only detective and judge but criminal, in a paradoxical world where the criminal connives in his temporary capture, the officers of the law in his escape.

In 1918 Freud published the last of the lengthy case histories, "From the History of an Infantile Neurosis," the famous case of the Wolf Man. The twenty-three-year-old Wolf Man had greeted Freud in 1910, Freud revealed to Ferenczi, with the genial offer to use Freud for anal intercourse and then to defecate on his head. By 1914, however, when the analysis terminated with the patient temporarily cured (he had several later relapses, one into a psychosis), the Wolf Man was so tractable that he asked Freud to write it all up. Freud comments:

> In spite of the patient's direct request, I have abstained from writing a complete history of his illness, of his treatment, and of his

recovery, because I recognized that such a task was technically impracticable and socially impermissible.

Freud therefore confines the case history to the infantile neurosis, which had ended thirteen years before Freud met the patient, consisting of a phobia about wolves at four, followed by an obsessional neurosis with ceremonials that included a compulsion to blaspheme and other interesting features. Freud explains in an introductory footnote:

> This case history was written down shortly after the termination of the treatment, in the winter of 1914–15. At that time I was still freshly under the impression of the twisted reinterpretations which C. G. Jung and Alfred Adler were endeavoring to give to the findings of psychoanalysis. This paper is therefore connected with my essay 'On the History of the Psychoanalytic Movement' which was published in the *Jahrbuch für Psychoanalyse* in 1914. It supplements the polemic contained in that essay, which is in its essence of a personal character, by an objective estimation of the analytical material.

Jung and Adler do at times seem to be more the subjects of the case history than the Wolf Man. Freud uses the case to demonstrate that Adler's will to power and "masculine protest" only mask deeper sexual motives, and to refute Jung's denial of the infantile aetiology of neurosis. "It is for this very reason, indeed, that I have chosen this case to report on," he writes. Freud's typical comment is: "But all the alleviations which the theories of Jung and Adler seek to afford us come to grief, alas, upon such paltry but unimpeachable facts as these." He adds a snarly footnote: "I did not require the contributions of Adler or Jung to induce me to consider the matter with a critical eye." The point of the Wolf Man is that he proves them both wrong.

The other problem that Freud uses to organize the case history is his old uncertainty whether a childhood event was real or fantasy. Here the event is not a seduction, but the Wolf Man's "primal-scene" memory of having, at the age of a year and a half, on a hot summer afternoon, witnessed the copulation of his parents, not once but three times, and in a fashion (which Freud delicately calls *"a tergo"* and *"more ferarum"*) which enabled him to observe their genitals. Freud introduces the account:

> I have now reached the point at which I must abandon the support I have hitherto had from the course of the analysis. I am afraid it will also be the point at which the reader's belief will abandon me.

Freud raises all the obvious arguments against the reality of the scene, and continues:

> Later on I shall carefully examine these and other doubts; but I can assure the reader that I am no less critically inclined than he towards an acceptance of this observation of the child's,

and I will only ask him to join me in adopting a *provisional* belief in the reality of the scene.

After assuming the reality of the primal scene for many pages, Freud switches to suggesting another possibility: that the Wolf Man witnessed the copulation of animals, probably sheepdogs, and displaced it onto his parents. "The scene was innocent," he concludes. Freud continues: "It is at once obvious how greatly the demands on our credulity are reduced." He then adds clinching information, that *whenever* his patients tell him of witnessing a primal scene it is always *a tergo*, the only fashion that will enable them to observe the genitals. and that they invariably recall interrupting it as the Wolf Man did, by soiling themselves and crying. "There is surely no need any longer to doubt," he concludes, "that what we are dealing with is only a fantasy, which is invariably aroused, perhaps, by an observation of the sexual intercourse of animals."

Having gotten us to this satisfactory point, Freud then backtracks: "This case history is not yet at an end; in its further course a factor will emerge which will shake the certainty which we seem at present to enjoy." The additional factor that eventually emerges is a memory of the Wolf Man's at the age of two and a half, of urinating at the sight of a serving-girl bent over to scrub the floor. Freud concludes:

> On these issues I can venture upon no decision. I must confess, however, that I regard it as greatly to the credit of psychoanalysis that it should even have reached the stage of raising such questions as these. Nevertheless, I cannot deny that the scene with Grusha, the part it played in the analysis, and the effects that followed from it in the patient's life can be most naturally and completely explained if we consider that the primal scene, which may in other cases be a fantasy, was a reality in the present one.

Whether or not such backing and filling is to the credit of psychoanalysis, it is certainly a fine dramatic way of expressing ambivalence, by coming out at different times for both sides of the argument. Freud begins "From the History of an Infantile Neurosis" with his familiar archaeology metaphor, talking of "descending into the deepest and most primitive strata of mental development." He concludes with the statement that the strongly bisexual Wolf Man had "a constitution which deserves the name of archaic," so that "his mental life impressed one in much the same way as the religion of ancient Egypt." Freud ends where he ended in *Totem and Taboo:* in the beginning was perhaps the myth, but he stubbornly prefers to believe in the deed.

———————————

T w o other papers followed the Wolf Man case in 1918. The first was another Contribution to the Psychology of Love, "The Taboo of

Virginity." Here Freud draws heavily on comparative anthropology, particularly the work of Ernest Crawley, who uses "terms that are hardly distinguishable from those employed by psychoanalysis." Freud finds a "general female tendency to ward off sexuality," and now a universal female "penis-envy." He writes:

> Now, upon this penis-envy follows that hostile embitterment displayed by women against men, never entirely absent in the relations between the sexes, the clearest indications of which are to be found in the writings and ambitions of 'emancipated' women.

He concludes that defloration is emotionally as well as magically dangerous, and that the deflowerer sacrificially takes on himself this enmity.

The other 1918 work is a lecture, "Turnings in the Ways of Psychoanalytic Therapy," delivered before the Fifth International Psychoanalytic Congress in Budapest, and published the next year. Its running theme is an elaboration of the familiar comparison with chemistry. Freud asks of psychoanalysis:

> Why 'analysis,' which means divellication and dissection and, by analogy with the work of chemists, suggests the substances they find existing in nature and bring into their laboratories?

He answers, "Because in an important respect there is really an analogy between the two." Freud then explains: "We point out to the patient these instinctual motives in his symptoms of which he has hitherto been unaware—just as a chemist segregates the fundamental substance, the chemical 'element,' out of the salt in which it had been combined with other elements and was thus unrecognizable." He continues:

> When we succeed in dissolving a symptom into its elements, in freeing an instinct from one concatenation, it does not remain in isolation, but immediately enters into combination again with something else.

Freud adds the footnote:

> Even in chemical analysis something very similar occurs. Simultaneously with the isolation of the various elements, which the chemist forces upon them, syntheses which are no part of his intention come into existence, owing to the liberation of the elective affinities in their substances.

He concludes the lecture on a related image of metallurgy: "It is very probable, too, that the application of our therapy to numbers will compel us to alloy the pure gold of analysis plentifully with the copper of direct suggestion." Freud phrases his recognition of the partial nature of metaphor like a proposition in geometry: "And the two objects in a comparison need only touch at a single point and may be entirely different from each other in all else." His account of the analytic relationship makes it precisely such a metaphoric contact between dissimilars. Freud writes:

> For I have been able, without affecting their individuality, to help people with whom I had nothing in common, neither nationality, education, social position nor outlook upon life in general.

In 1919 Freud published four papers, the first of them " 'A Child Is Being Beaten': A Contribution to the Study of the Origin of Sexual Perversions." This account of a common erotic fantasy admits that "at the present time theoretical knowledge is still far more important to us than therapeutic success," and without fully explaining the fantasy (which Freud was only able to do years later when he recognized its masturbatory content), took advantage of its relationship to the Oedipus complex to define the latter as "the nuclear complex of neuroses." Freud next published "The 'Uncanny,' " a scholarly exploration in applied psychoanalysis which follows the subject through a library of dictionaries and horror literature as well as case material, including a superstition of his own. Another essay, a preface to the anthology *Psychoanalysis and the War Neuroses*, contains a single striking image in which the war neuroses are shown trying to shout down Freud's theory of sexual aetiology, rather like Jung and Adler. Freud writes: "The traumatic neuroses and war neuroses may proclaim too loudly the effects of mortal danger and may be silent or speak only in muffled tones of the effects of frustration in love." It was followed by a second preface, "Psychoanalysis and Religious Origins," to Theodor Reik's *Ritual*. This repeats some of the *Totem and Taboo* material in more dramatic form, referring to what Freud was later to call the id as "the mental underworld," and again paralleling neurotic behavior with poetry, religion, and philosophy.

Two papers appeared in 1920. The first, "The Psychogenesis of a Case of Homosexuality in a Woman," explains sadly that homosexuality is extremely common, female as well as male, and almost impossible for psychoanalysis to cure, except in the rare cases where it can restore "full bisexual functions." The difficulty, the unwillingness to cooperate, Freud describes in vivid art-and-commerce metaphors. He writes:

> Situations like that of a proprietor who orders an architect to build him a villa according to his own tastes and desires, or of a pious donor who commissions an artist to paint a picture of saints, in the corner of which is to be a portrait of himself worshipping, are fundamentally incompatible with the conditions of psychoanalysis.

When he could get nothing resembling a positive transference, Freud broke off the treatment and advised the girl's father that if she tried again she should get a woman doctor. The other paper in 1920 is "A Note on the Prehistory of the Technique of Analysis," published semi-anonymously in a psychoanalytic journal over the signature "F." It begins with Havelock Ellis' claim that Freud's writings should be judged "not as a piece of scientific work but as an artistic production." "Resistance!" Freud answers sharply, habituated to attack in those terms and now unable to recognize praise. The essay goes on to discuss an early forerunner of psychoanalytic free association Ellis had dug up, a Dr. J. J. Garth Wilkinson, and counters with some forerunners of Wilkinson's, particularly Ludwig Boerne, whom "Professor Freud" was quoted as saying he had read as a child.

Freud's first book of metapsychology in the wider sense, *Beyond the Pleasure Principle*, was begun in 1919 and published in 1920. It centers in what Freud calls "this exquisitely dualistic conception of the instinctive life," as opposed to the monism of Jung and others. Like *Oedipus the King, Beyond the Pleasure Principle* is designed as a gradual revelation of its awful secret, with Freud taking full advantage of the mysterious "beyond" of his title. After explaining the "pleasure-principle" and its limitation by the "reality-principle," he hints in the last sentence of the first chapter at "a still more far-reaching limitation of the pleasure-principle." The last sentence of the second chapter hints even more sharply of "the operation of tendencies beyond the pleasure-principle, that is to say, tendencies which might be of earlier origin and independent of it." Finally, at the end of the third chapter, we learn that "repetition-compulsion" (an impulse to repeat the painful, which Freud had first discovered in 1915 in the behavior of his first grandson, Ernst) goes "beyond the pleasure-principle." It is as though Freud were slowly invoking spirits from the underworld, and he does in fact call repetition-compulsion "a pursuing fate, a daemonic trait in their destiny," and "this daemonic compulsion."

More than halfway through the book, after warning us that "What follows now is speculation, speculation often far-fetched," Freud suddenly confronts us sharply with his daemon: "The goal of all life is death." "The whole life of instinct," Freud continues, "serves the one end of bringing about death." Of the self-preservative instincts, he writes, "Even these watchmen of life were originally the myrmidons of death." Life consists of "detours to death." In this vision, the germ plasm, once perhaps a form of immortality, is now perhaps only "a lengthening of the path to death." In an infinitely poignant and suggestive phrase, the first protoplasm at the dawn of life "had death within easy reach." In an image that may have suggested Empson's villanelle "Missing Dates," with its ominous refrain "The waste remains, the waste remains and kills," Freud writes:

> Thus, left to itself, the infusorium dies a natural death from the imperfect disposal of its own metabolic products: perhaps all higher animals die ultimately from the same inability.

In another figure suggesting Hermes Psychopompos, Freud writes of "The instinctive forces which endeavor to conduct life to death." He concludes on "the most universal tendency of all living matter—to return to the peace of the inorganic world." This "nirvana-principle" is a third principle of mental functioning, along with the pleasure-princi-ple and the reality-principle. Freud never publicly gave the death-instinct a mythological name, as he named the life-instinct "Eros," but he named it often in conversation; it is that black Thanatos from whom Heracles wrestled Alcestis.

In *Beyond the Pleasure Principle*, for the first time, Freud breaks with the assumption of teleology that Darwin, Marx, and Frazer auto-matically assumed in their evolutions. Freud writes:

> The existence of a general impulse towards higher development in the plant and animal world can certainly not be established, though some such line of development is as a fact unquestionable. But, on the one hand, it is often merely a question of our own valuation when we pronounce one stage of development to be higher than another, and, on the other hand, biology makes clear to us that a higher development in one particular is often pur-chased with, or balanced by, retrogression in another.

He continues:

> Many of us will also find it hard to abandon our belief that in man himself there dwells an impulse towards perfection, which has brought him to his present heights of intellectual prowess and ethical sublimation, and from which it might be expected that his development into superman will be ensured. But I do not be-lieve in the existence of such an inner impulse, and I see no way of preserving this pleasing illusion. The development of man up to now does not seem to me to need any explanation differing from that of animal development, and the restless striving toward fur-ther perfection which may be observed in a minority of human beings is easily explicable as the result of that repression of instinct upon which what is most valuable in human culture is built.

Near the end of *Beyond the Pleasure Principle*, Freud writes: "I think this is the point at which to break off." He continues:

> I might be asked whether I am myself convinced of the views here set forward, and if so how far. My answer would be that I am neither convinced myself, nor am I seeking to arouse convic-tion in others. More accurately: I do not know how far I believe in them. It seems to me that the affective feature 'conviction' need not come into consideration at all here. One may surely give one-self up to a line of thought, and follow it up as far as it leads, simply out of scientific curiosity, or—if you prefer—as *advocatus diaboli*, without, however, making a pact with the devil about it.

"At all events," Freud writes, "there is no way of working out this idea except by combining facts with pure imagination many times in succession, and thereby departing far from observation." He con-cludes: "Where there are such good grounds for distrust, only a tepid feeling of indulgence is possible towards the results of one's own mental labors."

Freud's next book, *Group Psychology and the Analysis of the Ego,* was drafted in 1919, finished in 1920, and published in 1921. It is an odd flank attack on social psychology made by denying the distinction between individual and social psychology. Freud's old analogy of culture and neurosis from *Totem and Taboo* here becomes the statement that neurosis is the individual symbolic equivalent for the collective behavior of social institutions. Freud writes:

> If he is left to himself, a neurotic is obliged to replace by his own symptom formations the great group formations from which he is excluded. He creates his own world of imagination for himself, his own religion, his own system of delusions, and thus recapitulates the institutions of humanity in a distorted way.

Thus psychoanalysis becomes a kind of social psychology. Freud explains:

> In the individual's mental life someone else is invariably involved, as a model, as an object, as a helper, as an opponent, and so from the very first Individual Psychology is at the same time Social Psychology as well—in this extended but entirely justifiable sense of the words.

He rejects terms like "herd instinct" or "group mind" used by other social psychologists, although he is fascinated by the theory of Jones' best friend, Wilfrid Trotter, that "the tendency towards the formation of groups is biologically a continuation of the multicellular character of all the higher organisms." Eventually, Freud solves the problem by originating both studies in his earlier "Just-So Story": group psychology derives from the thinking of the primal horde, individual psychology from that of its old male leader.

What traditional social psychology neglects, of course, is the sex instincts. Freud explains that he might have avoided opposition by using a more genteel term than "sex," adding:

> But I did not want to, for I like to avoid concessions to faintheartedness. One can never tell where that road may lead one; one gives way first in words, and then little by little in substance too. I cannot see any merit in being ashamed of sex.

"A group is clearly held together by a power of some kind," he writes, "and to what power could this feat be better ascribed than to Eros, who holds together everything in the world?" In this affirmative mood, Freud describes the course of development of the erotic life of man as "astonishing," discusses hypnosis as a kind of love affair, and explains such collectives as the church and the army in libidinal terms. Freud's suggestion that the erotic ties of scientific groups might in the future replace these collectives shows that his mind is still not far from the emotionally-stormy history of the psychoanalytic movement, as do two other curious references. One is the old conundrum about St. Christopher, which Freud gives in both German and Latin: "Christopher bore Christ; Christ bore the whole world; Say, where did Christopher then put his foot?" The other, worked out with Rank, is an odd addition to Freud's origin myth, a myth of the primal artist, and Freud's self-image (as well as Rank's) in the heroic role is unmistakable. He writes of the situation after the horde father was slain:

> It was then, perhaps, that some individual, in the exigency of his longing, may have been moved to free himself from the group and take over the father's part. He who did this was the first epic poet; and the advance was achieved in his imagination. This poet disguised the truth with lies in accordance with his longing. He invented the heroic myth. The hero was a man who by himself had slain the father—the father who still appeared in the myth as a totemistic monster. Just as the father had been the boy's first ideal, so in the hero who aspires to the father's place the poet now created the first ego ideal. The transition to the hero was probably afforded by the youngest son, the mother's favorite, whom she had protected from paternal jealousy, and who, in the era of the primal horde, had been the father's successor.

Here epic father-slayer and scriptural father-slain merge, and Freud becomes the hero of his own epic poem.

Group Psychology was followed by a number of wide-ranging papers. "Dreams and Telepathy" was read before the Vienna Psychoanalytic Society and published in 1922. It is Freud's first public revelation of his occultism, although stated with such scientific caution as to constitute a fairly faint testimonial. (Freud had written and suppressed two earlier papers on the subject, which were not published until after his death.) He begins "Dreams and Telepathy" with the warning:

> You will learn nothing from this paper of mine about the enigma of telepathy; indeed, you will not even gather whether I believe in the existence of "telepathy" or not.

Freud admits that the material from which he is working "is very slight," that he himself has never had a telepathic dream, and that although he has had foretellings and forebodings, none has ever come true. After discussing a telepathic dream that had been sent to him, Freud writes: "It would be a great satisfaction to me if I could convince myself and others on unimpeachable evidence of the existence of telepathic processes, but I also consider that the data about this dream are altogether inadequate to justify any such pronouncement." The paper concludes:

> Have I given you the impression that I am secretly inclined to support the reality of telepathy in the occult sense? If so, I should very much regret that it is so difficult to avoid giving such an impression. In reality, however, I was anxious to be strictly im-

partial. I have every reason to be so, for I have no opinion; I know nothing about it.

The next paper, "Certain Neurotic Mechanisms in Jealousy, Paranoia and Homosexuality," shows Freud at the height of his literary powers. It begins like a novel: "Jealousy is one of those affective states, like grief, that may be described as normal." Freud's formulas for types of paranoid jealousy are capsule dramas, such as this: "As an attempt at defence against an unduly strong homosexual impulse it may, in a man, be described in the formula: 'Indeed I do not love him, *she* loves him!'" (Indeed, the whole of Joyce's *Exiles* is in that one.) A brief note written in 1922, apparently a sketch for a more extensive work, was published posthumously as "Medusa's Head." It makes the inevitable identification of the Gorgoneion with the female genitals, displayed "as an apotropaic act." That year Freud also wrote two encyclopaedia articles on "Psychoanalysis" and "The Libido Theory." The first is interesting for its offhand universalizing of the Oedipus complex, found "in every human being," and for its creedal listing of "The Corner-stones of Psychoanalytic Theory," of which Freud writes:

> The assumption that there are unconscious mental processes, the recognition of the theory of resistance and repression, the appreciation of the importance of sexuality and of the Oedipus complex—these constitute the principal subject-matter of psychoanalysis and the foundations of its theory. No one who cannot accept them all should count himself a psychoanalyst.

Freud now boasts that "analytic technique has attained a certainty and delicacy rivalling that of surgery," and that "analysis sets the neurotic free from the chains of his sexuality." The second article defines libido as "the dynamic manifestations of sexuality," and firmly distinguishes it from Jung's non-sexual use of the term.

Freud's jaw cancer first made its appearance in 1923. That year he published an historical reconstruction, "A Neurosis of Demoniacal Possession in the Seventeenth Century," working from a contemporary account of a pact with the devil made by a Bavarian painter named Christoph Haitzmann. He opens with a rhetorical paradox:

> Despite the somatic ideology of the era of 'exact' science, the demonological theory of these dark ages has in the long run justified itself. Cases of demoniacal possession correspond to the neuroses of the present day; in order to understand these latter we have once more had recourse to the conception of psychic forces. What in those days were thought to be evil spirits to us are base and evil wishes, the derivatives of impulses which have been rejected and repressed.

Eventually poor Haitzmann turns out to be suffering the consequences of the Oedipus complex, and Freud boasts that psychoanalysis is like the magical bow of Philoctetes; in the Freudian words of Sophocles:

"With these shafts alone can Troy be taken." A subsequent article, "The Infantile Genital Organizations of the Libido: A Supplement to the Theory of Sexuality," consists of supplementary material to the *Three Contributions*. Freud's account of infantile masturbation now makes it sound rather like dispassionate scholarship; the boy's penis, he writes, "never ceases to provide new problems for his epistemephilic impulse." The paper ends eloquently with female puberty: "The vagina become valued henceforth as an asylum for the penis; it comes into the inheritance of the mother's womb."

Freud's remaining 1923 paper consists similarly of supplementary material for *The Interpretation of Dreams*, "Remarks upon the Theory and Practice of Dream-Interpretation." He further develops the analogy of dreams to art, discussing a category of dreams "comparable to successful creative writings which have been artistically worked over and in which the basic themes are still recognizable though they have been subjected to any amount of rearrangement and transformation." A day-dreaming sequence is a "continued story (a novel in daydreams)." Having traced repetition-compulsion to the death instincts, Freud can now allow exceptions to the theory of wish-fulfilment. He writes:

> So far as I can at present see, dreams that occur in a traumatic neurosis are the only *genuine* exceptions, and punishment dreams are the only apparent exceptions, to the rule that dreams are directed towards wish fulfilment.

Eventually, traumatic dreams would turn out to be wish-fulfilments of Thanatos, and punishment dreams of a creature he was finally prepared to name in his next work.

The next book, published in 1923, is another venture into metapsychology, *The Ego and the Id*. In it Freud defines the ego, a familiar term in his writings, as the part of the personality dealing with the outer world. It is not equatable with consciousness, in fact, "not only what is lowest but what is highest in the ego can be unconscious." It *may* be equatable with the cortical homunculus of the brain, "the anatomical ego." The id (German *Es*, "it") is a term Freud borrowed from Georg Groddeck, who borrowed it in turn from Nietzsche. It is the "other," the primal mind out of which the ego and everything else develops. The third and equally-important part of the mind (although not, oddly enough, in the book's title) is the superego, which Freud had approximated as the ego-ideal or conscience as early as "On Narcissism" in 1914. The superego is another development out of the id, an irrational introjection of the voice of the parents, although in a mysterious passage Freud defines it as an inner rather than an outer representative. He writes:

> Whereas the ego is essentially the representative of the external world, of reality, the superego stands in contrast to it as the representative of the internal world, of the id. Conflicts between the

ego and the ideal will, as we are now prepared to find, ultimately reflect the contrast between what is real and what is mental, between the external world and the internal world.

The connections between these three sprightly entities (or nonentities) can of course best be expressed in metaphor. In its relation to the id, in an image borrowed from Plato's *Phaedrus*, the ego "is like a man on horseback, who has to hold in check the superior strength of the horse," and sometimes has to go where *it* wants to go. The ego courts the id, assuming the features of an erotic object-choice and saying: "Look, I am so like the object, you can as well love me." The ego submits to the superego "as the child was once compelled to obey its parents." In some cases the superego "displays particular severity and often rages against the ego with the utmost cruelty," or "rages against the ego with merciless fury, as if it had taken possession of the whole of the sadism available in the person concerned." In such cases the superego "often enough succeeds in driving the ego into death, if the latter does not protect itself from the tyrant in time by a revulsion into mania." At these times the superego is, "as it were, a pure culture of the death-instinct."

The poor ego is always caught in the middle. Freud writes:

Helpless in either direction, the ego defends itself vainly, alike against the instigations of the murderous id and against the reproaches of the punishing conscience.

He continues:

From the point of view of morality, the control and restriction of instinct, it may be said of the id that it is totally non-moral, of the ego that it strives to be moral, and of the superego that it can be hyper-moral and then becomes as ruthless as only the id can be.

In all of this, "the ego's position is like that of a constitutional monarch, without whose sanction no law can be passed but who hesitates long before imposing a veto on any measure put forward by Parliament." [1] The ego is the most miserable of monarchs, however. Freud continues:

From the other point of view, however, we see this same ego as a poor creature owing service to three masters and consequently menaced by three several dangers: from the external world, from the libido of the id, and from the severity of the superego.

His fullest account of the bedevilled ego is a blare of metaphor:

Like the dweller in a borderland that it is, the ego tries to mediate between the world and the id, to make the id comply with the world's demands and, by means of muscular activity, to accom-

---

[1] C. L. Barber reminds me that this is the familiar Shakespearian metaphor of "this little kingdom, man."

modate the world to the id's desires. In point of fact it behaves like the physician during treatment by analysis; it offers itself to the id as a libidinal object in view of its power of adaptation to the real world, and aims at attaching the id's libido to itself. It is not only the ally of the id; it is also a submissive slave who courts the love of his master. Whenever possible, it tries to remain on good terms with the id; it draws the veil of its Preconscious rationalizations over the id's Unconscious demands; it pretends that the id is showing obedience to the mandates of reality, even when in fact it is remaining obdurate and immovable; or throws a disguise over the id's conflicts with reality and, if possible, over its conflicts with the superego too. Its position midway between the id and reality tempts it only too often to become sycophantic, opportunist and false, like a politician who sees the truth but wants to keep his place in popular favor.

In the real world, however, the ego has the powerful ally it resembles. "Psychoanalysis," Freud concludes, "is the instrument destined for the progressive conquest of the id."

Freud published four clinical papers in 1924. The first, "Neurosis and Psychosis," announces itself as an application of *The Ego and the Id*. Freud writes:

> By applying it in this way we might also reap the advantage of turning away from the grayness of theory back to the ever-green realm of observation.

"Neurosis and Psychosis" repeats the book's basic distinction: neurosis arises out of a conflict between ego and id; psychosis out of a conflict between ego and the outer world. It then amplifies the distinction by finding some types of neurosis arising out of conflicts between ego and superego, calls for a study of ego psychology, and ends on a strong image of the mutilated ego. Freud writes:

> It is always possible for the ego to avoid a rupture in any of its relations by deforming itself, submitting to forfeit something of its unity, or in the long run even to being gashed and rent.

The next paper, "The Economic Problem in Masochism," distinguishes three types of masochism. They are "erotogenic," "feminine," and "moral," and rather oddly Freud says that he will limit his discussion of feminine masochism to men "for reasons connected with the material." Freud brings his types to dramatic life: "The true masochist always holds out his cheek whenever he sees a chance of receiving a blow"; sinful acts in the moral masochist "must then be expiated by the reproaches of the sadistic conscience (as in so many Russian character-types)." "The Passing of the Oedipus Complex" marks a major change in Freud's views by modifying his earlier absolute generalization. Now only "the majority of human children individually pass through the Oedipus complex," and in some cases their Oedipal wishes

then disappear permanently. Freud discusses the transition from
Oedipus complex to superego in charged language not too far from
that of the women's magazines: frustration "causes the love-lorn little
one to turn from its hopeless longing." The last paper, "The Loss of
Reality in Neurosis and Psychosis," having distinguished between the
two, reunites them as differing expressions of the id's refusal to bow
to necessity, *anangke*.

The publication of Freud's *An Autobiographical Study* in 1925
makes a convenient end to the period that began with the *History of
the Psychoanalytic Movement,* a period of war and postwar change
in the outer world, and comparable dissension and consolidation in the
psychoanalytic movement. The *Autobiographical Study* is surprisingly
impersonal, much more so than the *History.* In part, that is because
it was written for a volume of medical autobiographies, the emphasis
to be on professional rather than personal development. In large part,
however, its more impersonal tone reflects a substantial recovery from
the shock of the defections. Jung and Adler are dealt with moderately
and perhaps over-optimistically, Freud writing:

> The criticism with which the two heretics were met was a mild
> one; I only insisted that both Adler and Jung should cease to
> describe their theories as 'psychoanalysis.' After a lapse of ten
> years it can be asserted that both of these attempts against psy-
> choanalysis have blown over without doing any harm.

An Autobiographical Study reveals little about Freud personally.
Freud identifies himself, not as the "infidel Jew" of a later paper, but
with the flat statement: "My parents were Jews, and I have remained
a Jew myself." He remarks of his university days:

> Above all, I found that I was expected to feel myself inferior
> and an alien because I was a Jew. I refused absolutely to do the
> first of these things. I have never been able to see why I should
> feel ashamed of my descent or, as people were beginning to say,
> of my race.

One of the most revealing glimpses we get of Freud is his revelation of William James, whom he met at Clark in 1909, as a stoic ego-
ideal. Freud writes:

> Another event of this time which made a lasting impression upon
> me was a meeting with William James the philosopher. I shall
> never forget one little scene that occurred as we were on a walk
> together. He stopped suddenly, handed me a bag he was carrying
> and asked me to walk on, saying that he would catch me up as
> soon as he had got through an attack of angina pectoris which
> was just coming on. He died of that disease a year later; and I
> have always wished that I might be as fearless as he was in the
> face of approaching death.

For the first time, Freud publicly reveals his cancer, with the brief mention that "a grave illness warns me of the approaching end." In a 1935 postscript to the *Autobiographical Study*, he explains:

> Shortly before I wrote this study it seemed as though my life would soon be brought to an end by the recurrence of a malignant disease; but surgical skill saved me in 1923 and I was able to continue my life and my work, though no longer in freedom from pain.

Freud now refers to his theory of the primal horde as "the following hypothesis, or, I would rather say, vision." The book's concluding paragraph is equally moderate. Freud writes:

> Looking back, then, over the patchwork of my life's labors, I can say that I have made many beginnings and thrown out many suggestions. Something will come of them in the future, though I cannot myself tell whether it will be much or little. I can, however, express a hope that I have opened up a pathway for an important advance in our knowledge.

The end of the 1935 Postscript is less understated, and replaces the metaphor of cutting a path with a conclusion to the *History*'s metaphor of working down in the dark. Freud writes: "Nevertheless, the whole impression is a satisfactory one—of serious scientific work carried on at a high level." In his last years, Freud would briefly come out into the light.

Death Brings the Real Remedy

FREUD published half a dozen papers in 1925. One is a brief preface, "Psychoanalysis and Delinquency," to August Aichhorn's book *Wayward Youth*. It contains little of interest aside from Freud's statement that he accepts the old saw that there are three impossible professions—educating, healing, and governing—and that he has been too fully occupied with the second to know much about the first. Three long passages intended to be added to the next edition of *The Interpretation of Dreams* (although never in fact added) were published in Freud's collected writings that year as "Some Additional Notes upon Dream-Interpretation as a Whole." The first of them, "The Limits to the Possibility of Interpretation," shows Freud finally coming out from under the Stekel influence. He writes:

> This comment would not apply to someone who did without the dreamer's collaboration and sought to interpret dreams by intuitive insight. But dream-interpretation of such a kind, without reference to the dreamer's associations, would in the most favorable case remain a piece of unscientific virtuosity of the most doubtful value.

The second, "Moral Responsibility for the Content of Dreams," shows Freud still wrestling with the problem that concluded *The Interpretation of Dreams*, the guilt for his symbolic parricide. "Must one assume responsibility for the content of one's dreams?" he again asks. The answer is the same ambivalent reassurance. Freud writes:

> The ethical narcissism of humanity should rest content with the knowledge that the fact of distortion in dreams, as well as the existence of anxiety dreams and punishment dreams, afford just as clear evidence of his moral nature as dream-interpretation gives of the existence and strength of his evil nature. If anyone is dissatisfied with this and would like to be 'better' than he was created, let him see whether he can attain more in life than hypocrisy or inhibition.

The third supplement, "The Occult Significance of Dreams," returns to another favorite topic, telepathy, and this time comes out a little more boldly. "One arrives at a provisional opinion," Freud writes, "that it may well be that telepathy really exists." He admits that this is based on "experiments in my private circle," and concludes:

> In spite of the caution which is prescribed by the importance, novelty and obscurity of the subject, I feel that I should not be justified in holding back any longer these considerations upon the problems of telepathy. All of this has only this much to do with dreams: if there are such things as telepathic messages, the possibility cannot be dismissed of their reaching someone during sleep and coming to his knowledge in a dream.

Freud fortunately did not pursue the subject further.

The next paper, "The Resistances to Psychoanalysis," appeared in French in *La revue juive*. Its dualism is violently Manichaean in its account of the war between the forces of light, the psychoanalytic movement, and the forces of darkness, their opponents, who meet it with "outbursts of indignation, derision and scorn." The microcosm of this macrocosmic battle, and its motivation, Freud explains as the war within the personality between comparable armies. He explains in a parenthesis:

> These mutually opposing forces were described to begin with as the sexual instincts and the ego instincts. A later theoretical development changed them into Eros and the instinct of death or destruction.

Freud's metaphor of war extends to bloody revolution. He writes:

> Human civilization rests upon two pillars, of which one is the control of natural forces and the other the restriction of our instincts. The ruler's throne rests upon fettered slaves. Among the instinctual components which are thus brought into service, the sexual instincts, in the narrower sense of the word, are conspicuous for their strength and savagery. Woe, if they should be set loose! The throne would be overturned and the ruler trampled under foot.

In consideration of his special audience, Freud added one more dimension to the conflict, Jew against Gentile or anti-Semite. He concludes:

> Finally, with all reserve, the question may be raised whether the personality of the present writer as a Jew who has never sought to disguise the fact that he is a Jew may not have had a share in provoking the antipathy of his environment to psychoanalysis. An argument of this kind is not often uttered aloud. But we have unfortunately grown so suspicious that we cannot avoid thinking that this factor may not have been quite without its effect. Nor is it perhaps entirely a matter of chance that the first advocate of psychoanalysis was a Jew. To profess belief in this new theory called for a certain degree of readiness to accept a

position of solitary opposition—a position with which no one is more familiar than a Jew.

A brief paper, "A Note Upon the 'Mystic Writing-Pad' " is a single extended metaphor, unusually mechanist for Freud. Perceiving and remembering are not quite like making a note on a sheet of paper or a slate, Freud points out, but they are perfectly represented by the child's gadget for drawing and erasing that consists of a wax surface covered by sheets of waxed paper and celluloid. "On Negation" is a powerful account of the way repressed ideas first come into consciousness by being denied (the patient said the person in his dream was *not* his mother, so of course it was his mother). Only the affect remains unaltered. Denial thus becomes a form of affirmation, the negative is a mask for the positive, and we get an extension of the dream world into waking life in defiance of the categories of logic and reason.

The last of Freud's 1925 papers, "Some Psychological Consequences of the Anatomical Distinction Between the Sexes," was read to an International Psychoanalytic Congress by his daughter Anna. It makes a major alteration in Freud's theory, now seeing the female Oedipus complex as a secondary formation, preceded by a pre-Oedipal attachment to the mother and rivalry with the father. Freud introduces his account of the birth of the female castration complex, the girl's discovery that she lacks a penis, with the unconscious Freudian imagery that it is always amusing to find in his work; this analysis, he writes, "leads us into dark regions where there are as yet no sign-posts." [1] Freud's account of the boy's comparable discovery about girls is an extreme melodrama; it produces "horror of the mutilated creature or triumphant contempt for her." The little girl's reaction is calm and determined: she lacks a penis, wants one, and means to get one. From her special traumatic experience Freud derives differences of female character and personality. Jealousy "plays a far larger part in the mental life of women than of men," and in general women are inferior creatures. Freud concludes:

> I cannot escape the notion (though I hesitate to give it expression) that for women the level of what is ethically normal is different from what it is in men. Their superego is never so inexorable, so impersonal, so independent of its emotional origins as we require it to be in man. Character-traits which critics of every epoch have brought up against women—that they show less sense of justice than men, that they are less ready to submit to the great necessities of life, that they are more often influenced in their judgments by feelings of affection or hostility—all these would be amply accounted for by the modification in the formation of their superego which we have already inferred. We must not allow ourselves to be deflected from such conclusions by the denials

[1] How quickly Freud's innocence sophisticated the world! Thirty years later, Freudians were finding penis envy in the traditional female complaint, "I haven't a thing to wear."

of the feminists, who are anxious to force us to regard the two sexes as completely equal in position and worth; but we shall, of course, willingly agree that the majority of men are also far behind the masculine ideal and that all human individuals, as a result of their bisexual disposition and cross-inheritance, combine in themselves both masculine and feminine characteristics, so that pure masculinity and femininity remain theoretical constructions of uncertain content.

In 1926, when he was seventy, Freud published *The Question of Lay Analysis*, subtitled "An Introduction to Psychoanalysis." This pamphlet was occasioned by the prosecution of Theodor Reik for quackery under the Austrian law forbidding persons not medically qualified to treat the sick, and it constitutes an appeal for the modification or repeal of the law. Here for the first time the dramatic dialogue that had been covert in all of Freud's work, and which certainly represents a deep-seated ambivalence or split, becomes overt, and Freud writes the work as a Socratic dialogue between himself and a figure he calls the "impartial inquirer," apparently modelled on a high Viennese official. This antagonist begins in ignorance and scorn, remarking of psychoanalysis: "Then it is a kind of magic; you talk, and the patient's malady is blown away." He is soon revealed as intelligent and well-informed about most matters, although his mind is conveniently a fresh Magic Writing Pad about psychoanalysis. His insight sometimes enables him to get the better of the exchange, as when he says to Freud: "You are becoming aggressive, and I think you have been touched on a sensitive spot," forcing Freud into a franker admission than any flesh-and-blood opponent ever got from him: "If I seem aggressive, it is only my form of defense." When Freud strays, I. I. reminds him:

> This is getting worse still, and rather beyond me. You invited me to a discussion on whether laymen, meaning people not medically qualified, should be allowed to practise analysis. Why must we have these explanations of far-fetched and obscure theories, which I cannot find convincing?

When Freud complains that as an impartial inquirer he does not seem very impartial, I. I. seems hurt. He remarks:

> I am sorry to hear you say so. Your confidence in me seems shaken. Why did you not select someone else for the purpose?

Eventually Freud puts him to work summarizing psychoanalysis as far as he has learned it, which he does very well, kept in check by occasional remarks from Freud like "Gently—it is not so bad as that," but at the end he is still sharply critical of Freud's arguments and better equipped to attack them. Our final word from Impartial Inquirer, on the last page, is his comment on Freud's "*schnorrer*-fantasy" that "some American millionaire" will endow a corps of

analytically-trained social workers "to give battle to the neuroses."
"Aha, a new sort of Salvation Army!" he sneers, shuffling off into
the wings.

In *From Thirty Years With Freud*, Theodor Reik (whose misfortune had occasioned the book) argues that the dramatic form shows
Freud's scientific objectivity. Reik writes:

> This opponent and gainsayer is no stranger to us; he played the
> same part in Freud's earlier essays. He was not always personified,
> but he was always present. In all his works Freud anticipated
> objections, replied beforehand to arguments. This alternate
> examination and self-assertion was a sign of his strict self-criticism.

This would be more convincing if the impartial inquirer did not so
visibly function as a dramatic device, his role not to dispute the material but to strengthen it dialectically. As an aspect of imaginative
form, he is accompanied by Freud's usual troupe of metaphors. Freud
announces:

> We can only describe things in psychology with the help
> of comparisons. This is no peculiar feature—it is the same else-
> where. But we have to keep changing the comparisons, for none
> proves adequate for long.

Ego and id are now façade and structure, foreground and background,
bark and trunk, helm and screw, front and hinterland, and so forth.
Psychoanalysis is again a process of smelting out precious metal, or a
summoning-up of demons, or a path to a prospect with a beautiful
view. The imagery of war runs through the work, and a constant
sense of death. Freud's cynical comment on irresponsible and incompetent analysts is: "In the end, death brings the real remedy."
He makes fun of the German warning signs on high-tension wires that
read "To touch the wires is, because of danger to life, most strictly
forbidden," opposing them to the eloquent Italian notices: "Who
touches, dies." Ultimately, Freud's argument against the Austrian law
is a paradox: it is not lay psychoanalysts who are dangerous quacks,
but medical doctors who practise analysis without adequate training.
In short, nothing is what it seems, and although this quack is labelled
"Medical Doctor, Safe," in reality: who touches, dies.

The next year saw the publication of two papers. The first,
"Fetishism," explains the sexual fetish as a penis-substitute. "I hasten to
add," Freud writes whimsically, "that it is not a substitute for any
chance penis, but for a particular quite special penis that had been
extremely important in early childhood but was afterwards lost"—
the mother's. The second paper, "Postscript to a Discussion on Lay
Analysis," explains the pamphlet and its connection with the Reik case.
The charge against Reik was dismissed, Freud announces, but "I do
not believe that this was a result of my book." (It seems to have been
due to the fact that the complainant turned out to be unbalanced.)

What the paper does is extend the book's transvaluation of values, no longer defending the right of a lay analyst to be as good as a medical analyst, but boldly redefining the analyst's role so that a medical degree becomes irrelevant. The analyst now is a "secular spiritual guide," and his work is "spiritual guidance in the best sense of the words." Freud had come a long way since the days he spent stirring up the infernal regions and lancing figurative pus pockets.

Inhibition, Symptoms and Anxiety, written as early as 1925, appeared in 1927. It represents a considerable change of Freud's views, in reaction to Rank's theory of the importance of birth trauma, from the earlier theory that anxiety is caused by repression, to the more sophisticated theory that it causes the repression. Freud's tone at first is one of reluctant theoretical revision. He writes: "These are quite unwelcome complications for us"; "It is not pleasant to think of it, but there is no use in denying that I have repeatedly put forward the thesis"; "But I confess I thought"; "I supposed that I had recognized"; and so on. As the book goes along, Freud seems to recover his assurance. "This statement of mine is not incorrect," he writes of an old phrasing, "but superficial." He continues: "We now see that we need not dismiss earlier formulations as without value but have merely to bring them into line with our newer understanding." For the first time, Freud formally recognizes that some of his findings may be culture-bound. Discussing the neuroses of children, he adds the limitation, "so far at least as concerns upper-class urban children of the white race." Freud also returns to the concept of "defense mechanism," which he had discarded in favor of "repression" early in the century, now recognizing repression as only "one particular method of defense." [2] Freud begins the last section with the hope that "the diffident remarks which follow may bespeak critical indulgence."

None of this shilly-shallying extends to Freud's metaphors in the book, which are particularly bold. When an organ such as a finger or foot has acquired sexual associations, it behaves, Freud writes, "if we may hazard a somewhat scurrilous metaphor—like a cook who refuses to stay in the kitchen because the master of the house has embarked upon an affair with her." Freud's old friend little Hans, in the same sociological melodramatizing, becomes "a younger servant in a household who is in love with the mistress of the house and enjoys certain favors at her hands." The metaphors of war are so pervasive that for a stretch no page is without one. The ego and the id are "two opposing camps"; there are primary and secondary "defensive struggles"; hysterical symptoms are, "so to speak, frontier posts staffed from both sides of the border"; an ego with a symptom is like "a maimed war-veteran who had his leg shot away," now "peace-loving"; in the war against the repressed "the tide of battle turns increasingly against the repressing forces," and so forth. At other times Freud dramatizes these conflicts in a series of little playlets, so that we get typically:

[2] His daughter Anna's book, *The Ego and the Mechanisms of Defense*, later explored this new territory.

The superego behaves as if no repression had taken place, as if it were fully cognizant of the aggressive impulse in its true meaning and with its affective character undiminished; and it treats the ego on the basis of this hypothesis. The ego which knows on the one hand that it is innocent has on the other to experience a feeling of guilt and to carry a feeling of responsibility which it is unable to account for.

In Freud's increasingly paradoxical world, the familiar metaphor of illumination now becomes an oxymoron, illuminated darkness. "If we cannot see clearly," Freud writes, "at least we see the obscurities clearly."

Freud's next book, *The Future of an Illusion*, an attack on religion, was published in 1927. Like *Lay Analysis*, it is in the form of a dialogue with an opponent, but now the opponent is thoroughly familiar with psychoanalysis. The dialogue form appears at the beginning of the fourth chapter, when Freud suddenly interrupts his essay to write:

> An enquiry that proceeds uninterruptedly, like a monologue, is not altogether without its dangers. One is too easily tempted to push aside thoughts that would interrupt it, and in exchange one is left with a feeling of uncertainty which one will drown in the end by over-decisiveness. I shall therefore imagine an opponent who follows my arguments with mistrust, and I shall let him interject remarks here and there.

This antagonist uses his familiarity with Freud's writings to get in some telling blows, such as the charge that Freud has discarded his theory of the Oedipal origin of religion in *Totem and Taboo* for the more conventional theory of its origin in general human feelings of weakness and helplessness. Freud's answer—"In *Totem and Taboo* it was not my purpose to explain the origin of religions, but only of totemism"—is flatly untrue, and if Freud were a patient at this point we would say that he had become dangerously dissociated.[3] When the opponent charges that Freud's carefree demolition of religion will undermine ethics and is a piece of "purposeless cruelty," Freud can only answer that his remarks are "completely harmless and free from danger" because no one will be influenced by them. When Freud indulges in a utopian fantasy of a future freed from the superstition of religion, the opponent gets the last cynical word:

> That does sound splendid. A race of men that has renounced all illusions and has thus become capable of making its existence on earth a tolerable one! But I cannot share your expectations. And this, not because I am the pigheaded reactionary you perhaps take me for. No; it is because I am a sensible person. It seems to me that we have now exchanged roles; you prove to be the enthusiast, who allows himself to be carried away by illusions, and I represent the claims of reason, the right to be skeptical. What you have just

[3] Freud wrote to Ferenczi just before the book was published: "Now it already seems to me childish; fundamentally I think otherwise; I regard it as weak analytically and inadequate as a self-confession."

stated seems to me to be founded on errors, which after your precedent I may call illusions because they betray clearly enough the influence of your wishes. You indulge in the hope that generations which have not experienced the influence of religious teaching in early childhood will easily attain the wished-for primacy of the intelligence over the life of the instincts. That is surely an illusion; in this decisive point human nature is hardly likely to alter. If I am not mistaken—one knows so little of other civilizations—there are even today people who do not grow up under the pressure of a religious system, and they come no nearer your ideal than the others. If you wish to expel religion from your European civilization you can only do it through another system of doctrines, and from the outset this would take over all the psychological characteristics of religion, the same sanctity, rigidity and intolerance, the same prohibition of thought in self-defense.

Freud and his antagonist are not the book's only opponents. Everything is dualistic and shaped into antitheses. First we see the opposition between nature and culture, in which "every individual is virtually an enemy of culture," since it frustrates his natural instinctual wishes for incest, cannibalism, and murder. However, this frustration is really a benefit. Freud writes:

> But how ungrateful, how short-sighted after all, to strive for the abolition of culture! What would then remain would be the state of nature, and that is far harder to endure. It is true that nature does not ask us to restrain our instincts, she lets us do as we like; but she has her peculiarly effective mode of restricting us: she destroys us, coldly, cruelly, callously, as it seems to us, and possibly just through what has caused our satisfaction. It was because of these very dangers with which nature threatens us that we united together and created culture, which, amongst other things, is supposed to make our communal existence possible. Indeed, it is the principal task of culture, its real *raison d'être*, to defend us against nature.

In Freud's vision "nature rises up before us, sublime, pitiless, inexorable; thus she brings again to mind our weakness and helplessness, of which we thought the work of civilization had rid us." Beneath this dichotomy lies the deeper antithesis of life and death. Nature confronts us with "the painful riddle of death, for which no remedy at all has yet been found, nor probably ever will be." A valid *Weltanschauung* would reconcile to life and death equally, help one to "endure the troubles of life, the cruelty of reality." "And as for the great necessities of fate, against which there is no remedy," Freud adds, "these he will simply learn to endure with resignation." The only gods Freud recognizes in the book are Multatuli's twin gods, Logos and Anangke.

Ultimately, Freud's argument against religion is that it refuses to confront these dualities honestly. Freud asks of religious ideas: "What are these ideas in the light of psychology; whence do they derive the esteem in which they are held; and further, in all diffidence, what is their real worth?" He finds that the evidence for religious ideas is unsatisfactory and contradictory, and that we would not even believe that whales were mammals without better evidence (how characteristic of Freud to make his comparison an improbable *truth*). His answer to his first two questions is that religious beliefs "are not the residue of experience or the final result of reflection; they are illusions, fulfilments of the oldest, strongest and most insistent wishes of mankind; the secret of their strength is the strength of these wishes." "Thus religion would be the universal obsessional neurosis of humanity," Freud concludes. In another image (Marx's old image, in fact) religion is a narcotic. It is quite in keeping for "pious America," calling itself "God's country," to recognize that knowledge is the foe of religion and to have a monkey trial at Dayton, to prohibit alcohol to its citizens "and to satiate them with piety by way of compensation." Opposed to religion is an image of freedom, a vision full of "grandeur." This is not the free expression of instinct, a freedom to rape and murder, but a freedom to understand our natures and control them rationally for the social good. Freud's last word to his rhetorical opponent is that, while the latter is ultimately dependent on religious illusion, "From this bondage I am, we are, free." Freud's hope for his cause is an extraordinarily moderate one: "The voice of the intellect is a soft one, but it does not rest until it has gained a hearing."

F R E U D wrote nothing in 1928, the first such year in a quarter of a century. He published several significant papers, all written the year before. "Humor" is a reconsideration of the *Jokes* book, beginning with the admission that in that book, "I considered humor really from the economic point of view alone." As the book did not, "Humor" recognizes the humanistic affirmation of the subject. Freud writes:

> Humor is not resigned; it is rebellious. It signifies the triumph not only of the ego, but also of the pleasure principle, which is strong enough to assert itself here in the face of the adverse real circumstances.

Now in humor "one refuses to undergo suffering, asseverates the invincibility of one's ego against the real world and victoriously upholds the pleasure principle, yet all without quitting the ground of mental sanity, as happens when other means to the same end are adopted." As wit was the work of the unconscious in the book, humor is now recognized to be the work of the superego, but it is the superego at its most benign, the introjection of the good parent. Freud concludes:

> If it is really the superego which, in humor, speaks such kindly words of comfort to the intimidated ego, this teaches us that

we have still very much to learn about the nature of that agency. Further, we note that it is not everyone who is capable of the humorous attitude; it is a rare and precious gift, and there are many people who have not even the capacity for deriving pleasure from humor when it is presented to them by others. Finally, if the superego does try to comfort the ego by humor and to protect it from suffering, this does not conflict with its derivation from the parental function.

Freud's next paper, "Dostoevsky and Parricide," was first published as the preface to a volume in a German edition of Dostoevsky's works. It is one of Freud's most important literary analyses, but it is not itself very interesting for imaginative organization, and thus does not require much discussion here. Freud begins boldly with the statement that "Dostoevsky's place is not far behind Shakespeare," and that "The Brothers Karamazov is the most magnificent novel ever written." He describes Dostoevsky as a latent homosexual rather like his old case the Wolf Man (clearly, for Freud, the characteristic Russian personality) and does not spare the palette-knife in creating an unlovely portrait, but he always clearly and with great humility distinguishes the pathography from the art. "Before the problem of the creative artist," Freud begins, "analysis must lay down its arms." Before he is through, he admits, "We are laying ourselves open to the objection that we have abandoned the impartiality of analysis. . . . The objection is just." A brief essay, "A Religious Experience," was the remaining publication in 1928. Freud debunks a soupy religious experience, inspired by the corpse of a "sweet-faced dear old woman" on the dissecting-table, reported to him by an American physician. In the course of the paper Freud announces his famous self-identification, "an infidel Jew," and tells the American that his conversion is nothing more than surrendering to his Oedipus complex, "complete submission to the will of God the Father."

Freud's most important book in the last period of his life, *Civilization and Its Discontents*, was published in 1929. The day he finished it, Freud wrote cynically to Lou Andreas-Salomé: "While engaged in this work I have discovered the most banal truth." Three or four years later, however, he was enough impressed with it to tell H. D. (who describes the conversation in her beautiful *Tribute to Freud*):

> My discoveries are not primarily a heal-all. My discoveries are a basis for a very grave philosophy. There are very few who understand this, *there are very few who are capable of understanding this.*

It is true that Freud had known about the crippling burden of culture, and had written about it, since before the turn of the century. Now, after a decade of meditating on the death instinct, he faces it in its widest implications, with an impressive stoic acceptance. In Reik's words: "At times he seems even deliberately impassive when he is writing of

matters that rend every man at the heart." Everything that Freud has
to say in *Civilization and Its Discontents* arranges itself around his familiar dualities: culture and nature, life and death.

Freud begins his account of culture with metaphors of time and
space. Primitive feelings survive as evolutionary fossils, or like the
lower strata of an ancient city such as Rome. Freud's comment on the
first is "The analogy may be too remote"; he remarks of the second,
after trying it for a page or two:

> There is clearly no object in spinning this fantasy further; it
> leads to the inconceivable, or even to absurdities. If we try to rep-
> resent historical sequence in spatial terms, it can only be done by
> juxtaposition in space; the same space will not hold two contents.
> Our attempt seems like an idle game; it has only one justification:
> it shows us how far away from mastering the idiosyncrasies of
> mental life we are by treating them in terms of visual representa-
> tion.

"A town is from the outset unsuited for the comparison I have made of
it with a mental organism," he concludes. In *Civilization and Its Discontents* Freud comes close to admitting that his Primal Crime is an
essence he has temporalized into an origin myth. In a familiar dramati-
zation, he writes:

> Now, I should not be surprised if a reader were to cry out angrily:
> 'So it makes no difference whether one does kill one's father or
> does not, one gets a feeling of guilt in either case! Here I should
> think one may be allowed some doubts. Either it is not true that
> guilt is evoked by suppressed aggressiveness or else the whole
> story about the father-murder is a romance, and primeval man did
> not kill his father any more often than people do nowadays.'

Civilization or culture (Freud uses the terms interchangeably in
the book) is power over nature, but increase in this power seems to
produce no increase in satisfaction. Freud speaks of "profound long-
standing discontent" with civilization, and concludes that "power over
nature is not the only condition of human happiness." It is his intention,
Freud writes, "to represent the sense of guilt as the most important
problem in the evolution of culture, and to convey that the price of
progress in civilization is paid in forfeiting happiness through the
heightening of the sense of guilt." "Eros and Anangke," he explains,
"were the parents of human culture too." In his Freud Anniversary
Lecture, *Freud and the Crisis of Our Culture*, Lionel Trilling describes
this as "Freud's tragic sense of culture." Freud's appeal, in Trilling's
view, is ultimately to nature. Trilling writes:

> It suggests that there is a residue of human quality beyond the
> reach of cultural control, and that this residue of human quality,
> elemental as it may be, serves to bring culture itself under criti-
> cism and keeps it from being absolute.

Trilling explains that Freud's emphasis on biology is a liberating idea. He writes:

> It is a resistance to and a modification of the cultural omnipotence. We reflect that somewhere in the child, somewhere in the adult, there is a hard, irreducible, stubborn core of biological urgency, and biological necessity, and biological reason, which culture cannot reach and which reserves the right, which sooner or later it will exercise, to judge the culture and resist and revise it.

Freud's vision of nature in *Civilization and Its Discontents* seems at first wholly antagonistic. External nature, the harsh reality of life and death, brings no comfort. Inner nature, frustrated and guilty, seems hardly more promising. Yet the only true hope lies in the natural. The slim chance for happiness, Freud suggests, is "that way of life which makes love the center of all things and anticipates all happiness from loving and being loved." If Anangke is one of the parents of human culture, Eros is the other. If sexual love is socially fragmenting, it sublimates into brotherly love, which is not, although Freud shows it to be a very onerous demand. No love is pure, he says, going back to his deepest childhood experience, "possibly with the single exception of that of a mother for her male child." Returning to the reality of the body, Freud returns to a theme that had preoccupied him since 1905, the fact that the genitals "are hardly ever regarded as beautiful." He now makes them almost repulsive, writing:

> The genitals, too, excite the olfactory sense strongly in a way that many people cannot tolerate and which spoils sexual intercourse for them.

Now, however, we are saved by culture, in such defense mechanisms as repression, sublimation, and reaction-formation. Man the fire-maker is the victor over his own urethral erotism, as man the orderly and cleanly is the victor over his anal erotism. Salvation, in short, lies neither in nature nor in culture, and Trilling's formulation seems too limited. It inheres in the tension between the two, and in the swing back any time we swing too far in either direction.

In a famous and much-quoted passage, Freud writes:

> Life as we find it is too hard for us; it entails too much pain, too many disappointments, impossible tasks. We cannot do without palliative remedies. We cannot dispense with auxiliary constructions, as Theodor Fontane said. There are perhaps three of these means: powerful diversions of interest, which lead us to care little about our misery; substitutive gratifications, which lessen it; and intoxicating substances, which make us insensitive to it. Something of this kind is indispensable.

In this perspective, culture is not a tyranny but life-giving, and the instinctual hostility to it is opposed to life. Freud writes:

In all that follows I take up the standpoint that the tendency to aggression is an innate, independent, instinctual disposition in man, and I come back now to the statement that it constitutes the most powerful obstacle to culture. At one point in the course of this discussion the idea took possession of us that culture was a peculiar process passing over human life and we are still under the influence of this idea. We may add to this that the process proves to be in the service of Eros, which aims at binding together single human individuals, then families, then tribes, races, nations, into one great unity, that of humanity. Why this has to be done we do not know; it is simply the work of Eros. These masses of men must be bound to one another libidinally; necessity alone, the advantages of common work, would not hold them together. The natural instinct of aggressiveness in man, the hostility of each one against all and of all against each one, opposes this program of civilization. This instinct of aggression is the derivative and main representative of the death instinct we have found alongside of Eros, sharing his rule over the earth. And now, it seems to me, the meaning of the evolution of culture is no longer a riddle to us. It must present to us the struggle between Eros and Death, between the instincts of life and the instincts of destruction, as it works itself out in the human species.

The only alternative to turning the aggression outward is turning it inward against the ego, not as the loving superego that tells jokes but as the harsh, nagging superego that maddens and kills. (Franz Alexander would distinguish the former by Freud's old term "ego-ideal"). Freud asks: "Would not the diagnosis be justified that many systems of civilization—or epochs of it—possibly even the whole of humanity—have become 'neurotic' under the pressure of the civilizing trends?" Warning us against the seductive temptation of such analogies, he nevertheless proposes "the pathology of civilized communities" as a project for the future.

Thanatos is very much in the foreground of Freud's picture. He explains:

> The assumption of the existence of a death instinct or a destruction instinct has roused opposition even in analytical circles; I know that there is a great tendency to ascribe all that is dangerous and hostile in love rather to a fundamental bipolarity in its own nature. The conceptions I have summarized here I first put forward only tentatively, but in the course of time they have won such a hold over me that I can no longer think in any other way.

The ultimate vision is again of Manichaean conflict: "the eternal struggle between Eros and the destructive or death instinct." The best that Freud can hope for, in the powerful last sentences of the book, is a draw. He writes:

Men have brought their powers of subduing the forces of nature to such a pitch that by using them they could now very easily exterminate one another to the last man. They know this—hence arises a great part of their current unrest, their dejection, their mood of apprehension. And now it may be expected that the other of the two 'heavenly forces,' eternal Eros, will put forth his strength so as to maintain himself alongside of his equally immortal adversary.

(Four years later, even less optimistic, Freud added: "But who can predict his success and the final outcome?")

In 1930, in Freud's seventy-fourth year, his mother finally died, at the age of ninety-five, after long years of illness. Freud appeared to be much less affected than he was by his father's death so long before. He writes to Ferenczi:

Above all my warm thanks for your beautiful words about the death of my mother. It has affected me in a peculiar way, this great event. No pain, no grief, which probably can be explained by the special circumstances—her great age, my pity for her helplessness toward the end; at the same time a feeling of liberation, of release, which I think I also understand. I was not free to die as long as she was alive, and now I am. The values of life will somehow have changed noticeably in the deeper layers.

In 1930 Freud collaborated with Ambassador William C. Bullitt on a psychoanalytic study of Woodrow Wilson, still unpublished. He wrote little else that year, and only two papers in 1931. The first, "Libidinal Types," divides the possibilities into the erotic, the narcissistic, and the obsessional types, with a variety of possible combinations, including an erotic-narcissistic-obsessional type who would approach an ideal normality.

The other, "Female Sexuality," extends the conclusions of the earlier paper on the psychological consequences of anatomical differences into the pre-Oedipal phase in women. Freud's proud metaphor for his prehistory is that the discovery is "comparable in another field with the effect of the discovery of the Minoan-Mycenaean civilization behind that of Greece." In consequence of it Freud returns to one of the conventional ideas he began by repudiating, that hysteria is characteristically feminine (ah, Meynert!). Now the classic Oedipus complex is really only a male phenomenon. "It is only in male children," Freud writes, "that there occurs the fateful simultaneous conjunction of love for the one parent and hatred of the other as rival." By this time Freud had become somewhat snarly about analytic criticisms of his androcentric bias. He writes in a footnote:

It is to be anticipated that male analysts with feminist sympathies, and our women analysts also, will disagree with what I have said here. They will hardly fail to object that such notions have their origin in the man's 'masculinity complex,' and are meant to justify theoretically his innate propensity to disparage and suppress women. But this sort of psychoanalytic argument reminds us here, as it so often does, of Dostoevsky's famous 'knife that cuts both ways.' The opponents of those who reason thus will for their part think it quite comprehensible that members of the female sex should refuse to accept a notion that appears to gainsay their eagerly coveted equality with men. The use of analysis as a weapon of controversy obviously leads to no decision.

Freud refers to a variety of opinions on the topic by Helene Deutsch, Jeanne Lampl-deGroot, Melanie Klein, and Karen Horney, but he never mentions the more important female figure whose death had apparently again thrown him back into reliving his Oedipal phase.

The next year, 1932, Freud published his *New Introductory Lectures on Psychoanalysis*, seven lectures numbered serially to follow and supplement the *Introductory Lectures* of 1917. Freud explains in the Preface:

In contradistinction to them, these new lectures have never been delivered. My age has in the meantime relieved me of the duty of marking my membership of the University—even though the relation is only a peripheral one—by giving lectures; and a surgical operation has rendered me incapable of addressing an audience. It is therefore only in imagination that I picture myself once more in the lecture-room as I write out what follows; it may help me not to forget my duty to the reader as I delve deeper into my subject.

In the course of the work Freud gets almost carried away by the illusion of an audience. His closest friend in the analytic movement, Sandor Ferenczi, whom he addressed in correspondence as "my Paladin and secret Grand Vizier," had broken with him the year before, joining the great chain of betrayers: Breuer, Fliess, Stekel, Jung, Rank. For the first time Freud had no intellectual intimate in whom he could confide. When Freud interrupts a lecture to warn his audience that he is going to tell them a story, that "it will be long-winded," and then begins, "The story is this. One autumn day in the year 1919, at about 10:45 a.m. . . . ," the reader gets an uncanny sense of an audience.

Freud opens his first lecture with the announcement:

Ladies and Gentlemen—After a silence of more than fifteen years, I have brought you together again in order to discuss with you the new developments, or it may be improvements, which have taken place in psychoanalytic theory during the interval.

There is the familiar dialectic interplay, although now it is perhaps a little impatient. Freud writes:

That is a curious technique, is it not? It is not the usual way to treat a communication or an utterance. You guess, of course, that behind this procedure there lie concealed assumptions which have not yet been mentioned. But let us proceed.

Freud is still full of consideration for his illusory audience. Of one topic, he admits, "I do not know whether it will appeal to you in the same way as it appeals to me," and continues, "At this point I am quite prepared for you to ask scornfully whether our ego-psychology amounts to no more than taking abstractions literally." He admits to them that he cannot tell them something "because we ourselves do not feel that we have fully understood it." Later he expresses a polite wish that he has answered the earlier scornful question: "I hope you will by now feel that in postulating the existence of a superego I have been describing a genuine structural entity, and have not been merely personifying an abstraction, such as conscience." There are the familiar dramatic crises. Suddenly Freud interrupts:

'Stop!' you will exclaim, 'we cannot go so far as that with you.' You are right; I shall have to add something to what I have said, to make it seem acceptable to you.

His humility seems genuine enough. He writes:

I am afraid that this account will seem to you very difficult to follow, and you will guess that it is by no means a complete one. I am sorry to have caused you annoyance.

Freud summons up many of his familiar metaphors. There is the "powerful upward thrust" of the infantile wishes, with Freud working down there in the dark, "used as we are to the atmosphere of the underworld." We take the familiar walk that the *Interpretation of Dreams* developed: "Today we are to travel along a narrow path, but it may lead us to a wide prospect"; "we return to our starting-point"; when we come up from a journey underground "we have quite unexpectedly emerged into the open from the mental underworld." Mental processes are imaged in terms of monetary inheritances, so that the superego is "not merely the legatee of parental authority, it is actually the heir of its body." There are even a few pacific images of war: thought anticipates action "just as a general moves miniature figures over a map before setting his troops in motion"; the creation of the superego "is like introducing a garrison into a province that is on the brink of rebellion."

The rest of Freud's metaphors in the *New Introductory Lectures* are new, elaborate, and sometimes quite wild, reflecting the complex disorder of his subject matter. To justify a lack of neatness in his picture of the mental apparatus, Freud produces an image not unlike Darwin's tangled bank:

Let me give you an analogy; analogies prove nothing, that is quite true, but they can make one feel more at home. Let us picture a country with a great variety of geographical configurations, hills, plains and chains of lakes, and with mixed nationalities living in it. Germans, Magyars and Slovaks, who, moreover, are engaged upon a number of different occupations. Now the distribution might be such that the Germans lived in the hills and kept cattle, the Magyars on the plains and grew corn and vines, while the Slovaks lived by the lakes and caught fish and plaited reeds. If this distribution were neat and exact it would no doubt give great satisfaction to a President Wilson; it would also be convenient for giving a geography lesson. It is probable, however, that you would find a less orderly state of affairs if you visited the region. Germans, Magyars and Slovaks would be living everywhere mixed up together, and there would be cornfields too in the hills, and cattle would be kept on the plains as well. One or two things would be as you expected, for one cannot catch fish on the mountains, and wine does not grow in water. The picture of the region which you had brought with you might on the whole fit the facts, but in details you would have to put up with departures from it.

Freud's image for fragmentation of the personality is now equally elaborate. He writes:

Where pathology displays a breach or a cleft, under normal conditions there may well be a link. If we throw a crystal to the ground, it breaks, but it does not break haphazard; in accordance with the lines of cleavage it falls into fragments, whose limits were already determined by the structure of the crystal, although they were invisible. Psychotics are fissured and splintered structures such as these.

There is a violent new metaphor for the id: "We can come nearer to the id with images, and call it a chaos, a cauldron of seething excitement." More properly, it is an *ocean* of seething excitement, and Freud gives his Faustian slogan for strengthening the ego:

Where id was, there shall ego be. It is reclamation work, like the draining of the Zuyder Zee.

Freud's new metaphor for psychoanalytic diagnosis might be a metaphysical conceit. He writes:

Our diagnoses can very often only be made *ex post facto*. They are like the test for witch-finding applied by the Scottish king, of which I have read in one of Victor Hugo's books. This king declared that he had an infallible method for detecting witches. He put them to simmer in a cauldron of boiling water, and then tasted the soup. According to the taste he could say 'that was a witch,' or 'that was not a witch.' The same thing happens with us, except that it is we who are the sufferers.

Freud seems freer in letting his imagination go than ever before. "We are ready to believe whatever is made plausible to us," he writes, on the subject of occultism, adding:

Suppose we are dealing with the constitution of the interior of the earth. Admittedly we know nothing certain about it. We suppose that it consists of heavy metals in a molten condition. Now let us imagine that someone asserts that the interior of the earth is made of water impregnated with carbonic acid; that is to say, a kind of soda-water. We shall certainly say that it is very improbable, that it runs counter to all our expectations, and that it does not take into consideration the scientific data which have led us to put forward the metal hypothesis. But for all that it is not unthinkable. If any one shows us the way to prove the soda-water hypothesis, we shall follow it without any resistance. But now another person comes along who seriously asserts that the center of the earth is made of jam. We shall behave quite differently towards his theory. We shall say to ourselves that jam is not a product of Nature but of human cookery; moreover, the existence of that material presupposes the presence of fruit trees and their fruit, and we cannot see our way to placing vegetation and human cookery in the center of the earth. The result of this intellectual objection will be a diversion of our interests; instead of their being directed on to the investigation itself, as to whether the interior of the earth is really made of jam or not, we shall wonder what kind of man it must be who can get such an idea into his head, or at the most we shall ask him where he got the idea from. The unfortunate inventor of the jam hypothesis will complain that we are refusing to consider an objective evaluation of this theory out of what he calls scientific prejudice. But his complaints will be in vain.

"One does not expect any advances in our knowledge of pigeon-breeding," Freud writes, varying the metaphor, "from the tricks of a conjuror who produces pigeons out of an empty top hat." Sometimes Freud uses a startling oxymoron: "Poison is the nourishment that makes one ill." In a real flight of fancy, he finds the origin of plaiting and weaving in the attempt by women to create synthetic pubic hair. "If you repudiate this idea as being fantastic," he remarks genially, "I cannot of course defend myself."

By now, Freud's subject has openly become the whole complex richness of human life, rather than its psychological aspects alone. Consciousness is like life, he says, "it is not worth much, but it is all that we have." "Life is not easy," he remarks in another place. The last of the lectures is boldly entitled "A Philosophy of Life," and in it Freud concludes that psychoanalysis is in no position to create its own *Weltanschauung*, but as a branch of science can only subscribe to the general scientific *Weltanschauung*. Nevertheless, he does smuggle in a philosophy of life, and it is, as he told H. D., a gloomy one. Freud writes:

> It seems not to be true that there is a power in the universe, which watches over the well-being of every individual with parental care and brings all his concerns to a happy ending. On the contrary the destinies of man are incompatible with a universal principle of benevolence or with—what is to some degree contradictory —a universal principle of justice.

"Dark, unfeeling and unloving powers determine human destiny," he concludes.

———————————

OVER the next five years Freud produced half a dozen papers, several of them of the greatest importance. The first, "Why War?" in 1932, is a public exchange of views with Albert Einstein, sponsored by the League of Nations. The topic was set by Einstein. Although Freud has lost all the starry-eyed quality of the 1915 "Thoughts for the Times on War and Death," he still sees war as probably inevitable and perhaps even useful, since only war creates the larger units that might result in everlasting peace. After explaining the death instinct to Einstein, Freud writes:

> It may perhaps seem to you as though our theories are a kind of mythology and, in the present case, not even an agreeable one. But does not every science come in the end to a kind of mythology like this? Cannot the same be said today of your own Physics?

In the *New Introductory Lectures* Freud had referred to the instincts as "mythical beings, superb in their indefinitiveness." Later in "Why War?" Freud refers to "our mythological theory of instincts." The only real hope the mythologist can offer is the slow mobilization of Eros against Thanatos, and he recognizes the utopian nature of his hope. "An unpleasant picture comes to one's mind," Freud writes, "of mills that grind so slowly that people may starve before they get their flour." Freud's last word is, curiously, that "the lowering of aesthetic standards in war" is a major reason why "we pacifists" oppose it.

Another essay written the same year, "The Acquisition of Power over Fire," develops the vision from *Civilization and Its Discontents* of fire-making as the conquest of urethral erotism. Freud goes elaborately into the Greek myths of Prometheus stealing fire from the gods and Heracles killing the Lernean hydra, but since he has no idea how myths originate (he sees them as some sort of collective dream), he can only conclude hopefully:

> One has the impression that this approach might lead us quite a long way into the secrets of the myth, but, of course, we should not carry the feeling of certainty with us very far.

Freud's remaining 1932 paper, "My Contact with Josef Popper-Lynkeus," was written for a periodical commemorating the tenth anniversary of Popper's death. In it Freud explains his fascination with Popper, who discovered dream distortion about the time that Freud did, and praises him as a man so innocent and good as to live almost wholly free of repression.

During the next four years, Freud published little. He wrote much of *Moses and Monotheism* in 1934, but found himself unable to finish it.

In 1936, at the age of eighty, he published "A Disturbance of Memory on the Acropolis," a brief open letter to Romain Rolland on the occasion of Rolland's seventieth birthday. It tells of an odd reaction that Freud had had many years before, when he first saw Athens, introduced with the melancholy note:

> I am ten years older than you and my powers of production are at an end. All that I can find to offer you is the gift of an impoverished being, who has 'seen better days.'

The letter concludes:

> And now you will no longer wonder that the recollection of this incident on the Acropolis should have troubled me so often since I myself have grown old and stand in need of forbearance and can travel no more.

The point of the experience is that Freud had then felt guilt for excelling his father, who couldn't get to Athens. Now that Freud was, as he had called himself in a letter to Pfister some years before, "a travel cripple," he identified with the old man. The other paper published that year, "The Subtleties of a Parapraxis," is an analysis of a slip of the pen Freud made in arranging a gift for Lou Andreas-Salomé, which he attributed to his petty desire to keep the gift for himself. A slight production of two or three pages, the paper is nevertheless remarkable for the view it gives us of Freud at eighty still relentlessly scrutinizing his own behavior and motives, still engaged in the unsparing self-analysis he had begun in his youth.

In 1937 Freud published his last major paper, an amazing essay entitled "Analysis Terminable and Interminable." It is full of disillusionment. Freud for the first time admits that the effect of the reform in enlightening children about sex that he had called for many years before, and had seen achieved, "has been vastly overestimated." Such knowledge turns out to do the children no good. Freud writes:

> For a long time after they have been enlightened on these subjects they behave like primitive races who have had Christianity thrust upon them and continue in secret to worship their old idols.

With the same honesty, Freud asks the "deeply interesting" question: "Is there such a thing as a natural end to an analysis or is it really possible to conduct it to such an end?" He concludes that not only is analysis interminable, but that the analyst himself needs periodic reanalysis; "so not only the patient's analysis but that of the analyst himself has ceased to be terminable and become an interminable task." Analysis thus becomes a part of the organic process of living, rather than a means toward any such dramatic transformation as might be called "cure." [4] The only true termination of analysis is death. Freud had

---

[4] Freud had returned to the moderate hopes with which he began psychoanalysis. He had concluded the book with Breuer forty-two years before with the meagre promise to a hypothetical patient of "transforming your hysterical misery into everyday unhappiness."

made that point about incompetent analysis in *The Question of Lay Analysis*, but now he recognizes its wider application. Life and death are again very much in the foreground of the essay. "All that has once lived clings tenaciously to life," Freud writes. "In the psychical field," he concludes, "the biological factor is really the rock-bottom." Now death and life are inextricably intertwined, a Yang and Yin. Freud explains:

> It is not a question of an optimistic as opposed to a pessimistic theory of life. Only by the concurrent or opposing action of the two primal instincts—Eros and the death-instinct—never by one or the other alone, can the motley variety of vital phenomena be explained.

The year before, after his eightieth-birthday celebration, Freud had written to Stefan Zweig that he looked forward "with a kind of longing to the transition into nonexistence." In August of 1937, he wrote to Marie Bonaparte:

> I have an advertisement floating about in my head which I consider the boldest and most successful piece of American publicity. 'Why live, if you can be buried for ten dollars?'

Freud's metaphors in "Analysis Terminable and Interminable" are highly dramatic. Of speeded-up therapy, he writes:

> Probably it has not accomplished more than would be done if the men of a fire brigade, summoned to deal with a house set on fire by an upset oil lamp, merely removed the lamp from the room in which the conflagration had broken out.

In an analysis, infantile pathogenic material comes away "(the comparison is obvious) like sutures after an operation or small pieces of necrotic bone." One of Freud's metaphors is as elaborate as anything he ever attempted. Distinguishing repression from other defense mechanisms, Freud writes:

> I should like to make its relation to these other mechanisms clear by an analogy, but I know that analogies never carry us very far in such matters.
>
> Let us imagine what might have happened to a book at the time when books were not printed in editions but written out separately by hand. We will imagine that such a book contained statements which at a later time were regarded as undesirable—as, for instance, according to Robert Eisler (1929), the writings of Flavius Josephus must have contained passages about Jesus Christ which were offensive to later Christendom. At the present day the only defensive mechanism to which the official censorship would resort would be the confiscation and destruction of every copy of the whole edition. At that time other methods were employed to render the book innocuous. Either the offensive passages were

heavily scored through, so that they were illegible, in which case they could not be transcribed and the next copyist of the book produced a text to which no exception could be taken but which had gaps in certain places, probably making the passages in question unintelligible. Or, not satisfied with this, the authorities tried to conceal any indication that the text had been mutilated. They therefore proceeded to tamper with the text. Single words here and there were left out or replaced by others and whole new sentences were interpolated; at best, the passage was completely erased and replaced by another in exactly the opposite sense. When the book was next transcribed the text aroused no suspicion, but had, in fact, been falsified. It no longer contained the author's statement and very probably the correction was not in the interest of truth.

Without pressing the analogy too closely we say that repression is to the other methods of defence what the omission of words or passages is to the corruption of a text, and in the various forms of this falsification we can discover parallels to the manifold ways in which the ego may be modified.

Ultimately, Freud says, analysis is a process of strengthening the ego. It will be difficult or impossible if the instincts are strong and the ego is dislocated or crippled. "We shall achieve our therapeutic purpose," he writes, "only when we can give a greater measure of analytic help to the patient's ego." Freud concludes: "The business of analysis is to secure the best possible psychological conditions for the functioning of the ego; when this has been done, analysis has accomplished its task." The war is now on three fronts, and while Eros and Thanatos are locked in titanic combat, a third force, the mortal hero Self, can be nourished and strengthened for the battle.

Freud's last paper published in his lifetime was "Constructions in Analysis" in 1937. Its imaginative vision is a return to one of Freud's earliest metaphors, the archaeologist, but now with an amazing fullness. He writes:

His work of construction, or, if it is preferred, of reconstruction, resembles to a great extent an archaeologist's excavation of some dwelling-place that has been destroyed and buried or of some ancient edifice. The two processes are in fact identical, except that the analyst works under better conditions and has more material at his command to assist him, since what he is dealing with is not something destroyed but something that is still alive—and perhaps for another reason as well. But just as the archaeologist builds up the walls of the building from the foundations that have remained standing, determines the number and position of the columns from depressions in the floor and reconstructs the mural decorations and paintings from the remains found in the debris, so does the analyst proceed when he draws his inferences from the fragments of memories, from the associations and from the be-

havior of the subject of the analysis. Both of them have an un-
disputed right to reconstruct by means of supplementing and
combining the surviving remains. Both of them, moreover, are
subject to many of the same difficulties and sources of error. One
of the most ticklish problems that confronts the archaeologist is
notoriously the determination of the relative age of his finds; and
if an object makes its appearance in some particular level, it often
remains to be decided whether it belongs to that level or whether
it was carried down to that level owing to some subsequent disturbance. It is easy to imagine the corresponding doubts that arise
in the case of analytic constructions.

The analyst, as we have said, works under more favorable conditions than the archaeologist since he has at his disposal material
which can have no counterpart in excavations, such as the repetitions of reactions dating from infancy and all that emerges in connection with these repetitions through the transference. But in
addition to this it must be borne in mind that the excavator is dealing with destroyed objects of which large and important portions
have quite certainly been lost, by mechanical violence, by fire and
by plundering. No amount of effort can result in their discovery
and lead to their being united with the surviving fragments. The
one and only course left open is that of reconstruction, which for
this very reason can often reach only a certain degree of probability. But it is different with the psychical object whose early history the analyst is seeking to recover. Here we are regularly met
by a situation which in archaeology occurs only in such rare circumstances as those of Pompeii or the tomb of Tutankh-amen. All
of the essentials are preserved, even things that seem completely
forgotten are present somehow and somewhere, and have merely
been buried and made inaccessible to the subject. Indeed, it may,
as we know, be doubted whether any psychical structure can
really be the victim of total destruction. It depends only upon analytic technique whether we shall succeed in bringing what is concealed completely to light. There are only two other facts that
weigh against the extraordinary advantage which is thus enjoyed
by the work of analysis: namely, that psychical objects are incomparably more complicated than the excavator's material ones
and that we have insufficient knowledge of what we may expect to
find, since their finer structure contains so much that is still mysterious. But our comparison between the two forms of work can
go no further than this; for the main difference between them lies
in the fact that for the archaeologist the reconstruction is the aim
and end of his endeavors while for analysis the construction is
only a preliminary labor.

Freud writes at the end of the paper:

I am aware that it is of small service to handle so important a
subject in the cursory fashion that I have here employed. But none
the less I have not been able to resist the seduction of an analogy.

The individual delusions of patients, as well as the collective delusions of mankind, are like these analytic constructions, which in turn are like archaeological reconstructions. "They owe their power," he ends, "to the element of historic truth which they have brought up from the repression of the forgotten and primeval past." Ultimately everything is imaginative reconstruction of sherds, and we are all archaeologists together.

In 1931 Freud had confessed to Stefan Zweig that he had "actually read more archaeology than psychology." Eventually this passion for dredging up history from the past resulted in the last book published during Freud's lifetime, *Moses and Monotheism*. Freud had been working on it since 1934, when he wrote to Arnold Zweig:

> Faced with the renewed persecutions, one asks oneself again how the Jew came to be what he is and why he has drawn upon himself this undying hatred. I soon found the formula: Moses created the Jew. And my essay received the title: *The Man Moses, A Historical Novel* (with more right than your novel about Nietzsche). The material is divided into three parts; the first reads like an interesting novel; the second is laborious and lengthy, the third substantial and exacting. The enterprise foundered on the third section, for it contains a theory of religion which, although nothing new to me after *Totem and Taboo*, is nevertheless bound to be something fundamentally new and shattering to the uninitiated. Concern for these uninitiated compels me to keep the completed essay secret. For we live here in an atmosphere of Catholic orthodoxy. . . . And in addition to all this there is the feeling that the essay doesn't seem to me too well substantiated, nor do I like it entirely.

After some rewriting Freud published the first two parts in *Imago* in 1937, and the third part in 1939, after he was safe in England. It is his one thoroughly bad book, and one could wish that Freud's reluctance to publish had in this case been more powerful. The core of *Moses and Monotheism* is the paradox of the Family Romance, that Moses was not really the child of Jewish slaves in Egypt, but a highborn Egyptian; that is, the old joke that Pharoah's daughter found him in the bullrushes, "so she said." In a prefatory note to the third part, written while Freud was still in Vienna, he remarks:

> When I finished the last essay I said I knew full well that my powers would not suffice for the task. I was, of course, referring to the weakening of the creative faculties which accompanies old age.

(He had concluded the second part, "But I hardly trust my powers any further.") It is melancholy to observe that Freud was right.

The theory of Moses as an Egyptian follower of the monotheist Ikhnaton, who turned to the Jews when Ikhnaton died and the movement failed among the Egyptians, is intrinsically absurd, and Freud can do nothing to make it more credible. He has no understanding of the nature of myth, nor of its true relation to history. (See my discussion above, in the section on Frazer.) The ideas Freud produces to support his case, from a principle of phylogeny recapitulating ontogeny, to culture as "a sort of social contract," is merely the material of *Totem and Taboo* vulgarized. Freud admits to using the Bible "in an autocratic and arbitrary way," his slogan being "Draw on it for confirmation whenever it is convenient, and dismiss its evidence without scruple when it contradicts my conclusions." He excuses this practice with the argument that the text is very corrupt, and that everyone else does the same thing anyway. Freud defends his use of Robertson Smith's theories, admitting that they have been outmoded by later anthropology, with the childish argument:

> Above all, however, I am not an ethnologist, but a psychoanalyst. It was my good right to select from ethnological data what would serve me for my analytic work.

One of the problems is Freud's by-now-overpowering identification with the figure of Moses, who has become two separate historical Moseses in the book. Freud begins a section entitled "The Great Man" with the rhetorical question:

> How is it possible that one single man can develop such extraordinary effectiveness, that he can create out of different individuals and families one people, can stamp this people with its definite character and determine its fate for millennia to come?

Freud recognizes that the great man is a father image, and now this figure is described as looking suspiciously like Sigmund Freud:

> The decisiveness of thought, the strength of will, the forcefulness of his deeds, belong to the picture of the father; above all other things, however, the self-reliance and independence of the great man, his divine conviction of doing the right thing, which may pass into ruthlessness. He must be admired, he may be trusted, but one cannot help also being afraid of him.

"A terribly frightening old man," H. D. said of Freud, alternating love with awe. In a related manifestation, Freud's identification with Darwin becomes more overt. He writes:

> Let us take for an example the fate of any new scientific theory, for instance the Darwinian doctrine of evolution. At first it meets with hostile rejection and is violently debated for decades; it takes only one generation, however, before it is recognized as a great step towards truth. Darwin himself was accorded the honor of burial in Westminster Abbey.

At a few points in *Moses and Monotheism*, Freud does improve rather than vulgarize his *Totem and Taboo* material. He recognizes that the earlier book gave the impression that something that "in reality took centuries to achieve, and during that long time was repeated innumerably, had happened only once." Perhaps acquired experience is not inherited, only "a thought-disposition." If he is unwilling to renounce his Lamarckism, Freud *is* willing to concede: "Or at least I did not distinguish between the two, and was not quite clear about what a bold step I took by neglecting this difference." Freud concludes the book with his usual humility, writing:

> One cannot, however, reasonably demand or expect exhaustive answers of such enigmas. All that I can offer is a simple contribution, and one which should be appraised with due regard to the critical limitations I have already mentioned.

In 1938 Freud collaborated on several translations with his daughter Anna, including one of Marie Bonaparte's children's book about a chow named Topsy, and wrote his last book, *An Outline of Psychoanalysis*. Not quite finished, it was published posthumously in 1940. One chapter, left in the form of abbreviated jottings, was expanded by the editors. Freud opens the book with a curt Introductory Note, reading:

> The aim of this brief work is to bring together the doctrines of psychoanalysis and to state them, as it were, dogmatically—in the most concise form and in the most positive terms. Its intention is naturally not to compel belief or to establish conviction.
>
> The teachings of psychoanalysis are based upon an incalculable number of observations and experiences, and no one who has not repeated those observations upon himself or upon others is in a position to arrive at an independent judgment of it.

Much of the *Outline* is familiar material. One of its oddest features is Freud's return to believing in the reality of childhood seductions, which he had begun his science by repudiating. The focus, however, is no longer on the father. Freud now writes of "the sexual abuse of children by adults, their seduction by other children (brothers or sisters) slightly their seniors," as "common enough," and says of the figure of the mother: "By her care of the child's body she becomes his first seducer." The familiar metaphors once more appear: the dreamwork operates as "invading conquerors govern a conquered country"; the id behaves like "the non-commissioned officer who accepts a reprimand from his superior in silence but vents his anger upon the first innocent private whom he happens to meet"; the censor is again "that excellent fellow the night watchman"; and so forth. There are no important new metaphors, and only a few new ideas. The superego is no longer merely the introjection of the parental voice in the child, but now "takes over contributions from later successors and substitutes of his parents, such as teachers, admired figures in public life, or high social ideals." Freud is at last willing to accept Jung's name, "Electra complex," for the female Oedipus complex. He reaffirms his theory that "William Shakespeare" was a pseudonym for the Earl of Oxford (having publicly admitted it for the first time in the 1935 revision of his *Autobiographical Study*).

Freud's last two papers were also left unfinished. "Splitting of the

Ego in the Defensive Process," written late in 1937, remarks philosophically: "But everything has to be paid for in one way or another." "Some Elementary Lessons in Psychoanalysis," its title written in English, appears to be the beginning of a new attempt at an Outline of Psychoanalysis, but it ends after a few pages. Freud writes:

> But none of this implies that the quality of being conscious has lost its importance for us. It remains the one light which illuminates our path and leads us through the darkness of mental life. In consequence of the special character of our discoveries, our scientific work in psychology will consist in translating unconscious processes into conscious ones, and thus filling in the gaps in conscious perception. . . .

The manuscript breaks off there, at the heart of Freud's vision.

CONCLUSION

In some respects, the twentieth century is less attractive intellectually than the nineteenth. The entrenched enemy that Darwin, Marx, Frazer and Freud each battled in his own fashion, the bigoted ignorance and superstition that masks as religion, has survived their onslaughts and is apparently stronger than ever. It was Robertson Smith's dream, in his last years, to produce what his biographers call "a Dictionary of the Bible which should embody what he deemed to be the secure results of the labours of the Higher Critics." Smith died before he could do so, but two of his friends and followers, The Rev. T. K. Cheyne and John Sutherland Black, published the *Encyclopaedia Biblica*, dedicated to his memory, in the years from 1899 to 1903. This masterful work, which would be a classic in the history of thought if it contained nothing besides W. C. van Manen's article on "Paul," was meant to inaugurate a twentieth century of knowledge and reason, in the realm of Bible study at least. Instead, it is now visibly the end of something, a splendid monument to the nineteenth century's frustrated hopes for the rational intelligence. If one looks up a topic in the *Encyclopaedia Biblica* and then in such a work of our own day as the *Oxford Dictionary of the Christian Church*, published in 1957, it is as though the latter were published not sixty years later, but a thousand years earlier. All that a century of labor had painfully uncovered is once more buried under the sea of faith. The "secure results" of the Higher Criticism have become "curiosities" to the authors of the *Oxford Dictionary*. It is not that there has been a religious revival so much as an obscurantism revival, a disinterest in knowledge as a good in itself, perhaps a new failure of nerve. Where the ideas of Darwin, Marx, Frazer and Freud have been embraced by the church, it tends to be the embrace of the folklore witch, an embrace that castrates.

Apart from the influence of religious obscurantism, our century generally seems less interested in ideas than the last, seems to care about them less and to take them less seriously. Some of this is an unfortunate effect of the discounting Marx and Freud have taught us; it is so easy now to dismiss any idea as an ideology or a rationalization. Some of it is due to the fact that our sciences have become incomprehensible to the layman. Darwin's successors now write in genetic tabulations, Freud's in experimental statistics. The great twentieth-century revolution in physics inaugurated by Albert Einstein and Max Planck, at least as important as those we have chronicled, cannot be understood except in the dimmest and most general fashion without extensive training in science and mathematics. No layman can read Einstein's publications and agree or disagree, as he can with *The Origin of Species* or *The Golden Bough*. The fact that the true intellectual revolutions of our

427

century are going on behind the back, so to speak, of the humanisti-
cally-educated probably explains the popularity of such spurious historical lawmakers as Oswald Spengler and Arnold Toynbee, or such
intellectual shoddy as Immanuel Velikovsky's catastrophism or J. B.
Rhine's parapsychology. In some of our social sciences, particularly in
anthropology, the accumulation of data has become so overwhelming
that it can now be used to justify any generalization, and many anthropologists are so wary of any theory or law that they flee into atomism.

All four thinkers under discussion seem characteristically nineteenth-century (although Frazer and Freud did most of their work in
the twentieth century) because of their assumption of teleology. Even
Freud, who lacked the faith in the ever-onward-and-upward progress
of man that the other three shared, assumed without question an onto-
genetic teleology, a progress of the lucky individual to the ideal of
heterosexual genitality, productive sublimation, and ego capacity. Some
of the Freudian schismatics, in fact, sooner or later restored the phylo-
genetic teleology that Freud had bravely discarded. Adler writes in *Social Interest* in the 1930s: "The universal fact of the creative evolution
of all living things can teach us that a goal is appointed for the line of
development in every species—the goal of perfection, of active adaptation to the cosmic demands." It is precisely this secure faith in progress
toward an appointed goal that our century has lost. As Malcolm Cow-
ley demonstrates eloquently in his afterword to *Books That Changed
Our Minds*, we no longer make John Stuart Mill's assumption "that the
tendency of things, on the whole, is toward improvement," and we no
longer make it in large part because of what these nineteenth-century
thinkers, who did make it, have shown us. Helen Merrell Lynd writes
typically for our time in *On Shame and the Search for Identity* in 1958
that "the analogies based on the idea that evolution means inevitable
progress" are not "any longer possible for us." Where the nineteenth
century characteristically saw evolution, we characteristically see
only change.

In addition to their teleology, Darwin, Marx, Frazer and Freud
had many other things in common. Some are of the most trivial nature.
It does not particularly advance our insight into genius to discover that
they were all short-legged except Darwin (who was extraordinarily
long-legged), or that they all destroyed correspondence or manuscripts
at one time or another in their lives. Perhaps slightly more important is the fact that all four admired England, that sanctuary of the
free mind, and that all four died there, the two foreign-born as welcome (or in Marx's case, at least as unmolested) refugees from tyranny.
All but Darwin (who had never been there) loved France; Darwin's
preference for the Germanic was not shared by those who grew up in
it. (From his reluctance to return to *his* homeland, Scotland, we may
guess a similar antipathy in Frazer, but here as in a number of these
comparisons we lack adequate biographical information about Frazer.)
All four men were extraordinarily prudish even for their times and

cultures, and they wrote about sexual matters with various degrees of reluctance. All four were not only loving but faithful husbands, lifelong happily-married monogamists. All were unusually devoted fathers and grandfathers except Frazer, who was childless; deeply affected by the deaths of their own children and madly fond of children generally.

All four produced vast amounts of work, many thousands of pages in each case, despite crippling physical handicaps. There is some possibility, in fact, that the illness was essential. Marx writes in *Herr Vogt* of pain as an "antidote," and Freud, in a letter to Fliess, of "the moderate misery necessary for intensive work." If they required some ill health, these thinkers otherwise surrounded themselves with an impressive amount of creature comfort, including an ironclad schedule and the devoted care of a maternal wife and servants. The only one of them who experienced the seamy side of life, the pawnshop and the jail, was Marx, but even through the worst periods of poverty the Marxes had a servant, the loyal Helene Demuth.

Two characteristics are of particular interest and importance. The first is intellectual tenacity, held in varying degrees in proportion to the power of the formula used for discounting criticism and opposition. None was entirely tenacious, but where they were not they were lucky. Darwin, with no good formula for discounting any argument not obviously ignorant or bigoted, in the years after *The Origin of Species* fell away from his own ideas more and more into the Lamarckian inheritance of acquired characteristics. He was saved from undoing his own work by the fact that the world reacted to the first edition of the *Origin* and never noticed his later concessions, by the fact that his followers were purer in the faith than he, and by August Weismann's theory of the continuity of the germ plasm, which effectively saved Darwinism from merging with Lamarckism. Marx, with a fine formula for discounting every contradiction as the blindness of bourgeois ideology, fell away from his own faith only once, when he lost his faith in the revolution, around 1870. He was saved by the Paris Commune.

Frazer, stubborn rather than strong, deeply ambivalent, and with no machinery whatsoever for discounting criticism, changed his colors like a chameleon (as he acknowledged). He fully repudiated his great insight, and thus lost his chance to revolutionize thought on a scale comparable to the other three. Perhaps we can see Frazer best as an Engels who never found his Marx. Freud, with a formula for discounting, "resistance," as overpowering as Marx's, never fell away from his system in any major respect, once he got off the wrong road of confusing fantasy with experience. After revising his system so that it was stronger where it had been repaired, like a well-glued joint (it was this that Frazer could never do), Freud fell into only one un-Freudian heresy, Stekelian uniform dream symbolism, and this was a minor disease from which he recovered in his last years. All four men conceded to the world somewhat. Thus the 1859 edition of *The Origin of Species* is a better and stronger book than any later revision, the 1890 two-volume *Golden Bough* far outweighs the later enlarged editions, the 1899 *Interpretation of Dreams* is more persuasive than any later edition, and the first volume of *Capital* is enormously better than the later volumes.

The other important characteristic these writers share in varying degrees seems very close to the secret of their genius. It is a capacity for making their ideas a personal issue, for feeling themselves at stake, that resulted in peculiarly demanding personal relations and great vindictiveness toward deviationists. All, in short, needed what only Freud admitted to, the coexistence of a beloved friend who accepts and a hated enemy who rejects, preferably the same person at different stages in the relationship. For lack of information, we can only conjecture about personal factors behind Frazer's turnings. Freud's lengthy series of such cycles of love and betrayal has been explored above. Marx had the friend supremely and permanently in Engels, the enemy in Lassalle, Bakunin, and a hundred lesser figures. Darwin had something like an Engels in the combination of Hooker, Huxley, and Wallace. He had Engels' warmth of attachment in Hooker, his public battling in Huxley (who called himself "Darwin's bulldog"), and his self-effacement and even intellectual subservience in Wallace. If the gentle and inhibited Darwin never had a proper enemy, he nevertheless managed to have something like the whole Freudian cycle in Lyell, his earliest supporter and intellectual patron who infuriated him by never coming out publicly in support of the theory of evolution by natural selection.

The occasion of the death of a rejector is peculiarly revealing, as though its drama overcomes all repression. When Lassalle was killed in a duel, Marx, who had denounced him in the most vicious terms for a decade, was touched. He wrote to Engels:

> Lassalle's misfortune has been damnably in my head these days. He was, after all, one of the old stock, the enemy of our enemies. And then the thing came as such a surprise that it is hard to believe that so noisy, stirring, pushing a man is now as dead as a mouse, and must hold his tongue altogether.

But when Lyell died, that kindly man Charles Darwin was as cold as ice. He wrote to Hooker, expressing surprise at Hooker's grief: "I cannot say that I felt his death much, for I fully expected it, and have looked for some little time at his career as finished." And when Adler died, the unvindictive Freud was heartless. Like Darwin, he wrote to Arnold Zweig expressing surprise at Zweig's grief: "I don't understand your sympathy for Adler. For a Jewboy out of a Viennese suburb a death in Aberdeen is an unheard-of career in itself and a proof of how far he had got on."

T H E   influence and effects of Darwin, Marx, Frazer and Freud on the world can only be sketched in most superficially. There is general agreement that Darwin revolutionized not only biology, but the whole world of thought. "Psychology, Ethics, Cosmology were stirred to their foundations," Huxley wrote in 1885. The comparison generally made is with Newton. Darwin had himself made it rather modestly. As early as the 1837 notebook he compares the principle of natural selection to gravity, in its ability to subsume a great variety of phenomena under one law. A letter to Lyell in 1860 shows that Darwin had been reading a biography of Newton and had discovered several common factors in their situations, as does an 1868 letter to Hooker. Soon after the publication of the *Origin,* Wallace wrote to a friend: "It will live as long as the *Principia* of Newton." Thirty years later Wallace wrote in *Darwinism:*

> We claim for Darwin that he is the Newton of natural history, and that, just so surely as that the discovery and demonstration by Newton of the law of gravitation established order in place of chaos and laid a sure foundation for all future study of the starry heavens, so surely has Darwin, by his discovery of the law of natural selection and his demonstration of the great principle of the preservation of useful variations in the struggle for life, not only thrown a flood of light on the process of development of the whole organic world, but also established a firm foundation for all future study of nature.

Gerald Heard has made the same comparison (and added Freud) from the viewpoint of an opponent. He writes in *The Third Morality:*

> Newton banished God from nature, Darwin banished him from life, Freud drove him from the last fastness, the soul. It was all latent in Newton, in Descartes, in Galileo: mechanism would conquer all, once it had conquered nature, for man's body was sprung from nature and his mind from his body.

In biology since Darwin a few trends can be noted. Two props of Darwin's theory, developed by German zoologists, are the continuity of the germ plasm, popularized by Weismann, and Ernst Haeckel's theory that in embryology, ontogeny recapitulates phylogeny. Continuity has been challenged many times but never refuted, whereas Haeckel's recapitulation has been largely discarded, and in part replaced by its opposite, Walter Garstang's paedomorphosis (a resemblance of the adult descendant to the youthful ancestor, oddly anticipated by Darwin). The great modern readjustment of the theory of evolution by natural selection has been its integration with Mendelian genetics, after the simultaneous rediscovery of Mendel by three botanists in 1900. After brilliant experimental and mathematical work by W. Bateson, H. J. Muller, T. H. Morgan, J. B. S. Haldane, and others, this took final shape in Sir Ronald Fisher's *The Genetical Theory of Natural Selection* in 1930. Insofar as this synthesis is a modification of Darwinism, or neo-Darwinism, it is principally a recognition that natural selection operates by altering the hereditary qualities of a population.

For the most part, Darwin's theories have been strengthened rather than weakened by later scientific discovery. His theory of the origin of coral reefs seems to have been confirmed by borings, his general evolutionary theory has been greatly strengthened by immense progress in palaeontology (we now have whole fossil sequences), embryology, and other sciences. An evolution so rapid as to be visible in a lifetime, the phenomenon of melanism in British moths, has been discovered. Even Darwin's wildest theory, Pangenesis, is now recognized as an anticipation of modern cytology and taken seriously by geneticists (see p. 45 above). Reaction to Darwinism has somewhat divided by field. Thus botanists have tended to emphasize mutation rather than gradual modification, since they see the successful survival of radical mutations, while zoologists have tended to reject mutation, since their radical mutations are freaks that rarely survive and reproduce successfully. For the same reason geologists, with their still longer time perspective, have tended to be more sympathetic to Darwin's theory of the origin of coral reefs than zoologists. As the essence of Darwin's emphasis on slow-and-steady-wins-the-race is a temperamental expression, perhaps the reaction to ideas is temperamental too, and the more impetuous types prefer mutation theories (perhaps they *become* botanists for that reason, the less impetuous become zoologists, and the least impetuous, geologists). The most characteristic change between nineteenth and twentieth-century Darwinism (at least this one seems to be to our credit) is that its imagery has become pacific. In his foreword to *Evolution by Natural Selection,* a centenary reissue of the Darwin-Wallace statement of 1858 and Darwin's earlier drafts, Sir Gavin de Beer writes:

> In general, however, the 'struggle for existence' is wrongly pictured as nothing but a tooth-and-claw skin-game, for selection is mostly a matter of genes, competition between enzymes, and ecological efficiency, at the level of ions and molecules.

If Darwin's essential vision was of struggle and competition, he also saw combination, collaboration, and mutual aid in nature. In discussing the sociological or ethical applications of evolution by natural selection, there has been a tendency to see only the social Darwinism of Andrew Carnegie, that big-dog-eat-little-dog is natural and therefore right. Credit for this application is more properly Herbert Spencer's than Darwin's, although Darwin's son Leonard became a ferocious social Darwinian, according to Gwen Raverat's *Period Piece,* which quotes him as saying: "A man who can earn and keep money shows that he has the qualities essential to survival." Nor is it the only possible application, as Marx and Prince Kropotkin quickly realized. C. Bouglé writes in "Darwinism and Sociology," in *Darwin and Modern Science:* "Pessimistic and optimistic, aristocratic and democratic, individualistic and socialistic systems were to war with each other for years by casting scraps of Darwinism at each others' heads." Darwin's influence on literature has been similarly multiverse. If Darwinism first appeared in literature in the naturalism of Zola, the despair of Hardy, and the bleak determinism of Frank Norris, Jack London, and Theodore Dreiser, we can see a later humanistic and imaginative fiction that is equally Darwinian in such writers as William Golding in England and Bernard Malamud in the United States.

THE consequences of Karl Marx have been overwhelming. The Bolshevik revolution in Russia, and its sequels in Eastern Europe and Asia, have all been made in Marx's name, although what he would have thought of them is uncertain. The history of Marxist socialism and communism is too vast a subject for discussion here, and its literature alone is a life study. In our terms, Leninism is the taking-literally of metaphor, the concretization of imaginative vision into history, on the order of Christianity. There is no doubt that Marx wanted and demanded it, although that does not guarantee his delight in the result. Lenin's idea of revolution by a trained conspiratorial Communist party, inaugurating the dictatorship of the proletariat, is clearly implied in *The Communist Manifesto*, although Marx seems to have discarded it as impractical after 1850. Rather like mutation theory in biology, the Russian revolution was a triumph of saltation, violating Marx's rule of orderly progress through the necessary stages of historical development, advanced industrial capitalism being the last. In the final years of his life, in the preface to the Russian edition of the *Manifesto* in 1882, Marx formulated for some of his Russian followers the beginnings of a doctrine of Russian exceptionalism, based on the primitive Russian peasant commune, the *mir*.

With the Chinese revolution and agrarian communism, saltation has become even more pronounced, and Leninism and Maoism are thus truly neo-Marxisms, as much so as the mild deviationism of Polish and Hungarian communism, and the radical deviationism of Yugoslav communism. However much communism in practice differs from Marx's prescriptions, its ultimate appeal is always to his name (although Lenin often leaned toward Engels), and the sacred text is *Capital*. Berlin writes of *Capital:*

> It became the central objective of attack and defense. All subsequent forms of socialism hereafter defined themselves in terms of their attitude to the positions taken in it, and were understood and classified by their resemblance to it. After a brief period of obscurity, its fame began to grow and reached an extraordinary height. It acquired a symbolic significance beyond anything written since the age of faith. It has been blindly worshipped,

and blindly hated, by millions who have not read a line of it, or have read without understanding its obscure and tortuous prose. In its name revolutions were made; the counter-revolutions which followed concentrated upon its suppression as the most potent and insidious of the enemy's weapons. A new social order has been established which professes its principles and sees in it the final and unalterable expression of its faith. It has called into existence an army of interpreters and casuists, whose unceasing labours for nearly three-quarters of a century have buried it beneath a mountain of commentary, which has outgrown in influence the sacred text itself.

Marx's brutal and vitriolic polemic style, reinforced by Lenin's example in *Materialism and Empirio-Criticism* in 1909, has become the official communist prose style. Two decades earlier, Lenin wrote:

> The 'system of Marx' has a 'polemical character' not because it is 'tendentious,' but because it accurately portrays the theory of all the contradictions that exist in life. Therefore, incidentally, all attempts to assimilate the 'system of Marx' without assimilating its 'polemical character' remain and will remain unsuccessful: the 'polemical character' of the system is only the accurate reflection of the 'polemical character' of capitalism itself.

If the modern communist movement derives almost entirely from Marx, the modern democratic socialist movement derives from a combination of Marx and the independent tradition of Lassalle and British Fabianism. It began with the revisionism of the German Social Democrat Eduard Bernstein, whose book *Evolutionary Socialism*, published in 1899, is its manifesto. With the Russian revolution, the European socialist movement split into reformist parties along Bernstein's lines, who remained in the Second or Socialist International, and revolutionary parties along Leninist lines, who formed the Third. Scandinavian social democratic parties, the British Labour Party, and many others have at various times held governmental power, and have instituted such socialist measures as nationalization and confiscatory taxation. Other socialist measures have come into being where the socialist party was part of a governing coalition, or in opposition, or even tiny and powerless, as during Roosevelt's New Deal. In short, Marx's vision has considerably changed the world.

Beyond the confines of those calling themselves Marxists, Marx's ideas have been principally influential in historical theory and sociology. His economics has been generally discarded, and his philosophy quickly went out of fashion. The study of history, however, has been fundamentally altered by Marx's emphasis on material production and the struggle of classes, and it can never return to some of its earlier innocence. As for sociology, Marx is as much its creator as Comte, who named it. *Capital* is one of the great pioneering works in historical sociology, the history of social institutions, and Marx's stated intention in it was to found a science of society. He is equally a pioneer in the sociology of knowledge, where his insights were developed by Karl Mannheim and others. Some of these influential texts have been collected in *Karl Marx: Selected Writings in Sociology and Social Philosophy*, edited by T. B. Bottomore and Maximilien Rubel in 1956. From the generation of Emile Durkheim and Max Weber to that of Talcott Parsons and Robert Merton, sociologists are the sometimes-unwilling heirs of Marx.

In recent years there has been an attempt to rescue Marx and Engels from the Marxists, to see them as humanistic philosophers, moral preachers, even traditional Biblical prophetic voices. In *Science and Society*'s *A Centenary of Marxism* in 1948, the anthropologist Bernhard J. Stern dismissed Engels' *Origin of the Family* as anthropology to praise it as exhortation, "without doubt one of the most influential documents on behalf of the emancipation of women in the world's literature." With Engels, this has concentrated on his writings after Marx's death; with Marx, it emphasizes the young philosopher of alienation of 1844 and 1845, who rooted communist philosophy in love for mankind, and whose stated goal was the enrichment of human existence. Something of Marx's combination of humanism and intellectual rigor has been continued by such communist thinkers as Antonio Gramsci, the founder of the Italian Communist party, Georg Lucács, the Hungarian philosopher and critic, and Christopher Caudwell, the brilliant young English critic who died in the Spanish Civil War. Outside the Communist party, a line of French intellectuals has continued to take Marxist humanism seriously: Romain Rolland and Henri Barbusse, then André Malraux, then Jean Paul Sartre and Albert Camus, now such writers as Pierre Bigo, whose *Marxisme et Humanisme* in 1953 presented *Capital* as existentialist analysis.[1]

In England and America, the widespread Marxism of the 1930s produced little intellectual rigor. Its politics was soft-headed and sentimental, where it was not worse, and its literature was mostly poor and dull. There were a few exceptions, chiefly the poetry of Auden, Spender, and Day Lewis in England. Perhaps the best literature to come out of Marxism is marginal and ambivalent: the early novels of Ignazio Silone and the short stories of Isaac Babel, both torn between the rival pulls of socialism and folk religion. The Russians may yet produce a literature that makes the Marxist "leap into freedom," but

[1] Since this was written, Erich Fromm has published *Marx's Concept of Man*, an edition of the philosophical parts of the *1844 Manuscripts* in a new translation by T. B. Bottomore, accompanied by a long introduction in which Fromm interprets the work as spiritual existentialism in secular language, akin to Meister Eckhart and Zen. Fromm points out that "in the last fifteen years there has been an extraordinary renaissance of discussions on Marx in Germany and France, centered especially around the *Economic and Philosophic Manuscripts*." In Germany it has principally been the work of Protestant theologians, he notes; in France, of Catholic priests and socialist philosophers.

they still seem a long way from it. Marx, who preferred Shakespeare and Attic tragedy, would probably not have enjoyed socialist realism.

FRAZER'S influence and effect on the world has slowly shifted from anthropology to other areas. When *The Golden Bough* was first published, it was generally accepted as a work of scientific anthropology, even, as G. P. Gooch called it, "perhaps the most notable contribution of the age to our knowledge of the human race." The first generation of British anthropologists, including many of the great field ethnographers, took it as the fount of theory in their field. Malinowski, who was inspired to become an anthropologist by reading *The Golden Bough*, called Frazer "The greatest anthropologist of our age." In "Sir James George Frazer: A Biographical Appreciation," written in 1941, he lists some others influenced:

> Ethnographic field-work for the last half century or so has been under the spell of Frazer's suggestions. The work of Fison and Howitt, as well as of Spencer and Gillen in Australia; the famous Cambridge Expedition to Torres Straits led by A. C. Haddon in collaboration with W. H. R. Rivers, C. G. Seligman, and C. S. Myers; the African work of Junod, Roscoe, Smith and Dale, Torday, and Rattray—to mention only a few outstanding names— were carried on under the spiritual guidance of Frazer.

In the next generation, in England and America, a series of reactions set in against all of Frazer's assumptions. One of its leaders was Malinowski himself, who was inspired and spiritually guided by Frazer but had begun to disagree with him as early as his first published writing, on the economic aspect of Australian totemism, in 1912 ("His inability to convince seems to contradict his power to convert and to inspire," Malinowski writes in his memorial tribute). Within a short time Tylor's evolution became unfashionable and was replaced by the Ratzel-Boas history of diffusion; Smith's cross-cultural comparison gave way to Bastian's more restrained comparison within a culture area; Mannhardt's induction from a mass of amputated facts was succeeded by a new concern (led by Malinowski) with traits in their cultural context. Frazer's old-fashioned rationalist psychology, his assumption that motive and purpose are self-evident, was outmoded by the work of another man *The Golden Bough* had fundamentally influenced, Sigmund Freud. (Frazer had always refused to read anything by Freud or his followers.) Where Frazer was not ignored, his approach was derided. Evans-Pritchard writes typically in "The Intellectualist (English) Interpretation of Magic" in 1933:[2]

[2] Evans-Pritchard at least had the grace not to deliver his attacks as his Frazer Lecture. Not so Henri Frankfort, whose 1950 Frazer Lecture, "The Problem of Similarity in Ancient Near Eastern Religions," is a disgraceful attack on Frazer and his followers.

The apparent futility of Frazer's analogy between science and magic is due to the fact that he sees both as modes of thinking and not learnt modes of technical behaviour with concomitant speech forms. If he had compared a magical rite in its entirety with a scientific performance in its entirety instead of comparing what he supposes to go on in the brain of a magician with what he supposes to go on in the brain of a scientist, he would have seen the essential difference between science and magic.

In recent years, with evolutionary theory again fashionable in the form of neo-Evolutionism, and cross-cultural comparison no longer shameful, there seems to be something of a swing back. Max Gluckman, one of the newer British anthropologists, in his 1952 Frazer Lecture, "Rituals of Rebellion in South-East Africa," pays tribute to Frazer's "deep insight" into the nature and function of primitive ritual, and concludes: "But the answer to all these problems lies in comparative research, and here we must always follow in Sir James Frazer's footsteps." Although he is careful not to identify it as anthropology, M. F. Ashley Montague has acclaimed *The Golden Bough* as "one of the great books of our culture written by one of the great scholars of our time." Margaret Mead, in her introduction to the anthology *Primitive Heritage* in 1953, calls for a restoration of books like *The Golden Bough* to anthropological reading lists. It seems unlikely, for obvious reasons, that Frazer's naive assumptions will ever return to favor or that *The Golden Bough* will ever again be taken for modern scientific anthropology, but when rituals of rebellion in anthropology departments die away, there is no reason why it should not have a secure place as an early classic in the field, as magnificent and defective as the pioneering field studies.

It is in areas outside Anglo-American anthropology that Frazer's influence seems both lasting and growing. Malinowski writes:

> The first and lasting contributions of the French School under the leadership of the dominant and domineering figure of Durkheim, and carried on by Hubert and Mauss, Lévy-Bruhl, Bouglé, and Van Gennep, are unthinkable without the inspiration and achievement of Frazer. In Germany Wundt, Thurnwald, K. T. Preuss and many others have built on Frazer's foundations.

Here we are well into sociology, where Frazer has been received more sympathetically. The sociologist Donald G. MacRae, writing in *A Century of Darwin* in 1958, argues:

> The case for Frazer—who like Spencer is rather under a cloud today—is too complex and technical to be argued briefly here. His use of the comparative method on an enormous scale can be faulted, though the fascinating detail it reveals and the charm of his Augustan style ensure that he is still read. His industry was truly Darwinian, and I believe that his success in subsuming vast masses of data under a few leading ideas was con-

siderable. Unfortunately the anti-evolutionary reaction, largely led by Malinowski, has resulted in neglect of Frazer's achievement. Such a reaction was not surprising, for hypothetical yet untestable evolutionary theories had multiplied endlessly in the early years of the present century. In rejecting these a new freedom was gained, but, alas, much that was solid in the work of a Frazer or a Westermarck was forgotten.

The English anthropological compilers and theorists who were either Frazer's disciples, like Edward Westermarck, Ernest Crawley, and Edwin Sidney Hartland, or opponents very much influenced by him, such as R. R. Marett and Andrew Lang, are mostly recognizable now as outside the field of anthropology, as folklorists or comparative religionists. In these areas, Frazer's influence continues strong, and one such Frazerian compiler, E. O. James, is still anachronistically producing Frazerian compendia in enormous numbers. As Freud's anthropologist, Frazer is still enshrined in psychoanalysis, where a comparable anachronism, Theodor Reik, is still engaged in turning out books like *Totem and Taboo*, all heavily indebted to Sir James.

It is in his original field of classical studies, however, that Frazer may have produced his greatest effect. In *Reminiscences of a Student's Life* in 1925, Jane Harrison recalls the overwhelming effect of *The Golden Bough*. She writes:

> The happy title of that book—Sir James Frazer has a veritable genius for titles—made it arrest the attention of scholars. They saw in comparative anthropology a serious subject actually capable of elucidating a Greek or Latin text. Tylor had written and spoken; Robertson Smith, exiled for heresy, had seen the Star in the East; in vain; we classical deaf-adders stopped our ears and closed our eyes; but at the mere sound of the magical words 'Golden Bough' the scales fell—we heard and understood.

In a radio address printed in *The Listener* in 1954, Gilbert Murray recalls essentially the same experience. He writes:

> I remember the shock, the combined shock of interest and perhaps of horror, with which *The Golden Bough* burst upon classical scholars like me on its first appearance in 1890. Of course it was not absolutely our first introduction to anthropology. We knew something of Tylor and Andrew Lang and perhaps Mannhardt, perhaps even of Robertson Smith's sacred camel which had to be eaten alive before sunrise. But Frazer, for one thing, overpowered us with his mass of carefully ordered facts. We had heard of 'the beastly devices of the heathen' but had not realised their great number and variety, had not understood the method which underlay their madness.

There is validity in Malinowski's final judgment, that more than anything else Frazer was in the line "of great humanists and classical scholars." In the work of Murray and the Cambridge ritualists—Harrison, Francis Cornford, and A. B. Cook—the influence of Frazer permanently transformed and revitalized the field of classics, and however much it may appear to have returned to its old deaf-adder ways in recent years (and Frazer was the first to swing back from his own insights), it will never be the same again. The application of these ideas from classical to medieval and modern literature by a brilliant series of literary critics—William Troy, Francis Fergusson, Herbert Weisinger, John Speirs, C. L. Barber and others—has given Frazer an importance in literary criticism at least equal to that of Marx and Freud.

In 1959 a new one-volume abridgement of *The Golden Bough*, *The* New *Golden Bough*, was published under the editorship of Theodor Gaster. It is a thoroughly misguided work, attempting to rescue Frazer as up-to-date anthropology by gutting his text, translating his clear and simple terminology into Gaster's opaque terminology, dismissing his theories, and bringing his references up to date. What we need is not a face-lifting of Frazer, but a machinery for better using Frazer in his own terms. Criterion should have published, not Gaster's revision, but the *best Golden Bough*, the 1890 two-volume edition, for what it is, an 1890 book. In addition, we badly need the publication of Frazer's correspondence, an adequate biography, and a single comprehensive index of all of Frazer's books.

The Golden Bough is not primarily anthropology, if it ever was, but a great imaginative vision of the human condition. Frazer had a genuine sense of the bloodshed and horror behind the gaiety of a maypole or a London-bridge-is-falling-down game, akin to Darwin's sense of the war to the death behind the face of nature bright with gladness, or Marx's apocalyptic vision of capital reeking from every pore with blood and dirt, or Freud's consciousness of the murderous and incestuous infantile wish. The key image of *The Golden Bough*, the king who slays the slayer and must himself be slain, corresponds to some universal principle we recognize in life. It caught the imagination not only of Freud and Bergson, Spengler and Toynbee, but of T. S. Eliot, and produced *The Waste Land*. F. Beck and W. Godin explain Soviet managerial mobility in *Russian Purge and the Extraction of Confession* by "the theory of the grove of Aricia"; John McNulty in a newspaper column sees a prize ring at Madison Square Garden as the sacred wood at Nemi.

In his address on the occasion of the foundation of the Frazer Lectureship in 1921, A. E. Housman spoke of Frazer as though he were comparable to a psychoanalyst, dragging the repressed past back into consciousness. *The Golden Bough*, Housman said, has become a forest. He continues:

> There you have gathered together, for the admonition of a proud and oblivious race, the scattered and fading relics of its foolish childhood, whether withdrawn from our view among savage folk and in distant countries, or lying unnoticed at our doors.

Gaster's foreword makes the comparison directly. He writes:

> Indeed, what Freud did for the individual, Frazer did for civiliza-
> tion as a whole. For as Freud deepened men's insight into the
> behavior of individuals by uncovering the ruder world of the sub-
> conscious, from which so much of it springs, so Frazer enlarged
> man's understanding of the behavior of societies by laying bare
> the primitive concepts and modes of thought which underlie and
> inform so many of their institutions and which persist, as a sub-
> liminal element of their culture, in their traditional folk customs.

H. N. Brailsford, in "The Golden Bough" in the *New Statesman and
Nation* in 1941, adds the other two names. He writes:

> Darwin, whose disciple and continuer Frazer felt himself to be, had
> traced the origins and the evolution of our physical body: he
> gave us the record of our mental growth. He consciously used
> the same comparative method, and with Marx and Freud he ranks
> only after the founder of modern biology among the influences
> which have fixed the thinking of our day.

Frazer's revolution in human thought, Downie writes hopefully as the
conclusion to his biography, is "as yet scarce realized."

FREUD'S alteration of the world is as impossible a subject for discussion in a few pages as Marx's, and no single person could even
keep up with all the literature. Where psychoanalysis has been orthodox, from such early followers as Jones and Abraham to analysts who
were children when Freud died, it is in the application of Freud's
theory to new material, and although everyone has minor disagree-
ments with Freudian theory, the orthodox movement needs no discussion here.

The much-publicized rebels who broke away in personal terms—
Stekel, Adler, Jung, Rank, and Ferenczi—can be similarly skimped.
Each produced a body of new theory and each developed a movement and followers, but only Jung's analytical psychology seems influential enough to survive, perhaps because Jung himself survived for
so long, and it demands a few words. Christopher Caudwell, in *Studies
in a Dying Culture*, explains the defections simply: "Schism is the hallmark of religion." (He does not add that his own Marxism is the
only modern movement which has been more afflicted with schism and
heresy.) There is a truth in Caudwell's explanation, and personality
and temperament were at work too, but at least part of the truth is the
explanation Freud gives in the *History*, that resistance not only motivated but constituted the dissenting systems. In *Freud or Jung?*, Edward Glover concludes: "Jung's spiritual home is in the conscious
psychology of the pre-Freudian epoch," and "he seeks to get rid of

those embarrassing manifestations of unconscious function which call for explanation." Since the publication of Glover's demolition, the tendency has been, as I think quite properly, to dismiss Jung. Herbert Marcuse writes in *Eros and Civilization:* "Edward Glover's excellent analysis makes a further discussion of Jung's work unnecessary." Marcuse characteristically refers to Jungian psychology as "an obscurantist pseudo-mythology," while Norman O. Brown, in *Life Against Death*, simply calls it "Jungian *Schwärmerei*" (while reproaching the Freudians for leaving so large a range of their subject in Jungian hands).

The neo-Freudians or revisionists who broke away less completely by rejecting important Freudian concepts and retaining others —principally Karen Horney, Erich Fromm, Harry Stack Sullivan and their followers—warrant more space. I have criticized their revisions of Freudian theory in "Psychoanalysis and the Climate of Tragedy" in a forthcoming book of my essays, and I will not repeat it here. My opinion of the revisionists coincides with that of Marcuse and Brown. Marcuse has dismissed them as "retrogression," and observed that their inspirational style "suggests the Power of Positive Thinking to which the revisionist critique succumbs." Brown refers to "the catastrophe of so-called neo-Freudianism" and "the lullabies of sweetness and light which the neo-Freudians serve up as psychoanalysis."

However, the important question that the revisionists raise is the charge that Freudian psychology is ethnocentric or culture-bound, that it universalizes what is only true for our own culture or for Freud's subculture. The ambivalent villain here is again Malinowski. In a series of articles that culminated in *Sex and Repression in Savage Society* in 1927, he points out that the culture he had studied for many years, the Trobriand Islanders, did not even know of the father's role in procreation. The Trobriand male, he said, did not have Freud's Oedipus complex, but had instead an attachment to his sister and a rivalry with his maternal uncle. At the same time, Malinowski threw out *Totem and Taboo* as ethnocentric fantasy. He writes:

> It is easy to perceive that the primal horde has been equipped with all the bias, maladjustments, and ill-tempers of a middle-class European family, and then let loose in a prehistoric jungle to run riot in a most attractive but fantastic hypothesis.

Jones defended the universality of the Oedipus complex in controversy with Malinowski in *Imago*, arguing that the Trobrianders *did* understand paternity, but repressed the knowledge and displaced the love and hostility from mother and father to sister and uncle.

Jones never understood why anthropologists found *Totem and Taboo* so ridiculous. In his biography of Freud, he quotes Paul Radin's opinion in "History of Ethnological Theories" in the *American Anthropologist* in 1929: "For so keen a thinker as Freud his *Totem and Taboo* is really a woeful performance." Jones interprets this as resistance to the primal crime, "the horror aroused by what was considered to be a monstrous and improbable suggestion," rather than the proper scorn of field anthropologists for wild conjectural prehistory. Freud's usefulness for anthropologists is not in the theories of *Totem and Taboo* and *Moses and Monotheism* taken literally, nor even as the discoverer of the Oedipus complex, but as the pioneer explorer of the depths of the personality who made the triumphs of personality-in-culture anthropology possible.

Nor, it is beginning to be noticed, was Freud the cultural absolutist he has been made out to be. Heinz Hartmann, Ernst Kris, and Rudolph M. Loewenstein, in "Some Psychoanalytic Comments on 'Culture and Personality'" in *Psychoanalysis and Culture* in 1951, list a few examples of Freud's frequent cultural relativism. They call attention to the awareness in *The Psychopathology of Everyday Life* in 1904 that whereas self-destructiveness now takes the form of accident or illness, "formerly it was a customary sign of mourning; at other times it expressed itself in ideas of piety and renunciation of the world." In his paper on "A Neurosis of Demoniacal Possession" in 1925, Freud showed the demonological form neurosis took in seventeenth-century Europe. In a note added to his *Autobiographical Study* in 1935, he wrote:

> The period of latency is a physiological phenomenon. It can, however, only give rise to a complete interruption of sexual life in cultural organizations which have made the suppression of infantile sexuality a part of their system. This is not the case with the majority of primitive peoples.

Outside of psychoanalysis, bolder defenses have been made of Freud's superiority to the revisionists in cultural terms. Marcuse argues that Freud alone has revolutionary cultural implications, in that in his vision "the libidinal claims propel progress toward freedom." He adds:

> Conversely, the weakening of the psychoanalytic conception, and especially of the theory of sexuality, must lead to a weakening of the sociological critique and to a reduction of the social substance of psychoanalysis. Contrary to appearance, this is what has happened in the cultural schools.

Marcuse concludes: "Consequently, the revisionist emphasis on the influence of 'social conditions' in the development of the neurotic personality is sociologically and psychologically far more inconsequential than Freud's 'neglect' of these conditions."

If Frazer never read any Freud, and never even acknowledged the copy of *Totem and Taboo* that Freud sent him, Harrison was braver. She writes in *Reminiscences of a Student's Life:*

> By temperament I am, if not a prude, at least a Puritan, and at first the ugliness of it all sickened me. I hate a sick-room, and have a physical fear of all obsessions and insanity. Still I struggled on, feeling somehow that behind and below all this sexual mud was

something big and real. Then fortunately I lighted on *Totemism* (*sic*) *and Taboo*, and at once the light broke and I felt again the sense of release. Here was a big constructive imagination; here was a mere doctor laying bare the origins of Greek drama as no classical scholar had ever done, teaching the anthropologist what was really meant by his *totem* and *taboo*, probing the mysteries of sin, of sanctity, of sacrament—a man who, because he understood, purged the human spirit from fear.

"For generations," she concludes, "almost every branch of human knowledge will be enriched and illumined by the imagination of Freud." In her *Epilegomena to the Study of Greek Religion* in 1921, Harrison made the fertile marriage of Freud and Frazer that translates the origin-fantasy of *Totem and Taboo* into ritual reality. Among psychoanalysts, only Géza Róheim, the first analyst to acquire field anthropological experience, similarly went beyond Freud, in a series of books on the Australian aborigines and in a remarkable book of theory, *The Origin and Function of Culture*, published in 1943.

The important new movement in psychoanalysis since the death of Freud is the growth of ego psychology. Freud had always been aware of ego gratifications as well as of instinctual gratifications, as his accounts of his ambition-satisfying dreams in *The Interpretation of Dreams*, to take a single example, make clear. The emphasis of his earlier work, however, was largely on the id's primary drives. With *The Ego and the Id* in 1923, he finally turned to ego psychology, and in "Analysis Terminable and Interminable" in 1937, he fully defined ego therapy. The first significant work by others in the field was Anna Freud's *The Ego and the Mechanisms of Defense*, in 1936. The chief exponents of ego psychology have been Heinz Hartmann, a favorite pupil of Freud's, and Ernst Kris, one of the editors of his collected works. Hartmann's *Ego Psychology and the Problem of Adaptation*, published in 1939 and in English in 1958, is an eloquent reminder that "psychoanalysis, concerned as it is with the steering role of drive and thought, has lost sight of the steering done by the will," and is an attempt to redress the balance. Kris' *Psychoanalytic Explorations in Art*, published in 1953, bases itself on the concept of "regression in the service of the Ego." With Loewenstein, Hartmann and Kris have published a number of collaborative papers in ego psychology, the most significant "Some Comments on the formation of Psychic Structure" in *Psychoanalytic Study of the Child in 1946*. David Rapaport has specialized in systematizing ego theory, in a number of papers and in the anthology *The Organization and Pathology of Thought* in 1951. Other psychoanalysts who have devoted themselves to ego psychology range from the oldest, Paul Federn, whose *Ego Psychology and the Psychoses* appeared in 1952, in his fiftieth year of psychoanalytic practice, to some of the youngest and brightest.

It is sometimes hard to tell ego psychologists from revisionists, but the test seems to be that the ego psychologists do not deny Freud's primary drives, however much they may emphasize ego functions. Erik Homburger Erikson, the author of *Childhood and Society, The Young Man Luther,* and a number of important papers, is an interesting example of a borderline case. He is one of the most historically-minded of analysts, and one of the few with anthropological field experience. Sometimes, when Erikson balances ego-measure and id-wish in a dream, or the psychosocial and psychosexual in a disturbed child, he seems one with Hartmann or Rapaport. At other times he seems to deny the importance of the sexual or to translate it into ethical symbolism like Fromm, to get inspirational about "mutuality and considerate love" like Sullivan.

Beyond the deviant schools, the revisionists, and the variety of emphases within psychoanalysis itself, Freud's work has been enormously influential on every variety of psychology. It has revolutionized clinical psychology and psychiatry, not only directly, but through the projective tests of Hermann Rorschach and others. It has had equally profound effects on experimental and social psychology, and beyond them on every social science. If this has resulted in marvels of knowledge and insight, it has also resulted in marvels of vulgarization. One wonders what the fastidious stylist Freud would make of some of his consequences, of which the following, which appeared as a newsbreak in *The New Yorker,* is probably typical. It is an abstract from *Psychological Abstracts* of an article on "the life space interview" by Fritz Redl that appeared in the *American Journal of Orthopsychiatry* in 1959. It reads:

> The life space interview may be considered as the surrounding of a youngster's experience at a given time with some form of verbal communication for the purpose of regulating the impact of this experience on the child. It may be in the nature of clinical exploition of life events, for instance: reality rub-in, symptom estrangement, massaging numb value areas, new-tool salesmanship,[3] or manipulation of the boundaries of the self. Or it may be in the nature of emotional first aid on the spot, including such subcategories as: drain-off of frustration acidity; support for the management of panic, fury, and guilt; communication maintenance in moments of relationship decay; regulation of behavioral and social traffic; umpire services in decision crises as well as in cases of loaded transactions.

If the danger of applied psychoanalysis is vulgarization, the danger within the movement is dogmatic rigidity. It is not to the credit of psychoanalysis that the best recent books on it—Herbert Marcuse's *Eros and Civilization,* Philip Rieff's *Freud: The Mind of the Moralist,* and Norman O. Brown's *Life Against Death*—have all come from outside it, from a political scientist, a social scientist, and a professor of classics. Another classicist, E. R. Dodds, in *The Greeks and the Ir-*

[3] *There* is one that Freud would have understood, Howard Nemerov points out.

rational, in 1951, turned psychoanalysis on the ancient Greeks with revolutionary effect. It would be pointless to list the writers Freud has influenced, since no serious writer after the generation of Mann and Gide, Proust and Joyce, has been unaffected. It would in fact be hard to find any aspect of modern culture that has escaped Freud's influence.

"THE most challenging social science problem of our time," J. F. Brown wrote in *The Nation* in 1937, "lies in the antithesis between Freudian psychoanalysis and Marxian sociology." Perhaps they are not that antithetical. Marx's view of history is oddly like psychoanalysis in some respects. He wrote to Kugelmann in 1869, praising a predecessor: "In the past he rendered a great service by demonstrating how even the apparent accidents of social life possess, in their periodic recurrence and their periodic averages, an inner necessity." H. Stuart Hughes writes in *Consciousness and Society* of a group of modern thinkers, including Marx and Freud:

> Or, to put the matter in moral terms, they agree that the basic characteristic of human experience was the limited nature of its freedom. Men were masters of their fate, they argued, only for limited periods and in strictly limited segments of their activity. The eighteenth- or early nineteenth-century image of man as a self-consciously rational being freely selecting among properly weighed alternatives they dismissed as an antiquated illusion.

Freud apparently read some of Marx and Engels, although he disclaimed either "a thorough knowledge" or "a correct understanding" in a 1937 letter. Joseph Wortis reports in *Fragments of an Analysis with Freud* that in 1935 Freud praised Marx for elucidating the materialist side of history, adding, "But people go too far with it." "Communism and psychoanalysis go ill together," he concluded.

Efforts to combine Freud and Marx have been made from the psychoanalytic side principally by Alfred Adler, Wilhelm Reich, Erich Fromm, and their followers. Periodic efforts have also been made from the Marxist side, starting with Leon Trotsky and Karl Radek in the 1920s. These ventures, and their failures, are discussed in *The Armed Vision,* as are the more successful syntheses of a number of literary critics, principally Kenneth Burke, William Empson, Lionel Trilling, and Edmund Wilson. Since then the impulse has produced two extraordinary books. Marcuse's *Eros and Civilization* in 1955 creates a full-blown psychoanalytic socialism, with Marx's revolutionary "leap into Freedom" seen as a leap beyond the reality principle into the glorious world of the pleasure principle, resulting in the conversion of Thanatos into a life instinct. Brown's *Life Against Death,* published in 1959, asks for "a willing suspension of common sense," then goes on to define a future socialist society that will be entirely unrepressed, freed in polymorphous perversity from the tyranny of the genital, as it will be freed from the tyranny of capitalism by accepting its own anality without any necessity for sublimation.

These bold efforts to blend Freud and Marx characteristically demand the early humanist Marx of the *1844 Manuscripts* and the late tragic Freud of *Beyond the Pleasure Principle*. Brown writes:

> And thirdly, the psychoanalytical critique of quantifying rationality has an affinity with Marx, not the Marx of *Das Kapital*, which recognizes the irrationality of modern civilization but locates the irrationality in the 'system'; but the early Marx of the 'economic-philosophic manuscripts,' with his conception of the radical viciousness of the civilized mind, labeled 'the alienated consciousness.'

These thinkers refuse to accept the oversimplification that Marx and Freud represent two fundamentally incompatible lines of thought: Freud the line from Hobbes that despairs of the good society, Marx the line from Rousseau that expects it too easily. No one denies the existence of some incompatibilities. Where Marx saw work as the natural human condition, the fullest freedom being not idleness but productive labor, Freud assumes a "natural human aversion to work" that will always require a coercive society. Thrift, which Marx refutes as the "myth" of primary accumulation in *Capital*, Freud demands, so that for him culture is created by an elite capable of self-deprivation and sublimation. Fromm and Riesman have pointed out Freud's psychologizing of nineteenth-century market economy, with the mutual satisfaction of libidinous needs imaged in terms of expenditure and exchange. Some of these antitheses seem to represent a difference in emphasis rather than fundamental disagreement. The coercive and marketing libidinous relations Freud describes *do* exist, and *are* shaped by our culture and its economy (as Marx shows), but quite other relations are implicit in Freud's work, as Marcuse and Brown argue. Marx's leap into freedom is Freud's reclamation of the id (as it is Darwin's exaltation of lowly forms and Frazer's vision of totemic brotherhood). In their integration lies our future.

ULTIMATELY, the language of ideas is metaphor, and essentially metaphor. The arguments are not *clothed* in metaphor, they *are* metaphor. Joseph Schumpeter, in *Capitalism, Socialism and Democracy*, argues that Marx's metaphors always come when his thought is unclear and suggest "some weakness which must be screened." Patrick Mullahy, in *Oedipus: Myth and Complex*, insists that Freud's metaphors are "a very poor way of conceiving psychology." But for Aristotle in the *Poetics*, metaphor, the perception of likeness in dissimilars, is the sign of genius. Any book of ideas is to some degree metaphoric; a great book of ideas consists of profound metaphors in a realized form, analogous to the traditional forms of literature. If these metaphors are sometimes shocking and surrealistic—the children spun into silk, the cauldron of seething excitement—they are sometimes the ultimate commonplaces we have always known—the tangled bank of life, the web of thought.

These books, then, are literature, but are *The Origin of Species, Capital, the Golden Bough, The Interpretation of Dreams*, science, are they *true?* By Karl Popper's criterion for a scientific proposition, that it state the conditions whereby it may be refuted, they are all scientific, although perhaps erroneous science. In a deeper sense they are not scientific at all; one cannot refute a vision, although one can replace it by another vision, as we now see the universe through Einstein's eyes rather than through Newton's. The conventional canons of scientific reasoning are that a hypothesis enable one to subsume disparate phenomena under a simple formula that makes them more comprehensible, and to predict the occurrence of similar phenomena in a way susceptible of verification. By these canons, all four are scientific, or at least stated in a scientific fashion. But perhaps *all* science is ultimately metaphor, as Freud suggested in his open letter to Einstein, and even what we call comprehension and verification are only analogical processes. The ideas of Darwin, Marx, Frazer, and Freud are then as true as any ideas that explain our world to our satisfaction. If they arose out of the thinker's own nature, if Darwin projected his slow-and-steady personality on nature or Freud his wishful childhood, we can be sure of similar personal correlations underlying even Euclid's geometry and Newton's mechanics. Ideas come from minds, and minds are the products of an individual's nature and experience.

Our four thinkers produced four vast dramatic works for us, four dynamic visions of evolution, that is, of struggle, adaptation, and triumph. "Light can be thrown on this by our theory," Darwin wrote in his 1842 essay. "The Professor's explanations were too illuminating, it sometimes seemed;" H. D. wrote of Freud in the 1930s, "my bat-like thought-wings would beat painfully in that sudden search-light." In the century between those two remarks, four great illuminations, elucidations, enlightenments, were given to the world. In those powerful beams we can see our wriggling ancestor, the bloodstain on our fancy clothes, the corpse from which our grain sprouts, our lustful and murderous wish. If much of what has been dragged out into the light is evil and irrational, the heroic imaginative labor that dragged it out is benign and rational. These great enlightenings are humanist; philanthropic in the root sense, for the love of man.

ABRAHAM, KARL, *Dreams and Myths,* translated by William A. White, New York, 1913.
    Clinical Papers and Essays on Psychoanalysis, translated by Hilda C. Abraham and D. R. Ellison, London, 1955.

ADLER, ALFRED, *The Neurotic Constitution* (1912), translated by Bernard Glueck and John E. Lind, London and New York, 1917.
    The Practice and Theory of Individual Psychology, translated by P. Radin, London, 1925.

BAIRD, THEODORE, "Darwin and the Tangled Bank," in *American Scholar,* Autumn, 1946.

BARLOW, NORA, "Robert FitzRoy and Charles Darwin," in *Cornhill,* April, 1932.
    Charles Darwin and the Voyage of the Beagle, New York, 1946.

BARNETT, S. A. (ed.), *A Century of Darwin,* London, 1958.

BARTLETT, FRANCIS H., *Sigmund Freud: A Marxian Essay,* London, 1938.
    "The Limitations of Freud," in *Science and Society,* Winter, 1939.

BARZUN, JACQUES, *Darwin, Marx, Wagner,* Boston, 1941.

BERLIN, ISAIAH, *Karl Marx: His Life and Environment,* London, 1939.

BERNSTEIN, SAMUEL (ed.), *A Centenary of Marxism, Science and Society,* Winter, 1948.

BESTERMAN, THEODORE, *A Bibliography of Sir James George Frazer O. M.,* London, 1934.

"BIRRO, CELA," *The Ways of Enjoyment,* New York, 1957.

BISHOP, JOHN PEALE, "The Golden Bough" (1936), in *The Collected Essays,* New York and London, 1948.

BLACK, JOHN SUTHERLAND, and GEORGE CHRYSTAL, *The Life of William Robertson Smith,* London, 1912.

BRAILSFORD, H. N., "The Golden Bough" (1941), in *Turnstile One.* London, 1948.

BRILL, A. A., *Freud's Contribution to Psychiatry,* New York, 1944.
    Lectures on Psychoanalytic Psychiatry, London, 1948.

BROWN, NORMAN O., *Life Against Death,* New York, 1959.

BUCHANAN, SCOTT, *Poetry and Mathematics,* New York, 1929.

BUCHARIN, N. I., and others, *Marxism and Modern Thought,* translated by Ralph Fox, New York, 1935.

BURKE, KENNETH, *Attitudes toward History,* New York, 1937.
    The Philosophy of Literary Form, Baton Rouge, 1941.

BURNE, CHARLOTTE S. (ed.). Reviews of *The Golden Bough* in *Folk Lore,* June, 1901.

BUTLER, SAMUEL, *Evolution: Old and New.* London, 1882.
    Luck, or Cunning? London, 1887.

CAMPION, SARAH, "Autumn of an Anthropologist," in *New Statesman and Nation*, January 13, 1951.

"CAUDWELL, CHRISTOPHER," *Illusion and Reality*. London, 1937.
   Studies in a Dying Culture. London, 1938.

CLODD, EDWARD, *The Childhood of Religions*, London, 1876.
   Myths and Dreams, London, 1885.

COLE, G. D. H., *A History of Socialist Thought: The Forerunners 1789–1850*, London, 1953.

CORNFORD, F. M., *From Religion to Philosophy*, London, 1912.
   The Origin of Attic Comedy, London, 1914.

"D., H.," *Tribute to Freud*, New York, 1956.

DARWIN, CHARLES, *Diary of the Voyage of H. M. S. "Beagle"* (1831–36), edited by Nora Barlow, Cambridge, 1933.
   Journal of Researches (Voyage of the Beagle), London, 1839; revised, London, 1845.
   The Foundations of the Origin of Species: Two Essays Written in 1842 and 1844, edited by Francis Darwin, Cambridge, 1909.
   Geological Observations on the Volcanic Islands (1844) *and Parts of South America* (1846), London, 1876.
   with Alfred Russel Wallace, *The Linnean Society Papers* (1858), edited by Sir Gavin de Beer as *Evolution by Natural Selection*, Cambridge, 1958; edited by Bert James Loewenberg as *Darwin, Wallace and the Theory of Natural Selection*, Cambridge (Mass.), 1959.
   The Origin of Species. London, 1859; enlarged and revised: 1861, 1866, 1869, 1872. First edition reprinted, London, 1950. A variorum text edited by Morse Peckham, Philadelphia, 1959.
   On the Various Contrivances by Which Orchids Are Fertilised by Insects, London, 1862.
   The Movements and Habits of Climbing Plants (1865), London, 1875.
   The Variation of Animals and Plants under Domestication, London, 1868.
   The Descent of Man, London, 1871.
   The Expression of the Emotions in Man and Animals, London, 1872. With additions by Margaret Mead, New York, 1955.
   Insectivorous Plants, London, 1875.
   The Effects of Cross and Self Fertilisation, London, 1876.
   The Different Forms of Flowers, London, 1877.
   The Power of Movement in Plants, London, 1880.
   The Formation of Vegetable Mould, London, 1881.
   The Autobiography (1876, 1882), edited by Nora Barlow. New York, 1958.
   The Life and Letters, edited by Francis Darwin, London, 1887.
   More Letters of Charles Darwin, edited by Francis Darwin and A. C. Seward, London, 1903.
   The Darwin Reader, edited by Marston Bates and Philip S. Humphrey, London, 1957.

DARWIN, EMMA, *A Century of Family Letters 1792–1896*, edited by Henrietta Litchfield, New York, 1915.

DAWSON, WARREN R. (ed.), *The Frazer Lectures 1922–32*, London, 1932.

DOWNIE, R. ANGUS, *James George Frazer*, London, 1940.

DURKHEIM, ÉMILE, *The Elementary Forms of the Religious Life* (1912), translated by Joseph Ward Swain, Glencoe (Ill.), 1947.

EISELEY, LOREN, *Darwin's Century*, New York, 1958.

ELIADE, MIRCEA, *The Sacred and the Profane,* translated by Willard R. Trask, New York, 1959.

ELLIS, RICHARD W. (ed.), *Bernard Shaw and Karl Marx: A Symposium 1884–1889,* New York, 1930.

EMPSON, WILLIAM, *Some Versions of Pastoral,* London, 1935.

ENGELS, FRIEDRICH, *The Condition of the Working-Class in England in 1844* (1845), translated by Florence Kelley Wischnewetzky, London, 1892.

 The Peasant War in Germany (1850), translated by Moissaye J. Olgin, New York, 1926.

 Revolution and Counter-Revolution (1851), edited by Eleanor Marx Aveling (and attributed to Marx), Chicago, 1907; correctly attributed, London and New York, 1933.

 The Housing Question (1872), edited by C. P. Dutt, New York, n. d.

 Dialectics of Nature (after 1872), translated and edited by Clemens Dutt, New York, 1940.

 Herr Eugen Duehring's Revolution in Science (1877, 1878), edited by C. P. Dutt, translated by Emile Burns, New York, 1939. Translated in part as *Landmarks of Scientific Socialism* by Austin Lewis, Chicago, 1907. Translated in part as *Socialism: Utopian and Scientific* by Edward Aveling, New York, 1935.

 The Origin of the Family (1884), New York, 1942.

 Ludwig Feuerbach (1888), edited by C. P. Dutt, New York, n. d.

 Engels on Capital, translated and edited by Leonard E. Mins, New York, 1937.

 Engels as Military Critic, edited by W. H. Chaloner and W. O. Henderson, Manchester, 1959.

ERIKSON, ERIK H., *Childhood and Society,* New York, 1950.

 "The Dream Specimen of Psychoanalysis," in *Journal of the American Psychoanalytic Association,* January, 1954.

EVANS-PRITCHARD, E. E., *The Divine Kingship of the Shilluk of the Nilotic Sudan* (Frazer Lecture, 1948), Cambridge, 1948.

FERENCZI, SANDOR, *Sex in Psychoanalysis,* translated by Ernest Jones, London, 1916.

 Thalassa, translated by Henry A. Bunker, Albany (N.Y.), 1938.

FIRTH, RAYMOND (ed.), *Man and Culture: An Evaluation of the Work of Bronislaw Malinowski,* London, 1957.

FLIESS, ROBERT (ed.), *The Psycho-Analytic Reader,* London, 1950.

FRANK, PHILIPP G., *The Validation of Scientific Theories,* Boston, 1956.

FRANKFORT, H., *The Problem of Similarity in Ancient Near East Religions* (Frazer Lecture, 1950), Oxford, 1951.

FRAZER, JAMES G., *The Growth of Plato's Ideal Theory* (1879), London, 1930.

 Questions on the Manners, etc., London, 1887. Enlarged and revised: 1888, 1889, 1907.

 Totemism, Edinburgh, 1887.

 The Golden Bough, two volumes, London, 1890. Expanded to three volumes. London, 1900. Expanded to twelve volumes. London, 1911–1915. Abridgement by the author in one volume. London, 1922. Abridgement by Theodor H. Gaster in one volume as *The New Golden Bough.* New York, 1959.

 Passages of the Bible, London, 1895.

 Pausanias's Description of Greece, translated with a commentary, London, 1898. The commentary reprinted independently as *Pausanias and other Greek Sketches,* London, 1900. As *Studies in Greek Scenery, Legend, and History,* London, 1917.

Lectures on the Early History of the Kingship, London, 1905. Reissued as *The Magical Origin of Kings,* London, 1920.

The Scope of Social Anthropology (1908) and *Psyche's Task* (1909); as *Psyche's Task,* London, 1913; as *The Devil's Advocate,* London, 1927.

Totemism and Exogamy, London, 1910.

Letters of William Cowper, edited with a memoir, London, 1912.

The Belief in Immortality, Volume I, London, 1913, Volume II, London, 1922, Volume III, London, 1924.

Essays of Joseph Addison, edited with a preface, London, 1915.

Folk-Lore in the Old Testament, three volumes, London, 1918. Abridgement by the author in one volume, London, 1923.

Sir Roger de Coverley and other Literary Pieces, London, 1920. Expanded as *The Gorgon's Head and other Literary Pieces,* London, 1927.

Apollodorus, The Library, translated with an introduction, London, 1921.

The Worship of Nature, London, 1926.

Publii Ovidii Nasonis Fastorum Libri Sex, edited with a translation and commentary, London, 1929.

Myths of the Origin of Fire, London, 1930.

Garnered Sheaves, London, 1931.

Condorcet on the Progress of the Human Mind, Oxford, 1933.

The Fear of the Dead in Primitive Religion, Volume I, London, 1933, Volume II, London, 1934, Volume III, London, 1936.

Creation and Evolution in Primitive Cosmogonies, London, 1935.

Aftermath: a Supplement to the Golden Bough, London, 1936.

Totemica: A Supplement to Totemism and Exogamy, London, 1937.

Anthologia Anthropologica, edited by R. A. Downie, Volume I. London, 1938. Volumes II, III, and IV, London, 1939.

FREUD, ANNA, *The Ego and the Mechanisms of Defense,* London, 1937.

FREUD, MARTIN, *Glory Reflected,* London, 1957.

FREUD, SIGMUND, *On Aphasia* (1891). Translated by E. Stengel. London, 1953.

with Joseph Breuer, *Studies in Hysteria* (1895), translated by A. A. Brill, New York, 1937.

The Interpretation of Dreams (1899), enlarged and revised: 1909, 1911, 1914, 1919, 1921, 1925, 1930, translated by A. A. Brill, New York, 1938. Translated by James Strachey, London, 1954.

On Dreams (1901), translated by James Strachey, London, 1952.

The Psychopathology of Everyday Life (1904), translated by A. A. Brill, New York, 1938.

Three Contributions to the Theory of Sex (1905), translated by A. A. Brill, New York, 1938.

Jokes and Their Relation to the Unconscious (1905), translated by A. A. Brill as *Wit and Its Relation to the Unconscious.* New York, 1938. Translated by James Strachey. London, 1960.

Delusion and Dream (1907), translated by Helen M. Downey, New York, 1917.

"The Origin and Development of Psychoanalysis" (1909), translated by Harry W. Chase, in *Lectures and Addresses,* Worcester (Mass.), 1910.

Leonardo da Vinci (1910), translated by A. A. Brill, New York, 1947.

Totem and Taboo (1912), translated by A. A. Brill, New York, 1938.

The History of the Psychoanalytic Movement (1914), translated by A. A. Brill, New York, 1938.

Introductory Lectures on Psychoanalysis (1917), translated by Joan Riviere, New York, 1943.

Beyond the Pleasure Principle (1920), translated by C. J. M. Hubback, London, 1922.

Group Psychology and the Analysis of the Ego (1921), translated by James Strachey, New York, n. d.

The Ego and the Id (1923), translated by Joan Riviere, London, 1927.

An Autobiographical Study (1925), translated by James Strachey, London, 1935.

The Question of Lay Analysis (1926), translated by Nancy Procter-Gregg, London, 1947.

Inhibition, Symptoms and Anxiety (1927), translated by Henry Alden Bunker as *The Problem of Anxiety*, New York, 1936.

The Future of an Illusion (1927), translated by W. D. Robson-Scott, London, 1928.

Civilization and Its Discontents (1929), translated by Joan Riviere, London, 1930.

New Introductory Lectures on Psycho-Analysis (1932), translated by W. J. H. Sprott, New York, 1933.

Moses and Monotheism (1937, 1939), translated by Katherine Jones, New York, 1939.

An Outline of Psychoanalysis (1938), translated by James Strachey, New York, 1949.

Collected Papers, translated under the supervision of Joan Riviere by Alix and James Strachey and others. Volumes I and II, London, 1924, Volumes III and IV, London, 1925, Volume V, London, 1950.

The Origins of Psycho-Analysis: Letters to Wilhelm Fliess, edited by Marie Bonaparte, Anna Freud, and Ernst Kris, translated by Eric Mosbacher and James Strachey, New York, 1954.

Letters of Sigmund Freud, edited by Ernst L. Freud, translated by Tania and James Stern, New York, 1960.

FROMM, ERICH, *Sigmund Freud's Mission*, New York, 1959.

Marx's Concept of Man, New York, 1961.

GINGER, RAY, *Six Days or Forever?*, Boston, 1958.

GLOVER, EDWARD, *Freud or Jung?*, New York, 1956.

GLUCKMAN, MAX, *Rituals of Rebellion in South-East Africa* (Frazer Lecture, 1952). Manchester (England), 1954.

GRAY, ASA, *Darwiniana*, New York, 1876.

GREENE, JOHN C., *The Death of Adam*, Ames (Iowa), 1959.

HARRISON, JANE ELLEN, *Themis*, Cambridge, 1912. Enlarged, 1927.

Epilegomena to the Study of Greek Religion. Cambridge, 1921.

HARTMANN, HEINZ, *Ego Psychology and the Problem of Adaptation* (1939), New York, 1958.

HAYS, H. R., *From Ape to Angel*, New York, 1958.

HEGEL, GEORG WILHELM FRIEDRICH, *The Philosophy of History*, translated by J. Sibree, New York, 1899.

HIMMELFARB, GERTRUDE, *Darwin and the Darwinian Revolution*, London, 1959.

HITSCHMANN, EDUARD, *Freud's Theories of the Neuroses*, translated by C. R. Payne. London, 1921.

HOFFMAN, FREDERICK T., *Freudianism and the Literary Mind*, Baton Rouge, 1945.

HOLLITSCHER, WALTER, *Sigmund Freud: An Introduction*, London, 1947.

HORNEY, KAREN, *The Neurotic Personality of Our Time*, New York, 1937.

New Ways in Psychoanalysis. New York, 1939.

HUGHES, H. STUART, *Consciousness and Society*, New York, 1958.

HUNT, R. N. CAREW, *Marxism: Past and Present*, London, 1954.

HUXLEY, FRANCIS, "Charles Darwin: Life and Habit," in *American Scholar*, Autumn and Winter, 1959.
"Frazer within the Bloody Wood," in *New Statesman and Nation*, April 16, 1960.
HUXLEY, JULIAN, *The Living Thoughts of Darwin*, Philadelphia, 1939.
Evolution: the Modern Synthesis, New York, 1942.
HUXLEY, THOMAS H., *Darwiniana: Essays*, New York, 1893.
The Life and Letters of Thomas Henry Huxley, edited by Leonard Huxley, New York, 1900.
IRVINE, WILLIAM, *Apes, Angels and Victorians*, New York, 1955.
JACOBS, JOSEPH, "Recent Researches in Comparative Religion," in *Folk-Lore*, September, 1890.
JONES, ERNEST, *Essays in Applied Psychoanalysis*, London, 1923.
Sigmund Freud: Life and Work. Volume I, London, 1953, Volume II, London, 1955, Volume III, London, 1957. Abridgement by Lionel Trilling and Steven Marcus in one volume, New York, 1961.
Sigmund Freud: Four Centenary Addresses, New York, 1956.
Free Associations, London, 1959.
JUNG, C. G., *Psychology of the Unconscious*, translated by Beatrice M. Hinkle, New York, 1916.
Psychological Types (1920), translated by H. Godwin Baynes, London and New York, 1946.
KAUTSKY, KARL, *The Economic Doctrines of Karl Marx*, translated by H. J. Stenning, London, 1936.
KAYE, JULIAN B., *Bernard Shaw and the Nineteenth Century Tradition*, Norman (Oklahoma), 1959.
KEITH, ARTHUR, *Darwin Revalued*, London, 1955.
KEMPF, EDWARD J., *Psychopathology*, St. Louis (Miss.), 1920.
KRIS, ERNST, *Psychoanalytic Explorations in Art*, London, 1953.
LENIN, V. I., *Materialism and Empirio-Criticism* (1909), translated by David Kvitko, New York, 1927.
Marx-Engels-Marxism, edited by J. Fineberg, New York, 1933.
LEONTIEV, A., *Marx's Capital*, translated by Emily G. Kazakévich, New York, 1946.
LEWIS, JOHN (ed.), *1848–1948: Special Centenary Number, Modern Quarterly*, Spring, 1948.
LIEBKNECHT, WILHELM, *Karl Marx: Biographical Memoir* (1896), translated by Ernest Untermann, Chicago, 1901.
LINDNER, ROBERT (ed.), *Explorations in Psychoanalysis: Essays in Honor of Theodor Reik*. New York, 1953.
LORAND, SANDOR (ed.), *Psychoanalysis Today*, New York, 1944.
LYND, HELEN MERRELL, *On Shame and the Search for Identity*, New York, 1958.
McLENNAN, JOHN FERGUSON, *Studies in Ancient History*, London, 1876.
MAINE, HENRY SUMNER, *Ancient Law*, London, 1861.
MALINOWSKI, BRONISLAW, "Sir James G. Frazer: A Biographical Appreciation" (1941), in *A Scientific Theory of Culture*. Chapel Hill (North Carolina), 1944.
MALTHUS, THOMAS, "*A Summary View of the Principle of Population*" (1830), in *Three Essays on Population*, New York, 1960.
MANN, THOMAS, "Freud's Position in the History of Modern Thought," in *Past Masters*, translated by H. T. Lowe-Porter, New York, 1933.
Freud, Goethe, Wagner, translated by H. T. Lowe-Porter, New York, 1936.

MARCUSE, HERBERT, *Eros and Civilization,* Boston, 1955.

MARETT, R. R. (ed.), with T. K. Penniman, *Spencer's Scientific Correspondence with Sir J. G. Frazer and Others.* Oxford, 1932.

    Tylor, London and New York, 1936.

MARX, KARL, *The Jewish Question* (1843), translated by Edward Fitzgerald, London, 1935.

    Economic and Philosophic Manuscripts of 1844, translated by Martin Milligan, Moscow and London, 1959.

    with Engels, *The Holy Family* (1845), translated by R. Dixon. Moscow, 1956. London, 1957.

    with Engels, *The German Ideology* (1846), translated in part by R. Pascal, New York, 1939.

    The Poverty of Philosophy (1847), edited by C. P. Dutt and V. Chattopadhyaya, New York, n.d.

    with Engels, *The Communist Manifesto* (1848), with an introduction by D. Ryazanoff, translated by Eden and Cedar Paul, London, 1930. With an introduction by Harold J. Laski, London, 1948.

    Wage-Labour and Capital (1849), with an introduction by Frederick Engels, New York, 1933.

    The Class-Struggles in France 1848-50 (1850), with an introduction by F. Engels, New York, n.d.

    The Eighteenth Brumaire of Louis Bonaparte (1852), translated by Eden and Cedar Paul, London and New York, 1926.

    A Contribution to the Critique of Political Economy (1859), translated by N. I. Stone, Chicago, 1904.

    Value, Price and Profit (1865), edited by Eleanor Marx Aveling, New York, 1935.

    Capital, Volume I (1867), Volume II (1885), Volume III (1894), edited by Friedrich Engels. Translated by Ernst Untermann, Chicago, 1906-09. Volume IV published as *Theories of Surplus Value* (1905-10). Edited by Karl Kautsky. Translated in part by G. A. Bonner and Emile Burns, London, 1951.

    The Civil War in France (1871), with an introduction by Frederick Engels, New York, 1940.

    Critique of the Gotha Program (1875), edited by C. P. Dutt, New York, 1938.

    with Engels, *Selected Correspondence 1846-1895,* translated by Dona Torr, New York, 1942.

    Letters to Dr. Kugelmann, New York, 1934.

    with Engels, *On Malthus,* edited by Ronald L. Meek, translated by Dorothea L. Meek and Ronald L. Meek, New York, 1954.

    Selected Writings in Sociology and Social Philosophy. Edited by T. B. Bottomore and Maximilien Rubel. Translated by T. B. Bottomore. London, 1956.

    with Engels. *Literature and Art,* New York, 1947.

    with Engels. *On Religion,* Moscow, 1957; London, 1958.

    Capital and Other Writings, edited by Max Eastman, New York, 1932.

    Selected Works. Edited by V. Adoratsky and C. P. Dutt, Moscow and Leningrad, 1935.

    with Engels, *Selected Works,* Moscow and London, 1950.

    with Engels and others, *A Handbook of Marxism,* edited by Emile Burns, New York, 1935.

    On China 1853-1860, edited by Dona Torr, London, 1951.

    with Engels, *Revolution in Spain,* New York, 1939.

with Engels, *The Civil War in the United States*, edited by Richard Enmale, New York, 1937.

with Engels, "Unpublished Letters to Americans," edited by Leonard E. Mins. In *Science and Society*, Spring, 1938.

with Engels, *The Russian Menace to Europe*, edited by Paul W. Blackstock and Bert F. Hoselitz, London, 1953.

The Eastern Question, edited by E. M. Aveling and E. Aveling, London, 1897.

Secret Diplomatic History of the Eighteenth Century, edited by E. M. Aveling, London, 1899.

The Story of the Life of Lord Palmerston, edited by E. M. Aveling, London, 1899.

MEAD, MARGARET and NICHOLAS CALAS (ed.), *Primitive Heritage*, New York, 1953.

MEHRING, FRANZ, *Karl Marx: The Story of His Life* (1918), translated by Edward Fitzgerald, New York, 1935.

MILLHAUSER, MILTON, *Just Before Darwin: Robert Chambers and* Vestiges. Middletown (Conn.), 1959.

MOORE, RUTH, *Charles Darwin*, New York, 1955.

MORGAN, LEWIS H., *Ancient Society*, New York, 1877.

MORGAN, THOMAS HUNT. *A Critique of the Theory of Evolution*, Princeton, 1916.

The Scientific Basis of Evolution, New York, 1932.

MULLAHY, PATRICK, *Oedipus: Myth and Complex*, New York, 1948.

MURRAY, GILBERT, *Five Stages of Greek Religion*. London, 1935.

"Sir James Frazer," in *The Listener*, 1954.

MURRY, JOHN MIDDLETON, *Heroes of Thought*, New York, 1938.

NICOLAIEVSKY, BORIS, and OTTO MAENCHEN-HELFEN, *Karl Marx: Man and Fighter*, translated by Gwenda David and Eric Mosbacher, Philadelphia, 1936.

OBERNDORF, CLARENCE P., *A History of Psychoanalysis in America*, New York, 1953.

OSBORN, HENRY FAIRFIELD, *From the Greeks to Darwin*, New York and London, 1894.

OSBORN, REUBEN, *Freud and Marx*, New York, n.d.

PLEKHANOV, G., *Fundamental Problems of Marxism*, edited by D. Ryazanov, New York, n.d.

POULTON, EDWARD BAGNELL, *Charles Darwin and the Origin of Species*, London, 1909.

PUNER, HELEN WALKER, *Freud: His Life and Mind*, New York, 1947.

QUIGGIN, E. C. (ed.), *Essays and Studies Presented to William Ridgeway*, Cambridge, 1913.

RANK, OTTO, *The Trauma of Birth*, New York and London, 1929.

Psychology and the Soul (1932), translated by William D. Turner, Philadelphia, 1950.

RAVERAT, GWEN, *Period Piece*, London, 1952.

REICH, WILHELM, *Character-Analysis* (1928), New York, 1945.

The Sexual Revolution (1930), translated by Theodore P. Wolfe, New York, 1945.

REIK, THEODOR. *From Thirty Years With Freud*, London, 1942.

RIAZANOV, D., *Karl Marx and Friedrich Engels*, translated by J. Kunitz, New York, 1927.

(ed.) *Karl Marx: Man, Thinker and Revolutionist*, translated by Eden and Cedar Paul, London, 1927.

RICE, PHILIP BLAIR (ed.), "The Legacy of Sigmund Freud," *Kenyon Review*, Spring, 1940.

RIDGEWAY, WILLIAM, *The Origin of Tragedy*, Cambridge, 1910.
    The Dramas and Dramatic Dances of Non-European Races, Cambridge, 1915.
RIEFF, PHILIP, *Freud: The Mind of a Moralist*, London, 1959.
RÓHEIM, GÉZA, *Animism, Magic and the Divine King*, London, 1930.
    (ed.), *Psychoanalysis and the Social Sciences*, New York: Volume I, 1947, Volume II, 1950, Volume III, 1951.
ROMANES, GEORGE JOHN, *Darwin, and After Darwin*, Chicago, 1892.
ROSCOE, JOHN, *The Baganda*, London, 1911.
ROSENBERG, HAROLD, *The Tradition of the New*, New York, 1959.
RUEHLE, OTTO, *Karl Marx: His Life and Work* (1928), translated by Eden and Cedar Paul, New York, 1929.
SACHS, HANNS, *Freud: Master and Friend*, Cambridge (Mass.), 1944.
SCHOENWALD, RICHARD L., *Freud: The Man and His Mind 1856–1956*, New York, 1956.
SCHWARTZCHILD, LEOPOLD, *The Red Prussian*, translated by Margaret Wing, New York, 1947.
SEARS, PAUL B., *Charles Darwin*, New York and London, 1950.
SELIGMAN, C. G., with Brenda Z. Seligman, *Pagan Tribes of the Nilotic Sudan*, London, 1932.
    Egypt and Negro Africa (Frazer Lecture, 1933), London, 1934.
SEWARD, A. C. (ed.), *Darwin and Modern Science*, Cambridge, 1909.
SIMPSON, GEORGE GAYLORD, *The Meaning of Evolution*, New Haven (Conn.), 1949.
SMITH, W. ROBERTSON, *The Old Testament in the Jewish Church*, London, 1881.
    Lectures on the Religion of the Semites. Edinburgh, 1889.
SOOTIN, HARRY, *Gregor Mendel: Father of the Science of Genetics*, New York, 1959.
SPENCER, BALDWIN, and F. J. GILLEN, *The Native Tribes of Central Australia* (1899). Reissued with a preface by Frazer, London, 1938.
STALIN, JOSEPH, *Foundations of Leninism*, New York, 1932.
    Problems of Leninism, New York, 1934.
STEINER, FRANZ, *Taboo*, New York, 1956.
STEKEL, WILHELM, *The Interpretation of Dreams*, translated by Eden and Cedar Paul, New York, 1943.
SULLIVAN, HARRY STACK, *Conceptions of Modern Psychiatry*, Washington, n.d.
SWEEZY, PAUL M. (ed.), *Karl Marx and the Close of His System*, by Eugen von Boehm-Bawerk, and *Boehm-Bawerk's Criticism of Marx*, by Rudolf Hilferding, New York, 1949.
SYPHER, WYLIE, "Aesthetic of Revolution: The Marxist Melodrama," in *Kenyon Review*, Summer, 1948.
TAX, SOL. (ed.), *Evolution After Darwin*, Chicago, 1960.
THOMAS, NORTHCOTE W. (ed.). *Anthropological Essays Presented to Edward Burnett Tylor*, Oxford, 1907.
THOMPSON, CLARA, *Psychoanalysis: Evolution and Development*, New York, 1950.
TRILLING, LIONEL, *Freud and the Crisis of Our Culture*, Boston, 1955.
TROTSKY, LEON, *The History of the Russian Revolution*, translated by Max Eastman, Volume I, New York, 1932, Volume II, New York, 1933.
    The Living Thoughts of Karl Marx, Philadelphia, 1939.
TYLOR, EDWARD B., *Researches into the Early History of Mankind*, London, 1865.
    Primitive Culture, London, 1871.
VAN GENNEP, ARNOLD, *The Rites of Passage*, translated by Monika B. Vizedom and Gabrielle L. Caffee, London, 1960.

VAN TESLAAR, J. S. (ed.), *An Outline of Psychoanalysis*, New York, 1924.

WAELDER, ROBERT, *The Living Thoughts of Freud*, Philadelphia, 1941.

WALLACE, ALFRED RUSSEL, *Darwinism*, London, 1889.

    The World of Life, London, 1910.

WARD, HENSHAW, *Charles Darwin: The Man and His Warfare*, Philadelphia, 1927.

WEISINGER, HERBERT (ed.), *1859–1959: Darwin-Marx Centennial, Centennial Review*, Fall, 1959.

    "The Branch That Grew Full Straight," in *Daedalus*, Spring, 1961.

WEISMANN, AUGUST, *The Evolution Theory*, translated by J. Arthur Thompson and Margaret R. Thompson, London, 1904.

WEST, GEOFFREY, *Charles Darwin: A Portrait*, New Haven, 1938.

WILBUR, GEORGE B., and WARNER MUENSTERBERGER (ed.), *Psychoanalysis and Culture*, New York, 1951.

WILLEY, BASIL, *Darwin and Butler: Two Versions of Evolution*, New York and London, 1960.

WISDOM, J. O. (ed.), *Sigmund Freud Centenary, British Journal for the Philosophy of Science*, May, 1956.

WORTIS, JOSEPH, *Fragment of an Analysis with Freud*, New York, 1954.

WUNDT, WILHELM, *Elements of Folk Psychology* (1912), translated by Edward Leroy Schaub, London and New York, 1916.

Index of Names and Titles

(SUBJECT INDEX FOLLOWS)

Abel, Karl, 357
Abraham, Karl, 367, 440
Abstract of Morgan's "Ancient Society," 179
"The Acquisition of Power over Fire," 416
Adam, 41, 155, 272
Addison, Joseph, 232, 262
"Address on the Question of Free Trade," 98
"Address to the Working Classes of Europe," 84
Adler, Alfred, 298, 322, 369, 370, 384, 387, 396, 428, 430, 440, 445
Adonis, 240, 258, 260
Adonis Attis Osiris, 255, 256, 257, 259, 264
The Aeneid, 82, 247, 336
Aeschylus, 86
"Aesthetic of Revolution: The Marxist Melodrama," 146
"The Aetiology of Hysteria," 306, 321
Aftermath: A Supplement to The Golden Bough, 247, 251, 288, 290
Agrippa, Menenius, 162
Aichhorn, August, 398
Alcestis, 389
Alembert, Jean le Rond d', 126
Alexander, Franz, 410
Alexander the Great, 259
Alvarez, W. C., 13 n
American Anthropologist, 441

American Journal of Orthopsychiatry, 444
American Journal of Science and Arts, 30
Ampère, André Marie, 380
Anaitis, 244
Analogy of Revealed Religion, 37 n
"Analysis of a Phobia in a Five-Year-Old Boy," 353
"Analysis Terminable and Interminable," 417, 418, 443
Ancient Law, 6
Ancient Society, 178
Andreas-Salomé, Lou, 407, 417
"Anna O.," 303, 305
Annenkov, Paul, 138
Anthologia Anthropologica, 290
Anthropological Essays Presented to Edward Burnett Tylor, 270
Anti-Duehring, 176–178
Antigone, 138
Antike Wald- und Feldkulte, 7, 194
"The Antithetical Sense of Primary Words," 357
Apes, Angels, and Victorians, 14
Aphrodite, 258
Apollo, 258
Apollodorus, 275, 276, 281
Apsden, G., 139, 165
Arbeiterzeitung, 177
Areopagitica, 207
Argonauts of the Western Pacific, 276

459

Sand, George, 96
Santayana, George, 211
Sartre, Jean-Paul, 435
Saul, 273
Savage, Dr., 48
Scapegoat, 258, 261
Scatalogic Rites of All Nations, 363
Schelling, F. W. J. von, 88
Schiller, Friedrich von, 320, 341
Schliemann, Heinrich, 74
Schopenhauer, Arthur, 8, 82
Schreber, Judge, 360, 361
Schumpeter, Joseph, 446
Schurz, Carl, 82
Schwartzchild, Leopold, 160, 180
Science and Society: A Centenary of Marxism, 435
A Scientific Theory of Culture and Other Essays, 210
"The Scope and Method of Mental Anthropology," 273, 284
The Scope of Social Anthropology, 205, 229
Scorpion und Felix, 86
Scott, John, 68, 72
"Screen Memories," 309
The Secret History of Lord Palmerston, 115
Sedgwick, Adam, 11
Seligmann, C. G., 256, 268, 436
Semiramis, 258
Senior, Nassau W., 140, 141, 156, 162
Sex and Repression in Savage Society, 441
"The Sexual Enlightenment of Children," 350, 353
"Sexuality in the Aetiology of the Neuroses," 308
Shakespeare, William, 61, 137, 282, 308, 337, 365, 407, 423, 436
Shammuramat, 258
Shaw, George Bernard, 124, 127, 142, 146, 149, 159, 160, 169
Sigmund Freud: Life and Work (see also, Jones), 304, 360
Silone, Ignazio, 435
Simpson, George Gaylord, 28
"Sir James George Frazer: A Biographical Appreciation," 210
"Sir Patrick Spens," 199
Sir Roger de Coverly and Other Literary Pieces, 195, 200
Sismondi, Simonde de, 5

Sisyphus, 134, 264
Six Lectures to Working Men, 122
Sketch of an Historical Picture of the Progress of the Human Mind, 283
Smith, Adam, 6, 95, 118, 124, 127
Smith, E. W., 289, 436
Smith, William, 3
Smith, William Robertson, 6, 190, 191, 195, 196, 198, 199, 210, 215, 218, 219, 237, 239, 267, 422, 427, 438
Social Interest, 428
Socialism: Utopian and Scientific (see also, *Anti-Duehring*), 176
Socrates, 201, 376
Sombart, Werner, 100, 129
"Some Additional Notes upon Dream-Interpretation as a Whole," 398
"Some Character-Types Met With in Psychoanalytic Work," 374
"Some Comments on the formation of Psychic Structure," 443
"Some Elementary Lessons in Psychoanalysis," 424
"Some Points in a Comparative Study of Organic and Hysterical Paralyses," 302
"Some Primitive Theories of the Origin of Man" (see also, "Creation and Evolution in Primitive Cosmogonies"), 210
"Some Psychoanalytic Comments on 'Culture and Personality,'" 442
"Some Psychological Consequences of the Anatomical Distinction Between the Sexes," 400
"The Song of the Shirt," 166
Sophocles, 311, 312, 313, 337, 352, 392
Sorel, Georges, 131, 132
Speirs, John, 439
Spencer, Baldwin, 191, 212, 215, 219, 225, 228, 229, 230, 231, 285, 288, 291, 436, 437
Spencer, Herbert, 19, 27, 42, 300, 432
Spencer's Scientific Correspondence with Sir J. G. Frazer and Others, 228
Spender, Stephen, 435
Spengler, Oswald, 428, 439
Spinoza, 5, 142, 178
Spirits of the Corn and of the Wild, 237, 251
"Splitting of the Ego in the Defensive Process," 423

Subject Index

aesthetics, in *Origin*, 50 f
agon (s)
  Bible as series of, 200
  Bios against Thanatos, 2
ambivalence
  about reality of childhood events,
    384 f
  Breuer's, 303
  colloquy with audience as sym-
    bolic of, 378
  Darwin's, 24
  Engels', 169, 173
  Frazer's, 208 f, 209, 210
  Freud's, 326, 352, 357
  Freud's quarrel with his style as, 341
  in Freud's relationships, 322 f
  of life and death, 29
  represented in dramatic dialogue,
    401
analogy
  between analysis and chemistry,
    386
  between artists and analysts, 352
  between communist movement
    and early Christians, 186
  between criminal and neurotic, 350
  between culture and neurosis, 390,
    410
  between Darwin and "mad scien-
    tist," 66, 71
  between Darwin and Newton, 431
  between Darwin and St. Paul, 40 f
  between dreams and art, 393
  between Frazer and Darwin, Marx,
    Freud, 440
  between historical dialectics and
    evolutionary biology, 123, 124
  between magic and science, 235, 437

analogy (*continued*)
  between neuroses and caricatures,
    367
  between neurotic and worshipper,
    350
  between nursing child and sexu-
    ally satisfied adult, 350
  between psychoanalytic treatment
    and surgical operation, 381
  between savage and id, 386
  between worship of Osiris and
    worship of the dead, 257
  danger of, 279
  for future psychoanalytic society,
    358
  for politics, 112
  for repression, 418 f
  from natural sciences, 125, 234
  from photography, 363
  from picture language, 336
  in *New Introductory Lectures*,
    413 f
  literary, 337
  organic, 112
  religious, 135
  scientific, 126, 270
Anangke, 396, 405, 408, 409
animals
  as dramatic actors, 16
  humanizing of, 16, 31, 50, 59
  imagination in, 50
  sexuality of, 54
antagonists
  "impartial inquirer" as, 401
  in dialogue against religion, 404 f
  of Commune, 156
anthropology
  aim of, 206

comedy
    as dramatic form of *Class Struggles*, 108 f
    end of savagery as, 223
    in *Capital*, 148
    in Marx's style, 88
    of French history, 156
comparative method
    application to ethics, 238 f
    application to religion, 198 f
    as instrument for detecting savages, 270
    evaluation of, 198 f
    forms of, 199
    importance to anthropology, 275
    in Frazer's work, 194
    in *Pausanias*, 201
Coryanthes macrantha, 63, 68, 71
creation
    and evolution, 210
    as structure of Bible, 34
    as Western myth, 211
    evolutionary, 285
    of mood, 225
    of species, 21, 37
    Origin as drama of, 35
"Critical Criticism," 88–90
culture (see also civilization, society)
    and aggression, 410
    and guilt, 408
    and sublimation, 349
    as antithesis of nature, 405
    as human power, 51
    as life-giving, 409 f
    as opposed to "nature," 52
    compensatory, 51
    Darwin's acceptance of, 58
    evolution of, 410
    Freud's criticism of, 353
    Freud's implication for, 442
    "Freud's tragic sense of," 408
    ideal of, 246
    native, breakdown of, 288 f
    origin of, 366
    primitive, 197
custom
    and evolution, 205 f
    and motive, 237, 279
    of priesthood of Nemi, 234
    of sororate, 214
    origin of, 205 f, 242
    outside of time and space, 287

custom (*continued*)
    reflected in myth, 216
    reforming of, 208 f
cycle
    of death and rebirth, 254, 256, 280
    of nature, 211, 227, 254, 262
    of social institutions, 196
    tragic, 262

Darwinism
    in literature, 433
    reaction to, 432
    social, 19, 432
death
    and evolution, 41, 279
    and war, 372 f
    as antithesis of life, 405
    as dramatic action, 256
    as goal of life, 388
    as termination of analysis, 417 f
    essential to historical tragedy, 260 f
    in creationist cosmogonies, 211
    instinct of, 373, 399, 407 f, 410, 418
    June insurrection as, 109
    myth of origin of, 41, 270, 271
    of rejector, 430
descent of man, 31, 46, 47 f, 49 f
design of social organization, 220
detective story, as form of *Golden Bough*, 262
determinism, 341
dialectics
    analogy to sciences, 123, 124, 126
    Engels', 176
    Hegelian, 96, 130
    historical, 123
    Marx's, 96, 373
    materialist, 130
    Soviet, 160 n
drama
    farce, 113, 114
    historical, 103, 109, 222
    in Freud's agonistic form, 378
    movements of, 143
    of creation, *Origin* as, 35
    of death and resurrection of god, 256
    of Freud's psychology, 312
    of *Journal of Researches*, 27
    totemic ceremonies as, 223
dramatic action
    imaged in metaphors, 33

metaphor *(continued)*
  "giant body of the proletariat,"
    176
  Great Chain of Becoming, 125
  The Holy Family as, 89 f
  in *German Ideology*, 92
  inorganic, 117
  Marx's compared to Proudhon's,
    98
  menagerie of horrors, 134
  mixed, 103, 117, 126
  mutilations, 144
  mythological, 159
  of illusion, 103
  organic, 117, 124, 153
  rebirth, 134 f
  revolutionary, 115, 399
  scriptural sinfulness, 117 f
  social war, 164
  stripping away of veils, 97 f,
    102 f, 103, 108, 114, 135, 164 f
  theatrical performance, 108
  vampire, 106, 107, 290
  science as, 447
metapsychology, 361
method, Frazer's
  comparative (see comparative
    method)
  derivation of, 6 f, 195, 236 f
  of studying custom, 206
  use of historical perspective in,
    221
mistreatment of workers, 144
monism
  Darwinian, 46
  Jungian, 388
  totemic, 211
moral
  in *Class Struggles*, 108
  in *Fear of the Dead*, 287
  in *Wage Labor and Capital*, 105
  of *King Lear*, 365
  of *Medieval Faith*, 282
  of *The Peasant War*, 171
moral imperative
  Capital as, 131–133
  Darwin's, 58
moral indignation
  in *Eighteenth Brumaire*, 111
  in Engels' style, 167 f
  Marx's, 115, 143
moral themes of *Capital*, 97

morality
  disclaimer of, 168
  ethnocentric, 222
  of animals, 49
  of French bourgeoisie, 107, 157
  of humility, 42
  of primitive man, 49
  of the sexes, 55, 56
  sexual, 353
  supremacy of, 57
  "useless," 57
morphology, 33, 39, 124
mystery
  as totemic brotherhood, 42
  genetic theory as, 45
  in origin of species, 41
  of life, 280 f
myth
  and magic, 239
  as erroneous speculation, 281
  as history, 241, 281
  as rite, 241
  astrological, 364
  cognitionist theory of, 240, 275 f,
    281
  Edenic, 147
  euhemerist theory of, 216, 240, 241,
    257 f, 281
  Frazer's final position on, 275 f
  Freud on origin of, 416
  metaphoric, 134
  of the Cast Skin, 271
  of the Fall, Duehring's, 178
  of Heracles, 416
  of Kwoiam, 216
  of Moses, 421 f
  of Narcissus, 368
  of origin of death, 41, 270 f, 271
  of origin of fire, 281 f
  of origin of social institutions, 366
  of original expropriation, 129
  of original sin, Capitalism's, 147
  of the Perverted Message, 271
  of primal artist, 391
  of primitive origin, 285
  of Prometheus, 416
  of the Second Coming, 160
  of the Shilluk king, 268
  of the triumph of the saints, 160
  Old Testament stories as, 270 f
  origin, Primal crime as, 408
  Petty's, 134
  reflecting custom, 216

self-analysis, Freud's
  Interpretation of Dreams as ac-
    count of, 314
  stages of, 314–316
sexuality
  as aetiology of neuroses, 303, 305,
    307 f
  as evil spirit, 302 f
  Darwin's prudishness about, 52,
    54, 428 f
  Frazer's prudishness about, 221,
    226, 290, 428 f
  freedom of, under communism,
    181 f, 182
  Freud's prudishness about, 317,
    349, 428 f
  in animal terms, 54
  infantile, 348
  Marx's prudishness about, 100,
    428 f
  of animals, 54 f
  of plants, 70
  of worms, 77
  primitive, 227
slavery
  and social Darwinism, 19
  Darwin's reaction to, 17 f
society (see also civilization, culture)
  as dynamic vision, 94
  as organism, 124
  bourgeois, 107 f, 122, 168
  communist, 94, 125, 158
  English, 122
  French, 108
  Freud on, 365 f
  future, 125, 158 f, 175, 178, 181
  modern, 124, 137
  origin of, 218
  proletarian, 158
  Prussian bourgeois, 104 f
  scientific study of, 131
sociology
  and Frazer, 437 f
  Capital as, 130 f, 162
  Marxian, as antithesis of Freudian
    psychoanalysis, 445 f
  Marx's, as "social poetry," 131
  Marx's influence on, 434 f
  of female blushing, 59 f
  of institutions, 210
sources
  of Darwin's teleology, 40
  of *Expression of Emotions*, 58

sources (*continued*)
  of Frazer's notebooks, 290
  of Marx's metaphors, 134
  of Marx's *Tribune* articles, 114
  of *Totemism and Exogamy*, 221
species
  and creation, 21
  extinction of, 20
  immutability of, 20, 30
  modification of, 62
  mutability of, 20
  origin of, as gospel, 36
struggle
  and differential reproduction, 28
  as key image, 27, 44 f
  as poetic vision, 22
  of classes, 98 f, 104, 107, 109, 117,
    121, 146
struggle for existence
  as *agon* and *sparagmos*, 28
  as dramatic action, 28
  as metaphorical, 27 f, 28
  as tangled bank, 33
style, Darwin's, 26 f, 34, 68
style, Frazer's, 194, 202
style, Freud's
  dramatistic, 303, 304 f, 307, 312
  Freud's displeasure with, 312 f, 341
  rhetorical techniques in, 376–379
  simple-to-complex progression in,
    311
  tone of Great Detective in, 313
  tone of humility in, 313, 423
  use of debate form in, 376–378
  use of dialogue in, 300 f, 312, 340,
    371, 401, 404
  use of polemic in, 368, 369
style, Marx's
  abstract-concrete progressions in,
    118, 125
  change in, 152–154
  characteristics of, 136
  comic devices in, 88
  humor in, 114 f
  in *Class Struggles*, 106
  Marx in defense of, 136
  of ironic protest, 132
  of textbook, 116
  polemic, 137, 434
  scatological, 138, 142
  simple-complex progressions in,
    118 f, 124

Stanley Edgar Hyman

Stanley Edgar Hyman is a member of the literature faculty at Bennington College, a staff writer for *The New Yorker*, and book critic for *The New Leader*. Professor Hyman is the author of two books of literary criticism, *The Armed Vision* and *Poetry and Criticism*, and the editor of another, *The Critical Performance*. In 1959 he was awarded a fellowship by the American Council of Learned Societies. He lives in North Bennington, Vermont, with his wife, Shirley Jackson, and their four children.